Federal Tax Research

SEVENTH EDITION

William A. Raabe, Ph.D., CPA
The Ohio State University

Gerald E. Whittenburg, Ph.D., CPA
San Diego State University

Debra L. Sanders, Ph.D., CPA
Washington State University

THOMSON

SOUTH-WESTERN

Australia · Canada · Mexico · Singapore · Spain · United Kingdom · United States

Federal Tax Research, Seventh Edition

William A. Raabe, Gerald E. Whittenburg, and Debra L. Sanders

VP/Editorial Director:
Jack W. Calhoun

VP/Editor-in-Chief:
Alex von Rosenberg

Publisher:
Rob Dewey

Acquisitions Editor:
Charles E. McCormick, Jr.

Developmental Editor:
Craig Avery

Marketing Manager:
Chris McNamee

Production Editor:
Chris Sears

Manager of Technology, Editorial:
Vicky True

Technology Project Editor:
Christine A. Wittmer

Web Coordinator:
Scott Cook

Manufacturing Coordinator:
Doug Wilke

Production House:
Litten Editing and Production, Inc.

Compositor:
GGS Book Services

Printer:
WestGroup
Eagan, MN

Art Director:
Stacy Shirley

Internal Designer:
Joseph Pagliaro Graphic Design

Cover Designer:
Joseph Pagliaro Graphic Design

Cover Images:
© Getty Images

Library of Congress Control Number:
2005920274

For more information about our products, contact us at:

Thomson Learning Academic
Resource Center

1-800-423-0563

Thomson Higher Education
5191 Natorp Boulevard
Mason, OH 45040
USA

Asia (including India)
Thomson Learning
5 Shenton Way
#01-01 UIC Building
Singapore 068808

Australia/New Zealand
Thomson Learning Australia
102 Dodds Street
Southbank, Victoria 3006
Australia

Canada
Thomson Nelson
1120 Birchmount Road
Toronto, Ontario
M1K 5G4
Canada

Latin America
Thomson Learning
Seneca, 53
Colonia Polanco
11560 Mexico
D.F.Mexico

UK/Europe/Middle East/Africa
Thomson Learning
High Holborn House
50/51 Bedford Row
London WC1R 4LR
United Kingdom

Spain (including Portugal)
Thomson Paraninfo
Calle Magallanes, 25
28015 Madrid, Spain

This book is dedicated to our academic mentors:

William A. Raabe
Norton Bedford
Gerald Brighton
Christine Purdie
Joseph Schultz
Eugene Willis

Gerald E. Whittenburg
William H. Hoffman
James W. Pratt
John J. Willingham
Allan R. Bailey

Debra L. Sanders
William Raabe
Philip M. J. Reckers
Theodore Saldin
Robert Wyndelts

About the Authors

William A. Raabe, Ph.D., CPA, teaches graduate tax courses at the Fisher College of Business of The Ohio State University. He is a leader among business school tax faculty in incorporating developments in technology into curricula for the educational development of tax professionals.

Dr. Raabe's teaching and research interests focus on multijurisdictional taxation and financial planning, and he is recognized as the leader among business school academics in the fields of state and local income, sales, and property taxation. Dr. Raabe is the author or editor of approximately twenty book titles, including *West Federal Taxation,* and the *Multistate Corporate Tax Guide.* He has received university-wide recognition as the winner of the AMOCO Foundation Award for Teaching Excellence, and the Wisconsin Institute of CPAs named him the Educator of the Year.

Gerald E. Whittenburg, Ph.D., CPA, EA, is a Professor in the School of Accountancy at San Diego State University. A graduate of the University of Houston, Dr. Whittenburg's teaching and research interests include individual and corporate taxation, pension plans, and tax research methodology.

Dr. Whittenburg is also an author of *Income Tax Fundamentals.* In addition, he has published articles in journals such as *Advances in Taxation, Practical Tax Strategies, Taxes—The Tax Magazine, Journal of Taxation of Investments, Journal of Taxation of Employee Benefits, Journal of Taxation of Financial Institutions, Valuation Strategies, Journal of Small Business Strategy, The Tax Adviser,* and *Journal of Accounting Education.* Professor Whittenburg's professional designations include Certified Public Accountant (CPA) and Enrolled Agent (EA). He has received numerous teaching awards, including the Trustee's Outstanding Faculty Award for the entire California State University System. Recently, Dr. Whittenburg spent a sabbatical at the University of Adelaide in Australia. In his picture, he is shown with "Pumpkin" the koala.

Debra L. Sanders, Ph.D., CPA, is a professor in the Washington State University School of Accounting, Information Systems and Business Law. She has received numerous awards for outstanding teaching, research, and service including the Boeing Distinguished Faculty Research Award, the Shell Corporation Outstanding Teacher Award, and the College of Business and Economics Outstanding Service Award.

Dr. Sanders, a graduate of Arizona State University, publishes in both academic and professional journals. Her work has appeared in the academic journals *Behavioral Research in Accounting, National Tax Journal, The Journal of the American Taxation Association, Advances in Taxation,* and *The International Journal of Accounting.* Professional journals that have published her articles include *Taxation for Accountants, Taxation for Lawyers, The Review of Taxation of Individuals, Taxes, The Tax Adviser, and Journal of Financial Planning.*

Brief Contents

Contents

Preface

The Seventh Edition of *Federal Tax Research* reflects the increasing importance of online research databases in tax research practices. More than ever before, our text is *the* essential learning tool for tax research, both online and using standard library materials. From its new complete chapter on state and local tax research, to its *free* RIA Checkpoint® Student Edition tax database with each new copy, to its host of new and valuable tax links and up-to-date online tax news, *Federal Tax Research* 7e remains justifiably the market leader among tax research texts.

This popular book has been prepared as a comprehensive, stand-alone reference tool for the user who wishes to become proficient in Federal tax research. It is written for readers who are familiar with the fundamentals of the Federal income and transfer tax law, at a level that typically is achieved on the completion of two comprehensive introductory courses in taxation in either (1) the accounting program in a business school or (2) second- or third-year courses in a law school.

Nearly every accounting, tax, and tax law student can benefit from the strategies found in this book. The text is most appropriate for:

- Upper-level accounting students in a business school (i.e., seniors in a four-year program or those in the fifth year of a 150-hour program) who desire additional information concerning the practice of taxation.
- Those who are enrolled in a nontax graduate program in business administration (e.g., an MBA or MS—management program) and would like further practical training in the functions of taxation in today's business environment.
- Second- or third-year law school students, especially those who desire a more detailed and pragmatic introduction to a specialized tax practice.
- Those who are commencing a graduate degree program in taxation, in either a business school or a law school, and require a varied and sophisticated introduction to the procedures of tax research and to the routine functions and implications of a tax practice.
- Practicing accountants and attorneys who need an introduction, updating, or refresher relative to tax practice and research as an element of their career paths.

STRUCTURE AND PEDAGOGY

Too often, existing textbooks ignore the detailed, pragmatic approach that students require in developing effective and efficient tax research skills.

That is why we have included an unprecedented degree of **hands-on tax research analysis** throughout the text. This book does not simply discuss tax research procedures or the sources of the Federal tax law; nor does it provide a mere sample of the pertinent tax reference material. Rather, the Seventh Edition reflects our conviction that readers learn best by **active learning** and **real-world experience** with the most important elements of the Federal tax law. We have applied this conviction to the many important features of the Seventh Edition:

- **NEW:** A full chapter on **state and local tax research opportunities** reflects the importance of this type of tax work in today's practice.
- **NEW exercises, problems, and research cases** are included throughout that help students learn using actual online research tools and methods discussed in the text.
- **NEW Spotlight on Taxation** boxes in every chapter provide additional research tips, tax information, news, background, and factors to consider in developing a tax research solution.
- An **introduction to tax practice** continues to provide details on such valuable topics as preparer penalties, statutes of limitation, interest conventions, and return selection for IRS audits.
- The book's continuing focus on **tax planning** fits perfectly with this growing trend in tax practice.
- The text has been **thoroughly updated** with developments that affect those who conduct tax research, including **revisions to codes of ethics, IRS organizational structure and enforcement functions,** and other principles that control tax practice.
- Hundreds of **exercises and discussion questions** allow the reader to learn by exploring the reference materials in a well-developed tax library in their research strategies.
- Assignments allow students to **construct case briefs, file memos, client letters, and other elements of a comprehensive client file**—vital skills they will need in practice.
- Hundreds of pages of **reproductions and illustrations** have been excerpted from the most important tax reference materials and expose students to the real world of tax research.
- **Summary charts, diagrams, and other study aids** are integrated throughout the text that summarize the elements of primary and secondary sources of Federal tax law and encourage students to develop their own research routines and techniques.

FOCUS ON ONLINE AND COMPUTERIZED RESEARCH

The use of online databases and computerized research has become indispensable in tax practice, and the previous edition was at the forefront of coverage of these innovative tools. For the Seventh Edition, however, we focus the majority of our coverage on online and computerized research. Presenting and discussing these new tools, strategies, and research tactics now eclipses our discussions of traditional paper-based resources. We reviewed every internet and CD-ROM based research tool available, and the text now includes such new online coverage as:

- **RIA's Checkpoint® Student Edition Online Tax Research Database.** Each *new* textbook contains an RIA Checkpoint® Student Edition access code, good for six months of free access to content from the research database most widely used by tax professionals. As students use Checkpoint® to complete problems within the text, they build research skills and familiarity with the database—valuable preparation both for the CPA Exam and their professional future.

- **Tutorial for RIA's Checkpoint®.** This self-paced tutorial from RIA orients students to Checkpoint® and keeps instructors from having to use valuable lecture time to explain the same information. The tutorial walks through the application of RIA research techniques using sample problems similar to those on the CPA Exam.

- **Tax Tutor** online tutorials and interactive quizzes under the Student Resources page at the book's web site reinforce the tax research coverage in each chapter.

- **Ongoing news and updates to the tax law** are available at the text's web site: **http://raabe.swlearning.com**.

- The Instructors Manual, the Instructor Resource CD, and the instructors portion of the web site for the text **http://raabe.swlearning.com** include suggested solutions for assigned material, a generous test bank, multiple quizzes for each chapter, and lecture notes. The web site also offers templates for commonly used research documents, and sample syllabi so that the instructor can share in the learning approaches used by the text's many adopters.

As a result, we believe that <u>the Seventh Edition is indispensable to learning and performing real-world online and computerized tax research</u>.

NEW! TURBOTAX® BUSINESS

The market leading software for tax preparation comes free with all **new** texts, and provides access for all your tax preparation homework. **TurboTax® Business** software, the highest rated and best-selling tax software, is designed specifically for corporations, S-corporations, partnerships of up to 100 partners, and LLCs, as well as estates and trusts. It covers corporation, partnership, and fiduciary income texts and gives you practical, hands-on tax experience in tax preparation.

ACCESS AND DISCOUNT INCLUDED! Online Access to TaxBrain® Tax Preparation Software: TaxBrain® online individual tax preparation software is used by more than 2,500 tax professionals every year. You can use TaxBrain® to work the income tax form problems in the text with a real-world application, developing your skills as you master course information. To access, log on to **www.taxbrain.com**. Take advantage of a 20% discount when filing your 2004 return with TaxBrain®—enter promotional code **SWL947**.

USING THE TEXT

The text's exercises, cases, and advanced cases offer enough variety in both difficulty and subject matter that they may be assigned to individual readers, or to student groups of two or three, for their optimal use. The instructor also should consider giving each student in the course a different research case to complete, thereby both discouraging joint work and reducing the strain on the pertinent library resources.

Given both the nature of the tax research process and the limited tax library resources that are available to most firms and universities, the instructor must take care (1) to assign discussion materials for which the necessary resources are available and (2) to work through the assignment him- or herself, to ascertain that one's target solution to the assignment reflects the very latest in the development of the Federal tax law.

The instructor may want to defer the assigning of certain research cases until a specific electronic research service is discussed, which will provide additional illustrations. Alternatively, the reader could be encouraged to rework a previous assignment once the computerized tax reference tools have been introduced.

Instructors should see the online Instructor's Resource Guide for a list of resources.

ACKNOWLEDGMENTS

We are grateful to the reviewers of the Sixth Edition who provided valuable comments and insights, which guided us in the development of the Seventh Edition:

Adrian Allen, Shaw University
Rose Bailey, Gardner-Webb University
David R. Connelly, Western Illinois University
Patti Davis, Keystone College
Andrew Lafond, Philadelphia University
Tom Largay, Thomas College
Ernest Larkins, Georgia State University
Margaret Reed, University of Cincinnati
Robert Ricketts, Texas Tech University
Lee A. Sartori, Walsh College
James Trebby, Marquette University
Thomas C. Pearson, University of Hawaii at Manoa
Donald Williamson, American University

We wish to thank the **over 280 tax instructors** who participated in an e-survey on tax research and provided their detailed feedback. Without your responses our efforts would have been greatly diminished in scope. Any errors, of course, are the sole responsibility of the authors.

We welcome your comments and suggestions for further improvements to this text. Please feel free to use the following addresses to convey these remarks.

William A. Raabe
Fisher College of Business AMIS
The Ohio State University
Columbus OH 43210
614.292.4023
raabe.12@osu.edu

Gerald E. Whittenburg
School of Accountancy
San Diego State University
San Diego, CA 92182-0221
g.e.whittenburg@sdsu.edu

Debra L. Sanders
Department of Accounting and Business Law
Washington State University
Pullman, WA 99164-4729
dsanders@wsu.edu

William A. Raabe
Gerald E. Whittenburg
Debra L. Sanders

February 2005

The Tax Research Environment

Chapter 1

Introduction to Tax Practice

LEARNING OBJECTIVES

- Describe the elements of modern tax practice in the United States.

- Distinguish between open and closed transactions.

- Identify sources of legal and ethical standards that guide those who engage in tax practice.

- Examine in detail the major collections of ethical standards that bear upon tax practitioners today.

- Place tax issues in a broader context of ethics and morality.

- Understand the limitations on tax research by CPAs and other nonattorneys.

CHAPTER OUTLINE

Elements of Tax Practice
Tax Compliance
Tax Planning
Tax Litigation
Tax Research

Rules and Ethics in Tax Practice
Circular 230
Who May Practice
Enrolled Agents
Limited Practice without Enrollment
Tax Return Preparers
Conduct before the IRS
Due Diligence
Contingent and Unconscionable Fees
Solicitation and Advertising
Tax Return Positions
Best Practices

AICPA Code of Professional Conduct
Independence
Integrity and Objectivity
General Standards
Compliance with Standards
Accounting Principles
Confidential Client Information
Contingent Fees
Acts Discreditable
Advertising and Other Forms of Solicitation

Commissions and Referral Fees
Form of Organization and Name

Statements on Standards for Tax Services
Tax Return Positions
Answers to Questions on Returns
Certain Procedural Aspects of Preparing Returns
Use of Estimates
Departure from a Position Previously Concluded in an Administrative Proceeding or Court Decision
Knowledge of Error: Return Preparation
Knowledge of Error: Administrative Proceedings
Form and Content of Advice to Taxpayers

Sarbanes-Oxley and Taxation
ABA Model Code of Professional Responsibility

Nonregulatory Ethics
Morality
Social Responsibility
Business Ethics
Tax Planning Ethics
Other Ethical Standards

Tax Research by Certified Public Accountants
Historical Developments
CPAs and Other Nonattorneys

So you want to be a tax practitioner? For anyone interested in the tax aspects of doing business, answering this question will help determine if you want to pursue a career in the tax field. The practice of taxation is the process of applying the tax law, rules, regulations, and judicial rulings to specific transactions to determine the tax consequences to the taxpayer involved. There are many ways to practice tax. One can practice tax directly through jobs such as a Certified Public Accountant, tax attorney, Enrolled Agent, or commercial income tax return preparer. In addition, tax can be practiced indirectly by such individuals as controllers, accountants, CFOs, and others who do tax work as part of their other duties. An understanding of taxation and the tax practice environment is essential to the individual who wants to have a position in the tax area.

Taxation is the process of collecting revenue from citizens to finance government activities. In a modern technological society such as that of the United States, however, taxation comprises an interaction among several disciplines that is far from simple. The tax system is derived from law, accounting, economics, political science, and sociology (Exhibit 1–1). Principles of economics, sociology, and political science provide the environment, while law and accounting precepts are applied in a typical tax practice.

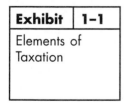

Exhibit	**1-1**
Elements of Taxation	

Tax policy questions concerning the effects that a specified tax law change will have on economic growth, the effects of projected inflation on the implementation of the tax law and vice versa, and the effects of the tax law on the United States' balance of payments are addressed by economists. Political scientists, economists, and sociologists, alternatively, examine issues such as who bears the ultimate burden of a tax, how a tax bill becomes law (including practical effects of the legislative process), the social equity of a tax, and whether a tax is discriminatory. Attorneys interpret (and often create) taxation statutes, and accountants apply the tax laws to current or prospective economic transactions.

ELEMENTS OF TAX PRACTICE

The tax laws of a democratic country such as the United States are created by a political process. In recent years, the result of this political process has been a law that levies taxes on income, sales, estates, gifts, and other items that usually are reflected by the accounting process. Thus, tax practice can be described as the application of tax legislation to specific accounting situations. The elements of modern tax practice can be separated into three categories: compliance, planning, and litigation, which are all supported by tax research. How these elements of tax practice fit together is illustrated in Exhibit 1–2.

Exhibit	1–2
Elements of Tax Practice	

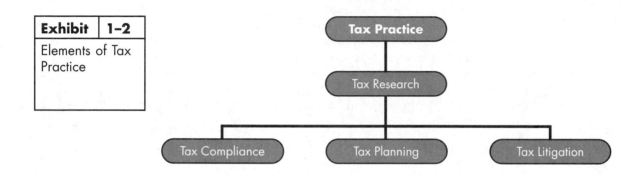

Tax Compliance

In general, **tax compliance** consists of the gathering of pertinent information, evaluation and classification of such information, and the filing of necessary tax returns. Tax compliance also includes other functions necessary to satisfy government requirements, such as representation at a client's Internal Revenue Service (IRS) audit. Commercial tax preparers, Enrolled Agents, attorneys, and certified public accountants (CPAs) all perform tax compliance to some extent. Noncomplex individual, partnership, and corporate tax returns often are completed by commercial tax preparers. Enrolled Agents, attorneys, and CPAs usually are involved in the preparation of more complex tax returns; in addition, they provide tax-planning services and represent their clients before the IRS. The elements of tax compliance and administration are examined in more detail in later chapters.

Tax Planning

Tax planning is the process of arranging one's financial affairs to optimize tax liabilities. However, whereas **tax avoidance** is the legitimate object of much of modern tax practice, **tax evasion** constitutes the illegal nonpayment of a tax and cannot be condoned. Fraudulent acts of this sort are unrelated to the professional practice of tax planning.

Tax planning can be divided into two major categories: **open transactions** and **closed transactions.** In an open transaction, the tax practitioner maintains some degree of control over the attendant tax liability because the transaction is not yet completed; for example, the title to an asset that has not yet passed. If desired, some modifications to an incomplete transaction can be made to receive more favorable tax treatment. In a closed transaction, however, all of the pertinent actions have been completed; therefore, tax planning may be limited to the presentation of the facts to the government in the most favorable, legally acceptable manner possible.

SPOTLIGHT ON TAXATION: Case Quotation

There is nothing inherently illegal or immoral in the avoidance of taxation (i.e., Tax Planning) according to the tax system's rules. The eminent judge Learned Hand best expressed this doctrine in the dissenting opinion of *Commissioner v. Newman*, 159 F.2d 848 (CA-2, 1947):

Over and over again, courts have said that there is nothing sinister in so arranging one's affairs as to keep taxes as low as possible. Everybody does so, rich or poor, and all do right, for nobody owes any public duty to pay more than the law demands: taxes are enforced extractions, not voluntary contributions.

TAX LITIGATION

A specialized area within the practice of law is the concentration on **tax litigation.** Litigation is the process of settling a dispute with another party (here, usually the IRS) in a court of law (here, a Federal court). Typically, a tax attorney handles tax litigation that progresses beyond the initial appeal of an IRS audit result. Accountants and other financial advisers can also serve in a support capacity. Later chapters contain additional discussions of the various opportunities and strategies available in tax litigation.

TAX RESEARCH

Tax research is undertaken to answer taxation questions. The tax research process includes the (1) identification of pertinent issues, (2) determination of proper authorities, (3) evaluation of the appropriateness of these authorities, and (4) application of these authorities to specific facts. Tax research techniques are examined in Chapters 2 through 10 of this text.

RULES AND ETHICS IN TAX PRACTICE

A person who prepares tax returns for monetary or other compensation, or who is licensed to practice in the tax-related professions, is subject to various statutes, rules, and codes of professional conduct. All tax practitioners are regulated by **Circular 230,** *Regulations Governing the Practice of Attorneys, Certified Public Accountants, Enrolled Agents, Enrolled Actuaries, and Appraisers* *before the Internal Revenue Service.* The ethical conduct of an attorney is also governed by the laws of the state(s) in which he or she is licensed to practice. Most states have adopted, often with some modification, guidelines that are based on the **American Bar Association (ABA)** *Model Code of Professional Responsibility* or the newer ABA *Model Rules of Professional Conduct.* CPAs who are members of the **American Institute of Certified Public Accountants (AICPA)** must follow its *Code of Professional Conduct* and any other rules generated by the state board(s) of accountancy. The AICPA has also produced a series of *Statements on Standards for Tax Services,* which contain advisory guidelines for CPAs who prepare tax returns.

Although CPAs who are not members of the AICPA are not bound by the *Code of Professional Conduct* and the *Statements on Standards for Tax Services,* those rules and standards are a useful source of guidance for all members of the profession. Statutory tax law also specifies certain penalties and other rules of conduct that apply to everyone (e.g., attorneys, CPAs, and Enrolled Agents) in addition to their respective professional standards, and also to commercial tax preparers who are not attorneys, CPAs, or Enrolled Agents. Chapter 13 addresses these rules. The basic overlapping sources of rules and ethics for tax practitioners are illustrated in Exhibit 1–3.

Exhibit	**1–3**

Sources of Rules and Ethics for Tax Practitioners

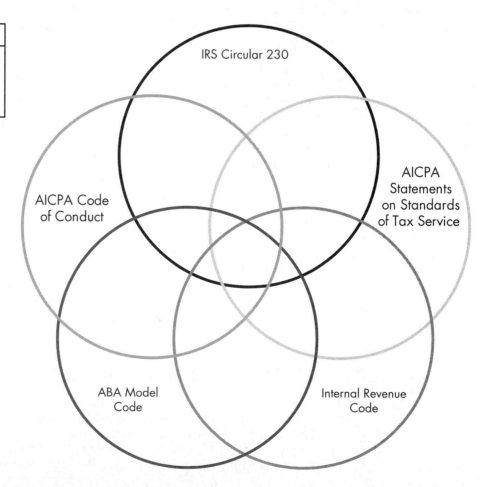

IRS Circular 230

AICPA Statements on Standards of Tax Service

AICPA Code of Conduct

ABA Model Code

Internal Revenue Code

CIRCULAR 230

Circular 230, which constitutes Part 31 of the Treasury Department Regulations, is designed to provide protection to taxpayers and the IRS by requiring tax preparers to be technically competent and to adhere to ethical standards. *Circular 230* contains the following definition of **practice before the IRS** in Section 10.2 of Subpart A.

> *. . . matters connected with presentation to the Internal Revenue Service or any of its officers or employees relating to a client's rights, privileges, or liabilities under laws or regulations administered by the Internal Revenue Service. Such presentations include the preparation and filing of necessary documents, correspondence with and communications to the Internal Revenue Service, and the representation of a client at conferences, hearings and meetings.*

Under this definition, practice before the IRS consists primarily of the representation of clients during audit procedures, such as a meeting with a revenue agent on behalf of a client to establish the correctness of a taxpayer's return. The preparation of tax returns or the furnishing of information to the IRS in response to a request for such information is not considered practice before the IRS. (Tax return preparation rules are addressed by various statutes discussed in Chapter 13.) *Circular 230* also states who may conduct such a practice and sets forth the disciplinary procedures that apply. In addition, Certified Public Accountants, lawyers, and tax return preparers are (or may be) regulated by the states. As a result, there can be additional statutes, regulations, and requirements that must be met by individuals who practice in certain states.

Who May Practice

Under Section 10.3, Subpart A, of *Circular 230,* the following individuals may practice before the IRS.

1. Attorneys

2. Certified public accountants

3. Enrolled Agents

4. Enrolled actuaries

To qualify under this rule, an attorney must be a member in good standing of the bar of the highest court in any state, possession, territory, commonwealth, or the District of Columbia. Likewise, CPAs and Enrolled actuaries must be qualified to practice in any state, possession, territory, commonwealth, or the District of Columbia. No further substantive examination is required.

Enrolled Agents

Individuals who are not attorneys or certified public accountants can qualify to practice before the Internal Revenue Service by becoming an Enrolled Agent (EA). An **Enrolled Agent** is someone who has either passed a special Internal Revenue Service examination (currently given once a year, in October) or worked for the IRS for five years. The procedures for becoming an Enrolled Agent are detailed in *Circular 230,* Subpart A, § 10.4, § 10.5, and § 10.6. Enrolled Agents have the same rights as attorneys and certified public accountants to represent clients before the Internal Revenue Service. Under *Circular 230,* an Enrolled Agent must renew his or her enrollment card on a three-year cycle. For each enrollment cycle, Enrolled Agents, like attorneys and CPAs, must meet certain continuing education requirements as defined in Subpart A, § 10.6. For an EA's enrollment card to be renewed, he or she must complete seventy-two hours (i.e., an average of twenty-four hours per year) of qualifying continuing education for each three-year enrollment period. In addition, a minimum of sixteen hours of continuing education credit must be completed during each year of an enrollment cycle. Subpart A, § 10.6(f) defines what qualifies as continuing education for Enrolled Agents.

Circular 230 allows an individual to be an attorney or CPA and an Enrolled Agent simultaneously. Being both an EA and an attorney or CPA might be useful to certain tax practitioners who practice across state lines. For example, a CPA in Texas who is also an Enrolled Agent can practice in any state. The Enrolled Agent's card is effectively a national license to practice before the Internal Revenue Service anywhere in the United States (including territories). In addition, most state taxing agencies grant an Enrolled Agent the right to practice before that state agency.

For more information on Enrolled Agents, see the following two web sites. The first site is Enrolled Agent information on the IRS's web page and the second is the web site of the National Association of Enrolled Agents.

http://www.irs.gov/taxpros/agents/

http://www.naea.org/

Limited Practice without Enrollment

In *Circular 230,* the Internal Revenue Service has authorized certain individuals to practice without being an attorney, CPA, or Enrolled Agent. Individuals (with proper identification) can represent themselves under § 10.7(a) and participate in Internal Revenue Service rule making as provided for under § 10.7(b). In addition, under § 10.7(c), individuals (with proper identification and authorization, IRS Form 2848) are allowed to represent taxpayers in the following special situations.

1. An individual may represent a member of his or her immediate family.

2. A regular full-time employee of an individual employer may represent the employer.

3. A general partner or regular full-time employee of a partnership may represent the partnership.

4. A bona fide officer or regular full-time employee of a corporation (including a parent, subsidiary, or other affiliated corporation), an association, or organized group may represent the corporation, association, or organized group.

5. A trustee, receiver, guardian, personal representative, administrator, executor, or regular full-time employee of a trust, receivership, guardianship, or estate may represent the trust, receivership, guardianship, or estate.

6. An officer or regular employee of a governmental unit, agency, or authority may represent the governmental unit, agency, or authority in the course of his or her official duties.

7. An individual may represent any individual or entity before personnel of the Internal Revenue Service who are outside the United States.

Tax Return Preparers

Any person who signs a tax return as having prepared it for a taxpayer is authorized to conduct "limited practice" before the Internal Revenue Service (with proper taxpayer authorization) under § 10.7(c)(viii). *Circular 230* requires that such person must not be disbarred or suspended from practice before the Internal Revenue Service or his or her profession. A tax return preparer can make an appearance as the taxpayer's representative only before the Examination Division of the IRS. A return preparer may not represent a taxpayer before any other Internal Revenue Service division, including the Appeals and Collection Divisions [IRS Publication 947]. In addition, the following actions are outside the authority of an unenrolled preparer [Rev. Proc. 81-38, 1981-1 C.B. 386].

1. Executing a claim for refund for the taxpayer

2. Receiving checks in payment of any refund of taxes, penalties, or interest for the taxpayer

3. Agreeing to later assessment or collection of taxes than is provided for by the applicable statute of limitations

4. Executing closing agreements with respect to tax liability or other specific matters for the taxpayer

5. Executing waivers of restriction on assessment or collection of a tax deficiency

Conduct before the IRS

Subpart B of *Circular 230* provides the rules of conduct for those individuals authorized to practice before the Internal Revenue Service. Attorneys, CPAs, and Enrolled Agents must observe the following rules of conduct when practicing before the IRS.

1. A tax practitioner must furnish information, on request, to any authorized agent of the Internal Revenue Service, unless the practitioner has reason to believe that the request is of doubtful legality or the information is privileged [§ 10.20(a)].

2. A tax practitioner must provide the Director of Practice of the IRS, on request, any information concerning the violation of any regulation pertaining to practice before the Internal Revenue Service. The tax practitioner must testify in a disbarment or suspension proceeding, unless there is reason to doubt the legality of the request or the information is privileged [§ 10.20(b)].

3. A tax practitioner who knows of client noncompliance, error, or omission with regard to the tax laws must advise the client of that noncompliance, error, or omission [§ 10.21].

4. A tax practitioner must exercise due diligence in preparing tax returns and other documents submitted to the Internal Revenue Service [§ 10.22].

5. Practitioners must not unreasonably delay matters before the Internal Revenue Service [§ 10.23].

6. Practitioners must not accept assistance from or employ a disbarred or suspended person or a former Internal Revenue Service employee disqualified from practice under another rule or U.S. law [§ 10.24].

7. Partners of government employees cannot represent anyone for which the government employee-partner has (or has had) official responsibility [§ 10.25]. For example, a CPA firm with an IRS agent as a partner cannot represent any taxpayer that is (or was in the past) assigned to the IRS agent/partner.

8. No former government employee shall, subsequent to his or her government employment, represent anyone in any matter administered by the Internal Revenue Service if such representation would violate other U.S. laws [§ 10.26].

9. No tax practitioner may act as a notary public for his or her clients [§ 10.27].

10. Fees for tax work must not be contingent or unconscionable [§ 10.28], and a practitioner must not negotiate a taxpayer's refund check [§ 10.31].

11. No tax practitioner can represent conflicting interests before the Internal Revenue Service unless he or she has the express consent of the directly interested parties [§ 10.29].

12. Tax practitioners who issue tax shelter opinion letters must comply with the complex requirements of § 10.33 of *Circular 230*.

Due Diligence

Section 10.22 of *Circular 230* requires tax practitioners to use due diligence in preparing tax returns and in their practice before the IRS. Due diligence is not defined in *Circular 230*. However, the Second Circuit in *Harary v. Blumenthal*, 555 F.2d 1113 (CA-2, 1977), has held that due diligence requires that the tax practitioner be honest with his or her client in connection with all IRS-related matters. In the view of the IRS, the failure to exercise due diligence involves conduct that is more than a simple error, but less than willful and reckless misconduct (*Coursebook Training 994-102*, IRS, December 1992). In determining if a practitioner has exercised due diligence, the IRS uses several factors, including the nature of the error, the explanation of the error, and other standards that apply (for example, the AICPA *Statements on Standards for Tax Services* that are discussed later in this chapter). In essence, due diligence means a tax practitioner should use reasonable effort to comply with the tax laws.

Example 1–1 Judy is a CPA who fails to include rental income on a tax return she completed for a client. The omitted rental income was from a new rental property purchased by the client this year and therefore had not been reported on prior years' tax returns. The taxpayer did not mention the new rental property to Judy in any communications with her. Under these circumstances, Judy has exercised due diligence in preparing the tax return. However, if Judy also kept the rental income records for the new rental property and still omitted the income from the tax return, she would not be exercising due diligence.

Contingent and Unconscionable Fees

Tax practitioners are prohibited from charging **contingent fees** on an original tax return by § 10.28(b) of *Circular 230*. Examples of contingent fees include a fee that is based on a percentage of the refund on a tax return or a fee that is a percentage of tax "saved." Although contingent fees are prohibited for the preparation of an original return, a practitioner may charge a contingent fee for an amended return or a claim for refund (other than a claim for refund made on an original return). The tax practitioner must reasonably anticipate, at the time of the fee arrangement, that the amended return will receive a substantive review by the IRS.

Example 1–2 Oak Corporation has been audited by the IRS for its tax return filed two years ago. The controller of the company completed the original return. The IRS is asserting that Oak underpaid its taxes by $100,000. Oak contacted Joe, a CPA, and engaged him to handle the appeals process with the IRS. In this situation, Joe can use a contingent fee arrangement. (For instance, Joe's fee could be 30 percent of any amount by which he could get the IRS to reduce the assessment.)

Section 10.28(a) also prohibits a tax practitioner from charging an unconscionable fee. This term is not defined in *Circular 230*. If a tax practitioner charges a fee that is out of line with some measure of the value of the service provided to a client, then the fee would be unconscionable. For example, a CPA could not charge a fee of $10,000 to an unsophisticated taxpayer (such as an elderly person) for simple tax work that most CPAs would complete for less than $500.

Solicitation and Advertising

An attorney, CPA, or Enrolled Agent may use public communication to obtain clients under § 10.30 of Subpart B. Types of public communication allowed by this provision include billboards, telephone books, and advertisements in newspapers, on radio, and on television. However, such public communications must not contain false, fraudulent, unduly influencing, coercive, or unfair statements or claims. If done in a dignified manner, examples of items that a practitioner may communicate to the public include (1) his or her name, address, and telephone number, (2) names of individuals associated with the practitioner, (3) a factual description of services offered, (4) credit cards accepted, (5) foreign language ability, (6) membership in professional organizations, (7) professional licenses held, and (8) a statement of practice limitations. Attorneys, CPAs, and Enrolled Agents also must observe any applicable standards of ethical conduct adopted by the American Bar Association (ABA), the American Institute of CPAs (AICPA), and the National Association of Enrolled Agents (NAEA).

Tax Return Positions

Tax practitioners under *Circular 230* must meet certain standards with respect to advice given to clients on tax return positions. Under § 10.34, a practitioner must not sign a tax return if he or she determines that the return contains a position that does not have a **realistic possibility** of being sustained on its merits if challenged by the Internal Revenue Service. The realistic possibility standard is met if analysis of the tax return position by a reasonable and well-informed person knowledgeable in the tax law(s) would lead such person to conclude that the position has approximately a one in three (or greater) likelihood of being sustained on its merits [§ 10.34(a)(4)].

A practitioner may recommend a position on a tax return that does not meet the realistic possibility standard if the position is not frivolous and the position is *disclosed* on the tax return. A frivolous position is one that is patently improper under the tax law. When analyzing the merits of a tax return position, the authorities applicable under IRC § 6662 and Reg. § 1.6662 should be used to decide if the realistic possibility standard has been met. See Chapter 13 for further discussion of pertinent restrictions on tax return positions. The complete text of *Circular 230* can be found on the IRS's web site at:

http://www.irs.gov/pub/irs-pdf/pcir230.pdf

Best Practices

In 2004, the IRS modified *Circular 230*'s rules of practice. The purpose of the changes was to specify the "best practices" standards for tax advisors and firms that provide tax opinions and opinions supporting tax-shelter-type transactions.

According to *Circular 230*, the best practices rules are aspirational. Thus, a practitioner who fails to comply with best practices will not be subject to discipline by the IRS. Still, tax professionals are expected to observe them to preserve public confidence in the tax system.

Best practices to be observed by all tax advisors include:

- Communicating clearly with the client about the terms of the engagement and the form and scope of the advice or assistance to be rendered;
- Establishing the relevant facts, including evaluating the reasonableness of any assumptions or representations;
- Relating applicable law, including potentially applicable judicial doctrines, to the relevant facts;
- Arriving at a conclusion supported by the law and the facts;
- Advising the client regarding the import of the conclusions reached; and
- Acting fairly and with integrity in practice before IRS.

In addition to the best practices standards, *Circular 230* was changed in 2004 to impose strict standards on "covered opinions." This is a new term that includes written advice (including electronic communications) concerning one or more federal tax issue(s) arising from:

- a listed transaction, i.e., a type of tax shelter;
- any plan or arrangement where avoidance or evasion of any tax is a principal purpose; or,

- any plan or arrangement where avoidance or evasion of tax is a significant purpose, if the written advice is: a reliance opinion; a marketed opinion; subject to conditions of confidentiality; or subject to contractual protection.

These changes indicate that the IRS expected a higher level of quality in the tax practice from attorneys, CPAs, and Enrolled Agents starting in 2005.

AICPA CODE OF PROFESSIONAL CONDUCT

Members of the American Institute of Certified Public Accountants (AICPA) are subject to the Institute's *Code of Professional Conduct*. The Code is relevant to all of the professional services performed by CPAs, including those services provided in the practice of public accounting, private industry, government, or education. It was previously referred to as the AICPA *Code of Ethics*. Changes adopted in 1988 were believed necessary to reflect the significant changes in the profession and the environment in which CPAs practice, although the basic tenets of ethical and professional conduct remained the same. One of the most significant changes was the expansion of the rules to apply to all members in all fields of practice, except where the wording of the rule limits the application to a specified field of practice. Under the prior *Code of Ethics,* only members engaged in the practice of public accounting were required to observe all of the rules. Other members, such as those in the fields of education, government, and industry, were subject only to the rules requiring integrity and objectivity and the rule prohibiting members from performing acts discreditable to the profession.

In addition, the rule prohibiting a CPA in public practice from engaging in a business or an occupation concurrently with the practice of public accounting, which would create a conflict of interest in rendering professional services, was deleted from the *Code of Professional Conduct.* The members of the Institute felt that such conflicts of interest are effectively prohibited under new Rule 102, Integrity and Objectivity.

The *Code of Professional Conduct* was designed to provide its members with the following.

1. A comprehensive code of ethical and professional conduct
2. A guide for all members in answering complex questions
3. Assurance to the public concerning the obligations and responsibilities of the accounting profession

The AICPA *Code of Professional Conduct* consists of two integral sections: the principles and the rules. The principles provide a foundation on which the rules are based. The principles suggest that a CPA should strive for behavior above the minimal level of acceptable conduct required by law and regulations. In addition to expressing the basic tenets of ethical and professional conduct, the principles are intended to provide a framework for the certified public accountant's responsibilities to the public, clients, and colleagues. Included are guidelines concerning the member's responsibility to perform professional services with integrity, objectivity, and independence.

The rules consist of a set of enforceable ethical standards that have been approved by a majority of the members of the AICPA. These rules are broad in nature and apply to all of the professional services that a CPA performs, whether in the practice of public accounting or in the fields of education, industry, or government. The only exceptions to the rules occur when their wording indicates that their application is limited to a specified field of practice only, or with respect to certain activities of those who are practicing in another country. In the latter case, however, the CPA must adhere to the ethical standards of the foreign country.

Any failure to follow the rules under the *Code of Professional Conduct* may result in the offender receiving admonishment, suspension, or expulsion from membership in the AICPA. The rules apply not only to the CPA, but also to those employees who are under his or her supervision, partners or shareholders in the practice of the CPA, and any others who act on the CPA's behalf (even if they are not compensated for their activities). As previously discussed, the *Code of Professional Conduct* is applicable to all of the professional services performed by a CPA, including services rendered in the fields of public accounting, such as tax and management advisory services, education, industry, and government.

In addition to the principles and rules, the *Code of Professional Conduct* provides for three additional promulgations. These are interpretations of rules, ethics rulings, and "ethics features." *Interpretations of Rules* are issued by the Division of Professional Ethics of the AICPA. They provide additional detailed guidelines for the scope and application of the rules. These guidelines are enforceable, and the CPA must be prepared to justify any departure from them.

The Division of Professional Ethics of the AICPA also issues *ethics rulings* to further explain the application and interpretation of the rules of conduct and to provide interpretations of the rules in specific circumstances. A member who, in similar circumstances, departs from the findings of these ethics rulings must be prepared to justify such departure. In addition, the Division of Professional Ethics publishes a column in the *Journal of Accountancy* dealing with issues of professional ethics. These informal articles are intended to address issues raised in questions submitted by members of the AICPA. The questions and answers contained in the articles are not considered formal rulings by the AICPA.

Rule 101: Independence

Under Rule 101, a CPA (or CPA firm) in public practice must be independent of the enterprise for which professional services are being provided. **Independence** is required not only for opinions on financial statements, but also for certain other reports and services where a body of the AICPA has promulgated standards requiring independence. A CPA is not independent if one or more financial relationships exist with a client during the period of professional engagement or at the issuing of the opinion. Thus, independence is impaired if a CPA:

1. has any direct or material indirect financial interest in the client's enterprise;

2. has any jointly held material investment with the client or with its officers, directors, or principal stockholders;

3. has any loan to or from the client, an officer of the client, or any principal stockholder of the client, except for loans, such as home mortgages, that were obtained under normal lending procedures;

4. is an officer, director, employee, or underwriter of the client during the period that is covered by the financial statements, during the period of the professional engagement, or at the time of expressing an opinion; or

5. is related as a trustee, executor, or administrator of any estate that holds a direct or material indirect financial interest in the client.

These independence standards also apply to a CPA who is restricted to doing tax work in a partnership with other CPAs who are examining related financial statements. For instance, a tax partner in a CPA firm should not own stock in a client whose financial statements are audited by her partners in the firm, even though she may have nothing to do with the audit of that client's statements.

Rule 102: Integrity and Objectivity

All professional services by a CPA should be rendered with objectivity and integrity, avoiding any conflict of interest. A CPA should not knowingly misrepresent facts or subordinate his or her judgment to that of others in rendering any professional services. For example, in a tax practice, the CPA may be requested to follow blindly the guidelines of a government agency or the demands of an audit client. Rule 102 prohibits such blind obedience. Prior to the most recent revision of Rule 102, a CPA in tax practice could resolve doubt in favor of the client. This phrase was omitted in the revised language because resolving doubt in favor of a client in an advocacy engagement is not considered as impairing integrity or objectivity and thus need not be specifically "allowed."

Rule 201: General Standards

The CPA must comply with the following general standards, as well as any interpretations of such standards, of the AICPA *Code of Professional Conduct*.

1. The CPA must be able to complete all professional services with professional competence.

2. The CPA must exercise due professional care in the performance of all professional services.

3. The CPA shall adequately plan and supervise the performance of all professional services.

4. The CPA must obtain sufficient relevant data to afford a reasonable basis for any conclusion or recommendation in connection with the performance of any professional services.

The standard requiring "professional competence" recognizes the need for members of the profession to commit to a program of professional development, learning, and improvement. Such a program of professional continuing education is also recognized in the standard of "due professional care."

Rule 202: Compliance with Standards

A CPA, whether providing tax, management advisory, audit, review, compilation, or other professional services, must comply with all standards promulgated by bodies designated by the AICPA Council.

Rule 203: Accounting Principles

A CPA is prohibited from expressing an opinion that financial data of an entity conform with Generally Accepted Accounting Principles if those statements or other financial data contain any material departure from the profession's technical standards. In some cases where a departure is present but the financial statement or other financial data would have been misleading without that departure, a member may be able to comply with this rule by describing the departure, the effect of the departure, and the justification for it.

Rule 301: Confidential Client Information

A CPA in the practice of public accounting must not disclose confidential client data without the specific consent of the client. Rule 301 does not, however, apply:

1. If there is a conflict with Rules 202 (Compliance with Standards) and 203 (Accounting Principles) as set forth by the AICPA *Code of Professional Conduct;*

2. If the CPA is served with an enforceable subpoena or summons, or must comply with applicable laws and government regulations;

3. If there is a review of a CPA's practice under AICPA or state society authorization; or

4. If the CPA is responding to an inquiry of an investigative or disciplinary body of a recognized society, or where the CPA is initiating a complaint with a disciplinary body.

In connection with this rule, members of the investigative bodies who may be exposed to confidential client information are precluded from disclosing such information.

SPOTLIGHT ON TAXATION: Confidentiality

A Texas District Court held that the identities of taxpayers who hired the accounting firm of KPMG to participate in a tax shelter later identified as potentially abusive by the IRS were not protected from disclosure under the § 7525 confidentiality privilege for communications between taxpayers and federally authorized tax practitioners. Disclosing taxpayers' identities to the IRS would only reveal their participation in these shelters, and it would not reveal any confidential communications made regarding these tax shelters. *John Doe 1 and John Doe 2 v. KPMG*, 93 AFTR 2d 2004-1759 (DC N. Tex.).

Rule 302: Contingent Fees

A CPA in public practice cannot charge or receive a contingent fee for any professional services from a client for whom the CPA or the CPA's firm performs audit, review, or compilation work. For example, a fee schedule of $5,000 for a qualified audit opinion and $35,000 for an unqualified opinion would not be allowed. Rule 302 also prohibits a CPA from preparing an original or amended tax return, or claim for a tax refund for a contingent fee.

A contingent fee is defined here as a fee established for the performance of any service pursuant to an arrangement in which no fee will be charged unless a specified finding or result is attained, or in which the amount of the fee is otherwise dependent on the finding or result of such service. Solely for purposes of this rule, fees are not regarded as being contingent if fixed by courts or other public authorities, or, in tax matters, if determined based on the results of judicial proceedings or the findings of governmental agencies.

Rule 501: Acts Discreditable

A CPA must not commit an act that is discreditable to the profession. This rule is not specific as to what constitutes a discreditable act; however, violations have been found when the CPA committed a felony, failed to return client records after a client requested them, signed a false tax return, or issued a misleading audit opinion.

Rule 502: Advertising and Other Forms of Solicitation

A CPA in public practice cannot seek clients through false, misleading, or deceptive advertising or other forms of solicitation. In addition, solicitation by the use of coercion, overreaching, or harassing conduct is not allowed. The Institute has placed no restrictions as to the type, media, or frequency of a CPA's advertisements, or on the artwork that is associated with them. Under Rule 502, an activity would be prohibited:

1. If it created false or unjustified expectations of favorable results;
2. If it implied the ability to influence any court, tribunal, regulatory agency, or similar body or official;
3. If it contains a representation that specific professional services in current or future periods will be performed for a stated fee, estimated fee, or fee range when it was likely, at the time of the representation, that such fees would be substantially increased and the prospective client was not advised of that likelihood; or
4. If it contains any other representations that would be likely to cause a reasonable person to misunderstand or be deceived.

For example, a radio spot that states a CPA firm "can beat the IRS every time" would be in violation of Rule 502.

Rule 503: Commissions and Referral Fees

A CPA in public practice cannot charge or receive a commission or referral fee from a client for whom the CPA or the CPA's firm performs audit, review, or compilation work. Thus, under Rule 503, a CPA who does only tax or other nonaudit work for a client may accept or pay a commission. The CPA must, however, disclose the commission to the client or other party in the transaction. In addition, a member who accepts or pays a referral fee for recommending or referring any service of a CPA must disclose that fact.

Rule 505: Form of Organization and Name

CPAs may practice public accounting only in the form of organization permitted by state law or regulation whose characteristics conform to resolutions of the AICPA Council. Under Rule 505, a CPA cannot practice under a firm name that is misleading. The names of one or more past owners may be included in the firm name of a successor organization. In addition, all partners or members of a firm must be members of the AICPA if a firm is to designate itself as "Members of the AICPA."

STATEMENTS ON STANDARDS FOR TAX SERVICES

To assist CPAs, the AICPA has issued a series of statements as to what constitutes appropriate standards for tax practice. These *Statements on Standards for Tax Services* (SSTS) delineate a CPA's responsibilities to his or her clients, the public, the government, and the profession. In August 2000, the SSTS replaced a set of prior statements called the *Statements on Responsibilities in Tax Practice* (STRP). Unlike the STRP, which was advisory in nature, the SSTS is a set of enforceable standards. They are intended to specifically address the problems inherent in the tax practitioner's dual role in serving the client and the public. The statements are intended to supplement, rather than replace, the AICPA *Code of Professional Conduct* and *Circular 230*. They are designed to address the development of tax practice as an integral part of a CPA's practice and the changing environment in which tax practitioners must operate, including the rapidly changing tax laws.

SSTS No. 1: Tax Return Positions

In providing professional services that involve tax return positions, a member should have a good-faith belief that a recommended position has a realistic possibility of being sustained if challenged; otherwise, such a position should not be recommended by the member. A member may reach a conclusion that a position is warranted based on existing law and regulations, as well as on other sources such as well-reasoned articles by tax specialists, treatises, IRS General Counsel Memoranda and written determinations, and explanations of revenue acts as prepared by the Joint Committee on Taxation. The tax professional should be aware that in this statement the members of the AICPA have adopted a standard that is similar to the substantial authority standard of IRC § 6662; however, the statement specifically states that the member may reach a conclusion based on authority as specified in the statement without regard to whether such sources are treated as "authority" under IRC § 6662. Thus, a member who is in compliance with SSTS No. 1 may still lack substantial authority for taking a position under § 6662. In cases where a taxpayer insists on a specific position, a member may sign the return even though the position does not meet the above standard, provided that (1) the position is adequately disclosed on the return by the taxpayer, and (2) the position is not "frivolous." Under no circumstances should a member recommend a tax return position that is exploitative or frivolous.

In cases where the member believes that the taxpayer may have some exposure to a penalty, the statement suggests that the member advise the taxpayer of such risk. Where disclosure of a position on the tax return may mitigate the possibility of a taxpayer penalty under the *Internal Revenue Code*, the member should consider recommending that the taxpayer disclose the position on the return.

SSTS No. 2: Answers to Questions on Returns

Before signing a return as the preparer, a member should make a reasonable effort to obtain from the taxpayer appropriate answers to all questions on the taxpayer's tax return. Where the taxpayer leaves a question on the return unanswered and reasonable grounds exist for not answering the question, the member need not provide an explanation for the omission. The possibility that an answer to a question may prove disadvantageous to the taxpayer, however, does not justify omitting the answer.

Reasonable grounds may exist for omitting an answer to a question on a return. For example, such an omission is acceptable where:

1. the pertinent data are not readily available and are not significant to the determination of taxable income (or loss) or the tax liability;
2. the taxpayer and member are genuinely uncertain as to the meaning of the question on the return; or
3. an answer to a question is voluminous (however, assurance should be given on the return that the data can be supplied upon examination).

In relying for reasonable grounds on the fact that an answer is voluminous, the taxpayer and member should be aware of a relevant IRS district newsletter, which states that a notation on Form 1120 and related schedules that information will be provided on request is not considered acceptable (*IRS Brooklyn District Newsletter* No. 47, 10/89).

SSTS No. 3: Certain Procedural Aspects of Preparing Returns

In preparing or signing a return, the member ordinarily may rely without verification on information that the taxpayer or a third party has provided, unless such information appears to be incorrect, incomplete, or inconsistent. A more formal audit-like review of documents or supporting evidence is generally not required for a member to sign the tax return. Where material provided by the taxpayer appears to be incorrect or incomplete, however, the member should obtain additional information from the taxpayer. In situations where the statutes require that specific conditions be met, the member should determine, by inquiry, whether the conditions have been met. For example, the Code and Regulations impose substantiation requirements for the deduction of certain expenditures. In such a case, the member has an obligation to make appropriate inquiries.

Although members are not required to examine supporting documents, they should encourage the taxpayer to provide such documents when deemed appropriate; for example, in the case of deductions or income from a pass-through entity, such as a partnership.

The member should make proper use of the prior year's tax return when feasible to gather information about the taxpayer and to help avoid omissions and errors with respect to income, deductions, and credit computations.

SSTS No. 4: Use of Estimates

A member may prepare tax returns that involve the use of the taxpayer's estimates if it is impractical to obtain exact data and if the estimated amounts appear reasonable to the member. In all cases, the estimated information must be supplied by the taxpayer; however, the member may provide advice in connection with the estimate. When the taxpayer's estimates are used, they should be presented in such a manner as to avoid the implication of greater accuracy than exists. Situations where the use of estimates may be appropriate include cases where the keeping of precise records for numerous items of small amounts is difficult to achieve, where data are not available at the time of filing the tax return, or when certain records are missing.

The use of estimates in making pertinent accounting judgments where such use is not in conflict with the *Internal Revenue Code* is not prohibited under this statement; such judgments are acceptable and expected. For example, the income tax Regulations permit the use of a reasonable estimate for accruals if exact amounts are not known.

Although in most cases the use of estimates does not necessitate that the item be specifically disclosed on the taxpayer's return, disclosure should be made where failure to do so would result in misleading the IRS about the accuracy of the return. For example, disclosure may be necessary where the taxpayer's records have been destroyed in a fire or where the taxpayer has not received a Schedule K-1 from a pass-through entity at the time the return is filed. Tax practitioners should make their taxpayers aware that the tax law does not allow estimates of certain income and expenditure items, and that more restrictive substantiation requirements apply in cases of certain expenditures, such as travel and entertainment expenses.

SSTS No. 5: Departure from a Position Previously Concluded in an Administrative Proceeding or Court Decision

The recommendation by a member as to the treatment of an item on a tax return should be based on the facts and the law as they are evaluated at the time during which the return is prepared or signed by the member. Unless the taxpayer is bound by the IRS to the treatment of an item in later years, such as by a closing agreement, the disposition of an item in a prior year's audit, or as part of a prior year's court decision, the member is not prevented from recommending a different treatment of a similar item in a later year's return. Thus, a member may sign a return that contains a departure from a treatment required by the IRS in a prior year, provided that the member adheres to the standards in SSTS No. 1.

In most cases, a member's recommendation as to the treatment of an item on a tax return will be consistent with the treatment of a similar item consented to in a prior year's **administrative proceeding** or as a result of the prior year's court decision. In deciding whether a recommendation contrary to the prior treatment is warranted, the member should consider the following.

1. Neither the IRS nor the taxpayer is bound to act consistently with respect to the treatment of an item in a prior proceeding; however, the IRS tends to act consistently in similar situations.

2. The standards under SSTS No. 1, Tax Return Positions, must be followed. In determining whether such standards can be met, the member must consider the existence of an unfavorable court decision and the taxpayer's consent in an earlier administrative proceeding.

3. In some cases, the taxpayer's consent to the treatment of an item in a prior administrative or judicial proceeding may have been due to a desire to settle the issue or a lack of supporting data, whereas in the current year these factors no longer exist.

4. The tax climate may have changed for a given issue since the prior court decision was reached or the prior administrative hearing concluded.

SSTS No. 6: Knowledge of Error: Return Preparation

The member must advise the taxpayer promptly, regardless of whether the member prepared or signed the return in question, when he or she learns of an error in a previously filed tax return or becomes aware that a required return was not filed. Such advice should include a recommendation for appropriate measures the taxpayer should take. However, the member is neither obligated to inform the IRS of the situation, nor may he or she do so without the taxpayer's permission, except as provided by law.

If the member is requested to prepare the current year's return, and the taxpayer has not taken action to correct an error in a prior year's return, the member should consider whether to proceed with the preparation of the current year's return. If the current year's return is prepared, the member should take reasonable steps to ensure that the error is not repeated.

A member may advise a taxpayer, either orally or in writing, as to the correction of errors in the prior year's return. In a case where there is a possibility that the taxpayer may be charged with fraud, the taxpayer should be referred to an attorney. If a member discovers the error during an audit or other nontax engagement, he or she should refer the taxpayer to the tax return preparer. If the item in question has an insignificant effect on the taxpayer's tax liability, the item should not be considered an "error" under this statement. In addition, the term "error" does not include a situation where the taxpayer's position satisfied the standards under SSTS No. 1 at the time the return was filed.

SSTS No. 7: Knowledge of Error: Administrative Proceedings

When a member represents a taxpayer in an administrative proceeding (such as an audit), and the member is aware of an error other than one that has an insignificant effect on the taxpayer's tax liability, the member should request the taxpayer's agreement to disclose the error to the IRS. Lacking such an agreement with the taxpayer, the member may be under a duty to withdraw from the engagement and may consider terminating the professional relationship with the taxpayer. Disclosure, once agreed on, should be made in a timely manner to avoid misleading the IRS.

SSTS No. 8: Form and Content of Advice to Taxpayers

In providing tax advice to taxpayers, the member must use judgment that reflects professional competence and serves the taxpayer's needs. The member must assume that any advice given will be used to determine the manner of reporting items on the taxpayer's tax return; therefore, the member should ensure that the standards under SSTS No. 1 are satisfied. When providing advice that will be relied on by third parties, the member's responsibilities may differ. Neither a standard format nor guidelines have been issued or established that would cover all situations and circumstances involving written or oral advice from a member. When giving such advice to taxpayers, in addition to exercising professional judgment, the member should consider each of the following.

1. The importance of the transaction and the amounts involved
2. The specific or general nature of the taxpayer's inquiry
3. The time available to develop and submit the advice
4. The technical complications that are presented
5. The existence of authority and precedents
6. The tax sophistication of the taxpayer
7. The possibility of seeking legal advice

Written communication is recommended in important, unusual, or complicated transactions, while oral advice is acceptable in more typical situations. In the communication, the member should advise the taxpayer that the advice reflects his or her professional judgment based on the current situation and that subsequent developments may affect previous advice, such as stating that the position of authorities is subject to change (see Chapter 10).

When subsequent developments affect the advice that a member has previously communicated to a taxpayer, the member is under no obligation to initiate further communication of such developments to the taxpayer unless a specific agreement has been reached with the taxpayer, or the member is assisting in the application of a procedure or plan relative to such advice.

Exhibit 1–4 summarizes the main topic of each of the AICPA *Statements on Standards for Tax Services*. The complete text of the SSTS can be found on the AICPA web site at:

http://www.aicpa.org/download/tax/SSTSfinal.pdf

Exhibit	1–4
Summary of AICPA Statements on Standards for Tax Service	

Statement	Summary of Contents
1	Specifies the standards for professional services that involve tax positions
2	Explains how a member should handle answering questions on a tax return
3	Describes the procedural aspects of preparing a tax return
4	Defines when a member can use an estimate in preparing a tax return
5	Explains what a member should do about items on a current return when similar items were audited on a prior year's return or were the subject of a judicial hearing
6	States what a member should do upon learning about an error in a prior year's tax return
7	Gives the procedure to follow if an error is discovered during an audit
8	Establishes standards for the giving of tax advice to taxpayers

SARBANES-OXLEY AND TAXATION

In 2002, Congress passed the Sarbanes-Oxley Act, which addressed the corporate management abuses that took place during the 1990s and early 2000s in publicly traded American corporations. These corporate governance breakdowns culminated in spectacular business failures such as with Enron, World-Com, Global Crossing, Waste-Management, Sunbeam, and others, and lead to the eventual failure of the Big Five CPA firm of Arthur Andersen.

The Sarbanes-Oxley Act made it "unlawful" for an auditor to provide any of the non-audit services listed in the Act. In addition, the Act provided that a registered public accounting firm "may engage in any non-audit service, including tax services, that is not described [in the list of nine specifically prohibited services] for an audit client only if the activity is *approved in advance* by the audit committee of the issuer" in accordance with the Act. The prohibited services are:

1. Bookkeeping or other services related to the accounting records or financial statements of the audit client

2. Financial information systems design and implementation

3. Appraisal or valuation services, fairness opinions, or contribution-in-kind reports

4. Actuarial services

5. Internal audit outsourcing services

6. Management functions or human resources

7. Broker or dealer, investment adviser, or investment banking services

8. Legal services and expert services unrelated to the audit

9. Any other service that the Public Company Accounting Oversight Board determines, by regulation, is impermissible

It should be noted that tax compliance work is not one of the prohibited services. However, tax work is subject to the pre-approval process. The requirement to pre-approve non-audit services says the audit committee simply needs to know about services in order to pre-approve them. However, since the passage of the Sarbanes-Oxley Act, many company managers take work to other CPA firms rather than seek approval of the audit committee. For example, a CFO or tax director may want to use the auditor for tax services, but instead will choose another firm rather than seek audit committee approval. As a result, many companies divide their audit and tax work between different firms. This appears to be an unintended result of the Sarbanes-Oxley Act.

Investors, on the other hand, would probably prefer that the audit committee be aware of everything that is going on within a company and actually pre-approve the work instead of having the work go elsewhere. Currently, the audit committee may not even be aware if someone other than the auditor is being used for non-audit work. Instead, decision-making remains hidden from audit committee review. Tax practitioners will have to wait to see how this contradiction plays out. Perhaps audit committees will get more comfortable with their Sarbanes-Oxley responsibilities and this division of traditional audit and tax work may decline in future years.

In addition to being a response to corporate governance and accounting transparency failures, the Sarbanes-Oxley Act is a response to the general failure of business ethics. For example, the proliferation of abusive tax shelters and super aggressive tax avoidance strategies (which are discussed shortly) are examples of other business ethical problems.

ABA MODEL CODE OF PROFESSIONAL RESPONSIBILITY

In 1969, the American Bar Association (ABA) adopted a revised set of guidelines for professional conduct, the *Model Code of Professional Responsibility.* The Code includes nine *canons,* which may be thought of as statements of principles. Canon 6, for instance, requires an attorney to represent a taxpayer competently. Each canon is followed by a series of *ethical considerations* (ECs), which in turn are supported by *disciplinary rules* (DRs). The ethical considerations are aspirational in character, setting forth objectives toward which all attorneys are to strive. The disciplinary rules set forth minimum standards of conduct. Any failure to abide by the disciplinary rules may subject the attorney to disciplinary procedures and punishment.

In nearly all jurisdictions, the ABA Model Code was adopted by the appropriate policy agency, although sometimes modifications were made. In August 1983, the ABA adopted the *Model Rules of Professional Conduct,* which, in a majority of the states, have substantially replaced the Model Code as the guide for attorney professional conduct.

The ABA has a Standing Committee on Ethics and Professional Responsibility that answers questions concerning ethics and professional conduct. Requests for opinions from the committee should be directed to the American Bar Association Center for Professional Responsibility in Chicago.

Neither the ABA Model Code nor the Model Rules have the force of law. Each was designed to be adopted by the appropriate agencies that govern the practice of law in the states. In many jurisdictions, the state supreme court is charged with policing the practice of law; in other states, the legislature bears this responsibility. Attorneys should consult their own jurisdiction's ethical guidelines to determine whether the provisions of the ABA Model Code or the Model Rules, or some modification of these doctrines, have been adopted.

The American Bar Association has not amended the Model Rules in more than twenty years. A commission called "Ethics 2000" has been established by the ABA to review the rules and to propose any needed adjustments. The specific charge of the Ethics 2000 Committee is to (1) conduct a comprehensive study and evaluate the ethical and professionalism precepts of the legal profession; (2) examine and evaluate the ABA *Model Rules of Professional Conduct* and the rules governing professional conduct in state and federal jurisdictions; (3) conduct original research, surveys, and hearings; and (4) formulate recommendations for action. The report of the Ethics 2000 Committee was released in November 2000. The current status of the ABA Model Rules and the Ethics 2000 Committee report can be found on the ABA web site at:

http://www.abanet.org/cpr/mrpc/mrpc_toc.html

NONREGULATORY ETHICS

There is substantially more to ethical behavior than just following the rules of ethics or conduct of professional organizations such as the AICPA or the ABA. Professional ethical behavior is the result of the interaction of personal morality, social responsibility, business ethics, and other general **ethical standards.** Exhibit 1–5 illustrates these ethical standards and shows possible business and accounting areas that could be impacted by ethical failures.

MORALITY

The subject of morality fills tens of thousands of books. Publications as diverse as the Bible and popular novels examine morality in one way or another. When something is judged to be morally right or wrong (or good or bad), the underlying standards on which such judgments are based are called moral standards.

According to some people's moral standards, cheating "just a little" in computing a tax liability is morally acceptable. Most people in the United States believe that everyone cheats a little on their taxes. Cheating significantly may be viewed differently, but where is the dividing line between morally "okay" tax cheating and morally wrong tax evasion? Under the self-assessed tax

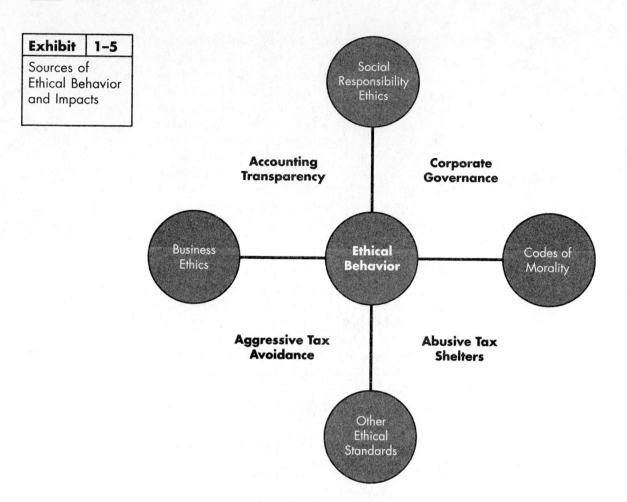

Exhibit | **1-5**

Sources of
Ethical Behavior
and Impacts

system in the United States, different moral standards provide different answers—from complete honesty to various degrees of dishonesty. The tax practitioner must be ready to work with clients holding various systems of morality and to accept the consequences of the moral choices made, including the possibility of losing a client, paying fines and penalties to the IRS, or even going to jail.

SOCIAL RESPONSIBILITY

The tax practitioner must be aware of social responsibility in areas such as environmental protection, equal opportunity, and occupational safety. Since World War II, society has held the business world increasingly responsible for meeting certain noneconomic standards. In 1970, Milton Friedman, the Nobel Prize-winning economist, said that the "social responsibility" of business is merely to increase profits. But the prevailing sentiment today is that business and the professions should return something to society to make it better, not just to make a profit. For the tax practitioner, this could mean going beyond the minimum legal responsibility to provide equal opportunity in the hiring of employees by making special recruitment efforts, or it could mean volunteering time to help charitable organizations with their tax problems.

BUSINESS ETHICS

In recent years, one of the major topics in the business world has been the question of business ethics. Many people believe that ethics has application only in one's personal life, not in the business or professional arena. Like Milton Friedman, they think the business of business is to make a profit. This view is popular because (1) people who work in business or professions must concern themselves with producing goods and services to earn a profit, and (2) it is easier to measure profit than to make value judgments. People are more comfortable discussing problems in terms of profits, rather than in terms of the ethical impact of the entity and its actions. Few business and professional people are trained in ethical analysis, and, therefore, they usually are not familiar with how to evaluate a problem in terms of ethics.

Example 1–3 Bruce owns a successful small business. The business is operated as a corporation. During the year, Bruce makes numerous personal long distance phone calls from the office, uses the company credit card to purchase gas for his family's personal automobiles, sends personal items using the company's FedEx account, and is reimbursed by the company for meals and entertainment expenditures that are primarily personal in nature. These items are deducted by the corporation on its tax return. Would you sign this company's Form 1120 as the tax return preparer? If you also audited this company, what would you do about these transactions?

That business and professional organizations have ethical responsibilities is readily apparent to anyone who reads the popular press. The lawsuits brought on by the savings and loan failures of the late 1980s and against the large international accounting firms in the last two decades are prime examples of society holding business to a standard of ethical conduct. Most of the big CPA firms have settled lawsuits (both in and out of court) against them for millions of dollars for what was, in part, a business ethics failure.

TAX PLANNING ETHICS

In addition to the previously discussed corporate governance issues addressed in the Sarbanes-Oxley Act, there are many examples of suspect ethics practices in the area of taxation. The following are some "classic" examples of the aggressive tax planning arrangements that have been promoted in recent years by CPAs, lawyers, and others:

Example 1–4 Cerveza Corporation is primarily in the beverage supply business. The taxpayer classified itself as a security dealer and then marks down (and claims a tax deduction) its accounts receivable based on the contention that they are not marketable and some of the accounts will not be paid. This practice was prohibited by Congress in 1998.

Example 1–5 Sneaky Inc., a United States-based corporation, pays $600,000 to buy an expiring foreign copyright that has one royalty payment left. The last payment is for $800,000, less $240,000 of foreign tax credit (30 percent of $800,000). On this deal the buyer has lost $40,000 ($600,000 payment less $560,000 net final royalty), but has purchased a $240,000 foreign tax credit that can be used to offset $240,000 of tax on Sneaky's other foreign income.

Example 1–6 Cheater Corporation borrowed $300,000 and used the proceeds to purchase a $2,000,000 single premium life insurance policy. The policy is a universal life insurance policy. Like many life insurance policies, this policy pays interest that is tax-free on the cash value of the policy. As a result of this transaction, the corporation receives an interest deduction for the loan and earns tax-free interest on the policy. This type of transaction was stopped by Congress in 1996.

For an expanded discussion of tax planning abuse during this period see, "Tax Shelter Hustlers," *Forbes* (December 14, 1998), p. 198.

SPOTLIGHT ON TAXATION: Ethics

The taxing authorities of the state of Georgia (along with several other states) post the names of delinquent taxpayers on their web site (**http://www.gatax.org**). The stated purpose of the postings is to "shame" the taxpayers who have not paid their Georgia state taxes into paying them. Although this posting clearly is legal, is it ethical? For example, suppose a family has a child with leukemia and has horrendous medical bills and simply cannot afford to pay their taxes. Should they be held up to ridicule because they are doing the right thing and taking care of their child, even if it prevents them from paying their taxes?

OTHER ETHICAL STANDARDS

The study of nonregulatory ethics could be expanded to cover such other issues as public policy, religious beliefs, and cultural values, issues that are beyond the scope of this text. Most of such topics would be addressed in a university course on ethics or business ethics. A tax practitioner can expand his or her understanding of the application of ethics to accounting and business situations by referring to the books on the following reading list:

- Armstrong, Mary Beth, *Ethics and Professionalism for CPAs* (Cincinnati: South-Western Publishing Co., 1993).
- Brooks, Leonard J., *Business and Professional Ethics for Directors, Executives, and Accountants* (Mason: South Western Business & Professional Publishing, 2004).
- Buchholz, Rogene, *Fundamental Concepts and Problems in Business Ethics* (Englewood Cliffs, NJ: Prentice Hall, 1989).

- Collins, Denis, and Thomas O'Rourke, *Ethical Dilemmas in Accounting* (Cincinnati: South-Western Publishing Co., 1994).
- Donaldson, Thomas, *Corporations and Morality* (Englewood Cliffs, NJ: Prentice Hall, 1983).
- Velasquez, Manuel, *Business Ethics: Concepts and Cases,* 5th ed. (Englewood Cliffs, NJ: Prentice Hall, 2002).

The following are examples of nonregulatory ethics dilemmas that could arise in a business, accounting, or tax setting:

Example 1–7 Hilary is a CPA who is a sole practitioner. This year, one of her clients, Gold Corporation, opened a new division in Europe. Gold is a long-time client of Hilary's, and she is anxious to keep it. However, Hilary has no experience in international tax and would not be able to give Gold the kind of tax advice needed for the new division. The ethical question is whether Hilary should inform the client of her lack of knowledge in this area and risk losing the client, or whether she should remain silent and "wing it" on the international tax issues. What should Hilary do in this situation?

Example 1–8 Patrick is a CPA who is a partner in a successful local CPA practice. The state in which Patrick lives has a forty-hour annual continuing professional education (CPE) requirement. If the CPE requirement is not met, a CPA will have his or her license suspended and will not be able to practice. Patrick is approached by the Flight-by-Night CPE Company about signing up for some of their CPE courses. The company representative tells Patrick that they will report that Patrick attended the courses so that he gets the CPE credit, even if he does not attend. Because Patrick is overloaded with work, he considers this a "low hassle" way to get his CPA license renewed. Would it be ethical for Patrick to obtain his CPE credit this way?

Example 1–9 Devona is an auditor in the Boston office of a large international CPA firm. She is sent on an inventory observation for a new client of the Houston office of the firm. The Houston office gives her a six-hour budget for the job. When she arrives at the client's office, Devona discovers that the Houston office has substantially underestimated the size of inventory to be counted. The client has a $20,000,000 inventory comprised of more than 6,000 different items. The client plans to take twenty hours to complete the count. Devona is up for promotion, and she does not want to have a negative personnel review because she overran the budget on this job. Therefore, she considers spending the budgeted six hours on the observation and signing off in the audit work papers that she completely observed the inventory. Devona thinks this would be OK since she perceives there is only a small risk of a material misstatement of the inventory. Would it be ethical for Devona to do this?

Example 1–10 Last year, one of Andy's clients, Trout Corporation, had a significant tax problem. Andy needed thirty-five hours of research time to arrive at an answer to Trout's problem. This year, another of Andy's clients, Bass Corporation, had the same problem. Because of his experience with Trout, Andy could solve Bass's tax problem in three hours. The ethical question is whether Andy should bill Bass for three hours or thirty-five hours of professional consulting time. There are two ways to look at this situation. Andy only spent three hours on the job, so he should only bill for three hours of time. Yet, there is "value" in Andy already knowing the approach to take on the Bass matter, so perhaps he should bill for that knowledge and not just for the actual time spent working on the problem. What should Andy do in this situation?

Example 1–11 Betty is negotiating a transaction on behalf of one of her clients, John Carp. During the process, Betty becomes aware that the other party to the transaction does not adequately understand the tax consequences of the proposed transaction, which are highly favorable to Carp. In fact, if the transaction were completed as proposed, the other side would suffer significant negative tax consequences. Ethically, should Betty inform the other party of the potential negative tax consequences of the proposed transaction?

As shown in the preceding examples, the application of ethics to business situations is not clear-cut. In many situations, doing what is right may not be possible. The tax practitioner is constantly faced with challenges on how to apply proper business ethics on a daily basis.

TAX RESEARCH BY CERTIFIED PUBLIC ACCOUNTANTS

Over the years, the tax community has addressed the issue of whether the practice of tax by a CPA or other nonattorney constitutes the **unauthorized practice of law.** The problem stems from the tax law itself, passed in 1913. The provisions of early tax law called for an income tax, but the statute was not specific about the accounting methods to be used in implementing it. In fact, not until 1954 was a formal statutory effort made to address accounting issues in the computation of taxable income. For this reason, many attorneys avoided tax work, allowing CPAs to fill the void and provide taxpayers with most of the professional-quality tax work.

When a CPA resolves an issue in most nonroutine tax situations, he or she is, to some extent, solving a legal problem. The issue is not whether the CPA is rendering legal service but, rather, how much legal service is provided. When does the CPA cross the mythical boundary and begin an unauthorized practice of law? Neither these professions nor the courts have promulgated binding guidelines on this issue. Instead, the Federal agencies seem to have taken the lead in attempting to solve this problem.

HISTORICAL DEVELOPMENTS

Lowell Bar Association v. Loeb, 315 Mass. 176, S2 N.E.2d 27 (1943), addressed the issue of the unauthorized practice of law by nonattorneys engaged in tax practice. The Lowell Massachusetts Bar Association sued Birdie Loeb, a commercial tax preparer, for her preparation of simple wage-earner tax returns. On appeal, the court held that the preparation of "simple" tax returns did not constitute the unauthorized practice of Massachusetts law because tax return preparation could not be identified as strictly within the legal discipline. Tax practice includes interaction among various disciplines, including law, accounting, economics, political science, and others.

Subsequent courts attempted to adopt the *Lowell* "wholly within the field of law" test in other jurisdictions, but they found that defining the boundaries of the legal profession was so difficult and the 1943 opinion was so general and vague that the *Lowell* precedent was of little value in other situations.

Probably the best known case concerning a tax accountant's unauthorized practice of law is *Bercu*, 299 N.Y. 728, 87 N.E.2d 451 (1949). Bercu was an accountant who consulted with a client concerning whether sales taxes that were accrued, but not yet paid, could be deducted on a tax return. The taxpayer who requested this advice was not one of Bercu's regular clients. Bercu advised the client that the sales tax could be deducted when it was paid. Bercu presented a bill to the client and, when it was not paid, sued the client to collect the fees.

Ultimately, the State Court of New York held that it was not proper for Bercu to render services in such a situation. The Court indicated that Bercu could have provided this type of service and answered the sales tax question had it been incidental to the tax return work he regularly performed for his clients.

This "incidental to accounting practice" test became the chief issue in several subsequent cases concerning the unauthorized practice of law. In a Minnesota case, *Gardner v. Conway*, 234 Minn. 468, 48 N.W.2d 788 (1951), a person who was neither an attorney nor a CPA attempted to answer difficult and substantial questions of law. The court held that the practitioner improperly gave advice to the client and rejected the "incidental to practice" test as an approach to providing guidelines for the definition of tax practice.

In a California case, *Agran v. Shapiro*, 127 Cal. App.2d Supp. 807, 273 P.2d 619 (1954), CPA Agran prepared returns, performed research, and represented his clients before the IRS. Agran's preparation of Shapiro's return involved extensive research—including more than 100 court cases, Code sections, and Regulations—concerning a question involving the proper treatment of a net operating loss. Upon completion of the work, the CPA presented his bill and, when he was not paid, sued Shapiro to collect. Agran was found by the court to have engaged in the unauthorized practice of law and, therefore, was unable to collect his fees. In its decision, the California Superior Court relied on *Gardner v. Conway* and rejected the "incidental to practice" test that Agran used in his defense. The Court did not decide, however, whether the authorization to practice before the IRS preempted the right of the state to regulate tax practice.

In *Sperry v. Florida*, 373 U.S. 379, 83 S.Ct. 1322 (1963), the U.S. Supreme Court held that a Federal statute that admitted nonattorneys to practice before Federal agencies (in this case, the Patent Office) took precedence over state regulation. In late 1965, Congress enacted Public Law 89-332, amending prior law and allowing CPAs to practice before the IRS. Although this law added to the force of the *Sperry* decision as it applied to CPAs, *Sperry* still provides for the preemption of Federal regulations and statutes in matters of practice before other Federal agencies.

In 1981, the AICPA and the ABA held a conference for attorneys and CPAs to address some of these definitional questions relative to tax practice and the unauthorized practice of law. The stated purpose of this session was to "promote understanding between the professions in the interests of the client [taxpayers] and the general public." This National Conference of Lawyers and CPAs issued a statement in November 1981, reaffirming that clients [taxpayers] are best served when attorneys and CPAs work together in tax practice. The text of the statement identifies eight areas related to income taxation and three areas related to estate and gift planning in which such professional cooperation should be encouraged. The statement lacks any form of exclusionary language. Indeed, it asserts the following:

> *Frequently, the legal and accounting phases (of tax practice) are so intertwined that they are difficult to distinguish. This is particularly true in the field of income taxation where questions of law and accounting are often inextricably intertwined.*

For a complete discussion of this conference statement, see the *Journal of Accountancy,* August 1982.

CPAs and Other Nonattorneys

Currently, CPAs and other nonattorneys who practice tax law before the IRS are in little danger of entering into the unauthorized practice of law provided they avoid providing general legal services. This can be accomplished if CPAs and other nonattorneys do not themselves engage in the following kinds of general law activities.

- Expressing a legal opinion on any nontax matter
- Drafting wills or trust instruments
- Drafting contracts
- Drafting incorporation papers
- Drafting partnership agreements

Taxpayers can draft any of these documents themselves without the services of an attorney. If a CPA's client wishes to handle personal legal affairs in this manner, the CPA (exercising caution) can render professional advice without running afoul of the case law concerning the unauthorized practice of law.

As long as CPAs and other nonattorneys stay within the practice of tax, and do not cross over into the practice of general law, the control exercised by *Circular 230* and the AICPA code should ensure that virtually all tax compliance, planning, and research activities that are provided by adequately trained nonattorney CPAs constitute the "authorized practice of law."

SUMMARY

In addition to the tax return preparation statutes that are discussed in Chapter 13, CPAs, attorneys, Enrolled Agents, and others who practice before the IRS are faced with various sets of overlapping rules of conduct. *Circular 230* applies to anyone who practices before the IRS. In addition, members of the legal and public accounting professions are subject to codes of ethics and conduct. Similarly, cultural codes of morality and social responsibility form general boundaries relative to acceptable behavior by a taxpayer or tax professional. When engaged in tax practice, one always must be aware of the appropriate rules of conduct and conduct oneself in accordance with those rules.

TAX TUTOR

Reinforce the tax research information covered in this chapter by completing the online tutorials located at the Federal Tax Research web site:

http://raabe.swlearning.com

KEY WORDS

By the time you complete this chapter, you should be comfortable discussing each of the following terms. If you need additional review of any of these items, return to the appropriate material in the chapter or consult the glossary to this text.

Administrative Proceeding	Open Transaction
American Bar Association (ABA)	Practice before the IRS
American Institute of Certified Public Accountants (AICPA)	Realistic Possibility
Circular 230	Tax Avoidance
Closed Transaction	Tax Compliance
Contingent Fees	Tax Evasion
Enrolled Agent	Tax Litigation
Ethical Standards	Tax Planning
Independence	Tax Research
	Unauthorized Practice of Law

DISCUSSION QUESTIONS

1. In a modern, industrial society, the tax system is derived from several disciplines. Identify the disciplines that play this role in the United States. Explain how each of them affects the U.S. tax system.

2. The elements of tax practice fall into what major categories in addition to tax research?

3. What is tax compliance as practiced in the United States? Give several examples of activities that can be classified as tax compliance.

4. Several groups of individuals do most of the tax compliance work in the United States. Identify these groups and describe briefly the kind of work that each group does. In this regard, be sure to define the term "Enrolled Agent."

5. What is tax planning? Explain the difference between tax evasion and tax avoidance, and the role of each in professional tax planning.

6. Tax planning falls into two major categories, the "open" transaction and the "closed" transaction. Discuss each type of transaction, and describe how each affects tax planning.

7. What is tax litigation? What type of tax practitioner typically handles tax litigation on a taxpayer's behalf?

8. In tax litigation, what is usually the role of a Certified Pubic Accountant?

9. Define tax research. Briefly describe the tax research process.

10. Who issues *Circular 230*? Which tax practitioners are regulated by it?

11. CPAs must follow the rules of *Circular 230*. In addition, CPAs in tax practice are subject to two other sets of ethical rules. Give the name and the issuer of both of these sets of rules.

12. The term "practice before the IRS" includes the representation of clients in the United States Tax Court for cases being handled under the "small tax case procedure." True or false? Explain your answer. (IRS adapted)

13. The rules that govern practice before the IRS are found in *Circular 230*. Discuss what entails practice before the IRS, and state which section of *Circular 230* contains the definition.

14. There are two ways to become an Enrolled Agent (EA). Briefly explain what they are and give the Subpart and section references in *Circular 230* where the details of becoming an EA are found.

15. Enrolled Agents (EAs) are subject to Continuing Education (CE) requirements. Briefly describe the CE requirements and give the reference to where the details can be found in *Circular 230*.

16. Leigh, who is not an Enrolled Agent, attorney, or CPA, is employed by Rose, a CPA. One of Rose's clients has been notified that his 2003 income tax return has been selected for audit by the IRS. Rose had prepared the return and signed it as preparer. Rose has been called out of town on a family emergency and would like for Leigh to represent the client. Leigh cannot represent the client even if she has Rose's written authority to do so and has the client's power of attorney. True or false? Explain your answer. (IRS adapted)

17. Regular full-time employees are allowed to represent certain organizations before the Internal Revenue Service without being an attorney, CPA, or Enrolled Agent. Name the organizations that can be represented by full-time employees, and cite where you found that authority in *Circular 230*.

18. Jane's mother is in a nursing home and cannot travel. There is a problem with her mother's last year's tax return, and the IRS needs to discuss the matter with her at the local IRS office. Is it possible for Jane to handle this matter without having to hire professional tax representation? Reference your answer to the appropriate part of *Circular 230*.

19. A practitioner could be suspended from practice before the IRS if the practitioner employs, accepts assistance from, or shares fees with any

person who is under disbarment or suspension from practice before the IRS. True or false? Explain your answer. (IRS adapted)

20. Tax practitioners must not sign a tax return under *Circular 230* if the return takes a position that does not have a "realistic possibility" of being sustained by the Internal Revenue Service.
    a. What is a realistic possibility as defined by the Internal Revenue Service?
    b. Is it possible for a tax practitioner to sign a tax return that takes a position that does not meet the realistic possibility standard? If so, what must be done to allow the tax practitioner to sign the tax return?

21. Under *Circular 230*, may an attorney, CPA, or Enrolled Agent advertise on television? On the Internet? If so, what standards are applied to the advertisements?

22. Can a tax practitioner who is a CPA form a CPA partnership with an IRS agent who is also a CPA? What limits (if any) would be placed on such a partnership?

23. If a tax practitioner finds an error in a prior year's tax return, what action must he or she take (if any) under *Circular 230*? What subpart and section addresses this situation?

24. Practicing CPAs generally are subject to the AICPA *Code of Professional Conduct*. What is its stated purpose?

25. The rules under the AICPA *Code of Professional Conduct* are a group of enforceable ethical standards. Broad in nature, they generally apply to all of the services that are performed by a CPA who is an AICPA member. Identify the two situations in which the application of the rules may be limited.

26. In what situation may a CPA under the AICPA *Code of Professional Conduct* accept a commission?

27. Under Rule 101 (Independence), a CPA (or CPA firm) in public practice must be independent of the enterprise for which professional services are being provided. Discuss situations in which the CPA's independence may be impaired.

28. Under Rule 102 (Integrity and Objectivity), a CPA who is engaged in tax practice may resolve a doubtful area in favor of his or her client. Explain.

29. A CPA must meet certain qualitative standards under Rule 201 (General Standards). Discuss the four general standards of this rule.

30. In each of the following independent situations, state which AICPA *Code of Professional Conduct* (if any) is violated by a CPA in public practice.
    a. The CPA opens a tax practice and names the new firm "Jill's Super Tax."
    b. In return for recommending a certain investment to an *audit* client, a CPA receives a 5 percent commission from the broker who sells the investments.
    c. A taxpayer is being assessed by the IRS for an additional $100,000 of tax. The CPA offers to represent the taxpayer for a fee that is equal

to 25 percent of any amount by which he can get the IRS to reduce its assessment.

d. A CPA places an advertisement in the local newspaper that states that she is the "Best CPA in the Western World." The advertisement further states that, because of her great skill, the CPA has considerable influence with the IRS and the United States Tax Court.

e. A CPA partnership has eight partners, six of whom are members of the AICPA. On its letterhead, the firm designates itself as "Members of the AICPA."

f. A CPA who is not in public practice is convicted of helping to run a large illegal drug operation.

31. Under Rule 301 of the AICPA *Code of Professional Conduct,* a CPA must not disclose confidential client data without the specific consent of the client. Under what conditions might a disclosure of confidential information without the client's consent be appropriate?

32. What are the *Statements on Standards for Tax Services?* Who issues them? Discuss their principal objectives.

33. What guidelines does SSTS No. 1 provide for a tax practitioner regarding tax return positions?

34. According to SSTS No. 2, a tax return should be signed by a member only after reasonable effort has been made to answer all of the questions on the return that apply to the taxpayer. What are some of the reasonable grounds under which a member may sign a return as the preparer even though some of the pertinent questions remain unanswered?

35. What guidelines are provided by SSTS No. 3 as to the reliance by a member on information supplied by the taxpayer for use in preparing the taxpayer's return?

36. A member may use estimates in completing a tax return according to SSTS No. 4. When might the use of estimates be considered appropriate?

37. Last year a taxpayer was audited by the IRS and an item of deduction on the tax return was disallowed. On this year's tax return, the taxpayer would like to deduct a similar item. Discuss the circumstances under which a member may allow the taxpayer to take the deduction on the current year's return and still be in compliance with SSTS No. 5. Under what conditions must special disclosure be made by the member?

38. When a member learns of an error in a previously filed tax return or learns of an error during an audit, how is he or she to respond and still be in compliance with SSTS No. 6 and No. 7?

39. What situations are addressed by SSTS No. 8?

40. The Sarbanes-Oxley Act prohibits CPA firms from providing certain services to publicly traded corporate audit clients. Is doing tax compliance work for an audit client one of the prohibited transactions? If such tax work is allowed, who must approve it?

41. Differentiate between the ABA *Model Code of Professional Responsibility* and that organization's *Model Rules of Professional Conduct.*

42. Who sets ethical rules for attorneys in the various states?

43. How does the term "the unauthorized practice of law" apply to CPAs?

44. List several services or products that a CPA or Enrolled Agent purposely should not make a part of a tax practice, so as to minimize exposure to a charge of the unauthorized practice of law.

EXERCISES

45. Summarize what is discussed in each of the following sections of *Circular 230*.
    a. Subpart A, § 10.4(b)
    b. Subpart B, § 10.21
    c. Subpart B, § 10.26
    d. Subpart B, § 10.32

46. Summarize what is discussed in each of the following sections of *Circular 230*.
    a. Subpart C, § 10.51(b)
    b. Subpart A, § 10.6(e)
    c. Subpart A, § 10.2(e)
    d. Subpart B, § 10.28

47. Summarize what is discussed in each of the following sections of *Circular 230*.
    a. Subpart A, § 10.2(e)
    b. Subpart A, § 10.7(c)(viii)
    c. Subpart B, § 10.24
    d. Subpart B, § 10.34

48. Which subpart and section of *Circular 230* discusses each the following topics?
    a. Solicitation
    b. Negotiation of a taxpayer's refund checks
    c. Depositions
    d. Authority to disbar or suspend from practice before the Internal Revenue Service

49. Which subpart and section of *Circular 230* discusses each the following topics?
    a. Conflicting interests
    b. Tax shelter opinions
    c. Disreputable conduct
    d. Assistance from disbarred or suspended persons

50. Which subpart and section of *Circular 230* discusses each of the following topics?
    a. Practice of law
    b. Information to be furnished
    c. Fees
    d. Who may practice before the IRS?

51. Summarize what is discussed in each of the following rules of the AICPA *Code of Professional Conduct*. Give a simple example of a transaction or an action relevant to each rule.
    a. Article VI, ¶ para 1
    b. Rule 201, ¶ .02 201-1
    c. Rule 502, ¶ .03 502-2
    d. Rule 504, ¶ .01

52. Summarize what is discussed in each of the following *Statements on Standards for Tax Services*.
    a. SSTS No. 1
    b. SSTS No. 4
    c. SSTS No. 6

53. What is the precedent-setting value of each of the following cases?
    a. *Lowell Bar Association v. Loeb*
    b. *Bercu*
    c. *Sperry v. Florida*

54. Ms. E is an Enrolled Agent who prepared the tax returns for Mr. A and Mr. B (buyer and seller, respectively). Ms. E may not, under any circumstances, represent A and B before the IRS with regard to this buy and sell transaction. True or false? Explain your answer. (IRS adapted)

55. A full-time employee of a sole proprietorship may represent his or her employer in an examination by the IRS without being an Enrolled Agent, attorney, or CPA. True or false? Explain your answer. (IRS adapted)

56. An unenrolled tax preparer who has not prepared the tax return of John Gomez may represent John before an IRS revenue agent in the conduct of an examination, provided that the unenrolled tax preparer has written authorization from John. True or false? Explain your answer. (IRS adapted)

57. Enrolled Agents, attorneys, and CPAs shall exercise due diligence in preparing or assisting in the preparation of documents and other papers relating to IRS matters. True or false? Explain your answer. (IRS adapted)

58. Which of the following statements may not be used when an Enrolled Agent advertises?
    a. Name, address, and office hours
    b. Names of associates of the firm
    c. Claims of quality of service that cannot be verified
    d. Membership in professional organizations
    Explain your answer. (IRS adapted)

59. The Director of Practice may take into consideration a petition for reinstatement from any person disbarred from practice before the IRS after a period of how many years?
    a. Never
    b. 2 years
    c. 3 years
    d. 5 years
    Explain your answer. (IRS adapted)

60. Inclusion of which of the following statements in a CPA's advertisement is *unacceptable* under the AICPA *Code of Professional Conduct*?
    a. Julie Adams, Certified Public Accountant, Fluency in Spanish and French
    b. Julie Adams, Certified Public Accountant, MBA, Big State University, 1992
    c. Julie Adams, Certified Public Accountant, Free Initial Consultation
    d. Julie Adams, Certified Public Accountant, I Always Win IRS Audits
    Explain your answer.

61. Which of the following situations would most likely result in a violation of the practitioner's ethical standards?
    a. A CPA is controller of a bank and grants permission to the bank to use his "CPA" title in the listing of the bank officers in the bank's publications.
    b. A CPA who is also a member of the bar represents on her letterhead that she is both an attorney and a CPA.
    c. A CPA, the sole shareholder in a professional accountancy corporation, uses the term "and company" in his firm's title.
    d. A CPA who writes a newsletter on financial management topics grants permission to the publisher to solicit subscriptions.
    Explain your answer.

62. Which of the following situations would provide an acceptable case for using a taxpayer's estimated figure in the preparation of a Federal income tax return?
    a. The taxpayer has the necessary data available, but is busy with a pressing public offering and has not had the time to look through her records for the information.
    b. The data are not available at the time of filing the return, and the estimated amounts appear reasonable to the CPA.
    c. The taxpayer has the data available at the time for filing the return but feels that the data do not fairly represent the results of her business operation and therefore desires to use an "estimate."
    d. The taxpayer, relying on the income tax regulations that allow the use of reasonable estimates under certain circumstances, desires to use an estimate to determine the amount of his deduction for entertainment expenses.
    Explain your answer.

63. According to the AICPA *Code of Professional Conduct*, CPAs in tax practice who are representing a taxpayer in a formal controversy with the government are permitted to receive contingent fees because
    a. this practice establishes fees that are commensurate with the value of the services rendered.
    b. attorneys who are in tax practice customarily set contingent fees.
    c. determinations by tax authorities are a matter of judicial proceedings that do not involve third parties.
    d. the consequences are based on the findings of judicial proceedings or the findings of a government agency.
    Explain your answer.

64. The AICPA *Code of Professional Conduct* states that a CPA shall not disclose any confidential information in the course of a professional engagement, except with the consent of the client. This rule should be understood to preclude a CPA from responding to an inquiry that is received from
    a. an investigative body of a state CPA society.
    b. the Trial Board of the AICPA.
    c. a CPA-shareholder of the taxpayer corporation.
    d. an AICPA voluntary quality review body.
    Explain your answer.

65. A taxpayer's records are destroyed by fire. A CPA prepares the tax return based on estimates and other indirect information she has obtained. Under the *Statements on Standards for Tax Services,* she should
    a. disclose the use of estimates to the IRS.
    b. not disclose the use of estimates to the IRS.
    c. charge the taxpayer a double fee.
    d. not prepare a return based on estimates.
    e. have an attorney prepare the return.
    Explain your answer.

66. With regard to the categories of individuals who may practice before the IRS under *Circular 230,* which of the following statements is correct?
    a. Only Enrolled Agents, attorneys, or CPAs may represent trusts and estates before any officer or employee of the IRS.
    b. An individual who is not an Enrolled Agent, attorney, or CPA and who signs a return as having prepared it for the taxpayer may, with proper authorization from the taxpayer, appear as the taxpayer's representative, with or without the taxpayer, at an IRS Appeals Office conference with respect to the tax liability of the taxpayer for the taxable year or period covered by the return.
    c. Under the limited practice provision in *Circular 230,* only general partners may represent a partnership.
    d. Under the limited practice provision in *Circular 230,* an individual who is under suspension or disbarment from practice before the IRS may not engage in limited practice before the IRS.
    Explain your answer. (IRS adapted)

67. If an Enrolled Agent, attorney, or CPA knows that a client has not complied with the revenue laws of the United States with respect to a matter administered by the IRS, the Enrolled Agent, attorney, or CPA is required under *Circular 230* to
    a. do nothing until advised by the client to take corrective action.
    b. advise the client of the noncompliance.
    c. immediately notify the IRS.
    d. advise the client and notify the IRS.
    Explain your answer. (IRS adapted)

68. Answer each of the following questions.
    a. What is found in Subpart A, § 10.7(a) of *Circular 230?*
    b. In *Circular 230,* where are the rules on tax shelter opinions found?

    c. Describe the requirements of Rule 301 of the *AICPA Code of Conduct*.

    d. Which *Statement on Standards for Tax Services* (SSTS) discusses the use of estimates in preparing a tax return?

    e. Under *Statement on Standards for Tax Service* (SSTS) No. 1, a member must have a good-faith belief that a recommended position has a ____ ____ of being sustained if challenged. (Fill in the blank.)

69. Answer each of the following questions.

    a. What is found in Subpart C, § 10.51 of *Circular 230*?

    b. In *Circular 230*, where are the rules on knowledge of client omissions found?

    c. Describe the requirements of Rule 503 of the *AICPA Code of Conduct*.

    d. Which *Statement on Standards for Tax Services* (SSTS) discusses the requirements for verifying a tax client's information?

    e. Under *Statement on Standards for Tax Services* (SSTS) No. 8, a member must use judgment that reflects ____ ____ and serves the taxpayer's needs. (Fill in the blank.)

70. The exam to become an Enrolled Agent has four parts. Go to the IRS web site (**http://www.irs.gov**) and determine what is tested on each part of the exam. Give the content of each part.

71. Go to the National Association of Enrolled Agents web site (**http://www.naea.org**). Who is the current president of the NAEA and in what city is the headquarters located?

72. Go the AICPA web site (**http://www.aicpa.org**). Find *Statement on Standards for Tax Services* (SSTS) No. 2 and print out the complete statement.

73. Go to the IRS web site (**http://www.irs.gov**). What is the form number of the Application for Enrollment to Practice before the Internal Revenue Service? Print out a copy of the form to hand in.

74. Go to the IRS web site (**http://www.irs.gov**). Do a publications search and find the most recent *Circular 230*. Print out the title page of the *Circular 230* you found to hand in.

RESEARCH CASES

75. You are a CPA in practice who has just obtained a new client. Another CPA did the tax returns for the prior three years. The client has operated his business as an S corporation during the three-year period. After starting work on this year's tax return, you notice that the S corporation has an October 31 fiscal year-end. After examining the file, you discover that three years ago, when the S corporation adopted the fiscal tax year, a § 444 election was not made. In addition, the S corporation has not maintained the proper required "minimum deposit account" with the IRS.

The client wants your advice on what to do now. You determine that there are three options: (1) you can do nothing and hope the IRS doesn't find out, (2) you can notify the IRS of the mistake and pay any interest and penalties, or (3) you can elect a calendar year and hope the IRS doesn't notice the current invalid fiscal year. What potential nonregulatory ethical issues do you see in this situation that could influence your decision on any recommendation?

76. You are a CPA in practice and have a long-term client who is involved in a nasty divorce proceeding with her husband. The client has assets she deposited in a bank account in the Grand Cayman Islands. There is U.S.-taxable interest on the deposits. Because she does not want her husband to know about the deposits, she asks you to report the interest on her tax return in such a way that it will not "tip off" her husband to the existence of the account. You can handle this request by reporting the interest through the Schedule C (instead of Schedule B) on her tax return and thus avoid making the source of the income known. What potential nonregulatory ethics issues do you see in this situation?

77. Ahi Corporation is one of your clients in Hawaii. The company had a good year last year and owes the IRS $100,000,000, due on March 15. There are no penalties or interest due to the IRS. One of Ahi's employees approaches you with the following plan to benefit from the so-called "float" on the large payment due to the government. First, Ahi Corp. will courier its tax return and payment to the U.S. Virgin Islands. There, the tax return will be mailed to the IRS Service Center in Fresno by certified mail on the return's due date, March 15. By doing this, the employee thinks it will take at least six days for the tax return to reach the IRS and for them to cash the $100,000,000 check. Ahi can earn 7 percent after tax on its money, so the interest earned during these six days because of the float is $19,178 per day [($100,000,000 × .07)/365 days]. Thus, the total interest earned on the float for six days would be $115,068 ($19,178 × 6 days).
a. Would you recommend Ahi complete this transaction?
b. What potential ethics issues do you see in this situation?

78. John Haddock owns 75 percent of Haddock Corporation. The other 25 percent of the stock is held by John's wife, Marsha. You are a tax manager assigned to prepare the corporate tax return for Haddock. While working on the return, you note that Haddock Corp. pays rent to John for a building he owns with his son, John, Jr. The rent being paid is at least three times the normal rate for rentals of similar property in that area of town. You report this observation to the partner on the engagement. She tells you that it is all right to deduct the payments because Haddock Corp. has been doing it for several years. Under your firm's policy, managers sign the tax return for clients.
a. Would you sign this tax return?
b. What potential ethics issues do you see in this situation?

79. You are negotiating a transaction for your client, Shark Corporation. Parties on the other side of the deal ask you for information about the structural stability of a building, which is a significant part of the transaction. Coleman, Shark's tax director, tells you to say "everything is OK," when, in reality, the building has substantial hidden damage. Cole-

man tells you to say this because it would be more favorable to Shark's position in the transaction.

a. How would you respond to Coleman's request?

b. What if you have already told the other side that the building is OK when you learn about the problems?

c. What other potential ethics issues do you see in this situation?

80. Big CPA Firm has many partners in one of its local offices. Two of these partners are Tom, a tax partner, and Alice, an audit partner. Because of the size of the office, Tom and Alice do not know each other very well.

Tom has a tax client, Anchovy Corporation, that is in severe financial trouble and may have to file for bankruptcy. Anchovy is a customer of Sardine Corporation, one of Alice's audit clients. Accounts receivable on Sardine's books from Anchovy are significant. If Anchovy goes bankrupt, it could cause serious problems for Sardine. Alice is unaware of the bad financial condition of Anchovy.

a. Can Tom disclose to Alice the problems at Anchovy?

b. What if Anchovy goes under and takes Sardine with it?

c. What potential ethics issues do you see in this situation?

81. You are the tax manager in a CPA office. One of your clients, Snapper Corporation, is also an audit client of the firm. The CFO of Snapper invites you and the audit manager for a one-week deep-sea fishing trip to Mexico, all expenses to be paid by Snapper. The audit manager says that you both should go and just not tell your supervisor at the CPA firm any details (like who paid the expenses) about the trip.

a. Would you go on the trip?

b. Would you tell your supervisors at the CPA firm if the audit manager went on the trip without you?

c. What other potential ethics issues do you see in this situation?

82. Clara comes to an attorney's office in need of assistance with her husband's estate. Her husband, Phil, a factory worker, had been a saver all his life and owned approximately $1,500,000 in stocks and bonds. Clara is relatively unsophisticated in financial matters, so the attorney agrees to handle the estate for 17 percent of the value of the estate. The normal charge for such work is 3–5 percent of the estate. The widow agrees to the 17 percent arrangement. The attorney then hires CPA Charles for $10,000 to compute Phil's estate tax on Form 706 and to prepare other appropriate documents.

a. Does Charles have any responsibility to inform the widow that she is being significantly overcharged by the attorney?

b. What potential ethics issues do you see in this situation?

83. Darlene works for Big CPA Firm. When she was being interviewed, Darlene was told by a partner in the firm that she was not to underreport her time spent on various engagements. However, after working for a few months, she discovers that everyone in her office "eats time." Because she is not eating time like everyone else, Darlene is always over

budget. She is beginning to get a reputation as a "budget buster." As a result, none of the senior tax staff wants her on their engagements. She is getting the worst clients and bad reviews from the people for whom she works. It appears that unless she starts eating time, Darlene's future with the firm is limited.

a. What would you recommend Darlene do?

b. What potential ethics issues do you see in this situation?

84. Freya is an accountant working on the tax return of a high-tech client. After reviewing the work papers, she discovers that there is a pattern of double billing the U.S. Navy for various projects done by the tax client. She brings this to the attention of her manager on the job, and he tells her that it is not the CPA firm's business what the client does since this is not an audit engagement.

a. What would you recommend Freya do at this point?

b. What potential ethics issues do you see in this situation?

85. Jenny is an accountant for an international energy corporation. She oversees the accounting for certain associated offshore entities. The amount of funds involved in the entities is substantial. At the end of the year she notices that the accounting information from the offshore entities is not included in the consolidated financial statements of the corporation, but is reported on the consolidated tax return. She inquires about this and she is told that the corporation does not report the financial information from the offshore entities since it would lower the earnings of the main corporation. Jenny is sure that this is not the proper accounting and tax treatment for the entities.

a. What would you recommend Jenny do at this point?

b. What potential ethics issues do you see in this situation?

86. Eric is a tax manager for a national CPA firm that audits Penny-Pinching Bank (PPB). Eric and his staff prepare and review the tax return for PPB. One day, at an alumni football tailgate party, he meets another alumnus who Eric discovers is on the Audit Committee of PPB. The Audit Committee member/alumni was unaware that Eric's CPA firm is doing PPC's tax return.

a. What would you recommend Eric do at this point?

b. What potential ethical and practice issues do you see in this situation?

87. Dodger Corporation has been in the manufacturing business in the United States for over 100 years. A tax consultant has proposed that Dodger use a corporate inversion to nominally move its headquarters to an island in the Atlantic Ocean. The operating headquarters will remain in the United States, along with all of its employees, its plant and equipment, and most of its customers. By undertaking this corporate inversion and technically moving its headquarters offshore, Dodger can avoid paying United States corporate income tax. However, for all practical purposes, it remains a U.S.-based company.

a. What would you recommend Dodger do about the proposed corporate inversion?

b. What potential ethics issues do you see in this situation?

Chapter 2

Tax Research Methodology

LEARNING OBJECTIVES

- Recognize the importance of a systematic approach to tax research.

- Delineate and elaborate on the steps of the tax research process.

- Appreciate the importance of gathering pertinent facts and identifying research issues.

- Discuss the sources of the federal tax law.

- Identify how computer resources affect the conduct of tax research.

CHAPTER OUTLINE

What is the tax research process and why should a tax practitioner become efficient at it? The obvious answer to the first question is that the primary purpose of tax research is to find solutions to tax problems. The primary consideration in answering the second part of the question can be summarized as "the cost of tax research." Tax research can be very expensive for the client, or it can take away valuable time that could be used for other activities from a tax practitioner. Unnecessary time spent doing tax research could be used by the tax practitioner to produce additional tax revenue, or to give him or her additional personal time for other activities.

SPOTLIGHT ON TAXATION: The Complexity of Taxation

The complexity of the tax system (and thus tax research) can be shown in a quote related from Pam Olson, the Treasury's Assistant Secretary for Tax Policy. When speaking to a group of tax specialists, she quoted an email sent to her by a tax lawyer that said:

It is difficult to predict the future of an economy in which it takes more brains to figure out the tax on our income than it does to earn it.

The tax research process is similar to that of traditional legal research. The researcher must find authority, evaluate the usefulness of that authority, and apply the results of the research to a specific situation. One can identify two essential tax research skills. The first is the ability to use certain mechanical techniques to identify and locate the tax authorities that relate to solving a problem. The second entails a combination of reasoning and creativity and is more difficult to learn. A tax researcher must begin with native intelligence and imagination and add training and experience properly to apply the information found. Creativity is necessary to explore the relevant relationships among the circumstances and problems at hand to find a satisfying (and defensible) solution. In many cases, no legal authority will exist that is directly on point for the problem. If such a situation exists, the researcher must combine seemingly unrelated facts, ideas (including those that he or she has derived from previous research work), and legal authority to arrive at a truly novel conclusion. This creative ability of the researcher often spells the difference between success and failure in the research process.

OUTLINE OF THE TAX RESEARCH PROCESS

As the tax problems of the client become more significant, the related tax research can become time consuming and thus expensive to the client. A moderate tax research problem often takes up to eight or ten hours of research time, and the bill for these services may approach or even exceed $2,000. Because of the costs that are involved, the tax researcher must work as efficiently as possible to obtain the solution to the client's problem. The researcher needs a framework for the research process, so that he or she does not waste time and effort in arriving at a solution to the problem.

The tax research process can be broken down into six major steps (Exhibit 2–1). Tax researchers (especially those without a substantial amount of experience at the task) must approach the resolution of a tax problem in a structured manner, so that the analysis of the problem will be thorough and the solution complete.

Exhibit	**2–1**
Steps in the Tax Research Process	

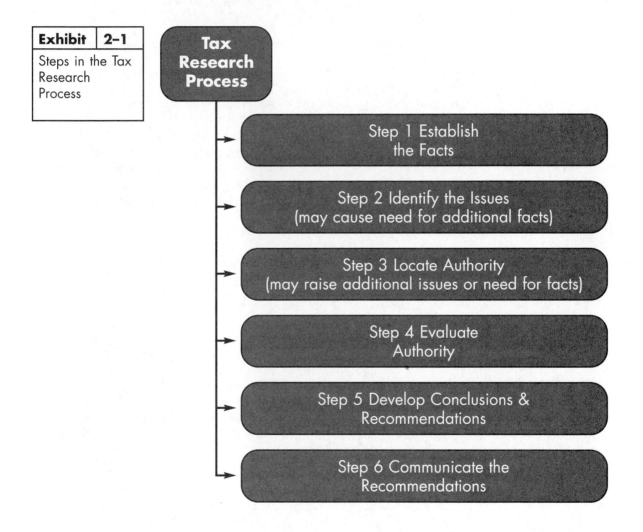

Tax Research Process

Step 1 Establish the Facts

Step 2 Identify the Issues (may cause need for additional facts)

Step 3 Locate Authority (may raise additional issues or need for facts)

Step 4 Evaluate Authority

Step 5 Develop Conclusions & Recommendations

Step 6 Communicate the Recommendations

STEP 1: ESTABLISH THE FACTS

All tax research begins with an evaluation of the client's factual situation. To find the solution to a problem, the researcher must understand fully all of the facts that could affect the related tax outcome. Many beginning tax researchers make the mistake of attempting to research a problem before they completely understand all of the relevant facts and circumstances.

Moreover, a tax researcher may approach the tax research process so rigidly that he or she ignores new factual questions that arise during the other steps of the research task. The tax researcher may engage in several rounds of fact gathering, including those necessitated by additional tax questions that arise as he or she is searching for or evaluating pertinent tax authority. These research "feedback loops" are not endless, although they might seem to be. The best tax researcher is one who can balance the need for efficiency against the need for thoroughness.

Significant tax facts that often influence the client's situation include:

- the client's tax entity, for example, individual, corporation, trust;
- the client's family status and stability;
- the client's past, present, and projected marginal tax rates;
- the client's place of legal domicile and citizenship;
- the client's motivation for the transaction;
- relationships among the client and other parties who are involved in the transaction;
- whether special tax rules apply to the taxpayer due to the type of business in which the taxpayer is engaged (he or she is a farmer, fisherman, or long-term contractor); and
- whether the transaction is proposed or completed.

Fact gathering can present many practical problems for the researcher. Often, the client will (wittingly or not) omit information that is vital to a solution. He or she may not believe that the information is important or may have personal reasons for not conveying the information to the practitioner. In such cases, the researcher must persist until all of the available information is known. In some cases, facts that initially appear to be irrelevant may prove to be important as the research project progresses. The researcher, therefore, should pay attention to and record all details that the client discloses. Efficient tax research cannot be completed until the factual situation is clear; without all of the facts at hand, the researcher could make costly false starts that, when additional pertinent facts become known, must be discarded or redone, often at the client's (or, worse, at the researcher's) expense.

In gathering facts relative to a research problem, the researcher also must be aware of the nontax considerations that are pertinent to the client's situation. For example, the client may have economic constraints (such as cash flow problems) that could preclude the implementation of certain solutions. In addition, the client may have personal preferences that will not accommodate the best tax solution to the problem. For instance, assume that the client could reduce his own income and estate tax liability by making a series of gifts to his grandchildren. However, because the client does not trust the financial judgment of the grandchildren, he does not want to make any such gifts to them during his lifetime. Accordingly, the researcher must look for alternative methods by which to reduce the client's total family tax burden.

STEP 2: IDENTIFY THE ISSUES

A combination of education, training, and experience is necessary to enable the researcher to identify successfully all of the issues with respect to a tax problem. In some situations, this step can be the most difficult element of a tax research problem.

Issues in a closed-fact tax research problem often arise from a conflict with the IRS. In such a case, one can easily ascertain the issue(s). Research of this nature usually consists of finding support for an action that the client has already taken.

In most research projects, however, the researcher must develop the list of issues. Research issues can be divided into two major categories, namely, fact issues and law issues. **Fact issues** are concerned with information having an objective reality, such as the dates of transactions, the amounts involved in an exchange, reasonableness, intent, and purpose. **Law issues** arise when the facts are well established, but it is not clear which portion of the tax law applies to the issue. The application of the law might not be clear because of an apparent conflict among code sections, because a genuine uncertainty as to the meaning of a term as used in the *Internal Revenue Code* may exist, or because there are no provisions in the law that deal directly with the transaction at hand.

When undertaking a research project where the issue may end up being challenged in court, the researcher must be sure to address all of the issues in the tax return. The legal concept of *collateral estoppel* bars relitigation on the same facts or the same issues. Therefore, the practitioner must make sure that his or her case is researched fully, and that no issues that could be resolved in the client's favor have been overlooked. If such an issue is not addressed in the original case, it may be lost forever.

In many situations, a research project may encompass several tax years. The researcher must be aware of any fact or law changes that occur during the period that might affect the results of the research project. The pertinent facts or law may be subject to changes that will cause the researcher to arrive at different conclusions and recommendations, depending on the tax year involved. For example, at one time, the question of whether property qualified for the regular investment credit was a common problem encountered by the tax practitioner. Since the investment credit was repealed for most property placed in service after 1985, subject to transitional rules for certain property, defining "qualified property" is no longer an issue for most taxpayers. Because the transitional rules and the recapture rules still apply where the investment credit was claimed, though, the researcher must still be aware of the provisions.

Seemingly, simple situations can often generate many tax research issues. In the process of identifying tax issues, the researcher might discover that additional facts are necessary to provide sufficient answers for the new questions. The taxpayer in the following example is used to illustrate the potential for complexities in merely identifying tax research issues.

Example 2–1 The KML Medical Group of Houston would like to hire a new physician from Atlanta. However, the new physician owns a home in Georgia on which she will sustain a loss if it is sold in the current housing market. KML approached the Happy Care Hospital, the institution at which the group practices, and asked whether they would reimburse the new physician for the loss to facilitate her move to Texas. The hospital agreed to reimburse the physician this year for her $20,000 realized loss.

A tax researcher might address or clarify at least the following issues in making recommendations concerning tax treatment of the reimbursement.

- Why did the hospital reimburse the physician?
- Is there any parent-subsidiary relationship between the hospital and the KML Medical Group?
- Do any members of the KML Medical Group have an equity or debt interest in the hospital?
- Does the reimbursement constitute gross income to the physician?
- If the reimbursement does constitute gross income to the physician, is it treated as active, passive, or investment income?
- Is the new physician classified as an employee of the hospital?
- Should the hospital report the payment to the physician on a Form 1099 or W-2?
- Should the hospital withhold any income or FICA tax on the reimbursement?
- Can the hospital deduct the reimbursement as a trade or business expense?
- Should the physician consider the reimbursement and/or the loss on the sale of her residence in computing her moving expense deduction?
- If the reimbursement is considered gross income to the physician, when should the amount be included in the physician's income?
- Is the reimbursement subject to any restrictions such as the physician's continued employment? For how long?
- Is the reimbursement to the physician considered an additional amount realized on the sale of her residence?
- Can the reimbursement be considered a gift from the hospital to the physician?

Imagine how the question concerning whether the physician's gross income (if any) was ordinary income might lead to further questions concerning her potential employee status, income tax and FICA withholding, and reporting issues.

Tax Research as an Iterative Process

The process of tax research is iterative in the sense that, once an answer is found, it often causes a new issue to appear and thus requires the gathering of more information. In other words, the tax research process is not strictly linear. This relationship between facts, issues, and answers is illustrated in Exhibit 2–2. The tax research process requires *mechanical skills* and *critical thinking*. Mechanical techniques are gained and sharpened through both knowledge and experience. *Knowledge* is usually gained through edu-

Exhibit | **2–2**

Interaction among Research Facts, Issues, and Solutions

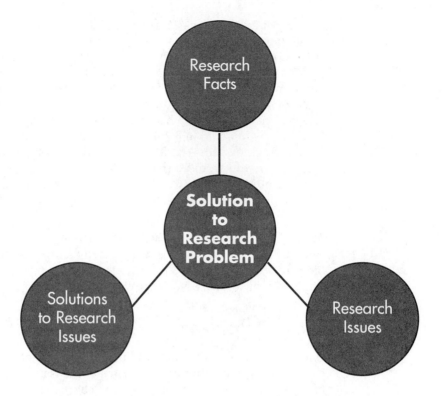

cation in universities and other formal class work. *Experience* is obtained through working in the field and dealing with real tax problems on a recurring basis. Critical thinking is the hardest skill for the researcher to develop. To some extent, it depends on native ability, but a person can be taught the elements of logical analysis and can learn to watch for common pitfalls in evaluating information. Being able to analyze and solve a problem is something the tax researcher must master if he or she is to earn a living in this field. Knowledge is useless when it cannot be applied to solve the problem at hand. The following example illustrates how both mechanical skills and critical thinking are used to solve a tax research problem.

Example 2–2 This year, Chris Lee, a client of your CPA firm, sold stock in Slippery Bank (a publicly traded company with a limited market) to Kolpin Corporation for $100,000. Chris has records that show the stock was acquired ten years ago and has a basis of $135,000. He personally owns 30 percent of Kolpin Corporation. At first glance, the tax researcher would conclude that Chris would have a capital loss of $35,000, which would be deductible against his current-year long-term capital gains of $50,000. This situation appears to be very straightforward. The problem could become complex, though, if someone at the CPA firm asked questions about the other owners of Kolpin. What if Chris's wife, Judy Lee, owns Kolpin stock? The researcher must back up in the research process and gather more facts to determine how many shares she owns.

Suppose Judy Lee owns 25 percent of the Kolpin stock. Now the tax practitioner (you) is faced with new facts and issues; § 267 of the *Internal Revenue Code* suggests that the loss might be disallowed. By looking at § 267(b)(2), you would find that losses between an individual and a corporation are disallowed if "more than 50 percent in value of the outstanding stock of which is owned directly or indirectly, by or for such individual." You then need to know what "indirect ownership" is. Looking further in the Code, you would find in § 267(c), "An individual shall be considered as owning the stock owned, directly or indirectly, by or for his family." Finally, in § 267(c)(4), you would discover, "The family of an individual shall include only his brother and sisters (whether by whole or half blood), spouse, ancestors, and lineal descendants."

Armed with this new information, it becomes clear that Chris is a related party to Kolpin Corporation within the meaning of § 267. He owns more than 50 percent of the stock, 30 percent directly and 25 percent indirectly through his wife. As a result, the $35,000 capital loss is not allowed to Chris, and he cannot use it to offset his other capital gains.

STEP 3: LOCATE AUTHORITY

Once facts have been gathered and the issues defined, the tax researcher must locate legal authority that relates to the issue(s). Authority comes from many sources, including Congress, the courts, and the IRS. Since the inception of the 1913 tax law, several hundred thousand pages of such authority have been produced. To solve a given problem, the researcher must find the appropriate authority in this massive amount of information.

In general, tax authority can be classified as either primary or secondary authority. **Primary authority** is an original pronouncement that comes from statutory, administrative, and judicial sources. **Statutory sources** include the U.S. Constitution, tax treaties, and tax laws passed by Congress. Statutory authority is the basis for all tax provisions. The Constitution grants Congress the power to impose and collect taxes, and authorizes the creation of treaties with other countries. The power of Congress to implement and collect taxes is summarized in the *Internal Revenue Code*, the official title of U.S. tax law. The *Internal Revenue Code* constitutes the basis for all tax law and, therefore, the basis for arriving at solutions to all tax questions.

The other primary sources of the tax law, administrative and judicial authority, function primarily to interpret and explain the application of the provisions of the *Internal Revenue Code* and the intent of Congress. **Administrative sources** include the various rulings of the Treasury Department and the IRS. These are issued in the form of Regulations, Revenue Rulings, and other pronouncements. **Judicial sources** consist of the collected rulings of the various courts on federal tax matters. The primary sources of the tax law will be discussed in detail in Chapters 3, 4, and 5. **Secondary authority** consists of interpretations of primary authority and is an unofficial source of tax information. Examples of secondary authority include tax services, journals, textbooks and treatises, and newsletters. The distinction between primary and secondary sources of authority has become more important since the enactment of § 6662, which imposes a penalty on substantial understatements of tax, except where the taxpayer has "substantial authority" for the position taken on the return. The regulations under § 6662 specify the sources of "substantial authority" to include the provisions of the *Internal Revenue Code*, temporary and final Regulations, court cases, administrative pronouncements, tax treaties, and congressional intent as reflected in committee reports. This list was expanded by the Committee Report for the Revenue Reconciliation Act of 1989 to include Proposed Regulations, Private Letter Rulings, Technical Advice Memoranda, Actions on Decisions, General Counsel Memoranda, Information or Press Releases, Notices, and any other similar documents published by the IRS in the *Internal Revenue Bulletin*. Treatises and articles in legal periodicals, however, are not considered substantial authority under this statute.

Secondary authority is useful when conflicting primary authority exists, when there appears to be no extant primary authority, or when the researcher needs an explanation or clarification of the primary authority. During the past fifteen years, as the support staff of government agencies and (especially) Federal courts has decreased in number or otherwise become inadequate, more dependence has been placed on the secondary authorities of the tax law, even by the IRS, the Treasury Department, and the court system. The beginning researcher must be careful, though, not to rely too heavily on secondary authority, and always to read any pertinent primary authority that is referred to in the secondary sources.

Because of the vast amount of tax authority that is available, the tax researcher would have a tremendous problem in undertaking a tax research problem for a client if it were not for commercial **tax services** and treatises. Several publishers have produced coordinated sets of reference materials that organize the tax authority into a usable format, making the *Internal Revenue Code* much more accessible. These commercial tax services are useful in that they often provide simplified explanations with footnote citations, as well as examples illustrating the application of the law. These tax services may lead the tax researcher, via the footnote references, to the primary source that is pertinent to the question at hand.

Traditionally, tax services have been classified as either annotated or topical. The annotated services are organized in *Internal Revenue Code* section order, while the topical services are arranged by topic, as defined by the publisher's editorial staff. However, the use of computers has significantly blurred the differences between the organization of commercial tax services. With computer hypertext linking, any of the tax services can be used from a Code or topical orientation. Exhibit 2–3 includes a listing of the current major commercial tax services. The tax services are discussed in detail in later chapters.

In 1992, Prentice Hall (and Maxwell Macmillan, an associated publisher) sold its annotated tax reporter and other research items to the Research Institute

Exhibit	2-3	Major Tax Services

Publisher	Title of Tax Service	Orientation
Research Institute of America (RIA)	*Tax Coordinator 2d*	Topic
Research Institute of America (RIA)	*United States Tax Reporter*	Code
Commerce Clearing House (CCH)	*Standard Federal Tax Reporter*	Code
Commerce Clearing House (CCH)	*Federal Tax Service*	Topic
Bureau of National Affairs (BNA)	*Tax Management Portfolios*	Topic
West Group	*Mertens Law of Federal Income Taxation*	Topic

of America (RIA). RIA has renamed and continued the former annotated Prentice Hall tax reporter, as well as its original topical reporter (*Tax Coordinator*). As the new products are phased into existing shelf space, some of the items mentioned in this book as produced by RIA, especially older material, may still appear in tax libraries as Prentice Hall or Maxwell Macmillan publications.

Court decisions are published in sets of bound volumes called *court reporters*. Examples of publishers and court reporters would include those produced by the Government Printing Office (GPO): *Tax Court of the U.S. Reports*, West Publishing Company: *Federal Reporter*, Research Institute of America (RIA): *American Federal Tax Reports*, and Commerce Clearing House: *United States Tax Cases*. Chapter 5 discusses in detail the means by which to find court cases in these (and other) reporters.

Both CCH and RIA provide "citators" as part of their tax services. A citator is a reference source that enables the researcher to follow the judicial history of court cases. The citators are discussed in detail in Chapter 8. The GPO prints many of the pronouncements of the IRS. The primary publication for IRS authority is in a set of bound volumes titled the *Cumulative Bulletin*. Chapter 4 includes a detailed discussion concerning the use of this authority.

Tax journals are another source of information that can be useful. By reading tax journals, a tax practitioner can become aware of many current problem areas in taxation. She can also increase her awareness of recent developments in the tax law, tax compliance matters, and tax planning techniques and opportunities. Numerous journals, ranging from law reviews to *Cosmopolitan*, publish articles on current tax matters. The tax researcher typically is interested in publications devoted to scholarly and professional discussions of tax matters. Among these publications, each tax journal usually is written for a specific group of readers. Exhibit 2-4 lists several useful tax journals, their publishers, and the target readership of each.

Exhibit	**2-4**	Selected Tax Journals

Journal	Publisher	Target Readership
Journal of Taxation	Warren, Gorham & Lamont—Thomson RIA	Sophisticated tax practitioners
Practical Tax Strategies	Warren, Gorham & Lamont—Thomson RIA	Tax practitioners in general practice
Estate Planning	Warren, Gorham & Lamont—Thomson RIA	Practitioners who are interested in estate and gift tax matters
The Tax Adviser	American Institute of CPAs	Members of AICPA and other tax practitioners
TAXES	Commerce Clearing House	General tax practitioners

STEP 4: EVALUATE AUTHORITY

After the researcher has located authority that deals with the client's problem, he or she must evaluate the usefulness of that authority. Not all tax authority carries the same precedential value. For example, the Tax Court could hold that an item should be excluded from gross income at the same time that an outstanding IRS Revenue Ruling asserts the item is taxable. The tax researcher must evaluate the two authorities and decide whether to recommend that his or her client report the disputed item.

In the process of evaluating the authority for the issue(s) under research, new issues not previously considered by the researcher may become known. If this is the case, the researcher may be required to gather additional facts, find additional pertinent authority, and evaluate the new issues. This interaction is illustrated in Exhibit 2–1.

STEP 5: DEVELOP CONCLUSIONS AND RECOMMENDATIONS

After several iterations of the first four steps of the tax research process, the researcher must arrive at his or her conclusions for the tax issues raised. Often, the research will not have resulted in a clear solution to the client's tax problems, perhaps because of unresolved issues of law or incomplete descriptions of the facts. In addition, the personal preferences of the client must also be considered. The "ideal" solution for tax purposes may be entirely impractical because of other factors that are integral to the tax question. In any of these cases, the tax practitioner must use professional judgment in making recommendations based on the conclusions drawn from the tax research process.

SPOTLIGHT ON TAXATION: Changing a Research Conclusion

The changing nature of a tax research conclusion can be illustrated as follows. When Congress created Roth IRAs, a procedure was set up for taxpayers to convert a regular IRA into a Roth IRA by paying the tax on the conversion over a four-year period. In spite of this, after making the conversion many taxpayers reexamined their tax situation and found that the Roth conversion was not as good a deal as originally thought. In this case, however, there was a way out. The tax law gave taxpayers a "second chance" by allowing them to "recharacterize" the Roth IRA conversion back to a regular IRA (within a certain period). Many taxpayers opted to change their converted Roth IRA back into a regular IRA.

Where unresolved issues exist, the researcher might inform the client about alternative possible outcomes of each disputed transaction and give the best recommendation for each. If the research involved an open-fact situation, the recommendation might detail several alternative courses of future action (e.g., whether to complete the deal, or how to document the intended effects of the transaction). In many cases, the researcher may find it appropriate to present his or her recommendation of the "best" solution from a tax perspective, as well as one or more alternative recommendations that may be much more workable solutions. In any case, the researcher will want to discuss with the client the pros and cons of all reasonable recommendations and the risks associated with each course of action.

STEP 6: COMMUNICATE THE RECOMMENDATIONS

The final step in the research process is to communicate the results and recommendations of the research. The results of the research effort usually are summarized in a memorandum to the client file and in a letter to the client. Both of these items usually contain a restatement of the pertinent facts, as the researcher understands them, any assumptions the researcher made, the issues addressed, the applicable authority, and the practitioner's recommendations. An example of the structure of a simple tax research memo is shown in Exhibit 2–5. The memorandum to the file usually contains more detail than does the letter to the client.

In any event, the researcher must temper his or her communication of the research results so that it is understandable by the intended reader. For instance, the researcher should use vastly different jargon and citation techniques in preparing an article for the *Journal of Taxation* than in preparing a client memo for a businessperson or layperson who is not sophisticated in tax matters. Chapter 10 provides additional guidelines and formats for client memoranda and other means of delivering the results of one's research. In addition, an excellent web site to help the tax researcher improve their written tax communication is: http://www.nc.gsu.edu/~accerl/.

Exhibit	2–5	Tax Research Memo Sample Format

Raabe, Whittenburg & Sanders
Certified Public Accountants
San Francisco, CA

Relevant Facts:

Specific Issues:

Conclusions:

Support:

Actions to Be Taken:

_____ Discuss with client.   Date discussed: _____

_____ Prepare a memo or letter to the client.

_____ Explore other fact situations.

_____ Other action. Describe:

Preparer: _____

Reviewer: _____

OVERVIEW OF COMPUTERIZED TAX RESEARCH

The body of knowledge that encompasses the field of taxation grows at a phenomenal pace. Since 1975, Congress has enacted more than two dozen major tax and revenue bills that have had a significant effect on U.S. taxpayers. In addition, each year hundreds of new Treasury Regulations, court decisions, Revenue and Private Letter Rulings, Revenue Procedures, and Technical Advice Memoranda are issued.

The avalanche of tax-related information is not expected to decrease during the foreseeable future. The abundance of available information, as well as the complexity of the tax laws that have been enacted since 1975, has made it even more difficult and time consuming to conduct thorough and effective research concerning a tax-related issue.

Whenever a diligent tax professional is providing advice or other services to a client, he or she must be cognizant of the latest legislative changes and judicial decisions. Furthermore, he or she must be able to draw upon, and sort through, the vast body of established tax knowledge and to apply statutes and administrative and judicial rulings to the current tax issue.

Most tax professionals conduct a significant portion of their tax research using computer resources. The vast amount of storage available on a computer, coupled with the computer's fast retrieval of information, has made electronic tax research invaluable for the tax profession. The tax practitioner has two chief ways to find computer information for tax research purposes: (1) **online** and **CD-ROM** subscription systems and (2) online free (nonsubscription) **Internet** sites.

Computerized tax online services are accessible through the Internet and several public telecommunications networks. The materials that are available with these services are contained in databases that are stored at centralized computer locations. These databases may be accessed from remote locations with the use of a variety of compatible video display terminals and keyboards. Usually, they can be accessed via compatible handheld devices and computers that the user already owns. Some popular computer subscription systems are shown in Exhibit 2–6, and examples of online free Internet sites are shown in Exhibit 2–7.

Electronic online tax research systems are relatively simple to operate. Normally, the user will have no trouble utilizing the system after he or she has devised an effective search command or query. Once the user is satisfied with the composition of his or her search query in an online system, it is transmitted over the Internet or a commercial network to a central computer, where it is processed and documents are identified that satisfy the search request. The text of the retrieved documents is then transmitted to the user and displayed for reading, printing, or saving. After the documents are received, the user must evaluate them and decide whether further research is required. As in using the tax research methodology itself, electronic searching requires a combination of technical knowledge, experience, and creativity in approach.

Exhibit	2-6	Examples of Online Tax Resources

Name	Description
RIA Checkpoint	A web-based computerized tax research service that contains all the RIA material on Federal, state, local, and international taxation. Checkpoint contains all RIA analytical material such as the *Tax Coordinator 2d* and the *United States Tax Reporter*. All public domain information such as the Code and Regulations, U.S. tax treaties, IRS publications and pronouncements, and court cases are available on Checkpoint.
CCH Tax Research Network	A web-based Internet system that contains all of CCH's tax services and other Federal and state legal and tax information. All government documents (IRS publications, court cases, etc.) are available on this system.
Kleinrock's	The Code, the Regulations, *Cumulative Bulletins*, Tax Court Regular decisions (since 1954), Tax Court Memo decisions and other court cases (since 1987), and all IRS publications.
Tax Analysts	The Code, the Regulations, *Cumulative Bulletins*, Court Regular decisions (since 1954). Tax Court Memo decisions and other court cases (since 1985), *Circular 230*, and all IRS publications.
LexisNexis	The largest of the commercial computer-based information systems. Besides containing all Federal and state legal and tax research material, Lexis has extensive libraries of newspapers, magazines, journals, patent records, and medical, economic, and accounting databases.
Westlaw	Offered by the major legal publisher, this system contains all Federal and state legal sources including court cases, administrative releases, and statutory information. All government documents (IRS publications, court cases, etc.) are also available on this system.
Practitioners Publishing Company	A practitioner oriented service that also contains a good free tax newsletter. Part of Thomson Publishing.

BENEFITS OF USING A COMPUTERIZED TAX SERVICE

Traditional tax research usually begins with the consultation of topical and annotated tax services or tax-related text. In most instances, the user first must consult a topical index to locate the appropriate page or pages on which to begin his or her research. However, any time that a tax service is accessed by way of its topical index, the user is relying on someone else's judgment (i.e., the service's editors) or performance (e.g., the staff of the database or library for proper treatment of update material) as to what is important with respect to the specific topic. Moreover, the desired information may not be located, even if it exists in the proper place in the database, because the keyword for which the user is looking is not the same word that was used by the editor in the index to discuss the issue that is the subject of the search. It is also possible that, when the index was prepared, the topic of the search was ignored because it was not as important a topic as it is today.

Exhibit	2–7	Examples of Online Free Tax-Related Internet Sites

Site Name	Internet Address	Description
Tax Sites	**http://taxsites.com**	Indexes to other tax, accounting, and legal web sites.
		Links to commercial, Federal government, state, local, and international web sites.
Internal Revenue Service	**http://www.irs.gov**	Taxpayers can find tax forms, instructions, publications, and other IRS information.
Ernst & Young	**http://www.ey.com**	A web site that contains a large amount of tax and accounting information from the staff of E&Y.
Deloitte Tax LLP	**http://www.deloitte.com**	The Deloitte Tax LLP web site contains a large amount of tax and accounting information from the staff of Deloitte Tax LLP.
Thomas	**http://thomas.loc.gov**	Legislative information from the Library of Congress.
Will Yancey's Home Page	**http://www.willyancey.com**	Indexes to other tax, accounting, and legal web sites.
		Links to commercial, Federal government, state, local, and international web sites.

The primary benefit of using a computerized tax service is that such a resource makes it possible for the *user* to index any significant term, that is, by using it as a search term in a query. By creating his or her own indexes, the researcher is not bound by the limitations that are imposed by a third party editor or data processor. Once the central computer or CD is accessed with a proper search request, the service's software will electronically scan the designated files and retrieve all of the documents that contain the word or words included in the query. Thus, the user is able to bypass the predefined list of topics that constitute the subject's index and perform his or her search directly on the documents themselves.

Another benefit of using a computerized tax research system is that the user can tailor his or her query to fit the requirements of a specific tax problem. Because the user defines the precise specifications of the query, computerized research is exceptionally flexible. Each search request can be made as specific or as broad as desired, depending on the issue to be researched. If they are properly structured, computerized search queries can result in the research process being conducted with greater speed and thoroughness, and they can reduce the amount of time spent on that phase of the research task.

Such speed and flexibility are best realized as the researcher moves among pertinent tax documents. Most of the electronic services allow this capability through **hypertext** linking. Generally, when a hypertext link is indicated, typically through a different color for the text, the user can move to the related document so indicated with a click of the mouse or keyboard. For instance, the researcher could be reading a court case that refers to § 2032A. By clicking on the hypertext link character, he or she is taken directly to the text of the Code section for direct perusal of the statutory language. Similarly, links can be made to pertinent Regulations or to similar court documents in a manner that the researcher could not accomplish by hand. As the number of available tax documents becomes more voluminous, the importance of moving among the documents quickly is met only with an electronic tax research tool.

Online services are updated many times a day. A researcher generally is able to retrieve recent court decisions and administrative rulings from a computerized service almost immediately upon release by the source of the document. In addition, the computerized services include one or more of the daily tax news summaries, such as BNA's *Daily Tax Report* or Tax Analysts' *Tax Notes Today*. In this regard, a computerized tax service allows a tax researcher to stay on top of the latest news and developments without incurring additional subscription costs for the stand-alone services.

Computerized services are particularly useful in researching case law. Every word that is contained in a case is included in the database of the computerized service. Thus, the user can save time by directly accessing only those cases that contain the key terms of his or her search. For example, all of the cases that deal with unreasonable compensation can be accessed within seconds, simply by using *unreasonable compensation* as a search request.

An additional benefit of using a computerized tax service is that certain documents no longer are available in print. For example, full printed transcripts of Actions on Decision and slip opinions normally are not published. However, these documents often may be obtained from the databases of an electronic tax service.

A computerized research service also can be used to obtain regularly published documents to which the researcher does not have access. For example, the full text of Private Letter Rulings is available on most computerized tax research databases. Thus, by using a target or filter feature in a computerized service, a tax practitioner can obtain only the ruling needed, without subscribing to an expensive loose-leaf service for the entire year.

FACTORS IN CHOOSING A COMPUTERIZED TAX SERVICE

In *Computer-Assisted Legal and Tax Research* (Prentice-Hall), Thomas and Weinstein propose that a potential subscriber consider the following factors when choosing a computerized tax database.

- *Database contents:* Does the service provide specialty libraries that will be important in the researcher's work and that are unavailable elsewhere?

- *Search capabilities:* While the search commands and requirements are similar among the commercial tax services, some of the electronic services allow direct reviews of editorial information, and others encompass the Shepard's citations service.
- *Training:* Each of the services offers some level of educational training, either at the user's office or at a regional training center. The proximity, depth, and quality of such seminars may differ among services and across the country.
- *Customer support:* Other forms of contact with the user, such as to develop more sophisticated search techniques or to provide necessary repair services, should be available to the subscriber.
- *Price:* One must consider the cost of the time required to perform the research itself, as well as that of necessary equipment or special software.

In the past, tax practitioners were faced with a choice of either a variable-cost online computer service (e.g., Lexis, Westlaw) or a fixed-cost CD-ROM tax service (e.g., RIA OnPoint). Recently, however, the advent of the Internet-based fixed-cost tax service (e.g., RIA Checkpoint) has changed what is the optimal computer tax subscription for many tax practitioners. With a web-based tax service, tax practitioners have all the features (e.g., fast updates, large databases) of the variable-cost online system with the fixed-cost structure of a CD-ROM system. In addition, a web-based computer tax service does not require any additional hardware, since most tax practitioners already have the hardware in the office. Because of all its inherit advantages, the web-based tax service will probably become the standard source for current and archival tax research material.[1]

Using a Computer in Tax Research

In the first part of this chapter, we presented a model of the tax research process. In this model, steps 1 and 2 of the tax research model are (1) to establish the facts and (2) to identify the issues related to the research question(s). The next step in the research model is to locate tax authority with which to solve the research question. In most situations, the tax researcher uses a computer in step 3 of the model in order to find the required authority (or to conclude that there is no authority on the subject). The process of finding tax authority using a computer can be broken down into several steps, as shown in Exhibit 2–8.

Step 1: State the Issue as a Question

After the tax researcher has established the facts and identified the issues that he or she needs to resolve, the issues should be stated as a question to be answered. For example, suppose the researcher has a client who is a self-employed attorney. As part of her trade or business, the attorney incurs substantial travel expenses during the year. She has learned that if she buys airline tickets in advance and extends her visit over a Saturday night, she will receive a large savings on airfare. Usually, an extra day of meals and

1. See also Dennis Schmidt, "Tax Information on the Web," *Practical Tax Strategies*, February 2004.

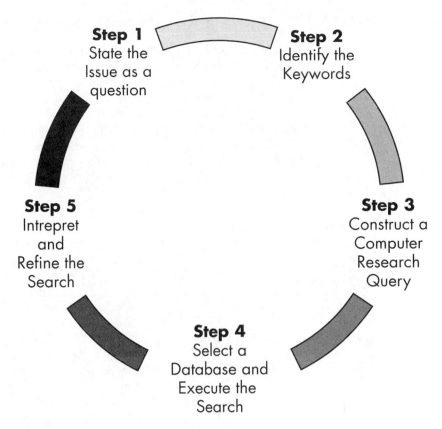

Exhibit | 2–8

Steps in the Computer Research Process

Step 1
State the Issue as a question

Step 2
Identify the Keywords

Step 3
Construct a Computer Research Query

Step 4
Select a Database and Execute the Search

Step 5
Intrepret and Refine the Search

lodging can save many hundreds of dollars in her airfare travel expenses. In the current year, she has spent $4,000 in extra Saturday night expenses to save $12,000 in airfare. The research question in this situation could be stated as:

Are the additional travel costs (primarily meals and lodging) of staying over a Saturday night in order to save substantial amounts on the business airfare deductible?

STEP 2: IDENTIFY THE KEYWORDS

Once the research question has been stated, the researcher must next identify the keywords to construct a proper query in the next step. In the preceding research question, the keywords would be as follows:

- meals and lodging
- travel
- Saturday
- deductible
- airfare

The researcher is looking for words that, when entered into a computer, will find tax authority that is "on point." If the correct keywords are not identified, tax researchers cannot find the authority needed or could be led down blind alleys.

STEP 3: CONSTRUCT A COMPUTER RESEARCH QUERY

Computer tax research systems use a **query** in order to begin the search for the authority needed by the researcher. The construction of the query varies for each commercial computer tax research system; however, there are many similarities between the systems. All tax computer research systems recognize various types of connectors to construct a research query. Generally, computer tax services, such as **RIA Checkpoint**, have ten to fifteen search connectors available, but most tax research searches can be accomplished by using several basic connectors. The syntax of the four most useful connectors in RIA Checkpoint is shown in Exhibit 2–9.

Exhibit	2–9	Selected RIA Checkpoint Search Connectors

Connector	Example	Description
and	stock and securities	Finds documents with both the term stock and the term securities in them.
or	stock or securities	Finds documents with either the term stock or the term securities in them.
/n	stock/15 securities	Finds documents where the term stock is within fifteen words of the term securities.
not	stock not securities	Finds documents with the term stock, but not the term securities.

In addition, the tax services allow the use of wildcard (universal) character(s). For example, in RIA Checkpoint, an "*" (asterisk) at the end of a root word finds all variations of that word. Thus, the word "deduct*" will find deduct, deducted, deduction, deductible, etc. Other computer tax services use similar methods to construct tax research queries.

Computer tax services are continually being updated. Users should check the appropriate help menu of whichever computer tax service is being used to determine how to construct a query and to find other new features.

STEP 4: SELECT A DATABASE AND EXECUTE THE SEARCH

Once the query is constructed, the researcher must log on to and choose a database to search. Each computer tax research system contains numerous databases. As an example, RIA Checkpoint contains the following databases (among many others).

- All Federal Databases
- Federal Editorial Material
- *Federal Tax Coordinator 2d* (a tax service)
- Source Material: Cases
- Source Material: Code, Committee Reports, Regulations, Tax Treaties

- Source Material: IRS Rulings and Releases
- Source Material: Tax Court and Federal Procedural Rules
- WG&L Journals

Continuing our example of the deductibility of Saturday night expenses, we could choose to search *"All Federal Databases"* using a query such as: *travel/25 Saturday*. See Exhibit 2–10. If we executed this search on RIA Checkpoint, we would find several references to the fact that the IRS has issued Private Letter Ruling 9237014 that states the extra expenses for staying over a Saturday to get a lower airfare are deductible as part of the expenses of the business trip.

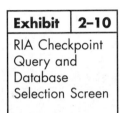

Exhibit | 2–10

RIA Checkpoint Query and Database Selection Screen

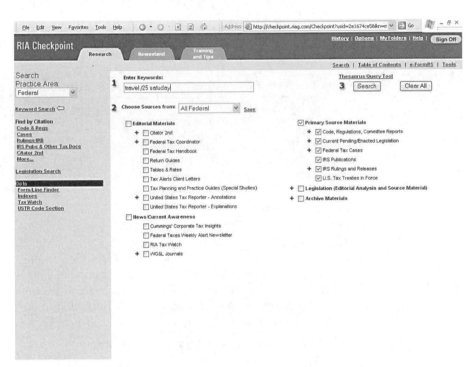

STEP 5: INTERPRET AND REFINE THE SEARCH

After executing a computer tax search, often the query produces too little or too much information. If there is too little information, the search query must be broadened. For example, other keywords may be used or proximity connectors may be relaxed. On the other hand, if the query generates too much information, the search should be tightened. For example, fewer libraries or more unique keywords may be used or proximity connectors may be used or narrowed.

Each computer tax service (e.g., Lexis, Westlaw, Kleinrock's, CCH Tax Research Network) uses its own format for conducting tax searches. However, all services (including those conducted on Google or Yahoo) use the same basic steps in executing such searches. In all computer tax systems, the researcher must state the issue, select the keywords, construct a query, choose a database, execute a search, and interpret and refine the search.

IRS WEB SITE RESEARCH

The IRS maintains an excellent web site where someone interested in tax information can conduct limited tax research. While the IRS web site is not a full-service site, it does contain searchable and downloadable tax information such as tax forms, instructions, publications (e.g., Publication 17), and other IRS information. The IRS web site also has a limited search engine that uses several of the basic connectors and recognizes wild card characters as shown in Exhibit 2–11.

Exhibit 2–11		
IRS Web Site Connectors		

Boolean Connectors	http://www.irs.gov Shortcuts
OR	Space
AND	+
NOT	—
ADJ	"enclose in quotes"

The wildcards "*" and "?" are also allowed by the IRS search engine. Using these wildcards, you can find documents that contain words that have similar spellings but are not stemmed variants. For example, air* finds documents that contain air, airline, and airhead. Entering "?at" finds documents that contain cat and hat, while "??at" finds documents that contain that and chat. For complete information on how to do IRS web site searches, go to:

http://www.irs.gov/help/search_help.html

Example 2–3 Last year, Doris's daughter and her (worthless) husband moved into her home. This year, Doris has supported both of them for the entire year. Doris would like to know if she can claim a dependency exemption for her son-in-law. Doris could go to the IRS web site (**http://www.irs.gov**) and click the search button. She could then search terms such as "son-in-law" and "dependent." See Exhibit 2–12. The IRS search engine should return several IRS publications (e.g., Pub 501) that will inform Doris she can claim a deduction for her son-in-law.

SUMMARY

Tax research is a complex process. The researcher must complete all of the steps in the research process to arrive at a solution to or recommendation for the client's tax problem. Moreover, the steps delineated in Exhibit 2–1

Exhibit | 2-12

Example of IRS Site Search

(or iterations of them) must be completed in their proper order to minimize the possibility of errors in evaluating the authority, arriving at conclusions, or making recommendations. If the process is abbreviated, the researcher risks failure to properly serve the client. This could result in the payment of unnecessary taxes by the client, or in the payment of damages by the tax practitioner to the client.

TAX TUTOR

Reinforce the tax research information covered in this chapter by completing the online tutorials located at the *Federal Tax Research* web site:

http://raabe.swlearning.com

KEY WORDS

By the time you complete this chapter, you should be comfortable discussing each of the following terms. If you need additional review, return to the material in the chapter or consult the glossary to this text.

Administrative Sources	*Internal Revenue Code*
CD-ROM System	Internet
Collateral Estoppel	Judicial Sources
Fact Issue	Law Issue
Hypertext	Online System

Primary Authority	Statutory Sources
Query	Tax Journal
RIA Checkpoint	Tax Service
Secondary Authority	

DISCUSSION QUESTIONS

1. What is the purpose of tax research?

2. What are the basic steps in conducting tax research? Briefly discuss each step in the tax research process.

3. What are the two chief tax research skills, as identified in this text? Explain the importance of each basic skill.

4. The tax researcher must find the facts as the first step in tax research. Give examples of the kind of information that a tax practitioner might want to obtain.

5. What are some of the potential pitfalls in the first step of the tax research process?

6. In each of the following independent situations, indicate whether the item generally would be a tax (T) or a nontax (NT) consideration in solving a tax research or tax planning problem.
   a. The taxpayer would like to set up a private foundation to reduce her annual income tax liability.
   b. The taxpayer has a very poor cash flow because of prior investments; therefore, he has a limited ability to make "tax-advantaged" investments.
   c. The taxpayer wants to transfer as much of her property to her grandchildren as possible. However, she does not want any of the property to fall into the hands of the grandchildren's mother (her daughter-in-law).
   d. The taxpayer lived through the Great Depression of the 1930s and does not like investments with any risk, such as owning stocks or bonds.
   e. The taxpayer likes to maintain highly liquid investments, such as money market funds and certificates of deposit in insured banks and savings and loan institutions.
   f. The taxpayer hates to pay Federal taxes. He will take any legal action to avoid paying any Federal income, estate, or gift taxes.

7. Identify and briefly describe the two major types of tax research issues.

8. What is *collateral estoppel*? How does it affect tax research and planning?

9. Tax law provisions tend to change over time. Explain how this might affect tax research and planning.

10. In the tax research process, the researcher has an obligation to the client to evaluate authority. Do the precedents in all tax authority carry the same value? Explain.

11. Primary tax authority can be classified as statutory, administrative, or judicial. Briefly describe each.

12. Classify each of the following items as a primary (P) or secondary (S) tax research authority.
    a. The *Internal Revenue Code*
    b. A Tax Court case
    c. A textbook on corporate taxation
    d. Treasury Regulations
    e. An IRS Revenue Ruling
    f. An article in *Journal of Taxation*
    g. *Taxes on Parade* (a newsletter)
    h. A Supreme Court decision on a tax matter

13. Briefly characterize and distinguish between annotated tax services and topical tax services.

14. Classify each of the following commercial tax services as either an annotated service (A) or a topical service (T).
    a. CCH's *Standard Federal Tax Reporter*
    b. RIA's *Tax Coordinator*
    c. BNA's *Tax Management Portfolios*
    d. *Mertens Law of Federal Income Taxation*
    e. CCH's *Federal Tax Service*

15. What is a court reporter? Name three organizations that produce court reporters.

16. Who publishes each of the following court reporters?
    a. *United States Tax Cases*
    b. *Federal Reporter*
    c. *American Federal Tax reports*
    d. *Tax Court of the U.S. Reports*

17. What kind of information can be found in a citator?

18. Name the primary bound publication where IRS pronouncements can be found.

19. Tax practitioners use the term "tax service" all the time. What is a tax service?

20. What is the target readership of each of the following tax journals?
    a. *TAXES*
    b. *Journal of Taxation*
    c. *Practical Tax Strategies*
    d. *The Tax Adviser*
    e. *Estate Planning*

21. Specific items of tax authority have different "values" in helping the tax researcher to solve his or her problem. Explain this statement and describe how it applies to the tax research process.

22. Step 5 in the tax research process is concerned with reaching a conclusion or making a recommendation. If one has not found a clear answer to a tax research problem, how is a conclusion or recommendation to be reached?

23. The final step in the research process typically involves a memorandum to the client file and/or a letter to the client communicating the results of the research. List the items that should be found in the body of both of these documents.

24. It has been said that the tax research process is more circular than linear. Do you agree with this statement? Explain your answer.

25. What is deemed to be substantial authority under the § 6662 Regulations? Why is this important?

26. Describe an online tax research system. What are two advantages of such a system over a standard printed tax service?

27. Give the web address of three free online Internet sites where someone could find information on various aspects of taxation.

28. What is computerized tax research, and why is it necessary for the tax professional to be able to use computerized techniques to conduct tax research?

29. Briefly describe what is contained in each of the following tax services.
    a. RIA CheckPoint
    b. CCH Tax Research Network
    c. LexisNexis
    d. Westlaw

30. What are the disadvantages of using a computerized tax service?

31. List four benefits of using a computerized service to conduct your tax research.

32. What are the major steps in developing an effective computerized tax research query?

33. If you were researching an issue and the computer informed you that it had located 1,000 pertinent documents, what would you do to reduce the number of retrieved documents to a more reasonable number?

34. What are the search connectors discussed in the text used by RIA Checkpoint? Describe how each operates.

35. For the following RIA Checkpoint databases state if they generally contain primary or secondary authority: (1) *Federal Tax Coodinator 2d*, (2) Source Material Cases, (3) Source Material IRS Rulings and Releases, and (4) WG&L Journals.

36. What is the Internet address of the Internal Revenue Service's server?

37. What are the connectors used by the IRS web site search engine?

38. What are the two "wildcards" used by the IRS web site search engine? Explain how each operates.

39. Where can someone find additional information on searching techniques available for use on the IRS web site?

EXERCISES

40. Use your university's tax library (or other library assigned by your instructor) to discover the breadth of tax journal offerings. List any five tax journals and the publisher of each.

41. The purpose of this exercise is for you to locate publications that frequently are used in tax research. Give the call number and location (i.e., floor, room, stack, etc.) in your library, and the major color of the binding of the publication, for each of the following references. If a publication is not available, state that it is not.
    a. RIA's *United States Tax Reporter*
    b. CCH's *Standard Federal Tax Reporter*
    c. BNA's *Tax Management Portfolios*
    d. *Mertens Law of Federal Income Taxation*
    e. RIA's *Tax Coordinator 2d*

42. Find out whether each of the following court reporters is available in your library. Give the call number and location (i.e., floor, room, stack, etc.) for each reference. If a reporter is not available, state that it is not.
    a. *American Federal Tax Reports*
    b. *United States Tax Cases*
    c. *Tax Court of the U.S. Reports*
    d. *Federal Reporter*

43. Determine if each of the following tax journals is available in your library. What is the most current issue in your library? List the author(s) and title of any two articles from the most recent issue.
    a. *Journal of Taxation*
    b. *Practical Tax Strategies*
    c. *Journal of International Taxation*
    d. *The Tax Adviser*
    e. *TAXES*

44. Is the *Internal Revenue Code* found in separate volumes in each of the following tax services? If so, in how many volumes?
    a. CCH's *Standard Federal Tax Reporter*
    b. BNA's *Tax Management Portfolios*
    c. RIA's *Tax Coordinator 2d*

45. Find a copy of the *Cumulative Bulletin* in your university's library. By looking in a volume, list three different tax research sources published in a *Cumulative Bulletin*.

46. Locate a copy of the *American Federal Tax Reports* in your library. List two courts that have decisions published in this court reporter.

47. Locate a copy of CCH's *United States Tax Cases* in your library. List two courts which have decisions published in this court reporter.

48. In your university's library, locate the CCH and RIA citators. How many volumes does each contain?

49. Determine if your campus has any of the following online or CD-ROM tax research services available for student use. If a service is available on your campus, describe how you would gain access to that system for research projects in your tax classes. If a service is not available on your campus, state where you might be able to find it.
    a. Kleinrock's
    b. Lexis
    c. RIA Checkpoint
    d. Westlaw
    e. CCH Tax Research Network

50. Go to the IRS web page (**http://www.irs.gov**) and print out a copy of the most recent Instructions for Form 3903 of Form 1040.

51. Go to the IRS web page (**http://www.irs.gov**) and print out a copy of the most recent Instructions for Form 4952 of Form 1040. You may first need to download the Adobe Acrobat Reader (© Adobe Systems) software to be able to view or print the form. The software is provided free of charge by Adobe through a link on the IRS page.

52. Go to the IRS web page (**http://www.irs.gov**). What IRS publication number addresses tax rules that apply to personnel in the armed forces? Print the first page of the IRS publication to hand in.

53. Go to the IRS web page (**http://www.irs.gov**). What IRS publication number addresses tax rules for pension and annuity income? Print the first page of the IRS publication to hand in.

54. Go to the IRS web page (**http://www.irs.gov**). Find information on abusive tax shelters. Give an example of an abusive tax shelter listed by the IRS.

55. Go to **http://taxsites.com** and give the complete web address for each of the following sites:
    a. The California Franchise Tax Board
    b. The New York Department of Taxation and Finance
    c. The American Institute of CPAs (AICPA)

56. Go to **http://www.willyancey.com** and give the complete web address for each of the following sites:
    a. The Hawaii Department of Taxation
    b. The Vermont Department of Taxes
    c. The American Taxation Association

57. Go to the Practitioners Publishing Co. web site (**http://www.ppcnet.com**) and locate the most recent Practitioners *Tax Action Bulletin*. Print out a copy of the bulletin.

58. Go to the IRS web page (**http://www.irs.gov**) and find the most recent IRS Publication 1542, Per Diem Rates. What is the maximum per diem rate for lodging and meals and incidental expenses (M&IE) for each of the following towns?

    a. Miami, Florida

    b. Palm Springs, California

    c. San Antonio, Texas

59. Go to the IRS Web page (**http://www.irs.gov**) and find the most recent IRS Publication 1542, Per Diem Rates. What is the maximum per diem rate for lodging and meals and incidental expenses (M&IE) for each of the following towns?

    a. Buffalo, New York

    b. Honolulu, Hawaii

    c. Spokane, Washington

60. Locate and print out the web site home page of each of the following CPA firms.

    a. Ernst and Young LLP

    b. Deloitte Tax LLP

    c. BDO Seidman LLP

    d. PricewaterhouseCoopers LLP

61. Jennifer owns 200 acres of land on which she grows flowers for sale to local nurseries. Her adjusted basis in the land is $30,000. She receives condemnation proceeds of $20,000 from the state for ten acres of her land on which a new freeway will be built. The state also pays her $30,000 for the harmful effects that the increased auto exhausts might have on her flowers. List as many tax research issues as you can to determine the tax consequences of these transactions. Do not attempt to answer any of the questions you raise. Simply identify the research issues.

62. Joey parked his car on the top of a hill when he went to watch the X games in San Diego. He did not properly set his brakes or curb the wheels when he parked the car. When he returned from the games, he found his car had rolled down the hill, smashed into Nick's house, and injured Nick, who was watching TV in his den. Joey does not have car insurance. List as many tax research issues as you can to determine the tax consequences of this accident. Do not attempt to answer any of the questions you raise. Simply identify the research issues.

63. John and Marsha are married and filed a joint return for the past year. During that year, Marsha was employed as an assistant cashier at a local bank and, as such, was able to embezzle $75,000, none of which was reported on their joint return. Before the defalcation was discovered, Marsha disappeared and has not been seen or heard from since. List as many tax research issues as you can to determine the tax consequences of this crime. Do not attempt to answer any of the questions you raise. Simply identify the research issues.

64. In the current year, Dave receives stock worth $125,000 from his employer. The stock is restricted and cannot be sold by Dave for seven years. Dave estimates the stock will be worth $300,000 after the seven years. List as many tax research issues as you can to determine the tax consequences of this transaction. Do not attempt to answer any of the questions you raise. Simply identify the research issues.

65. On December 1, 20x1, Ericka receives $18,000 for three months' rent (December, January, and February) of an office building. List as many tax research issues as you can to determine the tax consequences of this transaction. Do not attempt to answer any of the questions you raise. Simply identify the research issues.

66. Formulate a search query to determine whether your client is required to include in gross income the proceeds from a redemption of a tax-exempt bond, purchased in 1988 and called by the school district this year. Redemption proceeds were $90,000, and the 1988 purchase price on the secondary market was $76,000. Give an example of a computer search query using only the following RIA Checkpoint connectors: "and," "or," "/n," and "not."

67. Formulate a search query to determine the provisions of the United States' treaty with Germany relative to fellowship income received by a business student during a summer internship with the German Department of Price Controls. Give an example of a computer search query using only the following RIA Checkpoint connectors: "and," "or," "/n," and "not."

68. Formulate a search query to determine whether your client is required to capitalize fringe benefits and general overhead that is attributable to employees who are building an addition to your client's factory during a "slack time" at work. Give an example of a computer search query using only the following RIA Checkpoint connectors: "and," "or," "/n," and "not."

69. Formulate a search query to determine whether your client can retroactively elect to change its accounting method. Give an example of a computer search query using only the following RIA Checkpoint connectors: "and," "or," "/n," and "not."

70. Formulate a search query to find all of the cases in which the word *constructive* occurs within ten words of the word *dividend*. Give an example of a computer query using only the following RIA Checkpoint connectors: "and," "or," "/n," and "not."

RESEARCH CASES

71. Sam Manuel has been employed on a full-time basis as an electrical engineer for the past three years. Prior to obtaining full-time employment, he was self-employed as an inventor of complex electronic components. During this period of self-employment, most of his projects produced little income, although several produced a significant amount of revenue.

    Due to the large expenditures necessary and the failure of the majority of the products to produce a profit, Sam was forced to seek full-time employment. After obtaining full-time employment, he continued to work long hours to perfect several of his inventions. He continued to enjoy relatively little success with most of his products, but certain projects were successfully marketed and generated a profit. For the last two years, Sam's invention activity has generated a net loss.

a. List as many possible tax research issues as you can to determine whether the losses may be deducted.

b. After completing your list of tax research issues, list the keywords you might use to construct a computer tax research query.

72. Matthew Broadway was a partner in the law firm of Johnson and Smith, a partnership of twenty partners, for the past ten years. Without the knowledge or consent of the other partners, Matthew worked on a highly complicated acquisition and merger project for six months, at all times using the resources of the law firm. Several months later, the firm for which Matthew provided the professional services made out a check for $300,000 to the firm of Johnson and Smith. Matthew insisted that the fee should rightly be his, while the firm disputed his claim. Because of the dispute, the fee was held in escrow until the following year when the dispute was settled.

The dispute was settled with Matthew agreeing to withdraw from the partnership. Included as part of the withdrawal agreement was a clause that specified he would receive $45,000 of the $300,000 fee, with the law firm retaining the remainder. Six months later, Matthew received a total payment of $125,000, which included the $45,000 fee, from Johnson and Smith.

a. List as many possible tax research issues as you can to determine the tax treatment of the $125,000 payment received by Matthew.

b. After completing your list of tax research issues, list the keywords you might use to construct a computer tax research query.

73. Juanita Sharp purchased a large parcel of property for $120,000. A short time after purchasing the property, Sharp submitted plans for the division of the parcel into six lots and the construction of three single-family residences on three of the lots. The city permits required that the property be divided into six lots and that street improvements and water and sewer access be provided. Sharp spent $22,000 for the street, water, and sewer improvements. As a result of the improvements, the value of each of the three vacant lots increased by $1,000, based on an appraisal completed subsequent to the completion of the improvements. The costs of constructing the three single-family residences totaled $200,000.

a. List as many possible tax research issues as you can to determine how the original purchase price of $120,000, the $22,000 cost of the improvements, and the $200,000 cost of the construction of the homes should be allocated to the basis of each of the lots for purposes of determining gain or loss on the sale of the lots.

b. After completing your list of tax research issues, list the keywords you might use to construct a computer tax research query.

74. Tom and Donna were divorced three years ago. At the time of their divorce, they owned a highly appreciated residence. Tom remained half-owner of the house, but moved out and allowed Donna to continue

living in the house. In the current year, Tom and Donna sold the house for $300,000. Last year, Tom purchased a new house for $190,000.

    a. List as many possible tax research issues as you can to determine tax treatment(s) available to Tom on the sale and purchase of the residence.

    b. After completing your list of tax research issues, list the keywords you might use to construct a computer tax research query.

75. Vincent Vineyard, MD, is a very successful physician in Temecula, California. He earns approximately $800,000 per year from his medical practice. His two children have graduated from college and he and his wife are now "empty-nesters." Vincent, Jr., is an officer in the Navy and his daughter Valerie is an engineer in Texas. Vinny has had an interest in wine and grape growing for many years. Now, with more time to devote to other activities, Vinny recently started a winery with an initial investment of $1,000,000. Since the winery is new, he expects it to be eight to ten years before the winery makes a profit. Vinny would like your advice as to any potential tax problems he might have with his new winery investment.

    a. What additional information might you want in this situation?

    b. Where might that information come from?

    c. Are all the given facts pertinent? Which (if any) are irrelevant?

    d. What is the primary research question you would try to answer?

    e. Are there any additional research question(s) you want to address?

76. Ned Naive operated several franchised stores, and at the home office's suggestion, consolidated its payroll and accounting functions with Andy the Accountant. Andy is a not a CPA. Last year, Andy began embezzling taxpayer's escrowed tax withholdings and failed to remit required amounts for the four quarters. The IRS assessed Ned penalties for failing to make the proper withholding deposits during the year.

    a. What additional information might you want in this situation?

    b. Where might that information come from?

    c. Are all the given facts pertinent? Which (if any) are irrelevant?

    c. Where might that information come from?

    d. What is the primary research question you would try to answer?

    e. Are there any additional research question(s) you want to address?

77. Diego Dissolution is a new client. He is recently divorced and has some questions regarding payments he is making to his ex-wife (Mrs. D.). Dr. Diego is 45 years old and has a successful dental practice. Mrs. D. was previously divorced from her first husband six years ago. Diego is paying $12,000 per month to Mrs. D. He wants to know if the tax payments on the $12,000 per month payments are deductible.

    a. What additional information might you want in this situation?

    b. Where might that information come from?

    c. Are all the given facts pertinent? Which (if any) are irrelevant?

    c. Where might that information come from?

    d. What is the primary research question you would try to answer?

    e. Are there any additional research question(s) you want to address?

78. Your client, Barney Green, and his wife, Edith, attended a three-day program in Honolulu, entitled "Financial, Tax, and Investment Planning for Investors." The Greens went to Hawaii several days early so that they could adjust to the jet lag and be ready for the seminar. The $3,000 cost of the trip included the following expenses.

First-class air fare	$1,200
Hotel (7 days)	800
Program fee	300
Meals and other expenses	700

The Greens have records to substantiate all of the above expenditures in a manner that is acceptable under § 274.
    a. List as many possible tax research issues as you can to determine whether the Greens can deduct any or all of the $3,000 of expenditures on their current-year tax return.
    b. After completing your list of tax research issues, list the keywords you might use to construct a computer tax research query.
    c. Execute a computer search using your query. For simplicity, select the IRS Taxpayer Information Publications (TIPS) database from whichever computer tax service you use. Summarize your findings.

79. Ban Vallew was divorced in 2001. He has a son, Katt, by this marriage, who is in the custody of his ex-wife. Katt Vallew has a history of emotional disturbance. He has been sent to a psychiatrist for several years for this problem. This year he has become so disturbed, manifesting violence at home and school, that he had to be sent to a special school in Arizona for problem children. This school is very expensive ($2,000 per month), the cost of which Ban pays for. Ban would like to determine whether he is entitled to the medical expenses deduction (over 7.5 percent of adjusted gross income) for the cost of sending his son to this special school.
    a. List as many possible tax research issues as you can to determine tax treatment(s) available to Ban on the payments to the special school.
    b. After completing your list of tax research issues, list the keywords you might use to construct a computer tax research query.
    c. Execute a computer search using your query. For simplicity, select the IRS Taxpayer Information Publications (TIPS) database from whichever computer tax service you use. Summarize your findings.

80. Linda Larue suffered from arthritis. Her chiropractor advised her that she needed to swim daily to alleviate her pain and other symptoms. Consequently, Linda and her husband, Philo, purchased for $100,000 a new home that had a swimming pool, after selling their old home for $85,000. If the Larues had constructed a pool at their former residence, it would have cost $15,000 to build, and it would have increased the value of their home by $8,000.
    a. List as many possible tax research issues as you can to determine whether the Larues can deduct any of their current-year expenditures for Linda's arthritis.

    b. After completing your list of tax research issues, list the keywords you might use to construct a computer tax research query.

    c. Execute a computer search using your query. For simplicity, select the IRS Revenue Rulings database from whichever computer tax service you use. Summarize your findings.

81.   Gwen Gullible was married to Darrell Devious. They were divorced two years ago. Three years ago (the year before their divorce), Darrell received a $250,000 retirement plan distribution, of which $50,000 was rolled over into an IRA. At the time, Gwen was aware of the retirement funds and the rollover. The distribution was used to pay off the couple's mortgage, purchase a car, and for living expenses. Darrell prepared the couple's joint return, and Gwen asked him about the tax ramifications of the retirement distributions. He told her he had consulted a CPA and was advised that the retirement plan proceeds used to pay off a mortgage were not taxable income. Gwen accepted that explanation and signed the return. In fact, Darrell had not consulted a CPA.

One year ago (after the divorce), Gwen received a letter from the IRS saying they had not received the tax return for the last full year of marriage. On advice from a CPA, Gwen immediately filed the return (she had a copy of the unfiled return). The Internal Revenue Service notified Gwen that no estimated payments on the retirement distribution had been paid by Darrell, and that she owed $60,000 in tax, plus penalties and interest.

    a. List as many possible tax research issues as you can to determine whether Gwen is liable for the tax, interest, and penalties.

    b. After completing your list of tax research issues, list the keywords you might use to construct a computer tax research query.

    c. Execute a computer search using your query. For simplicity, select the IRS Revenue Rulings database from the computer tax service you use. Summarize your findings.

Part 2

Primary Sources of Federal Tax Law

Chapter 3

Constitutional and Legislative Sources

LEARNING OBJECTIVES

- Outline the primary and secondary sources of the Federal tax law.

- Describe in detail the nature and structure of the statutory sources of the tax law, including the Constitution, tax treaties, and the Internal Revenue Code.

- Delineate how statutory tax law is created and how tax research resources are generated in this process.

- Determine how to locate the statutory sources of the tax law.

- Discuss how the tax researcher can carefully interpret the Internal Revenue Code.

CHAPTER OUTLINE

Sources of Federal Tax Law

History of U.S. Taxation

U.S. Constitution

Tax Treaties

The Legislative Process
  Where to Find Committee Reports

Internal Revenue Code
  Organization of the Internal Revenue Code
  Where to Find the Internal Revenue Code

Interpreting the Internal Revenue Code

What are the **constitutional and legislative sources** of tax authority, and how can a tax researcher use them to solve tax questions? In simple terms, the constitutional and legislative tax sources are the foundation on which all other tax sources (e.g., administrative and judicial) are built. In this chapter, we take a closer look at the tax research process and how the primary tax law sources are used to help the tax researcher arrive at a solution to his or her client's tax problems.

Sometimes tax professionals state that there are three primary sources of the tax law, mirroring the constitutional division of the function of the Federal government.

• Statutory sources, or the legislative branch.
• Administrative sources, or the executive branch.
• Judicial sources, or the judicial branch.

Thus, the constitutional and legislative tax sources often are referred to as the "**statutory sources.**"

SOURCES OF FEDERAL TAX LAW

As mentioned in the previous chapter, the sources of the Federal tax law can be classified as **primary authorities** or **secondary authorities**. Chapters 3 through 8 of this text include detailed examinations of these various sources, discussing their nature, location, and use in the tax research process. The sources of the Federal tax law to be examined here are presented in outline form in Exhibit 3–1. In particular, we will examine the statutory sources of

Exhibit	3–1	Framework of Primary and Secondary Sources of Federal Tax Law

Primary Sources (Original Pronouncements)	Secondary Sources (Interpretations of Primary Authority)
Statutory Sources (Chapter 3)	
U.S. Constitution	**(Chapters 6–8)**
Tax Treaties	
Internal Revenue Code	***Tax Services***
Administrative Sources (Chapter 4)	*Annotated Services*
Treasury Regulations	*Topical Services*
Revenue Rulings	
Revenue Procedures	***Tax Citators***
Other written determinations	
Miscellaneous IRS publications	***Tax Journals***
Judicial Sources (Chapter 5)	
Supreme Court	***Tax Newsletters***
Courts of Appeals	
District Courts	***Tax Textbooks***
U.S. Court of Federal Claims	
Tax Court	***Tax Treatises***
Tax Court, Small Cases Division	

the U.S. Constitution, tax treaties, and the *Internal Revenue Code*. The reader should refer to this outline while reading this text to maintain perspective as to the relationships between each of the sources discussed.

HISTORY OF U.S. TAXATION

Although the Massachusetts Bay Colony enacted an income tax law in 1643, the first U.S. income tax was not created until the Civil War. An income tax law was passed at that time to help the North pay for the cost of fighting the war. This Federal income tax law was passed on August 5, 1861. Although the tax was not generally enforced, some limited collections were made under the law.

This first Federal income tax was levied at the rate of a modest 3% on income between $600 and $10,000, and 5% on marginal incomes in excess of $10,000. Later, in 1867, the rate was a flat 5% of income in excess of $1,000. The Civil War income taxes were allowed to expire in 1872. In 1894 another income tax act was passed by Congress. By this time, however, the income tax had become an important political issue. The southern and western states generally favored the tax, and the eastern states generally opposed it because the tax had developed into an important element of the Populist political movement. In *Pollock v. Farmers' Loan and Trust Co.*, 157 U.S. 429, 15 S.Ct. 673 (1895), the Supreme Court held that the income tax was unconstitutional because it was a constitutionally prohibited "direct tax."

The supporters of the income tax decided to amend the Constitution so that there would be no question as to the constitutionality of a Federal income tax, applying progressive rates to diverse sources of income. The proposed amendment was sent to the states on July 12, 1909, by the Sixty-first Congress; it was ratified on February 3, 1913. The new Sixteenth Amendment to the Constitution stated:

> *The Congress shall have the power to lay and collect taxes on incomes, from whatever source derived, without apportionment among the several States, and without regard to any census or enumeration.*

A copy of a 1913 individual tax return (Form 1040) is shown in Exhibit 3–2. It should be noted that individual taxpayers were allowed a $3,000 ($4,000 for married taxpayers) "specific exemption" before they had to start paying income tax at a 1% rate. The 1% bracket went up to $20,000 of taxable income before a surtax of an additional 1% percent was added. The surtax eventually reached 6% at a taxable income of $500,000. Thus, the maximum marginal tax rate in 1913 was 7% (1% regular tax plus 6% surtax).

The 1913 specific exemption is similar to the current standard deduction. If $3,000 in 1913 were price-level adjusted into today's dollars, it would be approximately $63,000. Thus, $63,000 is the minimum amount of taxable income an individual taxpayer would need before he or she had to start paying income tax if an equivalent exemption were in place today.

Before the Sixteenth Amendment was ratified, Congress passed a corporate income tax in 1909. This tax also was challenged at the Supreme Court level,

| Exhibit | 3–2 | 1913 Individual Form 1040 |

TO BE FILLED IN BY COLLECTOR.

Form 1040.

TO BE FILLED IN BY INTERNAL REVENUE BUREAU.

List. No. ....

.... District of ....

Date received ....

INCOME TAX.

THE PENALTY
FOR FAILURE TO HAVE THIS RETURN IN
THE HANDS OF THE COLLECTOR OF
INTERNAL REVENUE ON OR BEFORE
MARCH 1 IS $20 TO $1,000.
(SEE INSTRUCTIONS ON PAGE 4.)

File No. ....

Assessment List ....

Page .... Line ....

UNITED STATES INTERNAL REVENUE.

RETURN OF ANNUAL NET INCOME OF INDIVIDUALS.

(As provided by Act of Congress, approved October 3, 1913.)

RETURN OF NET INCOME RECEIVED OR ACCRUED DURING THE YEAR ENDED DECEMBER 31, 191 ....

(FOR THE YEAR 1913, FROM MARCH 1, TO DECEMBER 31.)

Filed by (or for) .... of ....
(Full name of individual.)   (Street and No.)

in the City, Town, or Post Office of .... State of ....
(Fill in pages 2 and 3 before making entries below.)

1. GROSS INCOME (see page 2, line 12) . . . . $

2. GENERAL DEDUCTIONS (see page 3, line 7) . . . . $

3. NET INCOME . . . . $

Deductions and exemptions allowed in computing income subject to the normal tax of 1 per cent.

4. Dividends and net earnings received or accrued, of corporations, etc., subject to like tax. (See page 2, line 11) . . . $

5. Amount of income on which the normal tax has been deducted
   and withheld at the source. (See page 2, line 9, column A)

6. Specific exemption of $3,000 or $4,000, as the case may be.
   (See Instructions 3 and 19) . . . .

Total deductions and exemptions. (Items 4, 5, and 6) . . . . $

7. TAXABLE INCOME on which the normal tax of 1 per cent is to be calculated. (See Instruction 3) . $

8. When the net income shown above on line 3 exceeds $20,000, the additional tax thereon must be calculated as per schedule below:

						INCOME.			TAX.		
1	per cent on amount over $20,000 and not exceeding $50,000 . .					$			$		
2	"	"	50,000	"	"	75,000 .					
3	"	"	75,000	"	"	100,000 .					
4	"	"	100,000	"	"	250,000 .					
5	"	"	250,000	"	"	500,000 .					
6	"	"	500,000	. . . .							

Total additional or super tax . . . . $

Total normal tax (1 per cent of amount entered on line 7) . . $

Total tax liability . . . . $

in *Flint v. Stone Tracy Co.* 220 U.S. 107, 31 S.Ct. 342 (1911). The Court held that this tax was constitutional because it was a special form of excise tax using income as its base, rather than a (prohibited) direct income tax.

SPOTLIGHT ON TAXATION: Who Pays the Income Tax?

The 1913 income tax was strictly a tax on wealthy and high income taxpayers (i.e., a "select tax"). The original post-Sixteenth Amendment income tax applied to less than 1% of the population (i.e., 1 in every 271 adults). It wasn't until the end of World War II that the income tax became a broad-based tax that applied to the majority of the population (i.e., a "mass tax").

In recent years, the income tax has been attacked in the courts on the basis that it is unconstitutional. For instance, some protesters have asserted that, since the U.S. currency no longer is based on the gold standard, the Sixteenth Amendment's measure of income, and therefore the tax itself, is invalid. Others have asserted that the Federal income tax law forces the taxpayer to surrender his or her Fifth Amendment rights against self-incrimination. Federal courts, however, have denied virtually all of the protesters' challenges.

Congress has passed several new laws to discourage tax protesters. For instance, a taxpayer is subject to a $500 fine if he or she files a "frivolous" tax return as a form of protest against the IRS or the U.S. budgetary process. This fine would be levied, for example, when the taxpayer files a blank tax return accompanied by a note suggesting that the Federal income tax is unconstitutional or that the taxpayer wishes to protest against tax revenues going to the creation of nuclear weapons. A number of lower courts have upheld the constitutionality of this fine [e.g., *Schull*, 842 USTC ¶ 9529 (D.C., Va.)].

The Tax Court can impose a penalty, not to exceed $25,000, if the taxpayer brings a "frivolous" matter before the Court. Under §§ 6673 and 6702, a frivolous matter is where the intent is to delay the revenue collection process and where the proceedings are found to be groundless, or where the taxpayer unreasonably failed to pursue available administrative remedies. Sanctions can also be imposed against tax practitioners who participate in the litigation of frivolous tax return positions.

U.S. CONSTITUTION

The Constitution of the United States is the source of all of the Federal laws of the country, including both tax and nontax provisions. In addition to the Sixteenth Amendment, however, the Constitution contains other provisions that bear upon the taxation process. For example, the Constitution provides that Congress may impose import taxes but not export taxes. Moreover, the constitutional rights of due process and of the privacy of the citizen apply in tax, as well as nontax, environments.

The Constitution also requires that taxes imposed by Congress apply uniformly throughout the United States. For instance, it would be unconstitutional for Congress to impose one Federal income tax rate in California and another rate in Vermont. Moreover, except as provided by the Sixteenth Amendment, the

Constitution still bars per capita and other direct taxes, unless the revenues that are generated from these taxes are apportioned to the population of the states from which they were collected.

The Federal courts have upheld the constitutionality of the estate and gift taxes because they are in the form of excise taxes on (the transfer of) property, rather than direct taxes on individuals. Thus, one can conclude that, for better or worse, most future judicial challenges to the constitutionality of the elements of the Federal tax structure probably will be fruitless.

One can find copies of the U.S. Constitution in many textbooks, encyclopedias, dictionaries, and in publications such as *The World Almanac* and the *Information Please Almanac*. The Constitution is also reproduced in Volume One of the *United States Code*, as published by the Government Printing Office.

The U.S. Constitution (Exhibit 3–3) can also be found at various nonsubscription Internet sites. An example of such a site is:

http://www.archives.gov

TAX TREATIES

Tax treaties are agreements negotiated between countries concerning the treatment of entities subject to tax in both countries. The United States has entered into treaties with most of the major Western countries of the world. The overriding purpose of such treaties (also known as *tax conventions*) is to eliminate the "double taxation" that the taxpayer would face if his or her income were subject to tax in both countries. In such a case, a U.S. citizen who has generated income from an investment in the United Kingdom (U.K.) usually would be allowed a credit on her U.S. income tax return to the extent of any related U.K. taxes that she paid.

Any tax matter can be covered in a tax treaty with another country. Many times, there are multiple tax treaties with a given country. For example, one treaty will address income tax issues, while another treaty covers estate tax, and a third treaty addresses excise taxes. An example of a portion of a tax treaty is shown as Exhibit 3–4.

In addition to the tax treaties, the U.S. government enters into nontax international agreements that are not formal tax treaties; however, in many respects they function like one. Along with other provisions, these agreements address tax issues involving the parties associated with the agreement. Examples of such international agreements include the North American Free Trade Agreement (NAFTA) and the General Agreement on Tariffs and Trade (GATT). Other agreements might address the exchange of tax, banking, and securities information among citizens of one or more countries.

Treaties are an important source of Federal law. Most treaties do *not* address tax issues, but the ones that do have a far-reaching effect. When dealing with a research problem that has international connotations, the researcher must locate, read, and evaluate any tax treaty that applies to the client's problem. The researcher cannot rely on the more typical sources of tax

Exhibit	3–3	United States Constitution

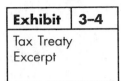

Exhibit   3–4

Tax Treaty
Excerpt

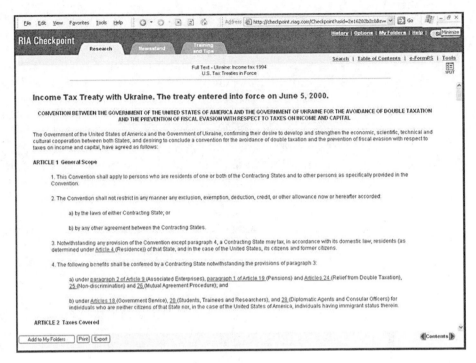

research information because these references usually address only domestic tax precedents. Tax treaties often address issues such as the following.

- How to treat the business and investment income of the visiting taxpayer
- When the visitor is subject to the host country's tax laws
- How to offset the possibility of taxing the same income or assets more than once
- How to compute the taxable amount in the host country
- To what extent host-country withholding taxes are applied to the visitor's transactions
- What tax disclosures must be made by the visitor

The Constitution provides that "Laws of the United States which shall be made in pursuance thereof; and all Treaties made, or which shall be made, under the Authority of the United States, shall be the supreme Law of the Land." An *Internal Revenue Code* provision and a provision under a treaty will sometimes conflict. In such a case, both of the provisions cannot represent the law; the one adopted later in time generally controls.

Example 3–1 Treaty Override. Prior to 1980, the United States negotiated treaties with several countries that allowed foreign taxpayers to sell U.S. real estate and not pay tax on gains. Under these treaties, nonresident aliens and foreign corporations could avoid U.S. taxes on real estate if the gains were treated as capital gains and were not effectively connected with the conduct of a U.S. business. Because of this favorable treatment for foreign investors, many U.S. farmers felt foreign investors were bidding up the price of farmland in the United States. This and other concerns led Congress to pass the Foreign

Investment in Real Property Tax Act (FIRPTA) of 1980. Under § 897, FIRPTA makes gains and losses by nonresident aliens and foreign corporations taxable by treating such transactions as effectively connected with a U.S. trade or business. This provision overrides any treaties in effect at that time by making foreign capital gains on real property taxable for transactions after 1984. If an existing treaty was renegotiated prior to 1985, the new treaty could designate a different effective date for § 897; however, the designated effective date could not be more than two years after the signing of the renegotiated treaty.

This later-in-time rule appears to be a simplistic approach to the complex interaction of the Code and treaty provisions. The courts have presented interpretive guidelines to be used in resolving interstatutory conflicts. One such guideline is that, where possible, equal effect should be given to both statutes; congressional intent to repeal a statute should not be assumed. A significant judicial history also exists for the interaction of treaties and the Code. In fact, as with conflicts between statutes, courts usually attempt to reconcile the apparent conflict in a way that gives consideration to both the treaty and the Code provisions.

The equality of the two types of provisions is indicated in § 7852(d) of the Code, which provides that neither a treaty nor a law shall be given preferential status by reason of its being a treaty or a law. The language of both the Code and the Constitution make this clear. The only codified exception to this rule is that treaty provisions in effect in 1954 and which conflicted with the 1954 Code as originally enacted are given precedence over the existing provisions of the 1954 Code, but not over later amendments to the Code. Section 894 states that due regard shall be given to any treaty obligation of the United States that applies to the taxpayer when applying the provisions of the *Internal Revenue Code*.

Treaties are authorized by the Constitution. Under Article II, Section 2, of the Constitution, the President of the United States is allowed to enter into treaties with other countries after receiving the advice and consent of the Senate. The President may also enter into other international agreements that have effects on the Federal tax structure. Such agreements need not be ratified by the Senate; however, they are implemented by Congress in accordance with existing Federal laws. But tax treaties usually are initiated by the State Department, not the Treasury. Generally, tax treaties do not address the state and local tax effects of the citizens and transactions covered by them.

Treaties may be terminated in several ways. They may expire because of a specific congressional time limitation, be superseded by a newer treaty, or be terminated by the countries' mutual actions.

Tax researchers often find it necessary to examine the provisions of tax treaties. Tax treaties can be found in both the online and printed versions of most tax services, at the government web sites of many countries, and in many legal publications such as West's *United States Code Annotated*.

THE LEGISLATIVE PROCESS

To understand how to research tax issues, the tax researcher must have a grasp of the Federal legislative process. The tax law of the United States, like automobiles and hot dogs, is created in a multistep process. At each stage in the creation of a tax law, Congress generates additional items of information, each of which may be useful in addressing a client's tax problem.

Most tax legislation begins in the House of Representatives. In the House, tax law changes are considered by the Ways and Means Committee. Upon approval by this committee, the bill is sent to the full House of Representatives for its approval. The bill then is sent to the Senate, where it is referred to the Finance Committee. When the Finance Committee approves the bill, the proposal is considered by the entire Senate.

If any differences between the House and Senate versions of the tax bill exist (which is almost always the case), the bill is referred to a Joint Conference Committee, where these differences are resolved. The compromise bill must be approved by both houses of Congress before it is forwarded to the President. If the President signs the bill, the new provisions are incorporated into the *Internal Revenue Code*. If the bill is vetoed by the President, however, it is not enacted, unless Congress overrides the veto with a sufficient revote. Exhibit 3–5 summarizes the usual steps of the legislative process as it is encountered relative to tax legislation.

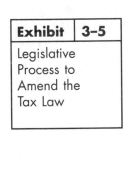

Exhibit 3–5

Legislative Process to Amend the Tax Law

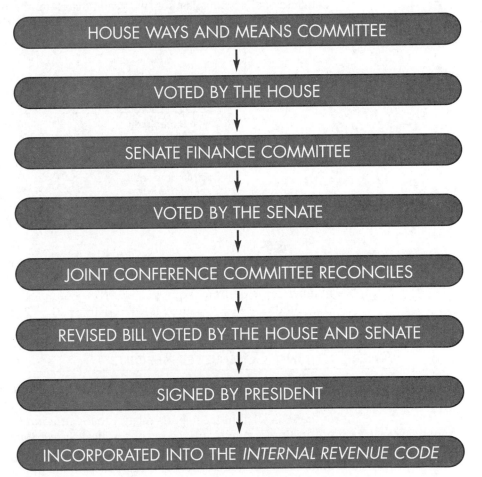

HOUSE WAYS AND MEANS COMMITTEE

↓

VOTED BY THE HOUSE

↓

SENATE FINANCE COMMITTEE

↓

VOTED BY THE SENATE

↓

JOINT CONFERENCE COMMITTEE RECONCILES

↓

REVISED BILL VOTED BY THE HOUSE AND SENATE

↓

SIGNED BY PRESIDENT

↓

INCORPORATED INTO THE *INTERNAL REVENUE CODE*

At each step in the legislative process, the appropriate committee of Congress produces a **Committee Report**, which explains the elements of the proposed changes and the reasons for each of the proposals. These Committee Reports are an important tool for tax researchers. In many situations where the tax law is unclear, or when recent legislation has been passed, they can provide insight concerning the meaning of a specific phrase of the statute or of the intention of Congress concerning a certain provision of the law. Committee Reports typically result from the deliberations of the Ways and Means Committee, the Finance Committee, and the Joint Conference Committee. A "General Explanation" of tax legislation occasionally is prepared by the Joint Committee on Taxation (the "Blue Book"). Exhibit 3–6 reproduces a portion of such a Committee Report.

Committee Reports generally are referred to by Public Law number. Every bill that Congress passes is assigned such a number. For example, the Tax Reform Act of 1986 was designated as P.L. 99-514. Public Law is abbreviated as "P.L." in this context. The prefix of the numerical designation (here, 99) refers to the session of Congress that passed the law. The suffix of the Public Law number (here, 514) indicates that this was the 514th bill that this session of Congress adopted.

Congressional sessions last for two years; therefore, the researcher may find it useful to construct a method by which to identify the two-year period in which a tax law was passed. The recent sessions of Congress are identified as follows.

Congressional Sessions	Years
One-hundred-sixth	1999–00
One-hundred-seventh	2001–02
One-hundred-eighth	2003–04
One-hundred-ninth	2005–06
One-hundred-tenth	2007–08
One-hundred-eleventh	2009–10
One-hundred-twelfth	2011–12

To convert a session number into the second year of the applicable congressional session, multiply the session number by 2 and subtract 212 (the number of years from 1788 to 2000). For example, the second year of the One-hundred-ninth Congress is 2006 [(109 $\times$ 2) − 212 = 06].

WHERE TO FIND COMMITTEE REPORTS

When a new tax law is passed, the pertinent Committee Reports are released in the Internal Revenue Service's weekly *Internal Revenue Bulletin*. The texts of the 1954 Committee Reports relative to the *Internal Revenue Code* are found not in the *Cumulative Bulletin*, but in the *United States Code Congressional and Administrative News*. All of the pre-1939 Revenue Act Committee Reports are reprinted in the 1939 *Cumulative Bulletin*.

Exhibit	3–6	Committee Report Excerpt

H. Rep. 108-126: JOBS AND GROWTH TAX RELIEF RECONCILIATION ACT OF 2003 (PL 108-27) INCREASE SECTION 179 EXPENSING (Sec. 202 of the House bill, Sec. 107 of the Senate amendment, and Sec. 179 of the Code)

PRESENT LAW

Present law provides that, in lieu of depreciation, a taxpayer with a sufficiently small amount of annual investment may elect to deduct up to $25,000 (for taxable years beginning in 2003 and thereafter) of the cost of qualifying property placed in service for the taxable year (Sec. 179). In general, qualifying property is defined as depreciable tangible personal property that is purchased for use in the active conduct of a trade or business. The $25,000 amount is reduced (but not below zero) by the amount by which the cost of qualifying property placed in service during the taxable year exceeds $200,000. An election to expense these items generally is made on the taxpayer's original return for the taxable year to which the election relates, and may be revoked only with the consent of the Commissioner. In general, taxpayers may not elect to expense off-the-shelf computer software.

The amount eligible to be expensed for a taxable year may not exceed the taxable income for a taxable year that is derived from the active conduct of a trade or business (determined without regard to this provision). Any amount that is not allowed as a deduction because of the taxable income limitation may be carried forward to succeeding taxable years (subject to similar limitations). No general business credit under Section 38 is allowed with respect to any amount for which a deduction is allowed under Section 179.

HOUSE BILL

The House bill provision provides that the maximum dollar amount that may be deducted under Section 179 is increased to $100,000 for property placed in service in taxable years beginning in 2003, 2004, 2005, 2006, and 2007. In addition, the $200,000 amount is increased to $400,000 for property placed in service in taxable years beginning in 2003, 2004, 2005, 2006, and 2007. The dollar limitations are indexed annually for inflation for taxable years beginning after 2003 and before 2008. The provision also includes off-the-shelf computer software placed in service in a taxable year beginning in 2003, 2004, 2005, 2006, or 2007, as qualifying property. With respect to a taxable year beginning after 2002 and before 2008, the provision permits taxpayers to make or revoke expensing elections on amended returns without the consent of the Commissioner.

EFFECTIVE DATE The provision is effective for taxable years beginning after December 31, 2002.

SENATE AMENDMENT The Senate amendment is the same as the House bill.

CONFERENCE AGREEMENT

The conference agreement follows the House bill and the Senate amendment, with modifications. The conference agreement provides that the increase in the dollar limitations, as well as the provision relating to off-the-shelf computer software, apply for property placed in service in taxable years beginning in 2003, 2004, and 2005. The conference agreement provides that the dollar limitations are indexed annually for inflation for taxable years beginning after 2003 and before 2006. With respect to a taxable year beginning after 2002 and before 2006, the conference agreement permits taxpayers to make or revoke expensing elections on amended returns without the consent of the Commissioner.

EFFECTIVE DATE Same as the House bill and the Senate amendment.

The Committee Reports and other legislative items can also be found in most subscription online tax services (e.g., RIA Checkpoint) and on various non-subscription Internet sites such as:

http://thomas.loc.gov

http://waysandmeans.house.gov/

http://www.senate.gov/~finance/

Commerce Clearing House and the Research Institute of America both publish, usually in paperback form, a collection of Committee Reports (or excerpts thereof) whenever a major new tax law is passed. If a tax researcher wants to find the Committee Reports that underlie a statutory provision, he or she also can use reference materials that are included in the bodies of most of the commercial tax services or in the index to the *Cumulative Bulletin*.

The Committee Reports Findings List in Commerce Clearing House's *Citator*, Volume M–Z, is a good place for the tax researcher to locate Committee Reports by P.L. number. See Part 3 of this text for a detailed review of the use of citators.

In addition to the Committee Reports, the Floor Debate Report may be of value to the tax researcher. The Floor Debate Report includes a summary of what was said from the floor of the House or Senate concerning the proposed bill. It may include some detailed or technical information that is excluded from the Committee Report. The Floor Debate Report is included in the *Congressional Record* for the day of the debate.

INTERNAL REVENUE CODE

After the Sixteenth Amendment was ratified in 1913, Congress passed a series of self-contained revenue acts, each of which formed the entire income tax law of the United States. For about two decades, Congress passed such a free-standing revenue act every year or two. By the 1930s, however, this series of revenue acts, and the task of rewriting the entire tax statute so often, had become unmanageable. Thus, in 1939, Congress replaced the revenue acts with the *Internal Revenue Code of 1939*, the first fully organized Federal tax law.

Although the concept of a free-standing tax code, as part of the entire *United States Code*, was a good idea, the organization of the *Internal Revenue Code of 1939* left little room to accommodate subsequent changes to the law. Accordingly, the 1939 Code was replaced with a reorganized, more flexible codification in 1954. Due to extensive revisions to the Code that were made as part of the Tax Reform Act of 1986, the statute was renamed the *Internal Revenue Code of 1986*. Thus, although the statute still follows the 1954 numbering system and organization, the official title of the extant U.S. tax law is the *Internal Revenue Code of 1986, as Amended*.

The principal sources of tax laws of the United States since 1913, then, have been identified as follows.

Period	Principal U.S. Tax Law
1913–39	Periodic Revenue Acts
1939–54	*Internal Revenue Code of 1939*
1954–86	*Internal Revenue Code of 1954*
1986–Present	*Internal Revenue Code of 1986*

Many provisions of the 1939 Code were carried over to the *Internal Revenue Code of 1954* without substantive change; some of these sections were adopted into the Code verbatim, although all of the sections were renumbered as part of the 1954 reorganization.

SPOTLIGHT ON TAXATION: Growth of the Code

If you think the tax law is getting more complex, you're correct. According to the Tax Foundation, in 1955 the *Internal Revenue Code* contained 106 Code sections and 409,000 words. Today there are 725 Code sections containing more than 1,670,000 words.

The *Internal Revenue Code* is part of the *United States Code*, which is a codification of all of the Federal laws of the United States. The elements of the *United States Code* are organized alphabetically and assigned title numbers. Accordingly, the *Internal Revenue Code* constitutes Title 26 of the *United States Code*; its neighbors in the *U.S. Code* include "Insane Asylums" and "Intoxicating Liquors."

ORGANIZATION OF THE INTERNAL REVENUE CODE

The *Internal Revenue Code* is organized into an outline form with multiple levels or subdivisions. The primary levels found in the Code are as follows.

Subtitles

Chapters

Subchapters

Parts

Sections

Subsections

Subtitles of the Code are assigned a capital letter to identify them (currently A through I are used). Generally, each subtitle contains all of the tax provisions that relate to a well-defined area of the tax law. Exhibit 3–7 identifies the subtitles of the current Code. The tax researcher spends most of his or her time working with Subtitles A, Income Taxes; B, Estate and Gift Taxes;

Exhibit	3–7	Subtitles of the *Internal Revenue Code*, as Amended

Subtitle	Tax Law Included
A	Income Taxes
B	Estate and Gift Taxes
C	Employment Taxes
D	Miscellaneous Excise Taxes
E	Alcohol; Tobacco; Miscellaneous Excise Taxes
F	Procedure and Administration
G	Joint Committee on Taxation
H	Presidential Election Campaign Financing
I	Trust Funds

and F, Procedure and Administration. The other subtitles typically are used only from time to time for special research problems.

Each subtitle contains a number of chapters, numbered, although not continuously, from 1 through 98. These chapter numbers do not start over at each subtitle; rather, they are used in ascending order throughout the Code. Thus, for example, there is only one Chapter 11 in the *Internal Revenue Code*, not nine of them. Each chapter contains the tax provisions that relate to a more narrowly defined area of the tax law than is addressed by the subtitles. Most of the subtitles include several chapters. Exhibit 3–8 examines the numbering system of the chapters of the *Internal Revenue Code*, concentrating on selected important chapters.

Exhibit	3–8	Key Chapters of the *Internal Revenue Code*

Chapter	Subjects Included
1	Normal Taxes and Surtaxes
2	Self-Employment Tax
6	Consolidated Returns
11	Estate Taxes
12	Gift Taxes
61	Administration/Information
79	Definitions

The chapters of the *Internal Revenue Code* are further divided into subchapters. Typically a subchapter contains a group of provisions that relates to a fairly specific area of the tax law. Subchapters sometimes are divided into parts, which may be divided into subparts. Letters are used to denote subchapters, and the lettering scheme starts over with each chapter. Thus, there may be a Subchapter A in each chapter.

Many times, tax practitioners use the subchapter designation as a shorthand reference to identify a certain area of taxation. For example, Subchapter C of Chapter 1 of Subtitle A of the *Internal Revenue Code* includes many of the basic corporate income tax provisions. Thus, when a tax practitioner wants to refer to a corporate tax matter, he or she often simply identifies it as a "Subchapter C" issue. Exhibit 3–9 identifies the subchapters of Chapter 1 (Income Taxes) of the Code.

Most of the Code's subchapters are divided into parts. The parts provide a natural grouping of provisions that address essentially the same issue. Not all subchapters are divided into parts, and occasionally the parts are not

Exhibit | 3–9

Subchapters of Chapter 1 (Normal Taxes), Subtitle A (Income Taxes), *Internal Revenue Code*

Subchapter	Topic(s) Included
A	Determination of Tax Liability
B	Computation of Taxable Income
C	Corporate Distributions and Adjustments
D	Deferred Compensation
E	Accounting Periods and Methods
F	Tax-Exempt Organizations
G	Corporate Accumulations/Personal Holding Companies
H	Banking Institutions
I	Natural Resources
J	Income Taxation of Estates and Trusts
K	Partnerships and Partners
L	Insurance Companies
M	Mutual Funds
N	International Taxation
O	Property Transactions
P	Capital Gains and Losses
Q	Readjustment of Tax between Years and Special Limitations
R	[Repealed]
S	S Corporations and Shareholders
T	Cooperatives and Patrons
U	[Repealed]
V	Bankruptcy Effects

numbered consecutively. For instance, the parts of Chapter 1, Subchapter A (i.e., normal income taxes), are

Part I   Tax on Individuals
Part II   Tax on Corporations
Part III   Changes in Rates during a Taxable Year
Part IV   Credits against Tax
Part V   Not Used
Part VI   Alternative Minimum Tax
Part VII   Environmental Tax

The most important division of the *Internal Revenue Code* for the tax researcher is the section, because the Code is arranged so that its primary unit is the section number. The sections currently are numbered 1 through 9800+, although not all of the numbers are used. Each section number is used only once in the Code. The researcher can refer to a specific provision of the *Internal Revenue Code* by its section number and not be concerned about duplication in another part of the law. Indeed, the most common element of the jargon of the tax practitioner community is the Code section number, and tax researchers must learn to identify important tax provisions merely by the corresponding section number.

Code sections can be divided into various smaller elements for the convenience of the drafter or user of the section. A section can contain subsections, paragraphs, subparagraphs, and clauses. Sections are denoted by numbers (1, 2, etc.), subsections by lowercase letters (a, b, etc.), paragraphs by numbers, subparagraphs by capital letters (A, B, etc.), and clauses by lowercase roman numerals (i, ii, etc.). In citing a Code section, one uses parentheses for each division that occurs after the section number.

There are some exceptions to the general formatting of Code section citations. For example, Congress has inserted Code sections in between other consecutive sections and has had to use a capital letter [e.g., or Section 25A(b)(1) or Section 280F(a)(1)] to accomplish this. Also, the Code skips the subsections in certain cases, such as Section 212(2). Exhibit 3–10 provides a specific interpretation of a Code section citation.

Although there are nearly a thousand Code sections, certain ones contain basic principles that affect most tax situations (Exhibit 3–11). The tax researcher should be familiar with this group of Code sections for efficient analysis of his or her clients' tax problems.

WHERE TO FIND THE INTERNAL REVENUE CODE

The amended *Internal Revenue Code* can be found in several places. National publishers such as Research Institute of America (RIA), West, and Commerce Clearing House (CCH) publish paperback versions of the Code for use by tax practitioners. In addition, the text of the Code may be found in most commercial tax services and as Title 26 of the *United States Code*.

The type of tax service will indicate the probable location of the original language of the Code in the service. Typically, an annotated tax service (refer

| Exhibit | 3-10 | Interpreting a Code Section Citation |

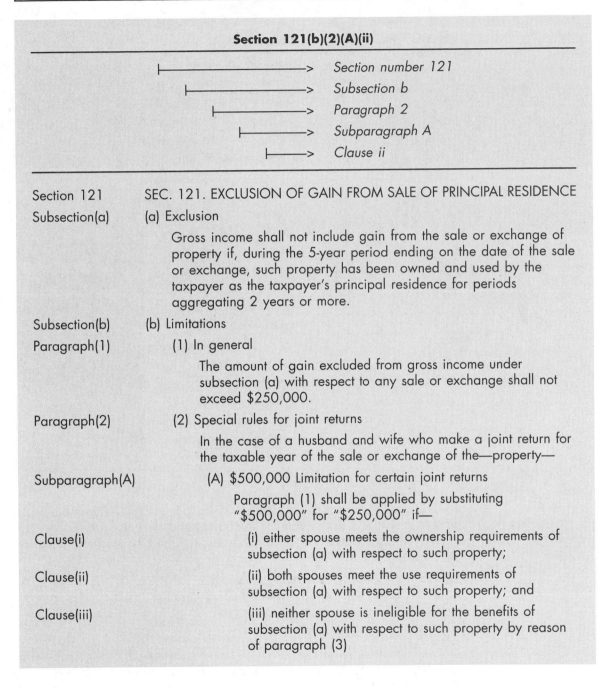

Section 121(b)(2)(A)(ii)

⊢————————————> *Section number 121*
⊢————————————> *Subsection b*
⊢————————————> *Paragraph 2*
⊢————————————> *Subparagraph A*
⊢————————————> *Clause ii*

Section 121	SEC. 121. EXCLUSION OF GAIN FROM SALE OF PRINCIPAL RESIDENCE
Subsection(a)	(a) Exclusion
	Gross income shall not include gain from the sale or exchange of property if, during the 5-year period ending on the date of the sale or exchange, such property has been owned and used by the taxpayer as the taxpayer's principal residence for periods aggregating 2 years or more.
Subsection(b)	(b) Limitations
Paragraph(1)	(1) In general
	The amount of gain excluded from gross income under subsection (a) with respect to any sale or exchange shall not exceed $250,000.
Paragraph(2)	(2) Special rules for joint returns
	In the case of a husband and wife who make a joint return for the taxable year of the sale or exchange of the—property—
Subparagraph(A)	(A) $500,000 Limitation for certain joint returns
	Paragraph (1) shall be applied by substituting "$500,000" for "$250,000" if—
Clause(i)	(i) either spouse meets the ownership requirements of subsection (a) with respect to such property;
Clause(ii)	(ii) both spouses meet the use requirements of subsection (a) with respect to such property; and
Clause(iii)	(iii) neither spouse is ineligible for the benefits of subsection (a) with respect to such property by reason of paragraph (3)

Exhibit	3-11	Some Important Code Sections

Section Number	Contents
1	Individual Tax Rates
11	Corporate Tax Rates
61	Definition of Gross Income
62	Deductions for Adjusted Gross Income
162	Trade or Business Deductions
163	Interest Deduction
164	Deduction for Taxes
165	Losses
167, 168, 179	Depreciation, Cost Recovery
212	Production-of-Income Expenses
312	Corporate Dividends
351	Forming a Corporation
368	Mergers, Acquisitions, Corporate Break-Ups
469	Passive Activities
501	Tax-Exempt Status
721	Forming a Partnership, LLC
861	Sourcing of International Income and Deductions
904	Foreign Tax Credit
1245	Depreciation Recapture
1504	Consolidated Taxable Income
6662	Penalties for Inaccurate Tax Filings

to Chapter 2 to review this definition) will include the text of the Code with the related section's discussion. On the other hand, a topical tax service typically reproduces the text of the Code in an appendix to pertinent chapters or volumes of the service.

The *U.S. Code* and the *Internal Revenue Code* (which is Title 26 of the *U.S. Code*) can also be found at various nonsubscription Internet sites. An example of such site would be:

http://uscode.house.gov/

Occasionally, a tax researcher needs to refer to a source that originated from the *Internal Revenue Code of 1939*. Many of the provisions of the 1986 (and 1954) Code can be found in the 1939 Code. Exhibit 3-12 gives examples of 1986 Code sections and their 1939 Code equivalents.

Other useful indices to the Code itself are provided by the editors of the tax services. For example, several useful tables are included in the Code volumes

Exhibit	3-12	Examples of 1986 Code Sections Derived from the 1939 Code

1986 Code Section	1939 Code Section
§ 61, Gross income defined	§ 22(a)
§ 71, Alimony and separate maintenance payments	§ 22(k)
§ 103, Interest on state and local bonds	§ 22(b)(4)
§ 151, Allowance of deductions for personal exemptions	§ 25(b)
§ 162, Trade or business expenses	§ 23(a)(1)
§ 172, Net operating loss deduction	§ 122
§ 212, Expenses for production of income	§ 23(a)(2)
§ 301, Distributions of property	§ 22(e), 115(a), (b), (d), (e)
§ 316, Dividends defined	§ 115(a) and (b)
§ 701, Partners, not partnership, subject to tax	§ 181

of the Commerce Clearing House tax service. In Cross-Reference Table 1, 1939 Code sections are cross-referenced to their 1954 (and 1986) counterparts. In Table 2 of the CCH service, current Code sections are cross-referenced to the 1939 Code.

Table III of this feature cross-references the Code sections within the current Code. These three tables can be useful to the tax researcher when he or she needs to find a 1939 Code section number, perhaps in interpreting a court case that addresses a pre-1954 Code issue, or in identifying situations where a Code section is referred to elsewhere in the current Code, or perhaps to find out whether other Code sections provide information bearing on the section being reviewed.

Most tax services also contain information about the history of each Code section. Typically, at the end of the text of each Code section, or as a related page that can be accessed by linking, the editors include a list of the Public Laws that have altered or amended the section. This listing generally includes a reference to the section as it existed prior to amendment, as well as the effective date of the amendment to the law. The tax researcher must be careful to consider the impact of any such amendments. Exhibit 3–13 illustrates the Public Law history with respect to a specific Code section.

One other publication will prove to be valuable if the researcher is addressing issues that predate the 1954 Code. *Seidman's Legislative History of Federal Income Tax Laws* details the historical evolution of the early tax law. It explains how certain provisions evolved into their current form in the Code.

Exhibit	3-13	Recent Amendments to Section 121

In 2003, P.L. 108-121, Sec. 101(a), redesignated para. (d)(9) as (10) and added para. (d)(9), effective for sales and exchanges after 5/6/97. For special rules, see Sec. 312(d)(2)-(4) of P.L. 105-34, reproduced below.

—P.L. 108-121, Sec. 101(b)(2), of this Act, provides:

"(2) Waiver of limitations. If refund or credit of any overpayment of tax resulting from the amendments made by this section is prevented at any time before the close of the 1-year period beginning on the date of the enactment of this Act by the operation of any law or rule of law (including res judicata), such refund or credit may nevertheless be made or allowed if claim therefore is filed before the close of such period."

In 2002, P.L. 107-358, Sec. 2, added subsec. (c) in Sec. 901 of P.L. 107-16 [see below], effective 12/17/2002.

In 2001, P.L. 107-16, Sec. 542(c), added para. (d)(9), effective for estates of decedents dying after 12/31/2009.

—P.L. 107-16, Sec. 901, of this Act [as amended by Sec. 2 of P.L. 107-358, see above], reads as follows:

"Sec. 901. Sunset of provisions of Act.

"(a) In general. All provisions of, and amendments made by, this Act shall not apply—

"(1) to taxable, plan, or limitation years beginning after December 31, 2010, or

"(2) in the case of title V, to estates of decedents dying, gifts made, or generation skipping transfers, after December 31, 2010.

"(b) Application of certain laws. The *Internal Revenue Code* of 1986 and the Employee Retirement Income Security Act of 1974 shall be applied and administered to years, estates, gifts, and transfers described in subsection (a) as if the provisions and amendments described in subsection (a) had never been enacted.

"(c) Exception. Subsection (a) shall not apply to section 803 (relating to no federal income tax on restitution received by victims of the Nazi regime or their heirs or estates)."

INTERPRETING THE INTERNAL REVENUE CODE

One of the greatest problems for a tax researcher is the interpretation of the *Internal Revenue Code*. Often, Code provisions are long, interrelated, and confusing. For example, several sentences in the Code exceed 300 words; one of them exceeds 400 words. In researching a client's tax problem, one must read each Code section that might apply. Many times, a single phrase or clause in the section may prevent the client from being subject to the provision or may contain other unexpected implications for the client's situation.

A researcher, in his or her initial review, may find the topical index, which is included by most publishers of the Code, a useful tool in locating a starting point or the relevant Code section. In reading, interpreting, and evaluating a selected Code section, the tax researcher must be especially critical of the language used throughout the section. Many, if not most, Code sections contain a general rule, followed by specific conditions that must be satisfied in order to apply the provision, and situations under which the taxpayer is excepted from the general rule. In some cases, the exceptions to the general rule are further modified to provide for exceptions to the general exceptions. Moreover, some exceptions to a Code section are addressed not within the same section, but in another section of the Code. Therefore, all relevant provisions must be read carefully.

In addition to being aware of the required conditions for application of a section, as well as the exceptions thereto, the researcher must be aware of the definitions of terms used in the section; pertinent definitions may be given within the section or in some other provision of the Code. These definitions may be significantly different from the common use of the term.

In § 7701, the text defines many of the terms used throughout the Code, but these definitions may be superseded by material contained within the applicable Code section. In addition, the researcher may need to look beyond the Code such as to the Regulations or other authority, to determine the conditions that a specific term may encompass. In all cases, the researcher should avoid jumping to premature conclusions until a thorough analysis of all relevant Code sections has been completed.

The tax researcher must be careful not to overlook words that connect phrases, such as "and" and "or." These words have very different logical meanings, and, even when the words are "hidden" at the end of the previous clause or subparagraph, they may significantly change the outcome of a research project. The word "and" is conjunctive; the word "or" is disjunctive. If the word "and" lies between two phrases, both of them must be true for the provision to apply to the client's problem. However, if the word "or" lies between two phrases, then only one of them must be true for the provision to apply.

The researcher also must be careful with words that modify percentage or dollar amounts. The phrases "less than 50%," "more than 50%," and "not less than 50%" have very different meanings in determining whether the provisions of a section apply. The researcher also must distinguish between such terms as "30 days" and "one month," because they usually identify different time periods.

Example 3–2 Conflicting Code Sections. Paul is a roofing contractor and has a truck he uses 100 percent of the time in his business. The truck cost $35,000 three years ago, and Paul has claimed ACRS of $24,920 on the truck, which leaves him an adjusted basis of $10,080. Paul sells the truck for $22,080 resulting in a gain of $12,000 on the truck. How is he to treat this gain for tax purposes?

In the *Internal Revenue Code*, Paul finds that when depreciable property used in a trade or business [§ 1231(b)] is sold, the gain is treated as a long-term capital gain [§ 1231(a)]. Thus, he might report the gain on his tax return as a long-term capital gain. However, in § 1245(a), Paul discovers that gain on depreciable personal property (in this case, the truck) is ordinary income to the extent of depreciation claimed since 1961. Thus, § 1245 would indicate the gain is ordinary, not long-term capital.

How is the problem resolved? In § 1245(d), Paul finds a directive that the recapture provision "shall apply notwithstanding any other provision of this subtitle [of the Code]." As a result, he must report the gain as ordinary income on his tax return, not long-term capital gain.

If Paul had read only § 1231 of the Code and not § 1245, he would have arrived at a different conclusion about the gain. In many situations, when Code sections conflict, the resolution of the conflict may not be as easy as in this example.

When analyzing a provision that recently has been changed by Congress, a researcher must be very careful to cross-reference all of the uses of terms whose definitions have been affected by the new law. Often, Congress does not use the care necessary to ascertain that all of the "loose ends" of the new provisions have been tied up. In recent years, almost every major change in the tax law has been followed by a "technical corrections act" to remove errors in implementing and interpreting the new provisions of the law, as well as to clarify problems that arise in integrating the new provisions with the existing provisions of the Code. Most of these corrections are identified by practitioners whose clients' situations are adversely affected by a given reading of the amended law; thus, the typical technical corrections act testifies as much to the thoroughness of the practitioners' research as to shoddy drafting of the law by Congress.

Because the provisions of the *Internal Revenue Code* change frequently, the researcher must be aware of the effective dates of the various changes to the law. A provision may not go into effect immediately upon its adoption by Congress. The date of the act with which the change in law is passed is not always indicative of the effective date of the provision. Often, various provisions under the same tax law will become effective on different dates and, in fact, may have effective dates that precede the date of the tax act. Similarly, when a provision of the tax law is deleted from the Code, the provision may be left in effect for a designated period of time before it actually expires. Transitional rules may also apply. The effective date for a change in the tax law usually may be found in the explanation of the Public Laws, which follows the pertinent Code section (see, for example, Exhibit 3–13). In some cases, the researcher may need to look to the explanation under another Code section for the effective date of a provision. The researcher must be careful to align the client's facts with the effective law at the pertinent dates, or a serious mistake could be made in the research conclusion.

Finally, the tax researcher must be aware that not *all* of the answers to a tax question will be found in the Code. The Code may be silent concerning the problem at hand, the application of Code language to the fact situation at hand may not be clear, or Code sections may appear to be in conflict. Thus,

Exhibit	3–14	Examples of Federal Laws Other Than the *Internal Revenue Code* That May Affect a Tax Transaction

Administrative Procedure Act

Alaska Native Claims Settlement Act

Atomic Energy Act Tax Provision

Bank Holding Company Act of 1956

Civil Rights Attorneys' Fees Awards Act of 1976

Financial Institutions Reform, Recovery, and Enforcement Act of 1989

Metric Conversion Act of 1975

Merchant Marine Act: Capital Construction Fund

New York City Pension Act

Organic Act of Guam

the researcher must look for an answer from other sources, such as tax treaties, administrative rulings (see Chapter 4), judicial decisions (see Chapter 5), or secondary sources of the law (see Chapters 6 through 8). Alternatively, the controlling law may be found in other parts of the Code, such as tariff or bankruptcy laws. Exhibit 3–14 lists examples of Federal laws other than the Code that affect specific tax matters.

SUMMARY

The three major sources of statutory tax law are the Constitution, tax treaties, and the *Internal Revenue Code*. The tax researcher must thoroughly understand each of these sources and the interrelationships among them. The Constitution is the basis for all Federal laws. The tax treaties are agreements between countries, negotiated by the President and approved by the Senate, that cover taxpayers subject to the tax laws of both countries. The authority of a tax treaty may equal or exceed that of a Code section. The greatest volume of tax statutes is found in the *Internal Revenue Code*, which is Title 26 of the *United States Code*. The Code contains the tax laws that Congress has passed, and it is the basic document for most U.S. tax provisions.

TAX TUTOR

Reinforce the tax research information covered in this chapter by completing the online tutorials located at the Federal Tax Research web site:

http://raabe.swlearning.com

KEY WORDS

By the time you complete this chapter, you should be comfortable discussing each of the following terms. If you need additional review of any of these items, return to the appropriate material in the chapter or consult the glossary to this text.

Committee Report   Secondary Authority
Constitutional and Legislative Sources   Statutory Sources
Internal Revenue Code   Tax Treaty
Primary Authority

DISCUSSION QUESTIONS

1. What are the three primary statutory sources of U.S. Federal tax law?

2. Discuss the effect of *Pollock v. Farmers' Loan and Trust Co.* on the development of U.S. income tax laws.

3. The Sixteenth Amendment to the Constitution had a significant effect on the U.S. income tax. What was it?

4. Discuss briefly the events leading to the passage of the Sixteenth Amendment to the U.S. Constitution.

5. What did the U.S. Supreme Court hold in *Flint v. Stone Tracy Co.* in 1911?

6. Tax protesters who file "frivolous" tax returns or bring "frivolous" proceedings before the U.S. Tax Court are subject to certain fines or other penalties. What are the grounds for imposing each penalty? What is the maximum amount of each penalty?

7. Discuss the powers of taxation that are granted to Congress by the U.S. Constitution. Are any limits placed on the powers of Congress to so tax?

8. Have the Federal courts ever held Federal estate and gift taxes to be unconstitutional?

9. What is a tax treaty? Explain the purpose of a tax treaty. What matters generally are covered in a tax treaty?

10. How is a tax treaty terminated?

11. When an *Internal Revenue Code* section and a tax treaty provision appear to conflict, which usually prevails?

12. Describe the ratification process for a tax treaty between the United States and another country.

13. The tax researcher must be able to find descriptions of tax treaties to solve certain tax problems. List different locations where a tax researcher might find a tax.

14. Briefly summarize the usual steps of the legislative process for development of Federal tax legislation.

15. As a bill proceeds through Congress, various Committee Reports are generated. List the three Committee Reports that typically are prepared for a new tax law.

16. When are Committee Reports useful to a tax researcher?

17. What is a Public Law number? In P.L. 100-203, what do the "100" and the "203" indicate?

18. Where would a tax researcher find pertinent Committee Reports? List at least four publications and their publishers that include tax-related Committee Reports. Is there an index that would help a tax researcher locate a specific Committee Report? If so, where might such an index be found?

19. In addition to the Committee Reports, which are a by-product to the development of tax legislation, what other report may be of value to the tax researcher analyzing a new provision of the tax law? Why?

20. Discuss the evolution of today's *Internal Revenue Code*.

21. The *Internal Revenue Code* is Title 26 of the *United States Code*. How is the *Internal Revenue Code* subdivided?

22. How are the subtitles of the *Internal Revenue Code* identified? What generally is contained in a subtitle?

23. In the citation § 101(a)(2)(B), what does the "a" stand for? What do the "2" and the "B" indicate to a tax researcher?

24. In the citation § 1031(a)(3)(B), what does the "a" stand for? What do the "3" and the "B" indicate to a tax researcher?

25. Are there any exceptions to the general formatting rules for a Code section? Give examples.

26. In what subchapter of Chapter 1, Subtitle A are the Code sections relating to corporations found? To mutual funds? To tax-exempt organizations?

27. What Code section contains the statute for the definition of gross income? The interest deduction? Depreciation and cost recovery?

28. The tax researcher must be careful not to overlook connecting words such as "and," "or," "at least," and "more than." Explain why this is important.

29. Not all statutory tax laws are found in the *Internal Revenue Code*. Is this statement true or false? Discuss briefly.

EXERCISES

30. What is found in each of the following subtitles of the *Internal Revenue Code*?
    a. Subtitle B
    b. Subtitle F
    c. Subtitle A
    d. Subtitle C

31. Each subtitle of the *Internal Revenue Code* contains several chapters. How are chapters identified? What generally is included in a chapter of the Code?

32. Identify the general content of each of the following chapters of the *Internal Revenue Code*.
    a. Chapter 11
    b. Chapter 61
    c. Chapter 1
    d. Chapter 12

33. Chapters of the *Internal Revenue Code* are subdivided into subchapters. How are subchapters identified? What generally is contained in a subchapter?

34. Correctly cite the italicized sentence indicated by the dart (▶) in the following passage from the Code.

    SECTION 74. PRIZES AND AWARDS
    (a) General rule
         Except as otherwise provided in this section or in section 117 (relating to qualified scholarships), gross income includes amounts received as prizes and awards.
    (b) Exception for certain prizes and awards transferred to charities
         Gross income does not include amounts received as prizes and awards made primarily in recognition of religious, charitable, scientific, educational, artistic, literary, or civic achievement, but only if—
         (1) the recipient was selected without any action on his part to enter the contest or proceeding;
    ▶ *(2) the recipient is not required to render substantial future services as a condition to receiving the prize or award; and*
         (3) the prize or award is transferred by the payor to a governmental unit or organization described in paragraph (1) or (2) of section 170(c) pursuant to a designation made by the recipient.

35. Correctly cite the italicized sentence indicated by the dart (▶) in the following passage from the Code.

    SECTION 263A. CAPITALIZATION AND INCLUSION IN INVENTORY COSTS OF CERTAIN EXPENSES
    (a) Nondeductibility of certain direct and indirect costs
         (1) In general—In the case of any property to which this section applies, any costs described in paragraph (2)—
              (A) in the case of property which is inventory in the hands of the taxpayer, shall be included in inventory costs, and
    ▶   *(B) in the case of any other property, shall be capitalized.*
         (2) Allocable costs

36. What is the general content of each of the following subchapters of Chapter 1, Subtitle A, the *Internal Revenue Code*?
    a. Subchapter C
    b. Subchapter K

c. Subchapter S
d. Subchapter E

37. What is found in each of the following subchapters of Chapter 1, Subtitle A, of the *Internal Revenue Code*?
    a. Subchapter D
    b. Subchapter H
    c. Subchapter P
    d. Subchapter L

38. What is the official name of P.L. 108-27? What year was that law enacted? Where did you find your answer?

39. What is the official name of P.L. 99-514? What year was that law enacted? Where did you find your answer?

40. The most important division of the *Internal Revenue Code* is the section. Sections usually are subdivided into various smaller elements. Name several of these elements and state how they are denoted.

41. Do section numbers repeat themselves or is each one unique?

42. Identify the general contents of each of the following *Internal Revenue Code* sections.
    a. § 61
    b. § 162
    c. § 1
    d. § 212

43. Identify the general contents of each of the following *Internal Revenue Code* sections.
    a. § 62
    b. § 163
    c. § 11
    d. § 164

44. Locate Section 217 of the Code. It is found in the:
    a. Subtitle of the Code
    b. Chapter
    c. Subchapter
    d. Part

45. Locate Section 2036 of the Code. It is found in the:
    a. Subtitle of the Code
    b. Chapter
    c. Subchapter
    d. Part

46. Use a computer tax service (e.g., RIA Checkpoint, Lexis, Westlaw, etc.) to answer the following questions.
    a. Which computer service did you use?
    b. What is the general content of *Internal Revenue Code* § 28?
    c. What is the general content of *Internal Revenue Code* § 141?
    d. What is the general content of *Internal Revenue Code* § 166?
    e. Print a copy (maximum of one page) of any one of the above Code sections and attach it to your assignment.

47. Use a computer tax service (e.g., RIA Checkpoint, Lexis, Westlaw, etc.) to answer the following questions.
    a. Which computer tax service did you use?
    b. What is the general content of *Internal Revenue Code* § 117?
    c. What is the general content of *Internal Revenue Code* § 165?
    d. What is the general content of *Internal Revenue Code* § 304?
    e. Print a copy (maximum of one page) of any one of the above Code sections and attach it to your assignment.

48. Use a computer tax service (e.g., RIA Checkpoint, Lexis, Westlaw, etc.) to answer the following questions.
    a. Which computer tax service did you use?
    b. What is the general content of *Internal Revenue Code* § 25A?
    c. What is the general content of *Internal Revenue Code* § 67?
    d. What is the general content of *Internal Revenue Code* § 280G?
    e. Print a copy (maximum of one page) of any one of the above Code sections and attach it to your assignment

49. Name several locations where a tax researcher would find the text of the current *Internal Revenue Code*.

50. If a tax researcher wants to know if there is an equivalent 1939 Code section for a specific 1986 Code section, how would he or she locate it?

51. One important problem that faces a tax researcher is interpretation of the *Internal Revenue Code*. Comment on each of the following interpretation problems.
    a. Exceptions to a Code section
    b. Words that connect phrases, such as "and" and "or"
    c. Recent changes in the Code
    d. Effective dates
    e. Words that modify percentages, dollar amounts, or time

52. Comment on the statement, "All tax questions can be answered using the *Internal Revenue Code*."

53. Does the United States have an income tax treaty with any of the following countries? If it does, in what year was the treaty signed? State where you found this information.
    a. Japan
    b. United Kingdom
    c. Egypt
    d. Germany

54. Does the United States have an estate tax treaty with any of the following countries? If it does, in what year was the treaty signed? State where you found this information.
    a. Canada
    b. Finland
    c. Hungary
    d. Italy

55. Does the United States have an estate tax treaty with any of the following countries? If it does, in what year was the treaty signed? State where you found this information.
   a. Ukraine
   b. Brazil
   c. Kenya
   d. Kazakhstan

56. Use a computer tax service (e.g., RIA Checkpoint, Lexis, Westlaw, etc.) to locate § 117 of the *Internal Revenue Code*. Answer the following questions.
   a. Which computer tax service did you use?
   b. How many subsection(s) does § 117 include?
   c. How many paragraph(s) does § 117(b) include?
   d. How many subparagraph(s) does § 117(d)(2) include?
   e. Print a copy (maximum of one page) of this section and attach it to your assignment.

57. Use a computer tax service (e.g., RIA Checkpoint, Lexis, Westlaw, etc.) to locate § 385 of the *Internal Revenue Code*. Answer the following questions.
   a. Which computer tax service did you use?
   b. How many subsection(s) does § 385 include?
   c. How many paragraph(s) does § 385(b) include?
   d. Print a copy (maximum of one page) of this section and attach it to your assignment.

58. Use a computer tax service (e.g., RIA Checkpoint, Lexis, Westlaw, etc.) to locate § 280C of the *Internal Revenue Code*. Answer the following questions.
   a. Which computer tax service did you use?
   b. How many subsection(s) does § 280C include?
   c. How many paragraph(s) does § 280C(b) include?
   d. How many subparagraph(s) does § 280C(b)(2) include?
   e. Print a copy (maximum of one page) of this section and attach it to your assignment.

59. When was each of the following sections originally enacted? State how you obtained this information.
   a. § 843
   b. § 131
   c. § 469
   d. § 263A

60. In which subtitle, chapter, and subchapter of the 1986 Code are each of the following sections found?
   a. § 32
   b. § 172
   c. § 2039
   d. § 6013

61. List the first three section numbers and titles of each of the following subchapters of Chapter 1 of the *Internal Revenue Code*.
    a. Subchapter B
    b. Subchapter E
    c. Subchapter J
    d. Subchapter S

62. Identify the equivalent section of the current Code for each of the following sections of the 1939 Code. If there is no equivalent section, say so.
    a. § 1
    b. § 113(a)
    c. § 22(a)
    d. § 115(a)
    e. § 181

63. Use a computer tax service (e.g., RIA Checkpoint, Lexis, Westlaw, etc.) to locate the following Code sections. What other Code sections reference each of the sections you found? State which computer tax service you used to complete this assignment.
    a. § 72
    b. § 307
    c. § 446

64. Name the article and section of the U.S. Constitution that gives Congress the power to tax.

65. Enumerate the Code sections that contain the chief tax law provisions on the following topics.
    a. S corporations
    b. Personal holding company tax
    c. Gift tax
    d. Tax accounting methods

66. Use a nonsubscription Internet site to determine how many Senators are on the Senate Finance Committee. Who is the Chair of the Finance Committee? State where you found this information.

67. Use a nonsubscription Internet site to determine how many Representatives are on the House Ways and Means Committee. Who is the Chair of the Ways and Means Committee? State where you found this information.

68. Use a nonsubscription Internet site to determine what is contained in each of the following. State where you found this information.
    a. U.S. Const. art. I, § 9 cl. 3
    b. U.S. Const. art. I, § 8 cl. 1
    c. U.S. Const. art. II, § 2 cl. 2

69. Locate and print the first page of a House Ways and Means Committee Report using only a nonsubscription Internet site. State where you found this information.

RESEARCH CASES

70. Private G.I. Jane was a soldier in the Gulf War. Her salary was $1,800 per month, and she was in the war zone for eight months. How much of her salary is taxable for the eight months? In answering this case, use only the *Internal Revenue Code* for your research. *Computer search keywords:* combat, pay, officers, enlisted

71. Carol received a gift of stock from her favorite uncle. The stock had a fair market value of $30,000 and a basis to the uncle of $10,000 at the date of the gift. How much is taxable to Carol from this gift? In answering this case, use only the *Internal Revenue Code* for your research. *Computer search keywords:* gift, gross income, exclusion

72. Maria is an independent long-haul trucker. She receives a speeding ticket for $125, which she pays. Can Maria deduct the ticket on Schedule C? In answering this case, use only the *Internal Revenue Code* for your research. *Computer search keywords:* fines, penalties, deduction

73. Julie loaned her friend Nathan $2,500. Nathan did not repay the debt and skipped town. Can Julie claim any deduction? In answering this case, use only the *Internal Revenue Code* for your research. *Computer search keywords:* loss, bad debt, worthless

74. In December of 20x1, Ann's twelve-year-old cousin, Susan, came to live with her after Susan's parents met an untimely death in a car accident. In 20x2, Ann provided all normal support (e.g., food, clothing, education) for Susan. Ann did not formally adopt Susan. If Susan lived in the household for the entire year, can Ann claim a dependency exemption for her cousin for the 20x2 tax year? In answering this case, use only the *Internal Revenue Code* for your research. *Computer search keywords:* dependent, household, support

75. John and Maria support their twenty-one-year-old son, Bill. The son earned $10,500 last year working in a part-time job. Bill went to college part time in the spring semester of the current year. To complete his degree, Bill started school full time in the fall. The fall semester at Bill's college runs from August 20 to December 20. Can John and Maria claim Bill as a dependent on the current year's tax return, even if Bill earns $9,000 gross income? Assume any dependency test not mentioned has been met. In answering this case, use a computer tax service with only the *Internal Revenue Code* database selected. State your keywords and which computer tax service you used to arrive at your answer.

76. George and Linda are divorced and own a house from the marriage. Under the divorce decree, Linda pays George $3,000 per month alimony. Since the real estate market has collapsed in the area where they live, George and Linda cannot sell the house. Since they are still friends, they decide to live in separate wings of the house until the real estate market recovers. If George and Linda live together for the

entire current year, can Linda claim a deduction for the alimony paid to George? In answering this case, use a computer tax service with only the *Internal Revenue Code* database selected. State your keywords and which computer tax service you used to arrive at your answer.

77. Juan sold IBM stock to Richard for a $10,000 loss. Richard is the husband of Juan's sister. How much of the loss can Juan deduct in the current year if Juan's taxable income is $55,000 and he has no other capital transactions? In answering this case, use a computer tax service with only the *Internal Revenue Code* database selected. State your keywords and which computer tax service you used to arrive at your answer.

78. Tex is a rancher. This year her herd of cattle was infested with hoof-and-mouth disease and had to be destroyed. Tex's insurance policy reimburses her for an amount in excess of the tax basis in the cattle, thereby creating an "insurance gain." After receiving the insurance proceeds, Tex buys a new herd of cattle. Can Tex defer the recognition of this insurance gain on the destroyed herd? In answering this case, use a computer tax service with only the *Internal Revenue Code* database selected. State your keywords and which computer tax service you used to arrive at your answer.

79. Betty owed Martha $5,000. In payment of this debt, Betty transferred to Martha a life insurance policy on Betty, with a cash surrender value of $5,000. The face value of the policy is $100,000. Martha names herself as beneficiary of the policy and continues to make the premium payments. After Martha has paid $15,000 in premiums, Betty dies and Martha collects $100,000. Is any of the $100,000 Martha received taxable? In answering this case, use a computer tax service with only the *Internal Revenue Code* database selected. State your keywords and which computer tax service you used to arrive at your answer.

80. On May 1, Rick formed a new corporation, Red, Inc. He spent $3,000 in legal fees and paid the state $600 in incorporation fees to set up Red Corporation. Red Corporation started operating its business on May 10. Can Rick or Red Corporation deduct either of these organizational fees? In answering this case, use a computer tax service with only the *Internal Revenue Code* database selected. State your keywords and which computer tax service you used to arrive at your answer.

81. This year, there were massive brush fires in the interior of Mexico. Amy gave $10,000 to the Mexican Relief Foundation, which is located in Mexico City. The funds were used to provide food, clothing, and shelter to the victims of the Mexican fires. Is Amy's charitable contribution deductible for income tax purposes? In answering this case, use a computer tax service with only the *Internal Revenue Code* database selected. State your keywords and which computer tax service you used to arrive at your answer.

82. Curtis is fifty years old and has an IRA with substantial funds in it. His son, Curtis, Jr., was accepted to Yale University upon graduating from high school. Curtis had not planned for this and needs to draw $25,000 per year out of his IRA to help pay the tuition and fees at Yale. What are the tax consequences of the withdrawals from the IRA? In answering this case, use a computer tax service with only the *Internal Revenue Code* database selected. State your keywords and which computer tax service you used to arrive at your answer.

83. Dennis is an executive of Gold Corporation. He receives a one-for-one distribution of stock rights for each share of common stock he owns. On the date of distribution the stock rights have a fair market value of $2 per right and the stock has fair market value of $20 per share. Dennis owns 10,000 shares of the stock with a basis of $5 per share. If Dennis does not make any special elections with regards to the stock rights, what is his basis in the rights?
    a. Locate the Code section(s) that deals with this situation. State the section number(s).
    b. Review the Code section(s). Does it raise a need for new information to solve this question?
    c. Are you able to reach a conclusion about the research question from this Code section? If so, what is your conclusion(s)?

84. Kurt purchased a new Toyota hybrid automobile that gets 50 miles per gallon of gasoline. Determine if Kurt gets any special Federal tax breaks for purchasing this energy-saving car. If so, how are such tax breaks calculated?
    a. Locate the Code section(s) that deals with this situation. State the section number(s).
    b. Review the Code section(s). Does it raise a need for new information to solve this question?
    c. Are you able to reach a conclusion about the research question from this Code section? If so, what is your conclusion(s)?

85. Monica purchased two acres of land with an old building on it for $1,000,000. The purpose of this purchase was to acquire the land for a new store she wanted to open on the property. Shortly after completing the purchase, Monica pays $80,000 to have the old building demolished. How does Monica treat the $80,000 demolition payment for tax purposes?
    a. Locate the Code section(s) that deals with this situation. State the section number(s).
    b. Review the Code section(s). Does it raise a need for new information to solve this question?
    c. Are you able to reach a conclusion about the research question from this Code section? If so, what is your conclusion(s)?

86. Lihue, Inc. sells timeshares in Hawaii. Gene buys a timeshare out of the inventory of timeshares for sale by Lihue, Inc. Gene agrees to pay them $10,000 down and Lihue, Inc. will finance a seven-year note for

the balance of the purchase price at the current market rate of interest. Can Lihue, Inc. use the installment method to report their gain on the sale of the Hawaiian timeshare to Gene?

a. Locate the Code section(s) that deals with this situation. State the section number(s).

b. Review the Code section(s). Does it raise a need for new information to solve this question?

c. Are you able to reach a conclusion about the research question from this Code section? If so, what is your conclusion(s)?

Chapter 4

Administrative Regulations and Rulings

LEARNING OBJECTIVES

■ Identify the most important administrative sources of the Federal tax law.

■ Distinguish among the structure, nature, and purpose of Regulations, Revenue Procedures, and IRS Rulings.

■ Describe how to locate, and how to interpret, the precedential value of administrative sources of the tax law.

■ Explain the elements of common citations for Regulations and other IRS pronouncements.

■ Detail the contents and publication practices of the Internal Revenue Bulletin and the Cumulative Bulletin.

CHAPTER OUTLINE

Regulations
Temporary Regulations
Effective Date of Regulations
Citing a Regulation
Assessing Regulations
Locating Regulations

Revenue Rulings
Revenue Ruling Citations
Locating Revenue Rulings

Revenue Procedures

Letter Rulings
Private Letter Rulings

Technical Advice Memoranda
Determination Letters
Public Inspection of Written Determinations
Written Determination Numbering System
Locating Written Determinations
Other IRS Pronouncements
Acquiescences and Nonacquiescences
Internal Revenue Bulletin
Chief Counsel Memoranda
Announcements and Notices
Miscellaneous Publications

How does a tax practitioner proceed once he or she has determined which statutory source(s) applies to an open research question? Many times the answer is to turn to administrative sources of tax authority. Most administrative sources of the tax law come from the Treasury Department. The head of the Treasury Department is the Secretary of the Treasury, who has the general responsibility for administering the tax law. The Secretary is a member of the President's cabinet and is not to be confused with the Treasurer of the United States. The Treasurer is another official in the Treasury Department, but is not concerned directly with tax matters.

The Internal Revenue Service is a division of the Treasury Department. It is assigned to manage day-to-day operations associated with administration of the provisions of the *Internal Revenue Code*. The chief operating official of the IRS is the Commissioner of Internal Revenue, a presidential appointee. The Treasury Secretary delegates most of the administrative responsibilities for the tax law to the IRS Commissioner.

To facilitate the IRS's administration of the tax laws, the Code authorizes the Treasury Secretary (or his or her delegate) to prescribe the Rules and Regulations necessary to administer the Code. According to § 7805(a),

> *Except where such authority is expressly given by this title to any person other than an officer or employee of the Treasury Department, the Secretary shall prescribe all needful rules and regulations for the enforcement of this title, including all rules and regulations as may be necessary by reason of any alteration of law in relation to internal revenue.*

This Code section gives the IRS general authority to issue binding Rules and Regulations concerning Title 26 of the *United States Code*. In practice, most of the IRS's pronouncements are written by IRS staff or by the office of the Chief Counsel of the IRS, who is an assistant General Counsel of the Treasury Department.

SPOTLIGHT ON TAXATION: The IRS Commissioner

Mark W. Everson was confirmed by the U.S. Senate on May 1, 2003, to be Commissioner of Internal Revenue. Mr. Everson is the 46th Commissioner since the agency was created in 1862. Mr. Everson was appointed by President Bush to a five-year term.

A native of New York, Mr. Everson was born on September 10, 1954. He began his career as a CPA with Arthur Andersen & Co. in New York. He received his bachelor of arts in history from Yale University and has a masters of science in accounting from the New York University Business School.

As IRS Commissioner, Mr. Everson presides over the continued reorganization and modernization of the nation's tax administration agency. His priorities include strengthening enforcement of the tax laws and improving services for taxpayers. The agency has approximately 100,000 employees and a budget of $10 billion. In 2002, the agency collected $2 trillion in tax revenue, processed 226 million tax returns and issued $283 billion in refunds.

The tax researcher must be especially familiar with the four major types of pronouncements that may be forthcoming under this authority, namely, Regulations, Revenue Rulings, Revenue Procedures, and Letter Rulings. Each of these categories of rulings is issued for a different purpose and carries a different degree of authority. The first three of these categories generally are published by the IRS, while the Letter Rulings (and other pronouncements) typically are not published by any government agency. The remainder of this chapter addresses the nature and location of each of these administrative pronouncements.

REGULATIONS

The **Regulations** constitute the IRS's and, thereby, the Treasury's official interpretation of the *Internal Revenue Code*. Regulations are issued in the form of **Treasury Decisions (TDs)**, which are published in the *Federal Register* and, sometime later, in the *Internal Revenue Bulletin*, discussed later in this chapter. At least thirty days before a TD is published in final form, however, it must be issued in proposed form, allowing interested parties time to comment on it. As a result of the comments received during this process of public hearings, the IRS may make changes in the TD before its final publication.

Before and during the hearings process, the TDs are referred to as **Proposed Regulations** and, unlike Final Regulations, do not have the effect of law. After the hearings are completed, and changes (if any) have been made to the text of the TD, the TD is published in final form. Final Regulations are integrated with previously approved TDs and constitute the full set of IRS Regulations. After this integration has occurred, the TD designation usually is dropped, and the pronouncement simply is referred to as a "Regulation."

Observers have identified two distinct categories of Regulations, general and legislative. **General Regulations** are issued under the general authority granted to the IRS to interpret the language of the Code, usually under a specific Code (or Committee Report) directive of Congress, and with specific congressional authority. An example can be found under § 212, Expenses for the Production of Income. This short Code section has many pages of interpretive Regulations, providing taxpayers with operational rules for applying this provision to tax situations.

With respect to **Legislative Regulations**, the IRS is directed by Congress to fulfill effectively a law-making function and to specify the substantive requirements of a tax provision. Regulations that are ordered by the Code in this manner essentially carry the authority of the statute itself and are not easily challenged by taxpayers. Such authority is granted because, in certain (especially technical) areas of the tax law, Congress cannot or does not care to address the detailed or complex issues that are associated with an otherwise-defined tax issue. Accordingly, Congress directs the IRS to pronounce Regulations on the matter. For example, Congress delegated to the IRS the authority to prescribe Regulations necessary to carry out the provisions of § 135, which grants an exclusion for interest on certain U.S. savings bonds used for higher education expenses, including Regulations requiring record keeping and information reporting. Another example of this legislative authority is found in § 385, which directs the IRS to prescribe Regulations to distinguish debt from equity in "thinly capitalized" corporations. Legislative Regulations bear the greatest precedential value of any IRS pronouncement.

TEMPORARY REGULATIONS

In addition to Proposed and Final Regulations, the IRS periodically issues **Temporary Regulations** in response to a congressional or judicial change in the tax law or its interpretation. Temporary Regulations are not subject to the public-hearings procedure that typifies the development of a Final Regulation, and they are effective immediately upon publication. Although they are effective immediately, the IRS must simultaneously issue the Regulations in proposed form; the Temporary Regulations expire three years after issuance pursuant to the statute.[1] Temporary Regulations are issued to provide the taxpayer with immediate guidance concerning a new provision of the law, perhaps concerning filing requirements that must be satisfied immediately or the clarification of definitions and terms.

Until a Temporary Regulation is replaced with the Final Regulation under a Code section, the tax researcher should treat the Temporary Regulation as though it were final. Thus, Temporary Regulations are fully in effect and must be followed until they are superseded, whereas Proposed Regulations, having been issued only to solicit comments and to expose the IRS's proposed interpretation of the law, need not be followed as if they were law.

EFFECTIVE DATE OF REGULATIONS

In general, a new Regulation can be effective on the date on which such Regulation is filed with the *Federal Register*.[2] However, there are certain situations in which a Regulation can be effective retroactively. These are:

- The Regulation is filed or issued within 18 months of the date of the enactment of the statutory provision to which the Regulation relates.
- The Regulation is designed to prevent abuse by taxpayers.
- The Regulation corrects a procedural defect in the issuance of a prior Regulation.
- The Regulation relates to internal Treasury Department policies, practices, or procedures.
- The Regulation may apply retroactively by congressional directive.
- The Commissioner also has the power to allow taxpayers to elect to apply new Regulations retroactively.

In situations where a Regulation applies retroactively, it technically can apply starting with the date of the underlying Code section to which it relates. However, the statute of limitations may limit the application of a retroactive Regulation in many situations.

1. IRC § 7805.
2. § 7805(b).

CITING A REGULATION

Tax practitioners use a uniform system for citing specific Regulations. Each Regulation is assigned a unique number by the Treasury, which is broadly based on the Code section being interpreted in that Regulation. An example of this citation system appears in Exhibit 4–1.

The number to the left of the period in a Regulation citation indicates the type of issue that is addressed in the pronouncement. The most commonly encountered types of Regulations include the following.

   1. Income Tax
  20. Estate Tax
  25. Gift Tax
  31. Employment Tax
301. Procedural Matters

By being familiar with this arbitrary numbering system used by the Regulations, the tax researcher immediately can identify the general issue that is

Exhibit | 4–1

Interpreting a Regulation Citation

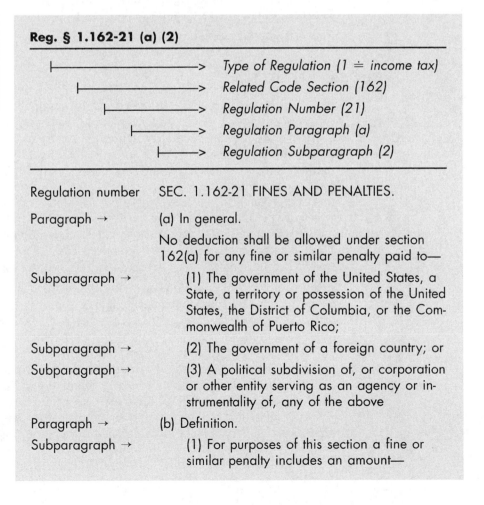

Reg. § 1.162-21 (a) (2)

$\longrightarrow$ *Type of Regulation (1 ≐ income tax)*

$\longrightarrow$ *Related Code Section (162)*

$\longrightarrow$ *Regulation Number (21)*

$\longrightarrow$ *Regulation Paragraph (a)*

$\longrightarrow$ *Regulation Subparagraph (2)*

Regulation number   SEC. 1.162-21 FINES AND PENALTIES.

Paragraph →   (a) In general.

No deduction shall be allowed under section 162(a) for any fine or similar penalty paid to—

Subparagraph →   (1) The government of the United States, a State, a territory or possession of the United States, the District of Columbia, or the Commonwealth of Puerto Rico;

Subparagraph →   (2) The government of a foreign country; or

Subparagraph →   (3) A political subdivision of, or corporation or other entity serving as an agency or instrumentality of, any of the above

Paragraph →   (b) Definition.

Subparagraph →   (1) For purposes of this section a fine or similar penalty includes an amount—

addressed in a pronouncement. Note that these numbers indicating the type of issue addressed in the Regulation do not necessarily correspond to the chapter numbers of the Code sections that address the same issues.

The number to the immediate right of the period in the citation of a Regulation indicates the Code section to which the Regulation relates. In the Exhibit 4–1 example of a full citation, one can determine that this is an income tax Regulation dealing with § 162 of the *Internal Revenue Code*. The numbers and letters to the right of the section number denote the Regulation number and smaller divisions of the pronouncement. Regulation numbers typically are consecutive, starting with 0 or 1, and follow the general order of the issues that are addressed in the corresponding Code section. The Regulation numbers, paragraphs, and so on, do not necessarily correspond, however, to the subsection or other division designations of the underlying Code section.

The numbering system for Temporary Regulations is similar to the numbering system for the Final and Proposed Regulations; however, usually the reference to or citation of a Temporary Regulation will include a "T" designating the temporary nature of the Regulation. An example of a citation for a Temporary Regulation under Code § 280H is:

Reg. § 1.280H-1T(b)(3).

ASSESSING REGULATIONS

In the course of tax practice, the researcher occasionally is faced with a question concerning the validity of a Regulation. If the practitioner disagrees with the scope or language of the Regulation, he or she bears the burden of proof of showing that the Regulation is improper. This can be difficult. Many Regulations simply restate the Code or congressional Committee Reports; they are known as "hard and solid" Regulations. Moreover, because of the authority delegated to the IRS, Legislative Regulations have the full force and effect of law. Finally, the Supreme Court views General Regulations as also having the force and effect of law, unless they conflict with the statute.[3] Thus, a taxpayer challenge to a Regulation typically must assert an improper exercise of IRS power, or an overly broad application of a rule.

In questioning the provisions of a Regulation, the tax researcher must be aware of several accuracy-related penalties Congress has enacted in the *Internal Revenue Code*. For example, a penalty is assessed equal to 20 percent of any underpayment of tax where the underpayment is found to be due to "negligence" on the part of the taxpayer.[4] Generally, negligence includes any failure to make a reasonable attempt to comply with the Code or any evidence of disregard of Treasury Rules or Regulations. Thus, if a practitioner chooses to ignore an administrative element of the tax law, he or she must possess substantial authority to do so to avoid this penalty or others of its kind. See Chapter 13 for a more detailed examination of these provisions.

3. *Maryland Casualty Co. v. U.S.*, 251 U.S. 342 (1920).
4. § 6662.

LOCATING REGULATIONS

When Treasury Decisions are final, they are published in the ***Internal Revenue Bulletin*** (IRB), a weekly newsletter of the IRS. Twice a year, the IRBs, reorganized by Code section, are bound into a set of volumes titled the ***Cumulative Bulletin***, which becomes the permanent IRS location of the Regulations.

Most commercial tax services also reproduce the Regulations in their materials; annotated services usually include the text adjacent to the language of the Code and the related court case notes, and topical services usually provide an appendix that includes the edited Regulations for the volume or chapter that discusses the pertinent issue. Paperback or hardbound editions of the tax Regulations also are available from several commercial publishers, including Research Institute of America (RIA) and Commerce Clearing House (CCH), typically as a companion to a similar edition of the Code. Exhibit 4–2 shows common places where the tax researcher can find the Regulations and most other sources of administrative tax research material.

Exhibit	**4–2**
Sources of Administrative Tax Law	

Computer Sources	
RIA Checkpoint	Research Institute of America
Westlaw	West Publishing Co.
CCH Tax Research Network	Commerce Clearing House
Kleinrock's	Kleinrock Publishing Co.
Lexis	LexisNexis

Printed Sources	
Tax Coordinator 2d	Research Institute of America
United States Code Annotated	West Publishing Co.
Standard Federal Tax Reporter	Commerce Clearing House
Cumulative Bulletin	Government Printing Office
Public Law Legislative History	Commerce Clearing House
Primary Sources (since 1968)	Bureau of National Affairs

REVENUE RULINGS

Revenue Rulings are second to Regulations as important administrative sources of the Federal tax law. A Revenue Ruling is an official pronouncement of the National Office of the IRS; it deals with the application of the Code and Regulations to a specific factual situation, usually one that has been submitted by a taxpayer. Thus, most Revenue Rulings indicate how the IRS will treat a given taxpayer transaction. Revenue Rulings do not carry the force and effect of Regulations.

Revenue Rulings provide excellent sources of information; in fact, they are published chiefly for the purpose of guiding taxpayers. Therefore, even for a tax researcher whose client did not submit the original request for the Ruling, the result of the Ruling is of value if it concerns a transaction similar in nature, structure, or effect to the client's situation. Reliance should, however, not be placed on a Revenue Ruling if it has been affected by subsequent legislation, Regulations, Rulings, or court decisions.

Revenue Rulings adhere to a general internal structure, as illustrated in Exhibit 4–3. The typical structure is as follows.

Issue: A statement of the issue in question.
Facts: The facts on which the Revenue Ruling is based.
Law and analysis: The IRS's application of current law to the issue in the Revenue Ruling.
Holding: How the IRS will treat the transaction.

About 100 Revenue Rulings are released by the IRS each year (e.g., 128 in 2003). Each is identified by the year in which it was released and the consecutive number of the Ruling for that year. The IRS publishes them in the weekly *Internal Revenue Bulletin* and, later, in the *Cumulative Bulletin*.

REVENUE RULING CITATIONS

Revenue Rulings bear both a temporary and a permanent citation. The temporary citation is structured as follows.

Rev. Rul. 2005-7, 2005-9 I.R.B. 712

where:
2005-7 is the Revenue Ruling number (the 7th Revenue Ruling of 2005).
2005-9 is the weekly issue of the *Internal Revenue Bulletin* (the 9th week of 2005).
I.R.B. is the abbreviation for the *Internal Revenue Bulletin*.
712 is the page number where the Ruling starts in the *Internal Revenue Bulletin*.

The permanent citation for the same Revenue Ruling would be as follows.

Rev. Rul. 2005-7, 2005-1 C.B. 712

where:
2005-7 is the Revenue Ruling number (the 7th Revenue Ruling of 2005).
2005-1 is the volume number of the *Cumulative Bulletin* (Volume 1 of 2005).
C.B. is the abbreviation for the *Cumulative Bulletin*.
712 is the page number where the Ruling starts in the *Cumulative Bulletin*.

Once the pertinent *Cumulative Bulletin* is published, the temporary citation is normally no longer used. The page number in the I.R.B. is the same as that in the C.B. Before 2000, Revenue Rulings were given a two-digit identification number instead of the current four-digit number (e.g., Rev. Rul. 98-23).

LOCATING REVENUE RULINGS

Generally, the tax researcher must examine every applicable Revenue Ruling before a tax research project is complete. Revenue Rulings can be found at

| **Exhibit** | **4–3** | Revenue Ruling |

REV. RUL. 2000-7

ISSUE

If the retirement and removal of a depreciable asset occurs in connection with the installation or production of a replacement asset, are the costs incurred in removing the retired asset required to be capitalized under Section 263(a) or 263A as part of the cost of the replacement asset?

FACTS

The assets of X, a telephone company, include telephone poles A and B. X placed Pole A in service in 1979 on land it owned. X placed Pole B in service in 1982 on land owned by Y under the terms of an easement permitting X to have one pole on Y's land. In 2000, X undertakes a project to replace telephone poles in the service area in which Pole A is situated. As part of that project, X incurs costs in 2000 in removing and discarding Pole A and installing a new telephone pole, Pole C, in the same location. X also undertakes a second project to replace telephone poles in the service area in which Pole B is situated. X installs a new telephone pole, Pole D, on Y's land, but not in the same location as Pole B. As part of this second project and to comply with the easement, X incurs costs in 2000 in removing and discarding Pole B.

LAW AND ANALYSIS

Section 162 of the *Internal Revenue Code* and Section 1.162-1 of the Income Tax Regulations generally allow a deduction for all the ordinary and necessary expenses paid or incurred during the taxable year in carrying on any trade or business.

Section 165 allows as a deduction any loss sustained during the taxable year and not compensated for by insurance or otherwise. For the allowance under Section 165(a) of losses arising from the permanent withdrawal of depreciable property from use in a trade or business or in the production of income, Section 1.165-2(c) cross references Section 1.167(a)-8(a), which permits, in part, a loss from physical abandonment of retired property.

Under Sections 263(a) and 1.263(a)-1(a), no deduction is allowed for capital expenditures, such as amounts paid for new buildings or for permanent improvements or betterments made to increase the value of any property. Section 1.263(a)-2(a) provides that capital expenditures include the costs of acquisition, construction, or erection of buildings, machinery and equipment, furniture and fixtures, and similar property having a useful life substantially beyond the taxable year.

Section 263A generally requires taxpayers that are producing real or tangible personal property to capitalize direct material costs, direct labor costs, and indirect costs that are properly allocable to the produced property. Section 263A(g)(1) provides that, for purposes of Section 263A, the term "produce" includes construct, build, install, manufacture, develop, or improve.

* * *

HOLDING

If the retirement and removal of a depreciable asset occurs in connection with the installation or production of a replacement asset, the costs incurred in removing the retired asset are not required to be capitalized under Section 263(a) or 263A as part of the cost of the replacement asset.

DRAFTING INFORMATION

The principal author of this revenue ruling is Beverly Katz of the Office of Assistant Chief Counsel (Income Tax and Accounting). For further information regarding this revenue ruling contact Ms. Katz at (202) 622-4950 (not a toll-free call).

most of the locations (i.e., published and computer tax services, the *Cumulative Bulletin*, and some Internet sites) shown in Exhibit 4–2. Prior to 1953, Revenue Rulings were known by different names, including Appeals and Review Memorandum (ARM), General Counsel's Memorandum (GCM), and Office Decision (OD). These early rulings still may have some application in client situations if the IRS has not revoked them or modified them in any way. A tax researcher cannot ignore such rulings simply because they are old.

The current status of a Revenue Ruling or other IRS ruling can be checked in the most current index to the *Cumulative Bulletin*. In addition, several of the printed commercial tax services, (i.e., Research Institute of America and Commerce Clearing House) present a variety of finding lists and other references with which to examine the status of a ruling.

REVENUE PROCEDURES

Revenue Procedures deal with the internal practice and procedures of the IRS in the administration of the tax laws. They constitute the IRS's way of releasing information to taxpayers. For example, when the IRS releases specifications for facsimile tax forms generated by a computer service, or informs the public about areas in which it will no longer issue Revenue Rulings, it issues a Revenue Procedure to that effect. Although a Revenue Procedure may not be as useful as a Regulation or a Revenue Ruling in the direct resolution of a tax research problem, the practitioner still should be familiar with all of the pertinent Procedures.

Revenue Procedures are issued in a manner similar to that for Revenue Rulings. They are first published in the weekly *Internal Revenue Bulletin* and later are included in the bound edition of the *Cumulative Bulletin*. The IRS issues approximately 100 Revenue Procedures per year (e.g., there were 86 in 2003).

SPOTLIGHT ON TAXATION: Factoid

Between 1954 and 2004, the Internal Revenue Service has issued approximately 20,000 Revenue Rulings and Revenue Procedures. This is an average of about 400 Rev. Ruls. and Rev. Procs. per year. But the average since 2000 has been only about one-half of that.

A Revenue Procedure is cited using the same system as that for Revenue Rulings, that is, adopting first a temporary and then a permanent citation. In this regard, the temporary citation refers to the location of the Procedure in the *Internal Revenue Bulletin*, and the permanent citation denotes its location in the *Cumulative Bulletin*. Thus, a typical Revenue Procedure would have the following permanent citation.

Rev. Proc. 2001-21, 2001-1 C.B. 742

A Revenue Procedure is reproduced in Exhibit 4–4. Revenue Procedures can be found in the same publications in which Revenue Rulings are located.

Exhibit	4–4	Revenue Procedure Excerpt

Rev. Proc. 2004-22, 2004-15 I.R.B. 727

SECTION 1. PURPOSE

This revenue procedure provides transition relief from Revenue Ruling 2004-38 for determining an "eligible individual" under section 223 who may make contributions to a Health Savings Account (HSA). The transition relief covers the months before January 1, 2006, in the case of an individual who is covered by both a high deductible health plan (HDHP) and by a separate plan or rider that provides prescription drug benefits before the minimum annual deductible of the HDHP is satisfied.

SECTION 2. BACKGROUND

Section 1201 of the Medicare Prescription Drug, Improvement, and Modernization Act of 2003, Pub. L. No. 108-173, added section 223 to the Internal Revenue Code to permit eligible individuals to establish HSAs for taxable years beginning after December 31, 2003. Generally, an "eligible individual" is an individual who is covered by an HDHP and no health plan that is not an HDHP. Revenue Ruling 2004-38, clarifies that an individual who is covered by a health plan that provides prescription drug benefits before the minimum annual deductible of an HDHP has been satisfied, is not an "eligible individual" under section 223(c)(1)(A) and may not make contributions to an HSA. Because of the short period between the enactment of HSAs and the effective date of section 223, many employers and health insurance providers have been unable to modify the benefits provided under their existing health plans to conform to the statutory requirements for an HDHP. Thus, it is appropriate to provide transition relief to allow individuals to contribute to an HSA who would otherwise qualify as eligible individuals but for coverage by a prescription drug benefit provided under a separate plan or rider that is not an HDHP.

SECTION 3. APPLICATION

For months before January 1, 2006, an individual who would otherwise be an "eligible individual" under section 223(c)(1)(A), but is covered by both an HDHP that does not provide benefits for prescription drugs and by a separate health plan or rider that provides prescription drug benefits before the minimum annual deductible of the HDHP is satisfied (i.e., the separate prescription drug plan is not an HDHP), will continue to be an "eligible individual" and may make contributions to an HSA based on the annual deductible of the HDHP.

SECTION 4. EFFECT ON OTHER DOCUMENTS

The holding of Revenue Ruling 2004-38 is suspended in part and replaced by the transition relief provided in this revenue procedure for months before January 1, 2006.

DRAFTING INFORMATION

The principal author of this notice is Shoshanna Tanner of the Office of Division Counsel/ Associate Chief Counsel (Tax Exempt and Government Entities). For further information regarding this notice, contact Ms. Tanner at (202) 622-6080 (not a toll-free call).

LETTER RULINGS

The tax researcher is also interested in the *letter rulings* that are issued by the IRS in several forms, including Private Letter Rulings, Determination Letters, and Technical Advice Memoranda. The IRS does not publish these items in any official collection, but they are available from several commercial sources, as will be discussed later in this chapter.

PRIVATE LETTER RULINGS

The National Office of the IRS issues **Private Letter Rulings** in response to a taxpayer's request for the IRS's position on a specified tax issue. The IRS has authority to decline to issue Letter Rulings under certain conditions, such as where the problem is one of an inherently factual nature. The content, format, and procedures that are used for Revenue Rulings apply with respect to Private Letter Rulings. The IRS does not publish its reply in the *Internal Revenue Bulletin* or *Cumulative Bulletin*, however. Rather, it sends its response only to the taxpayer who submitted the request. An excerpt of a Private Letter Ruling is shown in Exhibit 4–5.

The process is as follows. The taxpayer asks the IRS to disclose its interpretation of the Code, Regulations, and pertinent court cases for a transaction the taxpayer describes; the description should include a statement of the business purpose for the transaction. For instance, if two corporations plan to merge, one of them might request a Private Letter Ruling to find out

Exhibit	4–5

Private Letter Ruling Excerpt

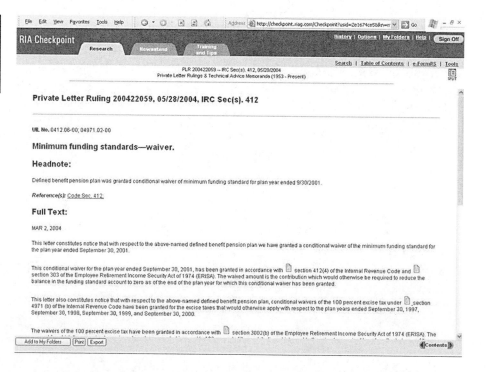

whether the IRS believes that the Code's tax-favored reorganization provisions will apply to the anticipated merger. In many cases, if the IRS asserts that the transaction will not receive a treatment favorable to the taxpayer, it will suggest means by which the transaction could be restructured to obtain the favorable treatment.

As mentioned, a Private Letter Ruling is issued only to the taxpayer who requested the ruling. However. Private Letter Rulings are included in the list of authorities constituting "substantial authority" upon which a taxpayer may rely to avoid certain statutory penalties.[5] Letter Rulings are, in any case, an important source of information, because they indicate how the IRS may treat a similar transaction.

Private Letter Rulings also constitute an important IRS stimulus for new Revenue Rulings. When the IRS comes across an unusual transaction that it believes to be of general interest, or when it receives a flurry of Letter Ruling requests concerning very similar factual situations, a Private Ruling may be converted into Revenue Ruling form and published in official administrative sources. The IRS must notify the taxpayer of its intention to disclose the ruling, and the taxpayer has the right to protest such disclosure. Before publication, all aspects of the new ruling, including the statement of facts, are purged of any reference to the taxpayer's name or other identifying information.

SPOTLIGHT ON TAXATION: Factoid

The IRS has issued over 88,000 Letter Rulings and Technical Advice Memoranda since 1980. As a result, a tax researcher is faced with an average of over 3,600 new research documents every year just from this one source of authority.

TECHNICAL ADVICE MEMORANDA

A **Technical Advice Memorandum** is issued by the IRS's National Office, making it similar in this regard to the Private Letter Ruling and different from the Determination Letter. The Technical Advice Memorandum, however, concerns a completed transaction. Whereas a Private Letter Ruling typically is requested by a taxpayer prior to completing a transaction or filing a tax return, a Technical Advice Memorandum usually is requested by an agent when a question arises during an audit that cannot be answered satisfactorily by the local office.

Similar to the Private Letter Ruling, a Technical Advice Memorandum applies strictly to the taxpayer for whose audit it was requested, and it cannot be relied on by other taxpayers. However, again, the information that is contained in the memorandum may be useful to the tax researcher for the

5. Reg. § 1.6662-4(d)(3)(iii).

insight that it gives concerning the thinking of the IRS relative to a given problem area in taxation.

These memoranda are not included in any official IRS publication, but they are open for public inspection, as we will discuss next. If the facts or the holding of a Technical Advice Memorandum are felt by the IRS to be of general interest, the memorandum may be converted into Revenue Ruling format and published by the IRS in the *Internal Revenue Bulletin* and the *Cumulative Bulletin*.

DETERMINATION LETTERS

A **Determination Letter** is similar in purpose and nature to a Private Letter Ruling, except that it is issued by the office of the local IRS district director, rather than by the National Office of the IRS. Because a Determination Letter is issued by a lower-level IRS official, it usually deals with issues and transactions that are not overtly controversial. For instance, the trustee of a pension plan might request a Determination Letter to ascertain whether the plan is qualified for the Code's tax-favored deferred compensation treatment.

Determination Letters usually relate to completed transactions rather than to the proposed transactions that typically lead to the issuance of a Private Letter Ruling. Determination Letters are not included in any official IRS publication, but they are available to the tax researcher from commercial and Internet sources.

PUBLIC INSPECTION OF WRITTEN DETERMINATIONS

The public can receive copies of any unpublished IRS Letter Rulings, e.g., in lieu of using a subscription commercial service.[6] Included under this provision are Private Letter Rulings, Determination Letters, and Technical Advice Memoranda. Before any public inspection is allowed, however, the IRS is required to remove the taxpayer's name and any other information that might be used by a third party to identify the taxpayer.[7] In addition, the IRS is required to purge the document of any items that could affect national defense or foreign policy, trade secrets, financial information, data relative to the regulation of financial institutions, geographical data, and items that could invade personal privacy. If the taxpayer opposes the disclosure of the written determination, he or she can bring the matter before the IRS and the Tax Court prior to the scheduled disclosure.

Once all of the required data have been removed from the written determination, it must be made open for public inspection at such places as the Treasury Secretary designates in the Regulations. Information of this type is available in Washington, D.C., and at selected other locations.

6. § 6110(f).
7. § 6110(c).

The precedential value of any of these written determinations is strictly limited.[8] Overall, such pronouncements may not be cited as authority in a tax matter by either the taxpayer or the IRS. However, Letter Rulings can be used as "examples" of IRS treatment of similar factual patterns when dealing with the IRS. For example, tax practitioners could suggest that a Letter Ruling be used as guidance in a similar situation during an audit. However, an IRS agent need not follow a Letter Ruling issued to a different taxpayer.

Taxpayers may rely on Private Letter Rulings, Technical Advice Memoranda, Actions on Decisions, General Counsel Memoranda, and other similar documents published by the IRS in the *Internal Revenue Bulletin*, to avoid certain understatement of tax penalties. But use of such pronouncements for this purpose does not expand the general precedential value of these pronouncements with respect to determining a taxpayer's tax liability.

WRITTEN DETERMINATION NUMBERING SYSTEM

Because the IRS issues thousands of Letter Rulings per year, it assigns a nine-digit document number to each written determination for identification purposes. The first four digits indicate the year in which the ruling was issued, the next two numbers denote the week, and the last three digits indicate the number of the ruling for the week. Thus, a lengthy but unique identifier is created for each pronouncement. For example, the number of a Letter Ruling can be interpreted as follows.

Ltr. Rul. 200517024

where:
2005 is the year the Ruling is issued.
17 is the week of the year the Ruling is issued.
024 indicates that this is the 24th Ruling issued that week.

Before 2000, only a two-digit date was used to signify the year in which the ruling was issued (e.g., 9814026).

LOCATING WRITTEN DETERMINATIONS

The tax researcher needs access to written determinations to complete many tax research projects. Selected written determinations can be found in summary form in the major tax services. However, if the tax researcher needs access to the full text of a large number of IRS pronouncements, an electronic database is the best approach. Consult Exhibit 4–2 for the online computer tax databases that contain the full text of IRS written determinations.

OTHER IRS PRONOUNCEMENTS

The IRS issues several other types of information that can be of value to the tax researcher, including acquiescences and nonacquiescences, the

8. § 6110.

Internal Revenue Bulletin, Chief Counsel Memoranda, and other miscellaneous publications.

ACQUIESCENCES AND NONACQUIESCENCES

When the IRS loses an issue or decision in court, the Commissioner may announce an acquiescence or nonacquiescence to the decision. An **acquiescence** indicates that the court decision, although it was adverse to the IRS, will be followed in similar situations. The Commissioner determines, at his or her own discretion, the degree of similarity required before the IRS will follow the result that is unfavorable to itself.

A **nonacquiescence** indicates that the IRS disagrees with the adverse decision in the case and will follow the decision only for the specific taxpayer whose case resulted in the adverse ruling. If the IRS wishes to express agreement with only part of the decision that is settled in the taxpayer's favor, the Commissioner may nonacquiesce with respect to certain issues. Finally, an acquiescence or nonacquiescence is not issued if the IRS prevails in a court case, because it likely agrees with all pertinent holdings.

Nonacquiescence may indicate to the tax practitioner that the IRS is likely to challenge a similar decision for the taxpayer in a case that has a similar factual situation. However, the issuance of an acquiescence does not necessarily mean that the IRS agrees with the adverse decision, but only that it will not pursue the matter in a (similar and) subsequent case. Each of these items of information can be useful when the practitioner prepares for, or anticipates, a court challenge to the client's position in a tax matter.

As mentioned, if the IRS has acquiesced to a case, then the taxpayer can rely on that decision as precedence that will be followed by agents for similar fact patterns. However, if the IRS has nonacquiesced, the taxpayer must evaluate whether to pursue a similar fact pattern in court. Such factors as the cost of litigation plus the probability of winning must be appraised before proceeding with a case similar to one with which the IRS has nonacquiesced.

Occasionally, the IRS changes (with an attendant retroactive effect on taxpayers) its acquiescence or nonacquiescence position by withdrawing the original pronouncement. For example, in *U.S. v. City Loan and Savings*, 287 F.2d 612 (CA-6, 1961), the court allowed the IRS to withdraw an acquiescence on an issue-by-issue, but not taxpayer-by-taxpayer, basis. This change may occur after only a short time passes or many years later. Such a change in the IRS's position typically is accompanied by a brief explanation of the reason for the change—for example, because of a contrary holding in a subsequent court case or a change in the agency's policy concerning the issue.

IRS acquiescence decisions are driven by related litigation costs, revenue effects, and administrative and policy directives. The Service issues acquiescences/nonacquiescences as **Actions on Decision(AOD)**, relative to the following court decisions.

- Regular Tax Court
- Memorandum Tax Court
- District Court

- Court of Federal Claims
- Courts of Appeal

IRS Actions on Decision are published in the *Internal Revenue Bulletin* and thereafter, in the *Cumulative Bulletin*. They are prepared by the office of the Associate Chief Counsel (Litigation). AODs are public documents, and they generally include:

- The issue decided against the government,
- The pertinent facts,
- A discussion of the reasoning supporting the acquiescence/nonacquiescence decision.[9]

Exhibit 4–6 reproduces an acquiescence from the *Cumulative Bulletin* in which the IRS indicates its position on a case. A citator (see Chapter 6)

Exhibit	4–6	Action on Decision

ACTION ON DECISION 2003-01

January 10, 2003

SUBJECT: *Doyle, Dane, Bernbach, Inc. v. Commissioner.*, 79 T.C. 101 (1982).

ISSUE: Whether an accrual method taxpayer must include in its gross income for 1975 amounts representing claimed refunds of New York State franchise taxes and New York City general corporate taxes paid for 1972 which became refundable by virtue of a net operating loss incurred in 1975 and carried back to 1972.

DISCUSSION: The Service issued an action on decision that non-acquiesced in the decision of *Doyle, Dane, Bernbach, Inc. v. Commissioner,*1 C.B. 1. In a revenue ruling published elsewhere in this issue of the *Internal Revenue Bulletin,* the Service has concluded that New York State's approval of corporate franchise tax refund claims resulting from net operating loss carrybacks is not ministerial but involves substantive review. Accordingly, a New York State corporate franchise tax refund attributable to a net operating loss carryback is includible in the income of a taxpayer using the accrual method of accounting when the taxpayer receives payment or notice that the refund claim has been approved, whichever is earlier. SEE Rev. Rul. 2003-3.

RECOMMENDATION: Acquiescence. The action on decision approved on June 27, 1988 is withdrawn and replaced with this action on decision.

Reviewers:
NORMA ROTUNNO
Attorney Branch 2
Associate Chief Counsel
(Income Tax & Accounting)

Approved:
By: B. JOHN WILLIAMS, JR.
Chief Counsel

9. *Taxation with Representation Fund v. IRS*, 485 F.Supp. 263 (DDC, 1980).

also can be used to locate and interpret acquiescence and nonacquiescence decisions.

After the IRS issues such a pronouncement, any reference to the citation for the case includes either the abbreviation "Acq" or "Nonacq" (or, occasionally, "NA") to indicate the subsequent development.

INTERNAL REVENUE BULLETIN

The IRS's official publication for its pronouncements is the *Internal Revenue Bulletin* (IRB). Most IRS Revenue Rulings and Revenue Procedures, and the agency's acquiescences and nonacquiescences to regular Tax Court decisions, first are published in the IRB. This reference bulletin also includes the following information, all of which can be useful to the tax researcher.

- New tax laws, issued by Congress as Public Laws
- Committee Reports underlying tax statutes
- Procedural rules
- New tax treaties
- Treasury Decisions (which become Regulations)
- Other notices

Interested parties can subscribe to the *Internal Revenue Bulletin* by contacting the Internal Revenue Service. Alternatively, some of the commercial tax services include subscriptions to, or reproductions of, all of the issues of the *Internal Revenue Bulletin*.

CHIEF COUNSEL MEMORANDA

The office of the IRS's Chief Counsel periodically generates memoranda that may be of use to the tax researcher. Although the IRS does not publish these memoranda in any official document, they are available from commercial publishers. A **Technical Memorandum** (TM) is prepared in the production of a Proposed Regulation. A **General Counsel's Memorandum** (GCM) is generated upon the request of the IRS, typically as a means to assist in the preparation of Revenue Rulings and Private Letter Rulings. In addition, the Chief Counsel's office gives various forms of advice to IRS offices and personnel. IRS Chief Council Pronouncements are summarized in Exhibit 4–7.

These documents are available for public inspection and can be found on most computer-based tax services.

ANNOUNCEMENTS AND NOTICES

The IRS issues **Announcements and Notices** concerning items of general importance to taxpayers. Announcements are public pronouncements that have immediate or short-term value such as an approaching deadline for making an election. Notices contain guidance involving substantive interpretations of the Code or other provisions of the law that usually have long-term application. Exhibit 4–8 reproduces a typical Notice. Both Notices and Announcements are published in the weekly *Internal Revenue Bulletin*.

Exhibit	4–7
IRS Chief Counsel Pronouncements	

Document	Purpose
Technical Memorandum (TM)	TMs are prepared in the production of a Proposed Regulation.
General Counsel's Memorandum (GCM)	GCMs assist in the preparation of Revenue Rulings and Private Letter Rulings.
Action on Decision (AOD)	AODs are prepared when the IRS loses a case in a court. They convey the IRS decision to acquiesce/nonacquiesce.
Field Service Advice (FSAs)	FSAs are nonbinding advice, guidance, and analysis provided by IRS National Office attorneys to IRS field personnel.
Chief Counsel Notices (CCNs)	CCNs are temporary directives the IRS national office uses to disseminate policies, procedures, instructions, and/or delegations of authority to Chief Counsel employees.
Service Center Advice (SCAs)	SCAs are guidance provided by the IRS National Office to IRS service centers and related IRS functions concerning their tax administration responsibilities.

Exhibit	4–8	IRS Notice

Notice 2004-5, 2004-7 I.R.B. 489

ELP PARTNER MAY TAKE INTO ACCOUNT SEPARATELY PARTNERSHIP INCOME THAT IS QD

Section 772(a)(11) of the *Internal Revenue Code* provides that, in determining the income tax of a partner of an electing large partnership (ELP), the partner shall take into account separately the partner's distributive share of partnership items [in addition to those listed in § 772(a)(1) through (10)] to the extent that the Secretary determines that the separate treatment of these items is appropriate.

Pursuant to this authority, the Secretary has determined that it is appropriate for a partner of an ELP to take into account separately the partner's distributive share of the partnership's dividends received that are qualified dividend income (QDI) as defined in § 1(h)(11)(B). This requirement to separately account for QDI takes into account the changes in the taxation of QDI under § 302 of the Jobs and Growth Tax Relief Reconciliation Act of 2003, Pub. L. No. 108-27, 117 Stat. 752. This requirement is effective for dividends received by a partnership after December 31, 2002.

The principal author of this notice is Bradford R. Poston of the Office of Associate Chief Counsel (Passthroughs and Special Industries). For further information regarding this notice contact Bradford R. Poston at (202) 622-3060 (not a toll-free call).

Miscellaneous Publications

The IRS publishes numerous general and specialized documents to help taxpayers. Some of the more common ones include the following.

Publication 3, *Armed Forces' Tax Guide*
Publication 17, *Your Federal Income Tax*
Publication 225, *Farmer's Tax Guide*
Publication 334, *Tax Guide for Small Business*
Publication 463, *Travel, Entertainment, Gift, and Car Expenses*
Publication 519, *U.S. Tax Guide for Aliens*
Publication 520, *Scholarships and Fellowships*
Publication 589, *Tax Information on S Corporations*

Each of these documents is available directly from the IRS, both in print and electronic formats. See Exhibit 4–9 for an excerpt from an IRS Publication from the IRS web site. In addition, several of the commercial tax publishers offer copies of these lay-oriented Publications. Furthermore, any library that is designated as a government depository receives all of these documents in hard copy. Finally, many of the above Publications can be ordered from the IRS in Spanish-language editions.

Although the IRS Publications contain useful information, the tax researcher must be careful when relying on them. IRS Publications typically do not cite

Exhibit	4–9	IRS Publication 3 (Armed Forces' Tax Guide) Excerpt

Armed Forces Reservists

If you are a member of a reserve component of the Armed Forces and you travel more than 100 miles away from home in connection with your performance of services as a member of the reserves, you can deduct your travel expenses as an adjustment to income on line 33 of Form 1040 rather than as a miscellaneous itemized deduction. The deduction is limited to the amount the federal government pays its employees for travel expenses. For more information about this limit, see Per Diem and Car Allowances in chapter 6 of Publication 463.

Member of a reserve component. You are a member of a reserve component of the Armed Forces if you are in the Army, Navy, Marine Corps, Air Force, or Coast Guard Reserve, the Army National Guard of the United States, the Air National Guard of the United States, or the Reserve Corps of the Public Health Service.

How to report. If you have reserve-related travel that takes you more than 100 miles from home, you should first complete Form 2106, Employee Business Expenses, or Form 2106-EZ, Unreimbursed Employee Business Expenses. Then include in the total on line 33 of Form 1040 your expenses for reserve travel over 100 miles from home, up to the federal rate, from line 10 of Form 2106 or line 6 of Form 2106-EZ. Write "RC" and the amount of these expenses in the space to the left of line 33 of Form 1040. Subtract this amount from the total on line 10 of Form 2106 or line 6 of Form 2106-EZ and deduct the balance as an itemized deduction on line 20 of Schedule A (Form 1040). See Armed Forces reservists under Miscellaneous Itemized Deductions, later.

the Code, Regulations, or other authority on which the information included therein is based. In fact, the IRS disclaims any responsibility for damages that the taxpayer may suffer in erroneously relying on its Publications, and it may, in fact, take positions that are contrary to those that are included in the Publications in certain court cases or appeals hearings.

These documents are prepared from the government's point of view. For instance, if a lower court has ruled against the IRS on a given matter that is addressed in a Publication, the text of the document probably will not mention the possibility that the IRS's official position will be found to be incorrect on appeal. Although IRS Publications can be the source of some basic information that is useful for laypersons, or in a tax compliance context, the tax researcher should not rely on or cite such a reference in a professional research report.

SUMMARY

Administrative pronouncements provide the tax researcher with a significant amount of information from and about the IRS. The primary IRS pronouncements that are of interest to the tax researcher include the Regulations, Revenue Rulings, Revenue Procedures, and Letter Rulings. The tax practitioner who performs competent research must be aware of the content and format of each of these items, know how to locate them, appreciate the precedential value of each, and understand how each might affect the client's tax problem. Exhibit 4–10 summarizes the most commonly encountered IRS pronouncements.

Exhibit	**4–10**	Common IRS Pronouncements

Pronouncement	**Purpose**
Regulation	The official Treasury or IRS interpretation of a portion of the *Internal Revenue Code*
Revenue Ruling	The IRS's application of the tax law to a specific fact situation
Revenue Procedure	A statement of IRS practice or procedure that affects taxpayers or the general public
Announcement	IRS release that has immediate or short-term value
Notice	Guidance involving substantive interpretations that has longer-term application
Private Letter Ruling	Statement issued by the National Office of the IRS at a taxpayer's request, applying the tax law to a proposed transaction
Determination Letter	Statement issued by the District Director in response to a taxpayer request, concerning the application of the tax law to a specific completed transaction
Acquiescence	Acceptance by the IRS of a court decision that was held in the taxpayer's favor. Published as an Action on Decision.
Nonacquiescence	Notice that the IRS still disagrees with a court decision that was held in the taxpayer's favor. Published as an Action on Decision.
Treasury Decision	A Regulation is promulgated or amended
Technical Advice Memorandum	A letter ruling issued on a completed transaction, usually during an audit

TAX TUTOR

Reinforce the tax research information covered in this chapter by completing the online tutorials located at the Federal Tax Research web site:

http://raabe.swlearning.com

KEY WORDS

By the time you complete this chapter, you should be comfortable discussing each of the following terms. If you need additional review of any of these items, return to the appropriate material in the chapter or consult the glossary to this text.

Acquiescence	Private Letter Ruling
Action on Decision	Proposed Regulation
Announcements and Notices	Regulation
Cumulative Bulletin	Revenue Procedure
Determination Letter	Revenue Ruling
General Counsel's Memorandum	Technical Advice Memorandum
General Regulation	Technical Memorandum
Internal Revenue Bulletin	Temporary Regulation
Legislative Regulation	Treasury Decision
Nonacquiescence	

DISCUSSION QUESTIONS

1. What department and agency of the U.S. government has the responsibility to administer the Federal tax laws?

2. Section 7805(a) of the *Internal Revenue Code* authorizes the IRS to perform what activities?

3. The IRS issues numerous pronouncements. Name the four that are the most important in conducting Federal tax research.

4. Define the terms *Regulation* and *Treasury Decision*. Where are Treasury Decisions published so that interested parties can comment on them?

5. "A tax researcher should not ignore Proposed Regulations." Comment on this statement.

6. Define and distinguish between *General* and *Legislative* Regulations.

7. In the citation, Reg. § 1.212-3, what do the "1," the "212," and the "3" indicate?

8. Answer the following questions about this citation: Reg. § 20.2039-1(a).
   a. What does the "20" stand for?
   b. What does the "2039" stand for?
   c. What does the "1" stand for?
   d. What does the "(a)" stand for?

9. Answer the following questions about this citation: Reg. § 1.274-6T(a)(2).
   a. What does the "1" stand for?
   b. What does the "274" stand for?
   c. What does the "6T" stand for?
   d. What does the "(a)" stand for?
   e. What does the "(2)" stand for?

10. Give the number that is associated with each of the following categories of Regulations.
    a. Estate Tax Regulations
    b. Income Tax Regulations
    c. Gift Tax Regulations
    d. Procedural Regulations
    e. Employment Tax Regulations

11. Give the type of Regulation associated with each of the following Regulation numbers.
    a. 31   d. 601
    b. 301   e. 20
    c. 25

12. What are Temporary Regulations? What weight do they carry in the tax researcher's analysis?

13. The burden of proof is on the taxpayer to prove that a provision of the Regulations is improper. How could this affect one's tax research?

14. In general, what is the effective date of a new Regulation?

15. Give at least three locations where a tax researcher can find the complete text of a Regulation.

16. What is a Revenue Ruling?

17. Describe the structure of a typical Revenue Ruling.

18. Where are Revenue Rulings initially published by the IRS? Where are the rulings permanently published in hardbound editions?

19. Explain each of the elements of this citation: Rev. Rul. 2004-32, 2004-12 I.R.B. 621.

20. Explain each of the elements of this citation: Rev. Rul. 96-41, 1996-2 C.B. 8.

21. What is the correct citation for Revenue Ruling 2002-55, which is found on page 529 of the second *Cumulative Bulletin* volume for 2003?

22. What is the correct citation for Revenue Procedure 94-36, which is found on page 682 of the first *Cumulative Bulletin* volume for 1996?

23. What resources are available to help the tax researcher who wishes to check the current status of a Revenue Ruling?

24. Of what relevance to the tax practitioner is a Revenue Procedure?

25. Where can a tax researcher find copies of Revenue Procedures?

26. Construct the permanent citation for the fifth Revenue Procedure of 2001, which was published in the second week of the year. It is published on page 164 of the appropriate document.

27. Identify three types of Letter Rulings that are of interest to the tax researcher. Indicate whether each of these rulings is published by the IRS.

28. Which office of the IRS issues Private Letter Rulings? Who requests such a ruling? What kinds of issues are addressed therein?

29. Sometimes a Private Letter Ruling is generalized and included in an official IRS publication. What form does this recast private ruling take?

30. What is a Determination Letter? Which office of the IRS issues Determination Letters? What kinds of issues are addressed therein?

31. What is a Technical Advice Memorandum? Who requests it? What kinds of issues are addressed therein? Does the IRS include Technical Advice Memoranda in any official publication?

32. Discuss the precedential value of Private Letter Rulings, Determination Letters, and Technical Advice Memoranda. What role do these items play in conducting tax research?

33. Which IRS documents are open to public inspection under § 6110?

34. What is the precedential value of an IRS written determination under § 6110?

35. Explain each of the elements of this citation: Ltr. Rul. 9615032.

36. Where can a tax researcher find copies of written determinations?

37. The most important IRS publications are the *Internal Revenue Bulletin* and the *Cumulative Bulletin*. How often is each of these documents published? Name six items that typically are published in the *Cumulative Bulletin*.

38. Explain each of the elements of this citation: Rev. Proc. 2004-16, 2004-10 I.R.B. 559.

39. Explain each of the elements of this citation: Rev. Proc. 2000-41, 2000-2 C.B. 317.

40. Distinguish between a citation with "I.R.B." in it and one with "C.B." in it.

41. Discuss the difference between a Revenue Ruling and a Revenue Procedure.

42. In what publication(s) would a tax researcher find the official listing of the IRS acquiescences and nonacquiescences to a Tax Court decision?

43. Can the IRS change its mind on acquiescences or nonacquiescences?

44. Must the IRS acquiesce or nonacquiesce to every issue in a court decision?

45. What is the purpose of each of the following?
    a. Technical Memorandum (TM)
    b. General Counsel's Memorandum (GCM)
    c. Action on Decision (AOD)

46. What is the purpose of each of the following?
    a. Field Service Advice (FSA)
    b. Chief Counsel Notices (CCN)
    c. Service Center Advice (SCA)

47. Give the title of each of the following.
    a. Publication 17
    b. Publication 225
    c. Publication 334

48. Give the title of each of the following.
    a. Publication 3
    b. Publication 463
    c. Publication 520

49. What is an IRS Notice? When is it used? In your opinion, could a tax practitioner rely on an IRS Notice as authority for a tax return position?

50. Why should the tax researcher exercise caution in relying on an IRS publication, such as published instructions to tax forms, in undertaking a research project?

EXERCISES

51. Locate Revenue Ruling 99-56. Explain the effect of that ruling on previous Treasury Department pronouncements.

52. Briefly describe the subject of each of the following Letter Rulings. State the type [Private Letter Ruling (PLR), Field Service Advice (FSA), Service Center Advice (SCA), etc.] of each Letter Ruling.
    a. 200034026   c. 200113020
    b. 200113016   d. 200113023

53. Correctly cite the italicized sentence indicated by the dart (▶) in the following passage from the Regulations.

    SEC. 1.162-21 FINES AND PENALTIES.
    (a) In general.
         No deduction shall be allowed under section 162(a) for any fine or similar penalty paid to—
         (1) The government of the United States, a State, a territory or possession of the United States, the District of Columbia, or the Commonwealth of Puerto Rico;
    ▶   *(2) The government of a foreign country; or*
         (3) A political subdivision of, or corporation or other entity serving as an agency or instrumentality of, any of the above

54. Correctly cite the italicized sentence indicated by the dart (▶) in the following passage from the Regulations.

    SEC. 1.1362-1 ELECTION TO BE AN S CORPORATION.
    (a) In general.
         Except as provided in section 1.1362-5, a small business corporation as defined in section 1361 may elect to be an S corporation under section 1362(a). An election may be made only with the consent of all of the shareholders of the corporation at the time of the election. See section 1.1362-6(a) for rules concerning the time and manner of making this election.

▶(b)   *Years for which election is effective.*
An election under section 1362(a) is effective for the entire taxable year of the corporation for which it is made and for all succeeding taxable years of the corporation, until the election is terminated

55.   Briefly describe the subject of each of the following Letter Rulings. State the type [Private Letter Ruling (PLR), Field Service Advice (FSA), Service Center Advice (SCA), etc.] of each Letter Ruling.
a. 200414014   c. 200411001
b. 200235002   d. 199950003

56.   What is the subject of each of the following IRS Notices?
a. 89-114
b. 99-51
c. 2000-28

57.   What is the subject matter of each of the following Technical Advice Memoranda?
a. 9015001
b. 199914034
c. 200050005

58.   Briefly describe the subject matter of each of the following Treasury Decisions.
a. 8346
b. 8780
c. 8915

59.   For each of the following Code sections, how many Treasury Regulations have been issued? Give the total number of such Regulations and the number of the last Regulation.
a. § 102   c. § 301
b. § 143   d. § 385

60.   What is the current status of each of the following Revenue Rulings?
a. Rev. Rul. 95-35
b. Rev. Rul. 94-17
c. Rev. Rul. 87-34

61.   Locate the pronouncement at 1989-1 C.B. 76.
a. What is the number assigned to this written determination?
b. What is the issue(s) addressed in this written determination?
c. What is the holding in this written determination?

62.   Locate the pronouncement at 2000-2 C.B. 333.
a. What is the number assigned to this written determination?
b. What is the subject matter discussed in this written determination?

63.   Locate the pronouncement at 2004-10 I.R.B. 550.
a. What is the number assigned to this written determination?
b. What is the subject matter discussed in this written determination?

64.   What is the current status of each of the following IRS pronouncements?
a. Notice 2001-26   c. Revenue Procedure 89-31
b. Revenue Ruling 2000-41   d. Announcement 99-110

65. What is the current status of each of the following IRS pronouncements?
    a. Notice 2004-29   c. Revenue Procedure 93-15
    b. Revenue Ruling 2004-28   d. Announcement 99-41

66. A member of a tax-exempt business league makes deposits into a strike fund. The contribution reverts to the taxpayer if the fund is terminated. Are these deposits tax deductible?

    Database to search: IRS Letter Rulings
    Keywords: business, league, strike, fund

67. Can proceeds from a life insurance policy be included in a decedent's gross estate if the policy was purchased by an S corporation for an employee-shareholder?

    Databases to search: the Code and IRS Letter Rulings
    Keywords: Sec. 2042, life, insurance, estate, inclusion

68. Is a veterinary medical corporation a "personal service corporation" for purposes of the required use of the flat 34 percent tax rate?

    Database to search: Revenue Rulings
    Keywords: veterinary, personal, service, corporation

69. Are homeowners who claim an itemized deduction for interest paid on adjustable rate mortgages (ARMs) and then receive refunds in a later year required to show the refunds as taxable income?

    Database to search: Notices
    Keywords: adjustable, rate, mortgage, refund

70. Are points paid by homebuyers on VA and FHA loans deductible in the year the house is purchased?

    Database to search: Revenue Procedures
    Keywords: loan, origination, fees, VA, FHA

RESEARCH CASES

71. Lance asks you to explain why his employer, the Good Food Truck Stop, an establishment that employs more than thirty waiters/waitresses, included $2,400 in tip income on his Form W-2 for the year. Lance always has kept track of the tips he actually received, and he has reported them in full on his tax return.

    Partial list of research material: § 6053; Rev. Proc. 86-2, 1986-1 C.B. 560

72. Joe incurred $38,000 of investment interest expense in the current year. He also generated $35,000 in dividend income and had a $65,000 passive loss for the year. What is the amount of Joe's interest deduction?

    Partial list of research material: § 163; Reg. § 1.163-8T; Announcement 87-4, 1987-3 I.R.B. 17

73. Georgia won the Massachusetts lottery, which means that she will receive $28,000 a year for the next thirty years. Georgia purchased the lucky ticket in March, and it was selected the winner in June. Georgia

regularly spent $100 a month on lottery tickets, one-third for Massachusetts tickets and two-thirds for Vermont tickets.

a. What is Georgia's gross income from this prize?

b. Is there any corresponding deduction?

Partial list of research material: § 74; Rev. Rul. 78-140, 1978-1 C.B. 27

74. Dieter won the lottery this year, which means that he will receive $400,000 a year for the next thirty years. The present value of Dieter's prize is about $3,750,000. Conscious of the tax benefits of income shifting, Dieter irrevocably assigned one-fifth of every annuity payment to his daughter Heidi. What are the effects of these events on Dieter's taxable income?

Partial list of research material: § 74; Rev. Rul. 58-127, 1958-1 C.B. 42

75. Ace High and Lady Luck live together and have pooled their funds for several months to purchase food and other household necessities and to buy an occasional state lottery ticket. Ace used part of these pooled funds to buy a lottery ticket that won $3,000,000. When they discovered that the lottery proceeds could be paid only to one recipient under state law, Ace and Lady executed a "separate ownership agreement." The agreement created an equal interest in the ticket for both Ace and Lady. Must Ace pay gift tax on the transfer of a one-half interest in the ticket to Lady? What is the value of the gift?

List of research material: Ltr. Rul. 9217004

76. Shaky Savings & Loan has a depositor named Olive who opened an account last year. At that time, Olive gave Shaky her Social Security number as a taxpayer identification number (TIN). The IRS notified Shaky that Olive's Social Security number was invalid. This year, Shaky asked Olive for a corrected number, which she provided. Later this year, the IRS notified Shaky that the new Social Security number also was invalid. What should Shaky do at this point about backup withholding on Olive's account? Prepare (in good form) a research memorandum to the file.

77. Alpine Corporation is a qualified small business corporation eligible to elect S corporation status. Albert is a shareholder in Alpine. On February 1 of the current year, Albert dies before signing the proper S corporation election form. The stock passes to Albert's estate. Ellen is appointed executor of Albert's estate on May 1 of the current year. On March 10 of the current year, Alpine filed Form 2553, the election form to be an S corporation, properly signed by all March 10 shareholders, and Ellen (the executrix) on behalf of Albert. Is this a valid S corporation election? Prepare (in good form) a research memorandum to the file.

78. Joe Bacillus, owns Bacillus's Italian Restaurant. A friend of Joe's who owns a sports bar comes to Joe and wants to form a partnership with Joe to buy an old building, renovate it, and then move both the restaurant and the sports bar into it along with other tenants. Joe would like to make this investment. He needs approximately $200,000 for his share of the buy-in of the partnership that will purchase, renovate, and manage the building. However, because of other recent large expenses, Joe

finds himself cash short at the present time. His only large liquid asset is his self-directed IRA, which currently owns $225,000 in stock and bonds. Joe proposes that he direct the IRA to sell the securities and to use the proceeds to invest in the building renovation partnership. Conduct appropriate research (including a computer search) to determine if Joe's plan is workable. Prepare (in good form) a research memorandum to the file.

79. The Pima and Southern Railroad (PSRR) is a small railroad operating in rural Arizona. It exists by carrying freight to remote areas of the southwest. This year the PSRR needs to replace a 30-mile section of its track. The PSRR has bids from a contractor to replace the track for the following amounts:

Cost of new track	$ 5,000,000
Installing new track	3,000,000
Road bed grading and improvements	2,500,000
Removing old track (net of salvage)	1,500,000
Total	$12,000,000

The old track is fully depreciated, and the cost shown is net of $200,000 salvage value received for the scrap metal. The new track is an improved type, and it is expected to last 35–40 years. The controller of PSRR, Casey Jones, comes to you and wants to know the tax treatment of the above expenditures. He specifically wants to know if any costs can be deducted or if all must be capitalized and written off over a period of years. He is also concerned about any potential problems with the uniform capitalization rules under Section 263A. Prepare (in good form) a research memorandum to the file.

80. Your client, Ned Bovine, purchased a $2 million life insurance policy from the Nickel Life Insurance Co. (NLIC) of Dime Box, Texas. Ned's wife is the beneficiary of the policy. The policy was purchased ten years ago when Nickel Life Insurance was a mutual insurance company. In the current year, Nickel Life Insurance converted from a mutual company to a stock company in a tax-free reorganization. As part of the conversion, Ned received 800 shares of the new publicly traded (NASDAQ) Nickel Life Insurance Company. Three weeks after receiving the shares, Ned sold all his shares at $15 each. The total premiums paid by Ned on the policy before the conversion were $20,000.
    a. Locate the IRS pronouncement(s) that deals with this situation. State the pronouncement number(s).
    b. Review the IRS pronouncement(s). Does it raise a need for new information to solve this question?
    c. Are you able to reach a conclusion about the research question from this IRS pronouncement(s)? If so, what is your conclusion(s)?

81. At age 65, Carlota's financial position was better than her health. She had a large balance in an IRA that she wanted to move to a different IRA. Carlota withdrew $100,000 from the IRA and planned to roll the funds over into another IRA. Unfortunately, she died before completing

the rollover. Carlota's son, Andres, discovered what his mother had done a week after her death. Andres was both executor of Carlota's estate and beneficiary of her IRA. Can Andres, in his role as executor, complete the rollover for his deceased mother by depositing the $100,000 in another IRA within the 60-day rollover period?

a. Locate the IRS pronouncement(s) that deals with this situation. State the pronouncement number(s).

b. Review the IRS pronouncement(s). Does it raise a need for new information to solve this question?

c. Are you able to reach a conclusion about the research question from this IRS pronouncement(s)? If so, what is your conclusion(s).

82. The Venganza Tribe is a federally recognized Indian tribal government described in IRC Section 7701(a)(40)(A). The Venganza Tribe would like to invest some of its cash resulting from its newly opened casino in a real estate development, Vista de Basura, Inc. Vista de Basura, Inc. is an S corporation. Is the Indian tribal government an eligible shareholder for S corporation purposes?

a. Locate the IRS pronouncement(s) that deals with this situation. State the pronouncement number(s).

b. Review the IRS pronouncement(s). Does it raise a need for new information to solve this question?

c. Are you able to reach a conclusion about the research question from this IRS pronouncement(s)? If so, what is your conclusion(s)?

83. Fred Forgetful parks his personal car on a hill in sunny California and fails to properly set the brake or curb the wheels. As a result of Fred's negligence, the car rolls down the hill, damages Lucky's front porch, injures Lucky (who was sitting on the porch), and damages Fred's car. Due to the accident, Fred is forced to pay the following unreimbursed amounts.

Medical expenses for Lucky's injuries	$5,500
Repairs to Fred's car	7,000
Repairs to Lucky's porch	8,500
Fine for traffic violation	275

Using only the Regulations and Code, determine which of these payments, if any, would qualify for casualty loss treatment (before any percentage limitations) as to Fred.

Chapter 5

Judicial Interpretations

LEARNING OBJECTIVES

- Describe the structural relationship among the Federal courts that hear taxation cases.

- Detail the constitution of, and procedures concerning, each element of the Federal court system hearing tax cases.

- Use proper citation conventions for each of the courts that hear tax cases.

- State where tax court cases are published for use by tax researchers.

- Describe conditions under which the practitioner might choose each of the trial-level courts for a client's litigation.

- Work with the format and content of a court case brief.

CHAPTER OUTLINE

Federal Court System
Legal Conventions
Burden of Proof
Tax Confidentiality Privilege
Common Legal Terminology

Tax Court
Tax Court Decisions
Small Cases Division
Locating Tax Court Decisions
Tax Court Rule 155
Scope of Tax Court Decisions

District Courts
Locating District Court Decisions

Court of Federal Claims
Locating Court of Federal Claims Decisions

Courts of Appeals
Locating Court of Appeals Decisions

Supreme Court
Locating Supreme Court Decisions

Case Briefs

The Internet and Judicial Sources
Computer Tax Service Example

Where does one turn, if after locating any Statutory and Administrative sources of authority, the tax researcher still does not have an answer to his or her tax problem? The answer may lie in a judicial interpretation of the Code or administrative rulings. Therefore, the tax researcher must have an understanding of the third primary source of tax law, judicial sources. Since the adoption of the Sixteenth Amendment to the Constitution in 1913, tens of thousands of Federal court decisions have been rendered concerning litigation between taxpayers and the Internal Revenue Service. Such court cases are of special interest to the tax researcher because they typically are concerned with controversial areas of taxation. In this chapter, we will examine the Federal court system, learn to locate various Federal tax judicial decisions, and discuss the use of those decisions in solving tax research problems.

FEDERAL COURT SYSTEM

When a taxpayer and the Internal Revenue Service cannot reach an agreement concerning a specific tax matter using the administrative review process (i.e., audits and appeals, which are discussed in Chapter 12), the dispute may be settled in the Federal courts. Either the taxpayer or the IRS may initiate legal proceedings in the Federal court system. A taxpayer may decide to initiate proceedings as a final attempt to recover an overpayment of tax the IRS refuses to refund or to reverse a deficiency assessment determined by the IRS. Alternatively, the IRS may initiate proceedings to assert its claim to a deficiency, to enforce collection of taxes, or to impose civil or criminal penalties on the taxpayer.

Judicial decisions are the third primary source of the tax law. The *Internal Revenue Code* is the basis for Federal tax laws, and the administrative pronouncements of the IRS interpret provisions of the Code and explain their application. Frequently, however, additional issues and questions arise regarding the proper interpretation or intended application of the law that are not answered either in the law itself or in the administrative pronouncements. The judicial system is left with the task of resolving these questions. In this process, additional tax law is generated that can carry the full force of the statute itself. Often, recurring litigation in an area of innovative or unexpected judicial decisions regarding tax matters will result in Congress enacting legislation codifying certain judicial decisions. The practitioner must be familiar with the workings of this judicial system, which has the ability to stimulate tax laws and influence future legislative developments. In addition, in the event an issue is litigated in the court system, the tax practitioner must be familiar with the precedential value of court cases and the process for review of the court's decision.

Most disagreements with the Internal Revenue Service are resolved through the administrative process of appeals. Judicial decisions should be given significant weight in arriving at a conclusion or recommendation to a tax problem; however, caution should be exercised when it is apparent from the IRS's prior actions that a given position is almost certain to result in litigation. The costs of litigation, in terms of both money and time, may be prohibitive for certain taxpayers.

All litigation between a taxpayer and the government begins in a trial court. If the decision of the trial court is not satisfactory to one of the parties, the trial court decision may be appealed to an appellate court. The appellate court will review the trial court decision, often hear new evidence and arguments, and then either uphold the trial court's decision, modify it in some way, or reverse it.

The Federal court system consists of three trial courts and two levels of appellate courts. The three trial courts are the U.S. Tax Court, the U.S. District Courts, and the U.S. Court of Federal Claims. The two appellate courts are the U.S. Court of Appeals and the U.S. Supreme Court. Each of the trial courts has different attributes and is designed to serve in a different capacity in the Federal judicial system. Exhibit 5–1 diagrams the existing Federal court system. An appeal from any of the three trial courts is to the appropriate U.S. Court of Appeals. The taxpayers and the IRS have no direct access to the Supreme Court or any Court of Appeals.

Exhibit	**5–1**	Federal Tax System—Tax Cases

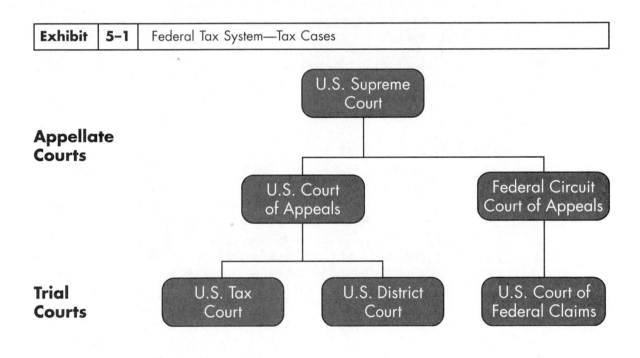

Appellate Courts

Trial Courts

LEGAL CONVENTIONS

Burden of Proof

In most litigation, the party initiating the case has the burden of convincing the court that he is correct with respect to the issue. Historically, however, in most civil tax cases the *Internal Revenue Code* placed the burden of proof on the taxpayer, whether or not he or she initiated the case, except in cases of such items as hobby losses, fraud with intent to evade tax, and the accumulated earnings tax.

However, the burden of proof shifts to the IRS in a few situations.[1] The IRS has the burden of proof in any court proceeding on income, gift, estate, or generation-skipping tax liability with respect to factual issues, provided the taxpayer:

- Introduces credible evidence of the factual issue,
- Maintains records and substantiates items as presently required under the Code and Regulations, and
- Cooperates with reasonable IRS requests for meetings, interviews, witnesses, information, and documents.

For corporations, trusts, and partnerships with net worth exceeding $7 million, the burden of proof remains on the taxpayer.[2] The burden of proof also automatically shifts to the IRS:

- If the IRS uses statistics to reconstruct an individual's income, or
- If the court proceeding against an individual taxpayer involves a penalty or addition to tax.

When reading a published opinion, the tax researcher should note whether the decision was based on the IRS's or the taxpayer's failure to meet a needed evidentiary burden, or whether the IRS or the taxpayer established his or her position with sufficient proof. The first situation should be considered a weaker precedent than the second. Understanding the "strength" of a court decision is an important part of tax research.

Tax Confidentiality Privilege

The attorney-client privilege of confidentiality also applies in tax matters to nonattorneys authorized to practice before the IRS (e.g., CPAs and enrolled agents), as identified in Chapter 1. The nonattorney-client privilege may be asserted only in a *noncriminal tax* proceeding before the IRS or Federal court.[3] The confidentiality privilege usually does not apply to the preparation of tax returns, or the giving of accounting or business advice.

The nonattorney-client privilege does not extend to written communications between a tax practitioner and a corporation in connection with the promotion of any tax shelter. Nor does it apply to the client's workpapers used to determine tax expense for financial statements.

Certified public accountants and enrolled agents need to understand the rules regarding tax confidentiality as they have been applied to lawyers so as to be aware of the privilege limits. Usually, these rules are determined by state law, and the federal confidentiality privilege cannot extend beyond the protection granted by state law, as it is currently interpreted.

Common Legal Terminology

Some of the common legal terms likely to be encountered by the tax researcher follow.

1. IRC § 7491.
2. § 7491(a)(2)(C).
3. § 7525(a)(1).

ad hoc For one particular or special purpose; for example, an ad hoc committee might be formed to solve a certain problem.

ad valorem According to value; used in taxation to designate an assessment of taxes based on property value.

appellant The party who appeals a decision, usually to a higher court.

bona fide In good faith and without fraud or deceit.

certiorari (writ of) The process by which the U.S. Supreme Court agrees to hear a case, based on the appeal of a lower court decision by one of the parties involved in that decision.

collateral estoppel When an issue of fact has been determined by valid judgment, that issue cannot be litigated again by the same parties in future litigation.

covenant An agreement or promise to do or not to do something.

de jure In law or lawful; legitimate.

de facto In fact or reality; by virtue of accomplishment or deed.

defendant In civil proceedings, the party who is responding to the complaint; usually the one who is being sued in some matter.

deposition A written statement of a witness under oath, normally taken in question-and-answer form.

dictum (dicta) A statement or remark in a court opinion that is not necessary to support the decision.

en banc A decision by all the judges of a court instead of a single judge or a selected set of judges.

enjoin To command or instruct with authority; a judge can enjoin someone to do or not to do some act.

habeas corpus (writ of) The procedure for determining if the authorities can hold an individual in custody.

nolo contendere A party does not want to fight or continue to maintain a defense; the defendant will not contend a charge made by the government; "no contest."

non obstante veredicto (n.o.v.) Notwithstanding the verdict; a judgment that reverses the determination of a jury.

nullity Something in law that is void; an act having no legal force.

parol evidence The doctrine that renders any evidence of a prior understanding of the parties to a contract invalid if it contradicts the terms of a written contract.

per curiam A decision of the whole court, instead of just a limited number of judges.

plaintiff The one who initially brings a lawsuit.

prima facie At face value; something that is obvious and does not require further support.

res judicata The legal concept that bars relitigation on the same set of facts. Because of this concept, taxpayers must make sure that all of the issues they want (or do not want) to be litigated are included in a case. Once the case is decided, it cannot be reopened.

slip opinion An individual court decision published separately shortly after the decision is rendered.

vacate A reversal or abandonment of a prior decision of a court.

TAX COURT

The U.S. **Tax Court** is a specialized trial court that hears only Federal tax cases. Established by the Code and not directly by the U.S. Constitution,[4] its jurisdiction is limited to cases concerning the various *Internal Revenue Codes* and *Revenue Acts* that were adopted after February 26, 1926. Before 1943, the Tax Court was known as the **Board of Tax Appeals** (BTA); it was an administrative board of the Treasury Department rather than a true judicial court. In 1943, the BTA became the U.S. Tax Court, an administrative court, and in 1969, its status was upgraded to that of a full judicial court, with enforcement powers.

Nineteen judges hear Tax Court cases. Each judge is appointed to a fifteen-year term by the President of the United States, with the advice and confirmation of the Senate. This appointment must be based solely on the grounds of the judge's fitness to perform the duties of the office. A Tax Court judge may be removed from his or her position by the President, after notice and opportunity for public hearing, because of inefficiency, neglect of duty, or malfeasance in office, but for no other reason.

To alleviate the heavy caseload of the appointed Tax Court judges, the Chief Judge of the Court periodically designates additional special trial judges to hear pertinent cases for a temporary period. Limited primarily by the budget granted by Congress, these temporary appointments are useful in decreasing the waiting period for taxpayers who wish to be heard before the Court. The decisions of these special judges carry the full authority of the U.S. Tax Court. Senior judges are retired judges who still hear cases from time-to-time by invitation of the Chief Justice.

SPOTLIGHT ON TAXATION: U.S. Tax Court Judges (2005)

At the time this edition was prepared, the roster of Tax Court judges included the following.

(some positions may be vacant)

Judges:

Joel Gerber, Chief Judge	Harry A. Haines	Stephen J. Swift
Carolyn P. Chiechi	James S. Halpern	Michael B. Thornton
Mary Ann Cohen	Mark V. Holmes	Juan F. Vasquez
Maurice B. Foley	Diane L. Kroupa	Thomas B. Wells
Joseph H. Gale	David Laro	Robert A. Wherry, Jr.
Joseph Robert Goeke	L. Paige Marvel	

Senior Judges:

Renato Beghe	Howard A. Dawson, Jr.	Robert P. Ruwe
Herbert L. Chabot	Julian I. Jacobs	Laurence J. Whalen
John O. Colvin	Arthur L. Nims, III	

Continued

4. § 7441.

Special Trial Judges:

Peter J. Panuthos, Chief Special Trial Judge	D. Irvin Couvillion	John J. Pajak
Robert N. Armen	John F. Dean	Carleton D. Powell
Lewis R. Carluzzo	Stanley J. Goldberg	

Tax Court judges are tax law specialists, not generalists. Typically, they have acquired many years of judicial or tax litigation experience before being appointed to the Tax Court. Thus, if a taxpayer wants to argue a technical tax issue with the IRS, the Tax Court usually is the best trial-level forum in which to try the case. Tax Court judges are better able to understand such issues than would be a judge in a more general court.

SPOTLIGHT ON TAXATION: Tax Law Complexity

We have from time-to-time complained about the complexity of our revenue laws and the almost impossible challenge they present to taxpayers or their representatives who have not been initiated into the mysteries of the convoluted, complex provisions affecting the particular corner of the law involved. . . . Our complaints have obviously fallen upon deaf ears.

—Arnold Raum, U.S. Tax Court Judge

The U.S. Tax Court is a national court, based in Washington, D.C. Its jurisdiction is not limited to a specific geographical region, as is the case with some other Federal courts. Taxpayers need not travel to Washington, D.C., to have a case tried before the Tax Court because some of its judges travel throughout the country and are available to hear taxpayer cases in every major city of the United States several times every year. See Exhibit 5–2 for a map showing cities where the Tax Court occasionally holds trials.

When a case is heard before the Tax Court, it usually is presented before only one of the nineteen Tax Court judges. Taxpayers cannot request jury trials before this court. After the judge hears the case, he or she prepares a decision that is reviewed by the Chief Judge of the court. In most instances, the trial judge's opinion stands, but the Chief Judge can designate the opinion for review by the other members of the Tax Court. Upon their agreement with the decision, the opinion is released.

If the case involves an unusual, important, or novel issue, more than one judge, or the entire Tax Court, might hear the case. This rare occurrence is identified as an *en banc* sitting of the court.

For a case to be heard, the taxpayer must petition the Court within ninety days of the IRS's mailing of a notice and demand for payment of the disputed

Exhibit	5-2
Tax Court Trial Locations	

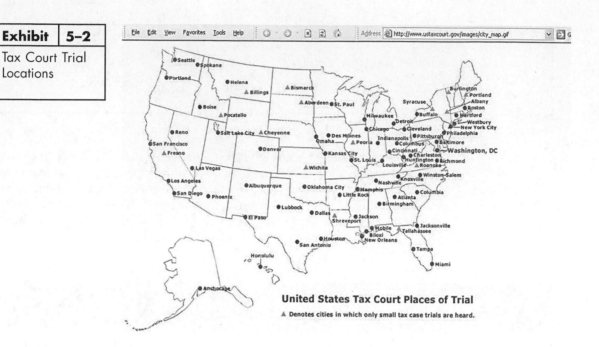

United States Tax Court Places of Trial

▲ Denotes cities in which only small tax case trials are heard.

amount. The taxpayer need not pay the disputed tax liability before the case is heard.

Tax Court Decisions

The Tax Court issues two kinds of decisions: regular and memorandum. A **Regular decision** (recently 50–100 cases per year) generally involves a new or unusual point of law, as determined by the Chief Judge of the court. If the chief judge believes that the decision concerns only the application of existing law or an interpretation of facts, the decision is issued as a **Memorandum decision** (300–400 cases per year). Over the years, however, this classification scheme has not always been strictly followed by the Court. Many of its Memorandum decisions address significant points of law or other issues important to the tax researcher. Accordingly, the researcher should not ignore Memorandum decisions. If issues or points of law pertinent to the problem at hand are addressed, both Regular and Memorandum decisions of the Tax Court should be considered by the taxpayer.

Because the Tax Court is a national court, it hears cases that may be appealed to Courts of Appeals (discussed later in this chapter) in different geographical regions, or *circuits*. Because these Courts of Appeals occasionally disagree on tax issues, the Tax Court is faced with a dilemma. For example, one Court of Appeals may have held that a specific item is deductible in computing taxable income, while another has held against such a deduction. Which precedent should the Tax Court follow? Under *Golsen*,[5] the Tax Court will follow the Court of Appeals that has direct jurisdiction over the taxpayer

5. 54 T.C. 742 (1970).

in question. If the Court of Appeals that has jurisdiction over the taxpayer has not ruled on the matter, the Tax Court will decide the case on the basis of its own interpretation of the disputed provision. This *Golsen* **rule** means the Tax Court may reach opposite decisions, based on identical facts, for taxpayers differentiated solely by the geographical area in which they live. The tax researcher must be aware of the *Golsen* rule in analyzing cases that may be affected by it.

Small Cases Division

The Tax Court maintains a **Small Cases Division**, which is similar to a small claims court. If the amount of a disputed deficiency, including penalties, or claimed overpayment does not exceed $50,000, a taxpayer may be heard before the Small Cases Division, upon approval of the Tax Court. The hearing is conducted as informally as possible, and the taxpayer may represent him- or herself, that is, acting *pro se*. (Of course, the taxpayer may be represented by an attorney if he or she so desires.) Neither elaborate written briefs nor formal oral arguments are required in the Small Cases Division. Issues brought before this forum generally are fact-based; for example, does the taxpayer have the necessary documentation to claim the earned income tax credit?

At any time before a decision is final, the Tax Court may interrupt a Small Cases hearing and transfer the case to the regular Tax Court for trial. This might occur, for example, when important facts or issues of law, more suitably heard in the more formal Tax Court context, become apparent only after the Small Cases proceedings have begun.

Small Cases decisions, called Summary Opinions, are not officially published by the government. Nevertheless, they are available for review by tax researchers and taxpayers through commercial publishers. Small Cases Division decisions cannot be used as precedents when dealing with the IRS; however, they do provide insight into how the Tax Court has treated similar tax situations. The decision of the Small Cases judge is final and may not be appealed by the taxpayer or the government. An excerpt from a sample Summary Opinion is presented in Exhibit 5–3.

Locating Tax Court Decisions

Tax Court regular decisions are published by the Government Printing Office (GPO) in a set of bound reporters called the *Tax Court of the United States Reports*. These volumes are cited as "T.C." The Board of Tax Appeals has its own reporter, called the *United States Board of Tax Appeals*, cited as "B.T.A."

Memorandum decisions are not published by the GPO. They are included in special-decision reporters that are published by Commerce Clearing House (CCH) and by Research Institute of America (RIA). The CCH reporter is titled *Tax Court Memorandum Decisions*, cited as "TCM," and the RIA reporter is known as *RIA Tax Court Memorandum Decisions*, cited as "RIA T.C. Memo." The Tax Court reporter is published twice a year, and both of the memorandum-case reporters are published once a year.

Exhibit	5-3	Tax Court Small Case (Summary Opinion) Excerpt

Estate of Stevens, Nicholas C., T.C. Summary Opinion 2003-163

Date Issued: 12/1/2003
Judge: Opinion by PANUTHOS

Pursuant to *Internal Revenue Code* Section 7463(B), this opinion may not be treated as precedent for any other case.

COUNSEL

Kim Patricia Bryan, pro se.
Clare J. Brooks, for respondent.

Opinion by PANUTHOS

This case was heard pursuant to the provisions of section 7463 of the *Internal Revenue Code* in effect at the time the petition was filed. The decision to be entered is not reviewable by any other court, and this opinion should not be cited as authority. Unless otherwise indicated, subsequent section references are to the *Internal Revenue Code* in effect for the year in issue.

Respondent determined a deficiency in decedent's Federal income tax of $1,324 and an addition to tax under section 6651(a)(1) of $121 for taxable year 2000. After respondent's concession, 1 the issue for decision is whether decedent is taxable on unreported income of $12,154 from wages and interest during the 2000 taxable year.

BACKGROUND

Some of the facts have been stipulated, and they are so found. The stipulation of facts and the attached exhibits are incorporated herein by this reference.

Nicholas Charles Stevens, Jr. (decedent) died in Baltimore County, Maryland, in October 2001 at the age of 18 years. Decedent's mother, Kim Patricia Bryan (Ms. Bryan), was directed to serve as personal representative of decedent's estate. At the time the petition was filed, Ms. Bryan resided in Baltimore, Maryland.

During the year in issue, decedent received wages of $1,048 from Maryland Car Care, Inc. and $4,719 from Mangione Enterprises of Turf Valley. Also during the year in issue, decedent was credited with interest income of $7,435 from custodial accounts at Farmers and Mechanics National Bank. Such accounts were established pursuant to the Maryland Uniform Transfers to Minors Act upon the death of decedent's father in 1992. Decedent, a minor, was 17 years old in 2000.

Decedent filed a Form 1040EZ, Income Tax Return for Single and Joint Filers with No Dependents, for the 2000 taxable year (2000 return). Decedent reported wages of $1,048 on his 2000 return. He did not report wages of $4,719 from Mangione Enterprises of Turf Valley. Nor did he report the interest income of $7,435 from custodial accounts.

Respondent issued decedent a notice of deficiency dated December 23, 2002, determining that decedent was taxable on unreported income of $12,154 from wages and interest during the 2000 taxable year. 2 Ms. Bryan contends that a deceased person should not be liable for any tax deficiencies.

| **Exhibit** | **5–3** | Tax Court Small Case (Summary Opinion) Excerpt—Concluded |

DISCUSSION

Decedent having filed his 2000 return after July 22, 1998, section 7491(a) is applicable in the instant case. However, neither party takes a position as to whether the burden of proof has shifted to respondent under section 7491(a). We conclude that resolution of the issue whether decedent is taxable on unreported income of $12,154 does not depend upon who has the burden of proof.

Gross income includes compensation for services. Sec. 61(a)(1). In the present case, decedent received wages of $4,719 from Mangione Enterprises of Turf Valley, and he did not report such amount in his 2000 return. Accordingly, we sustain respondent's determination that decedent received unreported income of $4,719 from wages in 2000.

Gross income also includes interest. Sec. 61(a)(4). In the present case, decedent was credited with interest income of $7,435 in 2000 from custodial accounts established pursuant to the Maryland Uniform Transfers to Minors Act (MUTMA). Under the MUTMA, interest income constitutes "custodial property" that generally transfers to a minor when he or she attains the age of either 18 years or 21 years, depending upon who originally transferred such property to the custodian. 3 See Md. Code Ann., Est. & Trusts secs. 13-301(f), 13-320 (2001). While decedent was only 17 in 2000, he enjoyed the economic benefit of interest income from the custodial accounts, and therefore, such interest is taxable in the year earned and not in the year of actual receipt by him. 4 See Anastasio v. Commissioner, 67 T.C. 814, (LEXIS through 2003 Sess.). 817-818 (1977), affd. 41 AFTR 2d 78-328, 78-1 USTC par. 9153 (2d Cir. 1977). We sustain respondent's determination that decedent was taxable on unreported interest income of $7,435 from custodial accounts in 2000.

Ms. Bryan nevertheless contends that a deceased person should not be liable for any tax deficiencies. "Death may be an avenue of escape from many of the woes of life, but it is no escape from taxes." Estate of Kahr v. Commissioner, 414 F.2d 621, 626 (2d Cir. 1969) (cited by United States v. Critzer, 498 F.2d 1160, 1163 (4th Cir. 1974)), affg. in part and revg. in part 48 T.C. 929 (1967).

Reviewed and adopted as the report of the Small Tax Case Division.

To reflect the foregoing, Decision will be entered for respondent with respect to the deficiency and for petitioner with respect to the addition to tax under Section 6651(a)(1).

Because many months may elapse between the release of a Tax Court decision and its publication in a bound reporter, such decisions receive both a temporary and a permanent citation. The **temporary citation** is structured as follows.

Hillman, D. H., 114 T.C. _____, No. 6 (2000), where:

114 is the volume number.
T.C. is the abbreviation for the Tax Court Reporter.
_____ indicates the page number, which is to be determined later.
No. 6 is the number of the case.
(2000) is the year of the decision.

The temporary citation includes no page number for the case because the opinion has not yet been published. All proper citations either italicize or underline the name of the court case; major elements of the citation are separated by commas. The **permanent citation** for the same case is reported as follows.

Hillman, D. H., 114 T.C. 103 (2000), where:

114 is the volume number.
T.C. is the abbreviation for the Tax Court Reporter.
103 is the page number.
(2000) is the year of the decision.

Most court case citations include the names of both parties involved. This convention is ignored for most Tax Court citations, however, because all such cases involve the taxpayer bringing suit against the government to avoid payment of disputed tax liabilities. Thus, a traditional citation for the above case would be *Hillman v. U.S.* (or, more precisely, *David H. Hillman v. Commissioner*). Nonetheless, common practice allows the tax researcher to omit the reference to the defendant in the action (i.e., the government), because such reference could be inferred from the notation for the court in which the lawsuit is heard.

Once the GPO publishes the decision in the permanent bound edition of the regular Tax Court cases, the temporary citation becomes obsolete. The same citation procedure is used with respect to Board of Tax Appeals cases, substituting "B.T.A." for the "T.C." identification. Indeed, this procedure for disclosing the citation for a case (i.e., Name–Volume Number–Reporter–Page Number–Year) is common among all American courts. Exhibit 5–4 is an example of a regular Tax Court decision, reproduced from the GPO Tax Court reporter.

Using the same citation conventions, the general and permanent citations, respectively, for a Tax Court memorandum decision would appear as follows.

General

Fields, Linda A., T.C. Memo 2002-320, where:

T.C. Memo is a reference to a Tax Court Memorandum decision.
2002 is the year of the decision.
320 is the decision number.

Permanent RIA

Fields, Linda A., 2002 RIA T.C. Memo ¶ 2002-320, where:

RIA T.C. Memo is the RIA Tax Court Memorandum reporter.
¶ 2002-320 is the paragraph number.

Permanent CCH

Fields, Linda A., 84 TCM 710 (2002), where:

84 is the volume number.
TCM is the CCH Tax Court Memorandum reporter.
710 is the page number.
(2002) is the year of the decision.

| Exhibit | 5–4 | Tax Court Regular Opinion |

Campbell, Edwina D., 121 T.C. 290, Code Sec(s) 6015.

Date Issued: 11/24/2003.

By Final Notice of Determination dated Nov. 6, 2001, R determined that P was not entitled to relief from joint and several liability relating to 1989 because the request was, pursuant to Sec. 6015, I.R.C., filed more than 2 years after R's [pg. 172] first collection activity against P. On Feb. 1, 2002, P filed, pursuant to sec. 6015(e)(1), I.R.C., a petition seeking review of R's determination. On Mar. 10, 2003, P filed a Motion for Partial Summary Judgment and on Mar. 31, 2003, R filed a Notice of Objection and Cross-Motion for Summary Judgment. The issue in both parties' motions is whether R's application of P's overpayment, relating to 1998, as a credit against P's 1989 tax liability is, pursuant to sec. 6015, I.R.C., a collection activity that bars P's request for relief relating to 1989.

Held: R's offset of P's overpayment is, pursuant to sec. 6015, I.R.C., a collection activity.

Held, further, P's Motion for Partial Summary Judgment is denied.

Held, further, R's Cross-Motion for Summary Judgment is granted. There is no genuine issue as to whether P is entitled to relief from joint and several liability relating to 1989 because P's election was, pursuant to sec. 6015, I.R.C., filed more than 2 years after R's first collection activity against P.

COUNSEL

Edwina Diane Campbell, pro se.
Erin K. Huss, for respondent.

FOLEY, Judge

OPINION

This matter is before the Court on Petitioner's Motion for Partial Summary Judgment and Respondent's Notice of Objection and Cross-Motion for Summary Judgment pursuant to Rule 121. 1 The sole issue for decision is whether respondent's application of petitioner's overpayment, relating to 1998, as a credit against petitioner's 1989 tax liability is, pursuant to section 6015, a collection action that bars petitioner's request for relief from joint and several liability relating to 1989.

BACKGROUND

On May 13, 1999, respondent applied, pursuant to section 6402(a), petitioner's overpayment, relating to 1998, as a credit against a portion of petitioner's 1989 tax liability and sent petitioner written notification thereof. On July 23, 2001, petitioner requested, pursuant to section 6015(b), (c), and (f), relief from joint and several liability relating to her 1989 joint Federal income tax return filed with Alvin L. Campbell.

By Final Notice of Determination dated November 6, 2001, respondent determined that petitioner was not entitled to relief from joint and several liability relating to 1989 because the request was, pursuant to section 6015, filed more than 2 years after respondent's first collection activity against petitioner.

Continued

Exhibit	5–4	Tax Court Regular Opinion—Concluded

On February 1, 2002, petitioner, while residing in Tucson, Arizona, filed a petition pursuant to section 6015(e)(1) seeking review of respondent's determination. Petitioner, on March 10, 2003, filed a Motion for Partial Summary Judgment, accompanied by a Memorandum of Points and Authorities, and Affidavit in support thereof. On March 31, 2003, respondent filed a Notice of Objection and Cross-Motion for Summary Judgment, accompanied by Declarations, and Memorandum of Law in support thereof. Petitioner, on April 16, 2003, filed an Opposition to Respondent's Cross-Motion for Summary Judgment.

DISCUSSION

An election pursuant to section 6015(b), (c), or (f) must be made within 2 years of respondent's first collection activity taken after July 22, 1998, against the individual making the election. 2 Internal Revenue Service Restructuring and Reform Act of 1998, Pub. L. 105-206, sec. 3201(g)(2), 112 Stat. 740; sec. 6015(b)(1)(E), (c)(3)(B); Rev. Proc. 2000-15, sec. 5, 2000-1 C.B. 447, 449.

Petitioner contends that respondent's offset of her overpayment is not, pursuant to section 6015, a collection activity. We disagree. The offset of an overpayment is by its plain and ordinary meaning a collection activity pursuant to section 6015. See Per [pg. 173] rin v. United States, 444 U.S. 37, 42 (1979) (stating that "A fundamental canon of statutory construction is that, unless otherwise defined, words will be interpreted as taking their ordinary, contemporary, common meaning"); Trent v. Commissioner, T.C. Memo. 2002-285 [TC Memo 2002-285] (stating that nonlevy collection actions include "offsetting overpayments from other tax years after the requesting spouse files for relief"). Because petitioner reported overpayments of tax on her 1998 return, she generally would be entitled to claim a refund. See sec. 6511(a), (b)(1); Commissioner v. Lundy, 516 U.S. 235, 240 [77 AFTR 2d 96-406] (1996). Pursuant to section 6402(a), however, respondent used petitioner's overpayment to partially satisfy her 1989 tax liability. Thus, respondent engaged, pursuant to section 6015, in a collection activity against petitioner. Because petitioner's election was filed more than 2 years after that collection activity (i.e., respondent applied the overpayment and sent petitioner written notification thereof on May 13, 1999, and on July 23, 2001, petitioner elected relief), there is no genuine issue as to whether petitioner is entitled to relief from joint and several liability relating to 1989. See Rule 121(b); Natl. Indus., Inc. v. Republic Natl. Life Ins. Co., 677 F.2d 1258, 1265 (9th Cir. 1982). Thus, Petitioner's Motion for Partial Summary Judgment is denied, and Respondent's Cross-Motion for Summary Judgment is granted.

Contentions we have not addressed are irrelevant, moot, or meritless.

To reflect the foregoing, An appropriate order and decision will be entered.

One can observe from the RIA citation that the opinion was issued in 2002 because all of the Tax Court Memorandum Decisions for that year are included in the RIA reporter using paragraph numbers that begin with "2002."

As we observed with respect to the regular Tax Court decisions, the temporary citation becomes obsolete when the permanent bound edition of the memorandum reporter is published.

Besides the traditional published sources for Tax Court decisions, these items also are available on computer tax services such as RIA Checkpoint, Lexis, Kleinrock's, etc. All of the computer services reference the general citation, and most give the parallel RIA and CCH reporter citations.

Tax Court Rule 155

When a court reaches a tax decision, it normally will not compute the tax that is due to the government or the refund that is due to a taxpayer. The computation of this amount is left to be determined by the IRS and the taxpayer. The court will compute the tax only if the government and the taxpayer cannot agree. When the Tax Court reaches a decision without calculating the tax, the decision is said to be entered under *Rule 155*. See *Estate of Wayne-Chi Young v. Commissioner*, 110 T.C. 24, for an example of when the Tax Court will enter a decision under Rule 155. For Tax Court decisions prior to 1974, this practice was referred to as *Rule 50*.

Scope of Tax Court Decisions

The Tax Court may examine an entire tax return for a taxpayer whose case it is hearing. On the other hand, the District Court and Court of Federal Claims can address only the specific issue or issues that are involved in the case. If a taxpayer wants only a specific issue (or issues) litigated in a case, then the District Court or Court of Federal Claims may be a better forum for him than the Tax Court.

DISTRICT COURTS

The U.S. **District Courts** are another trial-level forum that hears tax cases. Unlike the Tax Court, however, the District Courts hear cases involving legal issues based on the entire United States Code, not just the *Internal Revenue Code*. District Court judges typically are generalists, rather than specialists in Federal tax laws. The same District Court judge might render opinions concerning matters of tax law, civil rights, bank robbery, interstate commerce, kidnapping, and fraud.

The District Courts are further distinguished from the Tax Court in that a taxpayer who disagrees with the IRS may take his or her case to the appropriate District Court only after paying the disputed tax liability; thus, in the typical District Court taxation case, the taxpayer sues the government for a refund of the disputed tax liability.

Numerous District Courts are located throughout the United States, each assigned a geographical area. The designated district can be as small as one city (New York City) or as large as the largest state (Alaska). Typically, the taxpayer will request a hearing before the District Court that has jurisdiction over the location in which he or she lives or conducts business.

District Court cases are heard before one judge, not a panel of judges. In the appropriate District Court, the taxpayer can request a jury trial concerning a tax case (or certain other Federal matters). This opportunity may be useful if the taxpayer wants to argue an "emotional" issue rather than a technical one, or if the taxpayer or his or her associates are particularly credible witnesses (and thus have a good chance of winning a jury trial). Limited to decisions concerning questions of fact, juries apparently occasionally can be persuaded in a tax case to hold for the taxpayer when a judge might not be so inclined.

Because the District Courts are general in nature and do not specialize in tax matters, over time, their decisions can vary significantly among the districts. Some of their decisions have important precedential value and can be relied on by the tax researcher; however, many of these decisions are poorly structured or poorly conceived from a technical standpoint, and represent candidates for overturn on appeal. The tax researcher must examine these decisions carefully to assess their probable use as a precedent before using them to help solve a client's tax problem.

Locating District Court Decisions

District Court tax decisions are published in three different reporters. West Publishing includes such cases in its *Federal Supplement Series*; citations for these cases include the "F.Supp." or the "F.Supp.2d." abbreviation. The series contains all decisions of the District Courts designated for publication, including those for the numerous nontax cases. Most university and law school libraries subscribe to the *Federal Supplement Series*. However, it is a waste of money for the tax researcher to subscribe to this series to obtain just the tax decisions that are rendered in the District Courts. Instead, the tax researcher can use special tax case reporters that include only tax decisions selected from all of the decisions of the Federal courts except the Tax Court. (As we discussed earlier, the Tax Court's Regular and Memorandum Decisions are published in specialized reporters, so they do not present a budgeting problem of this sort.)

RIA's specialized tax reporter is titled *American Federal Tax Reports*, abbreviated in citations as **"AFTR."** Currently, the second series of this reporter is in use, with "2d" added to indicate that the cases therein usually relate to the current *Internal Revenue Code*. Accordingly, the abbreviation AFTR2d is commonly used. CCH's specialized Federal tax case reporter is known as *United States Tax Cases*, which is abbreviated as **"USTC"** in traditional citations. Do not confuse this abbreviation with that for the U.S. Tax Court, which we have identified as "T.C." Occasionally, the West citation (F.Supp.) is referred to as the primary citation for a case, and the CCH and RIA reporters are used for secondary citations. The AFTR2d and USTC reporters each publish 1,200–1,500 tax cases per year from courts other than the U.S. Tax Court.

Besides the traditional published primary and secondary court reporters, electronic court reporters are also available. For example, Kleinrock's publishes tax decisions as part of its computer service. The computer-based reporters have their own citations, and they usually cross-reference one or more of the standard printed reporters (West, RIA, and CCH). An illustration of various citations for a District Court case follows.

Court Reporters

West:	*Barber, Lori*, 85 F.Supp.2d 967 (N.D.C.A., 2000)
RIA:	*Barber, Lori*, 85 AFTR2d 2000-879 (N.D.C.A., 2000)
CCH:	*Barber, Lori*, 2000-1 USTC ¶ 50,209 (N.D.C.A., 2000)
Kleinrock:	*Barber, Lori*, KTC 2000-45 (N.D.C.A., 2000)

Each of these citations indicates both the specific District Court that heard the case and the year in which the opinion was issued. Given publication time lags, however, this may not match the year in which the reporter volume was published. Unless necessitated by such a delay, a proper citation need not include in the parentheses the year in which the opinion was issued, in all but a West citation.

Notice that more than one volume of the USTC reporter was published by CCH in 2000, as indicated by the volume number, and that this reporter uses paragraph numbers to organize the opinions. Other elements of the citations are familiar. A complete citation for this case, using traditional form, would appear as follows.

Barber, Lori, 85 F.Supp. 967; 85 AFTR2d 2000-879; 2000-1 USTC ¶ 50,209; KTC 2000-45 (N.D.C.A. 2000)

COURT OF FEDERAL CLAIMS

The U.S. **Court of Federal Claims** is the newest of the trial-level courts. It was created on October 1, 1982, by the Federal Courts Improvement Act (P.L. 97-164). In this act, the U.S. Court of Claims and the U.S. Court of Customs and Patent Appeals were reorganized into two new courts. The trial division of the U.S. Court of Claims became the new U.S. Claims Court, and the remaining divisions of both courts became the new Court of Appeals for the Federal Circuit, discussed later. The forum was renamed the U.S. Court of Federal Claims in 1992. Sixteen judges are appointed to the Court of Federal Claims. Its jurisdiction lies in hearing cases concerning all monetary claims against the Federal government, only one type of which is in the form of tax refunds. Thus, the taxpayer must pay the disputed tax and sue the government for a refund in order for the case to be heard in the Court of Federal Claims. Similarly, like the District Court but unlike the Tax Court, the Court of Federal Claims is composed of judges who, with only a few exceptions, are not specialists in technical tax law. The Court of Federal Claims does not allow jury trials on any matter.

The U.S. Court of Federal Claims is a national court located in Washington, D.C. However, because the Court of Federal Claims judges periodically travel to the major cities of the country and hear cases in these various locations, in a manner similar to that of the Tax Court, one need not go to Washington, D.C., to present a case before the Court of Federal Claims.

Moreover, because the Court of Federal Claims is a national court that must follow the decisions only of the Federal District of the Court of Appeals, it is not bound by the geographical Circuit Courts of Appeals that have ruled on similar cases, nor by the Court of Appeals for the circuit in which the taxpayer works or resides. This may be important to a taxpayer whose circuit has held adversely to his or her position on the disputed issue: if the case were presented to the appropriate District Court, or to the Tax Court (recall the *Golsen* rule), the precedent of the adverse ruling would be adopted by those trial courts, but the Court of Federal Claims is not so bound.

Locating Court of Federal Claims Decisions

Before October 1982, all U.S. Court of Claims decisions concerning both tax and nontax issues were published in West's *Federal Reporter*, second series (this reporter is now in its third series). Citations to the reporter use the abbreviations "F.2d" or "F.3d," as the case may be. Current decisions of the U.S. Court of Federal Claims can be found in West's primary reporter, *U.S. Court of Federal Claims*, which can be cited by using the abbreviation "Fed. Cl." In addition, tax decisions of the old U.S. Court of Claims and the new U.S. Court of Federal Claims are available through several secondary published and electronic reporters. U.S. Court of Federal Claims decisions are published in CCH's *United States Tax Cases* (USTC), RIA's *American Federal Tax Reports* 2d (AFTR2d), and other places.

Examine the following proper primary and secondary citations for decisions of the U.S. Court of Federal Claims. All of the elements of these citations are familiar to us. As is most often the situation, when a decision is issued and published in the same year, one need not be redundant in identifying the given year in the body of the citation because the reader can infer the year from other aspects of the listing. A complete citation of the case would include references to all of the publications, in the form indicated previously.

Court Reporters

West:	*Bennett, Courtney*, 30 Fed. Cl. 396 (1994)
CCH:	*Bennett, Courtney*, 94-1 USTC ¶ 50,044 (Fed. Cl., 1994)
RIA:	*Bennett, Courtney*, 73 AFTR2d 94-534 (Fed. Cl., 1994)
Kleinrock:	*Bennett, Courtney*, KTC 1994-647 (Fed. Cl., 1994)

As a general tax court, the U.S. Court of Federal Claims has generated decisions that cannot easily be anticipated. Practitioners usually should pursue a case in the U.S. Court of Federal Claims when the applicable U.S. District and U.S. Tax Court decisions are adverse to the taxpayer, or when a nontechnical matter lies at the heart of the taxpayer's case.

COURTS OF APPEALS

The first level of Federal appellate courts is the U.S. **Courts of Appeals**. Like the District Court and Court of Federal Claims, the Courts of Appeals consider issues in both tax and nontax litigation, although the Courts of Appeals generally will hear only cases that involve a question of law. Seldom will a Circuit Court of Appeals challenge the trial court's findings as to the facts.

Congress has created thirteen Courts of Appeals: eleven are geographical, in that they are responsible for cases that originate in designated states; one is assigned to Washington, D.C.; and one is known as the Court of Appeals for the Federal Circuit. This last court hears tax and other cases that originate only in the Court of Federal Claims. The other Courts of Appeals consider tax and nontax issues brought from the Tax Court or a District Court for an assigned geographical region.

The eleven geographical Courts of Appeals are organized into geographical *circuits*, each of which is assigned a number. Practitioners commonly refer to the circuit courts by this number. For example, the Court of Appeals designated to hear cases that originate in Seattle typically is referred to as the Ninth Circuit Court of Appeals. Exhibit 5–5 shows the jurisdiction of each of the Courts of Appeals. Approximately twenty judges have been appointed to each of the circuit courts. Typically, a three-judge panel hears a Court of Appeals case. Jury trials are not available in these courts.

A Court of Appeals decision carries precedential weight because each circuit is independent of the others and must follow only the decisions of the U.S. Supreme Court. Because the Supreme Court hears only about a dozen tax

Exhibit	5–5	Circuit and District Court Jurisdictions of the U.S.
		This map indicates the boundaries as of the end of 2004 for the U.S. District and Circuit courts. Reflecting population shifts, proposals are being considered to split the Ninth Circuit into at least two smaller areas, and to add another District to the state of California.

LEGEND
Circuit Boundaries
State Boundaries
District Boundaries

ADMINISTRATIVE OFFICE OF THE UNITED STATES SUPREME COURTS
APRIL 1988

cases annually, the Court of Appeals, in most situations, represents the final authority in Federal tax matters. Thus, a researcher generally must follow the holding of a tax decision issued by the Court of Appeals for the circuit in which the client works or resides if the controlling facts or issues of law are sufficiently similar.

Decisions by the circuit court in which the taxpayer works or resides should be given great consideration, even if the researcher has found that another circuit court has held in the taxpayer's favor in a similar case. For example, if a taxpayer lives in San Antonio, and the Fifth Circuit has held that an item similar to the taxpayer's does not qualify as a deduction, the deduction most likely should not be claimed, even if the Seventh or Eighth Circuit has held that the deduction is available. Under the *Golsen* rule, the unfavorable Fifth Circuit decision will apply to the taxpayer at the trial-court level, even though the U.S. Tax Court will be forced in this example to render opinions that are inconsistent among taxpayers.

If, in the same example, however, the Fifth Circuit had not yet ruled on the issue, and the favorable Seventh Circuit ruling is available, the researcher may be more comfortable in following the decision of the "outside" circuit. Prior decisions of Courts of Appeals are of great importance in the construction of subsequent decisions by another circuit, and the researcher rightly can place precedential value on the holdings of other circuits in anticipating the proper position for a client.

Therefore, in general, the Court of Appeals decisions most important to a given taxpayer are those issued by the circuit in which he or she works or resides. In addition, however, these observations can be made: Second, Ninth, and D.C. Circuit decisions are especially important, because of numerous innovative, unusual, and controversial judicial interpretations of the tax laws, and because their jurisdictions include the two most populous states in the nation and the nation's capital.

SPOTLIGHT ON TAXES—Do We Need More Courts?

There is a proposal before Congress to add at least one more circuit to the Courts of Appeals, by splitting up the Ninth Circuit. Because of population migration in the last several decades, the Ninth Circuit is seen by some as "too big," constituting almost 20 percent of the U.S. population. Another motivation for such a split-up might be political—the Ninth Circuit is historically the most progressive of the circuits, and this does not always sit well with citizens and their professional advisers in parts of the more conservative western states.

Locating Court of Appeals Decisions

Court of Appeals decisions are reported in several general and specialized tax publications. All of the decisions of the various Courts of Appeals designated for publication are included in West's *Federal Reporter* (F.2d or F.3d). Most tax cases from the Courts of Appeals are published in the *United States*

Tax Cases service (USTC), and in the *American Federal Tax Reports*. The familiar citation conventions are used in the following examples of primary and secondary citations for a Court of Appeals decision.

Court Reporters

West:	*Oxford Capital Corp.*, 211 F.3d 280 (CA-5, 2000)
RIA:	*Oxford Capital Corp.*, 85 AFTR2d 2000-1840 (CA-5, 2000)
CCH:	*Oxford Capital Corp.*, 2000-1 USTC ¶ 50,447 (CA-5, 2000)
Kleinrock:	*Oxford Capital Corp.*, KTC 2000-228 (CA-5, 2000)

A tax decision from the Court of Appeals is reproduced in Exhibit 5–6.

Exhibit	**5–6**	Court of Appeals Decision

Cziraki, Imre and Gizella v. Commissioner, 87 AFTR2d 2001-308; 2001-1 USTC ¶ 50,141.

Appeal from a Decision of the United States Tax Court

Before: GOODWIN, HUG, and PREGERSON, Circuit Judges.

Imre and Gizella Cziraki (the "Czirakis") appeal the tax court's decision denying their casualty loss deduction in the amount of $220,000 for the 1992 tax year for damage to a dirt road on their farm land. Specifically, the Czirakis challenge the tax court's determination that this road was a "single identifiable property" (SIP) as this limits their casualty loss deduction to the road's basis. We have jurisdiction to review the final order of the tax court under 26 U.S.C. Section 7482, and we affirm. Because the parties are familiar with the factual and procedural history of the case, we will not repeat it here except as necessary to explain the disposition.

The question of whether a dirt road is a SIP or is part of the surrounding land is untechnical and factual and, thus, subject to our review for clear error. See *Condor Int'l. Inc. v. CIR*, 78 F.3d 1355, 1358 (9th Cir. 1996). Tax deductions are a matter of legislative grace, and as such the burden of proving a deductible loss and its amount is always upon the taxpayer. *Clapp v. Commissioner*, 321 F.2d 12, 14 (9th Cir. 1963). A casualty loss deduction is allowed under I.R.C. Section 165(a) for "any loss sustained during the taxable year and not compensated for by insurance or otherwise." In this context, the amount of loss taken into account is the lesser of (1) the difference between the fair market value of the property immediately before and after the casualty or (2) the taxpayer's adjusted basis of the property. I.R.C. Section 165(b); Income Tax Regs. Section 1.165-7(b)(1). A loss incurred in a trade or business is determined in this manner, but by reference to the "single identifiable property" damaged or destroyed. Income Tax Regs. Section 1.165-7(b)(2).

The Czirakis maintain that the dirt road had no basis and rather than being a SIP it was inextricably part of the land and so their casualty loss deduction for damage to the road should be limited by their basis in the land. The tax court characterized the dirt road as a SIP and accordingly limited the Czirakis' deduction to the basis in that road. In doing so, the tax court considered the time, effort, expense and resources spent on constructing the road. The court also correctly considered that a taxpayer may not borrow basis from

Continued

| Exhibit | 5–6 | Court of Appeals Decision—Concluded |

unharmed property to increase the amount of a loss deduction for injury to other property. See *Rosenthal v. Commissioner*, 416 F.2d 491, 497-98 (2d Cir. 1969).

The tax court's finding that the dirt road was a SIP was not clearly erroneous. Accordingly, the decision of the tax court is AFFIRMED.

ENDNOTES

1. This disposition is not appropriate for publication and may not be cited to or by the courts of this circuit except as may be provided by 9th Cir. R. 36-3.

2. The Czirakis also contend that the tax court erred in commingling the basis in the dirt road and an adjacent asphalt road. If they are correct, then their entire deduction would be disallowed. Having noted that the Czirakis may have received a deduction to which they were not entitled, the Commissioner did not appeal the decision to allow the $6,844 deduction. Assuming the Czirakis prefer the limited deduction to no deduction at all, we leave the tax court's decision undisturbed.

SUPREME COURT

The U.S. **Supreme Court** is an appellate court and the highest court in the nation. Article III of the Constitution created the Supreme Court and extended to it judicial power "to all cases of law and equity, arising under this Constitution, the laws of the United States, and treaties. . . ." Thus, concerning all areas of Federal law, the Supreme Court is the final level of appeal and the sovereign legal authority.

The Supreme Court meets and hears cases only in Washington, D.C. If a taxpayer wants to have his or her case heard by the Supreme Court, the taxpayer and counsel must travel to the nation's capital to present the arguments. The Supreme Court is a nine-justice panel; all nine judges hear every case that the Court agrees to consider. The Court does not conduct jury trials.

A U.S. citizen has no automatic right to have his or her case heard by the Supreme Court. Permission to present the case must be requested by a **writ of certiorari**. If the Court decides to hear the case, the "certiorari is granted;" if the Court refuses, then "certiorari is denied." One must treat a Supreme Court decision as having the full force of the law; although Congress might repeal the challenged statute or the Federal administration might refuse to fund or enforce the underlying law and related activities, neither the citizen nor the government can appeal a Supreme Court decision.

As we have discussed, however, certiorari is granted in very few tax cases. Only about a dozen appeals relating to tax issues—state, local, and federal; income, property, sales, estate, and gift; individual, corporate, and fiduciary—are heard by the Supreme Court in a typical year. In most cases, those petitions granted involve an issue at conflict among the Federal circuits or a tax issue of major importance. For instance, the Court might hear a client's case concerning the inclusion in gross income of life insurance proceeds, if many similar cases had been brought before the various Federal courts and tremendous tax liabilities were under dispute, or if two or more of the circuits had issued inconsistent holdings on the matter.

In denying the petition for certiorari, the Supreme Court is not "upholding," or in any way confirming, a lower court decision. Rather, the Court simply does not find the appealed case to be interesting or important enough to consider during its limited sessions. The lower court's decision does stand, but one cannot infer that the decision necessarily is correct or that it should be followed in the future by other taxpayers whose situations are similar. These matters of open-fact tax planning must be analyzed using the tax researcher's professional judgment.

SPOTLIGHT ON TAXATION: The Supreme Court's Love Affair with Tax Law

If [a United States Supreme Court Justice is] in the doghouse with the Chief [Justice], he gets the crud. He gets the tax cases . . . .

—Harry Blackmun, Supreme Court Justice

Locating Supreme Court Decisions

At least five different general and specialized reporters publish all of the tax-related Supreme Court decisions. CCH includes such cases in the *United States Tax Cases* service (USTC), and RIA publishes them in the *American Federal Tax Reports* (AFTR, AFTR2d, or AFTR3d). The Government Printing Office publishes the *United States Supreme Court Reports*, which contains all of the tax and nontax decisions of the Court. In common citation convention, references to this service are abbreviated as "U.S." In addition, West Publishing includes all Supreme Court decisions in the *Supreme Court Reporter* (S.Ct.).

In the following examples of proper citations, one can infer from the GPO and West citations that the case was heard by the Supreme Court, and any further reference to that forum (e.g., as USSC) would be redundant. In addition, if a case involves an issue of pre-1954 Code tax law, the first series of the AFTR service would be cited. Exhibit 5–7 is an example of a tax decision of the Supreme Court.

Court Reporters

GPO:	*Indianapolis Power & Light*, 493 U.S. 203 (1990)
West:	*Indianapolis Power & Light*, 110 S.Ct. 589 (1990)
RIA:	*Indianapolis Power & Light*, 65 AFTR2d 90-394 (USSC, 1990)
CCH:	*Indianapolis Power & Light*, 90-1 USTC ¶ 50,007 (USSC, 1990)
Kleinrock:	*Indianapolis Power & Light*, KTC 1990-53 (USSC, 1990)

Exhibit	5-7	Supreme Court Decision Syllabus

SUPREME COURT OF THE UNITED STATES

Syllabus

O'GILVIE et al., Minors v. UNITED STATES

Certiorari to the United States Court of Appeals for the Tenth Circuit

Docket: 95-966, 95-977 – Decided December 10, 1996

519 U.S. 79; 117 S.Ct. 452

Petitioners, the husband and two children of a woman who died of toxic shock syndrome, received a jury award of $1,525,000 actual damages and $10 million punitive damages in a tort suit based on Kansas law against the maker of the product that caused decedent's death. They paid Federal income tax insofar as the award's proceeds represented punitive damages, but immediately sought a refund. Procedurally speaking, this litigation represents the consolidation of two cases brought in the same Federal District Court: the husband's suit against the Government for a refund, and the Government's suit against the children to recover the refund that the Government had made to the children earlier. The District Court found for petitioners under 26 U.S.C. Section 104(a)(2), which, as it read in 1988, excluded from "gross income," the "amount of any damages received . . . on account of personal injuries or sickness." (Emphasis added.) The court held on the merits that the italicized language includes punitive damages, thereby excluding such damages from gross income. The Tenth Circuit reversed, holding that the exclusionary provision does not cover punitive damages.

Held:

1. Petitioners' punitive damages were not received "on account of" personal injuries; hence the gross-income-exclusion provision does not apply and the damages are taxable. Pp. 2–11.

(a) Although the phrase "on account of" does not unambiguously define itself, several factors prompt this Court to agree with the Government when it interprets the exclusionary provision to apply to those personal injury lawsuit damages that were awarded by reason of, or because of, the personal injuries, and not to punitive damages that do not compensate injury, but are private fines levied by civil juries to punish reprehensible conduct and to deter its future occurrence. For one thing, the Government's interpretation gives the phrase "on account of" a meaning consistent with the dictionary definition. More important, in *Commissioner v. Schleier*, 515 U.S. 323, this Court came close to resolving the statute's ambiguity in the Government's favor when it said that the statute covers pain and suffering damages, medical expenses, and lost wages in an ordinary tort case because they are "designed to compensate . . . victims" id., at ____, n. 5, but does not apply to elements of damages that are "punitive in nature," id., at ____. The Government's reading also is more faithful to the statutory provision's history and basic tax-related purpose of excluding compensatory damages that restore a victim's lost, nontaxable "capital." Petitioners suggest no very good reason why Congress might have wanted the exclusion to have covered these punitive damages, which are not a substitute for any normally untaxed personal (or financial) quality, good, or "asset" and do not compensate for any kind of loss. Pp. 2–8.

(b) Petitioners' three arguments to the contrary—that certain words or phrases in the original, or current, version of the statute work in their favor; that the exclusion of punitive

Exhibit	**5–7**	Supreme Court Decision Syllabus—Concluded

damages from gross income may be justified by Congress' desire to be generous to tort victims and to avoid such administrative problems as separating punitive from compensatory portions of a global settlement or determining the extent to which a punitive damages award is itself intended to compensate; and that their position is supported by a 1989 statutory amendment that specifically says that the gross income exclusion does not apply to any punitive damages in connection with a case not involving physical injury or sickness—are not sufficiently persuasive to overcome the Government's interpretation. Pp. 8–11.

2. Petitioners' two case-specific procedural arguments—that the Government's lawsuit was untimely and that its original notice of appeal was filed a few days late—are rejected. Pp. 12–14.

66 F. 3d 1550, affirmed.

BREYER, J., delivered the opinion of the Court, in which REHNQUIST, C.J., and STEVENS, KENNEDY, SOUTER, and GINSBURG, JJ., joined. SCALIA, J., filed a dissenting opinion, in which O'CONNOR and THOMAS, JJ., joined.

* * *

CASE BRIEFS

Most court reporters contain a brief case summary at the beginning of a case called a **headnote**. Headnotes are usually inserted by the court reporter editors. They are useful to the researcher by helping to quickly determine if a particular case is of interest. A court case may contain several issues; therefore, there may be several headnotes for any one case. In addition to using headnotes, tax researchers have found that the construction of a concise **case brief** is of great value to them, both when they return to a client's research problem or planning environment after a period of time passes and in using the given case in constructing a research analysis for another client. The reader should be careful, though, to distinguish this concise research tool from the case briefs required as part of the procedure of most court hearings. The latter is a lengthy collection of documents that includes a detailed analysis of all parts of the litigants' arguments.

A proper tax research case brief presents in summary fashion, ideally not exceeding one page, the facts, issue(s), holding, and analysis of the chosen court case. From such a brief, the researcher can discover in a very short period whether the full text of the case is of further use in the present analysis. If the briefed case does warrant further examination, the researcher can locate it (or any other cases that are cited in the brief itself) very quickly.

Study carefully the format of the case brief in Exhibit 5–8. Notice that the indicated tax research issues correspond with each of the analyses and holdings of the court, as indicated by the numbers of the brief's outline format. Finally, notice that citations to other cases, or to administrative proclamations, are complete and somewhat detailed, helping to facilitate further research.

Exhibit	5-8	Court Case Brief Illustrated

CITATION   *U.S. v. Stephen W. Bentson*, 947 F.2d 1353; 92-1 USTC ¶ 50,048; 68 AFTR2d 5773 (CA-9, 1991).

ISSUE(S)   (1) Does the IRS's failure to comply with the Paperwork Reduction Act (PRA) preclude a taxpayer from being penalized for failing to file a tax return and cause charges against him to be dismissed?
(2) Could the IRS penalties be avoided because the Form 1040 had not been published in the *Federal Register*?
(3) Could the IRS penalties be avoided because of a lack of proof that Bentson had failed to file returns?

FACTS   For the tax year 1982, Bentson filed a "protest tax return." He refused to supply information other than his name, address, social security number, and signature. The rest of his Form 1040 was filled with asterisks, and he attached a statement asserting that to supply other information violated his Fifth Amendment constitutional right. No tax returns could be located for 1983 and 1984. Bentson was charged by the IRS with three counts of willful failure to file tax returns. A District Court bench trial was held. After the close of the government's case, Bentson moved for dismissal, relying on *U.S. v. Kimball*, 896 F.2d 1218, vacated, 925 F.2d 356 (CA-9, 1991).

HOLDING   The District Court granted Bentson's motion as to the first count only. He was found guilty on two counts and sentenced to eight months incarceration followed by three years' probation, and a $2,000 fine. The Ninth Circuit affirmed the lower court's decision.

ANALYSIS   (1) Bentson argued the IRS failed to comply with the Paperwork Reduction Act and relied on the original *U.S. v. Kimball*. This decision was reversed in 1991 (see 925 F.2d 356). The Ninth Circuit held that the public protection provision of the Paperwork Reduction Act is not a defense to prosecution under IRC § 7203 (willful failure to file a return, supply information, or pay tax).
(2) Bentson argued that Form 1040 and the instructions constitute a "rule" for purposes of the Administrative Procedures Act (APA) and therefore must be published in the *Federal Register* to be valid. The Ninth Circuit ruled this argument had no merit.
(3) Bentson argued the IRS had not proved he did not file tax returns for 1983 and 1984. This argument was rejected because Bentson had already made a binding judicial admission to the contrary.

THE INTERNET AND JUDICIAL SOURCES

The Internet and the World Wide Web provide a new way for tax researchers to access judicial sources of tax law. Many law schools, journals, tax publishers, and individuals have set up their own home pages (web sites) on the Internet. While not as user friendly as a commercial service, these home pages allow anyone with access to the Internet to locate many court decisions. Examples of some of these home pages that have links to other judicial sources are as follows.

Emory U. School of Law   **http://www.law.emory.edu**
Cornell U. School of Law   **http://www.law.cornell.edu**
U. of Texas School of Law   **http://www.utexas.edu/law**
Practitioners Publishing Co.   **http://www.ppcnet.com**
Will Yancey's Home Page   **http://www.willyancey.com**

COMPUTER TAX SERVICE EXAMPLE

The tax researcher can use a computerized tax service to find court cases of interest. If the researcher knows the case name or citation, he or she can enter it directly and obtain a copy of the case. However, if the case name or citation is not known, the researcher can use a computer query to find cases that have addressed the issue at hand.

Example 5–1 Your client is involved in a dispute with the IRS over the valuation for estate tax purposes of a closely held business. In the process of getting ready to go to the Tax Court on this matter, you have to hire an expert witness to justify the client's valuation of the business. During the interviews, one of the experts says that she will use the Capital Asset Pricing Model (CAPM) as the basis for her valuation. You are not sure what the CAPM is and how the courts will react to it. You therefore execute a computer search using RIA Checkpoint to see if there is any information available on the use of the CAPM in tax valuation. Exhibit 5–9 shows an

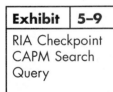

Exhibit | 5–9

RIA Checkpoint CAPM Search Query

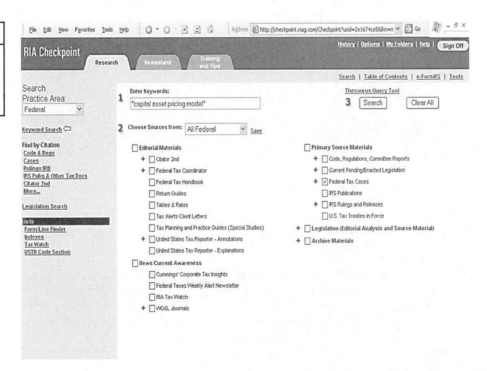

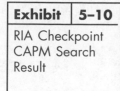

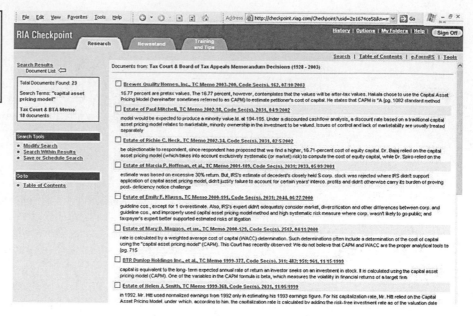

example of a search query that could be used to find any court cases that have discussed the CAPM. Exhibit 5–10 shows a listing of Tax Court Regular and Memo decisions discussing the use of CAPM in valuing closely-held business. After reviewing these cases, you would conclude that there is a lot of controversy about using the CAPM in non-publicly traded valuation situations. As a result, you should prepare your client's case using another method of valuation or be prepared to defend your use of the CAPM.

SUMMARY

The tax practitioner must possess a working knowledge of the Federal court system to address tax research problems. The researcher must understand the role of the courts in generating Federal tax law, the relationship of the courts to one another, the Constitution, and jurisdiction of each court, where to locate an appropriate decision, and how to interpret that decision.

Exhibit 5–11 offers a summary of some of the attributes of the trial-level and appeals courts discussed in this chapter. Because of differences among courts, the tax adviser may be inclined to choose one of the trial-level courts over the others to accommodate the special needs or circumstances of the client.

Exhibit 5–12 summarizes the decisions available in each of the tax case reporter services discussed in this chapter. With the variety of tax publications available, choices must be made so that the practitioner's tax research budget can be used effectively, without sacrifice of his or her ability to solve the client's problems.

Exhibit	5–11	The Judicial Obstacle Course: Selected Attributes of Trial-Level Courts

Item	Tax Court	District Court	Court of Federal Claims
Jurisdiction	Tax cases only	Legal issues based on entire *U.S. Code*	Monetary claims against U.S. government
Judges	Tax law specialists	Tax law generalists	Tax law generalists
Domain	National court, but judges travel	Limited geographical area	National court, but judges travel
Jury trial available?	No	Yes, if question of fact	No
Number of judges	One, reviewed by chief judge; *en banc* hearing for certain issues	One	One to five hearing case
Small Cases Division	Yes	No	No available?
Payment of tax	Trial, then payment	Payment, then trial	Payment, then trial
Precedents court must follow	Supreme Court; pertinent circuit court; Tax Court	Supreme Court; pertinent circuit court; own District court	Supreme Court; Federal Circuit Court; Court of Federal Claims

Exhibit	5–12	Court Decision Reporter Summary

I. BY REPORTER

Publisher, Common	Reporter, Common	Decisions Included
Primary Reporters		
T.C. (B.T.A.)	GPO	Regular Tax Court (BTA) decisions
TCM	CCH	Tax Court Memorandum decisions
RIA T.C. Mem. Dec.	RIA	Tax Court Memorandum decisions
F.Supp	West	District court decisions
Fed. Cl.	West	Court of Federal Claims decisions
F.3d (F.2d)	West	Court of Appeals and pre-1982 Court of Claims decisions
U.S.	GPO	All Supreme Court decisions
S.Ct.	West	All Supreme Court decisions
Secondary Reporters		
USTC	CCH	Tax cases from all Federal courts except the Tax Court
AFTR series	RIA	Tax cases from all Federal courts except the Tax Court
KTC	Kleinrock's	Tax cases from all Federal courts except the Tax Court

Continued

| Exhibit | 5–12 | Court Decision Reporter Summary—Concluded |

II. BY COURT

Court	Publisher	Citation	Reporter
Supreme Court			
All cases	West	S.Ct.	Supreme Court Reporter
	GPO	U.S.	U.S. Supreme Court Reports
Tax only	CCH	USTC	U.S. Tax Cases
	RIA	AFTR series	American Federal Tax Reports
	Kleinrock's	KTC	Kleinrock's Tax Cases
Court of Appeal			
All cases	West	F.3d (F.2d)	Federal Reporter, 3d (2d) series
Tax only	CCH	USTC	
	RIA	AFTR series	
	Kleinrock's	KTC	
Tax Court			
Regular	GPO	T.C.	Tax Court of the U.S. Reports
Memo	CCH	TCM	Tax Court Memorandum Decisions
	RIA	RIA T.C. MemDec.	RIA Tax Court Memorandum Decisions
	Kleinrock's	T.C. Memo	
District Courts			
All cases	West	F.Supp.	Federal Supplement Series
Tax only	CCH	USTC	
	RIA	AFTR series	
	Kleinrock's	KTC	
Court of Federal Claims			
All cases post-1982	West	Fed. Cl.	U.S. Court of Federal Claims
Tax only	CCH	USTC	
	RIA	AFTR series	
	Kleinrock's	KTC	

Finally, a number of observations concerning citation conventions can be made. Review the citation examples given in this chapter to verify the list shown in Exhibit 5–13 and to add your own observations to it.

TAX TUTOR

Reinforce the tax research information covered in this chapter by completing the online tutorials located at the Federal Tax Research web site:

http://raabe.swlearning.com

Exhibit	5-13	Citation Conventions and Observations

The common form of a citation is as follows: case name–volume number–reporter–page number–court–year.

The AFTR second series began with 1954 IRC cases.

The B.T.A. became the U.S. Tax Court in 1943.

The U.S. Court of Claims became the U.S. Claims Court in 1982, and the U.S. Court of Federal Claims in 1992.

Unless the case was published in a year different from that in which it was heard, the USTC volume number (and many AFTR page numbers) includes a reference to the year, so the year need not be repeated in the citation.

The S.Ct. and U.S. citations imply that the case was heard in the Supreme Court, so the court abbreviation need not be repeated in the citation.

The government need not be mentioned in a typical Tax Court citation.

Although they are not published in a printed court reporter, for tax years starting in 2001, U.S. Tax Court Small Case Summary Opinions are available for use on computer tax services (e.g., RIA and CCH).

KEY WORDS

By the time you complete this chapter, you should be comfortable discussing each of the following terms. If you need additional review of any of these items, return to the appropriate material in the chapter or consult the glossary to this text.

AFTR	Memorandum Decision
Board of Tax Appeals	Permanent Citation
Case Brief	Regular Decision
Court of Federal Claims	Small Cases Division
Courts of Appeals	Supreme Court
District Court	Tax Court
En Banc	Temporary Citation
Golsen Rule	USTC
Headnote	Writ of Certiorari

DISCUSSION QUESTIONS

1. Who can initiate a court case that deals with a tax matter—the taxpayer or the IRS?

2. Explain the general organization of the Federal court system for cases concerning Federal tax issues.

3. May a taxpayer take his or her tax case directly to the Supreme Court?

4. Who has the burden of proof in most cases involving the tax law? Why?

5. The U.S. Tax Court hears only certain types of cases. Identify those cases.

6. The U.S. Tax Court has undergone an evolution since it was founded. What happened to its structure in 1926, 1943, and 1969, respectively?

7. How many judges sit on the U.S. Tax Court? What is the length of time of the appointment of each judge?

8. The U.S. Tax Court is a national court that meets in Washington, D.C. Does this mean that the taxpayer and his or her attorney must travel to Washington to have a case heard?

9. May a taxpayer have a jury trial in the U.S. Tax Court?

10. What does the term sitting *"en banc"* mean?

11. Distinguish between a Regular, Memorandum, and Summary decision of the Tax Court.

12. The U.S. Tax Court is a national court that hears cases of taxpayers who may appeal to various geographical Courts of Appeals. How does the Tax Court reconcile the opposite holdings of two or more of these Courts of Appeals for taxpayers who work or reside in different parts of the country?

13. What is the Small Cases Division of the U.S. Tax Court? What is the maximum amount of the deficiency that can be the subject of a Small Cases hearing? Comment on the trial procedures in the Small Cases Division.

14. Where are regular Tax Court decisions published? Illustrate the elements of both a temporary and a permanent regular Tax Court citation. Explain what each part of the citation means.

15. Tax Court Memorandum decisions are not published by the Federal government. However, commercial reporters include these decisions. Illustrate the elements of both a temporary and a permanent citation for a Tax Court Memorandum decision, using both the CCH and RIA reporters. Explain what each part of the citation means.

16. What is the jurisdiction of a U.S. District Court?

17. Can Tax Court Summary Opinions be cited as precedent? Discuss.

18. Must the taxpayer pay the disputed tax deficiency to the government before his or her case will be heard in a District Court? In the U.S. Court of Federal Claims? In the U.S. Tax Court?

19. Which of the trial courts is most appropriate for a taxpayer who wishes to limit the judicial review of the relevant year's tax return to the specific issue(s) involved in the case?

20. Which of the trial courts would best serve a taxpayer litigating an issue of a technical tax nature? Why?

21. Is a Federal District Court a national court? How many judges hear a case brought before a Federal District Court?

22. Name the three court case reporters that publish tax and nontax District Court decisions. Illustrate the elements of a citation that might be found in each reporter. Explain what each part of the citation means.

23. Differentiate between a primary and a secondary case citation.

24. What type of cases are heard by the U.S. Court of Federal Claims?

25. How many judges are appointed to the U.S. Court of Federal Claims?

26. Is the U.S. Court of Federal Claims a national court? Must a taxpayer go to Washington, D.C., to present a case to this U.S. court?

27. Name the three court case reporters that publish U.S. Court of Federal Claims decisions. Illustrate the elements of a citation that might be found in each reporter. Explain what each part of the citation means.

28. Are the U.S. Courts of Appeals national courts? What type of cases do they hear?

29. Identify the circuit court that would hear the case of a taxpayer who lives or works in each of the following areas.
    a. Texas
    b. New York
    c. California
    d. Colorado
    e. Illinois
    f. A case that is appealed from the U.S. Court of Federal Claims

30. Identify the circuit court that would hear the case of a taxpayer who lives or works in each of the following areas.
    a. Florida   d. Puerto Rico
    b. Ohio   e. Guam
    c. North Carolina

31. Each Court of Appeals has approximately twenty judges. How many of these judges hear a typical case?

32. Name the three court case reporters that publish Court of Appeals decisions. Illustrate the elements of a citation that might be found in each reporter. Explain what each part of the citation means.

33. Can a taxpayer have a jury trial before a Court of Appeals?

34. What is the highest court in the United States? What is its jurisdiction? Where does it hear cases?

35. How does one petition the Supreme Court to hear one's tax case?

36. How many justices are appointed to the Supreme Court? How many hear each case?

37. Why does the Supreme Court hear so few tax cases?

38. Differentiate between the Supreme Court's overturning of a lower court's decision, and its denial of a writ of certiorari.

39. Name the four court case reporters that publish Supreme Court decisions. Illustrate the elements of a citation that might be found in each reporter. Explain what each part of the citation means.

40. Is it possible for a taxpayer to have a jury trial before any of the trial courts? Before a Court of Appeals? Before the U.S. Supreme Court?

41. Discuss the precedential value of a Court of Appeals decision. Which Court of Appeals decisions are most important to a specific taxpayer?

42. In the (fictitious) citation *Gomez v. U.S.*, 102 T.C. 123 (1999), what does the "102" stand for? The "T.C."? The "123"?

43. Which court would have issued the (fictitious) *O'Dell v. U.S.*, 66 TCM 86 (2000) decision? What does each element in the citation mean?

44. In the citation *Simons-Eastern v. U.S.*, 354 F.Supp. 1003 (D.Ct., Ga, 1972), the "F.Supp." tells the tax researcher that the decision is from which court?

45. *By using only the citation*, state which court issued each of the following decisions. If you cannot determine which court by looking at the citation only, say so.
    a. *Davis v. U.S.*, 43 Fed. Cl. 92 (1999)
    b. *D.C. Crummey v. U.S.*, 68-2 USTC ¶ 12,541
    c. *U.S. v. Goode*, 86 AFTR2d 2000-7273
    d. *James v. U.S.*, 81 S.Ct. 1052 (1961)

46. What is a case headnote? How might it be useful to the tax researcher?

47. *By using only the citation*, state which court issued each of the following decisions. If you cannot determine which court by looking at the citation only, say so.
    a. *Douglas, Christopher*, T.C. Memo 1994-519
    b. *Takaba, Brian G.*, 119 T.C. 285
    c. *Botts, Roy R.*, T.C. Summary Opinion 2001-182
    d. *American Airlines, Inc.*, 40 Fed.Cl. 712

EXERCISES

48. Find the court decision located at 100 T.C. 32.
    a. What court heard the case?
    b. Who was the judge(s)?
    c. In what year was the case decided?
    d. What was the issue(s) involved?

49. Find the court decision located at T.C. Memo. 2001-71.
    a. What court heard the case?
    b. Who was the judge(s)?
    c. In what year was the case decided?
    d. What was the issue(s) involved?

50. Find the court decision located at T.C. Memo. 1992-204.
    a. What court heard the case?

b. Who was the judge(s)?

c. What tax year(s) is in question and in what year was the case decided?

d. What Code section(s) was at issue?

e. What was the issue(s) involved?

f. Which party prevailed in the decision?

51. Find the court decision located at T.C. Summary Opinion 2003-168.
    a. What court heard the case?
    b. Who was the judge(s)?
    c. What tax year(s) is in question and in what year was the case decided?
    d. What Code section(s) was at issue?
    e. What was the issue(s) involved?
    f. Which party prevailed in the decision?

52. Find the court decision located at 2001-1 USTC ¶ 50,176.
    a. What court heard the case?
    b. Who was the judge(s)?
    c. What tax year(s) is in question and in what year was the case decided?
    d. What Code section(s) was at issue?
    e. What was the issue(s) involved?
    f. Which party prevailed in the decision?

53. Find the court decision located at 67 AFTR2d 91-718.
    a. What court heard the case?
    b. Who was the judge(s)?
    c. What tax year(s) is in question and in what year was the case decided?
    d. What Code section(s) was at issue?
    e. What was the issue(s) involved?
    f. Which party prevailed in the decision?

54. If your last name begins with the letters A–L, read and brief each of the following cases.
    a. *Sorensen*, T.C. Memo. 1994-175
    b. *Keller*, 84-1 USTC ¶ 9194

    If your last name begins with the letters M–Z, read and brief each of the following cases.
    c. *Washington*, 77 T.C. 601
    d. *Tellier*, 17 AFTR2d 633

55. If your last name begins with the letters A–L, read and brief each of the following cases.
    a. *Rownd*, T.C. Memo. 1994-465
    b. *Ames*, 93-1 USTC ¶ 50,016

    If your last name begins with the letters M–Z, read and brief each of the following cases.
    c. *Willie Nelson Music Co.*, 85 T.C. 914
    d. *Independent Contracts, Inc.*, 73 AFTR2d 94-1406

56. Read and brief each of the following cases.
    a. *Gregory v. Helvering*, 55 S.Ct. 266 (1935)
    b. *Hunt*, T.C. Memo. 1965-172

57. Read and brief each of the following cases.
    a. *Fulcher, Douglas R.*, TC Summary Opinion 2003-157
    b. *The Boeing Company and Consolidated Subs.*, 91 AFTR 2d 2003-1088 (123 S.Ct. 1099)

58. Use computer tax service to give two parallel citations for the *U.S. v. D'ambrosia*, a Seventh Circuit Court of Appeals case decided in 2002. Using only the headnote(s), what was the issue(s) in this case?

59. Use computer tax service to give three parallel citations for the *Baral v. U.S.*, a Supreme Court case decided in 2000. Using only the headnote(s), what was the issue(s) in this case?

RESEARCH CASES

60. Snidely Limited spent $1 million this year to upgrade its manufacturing plant, which had received several warnings from the state environmental agency about releasing pollution into the local river. Late in the year, Snidely received an assessment of $700,000 for violating the state's Clean Water Act. After he negotiated with the State, which cost $135,000 in legal fees, Snidely promised to spend another $200,000 next year for more pollution control devices, and the fine was reduced to $450,000. How much of these expenditures can Snidely Limited deduct for tax purposes?

    Partial list of research material: § 162; Rev. Rul. 76-130, 1976-1 C.B. 16; *Tucker*, 69 T.C. 675.

61. Last year, only four of thirty-two professional basketball teams turned a nominal accounting profit. Betty purchased such a team this year. Her taxable loss therefrom properly was determined to be $950,000. Can she deduct this loss?

    Partial list of research material: § 183; Reg. § 1.183-2; *Brannen*, 722 F.2d 695.

62. Herbert, a collector of rare coins, bought a 1916 Spanish Bowlero for $2,000 in 1984. He sold the coin for $4,500 in January. Herbert retired from his loading dock job in June and began actively buying and selling rare coins. By December, Herbert's realized gain from such activities was $21,500. What type of taxable income was January's $2,500 gain?

    Partial list of research material: § 1221; Rev. Rul. 68-634, 1968-2 C.B. 46; *Frankel*, 56 TCM 1156 (1989).

63. Steve is an usher at his local church. Can he deduct commuting expenses for the Sundays that he is assigned to usher for church services?

    Partial list of research material: § 170; Rev. Rul. 56-508, 1956-2 C.B. 126; *Churukian*, 40 TCM 475 (1980).

64. A new member of the San Diego Chargers wants the team to transfer $1,000,000 into an escrow account, in his name, for later withdrawal. The player suggests this payment in lieu of the traditional signing bonus. When is this income taxable to him?

    Partial list of research material: § 451; Rev. Rul. 70-435, 1970-2 C.B. 100; *Drysdale*, 277 F.2d 413.

65. Professor Stevens obtained tenure and promotion to full professor status many years ago. Yet, he continues to publish research papers in scholarly journals to satisfy his own curiosity and to maintain his professional prestige and status within the academic community. Publications are also necessary in order for Professor Stevens to receive pay raises at his university. This year, Dr. Stevens spent $750 of his own funds to travel to southern Utah to collect some critical pieces of data for his work. What is the tax treatment of this expenditure?

    Partial list of research material: § 162; Zell, 85-2 USTC ¶ 9698; *Smith*, 50 TCM 904.

66. The local electric company requires a $200 refundable deposit from new customers, in lieu of a credit check. Landlord Pete pays this amount for all of his new-to-town tenants. Can he deduct the $200 payments on his tax return?

    Partial list of research material: § 162; Hopkins, 30 T.C. 1015; *Waring Products*, 27 T.C. 921.

67. High-Top Financing charges its personal loan holders a 2 percent fee if the full loan principal is paid prior to the due date. What is the tax effect of this year's $50,000 of prepayment penalties collected by High-Top?

    Partial list of research material: § 61; *Hort*, 41-1 USTC ¶ 9354.

68. Cecilia died this year, owning mutual funds in her IRA worth $120,000. Under the terms of the IRA, Cecilia's surviving husband, Frank, was the beneficiary of the account, and he took a lump-sum distribution from the fund. Both Cecilia and Frank were age 57 at the beginning of the year.
    a. How does Frank account for the inheritance, assuming that he rolls it over into his own IRA in a timely manner?
    b. Would your answer change if Frank were Cecilia's brother?

    Partial list of research material: § 408; Rev. Rul. 92-47, 1992-1 C.B. 198; *Aronson*, 98 T.C. 283 (1992).

69. During a properly declared U.S. war with Outer Altoona, Harriet, a single taxpayer, was killed in action. Current-year Federal taxable income to the date of Harriet's death totaled $19,000, and Federal income tax withholding came to $2,300.
    a. What is Harriet's tax liability for the year of her death?
    b. What documentation must accompany her final Form 1040?

    Partial list of research material: § 692; Rev. Proc. 85-35, 1985-2 C.B. 433; *Hampton*, 75-1 USTC ¶ 9315.

70. Jerry Baker and his wife Hammi believe in the worship of the "Sea God." This is a very personal religion to Jerry and Hammi. To practice their beliefs, the Bakers want to take a two-week trip to Tahiti this year to worship their deity. The cost (airfare, hotels, etc.) of this religious "pilgrimage" is $5,250. Jerry wants to know if he can deduct the cost of this trip as a charitable deduction on the joint Form 1040, Schedule A.

    Partial list of research material: § 170 and *Kessler*, 87 T.C. 1285 (1986).

71. Willie Waylon is a famous country and western singer. As an investment, Willie started a chain of barbecue restaurants called Willie's Wonderful Ribs. Willie's friends and associates invested $500,000 in this venture. The restaurant chain failed, and the investors lost all their money. Because of his visibility and status in the entertainment community, Willie felt that he personally had to make good on the losses suffered by the investors, so he paid $500,000 to reimburse them all. What are Willie's tax consequences?

    Partial list of research material: § 162 and *Lohrke*, 48 T.C. 679.

72. Paul Preppie is an accountant for the Very Big (VB) Corporation of America, located in Los Angeles, California. When Paul went to work for VB, he did not have a college degree. VB required that Paul earn a B.S. degree in accounting, so he enrolled in a local private university's night school and obtained the degree. VB Corporation does not reimburse employees for attending night school, and because Paul attended a private university, the tuition and other costs were relatively expensive. Can Paul deduct any of the $5,500 he paid in tuition and other costs during the current tax year? Prepare (in good form) a research memorandum to the file. (See Chapter 2 for an illustration of the structure of a tax memo.)

73. Several years ago, Carol Mutter, a cash-basis taxpayer, obtained a mortgage from Weak National Bank to purchase a personal residence. In December 1999, $8,500 of interest was due on the mortgage, but Carol had only $75 in her checking account. On December 31, 1999, she borrowed $8,500 from Weak Bank, evidenced by a note, and the proceeds were deposited in her checking account. On the same day, Carol issued a check in the identical amount of $8,500 to Weak Bank for the interest due. Is the interest expense deductible for the 1999 tax year? Prepare (in good form) a research memorandum to the file. (See Chapter 2 for an illustration of the structure of a tax memo.)

74. Phyllis maintained an IRA account at the brokerage firm ABC. On February 11 of the current year, she requested a check for the balance of her account. She received the check made out in her name and deposited it the same day in a new IRA account at the brokerage firm XYZ. Phyllis then requested a check on May 8 from XYZ, which was deposited in another new IRA account 35 days later. Is the May 8 distribution taxable to Phyllis? Prepare in good form a research memorandum to the file. (See Chapter 2 for an illustration of the structure of a tax memo.)

75. Crystal Eros is a devout Pyramidist and a member of the Religious Society of Yanni, a Pyramidist organization. She adheres to the fundamental tenets of Pyramidist theology, including the belief that the Spirit of God is in every person and that it is wrong to kill or otherwise harm another person. Crystal's faith dictates that she not voluntarily participate, directly or indirectly, in military activities. Because Federal income taxes fund military activities, Crystal believes that her faith prohibits her from paying such taxes. Is there any legal substantiation for Crystal's position? Prepare (in good form) a research memorandum to the file. (See Chapter 2 for an illustration of the structure of a tax memo.)

76. Last year, your client, Robert Dinero, mailed an automatic extension for his tax return on April 15. He enclosed a check for $10,000 with the extension request. The IRS cashed the check on April 28. Later, the IRS assessed Robert late filing penalties of $2,900 because they claim he did not mail the extension request on time. On the same date, Robert mailed an income tax extension request and check to the state of California. The California check was cashed on April 16. You requested the IRS send you a copy of the extension request envelope showing the postmark: however, the IRS has lost it. The IRS recently attached Robert's bank account for the $2,900, thereby seizing the funds directly. You have known Robert for years, and he could be described as a good, law-abiding, taxpaying citizen. He always pays his taxes on time, has never been in trouble with the IRS, and is not a tax protester. Robert asks you to recommend whether he should engage a tax attorney and sue for a refund, knowing that the legal fees for such an action will probably exceed $10,000. After appropriate research, write a letter to Robert explaining your findings. His address is 432 Lucre Street, Tecate, CA 91980.

77. Your client, Luther Lifo, is an auditing professor who runs a CPA review course. He comes to you with the following tax questions.

    Question One. Luther teaches CPA review courses on either a guaranteed or nonguaranteed basis. Under the guaranteed program, students pay higher tuition and, if they fail the CPA examination, are entitled to a full refund within two weeks of the release of the results. The CPA review course contracts require him to place the tuition in a set-aside escrow account until the students pass the exam; he established the savings account as a trust account for this purpose. The registration fee and tuition must be paid in full before the classes begin. Thus, students enrolled in the class that started in January 20x1 paid their tuition in December 20x0. In 20x0, Luther deposited registration fees and tuition, including $30,000 in guaranteed tuition payments for the winter 20x1 courses, into a checking account. Also during 20x1, he paid refunds to guaranteed students who failed the 20x1 exams from that account. Does Luther report the $30,000 as income in 20x0 or 20x1? How are the refunds paid in 20x1 treated for tax purposes? State the authority for your conclusion.

    Question Two. Luther is a majority shareholder in a corporation that owns an office building. He leases space in the building for use in his

CPA review course. Luther pays approximately $20 per square foot in annual rent. The corporation leases the remaining space in the building to a LSAT, GMAT, SAT, and GRE review course run by other taxpayers for approximately $10 per square foot. Luther's main intent in negotiating the discounted lease was to secure the additional traffic generated by the other review courses in order to enhance the potential revenue for the CPA review course. What is the amount of rent that Luther can deduct in connection with the CPA review course? State the authority for your conclusion.

After appropriate research, write a letter to Luther explaining your findings. The address is 321 Fifo Street, Temecula, CA 91980.

78. Austin Towers is a convicted former spy for the former Soviet Union. Austin received a communication from a Soviet agent that $2 million had been set aside for him in an account upon which he would be able to draw. Austin was told that the money was being held by the Soviet Union, rather than in an independent or third party bank or institution, on petitioner's behalf. Over the next few years, Austin drew approximately $1 million from the account. During that period, Austin filed annual tax returns with his wife showing taxable income of approximately $65,000 per year. Conduct appropriate research to determine Austin's tax liability for the $1 million in spy fees. After appropriate research, write a letter to Austin explaining your findings. His address is Lompoc Federal Prison, Cell #123, Lompoc, CA 93401.

79. The Reverend Shaman Oracle is an ordained minister in the Church of Prophetic Prophecy in Palm Desert, California. In the current year, Shaman receives payments from the church for his services of $150,000. Of this amount, the church designates $60,000 for compensation and $90,000 as a housing allowance. Shaman and his wife own a home and have actual expenditures during the year for the home of $72,000. The house is located in a well-established rental market, and the fair rental value of the home for the current year is $55,000. Shaman wants to know how he and his wife should report these amounts on their current year's tax return. After appropriate research, write a letter to Shaman explaining your findings. His address is P.O. Box 1234, Palm Desert, California 92211.

80. Your client, Teddy Chow and his wife Abby filed a lawsuit to recover damages for personal injuries Teddy sustained in a 2000 auto accident. In 2004, a jury awarded Teddy $1,620,000 in damages. In addition, delay damages in the amount of $1,080,000 were then added to that award, resulting in a total judgment of $2,700,000. The defendants appealed the award, and while the appeal was pending, the parties reached a settlement, which provided for payment to Teddy of $2,550,000. In 2006, after attorney's fees of $850,000 were subtracted, Teddy received $1,700.000. Teddy wants to know how these amounts are treated for tax purposes. After appropriate research, write a letter to Teddy and Abby explaining your findings. Their address is 654 Hops Street, Golden, CO 78501.

81. Cabrito Ranch, Inc. is a family ranch owned and operated by two brothers, Billie and Bubba Cabrito. The corporation made in-kind bonus payments in the form of goats to its two officers (Billie and Bubba) in exchange for their performance of agricultural labor. The two brothers are the only employees to receive goat bonuses. The transfers of the goats to the officers occurred within days of the date Cabrito Ranch would have sold the goats within the ordinary course of its business. The two officers/brothers did not market their bonus goats separately from other Cabrito Ranch goats; rather, the bonus goats were loaded onto the same trucks and sold to the same goat buyer on the same terms as other Cabrito Ranch goats. The officer/brothers' goats were sold for $70,000 ($35,000 to each brother). Cabrito Ranch wants to know how to treat the cash from the goat bonuses for FICA purposes. After appropriate research, write a letter to Billie and Bubba explaining your findings. Their address is 247 Angora Road, Mohair, TX 77501.

82. Gwen Gullible was married to Darrell Devious. They were divorced two years ago. Three years ago (the year before their divorce), Darrell received a $250,000 retirement plan distribution, of which $50,000 was rolled over into an IRA. At the time, Gwen was aware of the retirement funds and the rollover. The distribution was used to pay off the couple's mortgage, purchase a car, and for living expenses. Darrell prepared the couple's joint return, and Gwen asked him about the tax ramifications of the retirement distributions. He told her he had consulted a CPA and was advised that the retirement plan proceeds used to pay off a mortgage were not taxable income. Gwen accepted that explanation and signed the return. In fact, Darrell had not consulted a CPA.

   One year ago (after the divorce), Gwen received a letter from the IRS saying they had not received the tax return for the last full year of marriage. On advice from a CPA, Gwen immediately filed the return (she had a copy of the unfiled return). The Internal Revenue Service notified Gwen that no estimated payments on the retirement distribution had been paid by Darrell, and that she owed $60,000 in tax, plus penalties and interest. The deficiency notice provided that the retirement distribution, less the amount rolled, was income to the couple. After appropriate research, prepare (in good form) a research memorandum to the file. (See Chapter 2 for an illustration of the structure of a tax memo.) Also, write a letter to Gwen explaining your findings. Her address is 678 Surprise Street, Houston, TX 77019.

83. Pealii Loligo owned and operated three "House of Calamari" restaurants from 1998 through 2000. His wife, Cleopatra Decacera, assisted with the management of the restaurants.

   In May 1999, Ms. Decacera and Mr. Loligo purchased a $900,000 home. In relation to this home purchase, in 1996 and 2000 they signed mortgage loan applications indicating joint annual incomes of $235,000 and $321,000, respectively. On their 1998 joint Federal income tax return, however, Ms. Decacera and Mr. Loligo reported that they earned no salaries and had net losses of $55,000; and on their 1999 joint tax return, they reported that Mr. Loligo earned a salary of $23,000, and that they had net losses of $77,000.

During 1998–2000, Ms. Decacera and Mr. Loligo paid approximately $70,000 for home furnishings, $30,000 for a swimming pool, and $40,000 for Ms. Decacera's jewelry. In addition, they leased two Mercedes-Benz automobiles and took Ms. Decacera's parents on vacations to Florida and Nevada.

In 2003, Decacera and Loligo were indicted and charged with filing false tax returns in 1998–2000. Loligo pled guilty, while Decacera signed a deferred prosecution agreement and admitted filing false returns. The couple divorced in 2005, and in 2006, the IRS issued a deficiency notice for the 1998–2000 taxes. In September 2006, Ms. Decacera filed a petition in which she requested relief from joint and several liability for 1998–2000 income taxes. During January 2007, Mr. Loligo filed his "notice of intervention." In July, an IRS Appeals officer determined that Ms. Decacera did not qualify for Innocent Spouse relief under Sec. 6015(f).

After appropriate research, prepare in good form a research memorandum to the file. (See Chapter 2 for an illustration of the structure of a tax memo.) Then, write a letter to Cleopatra explaining your findings. Her address is 4567 Whome Lane, Escondido, CA 92069.

84. Ned Naive (see research question Chapter 2, #76) operated several franchised stores, and at the home office's suggestion, consolidated its payroll and accounting functions with Andy the Accountant. Andy is a not a CPA. Last year, Andy began embezzling taxpayer's escrowed tax withholdings and failed to remit required amounts for the four quarters. The IRS assessed Ned $10,000 in penalties for failing to make the proper withholding deposits during the year. After appropriate research, prepare (in good form) a research memorandum to the file. (See Chapter 2 for an illustration of the structure of a tax memo.) Then, write a letter to Ned explaining your findings. His address is 4567 Brainless Street, Phoenix, AZ 91234.

Part 3

Research Tools

Chapter 6

Tax Services and Periodicals

LEARNING OBJECTIVES

- Understand the advantages and disadvantages of electronic tax services.

- Apply the research process to actual Federal research problems.

- Know the major features of electronic tax services.

- Understand the difference between annotated and topical tax services.

- Use the keyword, cite, and contents searches to find relevant materials in electronic tax services.

- Survey tax periodicals and the role they play in the tax research process.

- Use the correct citation forms for printed and electronic tax materials.

- Examine indexes to tax periodicals that can facilitate locating pertinent journal articles.

CHAPTER OUTLINE

Every tax researcher must have access to one or more commercial tax services. By organizing the vast array of primary and secondary sources of the tax law, these tax services facilitate more efficient, effective, and comprehensive research. Accordingly, the function of a commercial tax service is to act as an index for primary and secondary tax law source materials, not as an end in themselves. Generally, only reckless (or inadequately trained) tax researchers will confine their analysis to the commentary available in tax services. The tax services should efficiently direct the researcher to the germane primary sources of the controlling law. It is the professional duty of the researcher to undertake an evaluation of these sources. Furthermore, quality research is not completed until the latest developments in the relevant areas of the law have been assessed.

This chapter reviews the basic steps for developing effective and efficient tax research introduced in Chapter 2 while exploring the electronic versions of the major tax services, as well as some important tax newsletters and periodicals. Tax services offering legal as well as tax products are examined in Chapter 7.

BACKGROUND FOR ELECTRONIC TAX SERVICES

Traditionally, commercial tax services are classified into two general types, annotated and topical. **Annotated tax services** are organized by *Internal Revenue Code* section number. They may also be called **Compilations** because they compile an editor's explanation and evaluation with the Code section, its recent committee reports and Regulations, and they provide **annotations** (brief summaries) of related court cases and administrative rulings. **Topical tax services,** on the other hand, divide the tax law into transactions and related subject matter with underlying tax principles as an organizing format. Thus, the material follows logical threads that connect noncontiguous Code sections. Since the electronic services developed from published services, they are generally organized as topical and annotated databases; however, this structure may not be apparent.

Virtually all tax information is available in various electronic forms. However, the presence of this information does not translate into more effective research. This is because voluminous information takes more time to sort, read, and comprehend, which can lead to information overload and inefficiency. All this information must be managed; otherwise, using computers for tax research will become inefficient. With this caveat aside, electronic searching can greatly increase the effectiveness of tax research through instant access to an abundance of primary sources and explanations of the tax law.

One of the greatest benefits of any electronic tax service is the currency of the information provided. Most Internet services update in text on a daily or continuous basis. Keep in mind that daily updating does not necessarily mean that what happened yesterday will be accessible today. Processing time is still required. It does mean, however, that as soon as the information is processed it can be entered into the system.

The number of tax resources offered in electronic form has increased rapidly. Some tax services simply compile primary source information obtained from the government, while others originate information and include substantial analysis. While practitioners can retrieve many free primary tax sources through the Internet, this free access cannot substitute for the need to have access to comprehensive tax services. Besides checking the validity of primary tax sources, tax services furnish various methods of searching the tax sources, editorial analysis and comments, organization, and an integration of the tax resources.

ILLUSTRATIVE RESEARCH EXAMPLE

A sample research project will be used to explore the major features of the electronic tax services. It is important that *you* attempt the illustrative research project using the tax services available to you. The procedural knowledge necessary to use these tax services efficiently can only be acquired through hands-on practice. The remainder of this chapter is designed to guide you through the basic tax services and is *not* a substitute for your actually using the services.

Research Project 6–1   Our client, Ms. Sanski, an executive with International Marketing, was a guest professor at a local university for one semester. She found that one of the tenured professors, Dr. Nu, shared her interest in the acquisition and distribution networks for products during the European Renaissance. They decided to write a book on the subject and began working in March of the current year. Most of the documents they needed for the book, however, were located in Europe. In June, Ms. Sanski and Dr. Nu traveled to Italy, France, and Spain to examine documents germane to their book. Returning to the United States, they stopped in Washington, D.C., to gather more information at the Library of Congress. By the end of the current year, they expect to have collected most of the materials needed for writing the book. Ms. Sanski has incurred all of the expenses in obtaining these materials. The actual writing of the book will start next year and should be completed by the end of that year. When they have several chapters of the book written, they will contact a publisher. They hope the book will be in print within one year of completing the manuscript. Ms. Sanski wants to deduct all of the costs associated with data collection in the current year. Ms. Sanski asks you if it is possible to treat the costs as current business expenses.

APPROACHING THE RESEARCH PROBLEM

Regardless of the research method used, the starting point in approaching any tax research problem is to formulate the issues as tax questions being asked. The research questions for Project 6–1 appear to be: How should the current expenses for a book that may be published in the future be treated for tax purposes? Should the costs be immediately expensed or capitalized and deducted as the revenues from the book are received? This first formulation of the research questions should not be considered their final versions. As the research is performed, other issues will probably be identified that will require refinement of the questions. Recall the iterative nature of tax research as discussed in Chapter 2 relative to Exhibits 2–1 and 2–2.

Gradually research questions are refined to their final states. However, this refinement does not guarantee that a definite answer will be found which controlling authority substantiates. The final conclusion may be that one solution appears more supportable than another, or that the IRS or the courts will interpret the facts and circumstances in a particular manner when making a decision. Remember that in most tax decisions professional judgment is required because the controlling law is imprecise and can be interpreted differently by the taxpayer and the IRS.

Based on the initial questions formulated, the main issue in Research Project 6–1 appears to be expensing versus capitalization of the author's prepublication business costs. Therefore, relevant keywords appear to be "author," "business expenses," "prepublication expenses," and "capitalization." Through a basic knowledge of the Code, we know that capitalization of costs is governed by § 263A, the uniform capitalization rules. Finally, in prior research of other topics, you may have seen references to a case called *Hadley* that concerns an author's prepublication expenses. The case is old, but it may have some bearing on the situation.

ACCESSING ELECTRONIC TAX INFORMATION

The key to effective tax research is finding the pertinent material necessary to formulate an informed conclusion about the optimum treatment of the transaction. How the electronic tax services are entered will determine how efficiently the relevant materials are found. Most of the services allow researchers to choose whether to have retrieved documents presented in order of relevance to the search or listed by database sources. The latter lets the researcher decide which documents should be examined first. Regardless of the order displayed, a researcher unfamiliar with the topic should start with an editorial explanation of the topic. This overview will help identify the most pertinent elements of the project and introduce the primary tax law applicable to the research. It is easy to gain access to the primary sources from the explanation because they are generally hyper-linked to their citations.

From this initial analysis, a researcher may decide that a new, more targeted search is warranted. Once the relevant primary sources are identified, but before they are carefully read, it is necessary to determine which of the sources are still good law by checking them through a citator (see Chapter 8 for a full discussion of citators). The fact that the tax service locates a document and places it high on the relevance list does not mean the researcher can assume it is still valid law. The last step is to read carefully the germane primary tax law sources. After evaluating these sources, the researcher will be able to provide an educated suggestion as to the optimum treatment for the item in question.

Keep in mind that the commercial providers of tax services offer a plethora of tax products (databases) that can be bundled in a variety of ways. This chapter's description of the tax databases within any of the services may not be what is available to the reader. Each firm (or library) performs a cost–benefit analysis and purchases only those resources that it can afford and finds useful in its practice. Also, the tax services are constantly updating their products to maintain their competitive edges. Therefore, the current appearance of the tax services and products offered may differ from those presented in this text. Nevertheless, the basic methodology described in this chapter should apply to whatever tax databases and products are available to the reader and whatever their visual presentation.

RIA CHECKPOINT

Electronic tax services can be entered using three search methods: keyword, citation (Code section and case name), and content. How to use each method will be illustrated using **Checkpoint,** the Research Institute of America (RIA) Internet tax service. This is one of the most authoritative and well-known Internet tax services available. The general methodology that applies to RIA Checkpoint also applies to other tax services.

RIA Checkpoint provides a full gambit of Federal tax information with several different product packages available. The most inclusive package includes all primary tax sources, *Federal Tax Coordinator 2d, United States Tax Reporter, Citator 2nd Series,* Warren, Gorham & Lamont (WG&L) journals, WG&L textbooks, IRS publications, etc. With so much information available, it is important to limit a search to only those databases that are pertinent to the research project; otherwise, too many irrelevant documents will be retrieved.

Exhibit 6–1 shows the opening search screen appearing after the RIA Checkpoint log-on screen. The screen is organized to facilitate quick access to the research methods most frequently used by the practitioners. As can be seen, the focus of Checkpoint is on keyword searches; the keyword entry box is center screen. A table of contents search can be launched by clicking on the button so named at the top of the screen and searches by citation are accessed in the left frame. The discussion of searching in Checkpoint will start with keyword searching since that is emphasized and then move to table of contents and lastly citation searches. Before the searching can commence, a practice area needs to be selected. Among the choices are Federal, State & Local, Estate Planning, Pension & Benefits, International and All Practice Areas. The default area is Federal, and therefore, no changes need to be made for Project 6–1, because it involves a Federal income tax problem.

KEYWORD SEARCH

Checkpoint makes keyword searching appear to be easy as 1, 2, 3 (see Exhibit 6–1). First, enter keywords in the box provided. Second, select a database to search. Third, click on the "Search" button. If only it was that easy to find the perfect search terms, select just the right database, and have the

Exhibit | 6-1

RIA Checkpoint
Opening Screen

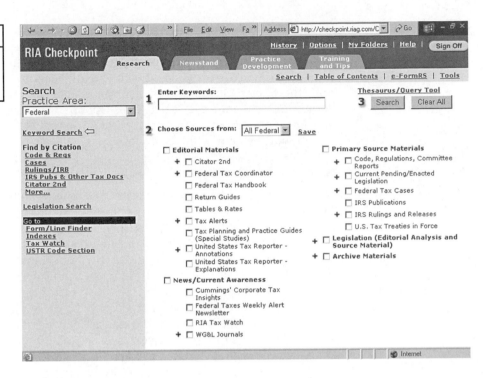

pertinent search results appear with the click of the mouse! Probably the most difficult part of a keyword search is finding the best words to use that are not so broad that too many irrelevant documents are retrieved and not so narrow that too few relevant documents are found.

For an initial search, the terms "author business expense" were entered in the Keywords box of Exhibit 6–1. Editorial Materials and Primary Source Materials databases were searched. Over 1,700 documents were referenced on the Source Documents screen. A full-text search looks for *"author"* anywhere in the text of the documents. It does not consider our desire that the document be about the taxation of business expenses of authors. The program literally only searches for a string of characters. Thus, every document about business expenses with the word "author" in it was identified. Regulations, for example, often have in their last paragraph "the authors of this Regulation are. . . ." If the Regulation discussed business expenses, it was included in the document list. The same would be true for documents containing comments about "the author." Approximately 1,000 of the search results are Regulations and IRS issuances, most of which are likely to refer simply to the authors of the document provided. This problem would not occur with an index search, because the individuals creating indexes take into consideration the meaning and context of keywords. The indexers know that the researcher is not interested in the authors of the documents, but rather in tax materials about authors.

Due to the number of the documents retrieved, the search was modified by selecting only Editorial Materials as the database. This database was selected because it was less likely to generate documents with irrelevant references to "authors." Running the search terms "author business expense" with the new database still identified more than seventy documents. Consequently, the term "business" was replaced with "prepublication" to narrow the search. From the Source Documents screen, the change can be made by selecting "Modify Search" from the Search Tools Options. The Search "Within Results" was not selected because the term "prepublication" is likely to appear in documents not containing the term "business" and thus may miss some relevant cites. The Search "Within Results" allows the researcher to further search the source documents already identified using additional terms.

Through this iterative research process, our final search terms became: "author prepublication expense" and we have reduced the retrieved documents to a reasonable number to examine. Our search terms were entered into the Keywords box in no particular order. However, if an order is desired, Boolean connectors may be used. A list of the RIA Boolean connectors is furnished in Exhibit 6–2. Not only can the researcher indicate order with these connectors, but words that constitute a phrase may also be identified. For example, if we want *prepublication expenses* to be treated as a phrase, we would type quotes around the terms. The spaces between words imply an "and" connection. Therefore, for our search, Checkpoint searched for documents containing all of these words anywhere in its text. If we want to search for expense, expensing, and expenditure, we could enter "expen*" where the asterisk is a holder for zero or more characters at the end of a word. The list of

Exhibit	**6–2**	RIA Checkpoint Boolean Connectors

Keyword Search Type	Connector to Use	Example
Containing all my keywords	Space, &, AND	earnings profits
Containing any of my keywords	I, OR	earnings OR profits
Contains one keyword but not the other	^, NOT	earnings NOT profits
Containing an exact phrase	" " (quotes)	"earnings and profits "
Containing variations of my keywords	* (asterisk)	deduct*
Showing order to perform commands	( ) (parentheses)	(earning profits) NOT retained
Within n words of other (any order)	/n (n equals a number)	consent /5 dividends
Within n words of other (in exact order)	pre/n	consent pre/5 dividends
Within same sentence (or 20 words) as other (in any order)	/s	consent /s dividends
Within same sentence (or 20 words) as other (in exact order)	pre/s	consent /s dividends
Within one paragraph (or 50 words) of other (in any order)	/p	consent /p dividends
Within one paragraph (or 50 words) of other (in exact order)	pre/p	consent pre/p dividends

connectors is available in Checkpoint by clicking on Thesaurus/Query Tool (see Exhibit 6–1).

If the researcher is not sure of the best terms to use, synonyms can be added to the keyword search terms, by using the thesaurus built into Checkpoint. The researcher has the option of selecting which of the synonyms displayed are added to the search or of including all of the alternatives. By being able to select only some or one of the terms, researchers can customize the search to their particular research project. For our Project 6–1, the only eliciting synonymous term is "expense". By selecting the synonyms we prefer, Checkpoint will automatically add the terms to the keywords box with vertical slashes between each term indicating an "or" connection for the synonyms. More information on formatting keyword entries can be found in the "Help" feature on the opening screen (see Exhibit 6–1).

Using the database and search terms described, our search results in documents being identified in three sources: Federal Tax Coordinator 2d—Analysis, Annotations (Code Arranged–USTR), and United States Tax Reporter Explanations. Clicking on anyone of the titles will display the list of documents found in these services. The **Federal Tax Coordinator 2d** (FTC), RIA's flagship service, is a topical service, whereas the **United States Tax Reporter** (USTR) is an annotated service which provides explanations as well as annotations to cases and rulings. The Analysis (FTC) has summaries of two documents: "Films, sound recordings, video tapes, books, etc." and "Writers" that appear to be pertinent to our research project. Clicking on the title of the document will retrieve its full-text entry. Exhibit 6–3 reproduces the document "Writers."

Exhibit	6–3

RIA Checkpoint
Document:
L-4110 Writers

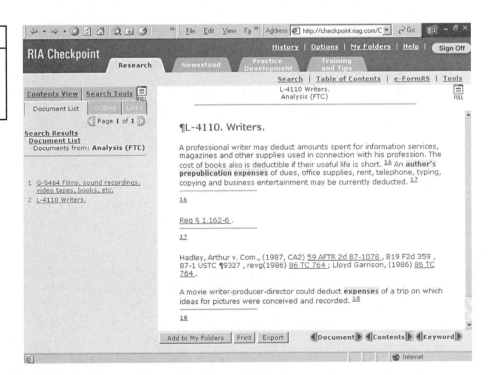

The document display screen provides easy access to the other documents in the FTC by listing them in the left frame. Others in the FTC and all documents found by the search are also accessible through the Document arrow. The Content arrows change the left frame to a Contents View. This allows the researcher to know where in the table of contents the current document is located. Also, through the view, the researcher can browse the service as one would flip through the pages of the published version. This is very handy when the researcher would like to read other explanations closely related to the topic of the research project. Lastly, the Keyword arrows find the occurrences of any of the keywords in the documents. The keywords throughout the text are highlighted for easy identification (see Exhibit 6–3). Also, any cites hyper-linked to full-text documents are indicated by being underlined and in colored type. Notice that such a hyper-link is available to the case we identified, *Hadley*, in footnote 17 at the bottom of the document (see Exhibit 6–3).

SPOTLIGHT ON TAXATION: Tax Service History

The *United States Tax Reporter*, the annotated tax service offered by RIA, didn't start out with this name. Prentice Hall published this tax service from 1924 to 1990 as the *PH Federal Taxes*. In November of 1989, Maxwell MacMillan bought the service and merely replaced Prentice Hall's name as the publisher. Then, in September 1991, Thomson acquired Maxwell MacMillian. The *PH Federal Taxes* became part of the RIA offerings in 1992 when its name was changed to the *United States Tax Reporter*.

To make sure we have found documents addressing the capitalization requirements for author's expenses, we enter a different keyword search using the terms "capitalization" and "author." The Source Documents screen indicates sources available in the Explanation–USTR and the Annotations–USTR as well as the FTC. One of the documents from Explanations is reproduced in Exhibit 6–4. Directly above the title of the document are a number of buttons which will lead the researcher to other documents related to this topic such as: annotations (Annot), the applicable Code sections (IRC), Regulations (Regs), Committee Reports (Com Rpts), history (Hist), and Compare It. When comparing this document with the FTC document in Exhibit 6–3, you will observe that these useful buttons are not present. This is because the FTC is a topical service and the USTR is an annotated service. Most of these buttons are self-explanatory with the exception of **Compare It**. This button offers a list in the left frame of where the topic in the right frame is addressed for each state (see Exhibit 6–4). Consequently, the researcher is able to determine Federal and state treatment of an item with just a click of the mouse.

We return to the Source Documents screen and select "Annotations–USTR." Most of the annotations summarized seem to be pertinent to our research. Upon opening each annotation, the researcher will notice that many of the

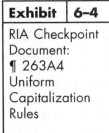

Exhibit | 6–4

RIA Checkpoint Document: ¶ 263A4 Uniform Capitalization Rules

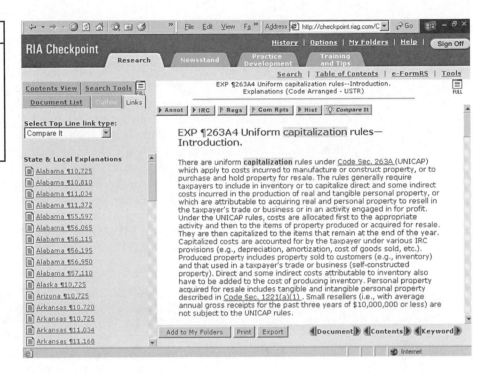

same buttons (IRC, Regs, Com Rpts) appear above the annotation title. In addition, the Expl button will take the researcher to the explanation portion of the USTR related to the annotation. Each annotation is hyper-linked to the related primary documents. Competent researchers will always read the primary documents and not rely on these exceedingly brief annotations when resolving a tax question.

CONTENTS SEARCH

One very important method of limiting the number of documents retrieved and guaranteeing their pertinence is to employ a contents search either in conjunction with a keyword search or as the only method of searching. This method basically treats electronic tax services as if they are their counterpart paper services. Accordingly, the researcher can "drill down" through the table of contents or indexes of the tax services just like they would "thumb through" these if they had books in front of them.

Table of Contents Search

A Table of Contents (TOC) search is launched from the opening screen by selecting the Table of Contents option (see Exhibit 6–1). For the illustrative Research Project 6–1, we could review the Federal Editorial Materials and in particular the FTC. Scanning the chapters in the FTC, both "Chapter G Tax Accounting: Periods, Methods, Inventories, Installment Sales" and "Chapter L Deductions: Business and Investment Expenses, Travel & Entertainment" appear to be relevant areas. Clicking on either of these will display the table of contents for the chapter. The researcher would continue to drill down through the contents until individual entries in the service are reached. All entries with a "+" in front of them may be expanded further. This drill-down method can be very efficient when the researcher has a good idea of where in the services the relevant documents are likely to be located. At any point in the drilling-down process, a keyword search may be performed by checking up to fifteen topics. This search is not limited to the table of contents titles as might be presumed; rather it searches the documents within the titles. Thus, using this method will lead to the same relevant documents as a general keyword. The advantage of this option, however, is that the researcher can limit the chapters of the tax service searched to only those that are pertinent to the issue being researched. The search shown in Exhibit 6–5, which was limited to Chapter L, was very efficient, as it led directly to the FTC explanation on "Writer" that was found using just the keyword search.

Exhibit   6–5

RIA Checkpoint *Federal Tax Coordinator 2d* Table of Contents

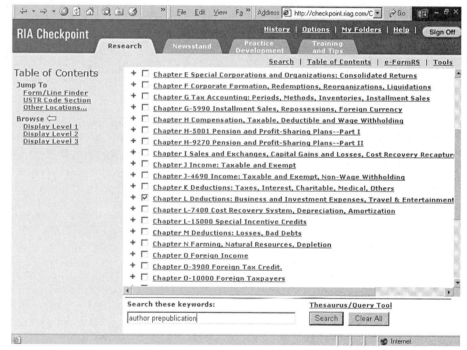

Index Search

An Index search starts with selecting its title under the Go To heading in the left frame of the opening screen (see Exhibit 6–1). The Federal databases indexes are the following.

- Federal Tax Coordinator 2d Topic Index
- Code Arranged Annotations & Explanations (USTR) Topic Index
- RIA's Federal Tax Handbook Topic Index

- Return Guide Indexes
- Current Code Topic Index
- Final & Temporary Regulations Topic Index
- Proposed Regulations Topic Index

Once a database is selected, the researcher has two options. Clicking on the database will display a listing of the alphabet. From this screen the researcher can select a letter and continue to drill down until the specific topic of interest and the documents are located. This method is similar to using an index for a published service.

As with the TOC, a keyword search is possible in the indexes. Unlike the TOC, the keyword search is restricted to the index entries. This differs from other keyword searches in that it is the index entries themselves, and not the underlying documents, that are being searched. The advantage of this approach is that the meaning of the words searched is relevant. This is because the entries within the indexes were created by individuals who considered the definitions of the words listed. Consequently, the keywords chosen for this type of search would likely be the same words the researcher would select for beginning a research project in a published service's index. Some researchers find it beneficial to start with an index search to help them identify effective terms for their general keyword searches.

CITE SEARCH

A third approach to electronic searches is a Citation search. To perform a search by Code section or case name, choose title under Find a Citation in the left frame of the opening screen (see Exhibit 6–1). If the type of document you wish to find is not listed, selecting More... contains an extensive list of documents that can be searched by citation. After selecting a type of document, Checkpoint provides templates for entering citations and examples for each template. These templates make entering a citation simple because the proper format is provided.

Code Search

Research Project 6–1 likely involves the capitalization of expenses rules under § 263A. A search on this section retrieves the full text of § 263A. The initial screen is reproduced in Exhibit 6–6. On careful examination of Exhibit 6–6, you will see a symbol for the four compass directions. Clicking on this symbol brings up a box in which the exact cite of document line is displayed. This small box is visible in Exhibit 6–6 for the § 263A(a)(2) paragraph. This is quite helpful when examining long Code sections or Regulations with complex paragraphing structures. If the researcher would like to know where the Code section fits within the *Internal Revenue Code,* the Contents View contains this information. It shows the exact location by providing the subtitle, chapter, subchapter, part, and section number for the section of interest.

Another useful feature offered in the left frame is the Outline. This gives an outline of the Code section by listing the subsection titles and their associated letters. By clicking on the title, Checkpoint will automatically present that

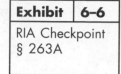

Exhibit 6–6

RIA Checkpoint § 263A

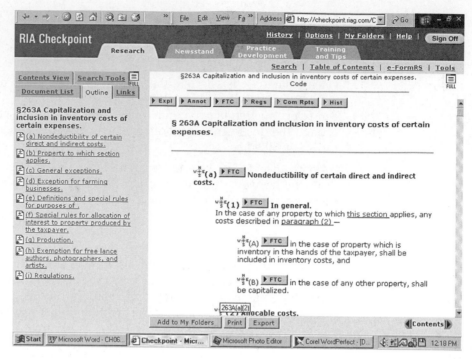

part of the Code section on the screen. With a section like § 263A, this is particularly helpful. It is easy to get lost as to where you are in sections that are as long as this one.

Using the Code section as the beginning point for identifying related documents is simplified by use of the buttons located above the Code section title and at each subsection or division thereof. These buttons will lead the researcher to explanations and annotations in the United States Tax Reporter (Expl and Annot), topical entries in the Federal Tax Coordinator 2d (FTC), relevant primary sources (Regs and Com Rpts), History (Hist), and to Warren Gorham & Lamont treatises (WG&L Treatises). Through these links, the researcher will find many relevant documents. However, relying exclusively on Code section searches may be more time consuming than contents or keyword searches when there are several Code sections involved in the research issue.

Case Search

Unlike the other major electronic citation services, Checkpoint allows the researcher to enter either the name of the case or its citation in the templates furnished. This is quite convenient when all you know is the name of the case as in Project 6–1. Entering the *Hadley* name retrieves all of the documents with Hadley as a taxpayer. The *Hadley* case pertinent to this research is 59AFTR 2d 87-1078. RIA lists the Code section to which the case applies which helps in identifying the *Hadley* case relevant to the research project. Click on this citation, and the case appears in full text. The complete RIA citation is given as the title for the document and, again, the Code section to which the case applies. Since the *Hadley* case is from 1987, we should check this case through the citator (using the citator button provided) to make sure that it is still good law (see Chapter 8 for a detailed discussion of citators).

As was true for a Code section document, a case document may furnish entry into the tax services. The buttons leading to explanations that appeared on the Code Section screen are also present on the Case screen. With these buttons, the researcher is led to the case's annotations in the United States Tax Reporter or explanations where the case is cited in the Federal Tax Co-ordinator 2d service. Selecting either of these buttons will lead the researcher to documents retrieved in the previous keyword searches.

With a case or Code section search, the specific case or section shows up as a result. These searches do not facilitate the retrieval of all documents that might be relevant to the research project. Case names or Code sections may be used as terms in keyword searches to locate relevant documents. It would be important in this type of search to include other keywords to ensure that every document containing the name or the Code section number is not re-trieved. These latter searches follow the same steps as any keyword search.

CCH TAX RESEARCH NETWORK

The Commerce Clearing House (CCH) Internet service, called **Tax Research NetWork** (NetWork) is visually quite different than RIA Checkpoint; however, the searching methods utilized with NetWork are similar to those applied in the Checkpoint section. The differences in the implementation of these methods will be illustrated in this section by using Research Project 6–1.

CCH is organized like a file cabinet with folders tabs for its major databases (see Exhibit 6–7). Since Network opens to the "My CCH" folder which con-tains current tax news, a folder must be selected before the researcher can begin searching. For Research Project 6–1, we will select the Federal folder and this will be the focus of the CCH section. The State and Sales Tax fold-ers will be discussed in Chapter 9.

SPOTLIGHT ON TAXATION: Tax Quote

"The difference between tax avoidance and tax evasion is the thickness of a prison wall."
—Denis Healey

KEYWORD SEARCH

As with RIA Checkpoint, CCH NetWork emphasizes keyword searching. The Keyword search box appears in the tools bar and therefore is available from

Exhibit 6-7

CCH Tax
Research
NetWork
Federal
Opening Screen

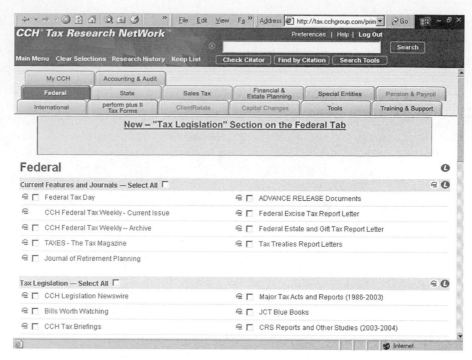

every screen (see Exhibit 6–7). The Search Tools button associated with the Keyword box enables the researcher to customize word searches. With this option, the researcher may select from the following search methods: all terms (the default setting), any term, near (terms to be within twenty words of each other), exact phrase, or Boolean connectors. The number of documents retrieved can set from 1 to 9999 with the default at 50. NetWork sorts the documents retrieved by relevance unless the researcher selects otherwise. The searching results in a list of documents. However, the researcher may change the display to list the documents based on the table of contents, by court reporters or tax services, for example. This is very helpful as it organizes the results and makes it easier to determine which documents are not relevant to the research project.

NetWork automatically applies a thesaurus to all the keywords. This may not be beneficial in all research situations as it may cause numerous unrelated documents to be retrieved. This feature may be turned off on the Search Tools screen. Recall that with RIA Checkpoint, the researcher must select which words the thesaurus suggests to be added to the keyword search. Application is not automatic. From this same Search Tools screen, the search databases can be restricted by date or by type of document. The Narrow by Date restriction option is especially convenient when the researcher is updating a previous research project.

Once the keywords and search options are entered, the databases within the folder must be selected. For our project, the Federal database was selected and within this folder there is a variety of resources groups, composed of numerous databases, from which to choose. Only a small portion of them may be seen in Exhibit 6–7. Researchers have the option of selecting all the databases within a resource group or only those databases applicable to their project. If a researcher decides to change the selection, using the Clear Selections option in the toolbar removes all choices, and the selection process starts over again. This clearing includes the choices made on the Search Tools screen. The researcher can also just unmark the database boxes not desired.

To locate documents related to Research Project 6–1, Primary Sources and CCH Explanations and Analysis databases were selected. Within the latter database those services such as Federal Estate and Gift Tax Reporter and Federal Excise Tax Reporter were deselected. As with RIA Checkpoint, CCH NetWork editorial materials provide a topical service, **Federal Tax Service** (FTS) and an annotated service, **Standard Federal Income Tax Reporter** (SFITR). However, unlike RIA, CCH's premier service is its annotated service.

The result of the search is a document list presented in order of relevancy by default. The presentation may easily be changed to a table of contents ordering, as was done for Exhibit 6–8, by selecting this option in a pull-down menu available in the upper right portion of this screen. Notice that at the top of this document list screen, CCH NetWork lists all of the terms searched, including those added by the thesaurus. For our search, the terms cost, expend, and expenditure were added. Interestingly no terms for author (such as writer) were added.

Exhibit | **6–8**

CCH Tax Research NetWork Standard Federal Income Tax Reporter Table of Contents View

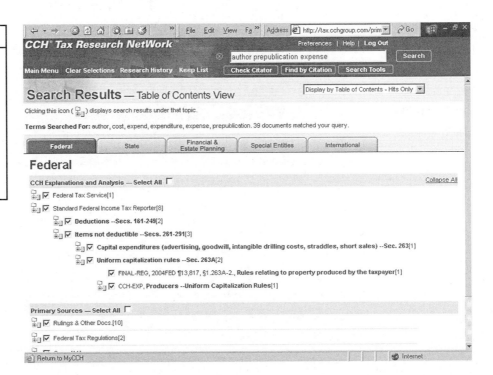

CITE AND CONTENTS SEARCHES

Citation

To search by Code section, case name, or other primary source, the researcher uses the Find by Citation option visible in Exhibit 6–7. This option offers templates for every type of primary and secondary source available through NetWork. If the complete citation is known, it can be entered in CCH recognizable format in the citation general box; otherwise, one of the citation templates is completed. Unlike RIA Checkpoint, names of cases may not be entered in the templates. Fortunately, if only the name of the case is known, the proper citation for a case is obtainable by selecting the Citator option and entering the taxpayer's name (see Exhibit 6–7).

Table of Contents

NetWork does not have a separate folder tax for table of contents searches. Rather, a contents search of a database begins by clicking on the *title* of the database of interest. The next screen will furnish the table of contents for the database. Continue to drill down in the same manner as in RIA Checkpoint until the documents of interest are recovered. As with RIA, a keyword search can be instigated at any point of the drill-down by marking boxes in front of databases. The same documents can be located using this method as were retrieved using only a keyword search.

Exhibit 6–9 reproduces one of the documents retrieved that is relevant to Project 6–1. Similar to RIA, NetWork offers links to other editorial materials

Exhibit   6–9

CCH Tax Research NetWork Document

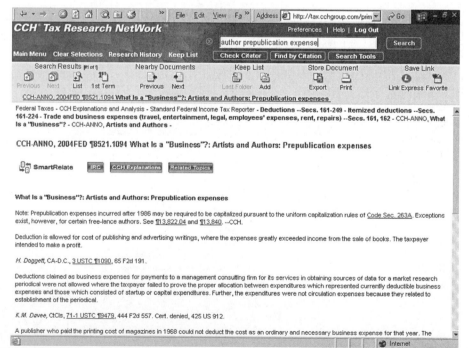

and primary sources through its SmartRelate button options. The Related Topics option yields a list of documents that would appear under the same heading in the index. These documents will vary greatly as to their applicability to the research project at hand. To jump to the next (or previous) document for the search results list, the researcher may click on the Search Results icons. To browse the materials that would be in close proximity to your document if in a printed service, select the icons for Nearby Documents. This option gives the ability to "flip through the pages" of the service. Finally, to find the first point at which one of the keywords appears in the document, use the icon for 1st Term.

Index

At the bottom of the Federal opening screen, the Topical Indexes lists all the services with indexes. An index search in NetWork can be conducted as a keyword search of the terms included in the index. Instead of using keywords, the researcher can drill down through an index of the selected service in a manner similar to that used with the table of contents. The statements in the RIA Checkpoint section regarding the usefulness of this searching method apply to CCH NetWork as well.

KLEINROCK

Kleinrock Publishing was originally known for its affordable, easy-to-use Federal **TaxExpert**® that was available on CD-ROM. It contained nearly a gigabyte of tax law sources on a single CD. Thus, not only was it comprehensive, it was also very portable. Kleinrock now supplies Internet access to its TaxExpert® service, while still offering the CD version and both at affordable rates. Besides this Federal service, Kleinrock offers many other products such as PLR and Tax Court Memorandum libraries, multi- and individual state tax services, employment tax service, and a full range of compliance products.

Kleinrock's Federal service includes twenty-five volumes of analysis and explanations that are similar to the CCH and RIA editorial tax services included in NetWork and Checkpoint. In addition, Kleinrock provides access to the Code, Regulations, IRS pronouncements and publications, U.S. tax treaties, Congressional Committee Report, and Federal tax cases (including Tax Court Memorandums). With the service, the subscribers receive daily online tax bulletins and biweekly printed issues of the Federal Tax Bulletin. The Total Tax Guide which is similar to the CCH Master Tax Guide is also sent in printed form to the subscribers of TaxExpert®.

Although Kleinrock has not been in the tax service business as long as RIA and CCH, it is rapidly developing product lines comparable to the established giants. Each year it is adding more features to its tax services and branching out into more areas of taxation. Kleinrock products are easy to use and very affordable, thus making them a choice of many practitioners. Access to Kleinrock products through Lexis/Nexis is facilitating awareness of what it has to offer.

SPOTLIGHT ON TAXATION: Freedom of Information Act

The Freedom of Information Act (FOIA), 5 USC § 552 gave the public the right to access IRS records unless they are protected from disclosure. Under this act, taxpayers have access to the non-published documents issued by the IRS such as Private Letter Rulings and Technical Advice Memorandums. The FOIA applies to records created by Federal agencies, yet records held by Congress and the courts are exempt. State and local government agencies are under each state's own public access laws.

The IRS complies with the FOIA by:

• Maintaining publicly available materials on the Internet in the IRS Electronic Reading Room
• Staffing the IRS Public Reading Room at 1111 Constitution Avenue, NW, Washington, D.C. 20224 [call (202) 622-5164]
• Responding to written requests for agency records not available in the Reading Room

Many IRS records are available for sale from the Government Printing Office. (http://www.gpo.gov/)

TAX PERIODICALS

Tax periodicals contain a variety of articles and news briefs that are designed to keep readers relatively knowledgeable of developments in specific or general areas of the tax law. These articles might contain, for example, an in-depth review of a recently decided court case, a broad analysis of the factors that should enter into the practitioner's decision on whether to make a certain tax accounting election, or a call for reform of a statute by a neutral (or biased) observer. Tax articles can suggest new approaches to tax problems, give guidance for solving complex problems, or just explain a new law in a readable form.

With an article that is right "on point" with tax issues, the practitioner is able to, in effect, use the author of the article as a research associate by capitalizing on the author's expert judgments and references on the relevant topic thereby saving hours of research time. Keep in mind, however, that tax periodicals are secondary sources of the tax law and therefore should not be cited as the controlling authority, especially when primary sources supporting the position are available. The article's references can lead the practitioner to the pertinent primary tax sources. With that caveat aside, researchers who ignore the tax periodicals might be accused, at best, of reinventing the wheel and, at worst, of professional malpractice.

Traditionally, citing articles in professional tax research is limited to two situations: (1) if the researcher is referring to the author's analysis and conclusions as stated in an article; (2) if the researcher cannot find any controlling primary sources of law and a secondary source addresses the issues. Tax articles are now being cited more frequently in case opinions than in the past.

When they are lacking both the appropriate primary law sources and adequate judicial staff, the authors of these opinions may draw on tax articles to support the views of the court. In any event, it is imperative that the researcher understands the practical implications of using secondary law sources.

CITING ARTICLES

A citation to a printed tax journal article should take the following standard form.

> Megaard, Susan L. 2004. Recent Corporate Scandals Focus Attention on Tax Treatment of Stock Losses. *Journal of Taxation* 101(Aug): at 102.

Notice the proper placement of capital letters, periods, and commas in the citation. The denotation "at 102" indicates that the researcher is referencing or quoting from a specific portion of the article. If the entire article were being referenced, the citation would merely contain the beginning page number of the article. For the citation above, this would be ". . . (Aug): 101."

Unfortunately, the proper citation for articles found on the Internet is not as well established as for printed materials. A problem that complicates the issue is deciding how to characterize the Internet material to be cited. For example, is the material a journal article, a newsletter, a report, who is the author, when was the resource generated? Once this information is deciphered (and deciphering this may not be easy), a generally safe citation format to follow that of a printed document with additions or deletions as necessary. The following would be an acceptable format for a journal article found on the Internet.

> Soled, Jay A. and Charles E. Falk. 2004. Cost Segregation Applied. *Journal of Accountancy Online*. 198 (August). Retrieved 9/10, 2004 from AICPA at: http://www.aicpa.org/pubs/jofa/aug2004/index.htm

Sites on the Internet are generally case and punctuation sensitive. Therefore, ignore normal grammar rules when providing uniform resource locators (URLs) and place no punctuation (such as a period or a comma) at the end of a URL. It is important to indicate the date on which the document was retrieved because documents and web site URLs may change or be removed over time.

TYPES OF PERIODICALS

Tax periodicals can be categorized according to the depth of the coverage of their articles and the audience for which they are written. From the most extensive coverage to the least, they are as follows.

- Annual proceedings
- Scholarly reviews
- Professional journals
- Newsletters

Although each publication has its unique characteristics, several general characteristics of each category will be identified. This discussion will provide an initial introduction to the broad market of secondary source tax commentary.

Annual Proceedings

A number of annual conferences for tax practitioners and academics are conducted every year. Usually sponsored by a professional organization, law school, or educational agency, these conferences generally last from two to five days. The agenda at these conferences may include any of the following: lectures, paper presentations with or without discussion, panel discussions, seminars, demonstrations, and luncheon addresses. Often, the conference speakers allow the sponsoring agency to publish their presentations as proceedings of the meeting. These **annual proceedings** are distributed to the participants at the conference, and later to the general public in the form of a collection of articles. Most of these papers exhibit considerable depth of coverage and practical insight by the authors. They can be a valuable resource for the tax researcher. A few of the more established tax conferences include the following.

- New York University Institute on Federal Taxation had its first annual meeting in 1942.
- Penn State Tax Conference was established in 1946.
- University of Chicago Law School's Annual Federal Tax Conference first met in 1947.
- University of Southern California's Major Tax Planning Institute began in 1948.
- Tulane Tax Institute started in 1952.

The proceedings and indexes to these conferences are widely available. For example, CCH publishes the proceedings of the University of Chicago law school's annual Federal tax conference as an issue of *Taxes—The Tax Magazine.*

While some conferences select different areas of tax each year as the theme of the meetings, other annual conferences focus on a specialized area year after year. Examples of specialized tax conferences include the Non-profit Legal and Tax Conference held in March in Washington D.C.; the Institute on Oil and Gas Law and Taxation, which meets in Dallas; the Great Western Tax and Estate Planning Conference of the National Law Foundation held in Las Vegas; the Asian Development Bank Organization's International Taxation Conference held in Japan; and the University of Miami Law Center's Heckerling Institute on Estate Planning, held each January in Miami Beach.

Scholarly Reviews

All major law schools and a few business schools produce publications referred to as **law reviews** or **academic journals.** These publications are edited either by faculty members or by graduate students under the guidance of the school's faculty. Most law reviews also use an outside advisory board comprised of practicing attorneys and law professors at other universities to aid in selecting and reviewing articles. The articles appearing in these **scholarly reviews** are usually written by tax practitioners, academics, graduate students, or other noted commentators.

Some law schools produce journals that are limited to a specific area of the law, such as constitutional or labor law, in addition to the regular multitopic law review. Most of the general law reviews feature one to three tax articles per year; however, some law reviews are dedicated exclusively to tax matters. The following are several of the law reviews that concentrate on taxation issues.

- *Akron Tax Journal* by University of Akron
- *Ohio Tax Review* by Capital University Law School
- *Florida Tax Review* by University of Florida
- *Tax Law Review* by New York University School of Law
- *Virginia Tax Review* by University of Virginia School of Law

Besides law schools, academic organizations such as the National Tax Association (NTA) and the American Taxation Association (ATA) publish scholarly journals. The articles appearing quarterly in its *National Tax Journal* and the proceedings from the NTA annual conference, published in *Proceedings of the Annual Conference,* tend to take an analytical or mathematical approach to identifying the broad economic and social implications of taxation on the population. The ATA, a subdivision of the American Accounting Association, publishes two regular issues of *The Journal of the American Taxation Association (JATA)* and, like the NTA, the ATA prints a special conference supplement containing the papers presented at its yearly national conference. This journal is a research publication that offers a combination of taxation articles that employ (1) quantitative or analytical, (2) empirical, or (3) theoretical methodologies in analyzing issues considered of interest to the tax community.

Professional Journals

A wide variety of **tax journals** are published for the purpose of keeping tax practitioners abreast of the current changes and trends in the tax law. This category of journals, commonly referred to as **professional journals** or **practitioner journals,** includes publications by professional organizations as well as commercial companies. Examples of the former are the AICPA's *Tax Adviser,* the ABA Section on Taxation's *Tax Lawyer,* and journals published by state CPA or law societies.

Because the commercial publications are numerous, the tax coverage of these journals can accommodate the needs of the general tax practitioner and those who specialize in a specific area of tax law. For example, journals such as Warren, Gorham & Lamont's (WG&L) *Journal of Taxation* and *Practical Tax Strategies* or Commerce Clearing House's *Taxes* cover a variety of tax areas, whereas journals such as Tax Management's *The Compensation Planning Journal* or WG&L *Journal of Taxation of Investments* cover singular topics. Further, the articles appearing in these journals also vary greatly in their coverage from very complex with an exceedingly narrow focus to extremely practical "how to" articles designed for immediate implementation. Since the editors of most professional journals presume that their readers have access to little, if any, other current tax resource material, any major change in the tax law or important Court tax decision will spawn numerous articles in the various periodicals on the same or similar topics.

To accommodate the tax practitioner's need for timely information, most of the multi-topic tax journals are published monthly, whereas the more specialized tax journals tend to be issued on a quarterly basis. Practitioners with subscriptions to Internet services may obtain their journal through their online services. For example, a subscriber to RIA Checkpoint may add subscriptions to the WG&L journals. The journals ensure the quality of their articles by accepting solicited and unsolicited articles prepared by appropriate tax experts. In each case, an editorial review board assesses the timeliness, accuracy, and readability of each article before it is accepted for publication.

Newsletters

The major tax services include a **tax newsletter** as a part of their service. The Internet and online services tend to have daily newsletters, whereas the published services send the newsletters weekly. These newsletters help the subscriber keep abreast of important tax law developments. They are designed to give the practitioner both a capsule summary of tax law modifications and a reference to the paragraphs in the compilation materials that contain a more detailed analysis. Some of these newsletters also publish information concerning tax seminars and professional meetings, short reviews of (or citations for) selected current tax articles, and editorial highlights concerning recent tax developments. Several of the most popular commercial tax newsletters are listed in Exhibit 6–10.

| **Exhibit** | **6–10** | Selected Tax Newsletters from Major Publishers |

Title of Newsletter	Frequency	Publisher
Daily Tax Report	Daily	Bureau of National Affairs
E-Commerce Tax Report	Daily	Bureau of National Affairs
Federal Daily Tax Bulletin	Daily	Kleinrock
Federal Tax Bulletin	Biweekly	Kleinrock
Federal Tax Weekly Alert	Weekly	Research Institute of America
Focus on Tax	Monthly	Commerce Clearing House
International Taxes Weekly	Weekly	Research Institute of America
State and Local Taxes Weekly	Weekly	Research Institute of America
State Tax Notes Today	Daily	Tax Analysts
State Tax Notes Weekly	Weekly	Tax Analysts
State Tax Review	Weekly	Commerce Clearing House
Tax Alert	Daily	Research Institute of America
Tax Features	Bimonthly	Tax Foundation
Tax News Headlines	Daily	Commerce Clearing House
Tax Notes	Weekly	Tax Analysts
Tax Notes International	Weekly	Tax Analysts
Tax Notes Today	Continuously	Tax Analysts
Tax Practice	Weekly	Tax Analysts
Tax Practice Series Bulletin	Biweekly	Bureau of National Affairs
Tax Tracker News	Daily	Commerce Clearing House
Tax Watch	Quarterly	Tax Foundation
Taxes on Parade	Weekly	Commerce Clearing House
TM Memorandum	Biweekly	Bureau of National Affairs
TM Weekly Report	Weekly	Bureau of National Affairs
Weekly State Reporter	Weekly	Bureau of National Affairs
Worldwide Tax Daily	Daily	Tax Analysts

RIA

Opening the RIA Newsstand folder generates the RIA Daily Updates. On this screen, the practitioner may access the most recent news briefs for the following services.

- RIA Tax Watch
- Federal Tax Updates
- State & Local Tax Updates
- Corporate Finance Updates
- WG&L Journal Previews

The RIA Tax Watch specifically reports tax legislative developments. Infrequently it will also contain articles by expert practitioners, giving commentary on various aspects of proposed and potential tax legislation. Another RIA tax news service is Tax Alerts. This service covers current tax developments impacting compliance. Besides supplying the news, it indicates which form(s) may be affected by the tax news, recommends actions to be taken for clients, and provides links to related materials in Checkpoint. It even contains a database of client letters, prepared to specifically explain the recent tax event.

CCH

Tax news is so important to CCH that the opening screen for NetWork is My CCH (see Exhibit 6–11). The Tax Tracker News appearing in My CCH can be personalized to focus on those areas of the tax law that are of particular interest to the practitioner. This time-saving feature alerts practitioners to tax law changes in their area of specialization without requiring that they wade

Exhibit | 6–11

CCH Tax Research NetWork Opening Screen

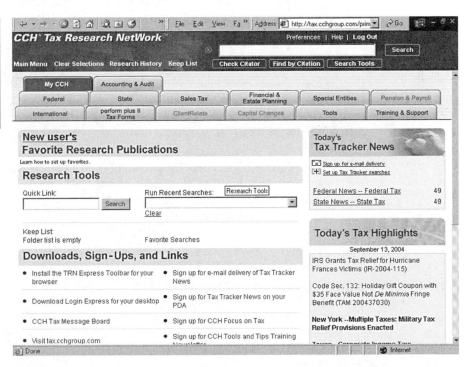

through all news articles for the day. The specialization can be for state news as well as Federal as both are provided in Tax Tracker.

Other news sources furnished on My CCH are Today's Tax Highlights and Tax Briefing Special Reports. Today's Tax Highlights contains a combination of Federal and state tax news. The number of news briefs varies from day to day with usually far fewer on the weekends. The Tax Briefing Special Reports are more specialized articles on topics such as new tax acts or multistate issues.

LOCATING RELEVANT TAX ARTICLES

The numerous published and computerized indexes available to tax researchers facilitate locating tax, business, and law journal articles that are pertinent to their research. However, the CCH *Federal Tax Articles* and the WG&L *Index to Federal Tax Articles* are the two indexes specifically designed for locating tax articles.

CCH Federal Tax Articles

The *Federal Tax Articles* (*FTA*) index, published by Commerce Clearing House, has many outstanding features that make it one of the best tax indexes available. However, its major drawback is that it is only available in a published format. It is not offered as part of its online tax service.

The *FTA* is known for its concise abstracts furnished for each article cited in the index. Reading these abstracts helps the practitioner reduce the false starts that commonly occur when trying to find pertinent articles based solely on their titles. The framework for organizing these abstracts is the *Internal Revenue Code.* This organization also facilitates finding articles addressing the Code section under investigation by the researcher. Lastly, CCH updates this index monthly so the citations are timely. Because the *FTA* current volume is a loose-leaf service, the updates either replace existing pages or are added to the end of the binder. Twice a year the updates are cumulated. A Report Letter is also provided each month. The first few pages of each monthly issue highlight the articles added to the index and present new developments.

Every four to six years, the CCH cumulative biyearly reports fill the loose-leaf volume and require the publication of a bound volume. At this time the article abstracts are reorganized, and the various indexes are consolidated for the entire period. In the bound volumes, the cited articles with their abstracts are arranged alphabetically by title under each Code section heading. The article citations are preceded by a new paragraph number that is tied to the Code section. Subsequently, a new loose-leaf volume is issued for articles that are published after the issuance of the bound volume.

Approximately 250 journals, law reviews, papers, and proceedings are included in the index. The topics covered in the *FTA* include Federal income, excise, estate, gift, and employment taxation. In the division called "Publishers and Publications," CCH provides the following information for each of the periodicals: publisher's name and address, frequency of publication, and the subscription cost. The cost of a single copy of each journal is also provided for those instances when the only source of a particular article is the publisher.

The main division of the index, called "Articles by Code Section," is where the full citation for each article and its abstract are located. This cumulative index gives Code section numbers with a brief description of the section as its headings. Articles can also be located by using the topic and author indexes. Each of these indexes refers the researcher to the "Articles by Code Section" division, through a system of paragraph numbers. The index's main cite number (i.e., to the left of the decimal point) provides the Code section paragraph number, and the numbers to the right of the decimal point refer to the specific article abstract. Note that the paragraph numbers for abstracts in the current binder will have no relation to the Code section number whereas in the bound volumes this is not the case.

As previously mentioned, the *FTA* is only available in print. As the loose-leaf volume accumulates a number of monthly updates, it becomes cumbersome to use. The twice a year consolidation and new paragraph numbers are assigned help somewhat but as the by-yearly reports become numerous, even reviewing them becomes a daunting task. Providing this service online would eliminate these problems with using the *FTA*.

WG&L Index to Federal Tax Articles

Warren, Gorham & Lamont's *Index to Federal Tax Articles* (*IFTA*) provides citations and occasional summaries for articles covering Federal income, gift, and estate taxation or tax policy that appear in more than 350 periodicals. The index surveys not only traditional tax journals, but also law reviews, major annual tax symposia, and certain economics, accounting, and finance journals. The *IFTA* is issued in bound volumes and includes permanent cumulations of references for the periods 1913–1974, 1974–1981, 1982–1983, 1984–1987, 1988–1992, and 1993–1996. A quarterly paperback cumulative supplement augments the main index volumes. Because the supplements are cumulative, the researcher need only consult one supplement for articles appearing in journals from 1997 to the present.

Unlike the CCH index, both the topic and the author indexes contain full article citations. Using the full citations in the author index, the researcher can identify other current articles by the same author pertaining to a specific topic. Authors with several articles on the same topic are more likely to have an expertise in that field, and, thus, their analysis may be more effectual. Further, the custom of listing citations for each author and topic heading in reverse chronological order (rather than in alphabetical order) expedites finding the most recent publications.

The *IFTA* contains a user's guide that explains how to use the index, lists the more than 1,500 topical index subject headings, supplies a key to abbreviations of periodical titles, and lists the periodicals included in the first three volumes. Further, each cumulative volume and the current supplement lists not only the periodical titles but also the volumes and issue numbers represented in that volume.

Whereas every citation in the CCH index is accompanied by an abstract, only articles judged by the compilers and Editorial Advisory Board to be of special interest are furnished a brief summary in the *Index to Federal Tax Articles*. Exceedingly few articles receive this distinction.

SUMMARY

There are many commercial tax services available and no one service is the best for all practitioners. While the services provide different features, all are most efficient when the organization of the service matches the issues in a client's tax situation. Thus, each tax service has its place in tax research, and practitioners must determine with which products they are most comfortable and which fit the research requirements of their firm. Changes in technology and the tax services happen on a continuous basis. The same changes occur in the practitioner's business. Consequently, the practitioner's comfort level with products and technology and the research needs will change over time. Practitioners should evaluate their tax resource choices often, at least once a year when it is time to renew their services.

The tax researcher should employ tax services as gateways to the primary sources and not as a substitute for primary source research. Tax services can make the research process more efficient and productive, but should not replace thorough review of primary sources and professional judgment.

Tax journals and other periodicals not only help researchers locate primary sources of the tax law, but also enlighten them as to other ways of analyzing a tax issue. Tax articles can synthesize information from the Code, Regulations, and pertinent court cases into a more logical presentation, which may be useful as the practitioner identifies relevant tax issues or precedents during the research process or prepares for litigation on behalf of a client. Finally, such publications are an integral part of the means by which the tax professional remains current with respect to the evolution of the Federal tax law.

TAX TUTOR

Reinforce the tax research information covered in this chapter by completing the online tutorials located at the Federal Tax Research web site:

http://raabe.swlearning.com

KEY WORDS

By the time you complete your work in this chapter, you should be comfortable discussing each of the following terms. If you need additional review of any of these items, return to the appropriate material in the chapter or consult the glossary at the end of this text.

Academic Journals

Annotated Tax Service

Annotations

Annual Proceedings

CCH *Federal Tax Articles*	Practitioner Journals
CCH *Federal Tax Service*	Professional Journals
CCH *Standard Federal Income Tax Reporter*	RIA *Federal Tax Coordinator 2d*
CCH Tax Research NetWork	RIA *United States Tax Reporter*
Checkpoint	Scholarly Reviews
Compare It	Tax Journals
Compilations	Tax Newsletters
Kleinrock's TaxExpert®	Topical Tax Service
Law Reviews	WG&L *Index to Federal Tax Articles*

DISCUSSION QUESTIONS

1. What is the function of commercial tax services?
2. Compare and contrast the general format of an annotated tax service with that of a topical tax service.
3. What are some of the benefits of electronic tax services?
4. Because the Internet services tend to update on a daily or continuous basis, they are current up to the minute. Comment on this statement.
5. What is the key to effective research?
6. What are some potential problems with all tax data being available electronically?
7. Why would a practitioner subscribe to a tax service when most of the primary sources are available for free on the Internet?
8. Why is it important for you to actually try research projects with the various tax services?
9. If a research question is formulated correctly, the researcher will be able to find a definitive answer to the question. Comment on this statement.
10. The fact that a tax service located a document and placed it high on the relevance list means you can assume it is still valid law. Comment on this statement.
11. Why is it important to limit the databases searched when using an electronic tax service?
12. What are the three methods for starting a research project with an electronic service? Which does RIA emphasize?
13. What functions do "Modify Search" and "Within Results" perform?
14. Explain the functions of the following special symbols in a keyword search: /s, " ", *.
15. Which annotated and topical tax services are included in RIA Checkpoint?
16. What function does the "Compare It" command perform?
17. What is the function of the directional symbol (compass) found in Code sections or Regulations reproduced in RIA Checkpoint? Why is it useful?

18. How does RIA Checkpoint differ from other electronic services with regards to case searches?

19. How do you perform a table of contents search in RIA?

20. Why can a table of contents search be very efficient?

21. What are the two options for conducting an index search?

22. Which annotated and topical tax services are included in NetWork?

23. What is the difference in the application of the thesaurus in Checkpoint and NetWork?

24. Explain the differences in conducting a table of contents search using Checkpoint and NetWork.

25. How is Kleinrock's TaxExpert® different from the other tax services discussed in this chapter?

26. Besides online at Kleinrock's web site how else can practitioners access TaxExpert®?

27. Why are the volumes of the annotated services called Compilation volumes?

28. Why are tax journals and newsletters generally not cited as authority in professional tax research? However, when is it appropriate to cite tax journals or newsletters as authority in professional tax research?

29. What does the denotation "at 407" indicate in the citation of a journal?

30. Briefly describe each of the following.
    a. Annual proceedings
    b. Scholarly reviews
    c. Professional journals
    d. Newsletters

31. What are some of the distinctive characteristics of law reviews and academic journals?

32. *Taxes—The Tax Magazine* published the conference proceeding from what annual meeting?

33. What type of articles would a reader find in the *National Tax Journal* and *The Journal of the American Tax Association?* What organizations publish these journals?

34. What type of articles would you expect to find in *Tax Advisor* versus the type you would expect to find in *Journal of Limited Liability Companies?* Which one of these would you expect to be published monthly and which quarterly?

35. How do newsletters of major tax services tie their stories to their service's editorial materials?

36. How is the news service on CCH's Tax Research NetWork different from RIA's Checkpoint news service?

37. What is one of the most outstanding features of the CCH *Federal Tax Articles* that is not available in most other journal indexes? How does

the organizational framework of the CCH *Federal Tax Articles* differ from the WG&L *Index to Federal Tax Articles?*

38. What are three methods that can be used to locate articles in the CCH *Federal Tax Articles?* Can these same three methods of locating an article be used with the WG&L *Index to Federal Tax Articles?* Explain your answer.

39. How frequently are the journal indexes *Federal Tax Articles* and *Index to Federal Tax Articles* updated?

40. On what electronic services are the journal indexes *Federal Tax Articles* and *Index to Federal Tax Articles* offered?

EXERCISES

41. Using the RIA Checkpoint opening screen, answer the following questions.
    a. Expand the *Federal Tax Coordinator 2d*. What are the subheadings listed?
    b. What is the earliest Congress listed in the Legislation materials available?
    c. What templates are available in the Form/Line Finder?
    d. What are the Practice areas available in Checkpoint?

42. Indicate the beginning year in which the following documents are included in RIA Checkpoint.
    a. Actions on Decisions
    b. Delegation Orders
    c. Notices
    d. Revenue Rulings

43. Use the Index to answer the following questions.
    a. What Federal Editorial Materials have indexes?
    b. In the FTC, determine what paragraph addresses farmers hedging transactions for marketing.
    c. In the Current Code Topic Index, determine what Code section discusses the depletion of Kyanite.
    d. In the Code Arranged Annotations & Explanations (USRT) Topic Index, determine which paragraph discussed rental pools.

44. Use the Tool function of Checkpoint to answer the following questions.
    a. With the savings tool, determine how much you need to start saving now (based on your current age) to have $1 million when you are sixty-five. Use an expected rate of return of 6 percent and expected inflation rate of 2.5 percent. Repeat the process adding ten years to your current age.
    b. With the auto tool, determine whether it would be better to buy or lease an automobile. The cost of the car is $30,000 and the down payment is $1,000. Assume a rate of return and interest rate of 8 percent, sales tax rate of 7 percent, and depreciation rate of 20 percent. The loan would be for five years. The lease option would be for three years with $100 in fees and $500 for a security deposit. The residual of the car would be 60 percent.

45. Use RIA Checkpoint to answer the following questions.
    a. What are the thesaurus alternatives for "car"?
    b. Using the Table of Contents, determine what section (paragraph) of the Pension Funding equity Act of 2004 allows airlines and steel companies to reduce certain single-employer defined benefit plans contributions for up to two plan years.
    c. What is the full citation for a Supreme Court case in 1977 involving GM Leasing Corporation?
    d. What Code section does Private Letter Ruling 200422053 involve?

46. Using the CCH NetWork, indicate what is the most recent entry for the following.
    a. Volume of *Taxes—The Tax Magazine* available
    b. Revenue Procedure available through Advance Release Documents
    c. State Court of Appeals case in the Advance Releases Documents for the state of Ohio (Hint: Use State tab)
    d. Volume of *Journal of Retirement Planning* Archive

47. Using the CCH Network Topical Indexes Database, determine the following.
    a. The listings for the letter "K" in the *Internal Revenue Code* index
    b. The number of listings under Bermuda in the *Tax Treaties Reporter*
    c. The letter "Q" in the *US Masters Tax Guide*

48. Under the Search Tools Options of CCH NetWork, determine the following.
    a. What date restriction options are available?
    b. When CCH Explanations and Analysis database is selected, which parts of a document may be searched? Does you response change if only the *Standard Federal Income Tax Reporter* is selected? Explain your response.
    c. Besides sorting results by relevance and indicating the maximum number of documents to show, what other options are in the Search Results section?

49. Use CCH Tax Research NetWork to answer the following questions.
    a. Who were the staff members (not legislatures) that participated in the issuance of the Joint Committee on Taxation "Blue Book" General Explanation of Tax Legislation Enacted in the 107th Congress, JCS 1-03 (January 28, 2003)?
    b. What is the most recent Private Letter Ruling Listed in Federal Tax Day? Give the full citation of the PLR and section to which it pertains.
    c. The Tax Practice Guides provide an explanation of using a doubt as to collectibility in an offer in compromise. What is this doubt based upon?
    d. Determine the maximum amount of § 179 deduction for 1999.

50. Use the CCH NetWork Tool Tab to answer the following questions.
    a. What is the per diem maximum for meals and lodging for a three-day stay (September 10–12, 2004) in Dublin, Georgia?
    b. Using the Federal withholding calculator, determine the estimated tax due (or refund) for yourself based on what you expect your income and family situation to be five years from now. Print the calculated page to turn in.

c. Using the Multistate Quick Answer Chart, determine the gasoline tax per gallon in the state of Oregon.

51. In Kleinrock TaxExpert®, determine the location where each of the following may be found.
   a. Compliance tip for filing child's return who is subject to the Kiddie Tax, when parents do not want to extend the child's return
   b. Qualified Tuition Reduction Programs
   c. Alimony Trusts
   d. Treatment of State death taxes for individuals dying after 2004

52. Using the Internet version of Kleinrock TaxExpert®, determine the function of each of these advanced search word operators and give an example of its use.
   a. The ? operator
   b. The < keywords > operator
   c. The * operator

53. Examine the latest edition of Kleinrock Federal Tax Bulletin.
   a. What is the volume and issue number?
   b. What are the titles of the articles?
   c. What is the most recent Revenue Ruling listed in the Briefs?
   d. Explain what is included in a "Highlight" entry.

54. Indicate the relevant information requested for CCH *Standard Federal Income Tax Reporter*, paragraph ¶ 12,623.025.
   a. What is the title for the paragraph and Code section?
   b. What Regulations apply to this paragraph? Where are the paragraph numbers for the Regulations?
   c. What are the current developments for this paragraph?
   d. What related topics are given for this paragraph?

55. Indicate the relevant information requested using RIA Checkpoint to locate § 521.
   a. What FTC paragraphs discuss the exemption of farmers' cooperatives [§ 521(b)(1)]? Provide paragraph number and title.
   b. What Regulations were issued on this Code Section? What are their titles?
   c. In what years and by what public laws was this section amended?
   d. What is the title of the Committee Report for PL 99-272?

56. Find the following Law Journals and provide the title to the article by the author indicated.
   a. *Akron Tax Journal*: Volume 19 by Stephanie Reinhart.
   b. *Virginia Tax Review*: Volume 23 by Nina J. Crimm.
   c. *Florida Tax Review*: Volume 6 by Erik M. Jensen.
   d. *Tax Law Review*: Volume 57 by Daniel N. Shaviro.

57. Locate the annual proceeding for *Institute on Federal Taxation* (New York University), Volume 62.
   a. For what year is Volume 62?
   b. Who is the publisher of the proceedings?
   c. What is the title of Chapter 9? Who is the author?

58. Locate the annual proceedings for *Major Tax Planning* (University of Southern California) for 2003.
    a. What is the volume number for 2003?
    b. Who is the publisher of the proceedings?
    c. What is the title of Chapter 9? Who is the author?

59. Use CCH's *Federal Tax Articles* index to answer the following questions.
    a. For the 2003 summary reports 491–496, give the proper citation of the second article listed that discusses § 2511.
    b. What is the most recent article discussing exempt entities organized as a Limited Liability Company (LLC)?
    c. Give the title of the September 2000 article listed for Eugene W. Seago. In what journal was it published?
    d. What is the date on the last update filed in your library's current binder of *Federal Tax Articles?* (Check behind the tab "Last Report Letter" to find the answer.)

60. Use CCH's *Federal Tax Articles* index to determine the publication schedule for the following journals.
    a. *CPA Journal*
    b. *Florida Law Review*
    c. *Today's CPA*
    d. *International Lawyer*

61. Use the WG&L *Index to Federal Tax Articles* to perform the following tasks. Include in your response the supplement and page number where each answer is located.
    a. Give the title and co-author of the 2003 article by Sanjay Gupta that is in the *Journal of Law and Economics*.
    b. Locate a 2000 article on holding offsetting positions in mark-to-market straddles by Hillary Johnson. Under what topical heading did you find an article? In what journal is the article printed?
    c. Who are the co-authors with Stephen T. Limberg of an article appearing in the *National Tax Journal?*
    d. What is the most recent article on Professional Responsibilities?

62. Find two current articles on assumptions of liabilities under § 357 using the CCH *Federal Tax Articles* index. Find the same two articles in the WG&L *Index to Federal Tax Articles.*
    a. List the title of the articles and provide the index name, volume, and page number on which each citation was found.
    b. Find two different articles on § 357 using the WG&L *Index to Federal Tax Articles.*
    c. Compare the search strategies in using each index. Which one provides easier access?

63. Find an article on constructive ownership of stock that appeared in *Taxes* in February 2003 using the CCH *Federal Tax Articles* index. Find the same article using the WG&L *Index to Federal Tax Articles.*
    a. List the article in standard citation format and provide the index name, volume, and page number on which the citation was found.
    b. Compare the search strategies in using each index. Which one provides easier access?

64. Find current articles written by Rolf Auster using the CCH *Federal Tax Articles* index. Now use the WG&L *Index to Federal Tax Articles* to determine the recent articles written by Rolf Auster.
    a. List the title of the most recent article and the journals in which it appeared. Provide the index name, volume, and page number on which the citation was found.
    b. Which index provided a more extensive list of articles by Rolf Auster written from 1998 to present?
    c. What would you guess that Rolf Auster's specialty area is?
    d. Compare the search strategies in using each index. Which one provides easier access?

65. Using the information collected in Exercises 61, 62, and 63, discuss the compatibility of the CCH *Federal Tax Articles* and the WG&L *Index to Federal Tax Articles* with the three methods of locating an article (by Code section, by author, and by topic).

RESEARCH CASES

The following research cases may be answered using either the electronic or published services discussed in this chapter.

66. Candidate Feldman ran for Congress in 2006, raising $1.7 million for the campaign, including $300,000 in Federal matching amounts. Seven months after his opponent had been sworn into office, auditors discovered that Feldman had kept $150,000 of campaign proceeds for a personal vacation, taken immediately after the unsuccessful campaign. What are the tax consequences of this unexpected use of election funds?

67. Brian is required under a divorce decree to pay alimony of $1,000 per month and child support of $1,500 per month. Brian has only been paying $2,000 per month because he thinks the child support requirement is too high. On Brian's tax return, what portion of the payments does he treat as alimony and what part is considered child support?

68. Which of the following items qualifies for the child care credit claimed by the Rodriguez family?
    - Salary for nanny
    - Employer's share of FICA tax for nanny, paid by Rodriguez
    - Employee's share of FICA tax for nanny, paid by Rodriguez
    - Health insurance premiums on nanny, paid by Rodriguez
    - One-half of nanny's hotel bill while on her own during a European vacation, paid by Rodriguez
    - Dry cleaning bills for nanny's clothes soiled by youngsters, paid by Rodriguez

69. Kenny has been a waiter at the Burger Pitt for four years. The Pitt treats its employees well, allowing them a 30 percent discount for any food that they buy and consume on the premises. This year, the value of this discount for Kenny amounted to $500 for days on which he was working, and $150 for days when he was not assigned to work but still

stopped by during mealtimes. How much gross income must Kenny recognize this year with respect to the discount plan?

70. Ollie died this year in September, after a long illness. His wages prior to death totaled $15,000, and his state taxes thereon came to $600.
    a. Who must file Ollie's last tax return?
    b. How is the return signed?
    c. Who collects Ollie's $440 Federal refund?

71. When Fifi, a sheriff's deputy, was injured on the job, she was allowed under her contract with the state to choose between a $1,000 weekly sick-pay distribution and a $700 weekly workers' compensation payment. What must Fifi include in gross income with respect to her $1,000 weekly check?

72. Willie was tired of cleaning up the messes that his wife made in their house. One morning, he found a crumpled Kleenex on the bathroom vanity, so he disgustedly flushed it down the toilet. Unfortunately, the Kleenex was wrapped around Barbara's engagement ring, which she had removed the previous evening after cutting her finger while shoveling snow. Is the couple allowed a deductible casualty loss for Federal income tax purposes under IRC § 165?

73. Louella was born into a poor family that lives in a poor section of town. She recently got a job as wardrobe consultant at High Fashions, Ltd., a retailer of expensive women's clothing at an Elm Grove shopping mall. Can Louella claim a § 162 business expense deduction on her Federal income tax return for the cost and upkeep of the expensive Yves St. Laurent outfits that she is required to wear on the job?

74. Harriet purchased a variety of birth control devices during the year. To what extent, and under what circumstances, do such items qualify under § 213 for a medical expense deduction?

75. Phyllis sued Martin's estate and won a $65,000 settlement. She showed the probate court that she carried out her end of a compensatory arrangement with her companion, where she provided "traditional wifely services" without benefit of matrimony during Martin's life in exchange for all of his estate. Martin left his entire estate to his faithful dog, via a trust. How much gross income is recognized by Phyllis?

76. How much gross income is recognized by Carol, who received $10,000 damages (two months' salary) for pain and suffering due to the school administration's critical reaction to her negative comments about ineffective recruiting of minority athletes?

77. Carol and Jerry, LLP, pay the monthly bill at the Good Eats Cafe. The two accountants eat lunch there every day and discuss business. Sometimes they invite friends who work at other CPA firms to join them so they can keep up with what is happening in the accounting community. Are these meals deductible?

78. Lila personally bought three insurance policies on her life. She borrowed $28,500 and prepaid the first five years' worth of annual payments on a whole life policy. In addition, she borrowed $4,200 and paid

one of the two required premiums on a group term policy through her professional organization. Finally, she borrowed $3,000 and bought into a utilities mutual fund; principal and interest of the fund's assets were to be appropriated in a timely fashion by Lila to make payments on a five-premium endowment contract. Interest charges for the three loans were $3,500, $420, and $310, respectively. How much of this interest can Lila deduct?

79. CPA Joe reimburses a client for a $75,000 tax liability that is traceable to Joe's bad tax advice. For fear of increasing his already steep malpractice insurance premiums, Joe does not file a claim with the insurer. Can Joe deduct the $75,000 loss?

80. Gardener Toni lent Harry a new $500 lawn mower. Harry ruined the lawn mower, but replaced it with a $425 model. Later in the same year, Toni lent Harry $5,000 for bail, $3,000 to start a fencing operation, and $15 for a meal. According to Harry's parole officer, none of these items ever will be paid back. Can Toni deduct any of these losses?

81. Geraldine bought a Kandinsky for her art collection from a mail-order advertisement for $310,000. The painting, however, was actually painted by Koepke and, according to Geraldine's dealer, was not worth more than $3,100. What is her deductible loss upon discovery of the forgery?

82. You were visiting the tax department of a CPA firm recently when you overheard two of the staff discussing "QTPs" and how distributions from them are now treated when "the credits" are involved. They mentioned that a tax act may have modified the treatment. You would like to know what "QTPs" are and what credits might affect the treatment of the distributions. Find two journal articles that discuss "QTPs" after the passage of the Economic Growth and Tax Relief Reconciliation Act of 2001. Write a one-page paper defining a "QTP" and describing the coordination of distributions from "QTPs" and educational credits and educational IRAs. Attach to your paper the first page of each article referenced.

83. It is 3 a.m. and your dog just ate your only copy of the Code. (Some dogs will eat anything!) Find a text version of the Code on the Internet and print § 61. Where did you find the Code? Who maintains the site? Send the site manager an e-mail message, expressing your appreciation for the manager's hard work in keeping the site up to date. Print your e-mail, and if you get an answer, print it also. Does the version of the Code you found use text hyper-links? What happens when you click on a hyper-link? Download and print a copy of a page with hyper-links, then click on several hyper-links and print the page to which it links.

84. Bob Carburetor is the new owner of Carburetor Cars. Bob's brother Bill has owned an auto dealership for years, Radiator Cars. Bob decides to adopt all of his brother's accounting methods. At Radiator Cars, when a vehicle is sold, the dealership tries to sell an auto service contract. The amounts received for these contracts are placed into an escrow account. The agreements grant the buyers the right to have parts or components covered by the contract repaired or replaced, whenever the

covered parts experience a mechanical difficulty. The dealer will provide the services or will reimburse the car buyer for the reasonable cost of repair or replacement. Normally, the buyer returns the vehicle to the dealer for repair, but this is not required. In either case, the repairs or replacements have to be authorized in advance by an administrator hired by Radiator Cars. Fees to the administrator of the contracts are paid out of the escrow account. Is this the proper tax treatment for these service contracts?

85. Betty Jo Harris lives in Maine with her son Rick and husband Walter Reed. Rick has Lou Gehrig's disease. Rick's physician encourages Betty Jo to go to a Lou Gehrig's disease conference at the Mayo Clinic in Rochester, Minnesota, so she can learn how to better take care of Rick. Betty takes the doctor's advice and flies to Rochester. Besides the cost of the plane ticket, Betty Jo incurs the following types of expenses: meals, lodging, phone calls home, cleaning (she dumps her taco salad on her lap at lunch) and conference registration fees. The leading speaker at the conference suggested that caregivers take their sick patients to destinations in warm climates to improve their state of mind and general condition. When Betty returns home, she arranges a two month trip (January and February) to the Bahamas for Rick and herself. One week after they have arrived in the Bahamas, Rick's father, Walter, arrives and stays for a couple of weeks. Advise Betty Jo as to whether any of these expenses are deductible as medical expenses.

EXTENSIVE CASES

86. Helen Hanks, who lives in San Francisco, California, has just been promoted to manager of the divisional office. However, the divisional office is located in Portland, Oregon. Helen's significant other, Tom Hunt, will be moving with her to Portland. Helen's children from a previous marriage will also be joining her in Portland. The children have been living with their father in Spain for the last year.

Helen easily sells the San Francisco house in which she and Tom live. Helen is the sole owner of the house. However, she has a harder time finding the right home in Portland. Helen has to make several trips to Portland before buying a house under construction. It won't be available for occupancy for at least 20 days after she arrives in Portland. Tom accompanied Helen on the house hunting trips to give his opinion on the houses and to look for a new job.

The actual move takes place as follows. The movers arrive on Wednesday to pack up Helen's and Tom's household items. Thursday, the movers pack up Helen's items from a storage unit located outside of the city and her sailboat. The movers then leave for Portland. Helen hires someone to drive her car to Portland; the driver leaves on Friday. On Saturday, after dropping Helen at the airport for her flight to Portland, Tom leaves to drive his car to Portland via Salt Lake City, Utah, where he visits his brother. Helen and Tom stayed in a hotel Wednesday to Friday while still in San Francisco and upon arriving in Portland until the house is ready for occupancy. The moving company stores their household items at its warehouse until Helen and Tom are ready to move in. Helen's children arrive two weeks after she and Tom have finally moved into the new house.

Helen pays for all of the costs involved in selling the San Francisco home and moving Tom, the children, and herself to Portland in November of the current year. Helen's employer eventually reimburses her (in March of the next year) for 75 percent of all costs of moving the household items (Helen's and Tom's), Helen's car, and two house hunting trips. The employer also reimburses Helen for 50 percent of the total hotel and meal costs while she and Tom were in Portland and waiting for the completion of their home. Advise Helen on the tax consequences of the above events.

87. Mark and Leslee Jones were married in 1995. Mark has an MBA from Harvard and worked in the financial markets in New York City. Leslee has a degree in Hotel Administration and worked for the Hilton Hotel until two years ago when Mark and Leslee moved to California. They moved to California because Mark lost his job. He had been accused of embezzlement and charges had been filed against him. However, the charges were dropped because the firm for which Mark worked did not want to be involved in a public scandal. Mark admitted the embezzlement to Leslee and promised if they stayed married and moved, he would never embezzle again. In California, Mark obtained a job as the chief financial officer of a mid-size company. His salary, while about 60 percent of his former salary, was still over $200,000.

Mark likes to gamble. He does so by betting on horse races, going to Las Vegas, playing in the stock market, and buying speculative real estate. The reason he had embezzled the money at his former job was to cover his gambling and stock market losses. While in California, he continued to bet on horse races and visit Las Vegas to gamble. Leslee accompanied him to the race tracks and to Las Vegas. Since Mark was known as a big gambler, their rooms were always provided for free, as were any costs associated with their stays in Las Vegas. Leslee would watch Mark gamble for a while, get bored, and then go to see shows or go shopping. Leslee liked to shop and spent thousands of dollars at a time.

As to the investment speculations, Leslee did not help in the decisions to purchase stock or real estate. However, she did sign all purchase and sell agreements for real estate, as California is a community property state. Any proceeds from the sales were paid to both Mark and Leslee. She endorsed all checks, which were deposited in their joint checking account. Leslee and Mark both wrote checks out of this account. What Leslee did not know is that Mark had a separate account into which he deposited much of his gambling winnings and stock gains.

In the current year, the Jones's prior two tax returns are audited and material omissions are found. The embezzled money was never reported, gambling gains were substantially understated, and gains on the sale of stock and real estate were omitted from the returns. Shortly after the notice from the IRS as to their findings regarding the audits, Leslee filed for divorce for obvious reasons. What tax-related advice do you have for Mark and Leslee? Leslee would like to apply for innocent spouse protection from the tax liabilities. She claims that she had no knowledge of any of the under reporting on their tax returns. Mark and Leslee always used a CPA to prepare their returns.

Chapter 7

Legal Services and Internet Sites

LEARNING OBJECTIVES

- Know the major features of legal services.
- Use the search methodologies that are available with each of the legal services.
- Understand the connectors, universal characters, and proximity commands applicable to each legal service.

- Know which legal services are most appropriate for different research objectives.
- Recognize the major tax newsletters and law reviews.
- Become familiar with Internet sources of tax information.

CHAPTER OUTLINE

Continuing with the survey of tax research tools, this chapter examines the tax products available through legal service providers and Internet sources. The services covered in Chapter 6 were designed strictly for tax research, whereas the major services covered in this chapter, Lexis and Westlaw, were originally developed for attorneys to provide research capabilities in a wide variety of legal arenas. Therefore, they are oriented toward legal research. Since tax is one of the legal domains, legal services are amenable to tax research. Further, the service providers are adapting their products to be user friendly to tax practitioners in the accounting profession. Both Lexis and Westlaw offer individual bundling of products, and for their larger accounting firm clients, create special web interfaces.

While there are numerous legal services that could be reviewed, the coverage in this chapter is limited to services most likely to be found in the "libraries" of tax practitioners. Only the tax products offered by these services will be discussed. Chapter 8 examines the case law products of these services, and Chapter 9 provides more detailed information regarding the state tax products available through the legal and tax services.

LEXIS

The amount of information available on the **LexisNexis** system is staggering. With more than 4 billion searchable documents, 2 billion U.S. public records, and 35,000 legal, business, and news sources included in LexisNexis, it is possibly the world's largest full-text information source. About the only tax services not obtainable on Lexis are RIA and Westlaw.

Lexis, for legal (tax) sources, was started in 1973 and **Nexis,** for news, financial, and business information, was started in 1979. The LexisNexis services were initially offered on dedicated terminals because they were developed long before the universal use of personal computers. These services are now offered on the Internet with yearly, weekly, or daily subscriptions and on a pay-for-document credit card system. Documents can be retrieved for a nominal cost and conducting the search is free.

SELECTING AND SEARCHING A DATABASE

Lexis is structured differently than the electronic services reviewed in Chapter 6. A researcher cannot access all the databases within Lexis in a single search, as is possible with the RIA and CCH services. Rather, Lexis is structured somewhat like a tree. The main libraries are located on the trunk of the tree, and the databases within the libraries are the various branches of the tree. At each level in the database selection process the branch is narrowing until the researcher reaches the end of the branch. For example, the opening screen in Exhibit 7–1 shows the major libraries (as folder tabs) within Lexis: Legal, News & Business, and Public Records. Selecting Legal leads to a listing of databases within the legal library. Taxation is one of the Areas of

Exhibit 7-1

Lexis Opening Legal Screen

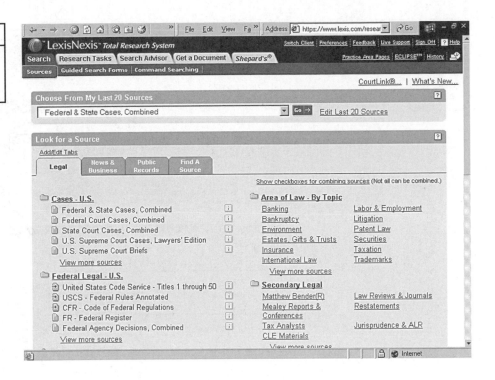

Law – By Topic that may be selected. Any of the topics listed may be added to the set of folder tabs by simply selecting the option when it is offered on screen.

The Search option provides three different methods for searching (see Exhibit 7–1). Users can search by Sources, Guided Search Forms, and Command Searching. To search using the Command Searching option the researcher must be familiar with database abbreviations, Lexis commands for searching, and dot commands for format. Using this option is beyond the introductory level and will not be covered further. A novice can master the other two methods of searching, however. The Guided Search Forms steers the researcher to the appropriate database to use by a process of drilling down through the series of headings. After a database is selected, keywords may be entered and date restrictions can be applied (see Exhibit 7–2). The problem with this method is that more than one tax database cannot be searched at a time. Exhibit 7–2 shows a partial list of the Lexis tax databases. Notice that the *Internal Revenue Code* is listed in a separate database from the other primary sources. This means that the researcher would have to perform a minimum of two searches with the same keywords to cover all primary sources.

The final method under the Search option is by Sources. This is again a process of locating the database of interest. As shown across the top of Exhibit 7–3, the drill down continued for several more iterations until a single

Exhibit	7-2

Lexis Guided
Search Forms:
Area of Law

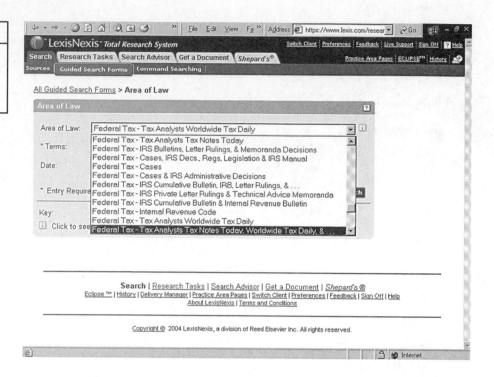

Exhibit	7-3

Lexis Search
Screen

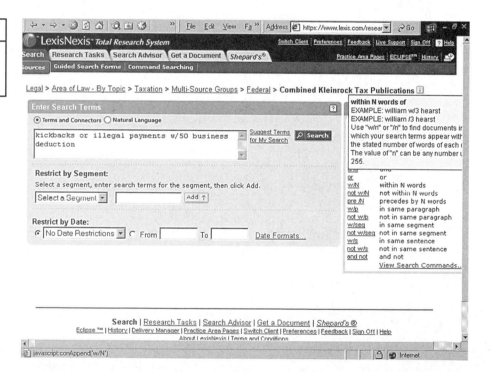

database, Combined Kleinrock Tax Publications, was reached. Rather than drilling through the library lists, the researcher can search for a database or library by entering the Find a Source tab shown in Exhibit 7–1. A source search can be located by either entering part or all of its title in the source entry box or selecting the first letter of the title.

Lexis offers the researcher a choice of natural language or **terms and connectors (Boolean)** types of searches (see Exhibit 7–3). With a **natural language** search, the tax question is entered in standard English (natural language) words, phrases, (entered within quotation marks), or sentences. The program determines the key terms for searching and relationships among the words (i.e., connectors to apply). This type of search is useful when the researcher is unsure as to which keywords would be the most effective.

Lexis supports numerous search connectors and **wildcard (universal) characters** in its terms and connectors searches. Many of the connectors and their definitions are listed on the right in Exhibit 7–3. Running the cursor over any of the terms displays an example and explains when to use the connector. Exhibit 2–9 in Chapter 2 also lists the most common connectors and their meaning. It is important to note that Lexis interprets a space between words as signifying a connection of words in a phrase and not as "and" in the usual sense. For example, if the researcher enters the words "kickback business deduction" with no connectors, Lexis identifies only documents with these three words appearing next to each other. To search for any occurrence of these words in the document, they must be entered with "and" in between them—"kickback and business and deduction."

Below the Search Term box are additional options to improve the search results. The options vary depending on whether terms and connectors or a natural language search has been selected. With a terms and connectors search, the researcher may restrict the search to a segment of the document (see Exhibit 7–3). The segments include title, author, headings, text, publication, footnotes, and endnotes. A date restriction is also available. The researcher selects either a previous period of time (e.g., previous week, month, year) or specifies a period (from . . . to . . .). The default is no date restriction. The date option is particularly beneficial when updating earlier research or when trying to locate tax law for a prior tax year.

Besides the two options for terms and connectors searches, a natural language search offers two other options. The Suggest Terms for My Search feature offers additional terms that can be added by the researcher as keywords to the natural language search. The terms suggested are based on the content of the natural search entered by the researcher. This option is useful when the researcher is having trouble identifying appropriate keywords. The other option available permits the researcher to restrict the search by requiring that certain terms appear anywhere in the document or in a specified document segment. These mandatory terms will restrict the documents retrieved to those pertinent to the project.

Another method of locating documents is by employing the Research Task feature. After selecting an area of law from the list provided, a search screen appears. If practitioners perform most of their searches in one area of the law, such as tax, this may be set as the default for the Research Task option. The search screen is full of choices, information, and search entry boxes. Exhibit 7–4 includes only part of this screen. The researcher can search tax sources, review tax news and legal developments, perform quick searches by citations or terms, search within a selected tax publisher, and learn more information. There are so many choices that it may take time to choose the best search to use!

The Search Advisor feature is designed to be used by someone needing help getting started searching. The Search Advisor is a finding tool for databases in the researcher's area of interest. It can help narrow the tax issue, identify the database to search, and formulate the query. The researcher can find a legal topic by either a keyword search or browsing the list of topics provided. At any point in the narrowing process of the legal topics, keywords may be entered and a search performed. The results give the drilled down locations of documents that may be relevant.

The last search feature is Get a Document. Documents can be retrieved by Citation, Party Name, or Docket Number. The citations must be entered in a format recognized by Lexis. If the researcher is not familiar with the Lexis format, one can use Citations Formats to provide a template for the citation. Since Lexis has thousands of document formats, the researcher can search for the format either by entering part or all of the title or by browsing by the first letter of the title. The Party Name option will find a case by plaintiff's and defendant's names. If only one name is known, such as the taxpayer's, it may be the sole entry. The jurisdiction for the case must also be selected.

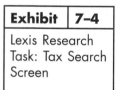

Exhibit 7–4

Lexis Research Task: Tax Search Screen

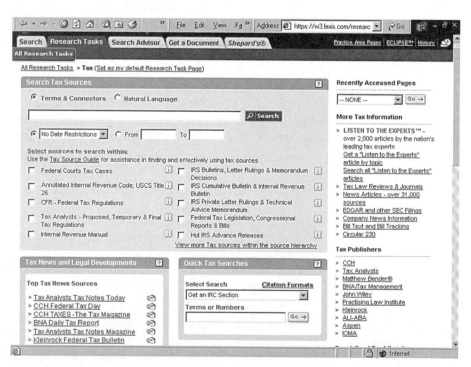

When the researcher is unsure, the combined Federal and state databases or just combined Federal should be selected. The third Get a Document option is to search by Docket Number. A jurisdiction must also be identified with this option. Obviously, this and the Party Name options are exclusively for case searches.

SPOTLIGHT ON TAXATION: The Huge Two

Two companies dominate the realm of providing legal and tax information, Reed Elsevier and Thomson. These corporations are two of the largest publishing and information providers in the world. Reed Elsevier, an Anglo-Dutch company, is the parent company of LexisNexis; Thomson owns Westlaw, RIA, and WG&L. Through LexisNexis and Westlaw, the tax practitioner has access to virtually every major tax publication. While CCH is a separate company owned by Wolters Kluwer, CCH has a longstanding relationship and multi-year agreement with LexisNexis. It is the only source, other than CCH itself, to offer web access to CCH products. In addition, LexisNexis offers BNA, Tax Analysts, Matthew Bender, Shepard's, and Kleinrock. Westlaw also offers access to BNA products as well as all of the RIA and WG&L products.

DOCUMENTS

Lexis offers four viewing choices for the documents identified by the search: Cite, KWIC, Full, or Custom. The **Cite** view lists the citations for the retrieved documents. Partial sentences are reproduced under each citation to give the researcher an idea of how the keywords are used within the document. Up to ten retrieved document citations will be listed on the initial screen.

With **KWIC** (keyword in context) view as seen in Exhibit 7–5, each document is presented on a separate screen. To move from one document to the next, click on either the "next" arrow at the top of the screen or the directional arrows for Doc at the bottom of the screen. The number of the document from the Cite view can also be entered in the Doc box. The keywords are displayed contextually in the document. The keyword being highlighted is designated in the Term box, also at the bottom of the screen (see Exhibit 7–5), and may be changed by the researcher. The researcher may set the breadth of the context. Clicking once on "KWIC + 25" term brings up the screen to set the context level. From one to 999 words can be displayed on either side of the highlighted keywords, the default being twenty-five words. Make sure the SuperKWIC is "On" when trying to set the number of context words in a natural language search.

Full view displays the full text of the document (cases, law, etc.) or a section of the document (treatises) with highlighted keywords. Lastly, the Custom view allows researchers to designate which parts of the documents are displayed. Thus, the Custom view is merely a modification of the Full view. If all segments are selected, the document view is Full. The list of segments

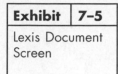

Exhibit   7-5

Lexis Document
Screen

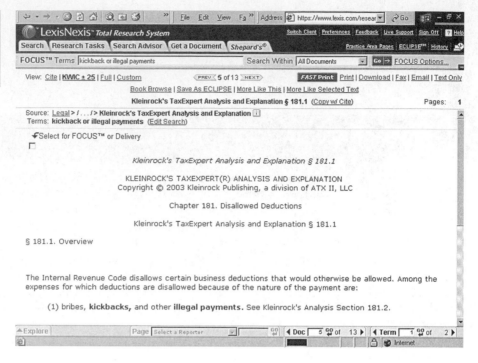

choices includes publication, cite, heading, section, supplement, text, footnotes, and endnotes. The Custom view option saves the researcher time when printing or downloading a document because only those segments of interest to the researcher need be included.

The document screen in Exhibit 7-5 will be the basis for the remaining discussion of Lexis. The "Book Browse" feature enables the researcher to browse the document as if it were in print. Browsing offers the researcher the ability to "flip through the pages" and find the area of interest without having to print the document. This can be more efficient when the researcher is acquainted with the document but does not remember the exact page where the pertinent information is located. Finally, two unique features of Lexis accessible on Exhibit 7-5 are the More Like This and More Like Selected Text options. Both of these options are offered only after an initial search has been completed. The More Like This derives core terms from documents with similar language patterns. The researcher can select any or all of these words as search terms. Additional terms or phrases and/or mandatory terms may also be included. The More Like Selected Text performs a similar search. A passage from a retrieved document is selected and entered into the search box by clicking on More Like Selected Text. Mandatory terms may also be added. The documents identified by this search will be utilizing the passage terms in a context similar to the original document. This helps to eliminate documents containing the terms of interest used in an entirely different manner.

LexisNexis Academic

LexisNexis offers a customized version of its services to academic institutions and public libraries called **LexisNexis Academic**. While the complete LEXIS/NEXIS service provides full-text documents from over 5,600 publications, most library subscriptions do not carry all of the offerings. The sources in Academic include the following.

- National and regional newspapers, wire services, broadcast transcripts, international news, and non-English language sources.
- Federal and state case law, Code, Regulations, law reviews, legal journals and international information.
- Shepard's citations for all U.S. Supreme Court cases from the late 1700s to present.
- Business news journals, company financial information, SEC filings and reports, and industry and market news.

To perform tax research using Academic, select Legal Research from the Academic Search Forms list (see Exhibit 7–6). The Legal Research libraries pertaining to tax law would be Case Law and Codes & Regulations. One of the options offered under Case Law, Area of Law by Topic, appears promising (see Exhibit 7–7). However, this choice leads to a dead end. Tax is not one of the topic areas listed. A more productive option is Tax Law found under Codes & Regulations. This library contains most of the primary tax sources (Code, Regulations, court cases, IRS pronouncements, etc.) and secondary sources of law reviews and journals by several different publishers (see

Exhibit	7–6

LexisNexis Academic Opening Screen

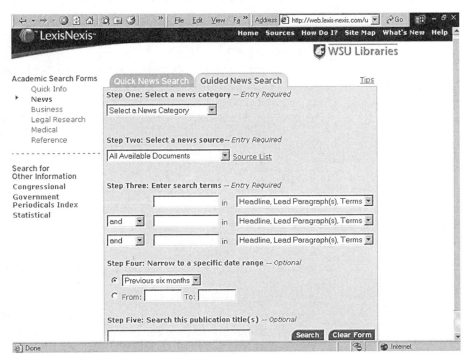

Exhibit   7-7

LexisNexis
Academic Tax
Law Search
Screen

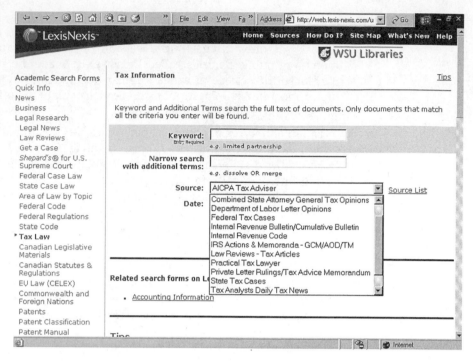

Exhibit 7-7). Each of these databases is keyword searchable, but only one database may be searched at a time. This can cause a search on Academic to be more time consuming than one in services that allow multiple database searches.

Since Tax Law uses a full-text search technique, the Quick search method is not an option in Exhibit 7-7. To view a brief description of each source, use the "Tips" button. More extensive information about the data source selected by the researcher is hyper-linked to Source List. The source selected may be searched by Keyword and Boolean connectors may be used. The Narrow Search with Additional Terms option (see Exhibit 7-7) is particularly useful when too many documents have been found on the target topic. Almost all of the documents retrieved through the Academic searches are full text and may be downloaded, e-mailed, or printed from the browser by the user.

TAX ANALYSTS

Tax Analysts is a nonprofit entity whose mission is to be "respectfully disagreeable" in order to create tax policy debate, support the debate with news and commentaries, and provide literary forums for the discussion of taxation for the purpose of facilitating taxation that is fair, simple and efficient. It disseminates timely and comprehensive state, Federal, and international tax information through its daily, weekly, and monthly print publications, scholarly books, and electronic database services. It also is known for its outstanding news publications, such as *Tax Notes* and *Tax Notes Today*.

RESEARCH LIBRARY

Federal

The **Federal Research Library** is available at two levels of service, Basic and Complete. The Basic service contains both primary and secondary sources that are updated on a frequent and regular basis to ensure that the most current and reliable information is available. The Basic Library includes the following.

- Code & Regulations.
- Documents issued by the IRS and publications such as *Circular 230*.
- Recent legislation and IRS Regulatory Agenda.
- More than twenty quick reference tables.
- Federal Tax Baedeker.
- Joint Committee on Taxation (JCT) Blue Book.

The Tax Analysts editorial service is **Federal Tax Baedeker**. This topical service is divided into twenty-six chapters that can be searched either by keyword or using the table of contents drill-down method. The explanations are basic plain-English guides to key Federal tax law. The coverage is not as in-depth as CCH or RIA furnishes, but it is more in the nature of the Kleinrock service. It is updated monthly.

The Complete service offers everything in the Basic plus the following.

- The Chief Counsel Advice Library including Private Letter Rulings, Technical Advice Memorandums, Field Service Advice, and other IRS guidance.
- The Court Opinions Library covering Federal tax cases.
- TaxPractice Magazine that provides weekly coverage of federal tax news.

The databases are organized into libraries. For the Basic service these libraries include Code & Regulations, All IRS Documents, and All Other Federal Tax Resources (see Exhibit 7–8). Any or all of these libraries may be searched using keywords. Also, within each library, the practitioner may select one, a few, or all of the databases.

Keywords, phrases, section numbers, or multiple terms with connectors, universal characters and proximity limits are permissible. As in the Lexis service, the program interprets a space between terms as signifying words in a phrase and not as the "and" connector. The "and" connector must be added to have the words searched as separate terms. The program searches for root words and finds common variations such as plurals, different tenses, and possessives.

Documents are retrievable by entering the citation, or by browsing a list of the documents of interest once the proper database is selected. For example, to find a specific Revenue Ruling, the researcher may enter the ruling number in the template provided for this database or select the ruling number from the dropdown menu for Revenue Rulings. For the Code, the title of each

Exhibit 7–8

Tax Analysts
Federal
Research Library
Opening Screen

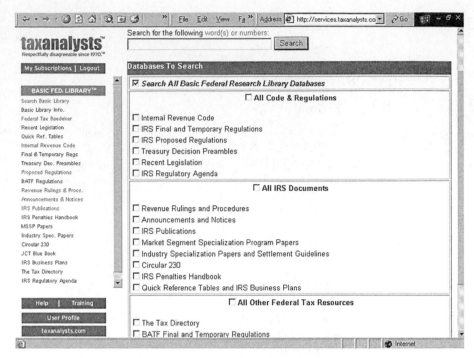

section is listed with the number, making it easier to find a section by browsing if the topic is known but not the exact section number.

State

Tax Analysts also offers a **State Research Library** that includes the following.

- Statutes and Regulations for all fifty states, the District of Columbia, and the Commonwealth of the Northern Mariana Islands. Statutes only are available for Puerto Rico (in Spanish), the U.S. Virgin Islands, American Samoa, and Guam. These are updated monthly.
- A Quick Reference State Tax Rate Chart for each state which lists corporate and personal income taxes, state sales and use taxes, estate, inheritance, and gift taxes, and gasoline taxes. This chart is updated biannually.
- State Supreme Court tax-related cases for all fifty states. Lower level cases are not currently available.

OneDisc

Tax Analysts developed a single-disc tax product, **OneDisc,** that contains an extensive list of primary Federal sources, IRS rulings and documents, full-text court cases, and the explanations of Federal Tax Baedeker included on one CD-ROM. The DVD version has 3.3 gigabytes of full-text source documents. In addition to what is on the CD-ROM, it includes more IRS documents and publications, tax cases, and U.S. Tax Treaties. Tax Analysts also offers a OneDisc with the same coverage as the State Research Library.

SPOTLIGHT ON TAXATION: Field Service Advice Memorandums

Field Service Advice (FSA) memorandums are available to the tax community thanks to Tax Analysts. In 1993, Tax Analysts filed a request under the Freedom of Information Act to have FSA memorandums be subject to public disclosure. The IRS declined this request, because these documents contained "return information" or were protected by the attorney-client privilege, and therefore were not available for public disclosure. Tax Analysts took the question to court and in 1996, a District Court ordered the IRS to release the FSAs to the general public. The court indicated that FSAs are similar to General Counsel Memoranda (GCMs) that are public information. They contain legal analysis and conclusions of the law and are not "return information" under any reasonable interpretation of § 6103. Further, just because an IRS attorney declares FSAs to be "return information" does not make them so. They are merely memorandums routinely used by the IRS as guidance in conducting audits and are therefore applied by the IRS in its dealings with the public.

NEWSLETTERS

Tax Analysts publishes an influential set of newsletters, including a daily tax news series and the periodical *Tax Notes.* **TaxBase** is the Internet service offering the newsletter databases covering up-to-the-minute Federal *(Tax Notes Today),* state *(State Tax Today),* and worldwide *(Worldwide Tax Daily)* tax news and the weekly *Tax Notes* and *State Tax Notes*. The Tax Analysts newsletters are available through Lexis.

Tax Notes Today (*TNT*) is updated continually throughout the day, not just once a day, so practitioners can be as up-to-date as they so desire. The amount of information included in these newsletters is staggering. The *TNT*, for example, includes the following.

- Commentary and analysis by experts
- IRS Private Letter Rulings, Chief Counsel advice, Revenue Rulings, Revenue Procedures, Field Service Advices, and Announcements
- IRS Final, Temporary, and Proposed Regulations, as well as public comments on Proposed Regulations
- All original full-text documents
- White House budget proposals, tax bills introduced in Congress, and coverage of other congressional action, as well as reports by the Congressional Budget Office (CBO) and the Joint Committee on Taxation (JCT)
- IRS and congressional hearing transcripts
- General Accounting Office (GAO) and Treasury Inspector General for Tax Administration (TIGTA) reports. (TIGTA was established under the IRS Restructuring and Reform Act of 1998 to provide independent oversight of IRS activities.)

The content of the weekly *Tax Notes* publication is similar to *TNT* and the *Weekly Report* published by BNA (discussed later in this chapter). However, *Tax Notes* includes in-depth analysis of court decisions, regulatory pronouncements, and policy-oriented research submitted by tax professionals and academics, as Exhibit 7–9 illustrates. Special sections provide news and practice tips just for accounting and tax practitioners. *Tax Notes* is available in published and on-line formats. The online version offers archives, links to full-text documents, PDF versions of all articles, full search capabilities, and multiple-user licenses.

To retrieve an article in *Tax Notes* the subscriber selects the document icon after the page number (see Exhibit 7–9). A document icon found within an article denotes that the preceding citation is linked to its full-text contents. The subscribers to the print version use the *Tax Notes* unique document identification numbers to facilitate retrieval of the full-text documents through an online service such as Lexis. To sample *Tax Notes* or any other Tax Analysts publication, visit the Tax Analysts web site at **http://www.taxanalysts.com.**

WESTLAW

The West Group, an authoritative legal publisher, offers tax research capabilities through its **Westlaw** service. This service is legally oriented because it was designed by attorneys for attorneys. Its orientation is evident in its structure and its emphasis on citators and citing. (The first two data entry boxes on the "Welcome" screen are for finding documents by citation.) Due to this orientation toward the legal profession, Westlaw is less represented than RIA and CCH in accounting firms. However, most international, regional

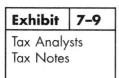

Exhibit   7–9

Tax Analysts
Tax Notes

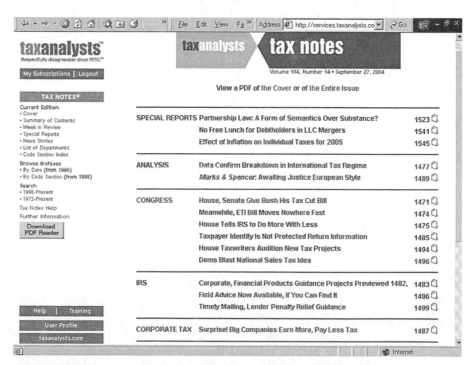

and large local CPA firms subscribe to Westlaw, especially those that hire attorneys into their tax service groups. Virtually all law schools train their students on the Westlaw system.

DATA AND ACCESS

Westlaw contains nearly 17,800 databases with information provided by numerous sources. Included in its databases are BNA *Tax Management Portfolios,* all of the RIA products including the *Federal Tax Coordinator 2d* and its citator, the Warren, Gorham & Lamont newsletters, journals, manuals, and treatises, law reviews, and various tax news services. The West Group's topical tax service, called *Mertens Law of Federal Income Taxation,* is also included in Westlaw.

As with Lexis, when Westlaw began in 1975, it required a dedicated online terminal. Now Westlaw is accessible via the Internet or with wireless and mobile devices (Westlaw Wireless). Westlaw offers tailored bundling of the databases to its customers and even provides access to its services without requiring a subscription. Using a pay-as-you-go system (credit card required), researchers can retrieve documents as necessary from Westlaw.

An attractive innovation of the West Group is customized Westlaw web sites to meet the specific professional needs of its different customers. Consequently, the appearance of the Westlaw service demonstrated in this chapter may vary from the customized site available to you through your school or employer. The basic searching strategies discussed in this section, however, are similar in all versions of Westlaw.

SEARCHING WESTLAW

When logging on to Westlaw, it may be necessary to enter a client name to proceed with the research project. This feature, included for the benefit of the tax professional, can be used to keep track of the time spent on each search by client for billing purposes.

The Welcome screen shown in Exhibit 7–10 provides access to the major features of Westlaw. The immediate options facilitate searching for a document by citation, perform a citator search, or locate a database. Also available is information about Westlaw's new products and interesting legal news. From this screen, the researcher may start a search by selecting one of the following options: Find, KeyCite, Directory, Table of Contents, or KeySearch. With the exception of KeyCite, each of these options is reviewed in this section. KeyCite is a citator and will be covered in Chapter 8, Citators and Other Finding Devices. As well as these options, Westlaw provides a file tab for accessing the news libraries. Further, the practitioner may add personalized tabs for those practice areas frequently searched. Notice, in Exhibit 7–10, a tab for the Tax practice area is given. Customizing the tabs is executed in My Westlaw (see Exhibit 7–10). Up to six personalized tabs may be added by selecting databases in the general, topical, Federal, or state jurisdictional

Exhibit | 7-10

Westlaw
Welcome Screen

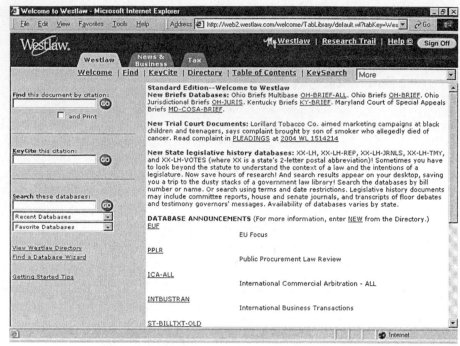

areas. The tabs can be further personalized to furnish direct access to databases most commonly accessed.

The first type of search offered in Westlaw is the Find a Document (the "Find" option). A document can be retrieved by typing the citation in the Find this Document by Citation box, if its citation is known (Exhibit 7–11). Exact spacing and punctuation is not necessary, but the Westlaw recognized citation must be known. Most Federal documents, topical materials, and law review or journal articles may be retrieved by citation. When the citation is not known, select one of the Find features: title, person, company, or database. Find Wizards helps researchers select a database to search if they are uncertain as to which database would be most efficient.

Another starting point for selecting databases to search is the Directory option. If the abbreviations of the databases desired are known, they are entered in the Search these Databases text box seen in Exhibit 7–12. Up to ten databases separated by commas or semicolons may be entered. Databases recently or frequently searched ("favorite databases") can be set up by the researcher. A list of Westlaw directories is also furnished as Exhibit 7–12 demonstrates. The researcher drills down through the directories until the topic databases desired are reached. For example, the tax practitioner would drill down to the taxation databases. To discover what is included in a database, the researcher may click on the "i" ball after the database abbreviation and a description of the scope of the database including a full listing of

Exhibit	7–11

Westlaw
Find Screen

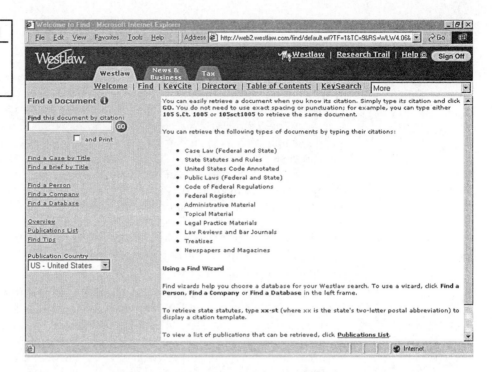

Exhibit	7–12

Westlaw
Directory Screen

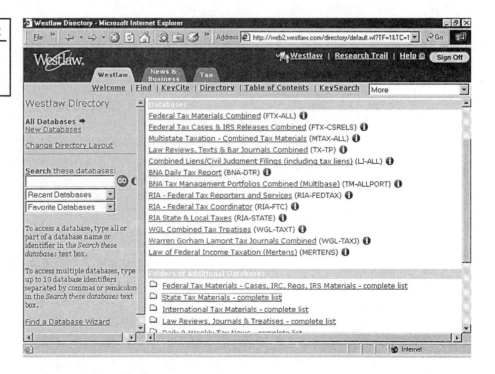

the items included will appear. As Exhibit 7–13 shows, the database selected appears at the top of the Search screen.

The researcher can search using either a natural language or terms and connectors (Boolean) keyword query. A thesaurus is conveniently available to help in selecting the best words for the search. The thesaurus is not automatically applied; however the synonyms must be added to the keywords by the researcher. The list of Westlaw connectors and expanders, which are furnished on the search screen, is similar to those of other services. Unlike other services, however, a space between two words is interpreted as an "or," not as an "and" or phrase connector. An "&" or the word "and" must be included to have an "and" connection. Westlaw likewise supports an expansive list of field restrictions such as judge, attorney, and references. Finally the date for the search documents can be limited either by selecting one of the period options provided or selecting Dates, which allows the researcher to enter specific dates for a period restriction. A list of Westlaw connectors, fields, and date options are presented in Exhibit 7–14.

The Table of Contents search option offers an expandable list of categories containing publications with tables of contents. Drilling down through the categories expands the lists. When the practitioner has reached the level of the publication desired, the document can be searched using the standard search methods. As discussed in Chapter 6, narrowing the list of databases searched can make the searching process much more effective and efficient.

Exhibit 7–13

Westlaw Search Screen

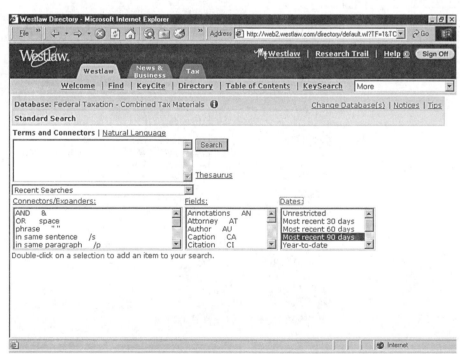

Exhibit	7–14	Westlaw Term Connectors, Fields, and Date Restrictions

Connector	Sign	Search Restriction Fields			Date Restrictions
Term Connectors					
AND	&	Annotations	Dissenting	Opinions	Unrestricted
OR	A space	Attorney	End	Prelim	Most recent 30 days
Grammatical Connectors					
	/p	Author	Docket Number	References	Most recent 60 days
	/s	Caption	Full Text	Source	Most recent 90 days
	+s	Citation	Headnote	Summary	Year-to-date
Numerical Connectors					
	/n	Concurring	Historical Note	Text	This year and last year
	+n	Court	Index	Title	Most recent 3 years
Phrase	" "	Credit	Judge	Topic	Most recent 10 years
BUT NOT	%	Digest	Notes	Year	

The results of the search will be more focused and fewer documents will be retrieved. Alternatively, the researcher may continue the drilling down until a document is identified. This is helpful when the researcher wants to read an entire chapter in a treatise, for example. Unfortunately, not all publications available through Westlaw can be accessed through the Table of Contents option.

KeySearch uses the West numbering system of key issues (topics) found in court cases as the backbone of this searching mode. The practitioner identifies the legal topic within which the research problem lies either by searching the list of topics with the word search or by drilling down through the topics presented. KeySearch formulates a query based on the underlying terms for the topic and adds the key numbers associated with the topic. The researcher can determine what type of cases will be searched as well as treatises, journals, law reviews and briefs. Other search terms can be added at the researcher's option to insure the results will be relevant. This type of search is especially effective when the researcher is unfamiliar with that particular area of the tax law.

Lastly, the More option (see Exhibit 7–13) is a pull down menu of other features available on Westlaw. Two of the more useful features are the Index and the Key Numbers & Digest. The Index feature offers indexes for United States Annotated Code and most state's statutes. Regrettably, indexes for other publications and documents are not furnished. The Key Numbers & Digest feature lists all of the West digest topics and key numbers. The legal issues in cases are assigned a topic and key number by West. These topics and key numbers can be used to find documents relevant to the question being researched.

NEWS & BUSINESS

Westlaw's Business Information and News offers a comprehensive list of news, business, and financial information from more than 8,000 sources only a few of which are visible in Exhibit 7–15. These sources include the following.

- *The Wall Street Journal*, including its European and Asian editions.
- Almost all of the top fifty daily newspapers plus thousands of international business sources.
- Newswires are continually updating the news on Westlaw.
- Business magazines such as *Barron's, Forbes, The Economist, Harvard Business Review, Business Week, Time,* and *Newsweek.*
- Company profiles and business intelligence reports for more than 450,000 companies.
- Stock quotes.
- Dun & Bradstreet Business Information Reports.

For a complete list of the Westlaw News offerings, select the View Westlaw Directory or View News & Business Directory (see Exhibit 7–15). These directories may be browsed or searched using the news source's name as a keyword. Alternatively, the full news library (ALL NEWS) may be searched for articles on a topic, using terms and connectors or natural language search (see Exhibit 7–15).

Besides all of these news sources, Westlaw offers access to the RIA and the BNA newsletters. The RIA newsletters are discussed in Chapter 6 and the BNA newsletters are discussed in this chapter. With all of these news and

Exhibit 7–15

Westlaw News & Business

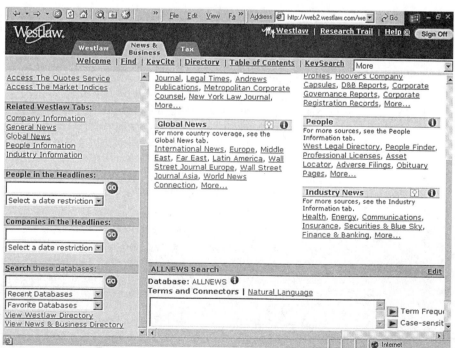

business information sources, a practitioner cannot plead ignorance to what is currently happening in tax due to lack of access to current data!

MERTENS SERVICE

Mertens Law of Federal Income Taxation (Mertens), developed by the West Group, is offered on Westlaw. It also is offered in a one-disc CD-ROM version, Tax Link, containing not only the entire Mertens service but also an annotated Code, Tax Court Rules, and recent issues of current newsletters. This version integrates with Westlaw, allowing the practitioner to access the full text of documents cited in the service. West updates Tax Link monthly by sending the subscriber a new CD-ROM.

The **Mertens** service has three main components: Mertens Treatise, Mertens Rulings, and Mertens Current Tax Highlights. The Treatise is a comprehensive topical service organized in over 100 chapters. While Mertens is comparable in its coverage and depth to the RIA and CCH topical tax services (see Chapter 6), it is much more oriented toward the legal profession. Consequently, courts cite it more than the other tax services. This legal orientation is evidenced by the text material being heavily footnoted. On occasion there is more footnote material than text material on a Mertens printed page. As Exhibit 7–16 illustrates, these footnotes provide more than mere citations to the relevant primary tax law sources; often they annotate cases, quote freely from the Code, Regulations, and Committee Reports, or review legislative history. Its in-depth analysis explains the intent of Congress in drafting the Code, what the Code

Exhibit	**7–16**
Mertens Footnotes	

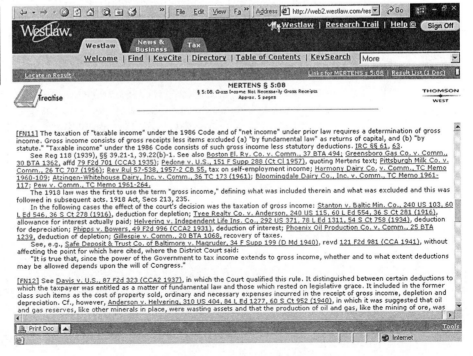

means and how the Internal Revenue Service has been interpreting it. Unlike other Internet services, Mertens is updated monthly rather than daily.

As part of the service, Mertens includes full text of every Revenue Ruling and Revenue Procedure since 1954. What makes this service unique is its indexing system, enabling a researcher to find every IRS document dealing with an individual code section. Thus, it is easy to determine the IRS's current stand on a particular issue.

Included in the Mertens Rulings is the Cumulative Bulletin Citations for Revenue Rulings and Revenue Procedures. This is a series of tables that provide the *Cumulative Bulletin* citation when all that is known is the official number of a ruling or procedure. In addition, the Code, Regulations, and Rulings volumes also contain Amendment Tables, which allow the researcher to trace the statutory or administrative evolution of any provision.

The Mertens Current Highlights component provides timely information on current developments in tax laws through newsletters, magazines, and alerts. Feature articles of special interest, and materials on recent developments, such as Committee hearings, new legislation, and breaking news from Capitol Hill are included as well as summaries of Code changes, cases, and recent IRS releases.

Finally, Mertens includes a Code Commentary, which furnishes contextual explanations of Code provisions and has "snapshot" versions of previous years' Code, Regulations, and Rulings volumes. This extremely useful feature of the Mertens service facilitates the analysis of the evolution of a law. For a client whose prior year's tax returns are under audit or at trial, the tax practitioner can use this feature of Mertens to reconstruct the details of the primary law sources that applied at the date of the original return.

BITTKER & LOKKEN SERVICE

Warren, Gorham & Lamont (WG&L) is the publisher of ***Federal Taxation of Income, Estates, and Gifts (B & L service)***, a treatise by Boris I. Bittker and Lawrence Lokken. Since WG&L is an affiliate of West, its products are offered through Westlaw and RIA. The five-volume B & L treatise is less comprehensive and more conceptual than many of the other topical tax services on the market. Its stated objective is "provid[ing] guidance and orientation [to income and transfer taxation] by emphasizing the purpose, structure, and principal effects of the *Internal Revenue Code*, without bogging down in the details." Due to its goals, the service sometimes reads like a collection of essays and journal articles rather than a systematic analysis of the workings of the Code. However, it is generally considered to be a leading authoritative treatise by professionals and even by the United States Supreme Court.

The B & L service may serve as a good starting point for the researcher who needs to obtain an initial grasp of a selected area of the tax law. Its citations can provide easy access into the other tax services or immediately direct the practitioner to the primary sources of tax law. Currently, it stands somewhere between a one-volume treatise or textbook and a freestanding comprehensive topical tax service.

SPOTLIGHT ON TAXATION: Humorous Quotes

"I am proud to be paying taxes in the United States. The only thing is—I could be just as proud for half the money." —Arthur Godfrey

"If you don't drink, smoke, or drive a car, you're a tax evader." —Thomas S. Foley

A tax loophole is "something that benefits the other guy. If it benefits you, it is tax reform." —Russell B. Long

"Taxation with representation ain't so hot either." —Gerald Barzan

"People who complain about taxes can be divided into two classes: men and women." —Unknown

"Next to being shot at and missed, nothing is really quite as satisfying as an income tax refund." —F. J. Raymond

"[A] tax lawyer is a person who is good with numbers but does not have enough personality to be an accountant." —James D. Gordon III

BNA

Tax Management, a subsidiary of the **Bureau of National Affairs** (BNA), offers a wide range of products covering all areas of Federal taxes. However, it is best known as the publisher of the BNA *Tax Management Portfolios* and its newsletter the *Daily Tax Report*. Both of these products are available on LexisNexis, Westlaw, and their own online service.

PORTFOLIOS

The almost 400 BNA *Tax Management Portfolios* (Portfolios) are classified into four series: U.S. Income Tax; Estates, Gifts, and Trusts; Foreign Income; and State. The size of the Portfolio library varies as topics are added, deleted, or combined. While the number of Portfolios appears vast, the series is not truly comprehensive. As with any topical service, it would be impossible to cover every issue that a practitioner may encounter in the course of business.

Each BNA Portfolio begins with a Portfolio Description, which gives a brief overview of the topic and the order in which the materials will be presented. The Table of Contents would follow this description. The remainder of the Portfolio contains three sections: (A) Detailed Analysis, (B) Working Papers, and (C) Bibliography and References. The printed page numbers of these sections are preceded by the letters (A, B or C) to indicate which portion of the Portfolio is being examined. The Portfolio sections are updated in response to important tax developments, and when necessary, the complete Portfolio is rewritten.

The Detailed Analysis section is, as the title suggests, a comprehensive examination of the topic. It is written by one or more tax practitioners who are experts on the topic. Practitioners are the preferred authors because they are more sensitive to the information requirements of the service users. For this reason, Portfolios are a favorite research tool with practitioners. As with other topical services, the Code, Regulations, Rulings, and court case opinions are integrated into the analysis with citations footnoted or included in the text. In addition, the authors identify potential pitfalls, probable IRS positions, effective tax planning techniques, and alternative means of structuring transactions in a tax-favorable manner. The value of these insights will vary by author.

The Working Papers section of the Portfolios is perhaps the service's most unique and useful feature. This portion includes practitioner checklists; reproduced IRS forms, occasionally filled in for an illustrative fact situation; computation worksheets; sample draft agreements and contract clauses; sample board or shareholder resolutions and employment contracts; reproductions of pertinent primary sources; and other practical materials that would assist the professional in implementing tax planning techniques and procedures.

The Bibliography section of a Portfolio has a comprehensive listing of the primary (Official) and secondary (Unofficial) sources of the tax law utilized by the author(s) in the preparation of the Portfolio. Finally, this section of the Portfolio often includes a listing of journal articles and treatises that are relevant to the Portfolio topic.

The published Portfolios have a comprehensive index to aid in the search process. For each series (Income, Estates, Gifts, & Trusts, and Foreign Income) the Master Index provides a list by topic and portfolio number of all the portfolios within the series. The topics section is a very broad-based index, whereas the numerical listing is like a table of contents for the series. The Master Index is updated at least quarterly.

The Index also contains a Code section guide that traces specific Code sections to the various Portfolios within which it is discussed. The asterisk in front of the Portfolio title indicates that it contains primary coverage of this Code section topic. Lastly, Portfolios may by identified by IRS Forms and Publications Finding Table. This part of the Index identifies Portfolios discussing the item and/or reproducing the form. It is particularly useful when the practitioner has questions regarding the proper completion of a particular form.

NEWS REPORTS

One of the most important tax newsletters available to practitioners is the BNA *Daily Tax Report* (DTR). Showing both breadth of topic and quality of analysis, the DTR offers the subscriber up-to-date information concerning statutory, administrative, and judicial tax law developments that affect state, Federal, and international taxation. In addition, the newsletter provides interviews with government officials, articles reviewing the day's events, and the full text of key documents discussed in the newsletter. In some instances these documents are not available from other tax services. Monthly indexes, including Private Letter Ruling and Code Section indexing, are provided and are cumulated quarterly.

The DTR is available through Lotus Notes, the web, e-mail (summaries and table of contents), fax (table of contents), LexisNexis, Westlaw, and by paper subscription, which is hand-delivered in most major cities. It offers the equivalent of thirty to fifty pages of single-spaced printed copy every weekday. Because this is clearly too much to digest every day, the DTR is organized to facilitate accessing only the material of greatest interest to the subscriber. While the content section lists only the title of each note by category, the highlights provide brief paragraphs describing the notes. Through the web, the listings in the contents and highlights sections are linked to the notes. Further, from the new notes or the highlights, the subscriber can access the actual government document on which the story is based.

A subscription to the DTR includes access to **TaxCore**, which is a web-based source of a wide variety of full-text primary tax materials. It provides a categorization of sources to facilitate accessing the document of interest. The source categories include: Congressional, Treasury, Court, IRS, State and Local, White House, and International. TaxCore is updated daily. For practitioners not subscribing to the DTR, TaxCore may be obtained separately for a modest fee.

As one would expect, receiving such extensive tax news on a daily basis is an expensive proposition. However, the DTR (as well as many newsletters produced by other publishers) is available online to subscribers of various electronic tax research services. Thus, by subscribing to one of the major tax database systems, the practitioner has access to the DTR at a small or no incremental cost.

Similar to Tax Analysts, BNA publishes a weekly newsletter as well as a daily. The **Weekly Report** coverage is similar to the DTR but more in depth. In addition, it contains articles on news and emerging tax topics. The comprehensive index makes locating items of interest easy. Besides other weekly, biweekly, and monthly newsletters, BNA publishes journals in the areas of financial planning, real estate, compensation planning, international, and estates, gifts and trusts. To sample any of the BNA tax publication, visit BNA's web site at **http://www.bnatax.com.**

INTERNET SITES

A growing source of tax materials that literally changes daily is the Internet. There is so much information available on the Internet that it can be overwhelming. Therefore, performing a "Google" search on a tax topic can return so many documents that the researcher does not know where to start. A more directed search, using a tax service, is usually more effective and efficient. The web sites for the tax services discussed in Chapter 6 and this chapter are listed in Exhibit 7–17. The web addresses in this list were accurate as of the date of publication. This list should by no means be considered a comprehensive list of tax services available to the practitioner.

As mentioned previously, most of the primary tax source documents are accessible free of charge on the Internet. The Federal government has numerous web sites to disseminate its documents to the general public. A list

| Exhibit | 7-17 | Web Sites for Commercial Tax Services |

Commercial Services	Web Sites
Bureau of National Affairs (BNA)	http://www.bna.com
Tax Management Resources (BNA)	http://www.taxmanagement.bna.com/tm/index.html http://www.bnatax.com/tm/index.html
Commerce Clearing House	http://tax.cchgroup.com
CCH Tax Research NetWork	http://tax.cchgroup.com/network http://tax.cchgroup.com/primesrc/bin/login.asp
LexisNexis	http://www.lexisnexis.com
LexisNexis Academic	http://web.lexis-nexis.com/universe
Lexis	http://www.lexis.com
Nexis	http://www.nexis.com
Kleinrock	http://www.kleinrock.com
Research Institute of America	http://ria.thomson.com/
RIA Checkpoint	http://checkpoint.riag.com
Tax Analysts	http://www.taxanalysts.com http://www.tax.org http://www.taxanalysts.org
Thomson	http://www.thomson.com
Thomson Tax and Accounting	http://www.thomson.com/taxacct
West	http://www.westgroup.com http://west.thomson.com
Westlaw	http://web2.westlaw.com

of web sites offering government documents is presented in Exhibit 7–18. There are also many web sites maintained by companies, organizations, and individuals that have links to the government sites to facilitate retrieval of primary sources of the tax law. One of the most useful of these sites is the **Tax and Accounting Sites Directory** (**http://www.taxsites.com**) shown in Exhibit 7–19. "Tax Sites" is a comprehensive index including links to Federal, state, and international primary sources as well as to most secondary source providers. It is designed to be a jumping off point for searching for tax information, products, and services. This site offers one-stop searching when looking for tax web sites.

SUMMARY

The market supports a variety of tax research products, all designed to facilitate locating relevant sources by practitioners. Whether the service is categorized as legal or tax, all have their place in tax research. The enor-

| Exhibit | 7-18 | Selected Primary Source Internet Sites |

Primary Source Information Available Web Site

Primary Source Information Available	Web Site
Code of Federal Regulations	http://www.gpoaccess.gov/cfr
Congressional Record	http://www.gpoaccess.gov/crecord/index.html
Federal Register	http://www.gpoaccess.gov/fr/index.html
Fedworld Info Network	http://www.fedworld.gov/
Financial Accounting Standards Board	http://www.fasb.org
Government Printing Office (GPO) Access	http://www.gpoaccess.gov/
House Ways and Means	http://www.house.gov/ways_means
Internal Revenue Code	http://www.access.gpo.gov/uscode/title26/title26.html
Internal Revenue Code Search (Title 26)	http://uscode.house.gov/search/criteria.php
Internal Revenue Service	http://www.irs.gov/ http://www.irs.ustreas.gov/
Internal Revenue Service Forms & Publications	http://www.irs.gov/formspubs/index.html
Joint Committee on Taxation	http://www.house.gov/jct/
Legislation Information	http://thomas.loc.gov
Office of the Law Revision Counsel	http://uscode.house.gov
Primary Sources	http://www.legalbitstream.com/
Revenue Rulings	http://www.taxlinks.com/
Senate Finance Committee	http://www.senate.gov/~finance/
Social Security Administration	http://www.ssa.gov
Tax Division Department of Justice	http://www.usdoj.gov/tax/
Tax Forms	http://www.irs.gov/formspubs/index.html
Tax Regulations	http://www.gpoaccess.gov/ecfr/ http://www.access.gpo.gov/nara/cfr/cfr-table-search.html
U.S. House of Representatives	http://www.house.gov
U.S. Senate	http://www.senate.gov
U.S. Treasury Department	http://www.ustreas.gov White House http://www.whitehouse.gov

mous databases of services such as Lexis and Westlaw make them very attractive. On the other hand, the ability to access materials on a single CD without having to connect to the Internet is appealing to many sole practitioners and small firms. There is a wide range of products between these extremes. Practitioners must decide which media and tax products best serve the needs of their business at a price they can afford. With technology and software advances occurring at a rapid pace, what seemed to be an innovative product when this text was written may be passé by the time

Exhibit 7-19

Tax and
Accounting Sites
Directory

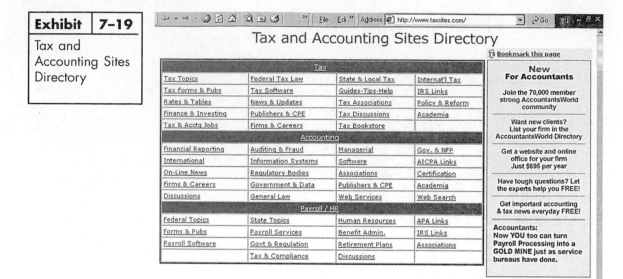

Exhibit 7-19

Tax and
Accounting Sites
Directory

it is read. The ability to be flexible and quickly adjust the changing technology to business needs is important to the success of tax practitioners.

TAX TUTOR

Reinforce the tax research information covered in this chapter by completing the online tutorials located at the Federal Tax Research web site:

http://raabe.swlearning.com

KEY WORDS

By the time you complete your work in this chapter, you should be comfortable discussing each of the following terms. If you need additional review of any of these items, return to the appropriate material in the chapter or consult the glossary to this text.

Boolean	KeySearch
Bureau of National Affairs	KWIC
Cite	Lexis
Daily Tax Report	LexisNexis
Federal Research Library	LexisNexis Academic
Federal Taxation of Income, Estates, and Gifts	Mertens
Federal Tax Baedeker	Natural Language
	Nexis

OneDisc
State Research Library
Tax Analysts
Tax and Accounting Sites Directory
TaxBase
TaxCore
Tax Management Portfolios

Tax Notes
Tax Notes Today
Terms and Connectors
Universal Characters
Weekly Report
Westlaw
Wildcard Characters

DISCUSSION QUESTIONS

1. When were Lexis and Nexis started? What topic areas are covered by each?

2. What tax sources are not included in the Lexis offerings?

3. How is the database structure of Lexis different from the RIA and CCH tax services?

4. What is a natural language search and when is it useful?

5. Explain the Command Searching method in Lexis.

6. Describe the Guided Search method in Lexis.

7. How is a space between keywords interpreted by Lexis and Westlaw?

8. Which of the legal services provides a thesaurus for their terms and connector searches? Is the thesaurus automatically applied? Explain your response.

9. Lexis allows the researcher to limit documents searched. What limitations are available for natural language and terms and connector searches?

10. Evaluate the following statement. The Search Advisor option in Lexis was created for researchers desiring advisory documents.

11. What information must the researcher know to use the Get a Document feature in Lexis?

12. What companies dominate the tax/law publications and services?

13. Lexis offers documents to be viewed in KWIC mode. What is KWIC?

14. Explain the More Like This and the More Like Selected Text features in Lexis.

15. What is LexisNexis Academic?

16. How does the LexisNexis Academic Narrowing Search function?

17. What is *Federal Tax Baedeker*? What services offer it?

18. What is the mission of Tax Analysts and for what publications is it known?

19. What is OneDisc?

20. What organization sued the IRS to gain access to Field Service Advice Memorandums?

21. What is the relationship between TaxBase, *Tax Notes* and *Tax Notes Today*?

22. What tax services are available through Westlaw? How does this compare with what is available through Lexis?

23. Which two legal services offer pay-for-document type services?

24. Who designed Westlaw and who is its target market?

25. How and why would a practitioner want to add personalized tabs to Westlaw?

26. How is a space between two keywords interpreted by Tax Analysts Federal Tax Baedeker?

27. Explain two methods of performing a table of contents search.

28. What is KeySearch?

29. How may a practitioner locate a news document in Westlaw?

30. What makes the footnotes in *Mertens Law of Federal Income Taxation* unique?

31. Why is the Mertens Rulings service unique?

32. What is the scope or objective of *Federal Taxation of Income, Estates, and Gifts*?

33. When would a practitioner likely start a research project by using *Federal Taxation of Income, Estates, and Gifts*?

34. What are the various tax services offered by the Bureau of National Affairs?

35. How is each volume of the BNA *Tax Management Portfolios* arranged?

36. Describe the Working Papers section of a BNA *Tax Management Portfolio*.

37. Compare the contents of Tax Analysts *Tax Notes* with BNA *Weekly Report*.

38. What is TaxCore? What is its purpose?

39. What information is available through the Tax and Accounting Sites Directory web site?

40. Why would a practitioner pay for tax service when most tax primary sources are available through the Internet for free?

EXERCISES

41. Using the Taxation topic area in Lexis, answer the following questions.
    a. In the Federal multi-source group, what sources are included in the combined Federal and state tax journals?
    b. Which accounting journals are available in the taxation library?
    c. Provide the citation, in proper format, for two Technical Advice Memorandums or Private Letter Rulings issued in 2003 discussing §83 and the Alternative Minimum Tax?
    d. Selecting the Tax Planning for Corporations and Shareholders database from the Taxation Topic screen, perform a natural language search to determine the tax treatment of stock redeemed from a deceased shareholder. Perform the same search using terms and con-

nectors. List your natural search question and the number of documents it retrieved. Provide the same information for the terms and connectors search. Explain why one was a more effective search.

42. Using Lexis, answer the following questions.
   a. Selecting the Guided Search Forms, Area of Law, which database provides searching of the Code, Regulations, Administrative Pronouncements, and cases?
   b. Selecting the Guided Search Forms, News, what are the U.S. regional sources offered?
   c. Selecting Research Tasks, Tax, what sources are provided by IOMA?
   d. Selecting Research Tasks, Tax, what is the most recent issue of the Kleinrock Federal Tax Bulletin? Provide the volume and issue number as well as the date.

43. Using Lexis, answer the following questions.
   a. Selecting Research Tasks, Tax, and Matthew Bender's Tax Havens of the World, determine the official language of Maderia.
   b. Are the State & Local listings found in Treatise & Analytical Materials the same as the State & Local listings found in Multi-Source Groups? Explain your answer.
   c. Selecting Search Advisor, then Tax Law, determine what is covered in the Federal Taxpayer Groups.
   d. Select in order Search Advisor, Tax Law, Federal Excise Tax, then Alcohol, Tobacco & Related Excise Tax database, then enter the following search terms: forfeitures automobile. What is the citation, in proper format, for the 1996 Supreme Court case deciding whether the IRS properly seized the taxpayer's jointly owned automobile used for criminal activity by her husband.

44. Using Lexis, answer the following questions.
   a. What is the Lexis recognized abbreviation for the Yukon Court of Appeals (Neutral Citation)?
   b. In a Terms and Connectors search, what segments are offered for limiting the search?
   c. When using the "w/n" proximity connector, what is the maximum number "n" can be?
   d. What are the date restrictions available for a terms and connectors search?

45. Using LexisNexis Academic, answer the following questions.
   a. What IRS pronouncements are included in the Tax Law database?
   b. Selecting Legal Research, then Federal Code, enter the terms: like-kind exchange. What sections are retrieved? Supply a title number and section number.
   c. After selecting legal research and legal news, enter the following search words: reorganization, technology, and tax. What is the title of the most recent article you find with these terms in the headline or lead paragraph?
   d. In the Tax Law library, select the *Internal Revenue Code* as the source and enter the terms: like-kind exchange. What sections are retrieved? Are these the same as what you found in part b. above?

46. Using LexisNexis Academic, answer the following questions.
    a. Select Business and Accounting to determine the ISSN for the *Journal of Accountancy*. What issues are available?
    b. Select Business News and Mergers & Acquisitions to determine the title of the most recent article with telecommunications in the headline or lead paragraph and "stock for stock" in the full text of the article.
    c. Select Today's News and enter the terms: income taxes. Select one of the articles and provide the title and author of the article.
    d. Select Tax Law and Law Reviews – Tax Articles as the source. Provide the title, author, and journal having the most recent article on stock redemptions.

47. Using Tax Analysts Federal Tax Baedeker, answer the following questions.
    a. What chapter and section discusses income averaging for farmers?
    b. Employ the Index to determine the chapter and section number that discusses a wash sale.
    c. Employ a keyword search using the terms: wash sale. List the chapter and section of the results.
    d. Explain why your responses to b. and c. above differ.

48. Using Tax Analysts, answer the following questions.
    a. The Basic Library includes BATF Final and Temporary Regulations. What is BATF and under what title of the Code of Federal Regulations do these regulations fall? Where did you find this information?
    b. The Quick Reference Tables provide information on the per diem deemed substantiation. What Revenue Procedure is most often listed as a source document? What time period does it cover?
    c. For what does the IRS acronym COGS stand? (Hint: Look in the Tax Directory.)
    d. What Market Segment Specialization Paper was released in April 2003?

49. Using Tax Analysts, answer the following questions.
    a. Examine the articles in the most recent issue of *Tax Notes*. Is the information in any of these articles essentially the same as a comparable article in *Tax Notes Today* for the same period? Elaborate.
    b. Provide the title and author of the most recent article in *Tax Notes* discussing Puerto Rico as a tax haven.
    c. Select an IRS Field Attorney Advice from a recent *Tax Notes Today*. Provide the Code section to which it applies and a brief synopsis of the issue and conclusion.

50. Using Westlaw, answer the following questions.
    a. List five of the options available from the More pull-down menu.
    b. What is the abbreviation for the *Journal of Cost Management*?
    c. Using the KeySearch, determine what the Key numbers 371k988.1 and 371k989 mean. (Hint: The subject under which these numbers appear is State Income Taxation of Corporate Dividends. Look for State & Federal Cases with these numbers.)
    d. Find a Tax Court case with a taxpayer named Ezo Products. Provide the citation in proper format.

51. Using Westlaw, answer the following questions.
    a. What symbol is used for the connector "but not"? Explain the use of the universal characters "*" and "!". What does " + n" mean and how large can "n" be?
    b. Using the Find search, locate the article in Volume 57 of the *Tax Law Review* starting on page 275. What is the title of the article, and who is the author?
    c. In the article found in part b. above, what Revenue Ruling is cited in the article?
    d. In the My Westlaw customizing command, what topics in the General choice tab options (besides Westlaw) would contain government documents?

52. Using Westlaw, answer the following questions.
    a. What is the database identifier (database abbreviation) for the WG&L combined tax treatises database? How many treatises with Bittker as the first author are included in this database?
    b. With the Directory search, find a Private Letter Ruling that discusses the taxability of gifts (cash payments) to clients of a tax exempt organization who participate in a new program.
    c. With Find the document by citation, determine the proper abbreviation used for finding Code sections, Regulations, and Revenue Rulings.
    d. Under what heading in the Table of Contents, Topical Secondary Sources & Forms, Taxation is *Mertens Law of Federal Income Taxation* listed?

53. Using Westlaw, answer the following questions.
    a. What synonyms does the Westlaw thesaurus provide for the following terms: kickback, casualty, and fuel?
    b. In what paragraph in WG&L treatise Federal Income Taxation of Real Estate (by Robinson) is the discussion of "At Risk" rules?
    c. What Federal materials have an index listed in the More pull-down menu Index?
    d. Determine what the Key number 371k1061 means using the Key Numbers & Digest in the More pull-down menu.

54. Using *Mertens Law of Federal Income Taxation*, answer the following questions.
    a. The sale of a patent by the original individual inventor generally is treated as a capital gain transaction. Is this true even for a professional inventor? Where was the relevant discussion of the law found?
    b. According to the historical development discussion of patent sales, when were substantial liberalizing revisions made to this area of the tax law? The Commissioner announced that for years beginning prior to the effective date and after May 31, 1950, he would adhere to the position he had taken prior to the enactment of the § 1235 changes. What did Congress do to foil the Commissioner's plan?

c. In what Chapter & Section is the relevant discussion found for the following?

Deduction of armed services uniforms.

Expenditures incurred in producing photographs.

Charitable contribution valuation of a business interest.

Redemption effects on Accumulated Earnings Tax.

d. How are the topics arranged in Mertens? (Hint: Look in the Introduction.)

55. Use Bittker & Lokken's *Federal Taxation of Income, Estates, and Gifts* to answer the following questions.

a. According to the Supreme Court case of *Diedrich v. CIR,* the payment of gift taxes by the donee may result in a taxable gain for the donor. State the circumstances that will cause this to happen. Where did you find this information? Provide the cite from the volume number to the subparagraph number.

b. What is the official citation for *Diedrich v. CIR?* Give the volume and page number of the *Iowa Law Review* that has a comment on this case.

c. List the titles of the volume through subparagraph of Volume 13, Chapter 92, Paragraph 92.3, Subparagraph 92.3.2. What is the first sentence of Subparagraph 92.3.2?

56. Using BNA's *Tax Management Portfolios,* answer the following questions.

a. Which *Portfolio(s)* discuss(es) the deductibility of gifts to clients?

b. On what worksheet found in which *Portfolio* is there information on how to elect out of the alcohol fuel credit?

c. In what section of which *Portfolio* is there a discussion of the tax treatment of transfers of appreciated property to political parties?

d. In which *Portfolio* do you find a worksheet sample of the § 173 election to capitalize newspaper circulation expenditures?

57. Use any available source to answer the following questions.

a. Find a recent article in BNA Tax Management *Weekly Report* that was also reported in *BNA Daily Tax Report.* What day did each article appear? What is the title of the article and the author(s)?

b. Find an article in *Daily Tax Report* explaining a recent Revenue Ruling. Provide a brief summary of the Revenue Ruling and its effect on taxation.

c. Find the March 2004 article in the *National Law Journal* that discusses the tax act of 2001 and its effect on Estate Taxes. What is the title of the article and the author(s)?

d. What is the title of the 2004 tax act that was H. R. 1308?

58. Use the Tax and Accounting Sites Directory (**http://www.taxsites.com**) to answer the following questions.

a. Where does the tax link for timber in Tax Topics take you?

b. What are the different headings under Tax Bookstore? Under what heading is this textbook listed?

c. What is the latest IR discussed on the IRS Newsroom web site?

d. Select Firms & Careers, then Career search: Tax & Accounting. Does Robert Half provide any free resources focused on accounting?

59. Surf the web and find three noncommercial tax sites that are not mentioned in this text. Provide the URL and a general description of the information provided on the site.

60. Visit the web sites of two commercial tax services discussed in this text. Describe the free news services they offer to the public. Evaluate the usefulness of these news services.

RESEARCH CASES

Support your answers for each case with citations to primary tax law sources.

61. Three friends form a small manufacturing partnership, each owning equal interests. Their contributions to the start-up entity are as follows.

    Glen: Cash $10,000; equipment, FMV $5,000, basis $4000.
    Alex: Land with a small building, FMV $70,000, basis $20,000, recourse mortgage $55,000 (assumed by the partnership).
    Debra: Neither cash nor other property, just extensive and valuable business knowledge.

    Determine the partners' bases in their respective partnership interests, and the partnership's basis in each of the assets transferred to it. State a general rule for deriving such computations.

62. Can a business traveler to your town use the high-cost-city meal allowance for travel away from home overnight? What would the meal allowance be for a business trip to Washington, D.C.?

63. Nancy and Curtis had not spoken to each other since their mother's funeral in 1971. Nancy broke the family discord this year by selling Curtis a family heirloom, basis to her $10,000, for $1,700. What are the tax consequences of this transaction?

64. Zarco, a very profitable corporation, was owned by three shareholders, Julio, Tilly, and Martinez. Julio and Martinez purchased all of Tilly's Zarco Corporation stock for $50,000 and a $100,000 promissory demand note that was guaranteed by Zarco. Tilly demanded payment on the note, and Zarco, rather than Julio and Martinez, paid the note. What are the tax consequences of this transaction?

65. Dolores is a limited partner in the Houston Hopes partnership. This year, she was forced under the terms of the agreement to make a $50,000 contribution to capital because the general partners were unable to meet the operating expenses of the entity. Dolores's basis in the partnership prior to the contribution was $40,000, but her at-risk amount was zero because of her limited partner status and her prior-year pass-through losses. What is her at-risk amount after the $50,000 cash call?

66. Steve is an usher at his local church. May he deduct as a charitable contribution the commuting expenses for the Sundays that he is assigned to usher?

67. Phil is a used-car manager. To obtain advanced skills in management and marketing, he enrolls in the weekend MBA program at Montana

State University, twenty miles from his home. Does Phil qualify for an educational credit? What items associated with Phil's education are deductible, assuming that he receives no reimbursements for any of them?

68. Jon and Mary have been married for twenty years. Without Mary's knowledge, Jon has been operating as a bookie at his local pub. This year's earnings from the operation were the highest ever. In fact, if Jon had reported any of the net gambling income, their joint Federal income tax liability would have increased by $140,000. When Jon finally is nabbed by the FBI, he is taken to jail. Mary is unable to locate any of Jon's earnings in bank or brokerage accounts. Can Mary fend off the IRS's charge that she should pay the $140,000 in tax, plus interest and penalties, from her salary as a physician?

69. Maria has an unusually strong constitution and the highest quality blood and plasma available for transfusion. She manages to stay healthy while donating blood at the hospital two or three times a week. For each donation, the Blood Center pays Maria $175 for the blood. Maria drives forty miles round-trip to the hospital to make her donation. Moreover, she spends about $35 every month for vitamins and other pills prescribed by her physician to ensure that her general health and blood quality do not degenerate in light of her frequent donations. Last year, Maria quit all of her part-time jobs and now survives financially solely by these blood donations. Specify the tax consequences of this regular activity.

70. Chang, a brain surgeon, pays for the *Journal of Brain Research* under the three-year plan; he paid $3,000 this year for a three-year subscription to the weekly scientific journal, which charges $1,500 for an annual renewal. In what year(s) can Chang deduct this $3,000?

71. Handy Corporation assists its relocated executives by buying their homes if an acceptable deal cannot be struck before the move. Purchase is made at the appraised value. What is the nature of Handy's gain or loss on the subsequent sale?

72. Walt was convicted of murder and sent to prison for life. Walt continued to profess his innocence. His sister, Wanda, believed him, and after spending three years in law school and two years gathering facts, she proved that he was innocent. Walt and Wanda assigned the book, movie, and photo rights concerning their story to Warner Brothers for $500,000. How is this payment treated by Walt and Wanda?

73. Hugo was burying his (dead) dog when he unearthed 100,000 certificates of ITT bearer bonds, current value $4,000,000. He speculated that they had been placed there by the (also dead) former owner of Hugo's home, at a time when they were worth nearly $400,000. Hugo did not sell the bonds by the end of the year. Must Hugo recognize any gross income with respect to the bonds?

74. Karla is a single parent with two children ages 7 and 11. She is a full-time student and earns $12,000. Both of her children receive dividends and capital gains from mutual funds started for them by their

grandparents. Karla has elected to include her children's income on her return for the kiddie tax computation. Since it is on her tax return, does her children's income affect the computation of Karla's earned income credit?

75. At gunpoint, Roger lent $2,000 from the cash register at his hardware store to four large youths who told Roger that they would set up their own store to compete with Roger's. Not having the phone number of any of the sprightly entrepreneurs, Roger could not recover any of the invested funds. Can Roger claim any deduction with respect to this loan? In what tax year?

76. Phyllis, a Virginia resident, owns some property in Florida. Every year, she travels to Florida (coincidentally, during baseball's spring training season) to inspect the property, initiate repairs, and look for new tenants and new properties in which to invest. She also attends about twenty ball games. Determine Phyllis's deductible travel expenses.

77. Bruce wanted to be an Olympic skater. His family paid $12,000 in 2002 and $14,000 in 2003 for travel and training expenses related to skating practices and competitions. Bruce made the 2004 U.S. Olympic team. The U.S. Olympic Committee is an exempt organization. How much of Bruce's expenses are deductible and when?

78. Harold installed a safe and an alarm system and bought a German shepherd dog to protect his vintage movie and video collection. What are his deductible items?

79. Donna's and Albert's children attend a parochial grade school. The school charges $1,500 annual tuition and $200 for uniforms for Donna's children, but only $500 tuition and $100 for uniforms for Albert's children because he is a member of the congregation. Albert contributed $800 to the church this year. Can Donna and Albert withdraw amounts out of their children's educational (IRA) savings accounts to pay for this private primary education? What is the amount of Albert's charitable contribution for the year?

80. Julie sings in the Seattle Symphony Chorus. The rules of the chorus require that its members wear traditional formal wear (i.e., $400 tuxedos for the men and $250 long black gowns for the women) during performances. In addition, because of her annual $15,000 contribution to the chorus's patron drive, Julie is a member of the symphony's board of directors. The board chooses the works to be performed, sites for the concerts, and the resident conductor. How much of Julie's $15,250 expenditures on behalf of the exempt orchestra this year can she deduct?

81. Tony, a single parent, spent $2,160 on after-school care for his six-year-old son. Tony received $900 from the Department of Social Services (DSS) for child care as part of the welfare assistance program in which he is enrolled. In determining his child-care credit, how much of the DSS payments are included in gross income, and what is the amount of Tony's child-care costs for computing the child-care credit?

82. Carmella really wants to be an actor but she is having trouble getting that "big break" that she so desparately needs. To keep food on the table, Carmella has a small tax preparation business and nets about $30,000 a year. She has received small parts in several movies and on television, earning about $10,000. However, she incurs substantial expenses associated with her acting career that amount to $12,000. Can Carmella deduct her acting expenses and/or can Carmella qualify for the qualified performing artist deduction?

83. Yukio was seriously injured when he fell through an open manhole. Yukio was awarded compensatory damages of $500,000 for his injuries, loss of current wages, reduced future earning ability, and suffering he incurred past, present, and in the future. Is any of the settlement taxable to Yukio? Specifically is the amount for lost wages taxable?

84. The Blue Fir Corporation has spent $50,000 on reforestation costs this year. The 100 acres being reforested to commercial and ornamental trees is government land that Blue Fir leases long-term. Naturally Blue Fir would like to deduct these costs as soon as possible. What is the proper treatment of these costs?

85. The farmers in Whitman County are concerned about the price they are receiving for their products. They have decided to create the Whitman County Farm Commission whose purpose will be to encourage farmers to band together when selling their products, educate the legislators on farming issues, and educate farmers on the best methods to control pests and weeds in the most environmentally safe manner. Will this organization qualify for exempt status?

ADVANCED CASES

These items require that you have access to research materials other than the Federal tax law and related services. For instance, you might need to refer to an international tax or multi-state service to prepare your solution for these cases. Consult with your instructor before beginning your work to be certain you have available to you all of the necessary research resources for the case(s) that you choose.

86. A friend of yours took a job in the air transportation industry. Knowing that you are taking tax courses, she asks you about the excise taxes that her firm must pay and some proposed changes in the deposit dates for those excise taxes. She is curious what the changes might be and whether the changes are in effect currently. Indicating that excise taxes for the air transportation industry are not generally covered in your research class, you tell your friend that you will see what you can find out about this for her. What did you learn about excise taxes for the air transportation industry?

87. Which of the following receipts are taxable to the state high school athletic association as unrelated business income?

- Ticket revenues from the basketball tournaments
- Advertising revenues from the programs sold at the tournaments
- Subsidy from the state budget for the tournaments
- Payment from Grand Central Limited to be the official sponsor of the tournaments

88. VanDelay, a citizen of the United States but a resident of Dulcinea, is an important sculptor. This year, he came to the United States to appear at a showing of his work in San Francisco. The United States has no tax treaty with Dulcinea. Does the $250,000 that VanDelay netted from the show qualify for the § 911 earned income exclusion?

89. Which of the following payments by International Partners, Inc., a Montana corporation, qualifies for the foreign tax credit?

- Income tax paid to Germany, covered by an existing treaty
- Income tax paid to Adagio, with which the United States has no income tax treaty
- Value-added tax paid to Largetto, with which the United States has no income tax treaty
- Oil extraction tax paid to Tedesco, with which the United States has no income tax treaty
- Transportation tax paid to Santa Lucia, with which the United States has no income tax treaty. The tax is reduced dollar-for-dollar when International provides consulting services in designing Santa Lucia's new bullet train system. This year, International incurred $1 million in taxes but earned a $600,000 reduction for its services.

90. Heather had named Brenda the executrix of her estate. Brenda had no experience in this domain, but she filed the return, and the estate paid a Federal death tax of $2 million. This year, Heather's son Dylan, studying for a master's degree in taxation, discovered that Brenda had not reported any of Heather's realty in the gross estate and that an additional $250,000 in tax and interest was due. The IRS then assessed various penalties, totaling $30,000. How can the estate, now administered by Dylan, avoid this penalty?

91. Popular Inc. has its corporate headquarters, plants, and warehouses all located in Vermont. Until this year, all of its sales have been in Vermont. Its first out-of-state sale of $1 million (cost of sales, $300,000) is shipped by a common carrier trucking firm from Popular's warehouse to the purchaser's dock in Indiana. The truck stops for gasoline in New York and Ohio, and its driver spends a night in Ohio. To which states must Popular apportion income from the sale? How much income is taxed in each such state?

92. The Ohio Government Employees Credit Union (Union) was created by merging the Ohio Teachers Bank, the Ohio Transit Credit Association, and the Federal Government Workers Credit Bank. The stock issued by the merged entity is held by those having deposits in Union. The Union believes that it is not subject to the Ohio franchise tax (an income tax) because immunity is implied under the Supremacy Clause of the U.S.

Constitution. The Union believes it is closely connected with the government and thus should be exempt from taxation. Is the Union correct in its conclusion that it is not subject to the Ohio franchise tax?

93. Last year, the Waltons were injured when an electrical cable that city workers were repairing landed in their swimming pool. The Waltons sued the city and were awarded damages as well as prejudgment interest. The state characterized all amounts paid to the Waltons as compensation for injuries. The Waltons assume that none of the amounts they received are taxable because of the state's treatment of the prejudgment interest as an element of the injury compensation. Are the Waltons correct in their assessment of the law?

94. Clyde Miller, a Mississippi resident, has lived with Lenora Waitsfield and her two children for the past five years. Clyde and Lenora are not married and her children are from a former relationship. The children have no legal relationship with Clyde, yet Clyde has supported the children and Lenora since they have been cohabiting. Clyde is claiming Lenora and the children as dependents on his tax return. He also has been claiming an earned income credit based on Lenora's children, who are both younger than age 17. Is Clyde correct in his treatment of Lenora and the children on his tax return? (State law considerations of the relationship between Clyde and Lenora are relevant.)

EXTENSIVE CASES

95. Thomas and Nicole Eirgo have been married for twenty years and have three children, Candice, age 18, and twin boys, Trevor and Julian, age 12. Nicole has an undergraduate degree in accounting and worked in public accounting while Thomas was obtaining his law degree. Five years ago they quit their jobs and started TechKnow, a C corporation that develops legal and tax software specifically for accountants and lawyers with hi-tech clients. Thomas and Nicole work more than full time at TechKnow and have received only modest salaries. No dividends have been paid. The business has finally started to make substantial profits, but success, unfortunately, has brought problems. Thomas and Nicole have very different opinions regarding TechKnow's future. Thomas would like to continue to reinvest most of the profits for the development of software for other specialties, whereas Nicole would like to focus on the lines they have and enjoy their success by distributing some of the profits. Since they cannot come to an agreement, the earnings are being retained, and no new software is being developed.

These business disagreements are having a disastrous toll on their marriage. The only solution Thomas and Nicole see is to divorce. As might be expected, Thomas and Nicole cannot decide on how to separate their ownership interests in TechKnow. Some options they are considering include redeeming Nicole's stock, having Thomas and/or the children buy the stock, or dividing the business in some manner between the two.

One thing Nicole has decided is to fulfill a lifelong dream of obtaining a doctorate degree in accounting. She will be entering a PhD program in the fall, at which time the divorce should be final. Since Candice will also be attending college, she will live in an apartment with her mother. Thomas will keep the house, and the boys will live with him. Thomas will pay Nicole alimony and child support while she and Candice are in school. The terms and amounts will be determined at the time the divorce is final.

Advise the Eirgos on the tax consequences of the above events. Support your conclusions with primary citations.

96. Chris and Sue are 50 percent shareholders in the BackBone personal service corporation. BackBone provides chiropractic services in four small towns: Troy, Union, Vista, and Willow. Chris is the main chiropractor in the Troy office, and Sue heads the Vista office. The two other offices have chiropractor employees running the practices. Herein is where Backbone's trouble lies. Charlie, the main chiropractor in the Willow office does not see eye-to-eye with Chris and Sue on management styles. Charlie does not take well to any interference in how he runs the office, the hours he keeps, or therapy techniques he employs. Firing Charlie is not an option for two reasons. First, it is difficult to find chiropractors who want to work and live in small towns. Second, and most important, if Charlie were to leave BackBone, he would start his own practice in Willow. He is very good with patients and would easily be able to take at least 80 percent of the clients in Willow. Sue and Chris have noticed that some of the patients in Union drive to Willow because they prefer Charlie to Joe, the chiropractor in their Union office.

Chris and Sue do not want to compete with Charlie and would prefer that they could come up with some arrangement that would make everyone happy. They already pay Charlie handsomely, so more salary is not the main solution. For Charlie, it seems to be a matter of control. Chris and Sue may be willing to give up control of the Willow office, but they do not want to completely lose the profits this office adds to BackBone.

Chris and Sue have come to you for some suggestions on how to solve this problem with the lowest tax cost. Provide BackBone with several options and the tax consequences of each. Support your conclusions with primary citations.

Chapter 8

Citators and Other Finding Devices

LEARNING OBJECTIVES

- Understand the function of the citator in the tax research process.

- Become adept at using the indexing systems in each of the most popular tax citators.

- Know the abbreviation and reference conventions used by the most popular tax citators.

- Efficiently use the update materials in the most popular tax citators.

- Know the comparative strengths and weaknesses of the most popular tax citators.

- Become familiar with the basic and advanced citator functions of Internet resources.

CHAPTER OUTLINE

Earlier chapters of this text discuss the tremendous number of legislative, administrative, and judicial sources of the tax law. This body of law is constantly changing because new laws are passed, administrative pronouncements are issued, judicial opinions are released, and old laws are superseded or overruled on a daily basis. This chapter addresses how tax practitioners can find the most up-to-date tax laws, cases, and administrative material.

BASIC RESEARCH GOALS

The goals of tax research are to define the research problem, find tax law that addresses the problem, apply the law to the problem, reach a conclusion about how the tax law affects the client, and communicate the findings to the client. Research serves different functions at different points in this process. In the beginning, the researcher is trying to obtain a basic understanding of the tax law pertaining to the client's problem. Reading journal articles or other authoritative explanations of the law, such as those found in tax services, is beneficial at this stage.

Next the researcher wants to determine how the primary source of tax law, the *Internal Revenue Code,* applies to the client's situation. Once the applicable Code sections are identified, they must be interpreted. Remember, if the Code is clear, practitioners need look no further because it is of the highest authority. However, in most cases the Code is not clear, and practitioners turn to other primary tax law sources such as Regulations, Rulings, or court cases to seek clarification. In this phase, the tax law is searched to find primary sources that interpret specific Code sections or contain facts resembling those in the client's case. Performing these research functions has been covered in Chapters 6 and 7.

Finally, once an opinion is formed as to the optimum application of the law to the client's situation, the practitioner needs to confirm that the primary tax law being relied upon has not been affected by subsequent developments. How to verify whether primary sources are still good law is addressed in this chapter. Lastly, the conclusions of the practitioner, based on the results of the research and verification of the sources, can then be communicated to the client by the methods covered in Chapter 10.

CITATORS

Law relies heavily on precedent, and tax law is no exception. Virtually every time a case is decided, the judge who writes the opinion refers to other cases and administrative rulings for guidance. The law attempts to maintain continuity so people can anticipate the application of the law to their situations. Each appellate opinion sets a precedent that applies to later cases.

WHAT IS A CITATOR?

The law is constantly in a state of flux, and, again, this is also true for tax law. The Code is changed frequently by passage of tax bills. Regulations are proposed, finalized, and withdrawn. Administrative rulings are issued, modified, superseded, and revoked or made obsolete by other changes in the tax law. A case decided at one level may be appealed by one or both parties. The higher court may overrule the lower court. Infrequently, a court may see a flaw in the reasoning it or another (equal or lower) court used to decide an earlier case or use a different reasoning to reach a distinct decision. When a court takes some action that relies on, rejects, or affects the holding of another case, it refers to that case in its opinion. All of this results in a tangle of inter-references among vast numbers of cases.

Along with statutory law, tax practitioners rely on administrative rulings and court decisions to interpret the law and argue the appropriate treatment of their clients' tax transactions. They must be able to determine if subsequent events have affected the validity of the law on which they rely. Thus, they need a tool to help them ascertain which rulings and cases are strong precedents and which have little to no value. One way would be to follow the reference threads from case to case or ruling to ruling, but this would be extremely tedious and would only identify earlier cases. Fortunately, citators do much of this work by following the threads in subsequent cases and summarize, in shorthand form, where the threads lead and what they mean.

A citator is a tool through which a tax researcher can learn the history of a case or ruling and evaluate the strength of its holdings. Before a researcher relies on the opinion in a case or analysis in a ruling, it is important to ascertain how later cases and rulings have treated the holdings. Thus, when a case or ruling relevant to a client's tax situation is found, this document's listing in the citator will indicate what later cases and rulings have said about its opinion. Some secondary sources such as law review articles may be included in the citators as well.

To avoid confusion, it is important to learn the specific terminology that describes references between cases. When one case refers to another case, it **cites** the latter case. The case making reference to another case is called the **citing case.** The case that is referenced is the **cited case.** The citing case will contain the name of the cited case and where the cited case can be found. The reference is called a **citation.** A **citator** is a service that indexes cited cases, gives full citations, and lists the citing cases and where each citing case can be found. A significant older case, one that establishes an important principle, may have been cited in hundreds of other cases. Thus, its entry in a citator would be extremely long and complex. A very recent or narrow case would have few cites and thus have a short entry.

A citator will not provide all types of information about a case or a ruling. For instance, it does not guide the researcher to documents related to the case or ruling that do not specifically cite it. Citators do not indicate when a case or ruling is no longer effective because of changes in the Code, unless the Code itself specifically identifies the document. This is because citators are created by searching primary sources for cites to the case or ruling. You can perform the same type of search by using the case name or its official cite in a keyword search of a database containing all primary sources. Imagine what an arduous task this would have been before the advent of electronically searchable databases! It is amazing that there were citators long before there were computers. Given the tremendous number of court cases issued annually, the citator is a vital element in the practitioner's tax research process.

The various commercial citators organize the lists of citing cases in distinctive ways. Depending on the researcher's purpose, one citator may be more appropriate than another. For example, one citator may only list citations that have a major impact on the logic or holding of the cited case. Another may list all citations. A researcher, initially checking to make sure a case has not been overruled, would prefer the former. The citations may be annotated to indicate the type of impact the citing case has on the cited case (e.g., modified, overruled, followed). A trial court case may be appealed, and it will generate a decision by each court that hears the case. Because each of these decisions may be cited in other documents, cases are generally organized by jurisdictional level. As each citator is discussed in this chapter, you should consider its suitability for specific research applications.

It is important for the practitioner to consider a case in context, to trace its judicially derived decision, and to monitor the reaction of subsequent court cases. This is even more important when the opinion is innovative. By using a citator properly, the practitioner reviews subsequent courts' reactions and determines the strength of the precedent established by the opinion. However, before turning to a case, the Code and Regulations that are the basis for the tax question being researched must be read and analyzed. Remember, cases and Rulings are reviewed to provide guidance in interpreting the law.

SPOTLIGHT ON TAXATION: Changing the Tax Law—Courts and IRS

There are ninety-four Federal District Courts. Each state has at least one district, and New York City and the District of Columbia have their own. Puerto Rico, the Virgin Islands, Guam, and the Northern Mariana Islands also have District Courts. These courts along with the other Federal courts over a two-year period (2002–2003) published almost 200 tax decisions giving guidance on taxes. Besides these decisions, the Tax Court gave more than 300 summary decisions for the same time period.

Revenue Rulings and Procedures

The IRS is much more productive than the courts in producing administrative tax law. For the two-year period 2002–2003, the IRS issued 380 Revenue Rulings and Revenue Procedures. Looking at the prior decade (1994–2003), the IRS produced about 1,400 Rulings and Procedures. This may seem like a tremendous number, but this is about 30 percent less than was produced from 1984 to 1993. In the mid-1990s the IRS decided to cut back on its issuances of Revenue Rulings thus causing the reduction in administrative rulings.

With so much tax law being promulgated on a yearly basis, practitioners are lucky there are citators to help determine which cases and rulings are still valid and which have been modified, reversed, revoked, and superseded.

When a case has been identified as pertinent to a research question, the first step in its review is an examination of a citator list of subsequent citing cases. For instance, say that a tax researcher has identified *Corn Products Refining Company* (a 1955 Supreme Court holding) as pertinent to a research project. The holding in the case might help or hurt the client's case. The task, then, is to find out how strong the holding in the *Corn Products* case is. The researcher must determine how subsequent cases evaluated the legal reasoning and findings of the *Corn Products* decision. In addition, the researcher must determine if changes in the Code made the case obsolete.

COMMERCIAL CITATORS

Of the four citators examined in this chapter, three exclusively cover tax cases— Commerce Clearing House (CCH), Research Institute of America (RIA), and Shepard's—and one includes tax cases in its law citator—Westlaw. The CCH, RIA, and Shepard's commercial citators are available in published or electronic formats, although the published format is less frequently available. Westlaw does not have a published counterpart. CCH provides its citator as part of its *Standard Federal Tax Reporter* tax service, whereas the *RIA Citator* is offered separately from its tax services. Both of these are available on CDs. *Shepard's Federal Tax Citator* is offered through the Internet exclusively by Lexis.

One of the advantages of the CCH and RIA electronic citators is that they allow the researcher to enter case names or citations; on the other hand, Shepard's and Westlaw accept only citations. All of the citators furnish templates and/or guidance for entering the citations of document of interest. The citations reproduced by CCH are general, directing the researcher to the first page of the citing case; whereas the other citators give local citations (also called pinpoint), directing the researcher to the exact page where the cited case is mentioned in the citing case. For example, *Corn Products* (350 US 46) is cited in *Kraft, Inc.,* (30 Fed Cl 739) on page 820. The CCH citation is *Kraft, Inc.,* 30 Fed Cl 739 (first page of the *Kraft* case), whereas the *RIA Citator* has *Kraft, Inc.,* 30 Fed Cl 820. Having local citations that pinpoint the discussion of the case of interest can be a real time saver when the citing case is long.

The discussion in this chapter concentrates on the electronic versions of the citators, and the *Upjohn Co., et al.* case (101 S. Ct. 677, 449 US 383, 47 AFTR 2d 81-523, 81-1 USTC ¶ 9138) will be used to demonstrate the citators. The published versions are briefly reviewed to give a sense of the origins and evolution of citators, as well as some concept of the physical scope of the information contained in citators. While the electronic versions tend to be just the paper publication in electronic form, this may not be evident to the user.

SHEPARD'S AND LEXIS CITATION SERVICES

Shepard's was the first major publisher to truly understand the commercial value of citators. It became the leading publisher of citators and thus its name has become synonymous with the act of citing. Many attorneys view

Shepard's as *the* citator service and all other services as imitations. This may have been true at one point in time, but the current competitors have just as much to offer as the original citator.

LexisNexis acquired Shepard's in 1998 and became the exclusive Internet provider of its citators in July 1999. Besides the *Shepard's Citators,* LexisNexis contains the Auto-Cite citator, Table of Authorities, and the LEXCITE search system. Each of these is a useful tool for the researcher when verifying a case's value as precedent. The accuracy of the case citations is very important; consequently, accuracy will be examined in this section.

SPOTLIGHT ON TAXATION: Factoid

Over 125 years ago, Frank Shepard of Chicago introduced his first citator as an aid to legal research. This citator gave references to citing cases for the Illinois judicial system. In 1900, Shepard's began to annotate the cases by indicating the treatment of the case by the citing cases (i.e., explained, overruled, etc.). Since that time, Shepard's has evolved into over twenty different citators which cover virtually every case reporter series, as well as for specialized areas of the law, such as *Shepard's Federal Tax Citator* for tax research. Because of its dominance in citator publishing and the breadth of its coverage, legal researchers often refer to the process of evaluating the validity of a case and locating additional authority as "**Shepardizing**" a case.

Shepard's Attributes

The **Shepard's Citators** (Shepard's) are currently available in print, on CD-ROM, and on the Internet exclusively through LexisNexis. Shepard's is the only major tax citator that is organized by case reporter series. Accordingly, the practitioner must know the court reporter citation for the case of interest, regardless of whether the paper or electronic version is used. This can be a problem if only the name of a case is known. However, the "Get a Document" button in Lexis supports retrieval of documents by citation, case names, or docket number. While viewing the retrieved case, clicking on the "Shepardize" button will display the Shepard's citator listing for the case.

Since citations must be entered in the proper format, Shepard's provides an exhaustive list of examples of citation formats for every possible document that can be Shepardized. There are so many sample entries that they are indexed themselves, as Exhibit 8–1 illustrates. For the letter "S," five pages of entries are provided. Once the document of interest is found, clicking on its associated abbreviation will display a template for entering the citation. The templates are all set up in the standard "volume, reporter, page" format. If the researcher knows these three elements of the citation, the program will be forgiving of punctuation, internal spacing, and capitalization variations.

The results of the citator search may be displayed in either the "Full" or "KWIC" view. Both displays begin with the case citation, followed by other

Exhibit   8–1

Shepard's Find
a Citation
Format Screen

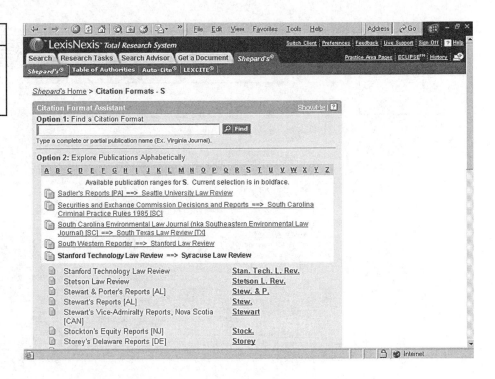

reporter locations of the case, called parallel citations. Shepard's includes cases reported in all of the court case reporter series discussed in Chapter 5 as well as any others that may be available. The "Full" view lists all of the prior history and subsequent appellate history. Preceding the prior history is the Shepard's summary. This contains a summary of all the citations generated for the case of interest. For example, Exhibit 8–2 indicates that out of the 2,677 total cites for the *Upjohn* case, one criticized *Upjohn*, 34 distinguished themselves from it, 103 followed it, and 786 law reviews cite it. This summary gives the practitioner a quick analysis of the general treatment of the case of interest by the citing cases plus a breakdown of the type of citing documents. For the *Upjohn* case, the majority of the citations are non-case documents. After the prior history of the case, the "Full" view lists all citing cases with or without an attached analysis, as well as statutes, law reviews, and legal periodicals citing the case of interest.

The other view choice, "KWIC" (keyword in context) retrieved fewer than 200 citing references. This option is generally selected for validating the citation of interest. It presents the subsequent appellate history and only those citing cases with editorial analysis. Even with these restrictions, the "KWIC" view may retrieve more cases than the researcher cares to review. To reduce the number of cases retrieved, researchers may narrow the search by choosing to view cases containing only negative evaluations ("All Neg") or positive evaluations ("All Pos") or may limit the search by designating headnote issues, applying date restrictions, specifying jurisdictions, or selecting analysis categories ("Custom"). All of these options are available with either the "Full" or the "KWIC" view (see Exhibit 8–2).

Exhibit | 8–2

Shepard's Full Citator List for *Upjohn* Case

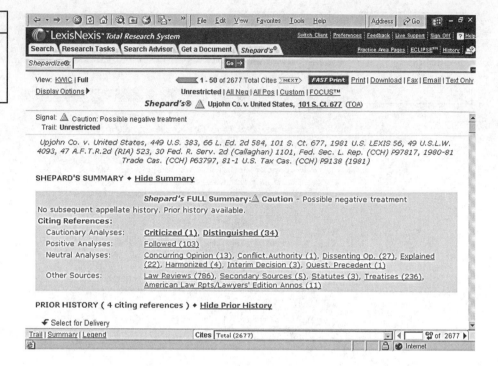

Shepard's Conventions

The information for a Shepardized case begins with the citation, then it gives prior direct history, and then it lists the citing cases. The prior direct history is prior judicial proceeding for the case of interest. For example, the prior direct history of the *Upjohn* case would include its Michigan District Court opinion and its appeal to the Sixth Circuit Court of Appeals. Cases may have prior direct histories that have more than two cases when the case has been remanded or other judicial proceedings were required.

Besides the citation of the citing case (and parallel citations), Shepard's hyperlinks the specific page where the citing case discusses the case of interest and indicates which headnote is linked to the discussion. **Headnotes** are the paragraphs in which the editors of the court reporter summarize the court's holdings on each issue of the case. They appear before the text of the actual court case. The numbered headnotes for a specific case will not necessarily correspond among the various reporters, due to differences in the editors analyzing the relevant legal issues. Thus, when using headnote numbers, the researcher must be cognizant of which court reporter headnote numbers are pertinent to each citator service.

Shepard's evaluates the discussion of the citing case and categorizes its treatment (e.g., criticized, distinguished, explained, followed, etc.) and the operation (amended, extended, revoked, etc.) of the citing cases. Further, Shepard's provides the following symbols as indications of the precedential status of the citing case.

- Red stop sign shape: Warning—Negative Treatment. The citing case has a history of strong negative treatment such as being overruled or reversed.
- Yellow triangle: Caution—Possible Negative Treatment. The citing case has a history of treatment that may have a significant negative impact such as having been criticized or limited.
- Green diamond with a "+" in the center: Positive Treatment. The citing case has had positive treatment such as being affirmed or followed.
- Blue circle with an "A" in the center: Neutral Analysis. The citing case has analysis that is neither positive nor negative.
- Blue circle with an "I" in the center: Information Available. The citing case has references available through Lexis, but the treatment is not categorized. Law review or treatise discussion would be an example of information available.

These symbols are not only assigned to citing cases but also to the case of interest. This makes it easy for the researcher to determine the judicial history of a case at-a-glance. Notice that the *Upjohn* case in Exhibit 8–2 has a yellow triangle associated with it. This means that there has been possible negative treatment of it by other cases and should likely not be relied on to support a client's position.

The citing cases begin with any Supreme Court citing cases and continue by Federal jurisdiction (Appeals Courts and District Courts), followed by the U.S. Court of Federal Claims, Tax Court, various state courts, statutes, law reviews and periodicals, treatises, and other secondary sources. Within each of these citing groups, the citations are listed in reverse chronological order (newest first). As Exhibit 8–2 indicates, the number of citing case references can be staggering; there are over 2,500 for the *Upjohn* case.

Lexis Services

LexisNexis developed its own citator, Auto-Cite, before it offered Shepard's. In addition, it furnishes the Table of Authorities and the LEXCITE search system. These services are accessed through the Shepard's button and can be seen in Exhibit 8–1. Lexis itself may also be used as a citator.

Auto-Cite First offered in 1979, the **Auto-Cite** citation service was originally available only through Lexis dedicated terminals. Now it is part of the Lexis Internet service. Auto-Cite was designed by Lawyers Cooperative Publishing to help their editors check the validity of citations. Therefore, its primary objectives are to provide absolutely accurate citations, and to do so within twenty-four hours of receipt of each case. Not only is Auto-Cite beneficial in determining whether a case is still good law, it also allows researchers to check the standing of Revenue Rulings and Revenue Procedures.

The information retrieved by Auto-Cite includes the correct spelling of the case name, its official citation, the year of the decision, and all official and most unofficial parallel cites. The prior and subsequent case history focuses on opinions relevant to the case's value as precedent. To help with analyzing whether the case is still good law, Auto-Cite uses the same at-a-glance symbol designations as Shepard's. Also, like Shepard's, Auto-Cite offers the researcher two views of the search results, a "Full" or "Abbreviated" version. The

"Abbreviated" version only provides the case, parallel citations, and the most damaging citing cases. The prior history of the case is not presented. In addition to the offerings of the "Abbreviated" view, the "Full" version contains article annotations from *American Law Reports* (ALR) and *Lawyers' Edition, 2d*. Lastly, an interesting feature of Auto-Cite that is not offered in Shepard's is a listing of documents negatively referenced by the case of interest.

The Auto-Cite is updated seven days a week and provides accurate information on cases that affect the strength of the cited case. Whereas Shepard's focus is on furnishing a comprehensive history of the case, Auto-Cite is a selective list of citing cases having a significant impact on the validity of the case of interest.

Table of Authorities The **Table of Authorities** is a citator service, but it is not like those previously discussed. Citators provide a history of a particular case and a list of cases citing it. The Table of Authorities, on the other hand, lists cases that are cited within the case of interest. The list of cases cited is organized by jurisdiction. For each case, the name of the case and its citation with parallel cites is given. The Table of Authorities also provides an assessment of how the case of interest evaluated the cited case and the page on which the cited case is discussed. The cited case itself is evaluated by its prior history and a Shepard's at-a-glance symbol (stop sign, triangle, etc.) indicating the status of the cited case. Clicking on the symbol will Shepardize the cited case. The Table of Authorities information is useful for finding deficiencies in a relevant case, whether or not it supports the client's preferred tax position. If the relevant case relies on other cases with negative or weak histories, the reasoning in a relevant case may be flawed. Hence, a case that itself has no negative history when cited and appears to be good law may be weak as precedent because it relies on cases that have been overruled or have other negative connotations.

LEXCITE When a researcher wants to search legal documents for references to a case of interest, **LEXCITE** is a useful tool. The citation for the case (not the name) must be entered in the standard "volume-reporter-page" convention. LEXCITE also offers the ability to enter keyword search terms, select the database, and restrict the search by date as can be seen in Exhibit 8–3. Once the case has been cited in a document, LEXCITE will identify and highlight subsequent *id.* or *supra* references.

For the case citation entered, LEXCITE ascertains parallel citations and then searches for all of the embedded cite references in documents such as cases, law reviews, journals, legal newspapers, the *Federal Register*, and *Cumulative Bulletins*. The LEXCITE feature actually searches the full text of the documents available in Lexis. Accordingly, the researcher is able to see the references to the case of interest in context and make a personal determination of how the case was evaluated by the document's author. One limitation should be mentioned, however; LEXCITE will not find references to case names only—a court reporter citation must be present for LEXCITE to identify the document as a source.

An advantage of using LEXCITE is that the practitioner can customize the search to retrieve documents that address only a particular point of law in the cited case by using other search terms in addition to the citation. The jurisdiction,

Exhibit | 8-3

LEXCITE Find Reference Screen

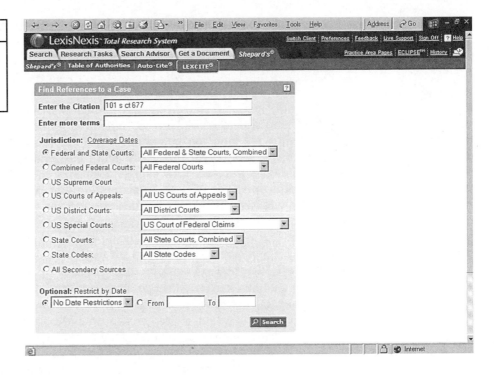

such as only 9th Circuit Court of Appeals or only Missouri state court cases, can be specified. Date restrictions are very helpful when updating previous research. This ability to customize the search is particularly useful when searching secondary sources, such as legal newspapers, journals, and law reviews.

Lexis Lastly, a Lexis keyword search may be employed as a citator when only the name of a case and not its citation is known. A regular Lexis search on the case name will locate every occurrence of the name within the chosen library. If the taxpayer has a common name, there may be many irrelevant references retrieved by Lexis. If the case name is long, it is best to use essential parts of the name, so the search won't miss an occurrence because the case name has been shortened in the documents. Further, the search can be tailored by using other search terms in combination with the name, as described for LEXCITE.

WESTLAW CITATOR SYSTEM

As discussed in Chapter 7, **Westlaw** is structured for legal research. It was designed by attorneys for attorneys. Since case law is very important in most areas of law, taxation included, the citation applications are the centerpiece of the Westlaw service. Westlaw's citators are also very effective in validating statutes and administrative rulings.

Westlaw launched its own major citator, called KeyCite, in 1997, while still offering other citator services such as Shepard's. With the loss of Shepard's, Westlaw has reorganized its citators and developed KeyCite into a comprehensive proprietary citator. Since it was developed solely for use by Westlaw customers, there is no published version of KeyCite.

Besides KeyCite, Westlaw also offers the *RIA Citator*. As its operation is not substantially different than when accessed through the RIA Checkpoint service, discussion of it will be held until the next section of this chapter.

KeyCite

As seen in the left frame of Exhibit 8–4, the **KeyCite** citator offers several options to the researcher. Those that will be examined are: History, Citing References, Full-Text Document, and Table of Authorities (TOA). Demonstrating just how "key" the KeyCite service is to Westlaw, it is accessible directly on the Westlaw Welcome screen (see Chapter 7, Exhibit 7–10) by entering a citation or by clicking on the KeyCite button in the Welcome screen and then entering a citation. As with *Shepard's Citator*, the citation of the document of interest must be known. Names of cases are not acceptable in KeyCite. Also like *Shepard's Citator*, the system has been designed to be flexible as to citation formats. Most formats are accepted as long as the general form of "volume-reporter-page" is used. If the researcher does not know the proper citation format for a document of interest, a publication list is available. The list contains over 2,600 documents; therefore, the list can be scanned by either entering words contained in the document title or entering letters or words starting the document title. Unlike Shepard's list, clicking on the title does not produce a template for entering the citation. The researcher must enter the citation in the KeyCite box using the abbreviation discovered in the publication list.

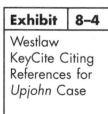

Exhibit	8–4

Westlaw KeyCite Citing References for *Upjohn* Case

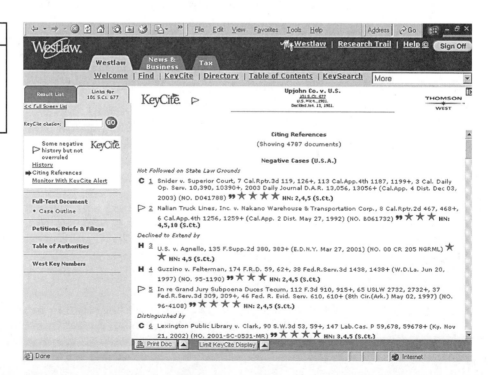

History The direct and negative indirect history for the case in the right-hand window is retrieved when the citation is initially entered into KeyCite. The case's progress through the courts is listed first in the **Direct History** section. The editors indicate the effects of this progression with words and symbols. Although the symbols employed are different from Shepard's, their meanings are similar. KeyCite's symbols are as follows.

- Red Flag: Warning—Negative Treatment. The case or administrative decision is no longer good law for at least one of the points of law it contains. For statutes or regulations, the law has been amended recently or repealed, superseded, or held unconstitutional or preempted in whole or in part.
- Yellow Flag: Caution—Some Negative Treatment. The case has negative history but has not been overruled. The statute or regulation has been renumbered, reinstated, corrected, or transferred recently or its validity has been called into doubt.
- Blue "H": Neutral Analysis. The case has some history but it is not known to be negative.
- Green "C": Information Available. The case or administrative decision has citing references but no direct or negative history. For statutes and regulations there are citing references, but no updating documents.

After the direct history, KeyCite presents the negative **Indirect History** section, which includes citing cases that adversely affect the precedent value of the case of interest. Phrases indicate whether the cases have criticized, distinguished, limited, questioned, or overruled the cited case's logic or holding. The negative cases are also evaluated as to whether they are still good law, using the same symbols as for the direct history (see Exhibit 8–4). Besides this evaluation, KeyCite determines the extent to which the citing cases discuss the cited case of interest. This feature is currently unique to KeyCite and greatly facilitates determining which citing cases should be reviewed. The symbols range from four stars to one star, with four denoting an extended examination of the case (usually more than a printed page in length) and one denoting a brief reference (such as in a string of citations). The final unique symbol supplied by KeyCite is quotation marks, indicating that the citing case has quoted the cited case. This symbol does not appear in the indirect history listing but is utilized in the Citing References (see Exhibit 8–4).

Citing References For a comprehensive list of citing cases, select the **Citing References** option. KeyCite retrieved over 4,700 documents for the *Upjohn* case, almost all of which are positive cites. The listing starts with the negative indirect history of *Upjohn*. These will be the same negative cases retrieved for the indirect history, but the most recent cases are presented first. The positive indirect history, next, is organized by the depth of coverage, starting with the four star examinations and leading to the one star citing cases. The last group in the list contains secondary source references by law reviews, *American Law Reports*, administrative materials, *Mertens* tax service, etc.

Since the number of documents retrieved can be overwhelming, KeyCite allows the researcher to limit those retrieved by headnotes (key numbers), location, type of jurisdiction, date, type of document, and depth of treatment (number of stars). A keyword search is possible if the KeyCite list is less than 2,000 documents.

As discussed previously, the headnote paragraphs represent a summary of each significant legal issue in the case. The interpretation of "significant issues" will vary by the editorial staff of each court reporter. The editors of these court reporters analyzed the judicial opinions to different degrees of detail. For example, the West's *Supreme Court Reporter* editors for the *Upjohn* case required ten headnotes to evaluate the law, whereas the RIA editors of the AFTR2d series needed just two. The drafting of headnotes and the breadth of the issue that each headnote addresses are a matter of style and editorial policy of the entity that publishes the reporter.

SPOTLIGHT ON TAXATION: Supreme Court Justices

The Supreme Court is made up of nine justices who are nominated by the President and approved by the Senate. Approximately 8,000 petitions are filed with the Supreme Court in the course of one year. In addition, some 1,200 applications of various kinds are filed each year that are acted upon by a single justice. As Supreme Court justices reside on the bench for life, the ability to nominate a Supreme Court justice accords the President tremendous power to influence future Supreme Court decisions by virtue of the person selected for nomination. Here is a list of the current (early 2005) Supreme Court justices. It is likely that this list will change in the next few years.

Name	Date of Birth Place of Birth	Nominating President	Year Installed
William H. Rehnquist (Chief Justice)	October 1, 1924 Milwaukee, Wisconsin	Nixon	1972
John Paul Stevens	April 20, 1920 Chicago, Illinois	Nixon	1970
Sandra Day O'Connor	March 26, 1930 El Paso, Texas	Reagan	1981
Antonin Scalia	March 11, 1936 Trenton, New Jersey	Reagan	1986
Anthony M. Kennedy	July 23, 1936 Sacramento, California	Reagan	1988
David H. Souter	September 17, 1939 Melrose, Massachusetts	Bush	1990
Clarence Thomas	June 28, 1948 Pinpoint, a community near Savannah, Georgia	Bush	1991
Ruth Bader Ginsburg	March 15, 1933 Brooklyn, New York	Clinton	1993
Stephen Breyer	August 15, 1938 San Francisco, California	Clinton	1994

The West headnote system has a particularly valuable feature for finding law, the West Key Number System. The points of law articulated in a case are editorially classified into Key Numbers that fit into an extensive system for organizing case law. West publishes a series of digests that organize the holdings of cases by Key Numbers. The Key Number & Custom Digests are also accessible on Westlaw via the drop-down menu found in the "More" option (see Exhibit 8–4) on the toolbar. The key number for a topic of interest can be found by either drilling down through the Key Numbers list or entering a broad topic in a search box (Tax for income taxes). Once the key number is identified, the search can be customized by jurisdiction, date restrictions, and additional search terms. The order in which the headnotes are displayed may also be specified. The result of the search is a list of cases with headnotes key numbered to the issue.

Full-Text Document Selecting **Full-Text Document** displays the text of the case entered in KeyCite. The full citation (all official cites and numerous unofficial cites) of the case, geographical location, and date of judgment are provided as well. After a summary of the case, the headnotes and key numbers assigned by the case reporter editors appear and then the official full-text of the document. Rather than retrieving the full-text, the researcher can select the outline option. With this option, the researcher can view the synopsis, headnotes, or opinions for the case.

Table of Authorities The Westlaw Table of Authorities (TOA) performs the same function as the Shepard's version. However, the Westlaw TOA reports more information. Not only does it indicate where the case of interest cites other cases in supporting its reasoning, Westlaw also denotes how much discussion was given to the case using its four-star depth of treatment symbols. Further, if the case of interest quotes other cases, this is designated with the quotation marks symbol. The cases listed in the TOA with negative history or that have been reversed or overruled are marked with either a yellow or red flag, making it easy for the researcher to determine the strength of the cases relied on by the case of interest as Exhibit 8–5 demonstrates.

RIA CITATOR

The **Research Institute of America Citator** and **Citator 2nd Series** were formerly published by Prentice-Hall and then Maxwell Macmillan. Many practitioners still refer to this service as the Prentice-Hall **(PH) Citators;** however, the name "Prentice-Hall" was eliminated from the *Citator 2nd Series* as of Volume 3. In this text, the Internet series will be called the **RIA Citator**, with the older published volumes referred to as the **PH Citators** and the newer published volumes as **Citator 2d Series**.

One of the significant advantages of the electronic *RIA Citator* over its published counterpart is that the need to consult multiple volumes is eliminated. The citations from the various published volumes are found with only one search. However, the *Checkpoint RIA Citator* does not include the older *PH Citators*; only the *Citator 2d Series* is available. Thus, if the case being

Exhibit 8-5

Westlaw KeyCite Table of Authorities for *Upjohn* Case

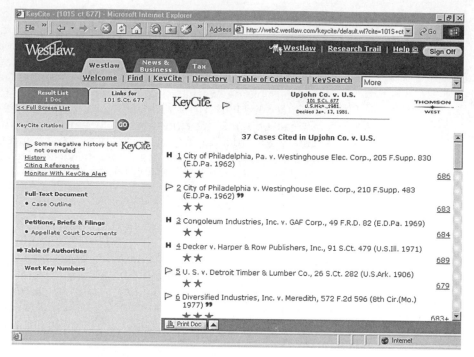

citated was decided before 1954, the researcher must resort to the published versions of the *PH Citators*.

RIA offers a comprehensive tax citator. Along with tax cases, Administrative Pronouncements (hereafter referred to as Rulings) and Treasury Decisions are evaluated. All District Court, Federal Claims, Court of Appeals, and Supreme Court cases reported in the AFTR, AFTR2d, and AFTR3d series are included, as well as Tax Court and Tax Court Memorandum decisions. The nonpublished Tax Court Summary Opinions are also contained in the *RIA Citators*. An abbreviated list of the Rulings covered by the *RIA Citator* is provided in Exhibit 8–6.

Using the RIA Citator

The *RIA Citator* is accessible from the opening Checkpoint screen (see Chapter 6, Exhibit 6–1). RIA supports citator retrieval by the name of the case, its citation, or through keyword searches. Templates are furnished for entering citations. The researcher has the option of receiving a list of cases and rulings that cite the case of interest (cited) or a list of "… all the cases and/or rulings which were cited by your search entry." (citing) From this definition, the researcher might expect a Table of Authorities like those found in Lexis or Westlaw; however, this is not the case. The "citing" option may evolve to become more like the Table of Authorities in the future.

The result of the *Upjohn* "cited" search is a list of all the tax cases citing *Upjohn*. Thus, the major difference between the *RIA Citator* and Shepard's or KeyCite is that only tax cases are cited. This may be beneficial as it reduces the number of citations retrieved to those citing the case of interest based on

Exhibit	8–6

RIA Citators Treasury Decisions and Rulings

Treasury Decisions and Rulings Cited in *RIA Citator*

Abridged List

Announc	Announcements
ARM	Appeals and Revenue Memorandum
ARR	Appeals and Revenue Recommendations
Ct D	Court Decisions
Del Order	Commissioner's Delegation Order
EO	Executive Orders
GCM	General Council Memorandums
IR	Internal Revenue News Releases
IT	Income Tax Unit Rulings
PLR Letter Ruling	Private Letter Rulings
LO	Law Opinions
News Release	News Releases
Notice	Notices
OD	Office Opinions
PS	Processing Tax Division Rulings
Rev Proc	Revenue Procedures
Rev Rul	Revenue Rulings
TAM	Technical Advice Memorandum
TD	Treasury Decisions
TD Cir	Treasury Decision Circular
TDO	Treasury Decision Order
TIR	Technical Information Release

its analysis of tax issues. Selecting on the underlined citation of any of the cases listed will produce the full text of the case. The case document provides full citations of the *Upjohn* case, Code sections addressed in the case, level of the court, date decided, prior history of the *Upjohn* case, and its disposition. The three buttons just above the *Upjohn* case name in Exhibit 8–7 access annotations of the case in the *United States Tax Reporter*, paragraph references of the case in the *Federal Tax Coordinator 2d*, or the case's listing in the *RIA Citator.*

RIA Conventions

When the plaintiff in a tax case is the U.S. Government, Commissioner of Internal Revenue, Secretary of the Treasury, or an IRS Director, the *RIA Citator* does not catalog the case under the plaintiff's name, as is the traditional legal convention. This is because there are thousands of cases in which Eisner, Helvering, Burnet, or other Commissioners or Secretaries of the Treasury initiated the litigation. Rather, the *RIA Citator* catalogs all cases by the taxpayer's name. This convention greatly facilitates the researcher's search for specific cases.

The *Upjohn* case was first decided in 1978 by the U.S. District Court (41 AFTR2d 78-796), which found for the IRS. The taxpayer appealed to the U.S. Court of Appeals for the Sixth Circuit. This case, decided in 1979 (44 AFTR2d 79-5179), found for the IRS on most issues. The taxpayer appealed again, this time to the U.S. Supreme Court. The Supreme Court decided the case in

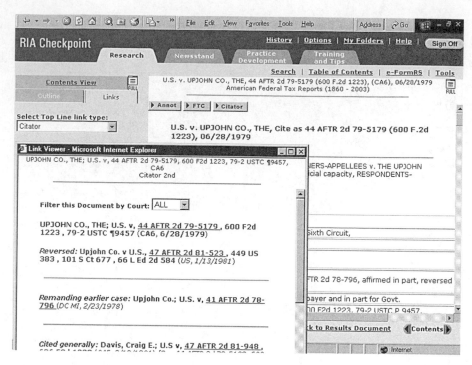

RIA Citator and Case—*Upjohn* Case

the taxpayer's favor in 1981 (47 AFTR2d 81-523). Consequently, there are three separate entries in the *RIA Citator* for this case because each of these courts wrote an opinion that can be cited by other cases. The Supreme Court opinion is the most cited, since it is the final decision on the issues. There is little reason for future decisions to cite the trial or appellate cases, since they were reversed. In fact, the 1979 Appeals Court case was last cited in 1990.

In Exhibit 8–7, after the *Upjohn* case name, the case's citation in RIA's AFTR2d series is listed, followed by its parallel citations. First, the official reporters (government publications) are listed and then other unofficial court reporters (commercial publishers). The first entries after the case name provide the judicial history of the case. Descriptions indicate the effects of the higher courts' decisions on the holdings of lower courts that previously heard the case. The Appeals Court case (44 AFTR2d 79-5179) was reversed by the Supreme Court case (47 AFTR2d 81-523). The trial court case was remanded by the Appeals Court.

After the judicial history, the *RIA Citator* first lists the citations for cases that are in complete agreement with the cited case. Next, citing cases are listed that discuss the holdings or reasoning of the cited case but do not refer to a specific paragraph or headnote. Lastly, cases are listed in order of the headnote issue that they address. The *RIA Citator* bases its headnote designations on the *American Federal Tax Reports* (AFTR, AFTR2d, and AFTR3d) series, which is also a product of RIA. For the *Upjohn* Supreme Court case, AFTR2d provides two headnotes. The researcher needs to make sure that with the *RIA Citator* the AFTR headnotes are utilized and not headnotes from other reporters, such as those published by West.

Within any of the citing groupings—complete agreement, no specific headnote, Headnote 1, Headnote 2, and so on—citing cases and rulings are listed in the following order.

- U.S. Supreme Court
- U.S. Courts of Appeal
- U.S. Court of Federal Claims (or predecessor court)
- U.S. District Court
- U.S. Tax Court (or predecessor court—BTA, regular then memorandum decisions)
- State courts
- Treasury Rulings and Decisions

Citing cases within any court or ruling group are arranged in chronological order.

In their listings, the *RIA Citator* includes all of the tax citing cases that mention the cited opinion. Therefore, the listings for important cases containing many issues can be several screens long. The headnote number references allow researchers to restrict their search to only those citing cases with issues that are relevant to their client's factual situation. Therefore, if the researcher is interested in the issue described in the second headnote of the *Upjohn* case, only cases thus designated need be reviewed.

Many researchers prefer to start their analysis of a case with the most recent citing cases and work backward to earlier cases. In this way, they can quickly identify the present status of the cited case. For example, a steady stream of recent favorable references probably indicates that the precedent of the original case is still valid and strong, whereas either a list of negative comments or a scarcity of references may indicate a weak decision. The citator portion of a research project is complete when the researcher is satisfied that the status of the case is sufficiently confirmed. At this point some of the citing cases should be examined because the facts of a client's situation are rarely identical to the cases initially located.

If the cases found initially support the client's position but the facts are somewhat different, the search should continue for a supportive case with more similar facts. Hence, those citations designated as "case reconciled," indicating that their facts or opinions are different from those of the cited case and require reconciliation, should be consulted. If the initial cases found have holdings adverse to a client's position, the practitioner should search for cases marked "case distinguished," to identify what factors are relevant to the issuance of an adverse opinion. The distinguished cases usually have facts that are actually different from those of the cited case, thus supporting a different holding. Some of these facts may resemble the facts of the practitioner's client and thus provide the desired support. Similarly, a case denoted as "citing generally" limits the holding of the cited case to a narrow set of facts.

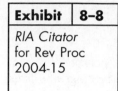

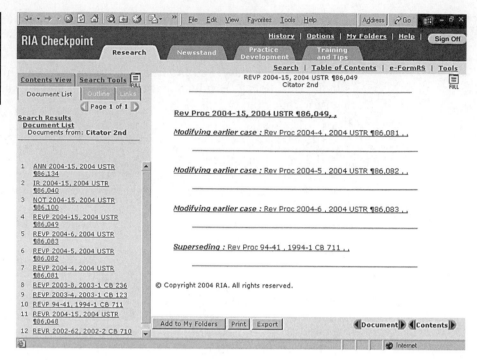

This may occur when a higher court has ruled differently on a case with somewhat similar facts or there has been a change in the tax law. Thus, the holding of the cited case may be inapplicable to the client's factual situation.

RIA Citator: Rulings

After identifying administrative rulings (Revenue Ruling, Revenue Procedure, Notice, etc.) that appear to support a client's tax position, it is critically important for a researcher to determine if they are still in effect and represent the current view of the IRS. Due to the constant state of change in the tax law, rulings are continually being modified, superseded, or invalidated. The *RIA Citator* furnishes templates for most IRS administrative rulings. The steps in checking the validity of a ruling are the same as with a court case.

Within each type of ruling, the entries are presented in chronological order, as is the citing ruling for the entry. If there are any cases citing the entry, these are listed after citing Revenue Rulings and before lesser pronouncements (such as Private Letter Rulings). As Exhibit 8–8 demonstrates, it is always important to check pertinent pronouncements through a citator. What is currently good law one week (Rev Proc 2004-6 issued January 7, 2004) may become unreliable at any point in the future (modified by Rev Proc 2004-15 on January 29, 2004).

CCH CITATOR

The *Commerce Clearing House Citator* (**CCH Citator**) is available in print as an integral part of CCH's *Standard Federal Tax Reporter* (discussed in Chapter 6) and is also accessible through CCH's Internet service Tax Research Net-Work (NetWork) in the Federal Tax library and the U.S. Master Tax Guide Plus. The computer versions are merely the paper version in electronic form. The *CCH Citator* is not offered by any of the other major Internet services (such as Lexis, Kleinrock, or Westlaw).

CCH Attributes

The *CCH Citator* differs dramatically from the other citators. First, the *CCH Citator* lists only those citing cases that the CCH editors believe will serve as useful guides in evaluating the cited case's effectiveness as precedent. Thus, the tax researcher is directed to those cases that may be most likely to develop, explain, criticize, or otherwise evaluate a rule of law. This is in contrast to the other citators, which provide all of the cases mentioning the cited case. Although the latter practice provides a level of thoroughness that may be useful, the CCH editorial screening procedure guards against the possibility of being overwhelmed by the sheer volume of citing cases presented. The more selective CCH approach, of course, forces the researcher to rely on an editor's evaluation concerning the usefulness of the citing cases.

Second, the *CCH Citator* covers only the Federal income tax decisions issued since 1913. Also, court decisions that are obsolete due to changes in the statutes are marked with a dagger symbol, and no citing cases are given for these cases. Estate and gift tax cases are listed by name, again with no citing cases. Tax Court estate and gift cases are not even listed by name. This is because CCH has other complete citator services for the estate and gift cases and also for excise tax cases.

Third, as Exhibit 8–9 illustrates, the *CCH Citator* acts as a Finding Table as well as a citator by giving paragraph references to where the case is reviewed in the *Standard Federal Tax Reporter*. This feature reduces the searching time required to locate supplemental information regarding a case or ruling of interest. The tax service discussions help the researcher evaluate the case or ruling in the context of relevant Code sections, Regulations, and administrative sources of tax law.

Finally, the *CCH Citator* does not provide evaluations of the citing cases (see Exhibit 8–9). This is a significant drawback of the citator. With a list of citing cases as long as that for the *Upjohn* case, knowing how each citing case interpreted to the *Upjohn* case could substantially reduce the number of cases the researcher reads.

CCH Conventions

As with other citators, the *CCH Citator* furnishes templates for entering the citation of the case or ruling of interest. However, AFTR (RIA Federal court reporter) citations are not supported by the *CCH Citator*, whereas the *RIA Citator* does include templates for USTC (CCH Federal court reporter) citations. This can cause problems when a journal article, for example, contains an AFTR 2d cite for a case with a common taxpayer name, but the practitioner has access only to the *CCH Citator* and CCH court reporters.

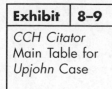

Exhibit | **8–9**

CCH Citator Main Table for Upjohn Case

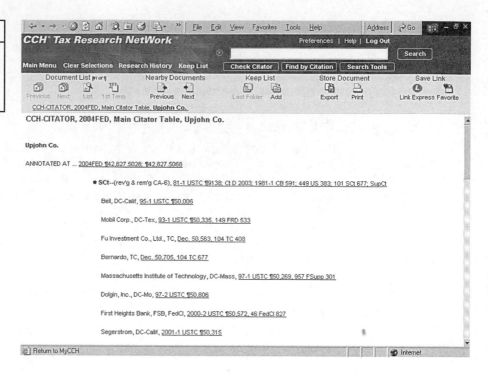

The first entry after the name of a cited case is the annotation paragraph number references to the *Standard Federal Tax Reporter* compilations (see Exhibit 8–9). The bold black bullets designate the court levels that have addressed the case. The highest level court to address the case is listed first, and the trial-level court is listed last. Hence, the citation for the *Upjohn* Supreme Court case is listed first followed by its citing cases, then the Sixth Circuit case followed by its citing cases, and lastly the District Court case. The advantage of this organization is that the researcher can easily determine the highest court that heard the case and the bullet headings clearly identify the levels of the court cases. Examining the entries in Exhibit 8–9, the citing cases under each court decision are not listed in any apparent order either by date or court.

The *CCH Citator* provides limited information about the judicial history of the case. The reference for the Supreme Court case denotes that it reversed the Sixth Circuit's holding and remanded the case. The Sixth Circuit reference indicates it affirmed some holdings of the District Court decision and reversed and remanded on other issues. Since the *CCH Citator* does not denote citing case evaluations, the researcher cannot determine if, for example, the *Bell* case followed, or explained, or distinguished itself from the *Upjohn* case.

Three methods for entering a case or ruling of interest into the *CCH Citator* are evident in Exhibit 8–10. If either the case name or a complete citation of the document is known, this data may be entered in the appropriate boxes. When the practitioner is unclear as to the proper form of the citation, the Citator templates may be used. For illustrative purposes, Exhibit 8–10 has entered the case name, complete citation, and cites using the case templates

Exhibit	8–10

CCH Check Citator with *Upjohn* Case Citations

for the *Upjohn* case. A researcher would actually provide data for only one of these searches. Lastly, while viewing a case on screen, selecting the "Check Citator" button on the main NetWork toolbar will display the Citator entries for the case being examined.

SUMMARY

The tax researcher's job of sorting through the thousands of potentially pertinent Federal tax authorities is facilitated by citators. When familiar with these research tools, the current status and precedential value of a specific case or ruling can be determined effectively and quickly. This determination is necessary for the researcher to evaluate the judicial and administrative sources of the tax law that pertain to a client's tax issue. The electronic services automate virtually all of the tedious mechanical aspects of Shepardizing cases and validating the formal correctness of citations. Further, they make the retrieval of cited and citing cases almost effortless. The overview of citators and the act of citing presented in this chapter demonstrate that research is not complete until all primary sources upon which the researcher is relying are found to be currently "good law."

TAX TUTOR

Reinforce the tax research information covered in this chapter by completing the online tutorials located at the Federal Tax Research web site:

http://raabe.swlearning.com

KEY WORDS

By the time you complete your work in this chapter, you should be comfortable discussing each of the following terms. If you need additional review of any of these items, return to the appropriate material in the chapter or consult the glossary at the end of this text.

Auto-Cite
CCH Citator
Citation
Citator
Citator 2nd Series
Cited Case
Cites
Citing Case
Citing References
Direct History
Full-Text Document

Headnote
Indirect History
KeyCite
LEXCITE
PH Citators
RIA Citator
Shepardizing
Shepard's Citators
Shepard's Federal Tax Citator
Table of Authorities
Westlaw

DISCUSSION QUESTIONS

1. What are the goals of tax research?

2. Describe the authority of the Code. What do practitioners do if the Code is not clear on an issue?

3. Why are subsequent cases important to the value of a prior case?

4. Describe the function of a citator in the tax research process.

5. Distinguish between the following terms: cited case, citing case, citation, and cites.

6. Citators do not provide all information related to a case. What kind of information do citators *not* provide?

7. Name three commercial citators that focus exclusively on tax cases, and indicate whether they are sold as part of a commercial tax service.

8. Explain the difference between a general directing and a local directing cite. Which service uses local directing cites?

9. What does "Shepardizing" mean?

10. Compare the coverage and organization of Shepard's with the RIA and CCH citator services.

11. With the *Shepard's Citator* a researcher can locate a case either by the case name or by its citation. Comment on this statement.

12. Evaluate the following statement. The headnotes for a given case are set by the court and thus are consistent across court reporting services.

13. What is the equivalent of the Shepard's Green Diamond symbol in Westlaw?

14. What is Auto-Cite, who developed it, and what is its primary objective?

15. What is the function of a Table of Authorities? Why is it a useful research tool?

16. What is LEXCITE, and when would a researcher use this Lexis service?

17. What is KeyCite? What event in 1999 caused a reorganization of KeyCite?

18. How does the information provided by KeyCite History differ from that retrieved using KeyCite Citing Reference?

19. What information regarding citing cases is provided by KeyCite that is not available from the other citation services discussed in this chapter?

20. What information about a case is available in the KeyCite full-text document option?

21. When is the West Key Number System useful to a researcher?

22. Compare the Shepard's (Lexis) Table of Authorities with the Westlaw KeyCite version.

23. Why is the responsibility of nominating Supreme Court judges an important presidential power? Which President appointed the greatest number of the current Supreme Court judges?

24. What company was the first to introduce citators as legal aids?

25. What publishers have been associated with the *Citator* and *Citator 2d Series*?

26. Name four types of Administrative Pronouncements covered by the *RIA Citator*.

27. What Internet service besides Checkpoint provides access to the *RIA Citator*?

28. What type of case retrieval does the *RIA Citator* support that is unavailable with Shepard's or KeyCite?

29. What is a drawback in the coverage of cases in the electronic version of the *RIA Citator*?

30. What information is provided in the full-text case document in Checkpoint?

31. The *RIA Citator* does not follow the traditional legal convention of listing cases under the plaintiff's name. What convention does it use? Why are the cases listed in this manner?

32. In what order does the *RIA Citator* list citations?

33. What is the benefit of a headnote when performing a citator search?

34. When is the citator portion of a research project finished?

35. Why must Revenue Rulings identified through a keyword search be checked in a citator?

36. What different Internet services offer access to the *CCH Citator*?

37. How is the *CCH Citator* different from the other citators discussed in this chapter?

38. How does the *CCH Citator* act as a Finding Table?

39. *CCH Citator* provides templates for most court reporter series. What series does CCH not support with templates?

40. When viewing a document in CCH NetWork, how can the document be easily run through the citator?

EXERCISES

41. State the proper Shepard's citation for the following documents.
    a. A 1992 article in *Florida State University Law Review*, volume 20 starting on page 196.
    b. The 4th Private Letter Ruling issued in the 26th week of 2000 (200026004).
    c. Arkansas Constitution, Article 16, Section 2.
    d. Field Service Advice 199952041.
    e. *Winthrop v. Union Insurance Co.* in volume 2 Washington's United States Circuit Court Reports, page 7.

42. Using the *Shepard's Citator*, Shepardize *C. G. Services Corp.* found in volume 73 of the Tax Court Reporter on page 406.
    a. What Shepard's evaluation symbol is associated with the case? What does the symbol mean?
    b. How many citing documents are listed for this case? How many of the citing cases followed *C. G. Services Corp.*?
    c. What is the subsequent appellate history of this case?
    d. There is an article in the 1989 Tennessee Law Review on page 661 that cites *C. G. Services Corp.* What is the title of the article and the name of the author?

43. Locate *City of New Britian*, 44 AFTR ¶ 798, using *Shepard's Citator*.
    a. What are the parallel citations for this case? In what year was this case decided?
    b. On what page does the case, *Estate of Romani*, 140 L. Ed. 2d 710, cite the *New Britian* case? What page would this be if you were using the United States Supreme Court Reports (U.S.)?
    c. The *Shepard's Citator* indicates that the *Kimbell Foods, Inc.*, case, 99 S. Ct. 1448, discusses the *New Britian* case on two different pages. What are the page numbers? Why does the United States Supreme Court Reports only indicate that the case is discussed on one page?
    d. What Lexis precedent symbol is associated with both the *Estate of Romani* and the *Kimbell Foods, Inc.* cases?

44. Locate *City of New Britian*, 1954 U.S. Lexis 2751, using Lexis Auto-Cite.
    a. What Lexis precedent symbol is associated with this case? What event caused the New Britian case to receive this symbol?
    b. What is this case's judicial history?

    c. What publication cites this case in its discussion of the provisions of 31 USCS §§ 3713 and 9309?

    d. What citing cases are listed in the subsequent treatment history section?

45. Using LEXCITE, enter the following citation: 5 L. Ed.2d 128 and select Combined Federal Courts as the Jurisdiction.

    a. What is the name of the case with the citation you entered? When was it decided? How many citing document are found?

    b. In the "Enter more terms" type "sweepstakes" into the box. Now how many citing documents are returned? There is a 1965 Tax Court case and its Second Court of Appeals case in the citing list. What is the name of this case?

    c. Remove the "sweepstakes" term and select Secondary Sources as the Jurisdiction. Use a date restriction of the previous five years. What is the full citation for the University of Colorado law review article citing the case of interest?

46. Using Lexis Table of Authorities, enter the following citation: 74 S. Ct. 367.

    a. What are the parallel citations for this case? In what year was this case decided?

    b. How many cases did it cite in developing its decision? Which cited cases have some type of warning associated with them?

    c. What are the jurisdictional levels in which the cases are divided?

    d. On which pages are the cases?

47. State the proper Westlaw KeyCite citation for the following documents.

    a. An article in *New York University Law Review*, volume 12 starting on page 137.

    b. The 4th Private Letter Ruling issued in the 26th week of 2000 (200026004).

    c. Arkansas Constitution, Article 16, Section 2.

    d. Field Service Advice 199952041.

    e. *Winthrop v. Union Insurance Co.* in volume 2 Washington Circuit Court Reports, page 7.

    f. Are these the same citation abbreviations and format as Shepard's uses?

48. Locate *Tank Truck Rentals, Inc.*, 78 S. Ct. 507, with Westlaw KeyCite.

    a. What are official parallel citations for this case? In what year was this case decided?

    b. Using KeyCite History, how many lower court cases are shown in the direct history? How was each treated?

    c. List the citing documents in the Negative Indirect History, and explain the depth of treatment by each.

    d. How many positive three- and four-star depth of treatment cases are listed for *Tank Truck Rentals, Inc.*? For the four-star cases, indicate what type of explanatory symbols were presented.

49. Use the Table of Authorities on Westlaw KeyCite to find the following information *for Tank Truck Rentals, Inc.*, 78 S. Ct. 507.

    a. How many cases does *Tank Truck Rentals, Inc.*, cite in its decision?

    b. Which case(s) does it quote that has three stars for depth of treatment?

      c. How many of the cases cited in *Tank Truck Rentals, Inc.*, have warning or caution symbols? How does this make you feel about the reasoning in this case?

      d. How many different pages have discussion of cases?

50.   Using the "More" pull-down menu in Westlaw, select Key Numbers & Digest.

      a. What is the key number for taxation?

      b. What are the roman numeral and "k" numerals associated with Inheritance and Gift Taxes?

      c. What are the three subsections for income taxes?

      d. How useful do you think the key numbering system will be in income tax questions?

51.   Use Shepard's on Lexis and KeyCite on Westlaw to locate *Algernon Blair, Inc.*, 441 F.2d 1379.

      a. How many citing *cases* does Shepard's list? How many citing cases have warning or caution symbols?

      b. How many citing *cases* does KeyCite list? How many citing cases have warning or caution symbols?

      c. What is the maximum depth of treatment the citing cases give *Algernon Blair, Inc.*? How many cases quote *Algernon Blair, Inc.*? Which service did you use to discover this information?

      d. Which service do you think provided you more useful information? Which provided you too much information (information overload)?

52.   Use Shepard's on Lexis and KeyCite on Westlaw to locate *Kirchner, Moore & Co.*, 448 F.2d 1281.

      a. Has this case been appealed? If yes, give the citation.

      b. What are the citing *cases* listed by Shepard's that KeyCite does not list?

      c. How many Fourth and Eleventh Circuit Court of Appeals cases cite *Kirchner, Moore & Co.*? List the names of the taxpayers in these cases.

      d. How much coverage did the *Ball* (54 TC 1207) case give to the *Kirchner, Moore & Co.* case? Should the *Ball* case be relied upon?

      e. Which service do you think was easier to use for each part of this question?

53.   Use the *RIA Checkpoint Citator 2d* to answer the following questions.

      a. Find the citing cases for the taxpayer Knetsch. Provide the citations for all the cases you retrieve.

      b. Which cases constitute direct history for the *Knetsch* Supreme Court case?

      c. How many headnotes does the case show? What does each headnote address?

      d. How many Eleventh Circuit Court of Appeals cases cite the *Knetsch* Supreme Court case? List the names of the taxpayers in these cases. What was the easiest method to find this information?

54. Use the *RIA Checkpoint Citator 2d* to answer the following questions.
    a. Perform a keyword search on the taxpayer name Algernon Blair. What is the citation for the Tax Court case with Blair as the taxpayer? In what year was the Tax Court case decided?
    b. How do the citing cases treat this Tax Court case?
    c. At what paragraph numbers in the *Federal Tax Coordinator* is this Tax Court discussed?
    d. At what paragraphs numbers is this Tax Court case annotated?

55. Use the *RIA Checkpoint Citator 2d* and Shepard's to cite *Deluxe Check Printers, Inc. v. U.S.* 62 AFTR 2d 88-5146.
    a. Explain the difference in proper citation form when entering the *Deluxe Check Printers* case in RIA versus Shepard's.
    b. Are the documents the same for RIA and Shepard's? Explain your response.
    c. Why are the court cases in a different order for RIA than they are for Shepard's?
    d. Which citator do you find easier to use? Explain your response.

56. Using the *CCH Citator*, locate *John Doe*, 74-1 USTC ¶ 9344, and answer the following questions.
    a. In what year was this decision rendered?
    b. What is the citation for *John Doe* in the F2d court reporter?
    c. What is the citation for *John Doe* in the AFTR2d court reporter?
    d. What was the court of original jurisdiction for this case?

57. Using the *CCH Citator*, locate the *William George* Tax Court case that was decided in 1956 and answer the following questions.
    a. What is the citation for the case?
    b. What is the title of the paragraph where *George* is annotated?
    c. What code section is related to the *George* case?
    d. A Revenue Ruling cites the *George* case. What is the citation and title? How does the Revenue Ruling evaluate the *George* case?

58. Locate Revenue Ruling 1979-162 and answer the following questions.
    a. What is its complete Cumulative Bulletin citation? Is it still a valid Revenue Ruling?
    b. What tax issue does the Revenue Ruling address?
    c. In what paragraph of the *Federal Tax Coordinator 2d* is this ruling discussed?
    d. In what paragraph of the CCH service was this ruling initially discussed?
    e. In what paragraph of the Code Arranged by Annotations (*RIA Checkpoint*) is this ruling discussed?

59. Using the *CCH* and the *RIA Citators*, locate the *Estate of Edward Kunze* case.
    a. What method did you use to find this case?
    b. Do the citators provide the same list of citing cases? Explain your response.
    c. How did the citing cases generally treat the *Kunze* case? Which citator did you use to determine this?
    d. What issues appear to be involved in this case? Which citator did you use to determine this?

60. Find Revenue Rulings 1999-49 and 2000-56 in a citator of your choosing.
    a. What are their full citations?
    b. Are these rulings still valid? Explain your response by referring to their administrative history.
    c. What effect did these rulings have on previously issued rulings?
    d. What causes the history of these rulings?

RESEARCH CASES

For each of the research problems locate court cases or administrative pronouncements (Revenue Rulings, Revenue Procedures, etc.) that support your position. Provide a list of cases or administrative pronouncements citing your authority that demonstrate your authority is still good law.

61. Jamie's adjusted gross income is $31,000. During 2003 and 2004, she spent $350 of her own funds on special school supplies for those children that could not afford to purchase the necessary supplies. She bought these supplies during a 75-mile round trip to a specialty educational store. Can she deduct any portion of these amounts?

62. Ted's sister, April, was injured while performing her duties as a police officer. She was in the hosited for three weeks before she died from her wounds. The city paid directly to Ted the workers' compensation benefits due to April before she died, as he is April's only surviving relative. How much gross income does Ted recognize upon receiving the benefits?

63. Peggy had been a heavy tobacco user until she joined the Norwood Tobacco Free Program. She had spent a substantial amount of money on nicotine patches and other nonprescription treatments without much success. Her father recently died from lung cancer. His death really made her realize that to kick the habit she would need to get professional help before her smoking created serious medical problems. While she is very pleased at being tobacco free for the first time in ten years, she is wondering whether any of the vast amounts spent on the cure are deductible.

64. Sally sells her home to Bob and pays the $9,000 in points by offsetting this amount against her sale proceeds. Determine the tax effects on both parties.

65. Ethel and Rick spent $4,500 in allocable interest and taxes and $1,100 in advertising and maintenance for their "bed and breakfast" inn. This year's rental income from the inn came to $4,900. Determine the tax effects of conducting the B&B as a one-third part of Ethel and Rick's residence.

66. The parents of this year's "Annie" (she is age 8) spent $8,000 in travel expenses for auditions and rehearsals of the popular play. When she got the part, her parents were designated in the Broadway contract to receive one-half of her total earnings. Discuss the proper recognition of gross income and related deductions concerning this arrangement.

67. Barbara's psychologist recommended that Barbara divorce her husband, Tom. Tom's dress and eating habits had led to Barbara's serious neuroses. Are the costs of the divorce deductible to Tom? To Barbara?

68. Newark Marine Food Service sells hot lunches and snacks to the crews of ships that dock at the Port of Newark. According to custom, the officers of the visiting ships receive a 5 percent "commission" from all sales, so that Marine can retain its "exclusive rights" to the seamen's business. Are the commissions deductible by the shipping firms?

69. Clara, a junior college graduate, works at the PamperU Hotel in Lake Tahoe. Clara's job is to provide relaxation demonstrations, teach yoga, provide massage therapy, and give lectures on stress management. Since Clara possessed no formal training in any of these subjects, she decided to attend seminars all over the United States on the topics related to her job. She also attended the local university and took physiology classes to learn more about the body and how it functions. Can Clara deduct these expenses as continuing educational expenses?

70. Joy accompanied her husband on a business trip to San Diego because he had been injured in a subway accident and could no longer drive an automobile. Joy was not associated with his business directly, but she did perform as his chauffeur on the trip. What is the tax treatment of Joy's incremental expenses for the trip?

71. After his divorce, Brown paid the expenses of maintaining the family home, which continued to be the principal residence of his ex-wife and their three daughters. He owned the house, but no longer lived there. Instead, he maintained another home as his principal residence. Can he claim head of household status, assuming that he is assigned the dependency exemptions for the daughters?

72. Alice, the chair of the School of Accountancy, entertains the faculty at her home each semester and has a holiday party at the end of December for the faculty and their families. When a faculty member is promoted or has a paper published in an exceptionally prestigious journal, she has a "social hour" at her house. She also sponsors a picnic for the faculty and graduate students at the start of the fall semester to let them get acquainted. To what extent are these expenses deductible?

73. Vandals caused $1,250 damage to Tricia's fully depreciated rental property. Determine her casualty loss or other deduction.

74. Buddy was injured by Matt in an automobile accident. The court awarded Buddy $30,000 in damages, but Matt was able to raise (and paid to Buddy) only $12,000. They both then considered the matter closed. Compute the amount of gross income to Buddy, and to Matt, from these transactions.

75. Con man Floyd sold Larry the Library of Congress for $15,000. Larry had embezzled the $15,000 he used to make the purchase from his employer.
    a. How much gross income should Larry and Floyd report as a result of these transactions?
    b. What is the tax treatment for Larry when he repays his (former) employer?

76. Reverend Ruth received an annual salary of $50,000 and a parsonage allowance of $12,000. She paid $9,000 rent on the home, and she spent $1,500 on housing-related purchases. What is her gross income from these items?

77. Jill received a research grant from the University of Minnesota in amounts of $10,000 for her time and $3,000 for related supplies and expenses. She purchased a $28,000 Audi the day after depositing the state's check. Jill is a candidate for a master's degree in philosophy and ethics. What is her gross income from the grant?

78. To what extent should Professor Dodd include in gross income the value of examination copies of books that he receives without charge from book publishers if he donates them to a local library in order and takes a charitable contribution deduction?

Chapter 9

State Tax Services

LEARNING OBJECTIVES

- Apply the research process to state and local research problems.

- Know the major features of state services.

- Understand the similarities and differences in Federal and state tax research.

- Use the search methodologies that are available with each of the state services.

- Know which tax services are most appropriate for different research objectives.

CHAPTER OUTLINE

State and local tax planning has become big business for accounting and tax law firms. All of the international and most of the regional CPA firms have specialized state and local tax departments. Even the large local CPA and law firms have individuals that are specialists in this area as well.

There are numerous reasons for the emphasis on state and local tax planning. For many businesses this is an untapped planning opportunity in which practitioners can provide value-added services. This is especially important as the Federal tax planning opportunities for businesses have been limited by law changes and previously taken advantage of with prior consulting work. While the amount of taxes paid to individual states may be small, the percentage of total state taxes paid by a business can be almost one-half of its tax bill. Coordinated state tax planning can substantially reduce this percentage, especially where the taxpayer operates in various state and local taxing jurisdictions and has some flexibility as to where its property and labor force are located.

The power to tax is an inherent attribute of state authority. Generally, local governments must be specifically authorized to impose taxes by state statutory or constitutional provisions. These authorizing provisions, in turn, regulate the rates and operation of local government taxes. Courts in some states, however, have ruled that the power to impose taxes can be implied from broad "home rule" grants. This grants partial autonomy to local taxing authorities under general state constitutional provisions.

This chapter explores state and local taxation and the resources available for state tax research. Since state and local taxing systems are separate from the Federal tax domain, an overview of state and local taxation is presented before delving into the tax products available to practitioners. Research projects then are used to demonstrate the major tax services.

IMPORTANCE OF STATE AND LOCAL TAXES

State and local taxes are playing an ever-increasing role in the tax planning of business and individuals alike. While Federal tax rates have declined in the past several years, state and local taxes have been on the incline. The necessity for greater revenues to meet the needs of constituents has caused states to raise the tax burdens of citizens. Tax increases for state and local governments is especially critical when the economy is in a down turn. During these times, the demands for social programs such as welfare and Medicaid build, while the tax bases for states are reduced due to the slow economy. Since most states constitutionally cannot operate at a deficit, the state and local tax obligations become more of a burden for the taxpaying businesses and individuals. Exhibit 9–1 illustrates the increase in the taxes over time. In 1970 the tax collected by states was $48 billion whereas by 2003 the amount had risen to almost $543 billion. This is more than a 1,100 percent increase in collections in thirty-three years!

State and local tax increases lead to those taxes becoming a greater proportion of the total tax burden for businesses and individuals. Exhibit 9–2 contains

Exhibit	9–1
State Tax Collections	

Year	Collections in Billions of Dollars	Year	Collections in Billions of Dollars
1970	48.0	1990	307.1
1975	80.1	1995	393.2
1980	136.9	2000	551.9
1985	214.9	2003	542.9

Source: U.S. Bureau of the Census.

Exhibit	9–2	State Tax Burdens in 2004

MEASURING TAXES AS A PERCENTAGE OF INCOME

States Ranked by Combined State and Local Tax Burdens

Rank	State	State Tax Burden	Federal & State Tax Burden	Rank	State	State Tax Burden	Federal & State Tax Burden
	U.S. Average	10.0%	27.8%	26	California	9.8%	28.4%
1	New York	12.9%	32.3%	27	Iowa	9.8%	25.6%
2	Maine	12.3%	28.9%	28	Montana	9.8%	26.0%
3	Ohio	11.3%	27.5%	29	New Mexico	9.7%	27.5%
4	Hawaii	11.3%	27.1%	30	Nevada	9.7%	28.4%
5	Rhode Island	11.1%	29.2%	31	North Carolina	9.7%	26.4%
6	Wisconsin	11.1%	28.2%	32	Illinois	9.7%	27.9%
7	Utah	10.8%	27.0%	33	North Dakota	9.7%	25.5%
8	West Virginia	10.6%	26.0%	34	Oregon	9.5%	26.5%
9	Connecticut	10.6%	32.3%	35	Pennsylvania	9.4%	26.5%
10	Minnesota	10.5%	28.1%	36	Massachusetts	9.4%	29.6%
11	Idaho	10.4%	26.2%	37	Virginia	9.3%	27.4%
12	Vermont	10.4%	27.6%	38	Missouri	9.3%	25.9%
13	Michigan	10.2%	27.4%	39	Oklahoma	9.2%	25.2%
14	Nebraska	10.2%	26.3%	40	Colorado	9.1%	27.8%
15	New Jersey	10.1%	29.9%	41	Alabama	9.1%	25.0%
16	Indiana	10.1%	26.7%	42	South Dakota	9.0%	25.4%
17	Kentucky	10.0%	26.1%	43	South Carolina	9.0%	25.1%
18	Georgia	10.0%	27.3%	44	Wyoming	8.9%	28.6%
19	Mississippi	10.0%	25.2%	45	Florida	8.8%	27.0%
20	Arizona	10.0%	27.2%	46	Texas	8.7%	26.8%
21	Washington	9.9%	28.8%	47	Tennessee	8.5%	25.1%
22	Kansas	9.9%	26.5%	48	Delaware	8.2%	26.3%
23	Louisiana	9.9%	25.4%	49	New Hampshire	7.5%	26.7%
24	Maryland	9.9%	27.7%	50	Alaska	6.3%	23.6%
25	Arkansas	9.8%	25.9%		District of Columbia	12.8%	32.1%

Source: Tax Foundation, State Finances (posted April 2004) http://www.taxfoundation.org/statelocal04.html
July 17, 2004.

the state tax burdens for each state as a percentage of income. The national average for state taxes is 10 percent, and the average for Federal and state taxes is about 28 percent. Thus, state taxes are more than one-third of the national tax burden. However, the tax burden varies across states, with New York having the highest percentage and Alaska having the lowest.

Businesses take the level of state and local taxation into consideration when deciding where to locate a new plant or headquarters. This analysis includes not only business taxes but also the personal taxes of the personnel relocating to the new location. Exhibit 9–3 reports the state taxes per capita for all fifty states and the national average. Consequently, the business and individual state and local taxing structure are crucial elements in fundamental business decisions.

Many state constitutions constrain the types of taxes imposed and/or on the upper limits which tax rates can assume. Therefore, states resort to alternative methods for generating more revenue, such as increasing compliance and imposing substantial penalties. As failure to comply with state and tax

Exhibit	9–3	Per Capita State Tax Collections in 2002*

Rank	State	Amt. in Dollars	Rank	State	Amt. in Dollars
	National Average	**1,854**	26	North Dakota	1,762
1	Hawaii	2,748	26	North Dakota	1,762
2	Delaware	2,692	27	Virginia	1,752
3	Connecticut	2,610	28	Oklahoma	1,732
4	Minnesota	2,577	29	Nebraska	1,731
5	Vermont	2,487	30	Ohio	1,718
6	Massachusetts	2,306	31	Iowa	1,705
7	New York	2,258	32	Utah	1,694
8	California	2,214	33	Idaho	1,693
9	Wyoming	2,195	34	Alaska	1,692
10	Michigan	2,175	35	Mississippi	1,647
11	Wisconsin	2,171	36	Louisiana	1,639
12	New Jersey	2,134	37	Indiana	1,623
13	Washington	2,081	38	Georgia	1,609
14	Maine	2,029	39	Montana	1,586
15	Rhode Island	1,989	40	Arizona	1,534
16	Maryland	1,983	41	Colorado	1,536
17	West Virginia	1,971	42	Alabama	1,533
18	New Mexico	1,955	43	Missouri	1,530
19	Kentucky	1,948	44	Florida	1,485
20	North Carolina	1,867	45	New Hampshire	1,478
21	Arkansas	1,858	46	Oregon	1,459
22	Nevada	1,815	47	South Carolina	1,400
23	Pennsylvania	1,795	48	Tennessee	1,345
24	Illinois	1,782	49	Texas	1,316
25	Kansas	1,770	50	South Dakota	1,283

Source: U.S. Bureau of the Census.

laws becomes more costly, businesses and individuals are requesting additional research from tax professionals to help reduce the significant state and local tax burdens.

HISTORICAL PERSPECTIVE

Since the time of the early American colonies, there have been payments made by citizens to local governing units. These payments may have been voluntary or required, but the purpose of the collections was to support community needs. Early taxing systems were based on the makeup of the local economy. Thus, in the southern states where cotton was the main commodity, taxes were based on imports/exports, whereas in the northern states taxes were based on the production from farmland. By the end of the eighteenth century, property taxes were becoming popular, and by the mid-nineteenth century, the cornerstone of state and local tax systems was taxation of property. In 1890, state tax collections had reached the $100 million mark.

States relying on property taxes then needed to supplement these revenue sources with other kinds of taxes. State income taxes were introduced in Wisconsin in 1911 and gradually spread to most other states and several municipalities. State sales taxes made an appearance in the early twentieth century and the first city sales tax was imposed by New York in the 1930s. The growth of tax base diversification helped to stabilize state and local governments' revenue yields over time.

In 1945 states were collecting almost $6 billion and by 2000 this amount had risen to over $550 billion (see Exhibit 9–1). In addition to the economic effects, state and local governments' financial burdens have escalated due to cutbacks in Federal aid at a time when public services demanded by citizens have increased. The combination of these effects has caused the burdens of state and local taxes to increase over the last fifty years.

SPOTLIGHT ON TAXATION: Tax Freedom Day

Every year the Tax Foundation determines "Tax Freedom Day," the hypothetical day when taxpayers have earned enough money to pay for all of their taxes and now can "work for themselves." In 2004, the national Tax Freedom Day was April 11, the earliest it had been in over thirty-five years.

The Tax Foundation also determines a Tax Freedom Day for each state. In 2004, the earliest dates were for Alaska (March 26) and Alabama, Tennessee, and South Carolina (April 1). The latest state dates were for Connecticut (April 28), New York (April 22), New Jersey (April 19), and Massachusetts (April 18). For details, go to http://www.tax foundation.org/taxfreedomday.html.

LEGAL PERSPECTIVE

Federal and state constitutional provisions play an integral role in state tax planning. The constitutional validity of state tax laws is commonly challenged in the courts today, whereas the Federal taxes are rarely questioned on their constitutionality any more. State and local tax challenges address not only whether the taxes fall within the purview of the state constitution, but also whether the laws are federally constitutional. The Federal clauses most frequently providing the basis for state taxation disputes are: supremacy, commerce, due process, equal protection, and privileges and immunities.

CONSTITUTION

Each state's taxing system is unique, yet they all are subject to the constraints of the United States Constitution and Federal laws. While many clauses of the U.S. Constitution are applied to state taxation, only two explicit restrictions seem to concern state taxation: the import/export clause and the very specific duty of tonnage clause. Both of these prohibit states from charging taxes on imports or exports without the consent of Congress. As import/export taxes have become less important at the Federal level, so have these clauses. Currently it is other Federal constitutional clauses that are invoked to limit a state's authority to impose taxes. Generally, states are afforded wide latitude in creating a taxing structure, as long as they meet the requirements contained in the Federal Constitution.

Although the Federal laws can seem to dominate the issue, it is each state's own constitution that is considered the fundamental law and places restrictions on the state's authority to assess taxes. Most state constitutions limit the rates and types of taxes a state can impose. They also generally require that taxes meet the public purpose, uniformity, and/or equal protection requirements. Because it is an elected legislative body that usually imposes taxes, there is an eminent presumption of validity. However, it is the ultimate role of the courts to insure that the legislature acts within the restraints of Federal and state constitutions.

PUBLIC PURPOSE

The constitutions of most states require that tax revenues be imposed only for **public purposes**. This is a lofty sounding requirement; however, the definition of "public purpose" is rarely supplied and thus the courts have rendered vague and broad interpretations when rendering decisions on challenges to specific taxes. Since the legislature is a representation of the state's citizens, Federal and state courts generally accept the legislative interpretation of the concept.

SUPREMACY

The supremacy provision in the Federal constitution confers superiority to Federal laws over state laws. That is, Federal laws are "the supreme law of the land" and trump state laws. If a state law or constitutional provision is in conflict with a Federal law, it is considered to be invalid. The **supremacy clause** is generally applied to tax conflicts involving the Federal commerce clause.

Another important application of the supremacy clause is to the taxation of the Federal government by states. If states were permitted to tax the Federal government, its supremacy would be impinged. Thus, the supremacy clause in the Constitution immunizes the Federal government from taxation by the states.

COMMERCE

The Federal Constitution **commerce clause** states that Congress shall have the power to regulate commerce with foreign nations, among states, and with Native American tribes. This clause contains the most significant Federal limitation on a state's capacity to impose taxes. It grants powers to Congress and places constraints on the states' ability to tax interstate trade.

The commerce clause has a long history of Supreme Court actions. The interpretation of the clause as it now stands is based on the case *Complete Auto Transit Inc. v. Brady.*[1] The case involved a tax imposed on a corporation for the privilege of conducting an interstate transportation business. The Court developed the four criteria now regarded as controlling whether a state may tax interstate commerce. A tax may be imposed if:

- The tax is applied to an activity with a substantial nexus (connection) with the taxing state
- It is fairly apportioned
- It does not discriminate against interstate commerce
- The tax is fairly related to the services provided by the state

Thus, one key for a state to have taxing authority over a business is for that entity to have established a nexus with the state.

DUE PROCESS

The Supreme Court has applied the Federal **due process clause**, found in the Fourteenth Amendment, to limit the territorial scope of a state's taxing authority in interstate commerce cases. States have lost cases in two key situations.

- They seek to tax out-of-state businesses whose connections with the state are not sufficient to constitute a nexus.
- The tax imposed does not fairly reflect the taxpayer's activities in the state.

To be successful in applying a tax, states must prove that the business has more than a *de minimis* existence within the state, and that the taxing base for the interstate enterprise includes only amounts fairly apportioned to its activities within the state. The *Complete Auto Transit* interpretation of the commerce clause also contains these two criteria for successful taxation of interstate commerce.

1. 430 U.S. 274 (1977).

A landmark case in determining the states' ability to have jurisdiction over out-of-state businesses under the due process and commerce clauses is *Quill Corp. v. North Dakota*.[2] The U.S. Supreme Court held in this case that the due process clause does not require a physical presence by the out-of-state entity for a state to have jurisdiction. An economic presence rising above the *de minimis* level is sufficient. The due process concern with "fairness" is satisfied when an out-of-state entity "purposefully avails itself of the benefits of an economic market in the foreign State."

The Supreme Court also indicated that mere contact with customers in a taxing state through U.S. mail or other common carrier does not create a substantial nexus. However, use by the out-of-state entity of direct marketing through retail outlets or personnel does create a nexus for taxing purposes. Thus, if a business's activity in any state goes beyond contacts by U.S. mail or common carrier, nexus may exist. Courts have also consistently ruled that out-of-state entities cannot skirt state jurisdiction by contracting with in-state persons to conduct company business that would have otherwise created nexus if the out-of-state company had used its own employees.

In the same year as the *Quill* case, the Supreme Court addressed a related *de minimis* issue in Wisconsin *Department of Revenue v. William Wrigley, Jr., Co.*[3] In this case, the Court clarified the definition of a *de minimis* with regard to the "solicitation of orders." Only activities considered ancillary or trivial to soliciting orders by an out-of-state business meet the definition of being *de minimis*. Whether an activity is ancillary should be determined by both qualitative and quantitative measures. If the activity is either quantitatively or qualitatively more than trivial, *de minimis* exception is violated.

The due process clause does not guarantee that the benefits received by the interstate enterprise will have any relationship to the amount of taxes paid to the state. As articulated in *Commonwealth Edison Co. v. Montana*,[4] "a tax … is a means of distributing the burden of the cost of government. The only benefit to which the taxpayer is constitutionally entitled is derived from his enjoyment of the privileges of living in an organized society, established and safeguarded by the devotion of taxes to public purposes."

UNIFORMITY AND EQUAL PROTECTION

The Federal and most state constitutions include an **equal protection** and/or a **uniformity clause**. These concepts are closely related and state courts often treat them as being interchangeable concepts. These rules require that similarly situated persons or property be treated for tax purposes in a similar manner. Although the Fourteenth Amendment equal protection clause does not reference taxation specifically, it has been relied upon to determine whether tax provisions treat different taxpayers equally.

The Supreme Court has construed the equal protection clause as barring states from creating arbitrary classifications for taxation. Yet, when the only

2. 504 U.S. 298 (1992).
3. 505 U.S. 214 (1992).
4. 453 U.S. 609 (1981).

Federal question is equal protection, the Court gives states wide latitude in delineating classifications in systems of taxation. The state legislature is considered to be in a superior position for devising its taxing system on an equitable and uniform basis. As long as the legislature can justify its treatment of classes of taxpayers differently, the Court typically will not second guess the wisdom of the state. Accordingly, the Supreme Court's approach to applying this Fourteenth Amendment clause insulates states taxes from most challenges under the Federal equal protection clause.

PRIVILEGES AND IMMUNITIES

Lastly, the Federal Constitution grants the citizens of each state all privileges and immunities of citizens in every other state. This means that a nonresident business has the right to engage in commerce within the state, without being subject to different or greater taxes than resident businesses. The main application of this clause has been to invalidate laws that imposed higher tax burdens on out-of-state businesses. Note that the **privileges and immunities clause** applies only to "citizens" of states. Since a corporation is considered a "person" but not a "citizen" under the law, corporations for the most part are covered by the equal protection clause but not the privileges and immunities clause.

STATE TAX STRUCTURE

The states have modeled their tax structure on the Federal tax system. All involve the three branches of government: legislative, executive, and judicial. Tax statutes are enacted by their legislatures. These statutes are signed by the state governor just as Federal tax laws are signed by the President. Regulatory agencies similar to the IRS issue regulations and rulings on tax matters and administer the tax law. Finally, state courts hear cases regarding tax matters.

LEGISLATIVE

State legislatures are responsible for enacting laws regarding the revenue sources of the state. With regard to taxes, the state legislatures pass bills amending and augmenting their state's taxing code. While Federal revenue bills must start in the House, this is not a requirement in all state legislatures. In fact, the jurisdictions of the state legislative houses vary from state to state, and there tends to be a significant overlap in their functions. One state, Nebraska, avoids this duplication by having only one legislative body. Once the tax bills are passed and signed by the Governor, they are incorporated into the state's statutory structure.

State tax codes can provide a challenge for tax practitioners to research. Each state organizes its tax code based on different criteria and has a different numbering system for its code. This means that the practitioner who is used to finding corporate tax laws in the 300s of the IRC must conduct a new search for the state corporate income tax laws, if they even exist!

States place varying reliance on the Federal tax code. Some states piggyback most of their individual and business income taxes on the IRC, whereas other states have adopted substantial differences. A current trend in state tax law is to avoid enacting all of the changes made by Congress—recent Federal changes reduced the tax base of the states in ways which many states cannot afford. Therefore, the practitioner must be diligent in finding possible differences in state and Federal law.

Income taxation is not the only tax that states utilize. In fact, there are several states that do not have income taxes. Rather, some states rely on a multitude of other taxes, including sales/use taxes, real and personal property taxes, excise taxes on a variety of products, severance taxes on natural resources, gaming/gambling taxes, and estate and gift taxes. Newer taxes often are assessed on the assets or transactions of service industries, communication and computer operations, and financial enterprises. The mix of taxes varies greatly from state to state. Exhibit 9–4 summarizes the major taxes imposed by each state.

ADMINISTRATIVE

Once tax statutes are enacted, they must be interpreted and enforced. These duties fall to the administrative agencies created by either statute or constitutional provision. In most states, the Department of Revenue (Department of Taxation, State Tax Commission, etc.) is the main administrative agency for this purpose. Other smaller agencies administer the more specialized taxes such as employment, tobacco, or fuel taxes. California is an exception in having two revenue agencies, the Franchise Tax Board (income and franchise taxes) and the State Board of Equalization (most other taxes).

Exhibit	9–4	Selected Taxes Imposed by Each State

	Income			Sales & Use	Property	Estate and/or Inheritance	Gift	Severance
	Ind.	Corp.	Franchise					
Alabama	Yes	Yes	Yes	Yes	Yes	Yes	No	Yes
Alaska	No	Yes	No	No	Yes	Yes	No	Yes
Arizona	Yes	Yes	No	Yes	Yes	Yes	No	Yes
Arkansas	Yes	Yes	Yes	Yes	Yes	Yes	No	Yes
California	Yes	Yes	No	Yes	Yes	Yes	No	Yes
Colorado	Yes	Yes	No	Yes	Yes	Yes	No	Yes
Connecticut	Yes	Yes	Yes	Yes	Yes	Yes	Yes	Yes
Delaware	Yes	Yes	Yes	Yes	No	Yes	No	No
District of Columbia	Yes	Yes	No	Yes	Yes	Yes	No	No
Florida	No	Yes	No	Yes	Yes	Yes	No	Yes

Exhibit	9–4	Selected Taxes Imposed by Each State—Concluded

	Income		Franchise	Sales & Use	Property	Estate and/or Inheritance	Gift	Severance
	Ind.	**Corp.**						
Georgia	Yes	Yes	Yes	Yes	Yes	Yes	No	No
Hawaii	Yes	Yes	No	Yes	No	Yes	No	No
Idaho	Yes	Yes	Yes	Yes	Yes	Yes	No	Yes
Illinois	Yes	Yes	Yes	Yes	No	Yes	No	Yes
Indiana	Yes	Yes	No	Yes	Yes	Yes	No	No
Iowa	Yes	Yes	Yes	Yes	No	Yes	No	Yes
Kansas	Yes	Yes	Yes	Yes	Yes	Yes	No	Yes
Kentucky	Yes	Yes	Yes	Yes	Yes	Yes	No	Yes
Louisiana	Yes	Yes	Yes	Yes	Yes	Yes	Yes	Yes
Maine	Yes	Yes	No	Yes	Yes	Yes	No	Yes
Maryland	Yes	Yes	No	Yes	Yes	Yes	No	No
Massachusetts	Yes	Yes	Yes	Yes	Yes	Yes	No	No
Michigan	Yes	Yes	No	Yes	Yes	Yes	No	Yes
Minnesota	Yes	Yes	No	Yes	Yes	Yes	No	Yes
Mississippi	Yes	Yes	Yes	Yes	Yes	Yes	No	Yes
Missouri	Yes	Yes	Yes	Yes	Yes	Yes	No	Yes
Montana	Yes	Yes	No	No	Yes	Yes	No	Yes
Nebraska	Yes	Yes	Yes	Yes	Yes	Yes	No	Yes
Nevada	No	No	No	Yes	Yes	Yes	No	Yes
New Hampshire	Yes	Yes#	No	No*	Yes	Yes	No	No
New Jersey	Yes	Yes	No	Yes	Yes	Yes	No	No
New Mexico	Yes	Yes	No	Yes	Yes	Yes	No	Yes
New York	Yes	Yes	Yes	Yes	No	Yes	No	Yes
North Carolina	Yes	Yes	Yes	Yes	Yes	Yes	Yes	Yes
North Dakota	Yes	Yes	No	Yes	Yes	Yes	No	Yes
Ohio	Yes	Yes	Yes	Yes	Yes	Yes	No	Yes
Oklahoma	Yes	Yes	Yes	Yes	Yes	Yes	No	Yes
Oregon	Yes	Yes	No	No	Yes	Yes	No	Yes
Pennsylvania	Yes	Yes	Yes	Yes	No	Yes	No	No
Rhode Island	Yes	Yes	Yes	Yes	Yes	Yes	No	No
South Carolina	Yes	Yes	Yes	Yes	Yes	Yes	No	No
South Dakota	Yes	No	No	Yes	Yes	Yes	No	Yes
Tennessee	Yes	Yes#	Yes	Yes	Yes	Yes	Yes	Yes
Texas	No	No	Yes	Yes	Yes	Yes	No	Yes
Utah	Yes	Yes	No	Yes	Yes	Yes	No	Yes
Vermont	Yes	Yes	No	Yes	Yes	Yes	No	No
Virginia	Yes	Yes	No	Yes	Yes	Yes	No	Yes
Washington	No	No	No	Yes	Yes	Yes	No	Yes
West Virginia	Yes	Yes	Yes	Yes	Yes	Yes	No	Yes
Wisconsin	Yes	Yes	No	Yes	Yes	Yes	No	Yes
Wyoming	No	No	Yes	Yes	Yes	Yes	No	Yes

*Sales tax on meals, rooms, and telecommunications only.
#On income from intangibles only.

It has been said that whoever has authority to interpret the law is really the lawmaker, and it is the state revenue agencies that are first authorized to interpret the state tax laws. These agencies issue published regulations, rulings, and various other authoritative pronouncements to aid tax practitioners and taxpayers in interpreting and applying the law to a specific situation. As in the Federal system, it is the courts' duty to ensure that the administrative agencies do not overstep their authority.

Most state revenue agencies issue rulings for specific taxpayers, similar in nature to Private Letter Rulings issued by the IRS. As with PLRs, the letters are for the exclusive use of the taxpayer requesting the guidance and usually cannot be relied upon by other taxpayers as authority. Private issuances, however, may provide taxpayers hints as to the revenue agency's position on a particular issue and therefore are useful to the researcher.

Oddly, Federal regulations and rulings may be pertinent to state tax issues. For states that piggyback income, estate, or other taxes on Federal statutes, guidance in interpreting the law will come from the Federal pronouncements. As previously stated, the degree to which states follow Federal law varies greatly.

JUDICIAL

Most state judicial systems are, for the most part, patterned on the Federal system. There often are three levels of courts: supreme courts, appeals (appellate) courts, and trial courts. The functions of the three levels of state courts are similar to the Federal functions. The trial courts establish the facts and apply the law to these facts. The appeals courts review the trial court's application of the law to the set of facts. The appeals courts generally rely on the trial courts' accounts of the facts. The state's supreme court has power corresponding to the Federal Supreme Court; it develops the law of the state, but precedents apply only for that state. For those states that only have two levels of courts, the functions of the appeals and supreme courts are conjoined.

Although most state have a three-tier judicial system, it may not be inherently obvious from the court names what their precedential values are. A "superior court" is likely to be a trial court or can be an appellate court but probably is not the highest court of the state. Most of the intermediate courts have the words "appeals" or "appellate" in their names. However, the highest court of a state can also be called the "court of appeals." The most diversity among states is with the trial courts. There are country, municipal, circuit, district, and superior trial courts to name a few. Each state has organized its trial courts to meet the needs of its citizens and judicial system.

Whereas the Federal judicial system includes a court specifically for tax cases, the Tax Court, most states do not have an equivalent. Rather, there may be administrative (quasi-judicial) tribunals authorized to expedite settlements of tax disputes. The findings of these settlements are generally available to the public; however, they tend to carry little precedential value. The findings apply only to the taxpayer bringing the dispute. As with other such documents, they can shed light on the state's position on a particular issue.

None of the tax services cull the tax cases from state court reporters and accumulate them into a state tax court service, like the CCH USTC or the RIA AFTR reporters. The tax cases are intermixed in the state reporters with all of the other types of cases that state courts hear. Fortunately, the ability to search electronically eliminates any inconvenience that not having dedicated reporters might cause.

MULTISTATE

Companies conducting business in more than one state are subject to multistate taxation. The income of the company must be apportioned among the states in which it conducts business. To create a greater uniformity and consistency in the measurements of business income, the **Uniform Division of Income for Tax Purposes Act (UDITPA)** was drafted by the **National Conference of Commissioners on Uniform State Laws** in 1957. This exercise received a mixed reception among the states.

Then in 1967, the **Multistate Tax Commission (MTC)**[5] was created through an organization of state governments called the **Multistate Tax Compact**. The MTC adopted the UDITPA as part of its Articles and issued regulations interpreting the UDITPA in 1971 and 1973. It continues to issue apportionment rules. Special industries which have been addressed include the service industries, interstate trucking, airlines, television and radio broadcasters, publishers, and, most recently, financial institutions. The MTC has strongly encouraged states to adopt the uniform tax laws and abide by the regulations. It has been successful in this endeavor as forty-five states are members or participants in MTC. The states not associated with MTC are Delaware, Indiana, Nevada, New York, Vermont, and Virginia.

The stated purpose of MTC is to "improve the fairness, efficiency and effectiveness of state tax systems as they apply to interstate and international commerce and preserve state tax sovereignty." The MTC believes that greater uniformity in multistate taxation will ensure that interstate commerce is more fairly taxed, lessen compliance costs for taxpayers and revenue agencies, and reduce the potential for Congress to intervene in the state's fiscal authority.

Participating states may take advantage of the **Joint Audit Program**, which allows the MTC to perform a comprehensive audit of a business's taxes for several states simultaneously. This obviously saves the states and the taxpayer time and compliance costs. Another program offered by MTC is the National Nexus Program. The central function of this program is to facilitate information sharing among participating states. For taxpayers, MTC provides the Multistate Alternative Dispute Resolution Program. This unique program affords taxpayers the opportunity to resolve common tax issues with several states at once. Further, the MTC will assist taxpayers with negotiations and drafting settlement agreements to be submitted to participating states.

5. http://www.mtc.gov.

SPOTLIGHT ON TAXATION: Quotation

"The thing generally raised on city land is taxes." Charles Dudley Warner

ILLUSTRATIVE RESEARCH EXAMPLES

Sample research projects will be used to demonstrate state research methods. It is important that *you* attempt this research project using the various tax services available to you. The procedural knowledge necessary to effectively perform state tax research can only be acquired through hands-on practice. The remainder of this chapter is designed to guide you through the basic tax services and is *not* a substitute for your actually performing the research yourself.

Research Project 9–1 We have a client that will be opening a new funeral parlor in Colorado. The client would like to know the sales tax implications for this business. Are morticians considered to be rendering services or are they selling tangible personal property or a combination of both? Specifically, the client would like to know whether to contract funeral services as one lump sum or whether it would be more beneficial to itemize the charges for caskets, urns, etc., separately from the services offered.

Research Project 9–2 We have a client that is considering locating a manufacturing plant in the Northwest. It is trying to decide which state would be best for tax purposes—Washington, Oregon, or Idaho. Its main concern is with regard to income taxes, state sales tax rates, and property taxes on inventory and personal property.

These two projects are very common types of state research projects. The first project requires locating specific tax information for a single state. The second project involves multiple states and calls for a comparison among the states for a number of taxes. While each can be researched in the same services, the method for searching the services will be quite different.

RIA STATE AND LOCAL SERVICE

Research Institute of America's **Checkpoint State & Local Tax (SALT)** service is a comprehensive analysis of state and local taxes for all fifty states and the District of Columbia. The service is designed to let the researcher designate the states, type of taxes, and documents to scan. Any or all of the states' taxes and documents may be searched simultaneously. Essentially all of the taxes imposed by states and most enacted by localities are covered in the service. For a complete list of the taxes and documents included in the RIA SALT service, see Exhibit 9–5. A practitioner would be hard pressed to find another service that affords better access to state and local tax materials.

Exhibit	**9–5**
RIA State Tax & Document Coverage	

RIA State Tax Databases

Corporate Income Tax	Limited Liability Partnerships
Corporate Licenses	Loans Tax
Corporate Reports	Mortgage Tax
Estate & Gift Taxes	Motor Vehicles Tax
Financial Institutions Taxes	New York City Taxes
Franchise Tax	Personal Income Tax
Fuels & Minerals Taxes	Public Utilities Tax
General Administrative Provisions	Real Property Tax
Initial Taxes	Recordation Tax
Insurance Companies Taxes	Sales & Use Taxes
Intangibles Tax	Special Local Taxes
Licenses & Occupations Taxes	Stamp Tax
Limited Liability Companies	Stock Transfer Tax

Document Types

State Statutes
State Regulations
Federal Laws on State Taxation
Official State Materials
State Cases and Rulings
    State Supreme and Appellate Courts Cases since 1950
    Attorneys General Opinions
    Primary and Secondary Rulings since 1988
    General State Administrative Rulings since 1980
Federal Court Cases involving State Issues since 1860
Selected Forms Instructions
Editorial Explanations & Annotations

As with the Federal Checkpoint, editorial explanations and annotations have been developed for this service. The explanations are particularly useful when investigating a state's taxes with which you are unfamiliar, such as the Single Business tax (a VAT) in Michigan or the Business and Occupation tax (gross revenue tax) of Washington. The explanations contain links to all the supporting materials to make retrieval a seamless process. The annotations for court and agency decisions are also linked to their primary sources.

SPECIAL FEATURES

Some of the special features of RIA's SALT service are discussed next.

StateNet

StateNet is a database consisting of all proposed and current enacted legislation in full text. For proposed legislation, current status can be tracked through StateNet. This is extremely valuable when proposed legislation could have a major impact on a practitioner's clients. The effective date calendar lists each state's enactment conventions. For example, California's effective date for passed legislation is the following January 1 or as provided in the Act, whereas Colorado's is immediately upon approval or as provided in the Act. However, if the bill becomes law without the Governor's signature, it becomes effective in thirty days. Lastly, the current legislative calendar is reproduced on StateNet.

All State Tax Guide

The **All State Tax Guide** is a concise state-by-state analysis of all major taxes, with citations to state materials. It offers numerous tables, charts, and checklists for a variety of tax data. The list of official state contacts makes it easy to find an address or phone number for tax authorities for states in which the practitioner does not reside.

State Newsletters and Journals

The latest news on state tax developments is available through the *State & Local Taxes Weekly* newsletter, a part of the SALT service. Also offered with the SALT service is the *Journal of Multistate Taxation and Incentives*. These periodicals are discussed in more detail in the "Periodical and Internet Sites" section at the end of this chapter.

Create-a-Chart

RIA offers **Create-a-Chart** that facilitates the creation of charts from various tax materials. The purpose of this feature is to enable the practitioner to summarize pertinent multistate tax information in a convenient chart that can be exported to a word processing document. The product supports linking information on the charts to controlling authority and/or RIA's explanation paragraphs. These links will be maintained when the chart is exported. The practitioner can designate the type of tax (income, etc.), a chart type (tax rates, starting point for computing taxable income, etc.), and which states to include in the comparison. There are currently over 100 chart types offered in Create-a-Chart.

Compare It

A new feature that RIA has added exclusively to Checkpoint is **Compare It**. This feature enables the researcher to link to the same topic material for one state in another state and return. This makes comparing the tax treatment of an item in multiple states easy, and it eliminates the need to return to the list of documents when performing multiple state searches. The Compare It icon appears on the explanatory material screens for sales and use, corporate income, LLCs, LLPs, and property tax areas. This feature is available only for explanatory materials and not for state statutes or regulations.

As with the Federal databases, the SALT databases can be entered using the three search methods: search, link, and browse. What is different for the SALT is the multistate search option. Since the multiple-source search is just a variant of a keyword search, it will be presented under the Keyword Search heading.

KEYWORD SEARCH

The opening screen for RIA Checkpoint (Exhibit 6–1, Chapter 6) allows the user to choose a practice area. Upon selecting "State & Local," the Checkpoint offers a list of the states. All the states or any number of separate states may be designated for the search. At this juncture there is no box to enter keywords. Checkpoint requires that a type of tax and document be specified before a keyword search may occur. Exhibit 9–6 reproduces the choices for taxes and documents. Again, any or all of the tax and document databases may be marked for the search.

Exhibit	9–6

RIA State & Local Document Choices

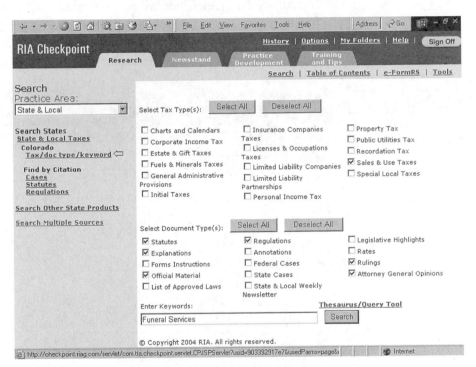

Rather than designating taxes and documents, the "Search Other State Products" option is available (see Exhibit 9–6). This option accesses secondary sources such as RIA newsletters and journals as well as StateNet and Federal cases on state topics. These databases may be searched using keywords or citations, depending on the nature of the database.

To work with Research Project 9–1, Colorado was picked in the list of states, sales taxes was checked for the taxes, and several document types were marked in the document type section (see Exhibit 9–6). The search results in links to explanations, regulations, and rulings pertaining to the sales taxes on funeral services in Colorado. By reading these documents, Research Project 9–1 can be fully analyzed.

Multiple Sources Search

As can be seen in Exhibit 9–6, one of the search options offered is Multiple Sources. Using this option while in the SALT practice area opens the screen for keyword searching. A comparison of Exhibit 9–6 with 9–7 reveals that the document categories are not identical for these two keyword search versions. One offered only in Multiple Sources is the Miscellaneous Multistate Materials database. This database includes the following documents.

- Multistate Tax Compact
- Multistate Tax Commission documents
- Federation of Tax Administrators Uniform Exchange of Information Agreement
- Multistate Statements of Information
- Formulas for the Apportionment and Allocation of Net Income of Financial Institutions
- Federal Laws on State Taxation

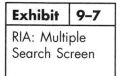

Exhibit	9–7

RIA: Multiple
Search Screen

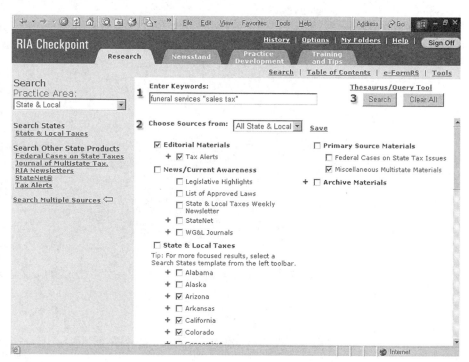

While the Multiple Sources search option contains the multistate materials it lacks a tax type indicator. Consequently, the type of tax must be included as one of the keywords, to narrow the results to the particular tax of interest. For Research Project 9–1, the terms funeral services and "sales tax" were entered. *Sales tax* has quotes around it to make sure that Checkpoint searches for it as a single term.

If the research undertaken involves only one state, the Multiple Source search is not necessary, and the keyword in the prior sections is preferable. However, if Project 9–1 is expanded beyond Colorado, to include Arizona and California, the Multiple Sources option is more beneficial. On the initial Multiple Sources screen, the states of Arizona, California, and Colorado (see Exhibit 9–7) are checked. If no states are marked for the search, all the states will be scanned. This finds documents for California and Colorado. Apparently, Arizona law does not specifically address funeral services, at least as of the date of our review.

Exhibit 9–8 is the result from drilling down to the Checkpoint explanation for California on "Funeral Items and Burial Services." Selecting Compare It displays in the left frame links to RIA's explanation of this same topic for each state. The researcher merely selects the state of interest, and the explanation for that state appears in the right frame. This makes comparing the state treatment of funeral services effortless. The explanations hyperlink state statutes and regulations for seamless access to the primary sources.

Exhibit	9–8

RIA California Explanations Screen & Compare It

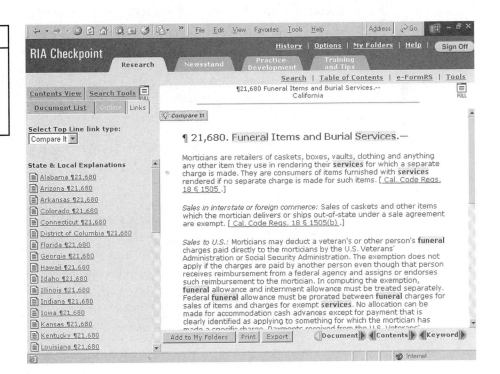

CITATION SEARCH

Unlike the Federal practice area opening screen, SALT does not allow citation searches directly on its opening screen. A single state must be earmarked for the search before the citation search option is offered. Based on the state, the citation search options will vary. For example, some states include rulings in the list of possible citation searches whereas others are limited to cases, statutes, and regulations. Once the state and type of primary document are specified, templates are furnished for entering the citation.

CONTENTS SEARCH

RIA supports table-of-contents searches for state research. This method allows the researcher to treat the tax services as if it were in a printed book. Thus, as in a book, the Table of Contents and Index can be browsed for the topic of interest. In many cases, this methodology for searching is more efficient than the keyword search. By narrowing the search through focusing on the contents of databases, fewer extraneous documents will be retrieved. The limitation with this type of search is that only those databases containing tables of contents or indexes are searchable. As with a Federal contents search, one selects the "Table of Contents" button to start a contents search.

Table of Contents Search

Exhibit 9–9 reproduces the expanded Table of Contents (TOC) for state available materials. At this point, the state databases may be searched using a keyword search by selecting the databases of interest and entering the keywords. This would be practical when the search involves more than one state or more than one of the main databases. The databases available in the State & Local Tax Library are shown in Exhibit 9–9.

From the expanded TOC, the researcher can drill down to the information of interest in a variety of ways. Using Research Project 9–1 to demonstrate, the researcher could select Colorado under the State & Local Tax heading and enter the keyword "funeral services" (see Exhibit 9–9). This search indicates that documents can be found in Explanations, Regulations, Official Material,

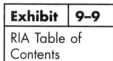

Exhibit | 9–9

RIA Table of Contents

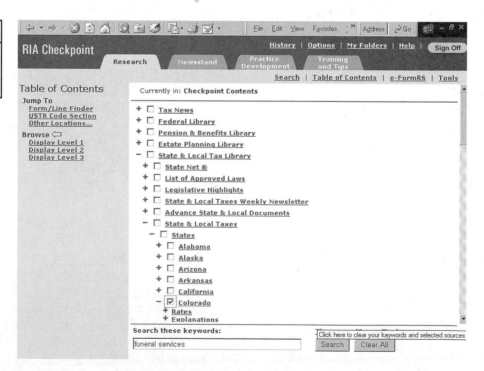

and Forms Instructions. Selecting Explanations or Regulations will retrieve the same document identified using the keyword search. The Official Material document is the 1996 Tax Publication regarding the Special Regulation on Morticians. A list of the other documents for this search appears in the left frame of the screen. Each is hot linked to the documents for easy access. The researcher does not need to return to the prior screen list in order to retrieve any of the other documents.

Rather than performing the keyword search, the researcher could drill down within the state subheadings, which include the following:

- Rates
- Explanations
- Forms Instructions
- Annotations
- Statutes
- Regulations
- Cases
- Official Material
- Index

The subheadings in this list cannot be searched using keywords. Only the drill-down method is possible. One of the most useful subheadings given for each state is Index. Through the Index, the same documents identified for Research Project 9–1 by the other methods can be found if State & Use tax is selected and Funerals is located. Since the listing under Sales & Use Tax is quite long, using the "Ctrl-F" command to bring up the "Find" box and entering in "funeral" will display the entries desired. These drill-down techniques are efficient in locating pertinent documents; however, the drawback is that each subheading must be examined separately.

Research Project 9–2, on the other hand, requires the comparison of various taxes in three states, Idaho, Oregon, and Washington. Using the drill-down method in the State & Local Taxes (see Exhibit 9–9), selecting Idaho, Explanations, Charts and Calendars, and then Chart of State Tax System, displays a chart covering the major taxes in Idaho. The Idaho tax data necessary for Project 9–2 is available in this chart. Applying the same method for the other two states, all the essential information on corporate income tax rates, state sales taxes, and property taxes on inventories and tangible personal property can be retrieved.

CCH NETWORK STATE SERVICE

Like RIA Checkpoint, Commerce Clearing House's NetWork tax service includes a complete state tax service. Unlike RIA, CCH features Sales Tax as one of its practice area Tabs that is available from its opening window (see Exhibit 6–7, in Chapter 6). The State Tab provides access to all of the state materials offered by CCH. This makes the initial screen of the State Tab quite lengthy. Due to this length, a very useful search option, the Topical Indexes, may be overlooked by researchers. Since all of the material in the Sales Tax

Tab is also retrievable through the State Tab, the focus in this section will be solely on the State Tab.

STATE TAB

State Tax Reporter

The backbone of the CCH state tax services is the **State Tax Reporters**. This service combines detailed explanations, primary source materials, and practical compliance guidance. All of the major taxes imposed by states and localities are covered by the service. Although, the CCH explanations are organized by tax type, with links to related primary sources, state material is retrieved by selecting the state(s) of interest. Unlike RIA which required the researcher to identify the type of documents to be searched, CCH assumes all materials are of interest. The list of document types searched can be reduced in the Search Tools feature. A list of what is being searched is summarized on this page.

Keyword Search: Researching the expanded Project 9–1 (Colorado, Arizona, and California) begins by selecting the state on the opening State Tab Screen. Always click Clear Selections before starting a new search, to make sure only the databases of interest are reviewed. Since there is no method to indicate an interest solely in sales tax, this term will need to be added to the keyword search (see Exhibit 9–10). CCH automatically applies a thesaurus to the keywords entered unless the researcher turns it off. In this search, using the word "service" will be interpreted as including all the derivations of the

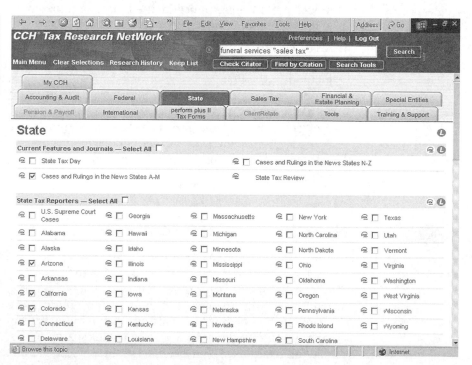

Exhibit 9–10

CCH State Opening Screen

Internal Revenue Service. Therefore, turning off the thesaurus would be helpful. To do so, use Search Tools. This is also where the type of search may be changed in case a Boolean search would be preferred.

Exhibit 9–11 is the result of retrieving one of the CCH documents for Colorado. The buttons supplied above the annotation have links to the Statutes, Regulations, Explanations, Cases and Rulings, and Related Topics—State. This last button is the state version of the Federal Smart Relate feature and functions similar to the Compare It in RIA Checkpoint. Clicking on the button displays a list of related topics for the state of interest. Further drilling down will generate a list of the states with similar provisions.

Content Search: Rather than checking the box before a state in the State Tax Reporters, clicking on the name will display a list of the information available for the state. The contents are organized by types of taxes and contain other related topics. This makes it possible for the user to pick a state and a tax type, and then perform a keyword search. Using this method, checking Colorado, Sales & Use taxes, and entering the term "funeral services," results in the same document list as keyword search from the opening screen.

Multistate Publications

CCH offers several multistate databases including a corporate income tax, property tax, and sales tax guides. Each is designed to be an all-in-one guide emphasizing multistate planning yet delivering state-by-state details for every topic. Cost-effective planning ideas are presented and the "at-a-glance" charts are efficient for finding quick answers to each state's treatment of key taxes.

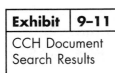

Exhibit	9–11

CCH Document
Search Results

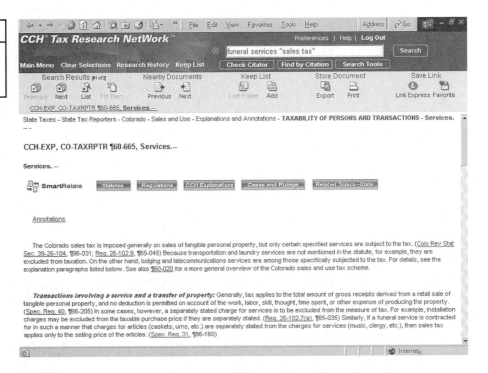

Included with the specialized multistate databases is the State Tax Guide. This is similar to the Master Tax Guide, as it is intended for finding quick answers to everyday questions on taxes levied in every state. Thus, its treatment of tax issues is very concise—state taxes are summarized rather than being reproduced. Each state has a page listing its major taxes, basis & rates, and due dates. This publication is very efficient when all that is needed is a short answer to a simple question.

In searching for information on Research Project 9–2, the **Multistate Quick Answer Charts** database is selected. Of the options offered in Exhibit 9–12, the Multistate corporate income tax, sales tax, and property tax guides will be most useful. These charts list each state having the tax of interest, the rates imposed, and/or the tax base to which the tax is applied. The databases offered under the Multistate heading facilitate efficient searching for the necessary data to respond to Project 9–2. The results are given in Exhibit 9–13.

News Services

CCH has numerous state news services. The *Tax Tracker News* is found on the My CCH Tab, whereas State *Tax Day* can be accessed on either the State and Sales Tax Tabs. Both of these news sources are updated daily. *State Tax Review* is a weekly newsletter that covers current changes in laws, new administrative rulings, and pertinent court decisions in every state. CCH also has a series of Tax Alert newsletters. These periodicals are discussed

Exhibit | 9–12

CCH Multistate Data Options

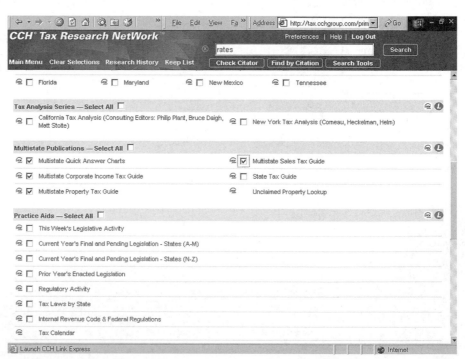

| Exhibit | 9-13 | CCH Results for Research Project 9–2 |

Tax	Idaho	Oregon	Washington
Corporate Income Rates	The tax rate is 7.6% of Idaho taxable income (IC Sec. 63-3025). Under no conditions will the tax be below $20 (IC Sec. 63-3025A). A multistate corporation transacting business in Idaho may elect to be taxed under the provisions of the Idaho Income Tax Actor pursuant to the Multistate Tax Compac (1%) (IC Sec. 63-3702, Rule 35.01.01.310).	The excise rate tax is 6.6%, imposed on Oregon taxable income (Sec. 317.061, ORS). The law defines "excise tax" to be a tax measured by or according to "net income" (Sec. 317.010(5), ORS). The rate of the corporation income tax is the same as that of the excise tax.	This state does not have an income tax. Rather, it has a tax on gross receipts (business and occupation tax). Manufacturers are taxed at the rate of 0.484% of the value of products, including byprod-ucts, manufactured. The measure of the tax is not affected by the place of sale or the fact that deliv-ery may be made out of state (RCW 82.04.240).
Property Tax on Inventories	Exempt	Exempt	Exempt
Tangible Personal Property	Taxable absent a specific exemption.	Only personal property used in a trade or business is taxable.	Taxable absent a specific exemption.
State Sales Tax Rates	Effective May 1, 2003, through June 30, 2005, the rate is increased to 6%. Thereafter, the rate decreases to 5%.	No sales tax	State rate is 6.5%.

in more detail in the "Periodicals and Internet Sites" section at the end of this chapter.

Practice Aids

The latest in state legislation actions is found in the Practice Aids section of the State Tab. This Week's Legislative Activity, Regulatory Activity, Current Year's Final and Pending Legislation, and Prior Year's Enacted Legislation are all located in the Practice Aids.

Interesting additions to Practice Aids are the **Ernst & Young (EY) Online Tax Advisor** and the **Ernst & Young Commonly Asked Questions**. Tax professionals wanting to use the EY Online Tax Advisor must pay separately for this option. The practitioner fills out a form online that provides relevant facts of the transaction—EY then delivers a response within a suggested time frame. The EY Commonly Asked Questions is a database of questions with answers that can be searched by keyword or the drill-down methods.

Topical Indexes

As previously mentioned, the last option on the State Tab is the Topical Indexes. The list of indexes is by state. Within each state, the number and choice of major topics differ. However, the major state taxes are topics, as is practice and procedures. The advantage of using an index is that the definition of the term is considered, not just its occurrence in the document. This is particularly of concern for Project 9–1, as to the term "service." With a keyword search, one can select more than one state for the inquiry. With the drill-down method, only one state can be accessed at a time. Either method will return the same CCH explanations that were uncovered by the prior searches.

CITATION SEARCH

State citation searches are conducted in the same manner as a Federal citation search. Once in the State Tab, the Find by Citation will present templates that are appropriate for state citation searches. Templates are supplied for State Tax Day, United States Supreme Court, pending and enacted legislation, and for every state's possible primary sources. If a state is selected in the State Tax Reported section, only the templates for that state will appear, as can be seen in Exhibit 9–14. Entered in the Regulation template is "1505," which is the California regulation addressing morticians.

Exhibit 9–14

CCH California State Citation Templates

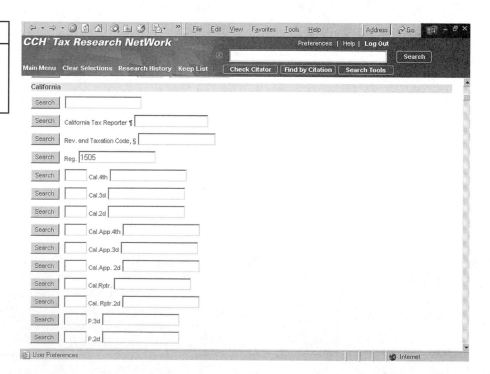

SPOTLIGHT ON TAXATION: Disposable Income

The Bureau of Economic Analysis computes the per capita disposable personal income based on the most current data available. For 2002, the top five states are located in the Northeast and bottom five states are in the Southeast and West.

Ranking	State	Per Capita Income
1	Connecticut	$35,859
2	New Jersey	33,995
3	Massachusetts	33,379
4	Maryland	31,166
5	New York	30,778
46	New Mexico	21,461
47	Utah	21,438
48	West Virginia	21,282
49	Arkansas	21,065
50	Mississippi	20,410

Source: U.S. Bureau of Economic Analysis, http://www.bea.doc.gov.

WESTLAW STATE SERVICES

Westlaw contains an extensive library of databases for state tax research. Exhibit 9–15 lists these databases. Note that the list includes the Bureau of National Affairs (BNA) Tax Management Portfolios devoted exclusively to state taxes and the RIA state series. Besides furnishing access to all state tax statutes, regulations, court cases, and administrative pronouncements, Westlaw enhances the tax practitioner's ability to stay ahead of the curve on new state legislation by providing databases to track current, pending, and proposed state bills. Newsletters such as the BNA *Daily Tax Report* and the RIA *State and Local Taxes Weekly* also help keep the practitioner up-to-date.

FIND AND KEYCITE

The Find option, on the opening screen (see Exhibit 7–10 in Chapter 7) allows the researcher to enter the citation for a state statute or the regulation. The citation, however, must be in a format recognized by Westlaw. A template for entering citations can be found by using the publication list feature (see Exhibit 9–16). Since there are more than 17,800 publications included in the Westlaw databases, searching for the item of interest is facilitated by being able to enter the first few letters in the "Starts with" box. As shown in Exhibit 9–16, the publication title is accompanied by the approved Westlaw abbreviation. Clicking on the publication title produces a template for

Exhibit | **9–15**

Westlaw State Databases

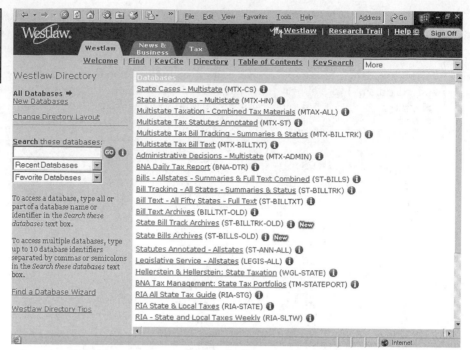

Exhibit | **9–16**

Westlaw Publication List Feature

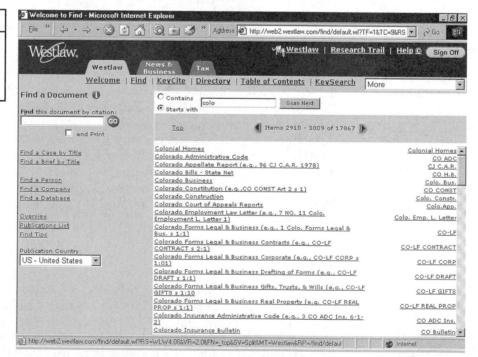

entering the citation. Thus, accessing state law primary sources is not complicated.

Another method for entering state law citations is with **KeyCite**. This option has a significantly smaller publication list (fewer than 3,000 items) than the Find option. For example, the Colorado Administration Code was not in-cluded in the KeyCite publication list on the date of our review. Therefore, referring to the publications list is important when using KeyCite. Unlike Find, the KeyCite publication list is not linked to templates for entering the citations.

DIRECTORY

There are two ways to access the state databases through the Directory Option. The first is to use the Tax Directory. It lists some of the state data-bases with the Federal selections and provides access to the complete list of state materials, as seen in Exhibit 7–12 in Chapter 7. Westlaw offers combined selections which include all the states' materials in a single data-base and materials segregated by state. In Exhibit 9–17, the separate state databases are found under the "Folders of Additional Databases" and the combined are located above this heading. Selecting the "State Taxation Statutes" title, for example, displays the states statutes in alphabetical or-der. After selecting the state of interest, a keyword search screen appears. This is the same screen as for Federal tax searching (see Exhibit 7–13 in Chapter 7).

The second Directory heading leading to a complete list of state tax materials is the "U.S. State Materials." Selecting the "Other U.S. States" subheading lists the states in alphabetical order. The accessible legal topics are listed

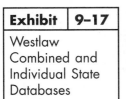

Exhibit | 9–17

Westlaw Combined and Individual State Databases

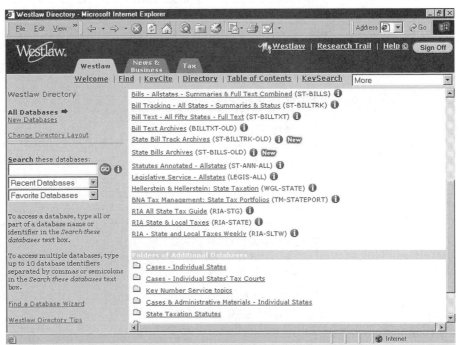

after choosing the state of interest. Tax materials will generally be one of the topics listed for each state. Rather than selecting "Other U.S. States," the researcher can select from the numerous topics under "U.S. State Materials" such as "Statutes & Legislative Services." This information is available for all states together and for individual states.

TABLE OF CONTENTS

The Table of Contents lists several headings for state taxation. Expanding any of the state headings presents a list of the states in alphabetical order. For each state, there is a table of contents for the specific topic. For instance, selecting Colorado from the "State Statutes & Constitutions" heading, exhibits a list of the Colorado Constitution and Statutes contents. Drilling down through the list the researcher will arrive at the statute addressing sales taxes on services.

The **KeySearch** system, as explained in Chapter 7, is a West numbering system of the key issues in court cases. The researcher identifies the legal topic applicable to the search and KeySearch formulates a query based on the underlying terms for the topic based on the key numbers system. Fortunately, KeySearch has a heading specifically for state and local taxation. Selecting one of the taxation areas displays the search screen for KeySearch. The researcher can determine what type of cases will be searched as well as treatises, journals, law reviews, and briefs. KeySearch develops a list of search terms from the selections made by the researcher. The list of search terms can be added to or modified to insure the results will be relevant to the particular project.

Practitioners performing state research frequently will want to create State and/or Federal circuit case tab(s) for easy access to these databases. The tabs are created using the Jurisdictional categories in the My Westlaw customizing option.

BNA STATE SERVICES

The Bureau of National Affairs (BNA) complements its U.S. **Tax Management Portfolios** with a **State Tax Series**. As with their other Portfolios, the state series is topic-driven and features analysis, insights, and guidance from leading state and local tax authorities on a variety of state issues. Some of the Portfolios offer an overview of the tax or topic while others focus on complex income tax, sales and use tax, and property tax issues. For topics such as credits and incentives or income taxation, it may take several Portfolios to cover all of the states. The state taxes and a sampling of the types of issues covered by the more than sixty State Portfolios are presented in Exhibit 9–18.

The State Portfolios have the same format as the U. S. series. Each State Portfolio begins with a Portfolio Description, presenting a brief overview of the topic and the order of presentation of the materials. The Portfolios contain

Exhibit	9-18	BNA State Portfolio List

BNA STATE PORTFOLIO TOPICS

Taxes and Issues Covered	Issues Covered
Corporate Income & Franchise Taxes	Procedures and Administration
Gross Receipts Taxes	Managing State Tax Audits
Personal Income Taxes	State Tax Appeal Systems
Property Taxes	State Tax Audit and Collection Procedures
Sales and Use Taxes	Definition of a Unitary Business
Excise Taxes	State Formulary Apportionment
Special Industry Taxes	Choice of Entity
State Environmental Taxes	State Taxation of Pass-Through Entities
State Taxation of Electronic Commerce	Consolidated Returns and Combined Reporting
State Taxation for Specific Industries	Mergers and Acquisitions
State Taxation for Specific States	Business Credits and Incentives
Business Operations in Puerto Rico	State Tax Aspects of Bankruptcy
Federal Constitutional Limitations on State Taxation	State Taxation of Compensation and Benefits
Limitations on States' Jurisdiction to Impose Taxes	Unclaimed Property

Source: http://www.bna.com.

the three usual BNA sections: (A) Detailed Analysis, (B) Working Papers, and (C) Bibliography and References. The Portfolio sections are updated in response to state tax changes, and, when necessary, the complete Portfolio is rewritten. BNA has been adding new Portfolios to cover emerging issues and to round out the State Portfolios offerings.

When unfamiliar with a state topic, the overview Portfolios furnish a thorough but easy to comprehend introduction to the topic. Those Portfolios focusing on a specific technical state topic may assume a certain level of practitioner sophistication and therefore may be more difficult for the state researcher novice. As with the Federal portfolios, the state statutes, regulations, rulings, and court case opinions are integrated into the analysis with citations footnoted or included in the text. The critical documents cited are reproduced in the working papers section. Other useful aids furnished in the State Portfolios include the following.

- Interactive state forms
- Reproductions of model acts
- Sample sales and use certificates
- Tables, charts, and lists
- State tax administrations' addresses and telephone numbers
- Keyword indexes, state-by-state indexes

Although BNA does not offer a full state tax service like RIA, CCH, or Westlaw, the State Portfolios and its news reports can compete with any provided by other services. If the practitioner can find a Portfolio that covers the state tax issue of interest, BNA has performed the key research, and all that needs to be done is to apply the results to the facts of the client's situation.

OTHER RESOURCES

Warren, Gorham & Lamont publishes the *State and Local Taxation* treatise by Jerome R. Hellerstein, Walter Hellerstein, and Joan M. Youngman. This treatise, currently in its seventh edition, is possibly the most comprehensive single work on state and local taxation. The authors have undertaken the ambitious task of assembling a comprehensive review of all state and many local tax laws and the decisions interpreting those laws. Because few other published works address state and local taxation in such a thorough manner, *State and Local Taxation* can be used as a textbook in law schools and masters of taxation programs.

The treatise analyzes, interprets, and integrates state and local tax laws in a manner that is understandable, illuminating, and sometimes very creative. A unique characteristic of the treatise is its discussion and evaluation of the strengths of many states' policy arguments regarding the taxation of an entity in a jurisdiction. These policy arguments can be important in state tax issues, and this makes this treatise a valuable resource.

The treatise includes a corresponding discussion of foreign commerce implications, where applicable. *State and Local Taxation* is available in print and through Internet services such as Westlaw and RIA Checkpoint.

Aspen's *Multistate Corporate Tax Guide* is another useful resource. The two volumes concentrate on key corporate tax issues in sales and use taxation and income-based taxes in 47 states, New York City, and the District of Columbia. The volumes provide quick access to each state's position statements on tax issues though numerous charts. Much of the analysis is based on data collected through questionnaires completed by the top state officials who interpret and apply the state laws. To assure timeliness and relevancy of the information, the treatise is updated mid-year with a supplement.

The *Guide* includes articles and white papers on nexus issues and the Multistate Tax Commission's guidelines for uniform taxes. Directories of state income, franchise, and sales/use tax office addresses, telephone numbers, and state Internet addresses are provided, as well.

PERIODICALS AND INTERNET SITES

State tax journals and newsletters contain a variety of articles and news briefs that are designed to keep readers current with regard to developments in specific or general areas of the state and local taxation. These articles might contain, for example, an in-depth review of a recently decided court case, a broad analysis of the factors that should enter into the practitioner's decision, or a call for reform of a statute by a neutral (or biased) observer. Tax articles can suggest new approaches to tax problems, give guidance for solving complex problems, or just explain a new law in a readable form.

JOURNALS

Two important journals in the state taxation arena are *Journal of Multistate Taxation and Incentives* (Warren, Gorham & Lamont), with ten issues per year, and *Journal of State Taxation* (Aspen/CCH) published quarterly. Both of these journals focus on practical solutions to state and local taxation, as well as creative planning strategies for multistate business operations and individuals with multistate tax liabilities. These journals keep the subscriber informed in critical areas of state and local taxation nationwide as well as providing expert assessments of important cases and their potential impacts. Generally there are reviews of current state legislative issues to keep the reader up-to-date on state proposed, pending, or enacted legislation. Articles may cover legal, accounting, and business aspects of multistate entities. Both of the journals also focus on incentives offered by states to encourage business growth and expansion.

NEWSLETTERS

Tax Analysts publishes two important state tax periodicals, *State Tax Notes* and *State Tax Today*. Like Tax Analysts flagship offering, *Tax Notes* (see Chapter 7), *State Tax Notes* is an authoritative source for news and commentary on state and local taxation. This weekly publication provides the latest news from all fifty states and the District of Columbia, as well as in-depth analysis from leading experts in state taxation. Summaries of all judicial, administrative, and legislative developments are also included in *State Tax Notes.*

The purpose of *State Tax Today* is to furnish the latest breaking state tax news on a daily basis. It includes tax news for every state, D.C., and U.S. territories. There are links to full-text state documents and decisions of the U.S. Supreme Court, and state supreme and appellate courts. Beside news briefs, *State Tax Today* has in-depth analytical articles, commentaries, and special reports.

Many of the other tax publishers provide state newsletters. For example, the *Tax Management Weekly State Tax Report* is the BNA equivalent to the Tax Analysts *State Tax Notes*. It gives a state-by-state analysis of state code and regulations, state administrative and judicial court decisions, and state administrative pronouncements as does *State Tax Notes*. Other state newsletters published by BNA include:

- Daily Tax Report Highlights
- Weekly State Tax Regulatory Alert
- Weekly State Tax Report
- Multistate Tax Report
- Email Highlights notification of the week's state tax highlights

The CCH newsletter is called *State Tax Review* and RIA's is *State & Local Taxes Weekly*. Both are offered through their Internet tax services.

INTERNET SITES

As described in Chapter 7, the *Tax and Accounting Sites Directory* web site[6] contains links to numerous tax sites. The state and local listing has links to each state's taxing agency, legal information, organizations, and government sites. As can be seen in Exhibit 9–19, general links to locators, sales & use tax, news & topics, organizations, rates & data, state tax guides, and e-commerce tax are also included in the state and local screen.

Exhibit	9–19

Tax and Accounting Sites Directory for State and Local Taxes

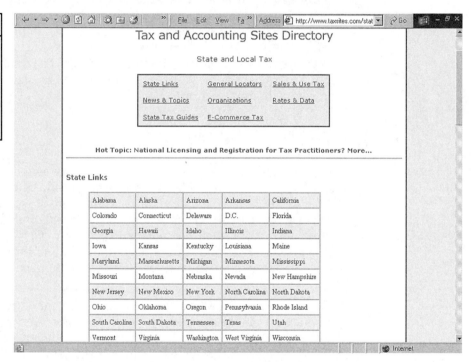

SUMMARY

With perhaps one-half of a business's tax bill being paid to the states, tax planning for state and local taxation has become more important to taxpayers and therefore to tax researchers. The research service industry has responded to this escalating need by providing a variety of tax research products, all designed to improve the practitioner's efficiency and effectiveness in state and local research. As state and local taxation consulting becomes more of a mainstay for practitioners, tax services will provide more options for re-

6. http://www.taxsites.com.

search. Consequently, state and local tax research tools will likely be among the fastest changing components of the major tax services.

TAX TUTOR

Reinforce the tax research information covered in this chapter by completing the online tutorials located at the Federal Tax Research web site:

http://raabe.swlearning.com

KEY WORDS

By the time you complete your work in this chapter, you should be comfortable discussing each of the following terms. If you need additional review of any of these items, return to the appropriate material in the chapter or consult the glossary at the end of this text.

All State Tax Guide
Checkpoint State & Local Tax (SALT)
Commerce Clause
Compare It
Create-a-Chart
Due Process Clause
Equal Protection
Ernst & Young Commonly Asked Questions
Ernst & Young (EY) Online Tax Advisor
Joint Audit Program
KeyCite
KeySearch
Multistate Quick Answer Charts
Multistate Tax Commission (MTC)
Multistate Tax Compact
National Conference of Commissioners on Uniform State Laws
Privileges and Immunities Clause
Public Purpose
State and Local Taxation
State Tax Reporters
StateNet
Supremacy Clause
Tax Management Portfolios State Tax Series
Uniform Division of Income for Tax Purposes Act (UDITPA)
Uniformity Clause

DISCUSSION QUESTIONS

1. Why are taxpayers emphasizing state and local tax planning?

2. Why have state and local taxes been increasing over recent years?

3. Approximately what percentage of the national tax burden is state taxes?

4. On what were the early taxing systems based in the southern states? The northern states?

5. What state was the first to introduce an income tax? In what year?

6. Describe the different constitutionality challenges with regard to Federal and state taxes.

7. What is the definition of "public purpose" for state tax law?

8. Discuss the supremacy provision in the Federal Constitution.

9. Which clause in the Federal Constitution contains the most significant limitation on state taxing authority?

10. What are the four criteria for imposition of state taxation set forth in *Complete Auto Transit Inc.?*

11. List two situations where the due process clause has limited the scope of a state's taxing authority.

12. What is the importance of the *Quill* and *Wrigley* cases?

13. What do the equal protection and the uniformity clauses of most state constitutions require?

14. Why are corporations not covered by the privileges and immunities clause?

15. Explain how the passage of a state tax bill is similar to the passage of a Federal law.

16. When would Federal rulings be pertinent to state tax issues?

17. What is UDITPA and what is its significance with regard to the Multistate Tax Compact?

18. What is the Joint Audit Program provided by the Multistate Tax Commission?

19. What is included in Checkpoint's StateNet?

20. Where can you find lists of official state contact information?

21. Describe the RIA Create-a-Chart function.

22. What is the function of the Compare It feature in RIA?

23. Compare the Multiple Sources search with the state and local initial search option in RIA.

24. Discuss the citation search capabilities in the RIA state and local tax practice area.

25. Why might a table of contents search be more efficient than a strict keyword search?

26. Which service provides tabs for state taxes and sales taxes? Discuss the differences in the materials provided in these two tabs.

27. In the CCH Network state tax service, how can a researcher reduce the list of documents searched? How is this different than the RIA method?

28. What is the CCH equivalent to the RIA Compare It function?

29. Describe the differences in locating a table of contents for a data set in RIA and CCH.

30. What is the function of the State Tax Guide offered by CCH?

31. Explain how a practitioner would use the EY Online Tax Advisor offered through CCH.

32. Compare the use of the Federal citator and the state citator in CCH.

33. How does a researcher access a template for entering state citations in Westlaw?

34. What is the difference between the publication lists for Find and KeyCite in Westlaw? Why is it important to check these lists before searching for a document?

35. Explain how the KeySearch system aids in searching on Westlaw.

36. What are the different sections in a BNA State Portfolio? How similar are these to the sections provided in the U.S. Income series?

37. Comment on the coverage and usefulness of the treatise *State and Local Taxation*.

38. Name two state taxation journals and indicate who publishes each.

39. Compare the state tax newsletters published by Tax Analysts and BNA.

40. Why does this chapter not provide a listing of state and local tax web sites?

EXERCISES

41. Locate the web site for the Multistate Tax Commission.
    a. What are the four items listed as the function of the Commission?
    b. Provide a brief summary of the latest News Release list on the web site.
    c. What is the "Multistate Tax Commission Review"? (Hint: Look in Publications.)
    d. How does a taxpayer initiate joint audits?
    e. The MTC provides a line to the Streamline Sales Tax Project. Use this link to discover what the mission is of this project. What is the mission?

42. Using RIA Checkpoint, locate the *Manz v. California State Board of Equalization* case using the Federal Cases in the State Taxes option.
    a. Provide the docket number, the court hearing the case, and the date the decision was issued.
    b. What types of taxes were involved in this case? What was the holding of the Court?
    c. Must the plaintiff and defendant names in the case be entered in order to find the case? Explain your response.
    d. Read this case. Perform a keyword search to locate the case without using the plaintiff or defendant names. Also use the "Search Within Results" feature. What keywords did you use for the general search and for your follow-up?

43. Using the RIA Checkpoint State & Local Search option, answer the following questions.
    a. Select Kentucky as the state and go to the next screen. What corporate items are provided in the tax type list? What is the database title for individual income taxes?
    b. Select Washington as the state and go to the next screen. What is the first tax type listed? What corporate items are provided in the tax type list? What is the database title for individual income taxes?
    c. Are the tax types the same for Kentucky and Washington? Explain your response.
    d. In what order are the Tax Types listed? In what order are the Document Types listed?

44. Use RIA Checkpoint to answer the following questions regarding the state of Illinois.
    a. Select State & Local Taxes in the Table of Contents (TOC). Compare the listing of documents available to the listing provided by the search option.
    b. Using the Index in the TOC, what are the listings for the letter "H" under the "stamp" heading?
    c. In the TOC under "Advance State & Local Documents" what are the listings for "Official Material"?

45. Use CCH NetWork to answer the following questions regarding the state of Rhode Island.
    a. What is the title of the most recent article in State Tax Day related to this state?
    b. What is the most recent court case for this state?
    c. In the State Tax Report, perform a keyword search using the term "escheat." What does this term mean and to what does it apply? In what paragraph did you find the answer?
    d. Using the Topical Index, perform a keyword search for "dining car." Under what headings are there entries for this term?

46. Perform a keyword search in CCH NetWork to answer the following questions.
    a. Does Hawaii allow estates a personal exemption? If yes, what is the amount and what is the state statute?
    b. Use the Smart Relate: Related Topics—States while in a document found in part a. What states appear to give a standard deduction or personal exemption to estates?
    c. Select all states to determine which states provide a personal exemption for estates. Use the keywords: estate personal exemption. Was this method as effective as the method used in part b? Explain your response.
    d. Turn on the Thesaurus (use Search Tools). Does the order in which you enter the keywords make a difference in the documents retrieved? Try entering the keywords in each of the following orders: estate personal exemption versus personal estate exemption. Explain the results.

47. Perform a Table of Contents (TOC) search using CCH NetWork to answer the following questions.

a. Did Alaska ever have a personal income tax? If yes, what was the last year to have a tax?

b. What is the aviation fuel tax rate in the state of North Dakota?

c. Using Multistate Quick Answer Charts, which state has the highest cigarette tax per pack? Which state has the lowest tax?

d. Using the Topical Indexes for locating information about targeted business zones in Delaware, which method is more efficient: a TOC search of Delaware or a TOC of Multistate Corporate Income Tax Guide?

48. Compare the efficiency of RIA Checkpoint with CCH NetWork when finding the answers to the following questions. It is each service's searching capability, not the tax issue, which should be compared.

a. What is the penalty rate in Texas for producers of sulfur for not timely reporting and paying their severance tax?

b. What is the kilowatt-hour excise tax rate in Ohio?

c. Could the potential purchaser of an operating plant qualify for reimbursement under the Maine Employment Tax Increment Financing Act by employing persons currently employed at the plant? (Hint: Look at an insurance tax.)

d. Which state has the highest state sales tax?

e. Which service is more effective for state tax research?

49. Use Westlaw to answer the following questions regarding the *Village Bank and Trust Co.* (471 A. 2d 1187) case.

a. What year was the case decided and by what court?

b. Clicking on the KeyCite Notes located in the West Headnotes provides access to three cases. What are the three cases and what KeyCite "flags" are associated with each?

c. Using KeyCite, is the list of cases presented the same as that found in part b? What KeyCite "flag" is associated with the *Village Bank* case?

d. What are the cases listed in the Table of Authorities for the *Village Bank* case? How much reliance does it place on these cases?

50. Using Westlaw Table of Contents (TOC), answer the following.

a. What is the New York statutory authority for the Amnesty Program of 2002–2003?

b. In the Statutes & Constitution, what is the title, division, section and article number for the alcohol beverage business privilege tax for Guam?

c. Are there any treatises listed in either the Thomson-West or the WG&L treatise headings that cover state taxation? If yes provide the names of the treatise and their authors.

51. The Westlaw Tax Directory State Materials—Complete list should be used to answer the following questions.

a. What statutes are covered in the Multistate Tax Statute database?

b. What is the West Key Number for state taxation?

c. What cities are covered in the Administrative Decisions—Individual States & Cities?

d. Search for a 1919 case involving the City of Richmond, Virginia, and a tobacco tax. Provide the citation for the case. What other city was involved?

52. Locate *Buchanan County v. Ritter Lumber Co.* 100 S. E. 546. For each question, indicate which service you used (RIA, CCH, or Westlaw).
    a. When was the case decided? What court decided the case?
    b. Is this case still valid for all points of law it covers?
    c. What cases did it cite in its decision?
    d. Which of the three services provided the most efficient access to the information requested in parts a, b, and c?
    e. If all you had was the name of the case and not the citation, what would you do?

53. Use the BNA Tax Management Portfolios, State Series for the following questions.
    a. Is there a portfolio on each state? Which state has the most portfolios?
    b. Generally what are the Portfolio Series numbers for the portfolios that address multistate issues?
    c. What is the title of the Portfolio that covers the limitations on state taxes imposed by the Federal Constitution?
    d. The portfolios covering state credits and incentives are unique. Explain why this statement is true. Who wrote each of these portfolios?

54. Use the BNA Tax Management Portfolios, State Series for the following questions.
    a. What is the title of State Portfolio 1550? How many worksheets are included in this Portfolio?
    b. Which Portfolio explains the QSSS election for S corporations?
    c. How many parties are usually involved in a drop shipment transaction? In which Portfolio did you find your answer?

55. Locate state tax newsletters to answer the following questions.
    a. What is the most recent article in Tax Analyst *State Tax Today* discussing Real Estate Investment Trusts (REITs)?
    b. In an Iowa case reviewed in CCH *State Tax Day*, the purchaser of property was entitled to recover property taxes paid subsequent to the tax sale and to the partition of the property. What case is cited in the article?
    c. What is the most recent article in CCH *State Tax Day*, All States on gasoline taxes?
    d. How many months of articles are kept on the Internet of CCH *State Tax Day*? How many years of CCH *State Tax Review* are maintained in the Archives?
    e. Give a summary of the latest Newsstand brief from the RIA State & Local Updates for your home state.
    f. How many years of RIA *State & Local Taxes Weekly* are archived?

56. Find an article in the *Journal of Multistate Taxation and Incentives* on the following topics. Provide the authors, title of the article, and date published.
    a. The treatment of electronic commerce by the Streamlined Sales and Use Tax Act.
    b. A two-part article that reviews state enterprise zone programs.
    c. Credits and exemptions used by Mississippi to promote development of broadband technology.
    d. The most recent current development for your home state.

57. Use the *Journal of State Taxation* to answer the following questions.
    a. What is the title of the article in the Winter 2004 volume written by Debra Pasdera Demmitt? How long is the article?
    b. What is the volume and number of the Spring 2003 issue? What article appears on page 20?
    c. Who is the current editor and what is his/her affiliation?
    d. Which international accounting firms (the Big 4) are represented on the editorial board?

58. Use Internet sites to answer the following questions.
    a. What links to news and topics does Tax Sites (http://www.taxsites .com) provide?
    b. Visit three national associations that are concerned with state tax issues. Provide their URLs.
    c. Visit the web site of your state's agency responsible for taxation (Department of Revenue for many states). Provide the URL for this agency. For California, provide both agencies' URLs.
    d. Select an adjacent state and give a summary of one of its taxes. (Alaska and Hawaii use each other.)

59. In Oklahoma, what types of documents are subject to a stamp tax? Indicate what tax service or Internet site you used to answer this question.

60. Which state has the highest marginal income tax rate for individuals (exclude AMT tax rates)? Indicate what tax service or Internet site you used to answer this question.

RESEARCH CASES

For each of the research problems locate court cases or administrative pronouncements (Revenue Rulings, Revenue Procedures, etc.) that support your position. Provide a list of cases or administrative pronouncements citing your authority that demonstrate your authority is still good law.

61. Tom and Verna are going to combine their fishing businesses to become more profitable. Tom currently lives in Mississippi and Verna lives in Louisiana. They would prefer to set up the business as an S corporation, but only if it will not be subject to state taxation. Since Verna and Tom live within twenty miles of each other, they don't have a preference as to the state of incorporation. Does it make a tax difference which state they choose?

62. NewCity, California, charged Rick a real estate transfer tax when his property was relinquished to the Federal Housing Administration in its capacity as his loan guarantor. The amount charged was the same as the amount Rick was required to pay the county. Can Rick be required to pay this tax, or should the FHA pay it?

63. TimberCut Corporation transferred all the rights to timber growing on its land located in Spokane County, Washington, to its wholly-owned subsidiary, PineCo. The Department of Revenue has imposed a real estate excise tax on TimberCut because PineCo transferred $1 million

cash to TimberCut. Is this transfer a sale of timber land and therefore TimberCut owes the taxes imposed?

64. WaterWorks Corporation has decided to sell off one of its amusement parks located in Texas. Several businesses have been identified as possible buyers. It is unlikely that one of these businesses will purchase all of the assets of the amusement park, but WaterWorks is confident that it can sell all of the assets within a six-month period. Will this sale be subject to Texas sales tax?

65. A tribal nation in Kansas is considering building a gas station to accommodate travelers through their reservation. Before undergoing the considerable expense for construction, the tribal members want to know whether the fuel sold will be subject to state fuel taxes. This will make a difference in the profitability of the project. Is gasoline sold on a federally recognized reservation subject to the fuel tax imposed by Kansas?

66. A town in Vermont wants to charge property tax on a lot and building used by a not-for-profit organization as its administrative office. To be exempt from property taxes, the property must:

   • be dedicated to public use;
   • have its primary use directly benefit a class of persons who are part of the public; and,
   • be owned and operated on a not-for-profit basis.

   Does the administrative use of the building meet the definition for the exemption?

67. Iowa imposes a tax on the operation of slot machines. The rate is graduated, based on slot machine revenues. Can Iowa charge a higher maximum rate to racetrack owners than it does to riverboat owners and not violate the equal protection clause of the U.S. Constitution?

68. The Pluto Corporation has been mining ore in Oklahoma for many years. A new mine just developed is producing ore containing uranium. Pluto would like to know what the rate of the severance tax is on mined uranium and upon what base the tax is assessed.

69. The Peppermint Partnership has been quite successful in its candy business. It is considering taking the partnership public and becoming a master limited partnership. If it does so, will it be subject to the corporate franchise in New York, where its headquarters and operating plant are located?

70. Rodney has been in the South Carolina National Guard for the last twenty years. This is his last year as an active member. Since Rodney turns sixty-five in August of this year, he will begin collecting Social Security benefits and Guard retirement pay. His employer laid him off in January, and Rodney qualified for unemployment compensation. Rodney received severance pay of $50,000 when terminated by his employer. Which of these amounts are taxable to Rodney in South Carolina?

Part 4

Implementing the Research Tools

Chapter 10

Communicating
Research Results

LEARNING OBJECTIVES

■ Produce a standard format for the construction of a file memorandum to contain the results of one's research efforts and professional judgment.

■ Develop other forms of communicating research results, including oral presentations and client letters.

CHAPTER OUTLINE

Once the practitioner has begun to develop effective tax research skills, he or she must hone them with practice—whether by working through tax research cases presented as a class exercise in a university course, or immediately beginning work for professional clients. Accordingly, the overriding purpose of this chapter is to provide the reader with guidance and opportunities to apply the research skills and examine the tax research resources that have been discussed in previous chapters.

In addition, this chapter will discuss the means by which the tax professional conveys the results of a tax research project—in other words, applying some of the judgment and communications skills required. Direction as to the proper format and content of memorandums to the file, of client letters, and of oral presentations is addressed, with development of professional skills the overriding goal.

COMMUNICATIONS AND THE TAX PROFESSIONAL

As we suggested in our initial discussions of the tax research process, illustrated in Exhibit 2–1, a tax research assignment often concludes with some form of communication by the tax professional. The audience for this communication often is the practitioner's supervisor or client, but tax-related communications can take many forms.

- A telephone call or instant message
- An informal discussion in person or via e-mail
- A letter prepared for reading by someone at least as familiar with the tax law as the writer
- A letter prepared for reading by someone less familiar with the tax law than is the writer
- A letter prepared for reading by someone who is essentially untrained in the tax law
- An article for publication in a newspaper or magazine directed at the general public
- An article for publication in a professional journal read by tax generalists
- An article for publication in a professional journal read by tax specialists
- A speech to a general audience
- A speech at a conference of tax professionals
- A memorandum to be read in the future by the writer or by a peer with similar training
- An appearance on a news broadcast or program with a serious tone
- An appearance on a broadcast with a less serious tone
- A posting on an Internet bulletin board or news group

For the most part, the tax professional's preparation for these communications is similar. For the purposes of this chapter, we assume that all of the pertinent tax research techniques developed in earlier parts of this text have been planned and conscientiously applied, so the practitioner is qualified and current enough with respect to prevailing tax law to address the audience in terms of the content of the communication. The challenge then becomes how to deliver this information in a manner that will be accepted and understood by the audience.

Actually, though, one's preparation for the delivery of tax communication must go far beyond obtaining control over the technical tax knowledge required for the assignment. As illustrated in Exhibit 10–1, communication truly occurs only when the message desired to be sent by the speaker or writer is received by the intended audience. Distractions of all sorts can make this process difficult to accomplish. Thorough research into the nature and expectations of the audience, factors that may interfere with the delivery of the message, and feedback and corrective measures must make up a critical part of the communicator's preparation.

Examples of "noise" that can disrupt the communications process include a mismatching of expectations as to the message, the chosen delivery method, the identity and nature of the sender and receiver of the message, other events competing for the attention of those involved, logistical difficulties, and technological problems. Feedback and corrective devices that can aid in accomplishing the delivery of the desired message include formal and informal evaluation processes, "real-time" opportunities such as question-and-answer periods and written comments received during the drafting of the document, and the sending and receiving of intended and unintended body language or other communicative signals.

Tax professionals generally are virtually untrained as to the application of communication methods in conveying tax messages, but this shortcoming can be remedied. The chief ingredients necessary to become an effective tax-content communicator are the desire to learn and improve as a communicator in general, and the use of every opportunity possible to obtain

| Exhibit | 10–1 | The Communication Process |

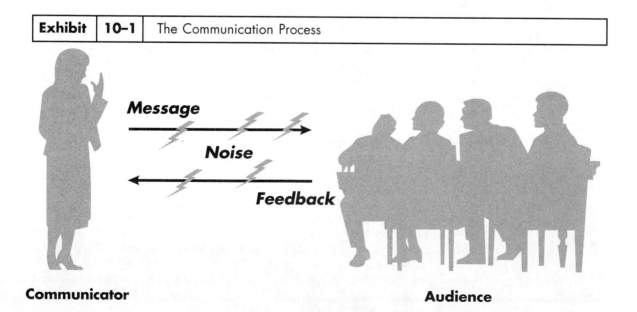

Communicator   **Audience**

and develop skills in the delivery of tax information. Given the nature of today's competitive tax profession, plenty of such opportunities for practice exist, and pressures from others who are competing for clients and promotions provide most professionals with more than enough motivation to make improvements in their communication skills a lifelong process.

SPOTLIGHT ON TAXATION: A Career in Taxation

"When I was young, I was taught the story of Jesus and the taxman. The point was that Jesus was good to everyone; so much so that he would even eat with the taxman. The story tells a lot about being good, but it also tells a lot about historical perceptions of the tax collector."

—Christopher Bergin

We begin a more detailed review of the communication process with an examination of the most commonly encountered written communications demanded in the tax practice. The chapter concludes with a discussion of skills needed in delivering spoken communications. In either case, the structure of the communication follows the basic format delineated in Exhibit 10–2.

Exhibit	10–2	The Structure of Technical Tax Communications

Element of the Message	Purposes	Comments
Introduction	Provide a roadmap for what is to come. Place the message in context. Generate audience interest, if necessary. Set the tone for the message.	**10% of allotted time/space.** Could include a story/anecdote, current news development, or "object lesson."
Body	Generally, the technical tax material is presented here. Usually follows an order suggested by the hierarchy of the sources of the tax law. Alternative ordering methods: historical, strengths/weaknesses, cost/benefit.	**80% of allotted time/space.** Must be brief, to the point, hard-hitting; not trite or condescending. Identify three to six key points that all readers/listeners must take away from the message.
Conclusion	Tie back to the introduction. Reinforce key elements of the message. Bring the presentation to a climax. Indicate next steps and follow-up action.	**10% of allotted time/space.** Tip off the reader/listener that the conclusion is starting, with "In closing," "To sum up," or "I'll conclude with. . . ."

THE HEART OF TAX RESEARCH COMMUNICATION: THE FILE MEMO

The tax researcher spends most of his or her time reviewing primary and secondary sources of the Federal tax law, redefining pertinent issues, and attempting to discover additional facts concerning the client's situation. On completion of this review, the researcher must integrate the disparate results of the research process into a more usable form. Thorough practitioners generate a memorandum to the client's file for this purpose. This **file memorandum** is designed to:

- organize the facts, issues, and conclusions of the project,
- facilitate a review of the research activities by the practitioner's supervisors or colleagues, and
- allow for a subsequent examination of the research issue, by the original researcher or by his or her successor, with respect to the same or another client's identical or related fact situation.

Accordingly, the file memo should be constructed in a general, usable format that lends itself to a quick perusal of the pertinent tax facts and issues. Many accounting and law firms impose a standardized format. If the reader's employer has enacted no such requirement, he or she should consider adopting the format illustrated in Exhibits 2–5 and 10–3. A template for this memo format is available at the web site for this text, **http://raabe.swlearning.com**.

A file memo should include a brief introductory summary of the facts and issues that face the client. In all but the most complex instances, this statement

Exhibit	10–3	File Memorandum for Tax Research

Raabe, Whittenburg & Sanders, CPAs
San Francisco, CA

September 30, 20XX

Relevant Facts

The Browns live in South Dakota. They own their home and hold investments in the debt of several domestic corporations. The interest that they received on this debt was gross income to them. To diversify their portfolio, the Browns took out a sizable second mortgage on their home and applied a portion of the proceeds to some City of Chandler School Bonds. The remainder of the proceeds was used to expand the facilities of Mrs. Brown's dental clinic.

Specific Issues

How much of the mortgage interest paid can be claimed as an itemized deduction by the Browns?

Conclusions

That portion of the mortgage proceeds applied to the dental clinic generates an interest deduction to be claimed against clinic income on Schedule C. No other deduction is allowed.

Exhibit	10–3	File Memorandum for Tax Research—Concluded

Support

The Code disallows the deduction of interest on indebtedness that is incurred or continued to purchase or carry obligations, the interest on which is exempt from the Federal income tax. IRC § 265(a)(2). This provision denies the double benefit that would be enjoyed by the taxpayer who would receive tax-exempt income while simultaneously claiming an investment interest deduction for the interest expense paid, e.g., by incurring a bank loan and using the proceeds to purchase municipal bonds.

The IRS examines evidence to infer the intent of the taxpayer who is incurring the indebtedness. Under Rev. Proc. 72–18, 1972–1 C.B. 740, a taxpayer who purchases exempt bonds can claim an interest deduction if the debt in question has been incurred (1) for personal reasons (e.g., via a mortgage to finance the purchase of residential property) or (2) for valid business reasons, as long as the borrowing does not exceed legitimate business needs.

Several court decisions have emphasized that the existence of such business motives must be documented clearly, as to both presence and amount. *Wisconsin Cheeseman v. U.S.,* 388 F.2d 420 (CA-7, 1968); *Bradford,* 60 T.C. 253 (1973); *Israelson v. U.S.,* 367 F.Supp. 1104 (D.Md., 1973). However, if the taxpayer's holdings of tax-exempt securities are deemed to be immaterial in amount, the § 265(a)(2) disallowance will not be invoked. *Indian Trail Trading Post, Inc. v. Comm.,* 503 F.2d 102 (CA-6, 1974). Typically, if the average adjusted basis of the exempt bonds does not exceed 2 percent of the average adjusted basis of the entire investment portfolio, the entire interest deduction is allowed. *Batten v. U.S.,* 322 F.Supp. 629 (E.D.Va., 1971); *Ball v. Comm.,* 54 T.C. 1200 (1970).

Mortgage indebtedness is a classic illustration of an investment that will generate deductible interest expenses for the taxpayer who holds exempt bonds. However, the timing of such a mortgage transaction must be monitored to exhibit the proper motives for the benefit of the IRS. In one case, the taxpayer paid for his home with cash. Only later was an investment program (that included municipal bonds) initiated and a residential mortgage secured. The IRS inferred that the mortgage proceeds were in indirect support of the exempt indebtedness, and the deduction for the mortgage interest was disallowed. *Mariorenzi v. Comm.,* 490 F.2d 92 (CA-8, 1974), 32 TCM 681 (1973). Had the taxpayer secured a mortgage before the home was completed, purchasing the exempt bonds out of savings, it appears that the deduction could have been preserved. The IRS has applied this doctrine outside of the Eighth Circuit, in PLR 80041291.

Because the Browns live in the Eighth Circuit, the *Mariorenzi* doctrine prevails, and no itemized deduction is allowed at all, i.e., for that portion of the loan that is applied to the school bonds. Rev. Proc. 72-18 is insensitive to portfolio diversification motives, and no personal motive appears to exist that supports any other possible deduction. According to the logic of these precedents, the Browns should have sold the exempt bonds and then used the proceeds to finance their portfolio acquisitions.

Actions to Be Taken

Prepare letter, review results with client.

Suggest changes in portfolio holdings to re-gain the deduction.

Preparer: Mary H. Polzin

Reviewer: Teri D. Cardwell

should require no more than two paragraphs. Similarly, the rare file-memo footnote should be restricted to current developments, for example, with respect to an appeal relative to one of the critical cases that is cited in the memo or a statutory amendment.

The file memo then includes a listing of the tax issues that are in dispute and a matching conclusion for each identified issue. This format allows the subsequent reader to determine quickly whether each issue is "pro" or "con" for the taxpayer and limits the time required to sort through a number of such memos. In the support section, a detailed review and evaluation of controlling laws is derived, with full citations presented in the standard forms. The "meat" of the memo is presented here, and the strengths and weaknesses of both sides of the tax argument are developed and discussed. Finally, recommendations for subsequent actions with the client may be enumerated, and other strategies as to tax return or audit positions are identified.

Often, the gathering of the pertinent facts is the most challenging of the tax professional's tasks. Tax engagements typically begin with client contact in the form of a phone call or meeting, followed by an exchange of copies of pertinent documents such as letters, spreadsheets, trusts or wills, contracts, life insurance or annuity agreements, employer handbooks, and diaries or logbooks belonging to the client. In reality, though, the initial determination of the facts is likely to be incomplete.

- Taxpayers tend to see the dispute only from their side, so that facts and circumstances that may cast doubt on the ability to determine or document the pro-taxpayer position may be hidden or "forgotten."
- Taxpayers are not trained in the details of the technical tax law, so they may be unable to determine which documents or other evidence of the facts are important in determining the controlling tax law.
- For tax research that requires the full professional judgment and experience of the practitioner, there may be no clearly controlling tax statute or precedent, facts may be truly incomplete, or they may unfold as the evaluation of tax law occurs. The researcher may discover that issues of taxpayer motive, knowledge, or other circumstances turn on facts that were not immediately known to be critical.

Moreover, fact gathering often turns on such intangible factors as the reliability of the memories of the taxpayers and key witnesses, the ability of witnesses to withstand scrutiny in the deposition and testimony phases of the case, the unanticipated death or disappearance of key parties, the destruction of records due to casualty or computer mismanagement, and the tendency of some taxpayers to "fix the truth" after the fact. Recalling our language in Chapters 2 and 3, more research engagements entail closed-fact settings than open-fact situations by far, but those facts may be fairly difficult to determine and support in a manner that will satisfy the IRS or the courts. Such fact-gathering travails make for interesting anecdotes at conferences of tax practitioners, and they seldom are apparent from the clean, black-and-white statements of facts that accompany file memos and case briefs.

The tone and nature of the file memo should recognize that its readers will be restricted to fellow tax practitioners who are well versed in the Federal tax law. Thus, references to primary and secondary sources of the tax law should be frequent and complete, but usually limited to the tax case reporters that are available in the office of the researcher's firm. One must presume that the ultimate reader of the memo's comments will need no introduction to the hierarchy of the Federal tax system nor to statutory citation practices. In addition, it often is helpful to include pertinent references to one or more of the commercial tax services to which the researcher's firm subscribes, perhaps on a "sticky note" or other attachment to the memo, providing a clear paper trail to facilitate subsequent review and commentary concerning the tax issue.

Seldom will the researcher's efforts result in merely the preparation of a research memorandum to the file. In general, the memo will be accompanied in the file by links to and briefs of one or more pertinent court cases or administrative pronouncements. (Review Exhibit 5–8 and your related class exercises concerning the format and content of a well-constructed court case brief.) In addition, many practitioners append to the file memo photocopies of or hot links to prior-year documents, in-house memos, various IRS rulings, and journal articles, much of which features "highlighting," i.e., markup with a pastel marker. These practices were illustrated in Exhibit 10–3.

The authors recommend that practitioners restrict such appended material to only those resources that are of utmost importance to reduce both the associated client costs and the volume of the typical memo. In this regard, we believe that an effective statement of facts and issues, followed by a concise synthesis of the controlling law, is far more valuable than a mass of duplicated, small-print tax reference materials.

SPOTLIGHT ON TAXATION: The Tax Profession

The file memo and supporting documents also come under review by the audit department and others in the firm, so technical tax material might be accompanied by a set of nontechnical objectives and timetables for the client engagement. Information that could be used by those dealing with the creditors of the taxpayer also might be available in the file.

EVALUATING THE SOURCES OF LAW

The tax researcher will have made a number of judgments and creative applications concerning the client's fact situation before preparing the file memo. For instance, the researcher may select and eliminate competing issues and direct the research process onto one or more pathways to the exclusion of others. Nonetheless, in deriving an analysis of the various elements of the controlling sources of the tax law, the practitioner must choose from among a number of varied interpretations of the statute and of its (interpretive) regulations and court case opinions.

Often the researcher will be guided in this regard by the opinions of the most recent of the court cases discovered. Well-written case opinions typically provide a summary of the evolution of the pertinent tax law and a discussion of the competing interpretations thereof by the parties to the lawsuit. In this manner, the researcher regularly can obtain an indication of both the critical facts and issues that the court has identified in the present case and its interpretation as to the distinguishing features of seemingly relevant precedents. (In reality, most of these sections of the opinion are written by law clerks or law school students who obtain and retain their positions by preparing thorough and insightful file memos of their own!) Moreover, court case opinions often include lengthy dissenting or concurring opinions, from which the researcher can further identify the pertinent facts and issues relative to the opinion.

Lacking (or in lieu of) such judicial direction, the researcher's evaluation of the efficacy of a precedent or pronouncement often is guided by no more than a review of the hierarchy of the sources of the Federal tax law. (For a review of these sources, see Chapters 3 through 5.)

In addition, we offer the following points to be considered in the evaluation of a series of apparently conflicting tax laws.

- Regulations seldom are held to be invalid by a court. In the typical year, fewer than a dozen such holdings are issued. Thus, challenges to the provisions of a Regulation should be based on more than a simple challenge to the Treasury's authority or a self-serving competing interpretation of the statute offered by the taxpayer.
- Revenue Rulings and Revenue Procedures, however, are frequently modified or otherwise held to be invalid by a court. Accordingly, the taxpayer's attempted restructuring of the pertinent law in his or her favor with respect to such an administrative pronouncement is more likely to be heard openly by the court and, therefore, to be based on the weight of the competing arguments rather than simply on the Treasury's preemptive interpretive rights.
- The decisions of courts that are higher in the judicial hierarchy should receive additional precedential weight. Given an adequate degree of similarity in fact situations, district and circuit court opinions have direct bearing on the taxpayer only if they were issued in the corresponding jurisdiction. On the other hand, opinions of the Court of Federal Claims and Tax Court are binding on the taxpayer, even though they were issued with respect to a taxpayer who works or resides in another jurisdiction, unless they are overturned in a pertinent appeal.
- Thus, a taxpayer who works in Wyoming is not bound by decisions of, say, the Seventh Circuit or Alaska District courts. The practitioner should not feel restricted in a trial or appeal hearing by the doctrine of *stare decisis*. Conversely, an Alaska taxpayer's Court of Federal Claims decision is binding on the Wyoming citizen's Court of Federal Claims case. If this Court

of Federal Claims decision was held in a manner that is detrimental to the Wyoming taxpayer, another trial court should be pursued.

- Other factors being equal, decisions of the Second, Ninth, and Federal Circuits should be assigned additional precedential value. Among other reasons, this additional weight can be attributed to the inclusion of the cities of New York and Washington and the state of California in these circuits. Typically, the Ninth Circuit is the first to introduce an innovative or otherwise unusual interpretation of the law, and the Second and Federal Circuits are authoritative in a more traditional vein.

- Older court decisions should be assigned a geometrically declining degree of importance unless (1) they are Supreme Court cases, (2) they are Second, Ninth, or Federal Circuit cases, or (3) they are the only precedents available. The roster and philosophical makeup of a court change over time and often reflect the changing societal culture and philosophies. Thus, recent case opinions are more likely to identify issues that are held to be critical by the sitting judges that the taxpayer will face, and they are likely to be better predictors of the outcome relative to the current taxpayer's issues.

- Tax treatises and journal articles are a useful source by which to identify current, critical tax issues. They also can be utilized in the formation of the practitioner's research schedule, because they often include both a comprehensive summary of the evolution of the controlling law and a thorough list of citations concerning prior interpretive court decisions.

- IRS agents are bound only by the Code, administrative pronouncements, and Supreme Court decisions. Some of the most difficult decisions a tax practitioner must face include those in which one must determine whether the time, effort, and expense of litigation will generate a reward that is sufficient to justify, in essence, the construction of new (judicial) tax law, that is, to overcome this narrow scope of the agent's concern.

- Court decisions are never completely predictable. Thus, even if absolutely all of the judicial precedent that is available supports the taxpayer's position, the court still may hold against him or her. Negative decisions may be the result of a poor performance by the attorney, other tax adviser, or witnesses that are heard by the court; changes in the makeup or philosophy of the members of the court; changes in societal mores, as reflected by the court; or an incorrect interpretation of the law by the court that hears the present case. The practitioner, however, can do little more than conduct a thorough tax research analysis concerning the case, identify convincing witnesses, and trust that justice will prevail.

CLIENT LETTERS

Our discussion to this point in the chapter has concentrated on the communication of tax research by the practitioner to him- or herself or to other tax professionals in a fairly sophisticated document—a memorandum to the file. We now shift the focus for the communication to a different audience, namely, the client, and to a different setting, the written or oral presentation.

By far the most common form of communication between the tax professional and his or her client is the telephone call. We must stress the danger inherent in placing too great a dependence on the phone call to convey the results of tax research, given the intricacies of both the fact situation and the (tax adviser's interpretation of) controlling law, in most professional situations. If the telephone must be used (perhaps because of time pressures or convenience) to convey tax research results, the practitioner should always send a fairly detailed follow-up **client letter,** in hard copy, not just e-mail, confirming his or her understanding as to the information that was conveyed and the actions that are to be taken as a result of the call.

Foremost among the attributes of the client letter is its brevity. Except in the most unusual circumstances, it should not exceed two pages. This rule should only be violated when the subject of the research is especially complex or grave, perhaps in anticipation of extended litigation or with respect to a more sophisticated client, where, for instance, one might be tempted to attach a copy (or a "client version") of the research file memo.

The brevity of the client letter is, most often, in response to the desire of the client for "the answer" that has been found concerning the extant tax issues. Clients do tend to see tax issues as black-and-white ones, and they want to know whether they will win or lose with the IRS. Of course, tax practitioners are aware of the colorful world that tax practice presents, and the various shades of emphasis and interpretation sometimes make the view quite murky. Thus, to accommodate the desire of the client, one typically must convey no more than the absolute highlights of the research process.

Another factor that leads to brief client letters is the tax practitioner's professional responsibilities. Responding to client questions is generally easier in a face-to-face meeting. Thus, most practitioners use the client letter to deliver the general conclusions of the research project and to request a follow-up meeting in which questions, comments, and the need for more detail can be addressed.

Exhibits 10–4 and 10–5 illustrate the format and content of typical client letters. The sole difference between these two letters is the degree of sophistication that is possessed by the receiving party.

In general, the client letter should be structured as follows, perhaps allowing one paragraph for each of the noted topics.

- Salutation/social graces/general conclusion
- Summary of the research project results
- Objective of the report
- Statement of facts and disclaimer as to the scope of the tax professional's knowledge base
- Summary of critical sources of law that lead to result
- Implications of the results
- Assumptions/limitations
- Closing/reference to follow-up meeting/social graces
- Attachments, if any (e.g., engagement letter, file memo, illustrative charts, bibliography), on a separate page

Effective written business communication often makes use of the following guidelines. Notice that most of these elements are present in each of the two sample client letters that we have included in this chapter.

Exhibit	10–4	Sample Client Letter—Sophisticated Client

Raabe, Whittenburg & Sanders, CPAs
San Francisco, CA
November 19, 20XX

M/M Dale Brown
2472 North Mayfair Road
Fillingham, SD 59990

Dear Dale and Rae,

Thanks again for requesting my advice concerning the tax treatment of your interest expenses. I am sorry to report that only a portion of your expenses can be deducted this year.

I have uncovered a series of court cases in which the IRS has prevailed over the taxpayer's requests for a deduction that is similar to yours. Unfortunately, the Tax Court's position is that interest such as yours is nondeductible, and additional litigation would be necessary to bring about a more favorable result for you.

My efforts have concentrated on the treatment of interest expenses that are incurred by taxpayers who hold exempt bonds while maintaining a bank loan that requires interest payments.

Over the last thirty years or so, a number of Circuit Court decisions have held that a taxpayer effectively must divest him- or herself of investments in such municipal bonds, regardless of portfolio diversification objectives, before a deduction for the interest payments to the bank is allowed. Fortunately, however, an exception exists relative to business-related loans, so that interest that is related to Rae's clinic will be allowed as a deduction. Conversely, that portion of the loan that relates to your school bond investment is nondeductible, even though it is secured by your residence.

You may wish to reconsider your use of the mortgage for this purpose, as your tax advantages therefrom are somewhat limited. This appears to be more palatable for you than would be the alternative of expensive further (and, probably, fruitless) litigation of the issue.

My conclusion is based upon the facts that you have provided me, and upon the efficacy of these somewhat dated court decisions. As you've requested, I've attached a copy of my research memo for you to read and from which you might develop subsequent inquiries.

I'm sorry that the news from me wasn't more favorable. I look forward to seeing you, though, at the firm's holiday reception!

Sincerely,

Mary H. Polzin, for Raabe, Whittenburg & Sanders, CPAs

- Make your main point(s) in the first paragraph of the communication.
- State a well-defined purpose for the document, and stick to it.
- Avoid "filler" language, e.g., "at the present time," "the fact that," "as you know," and "enclosed please find."
- Avoid cliches and trendy jargon, e.g., "interface," "input," "seamless," "hands-on," "state-of-the-art," and any number of sports analogies.

Exhibit	10–5	Sample Client Letter—Less Sophisticated Client

Raabe, Whittenburg & Sanders, CPAs
San Francisco, CA·
November 19, 20XX
M/M Dale Brown
2472 North Mayfair Road
Fillingham, SD 59990
Dear Dale and Rae,

Thanks again for requesting my advice concerning the tax treatment of your interest expenses. I am sorry to report that only a portion of your expenses can be deducted this year.

My research has uncovered a series of successes by the IRS in convincing several important courts that interest such as yours should not be allowed as a deduction to reduce your taxes. Unfortunately, the court whose decision initially would prevail upon us would hold against you, and a series of court hearings, over two or three years or so, would be necessary for you to win the case.

This research has been restricted to situations that are similar to yours, that is, in which the taxpayer both owns a municipal bond and owes money to the bank from an interest-bearing loan.

It seems that the IRS would rather have you purchase the municipal bonds with your own money, rather than with the bank's. It maintains that you get a double benefit from the nontaxability of the school bond interest income and the deductibility of the interest expense that is paid to the bank. Thus, that portion of the interest that relates to the bond investment is not allowed. A business purpose for the loan salvages the deduction, however, so you can deduct the interest from the loan that relates to Dr. Rae's clinic.

You may just have to live with this situation, as the IRS has been winning cases like these for about thirty years. Yours is not likely to be the one that changes their mind, so you might reconsider your investment in the municipals in the near future.

My conclusion is based upon the facts that you have provided me, and upon the reliability of the court cases that I found.

I'm sorry that the news from me wasn't more favorable. I look forward to seeing you, though, at the firm's holiday reception!

Sincerely,

Mary H. Polzin, for Raabe, Whittenburg & Sanders, CPAs

- Don't be afraid to revise the letter several times to improve its format or to expand or narrow (as needed) its content. In this regard, allow enough time for the preparation of the document in a professional manner.
- Use the social amenities to your advantage by spelling names correctly, keeping current on the recipient's promotions and current title, and adding handwritten messages at the beginning or end of the document.
- *Practice writing* until it becomes easier and more enjoyable for you to do. Word processing programs, with the editing and proofreading capabilities that they provide, will aid you in this task.

COMPREHENSIVE ILLUSTRATION OF CLIENT FILE

Exhibit 10–6 provides a comprehensive illustration of the two major elements of a client file: a client letter and a file memo. Notice the degree of correspondence between the two documents in that some portions of the client letter are no more than quotations or paraphrases of the file memo.

Exhibit	10–6	Client File Illustration

CLIENT LETTER

Tax Jockeys Limited
Newport, RI

December 10, 20XX

Harold and Frieda van Briske
2000 Fox Point Heights
Whitefish Bay, RI 02899

Dear Harold and Frieda,

Congratulations on your recent marriage! I hope that you found your honeymoon at Club Med to be an enjoyable and memorable experience.

Thank you again for requesting my advice concerning the tax treatment of your prenuptial agreement. I understand that Frieda transferred some appreciated stock to Harold on the morning of the wedding, under the prenuptial agreement. I am happy to report that the transaction will not result in the imposition of any Federal tax for either of you.

My research has uncovered a series of successes by the IRS in convincing several important courts, including the Supreme Court, that an agreement such as yours is not supported by "full and adequate consideration," and, therefore, that it is to be treated as a gift. Although you did not intend for your property transfer to be a gift, the intent of the parties in such agreements does not control for Federal tax purposes.

Fortunately, however, the treatment of your transaction as a gift will result in the imposition of neither Federal income tax nor Federal gift tax upon you. Federal income tax is not imposed upon the transfer because gross income is not recognized by either the donor or donee when a gift is made. Although a gift has occurred, no gift tax is due, because the unlimited gift tax marital deduction neutralizes the transfer.

This research has been restricted to fact situations that are similar to yours, that is, in which, pursuant to a prenuptial agreement, a taxpayer surrendered his or her other marital rights in exchange for a sum of money or other property.

My conclusion is based upon the facts that you have provided to me and upon the reliability of the court cases that I found.

I look forward to seeing you at the Christmas Charity Ball!

Sincerely,

Karen J. Boucher, CPA, JD, MST, for Tax Jockeys Limited

Continued

Exhibit	10–6	Client File Illustration—Continued

FILE MEMO

December 10, 20XX

Tax Jockeys Limited
Newport, RI

Relevant Facts

On the morning of their wedding, Frieda gave to Harold $400,000 of appreciated stock, pursuant to a prenuptial agreement. Frieda's basis in the stock was $150,000. In exchange for these securities, Harold surrendered all other marital rights and claims to Frieda's assets, under the terms of the agreement. Harold and Frieda both are residents of Arizona.

Specific Issues

(1) What are the gift tax consequences of this exchange?
(2) What are the income tax consequences of this exchange?

Conclusions

(1) Frieda incurs no gift tax liability as the agreement is executed and implemented.
(2) Asset basis carries over to Harold, the new owner of the securities. Neither Frieda nor Harold recognizes gross income as a result of the exchange.

Support
Issue One

Donative intent on the part of the donor is not an essential element in the application of the gift tax. Reg. § 25.2511-1(g)(1).

The Supreme Court has held that prenuptial transfers in relinquishment of marital rights are not adequate and full consideration in money or money's worth for the transfer of property, within the meaning of IRC § 2512(b). *Merrill v. Fahs*, 324 U.S. 308, 65 S.Ct. 655 (1945); *Comm. v. Wemyss*, 324 U.S. 303, 65 S.Ct. 652 (1945); Reg. § 25.2512-8. However, the Second Circuit has held that a prenuptial agreement was acquired for valuable consideration and did not constitute a gift, for income tax (basis computation) purposes. *Farid-Es-Sultaneh v. Comm.*, 160 F.2d 812 (CA-2, 1947). This decision is not critical to the present analysis, though, because the van Briskes do not live in the Second Circuit, and because the somewhat dated decision may be aberrational.

Continued

The remainder of the internal file for this hypothetical client would include, among many other possibilities:

• an engagement letter,
• a billing and collection history,
• case, regulation, and ruling briefs that are pertinent to the file memo, and
• links to important analyses of the client's prevailing tax issues from treatises, journal articles, and other resources.

Each consulting firm or tax department has its own formatting requirements with respect to client files. Because document and browser software is so

Exhibit	**10–6**	Client File Illustration—Concluded

Although the van Briske transaction resulted in a gift, no gift tax is imposed due to the application of the annual exclusion and the unlimited gift tax marital deduction. IRC §§ 2503(b) and 2523; Reg. § 25.2511-2(a); Rev. Rul. 69-347, 1969-2 C.B. 227.

IRC § 2501 imposes a tax on the transfer of property by gift; the gift tax is not imposed, though, upon the receipt of property by the donee. Rather, it is the transfer itself that triggers the tax. Since the prenuptial agreement here is enforceable by state law only when consummated by marriage, the transfer has not taken place until after the marriage occurred. Thus, the transfer appears to be eligible for the gift tax marital deduction, regardless of the timing of the transfer relative to the marriage ceremony on the wedding day. Even if the securities had been physically transferred to Harold prior to the completion of the ceremonies, the agreement was only enforceable after the couple was married. The IRS likely would not need or attempt to establish the exact moments of both (1) the transfer of the securities, and (2) the consummation of the marriage. *C.I.R. v. Bristol*, 121 F.2d 129 (CA-1, 1960); *Bradford*, 34 T.C. 1059 (1960, A); *Archbold*, 42 B.T.A. 453 (1940, A in result only); *Harris v. Comm.*, 178 F.2d 861 (1949).

Issue Two
Neither Harold nor Frieda recognize any gross income upon Harold's release of his marital rights. Gross income does not include the value of property that is acquired by gift. IRC §102(a); Reg. §1.102-1(a); Rev. Rul. 79-312; Rev. Rul. 67-221; *Howard v. C.I.R.*, 447 F.2d 152 (CA-5, 1971).

The transfer of securities is not deductible in any way by Frieda, but under the *Farid* decision, Harold's basis may be stepped up to fair market value. Recall our earlier comments, though, concerning the reliability of this precedent. *Illinois National Bank v. U.S.*, 273 F.2d 231 (CA-7, 1959), cert. den. 363 U.S. 803, 80 S.Ct. 1237 (1960); *C.I.R. v. Marshman*, 279 F.2d 27, cert. den. 364 U.S. 918, 81 S.Ct. 282 (1960); Rev. Rul. 79-312. In the typical gift situation, the donee takes the donor's income tax basis in the transferred property. IRC §§ 1015(a) and 1041(a)(1).

Actions To Be Taken
Prepare letter, review results with client.
Place copy of prenuptial agreement in the client file.
Alert the New York and New Jersey offices that their conclusions may differ, under the *Farid* decision.

Preparer: *Karen J. Boucher*
Reviewer: *Willie Schroeder*

easy to use, the temptation is for the tax researcher to reduce the thickness of the client file, as paper duplications of controlling law and other precedent are deemed unnecessary. This paper reduction movement constitutes a laudable goal. Yet one must not shortchange the importance of the client file as a roadmap by which to retrace the researcher's line of thinking that leads to the conclusions and recommendations evidenced in the file memo and client letter. Electronic equivalents of the mind-map of the researcher and of underlining or pastel highlighting of portions of lengthy legal documents must be developed.

Accordingly, every tax researcher must develop or work with a scheme by which to cross-reference the steps of the professional critical thinking model undertaken on the client's behalf. This might entail a listing of legal citations and computer files that would bear upon a reconstruction of the researcher's analysis, perhaps in the form of a decision tree or project management summary. Various software applications will be useful in this regard, not the least of which is the "research trail" feature of many electronic tax research products, which records the detailed sequencing of commands and decisions made during the online or CD-based project. Regardless of the form this project diary takes, its importance for professional quality control cannot be overstated.

ORAL PRESENTATIONS OF RESEARCH RESULTS

Psychologists tell us that most people's greatest fear is speaking before groups of other people. Indeed, the thought of being the only one in the room who is standing, of having your listeners whispering their evaluations of you to each other, of having members of the audience taking notes on (or tape recording) your comments (certainly so that your errors of omission and commission can be parroted back at a later date), and of fielding extemporaneous questions is enough to bring many people to tears.

Yet public speaking is an important part of the tax practitioner's professional life. In many ways, it is the most accurate predictor of success. As politicians have long known, when one is delivering an oral presentation in an effective and professional manner, the audience becomes convinced that all of the other professional qualities that they desire from the speaker are also present. Conversely, an ill-prepared or ill-delivered message can do much to erode the audience's confidence in the speaker, not just with respect to the topic of the presentation, but in general.

Thus, it behooves the tax professional to develop skill in public speaking. In contexts that range from the presentation of an award to a colleague or the conduct of a staff meeting to the presentation of a keynote address at the annual tax conference of your peers, such skills can mean the difference between enhancing and damaging your reputation.

SPOTLIGHT ON TAXATION: Observation

Jerry Seinfeld noted that peoples' fear of public speaking is greater even than the fear of death. Under this ranking, he thought, someone attending a funeral would rather be in the casket than delivering the eulogy!

What is advised here is not a series of "tricks" to fool the audience into believing that you are more knowledgeable than you really are. Rather, we convey here some time-tested techniques leading to an effective communication of ideas—from one who has developed a secure base of knowledge in a subject to an audience with a specified background that has a desire to learn more about that subject. Whether making a presentation of one's results to a supervisor in one's own firm or elaborating on a research project with the client's board of directors, the communication of tax research results poses special problems that make a review of oral communications procedures all the more valuable. Specifically, we can make the following suggestions concerning **oral presentations** of tax research.

- General preparation for the talk should include a thorough, frank examination of the following set of questions by the presenter. Nearly all of these observations can be characterized as knowledge of the makeup of the audience.
  Why me? Why was I asked to speak? What knowledge or celebrity do I bring to the event?
  What do they want? What does the audience hope to take away from the presentation? Technical knowledge? Relief from stress? Inspiration? Skill development? Amusement or entertainment? Should I present an overview or a detailed technical update or analysis?
  What is their attitude? Is the audience coming to the event curious or anxious to hear from me, or must they be persuaded of the relevance or importance of my topics?
  From what should I stay away? Are there topics that are taboo for this audience, due to their age, experiences, or existing attitudes? One must not alienate the audience, wittingly or unwittingly, in any way if the message is to get across.
  What do they already know? What is the knowledge base of the audience? It would be ideal to speak to a homogeneous audience, especially in the level of knowledge that it brings into the event, but this seldom is the case. One must decide, then, whether to aim at the median knowledge base, above, or below. The stakes are high in exercising this judgment, though, and either repeating what is common knowledge to the group, or presenting information at a high level that is accessible to only a few in the audience, can make communication impossible.
  Who is the audience? Details as to the audience's demographic characteristics such as age, education and income level, political leanings, and so forth can be vital for tailoring one's style, presentation speed and media, references to literature and popular culture, and use of humor in an effective manner. Remember to play to as many members of the audience as possible, not just the majority of those in attendance or those who were involved directly in hiring or retaining your services.
- Be prepared in the technical aspects of your discussion, particularly the basic research. Spend most of your preparation time on your main points and conclusions rather than on the fine points. If you are caught without a piece of technical information, it is clearly better for you if that information is specific (so that you can refer the questioner to a more detailed reference or to a later, private conversation with you), rather than basic in nature.

- Resist the temptation to tell the audience all that you know about the subject. You almost certainly have neither the time nor the organizational abilities that are necessary to command the attention of the audience for that long a time. Direct your remarks to the highlights and general results of the research, and allow a questions-and-comments period in which more detailed subjects can be addressed. In this manner, you will provide the greatest amount of information to the greatest number of listeners in the audience.
- Use visual aids effectively. Handouts, slides, or videotapes can serve to clarify or emphasize your key points (and, not incidentally, to transfer the "spotlight" of the presentation away from you). Most advisers recommend that you not look at the screen repeatedly, or read the text of the visual aid word for word along with the audience, but, rather, that you use the visual aid as a means of keeping the audience focused on the discussion points by the use of a pointer or other highlighter. Avoid a sequence that allows a "blank screen" for more than a second or two. Inexpensive computer software will assist you in preparing electronic presentations, slides, or transparencies, delivering your talk, and staying on schedule. Use your ink-jet or color laser printer to prepare your visual aids.
- If you are a frequent public speaker, purchase a moderately priced, easy to carry projector, so that you need not depend on conference center staff to present your slides.

Many speakers are tempted to overuse visual aids, especially because they are so easy to create, even at professional-quality levels, given today's software packages. Visual aids, though, generally should be used only for the following purposes.

- To illustrate things that are difficult to convey strictly with words by using a photograph, videotape, map, blueprint, or flowchart.
- To save time by consolidating ideas, committing to a time frame or strategy, or listing conflicting viewpoints or tactics.
- To create interest in a subject, perhaps by presenting the concept in a manner with which the audience is unfamiliar (e.g., an extra-large view, a view from "the other side of the issue," or an evolutionary time or growth line).
- To emphasize a point or concept by highlighting a graphic, picture, mnemonic, or list of key words or concepts.
- To organize the introduction, body, or conclusion of the presentation.
- To introduce humor to the event with a tasteful quotation or cartoon.
- To place ideas in the audience's memories, through a visual "take away" item.

A speaker's prepared slides should be designed with care and diligence. When using this technology, as opposed to the hand-drawn flip chart or on-the-fly whiteboard drawing, one essentially is competing with professional graphic and television artists, and the audience will hold your efforts to these high standards. Most visual and graphic artists offer guidelines for presentation layouts, including the following.

- Use the slide to emphasize pictures, not text or numbers. Except to be able to point to a specific position on the page and keep the members of the audience in the same spot throughout the presentation, do not use transparencies to duplicate pages of text or spreadsheets with voluminous numbers. Employ graphs, charts, arrows, and other pictorial devices instead.

- When text is involved, use the "six and six" rule: No more than six lines of type, and no more than six words on a line. This directive will help to dictate the font chosen and the corresponding size of print.
- Keep the font style simple. Use sans serif or newspaper-type fonts, not script or modern fonts, unless corporate logos or other protected styles are used. Most designers recommend that no more than two colors of text be used on a slide and that the color scheme of the graphics blend well with that of the text. Be conservative—stick to the primary colors, colors of local sports teams, and multiple shades of gray, so as not to frustrate the duplication process for related handout materials.
- Similarly, try to use some background music if your available technology will support it at a professional-quality level. In this regard, select audio clips that do not draw attention to themselves, but are memorable in a more subtle way. Music can signal the start or end of a presentation or its subunits, a change in direction, or a specific idea (e.g., a Frank Sinatra clip sends a different message than does one by Jimi Hendrix or a New Age group).
- On the average, allow at least three minutes of spoken presentation for each slide. Accordingly, limit the number of your slides to the length of your talk in minutes, divided by three. In this way, you will not overproduce your number of slides. If you want to provide your audience with a content outline, use some other medium, not the slides.
- Prepare for the worst: E-mail yourself an extra copy of the slides in case of emergency, and carry your files to the site on a floppy and a thumb drive. Bring a few sets of hard copy slides, as well.

Without exception, determine ahead of the presentation how long your talk is supposed to be and be absolutely certain not to exceed it. You need to be fair to the other speakers, if any, who follow your presentation. Moreover, with very few exceptions, the audience also is aware of the schedule for the session, and if the speaker exceeds the allotted time, the audience, at best, will stop paying attention and, at worst, will become restless or angry. Because of their technical nature, most tax presentations should not exceed 45 minutes, and one-half of that time might be ideal for both speaker and audience.

Have an outline for your discussion that includes miniature versions of slides and transparencies and your business address, phone and fax numbers, and Internet addresses. Use the visual aids to convince the audience that you are following the outline. This will (1) ensure that you will cover the material that you desire, (2) build confidence among the audience as to your speaking abilities, and (3) convince yourself that you are doing a good job in leading the discussion of the assigned topic.

Rehearse your presentation, word for word, at least once. The most effective means of preparing yourself in this manner probably is with a video recorder, because your distracting mannerisms (e.g., clearing the throat repeatedly, saying the words "ah" or "you know" too often, or pounding on the lectern) quickly will become apparent. Lacking such a device, use an (audio) tape recorder. Family members or colleagues should not be used for this rehearsal.

Be kind to yourself in evaluating your video performance, but be observant for the following "I didn't know I did that" items.

- In all but the very largest presentation venues, get as physically close to the audience as you can, ideally removing the lectern, stepping down from the stage or platform, and moving to a series of different spots in the room throughout your speaking time.
- Eliminate nervous and visual distractions, such as jingling coins, playing with pen and marker tops, and adjusting clothing. Minimize the use of crossing your arms, pounding the table, and finger-pointing, reserving them as means of emphasizing key points or declaring victory over competing viewpoints.
- Vary the pitch of your voice, avoiding both a dry monotone and a "classic actor" dramatic approach. Many speakers talk too fast or too loud; check yourself throughout the talk on these matters. Test the microphone system before the audience arrives, so that you don't need to ask, "Can you hear me in the back?"
- Don't be afraid of silence. Pauses invariably seem longer to the speaker than they do to the audience, so don't let natural breaks in the talk add to your anxiety. In fact, well-paced pauses can relieve tension (both yours and the audience's), signal changes of pace, and allow you to emphasize the importance of certain ideas.
- Don't read directly from your outline, except for a selected quote of three lines or so from the material once or twice in the presentation. Try not to have a separate set of note cards, because the tendency again is to break your contact with the audience and hide behind the scripting device. Disguise your notes in the form of comments on hard copies of transparencies and flip charts and notes in the margin of your copy of the outline. Keep your eyes up and on the audience.

Avoid references to administrative or "housekeeping" aspects of the event—leave these to be conveyed by the host of the event. Be enthusiastic and positive about your comments—don't apologize for a lack of discussion on a tangential point, a logistical snafu, or a misstatement of fact or law. The audience generally wants you to succeed, so don't undermine this trust with self-destructive comments. Don't refer to the schedule for the event or other timing issues, because they can distract the audience or otherwise detract from conveying your message (e.g., "Only 10 minutes to go," "We may be out of here early," "The previous speakers ran over into my time slot," or "I'll try to get through this quickly, so we can finish on time").

Rehearse the logistical aspects of the presentation, such as the lighting, projectors, or computer presentation software and terminals, before you begin to speak, ideally both the night before and one hour before your presentation. Have adequate numbers and varieties of markers, pointers, flip chart pads, and remote control devices. You don't want to encounter any surprises after it is too late to do anything about them! On your script, note cards, or transparency masters, make notes to yourself as to when, for instance, to pass out the handout material, turn on or turn off the projector, or refer to a flip chart.

Avoid clichés, such as opening with a joke, or saying, "It's a pleasure to be here." Don't take the risk of boring or offending the audience with a joke that (1) they may have heard already or (2) you may not tell effectively under pressure. This is not to suggest that you avoid humor altogether, however. Audiences, and speakers' reputations, thrive on it. If you are sure of your skill in this area, you might venture a joke, but it would probably be wiser to open with a "punch line" summary of some of the most interesting of your results or fact situations.

Have a "Plan B" ready to go—flexibility is the watchword of the effective speaker. If the time actually allowed for your talk is shorter than you had thought, due to a misunderstanding or unanticipated events, have a list of topics, videos, or slides that can be eliminated without changing the nature of the talk. Practice your question-and-answer-session skills, especially for occasions where there is more time available than you had anticipated. Do not mention any of these on-the-fly adjustments to the audience—make the changes, don't talk about them.

Observe audience body language, and use signals conveying interest, enthusiasm, boredom, or restlessness to your advantage. Make consistent eye contact with the audience, smile when appropriate, and take a few seconds at the completion of the presentation to accept the audience's show of thanks and savor your job well done.

SUMMARY

The tax professional must become proficient in communicating his or her research results. Recipients of these communications might include oneself or one's peers, via the file memorandum; the client, via a brief letter; or a number of other listeners, via an oral presentation. In each case, the practitioner must be sensitive to the needs, backgrounds, and interests of the recipients of the messages, without sacrificing professional demeanor or responsibilities.

TAX TUTOR

Reinforce the tax research information covered in this chapter by completing the online tutorials located at the Federal Tax Research web site:

http://raabe.swlearning.com

KEY WORDS

By the time you complete your work relative to this chapter, you should be comfortable discussing each of the following terms. If you need additional review of any of these items, return to the appropriate material in the chapter or consult the glossary to this text.

Client Letter   Oral Presentation
File Memorandum

TAX RESEARCH ASSIGNMENTS

As we have discussed them in this chapter, develop solutions and appropriate documentation for one or more of the problems that you have worked on in previous chapters or for the following fact situations. In this context, proper format and professional content are of equal importance, so that the development of the reader's tax research communication skills will be facilitated.

Specifically, as assigned by your instructor, prepare one or more of the following means of communicating your research results for your chosen problem or case.

- File memorandum
- Letter to tax-sophisticated client
- Letter to unsophisticated client
- Article for local business news weekly
- Speech to local chamber of commerce
- Article for *Practical Tax Strategies*
- Speech to State Bar Association conference
- Presentation to client's board of directors
- Presentation to client's senior counsel
- Posting to the Internet Tax Forum for Practitioners
- Posting to the Internet Tax Help group for taxpayers

PROBLEMS

1. Sarah came home one day to find significant water damage in her home. Apparently one of the hoses to her washing machine had worn out and split, spilling water all over the place. Over the next month, mildew appeared as well. Is there any casualty loss deduction for Sarah? Ignore any computational floors and assume that she did not have any homeowners' insurance.

2. Richie is a wealthy rancher in Texas. He operates his ranch through a grantor trust set up by his grandparents. Richie does not like to get his hands dirty, so he hires a professional management company to run the ranch. The property generated a $500,000 loss this year. Can Richie deduct this loss on his Schedule E, given the material participation rules of § 469?

3. Maggie could not conceive a child using natural means, so she sought out a woman who would donate an egg to be surgically implanted in Maggie, so that Maggie could become a mother. Which of the following items are deductible by Maggie in her process to find an egg donor?
   a. Payment to a search firm to find donor candidates.
   b. Payment to Maggie's attorney.
   c. Payment of a fee to the egg donor.
   d. Payment to medical staff to run physiological and psychological tests on the prospective donor.

4. Larry and Mo were in the process of being divorced, and the decree as negotiated allowed alimony payments to Mo of $3,000 on the fifteenth of each month. The divorce was final on July 5, 2006, but Mo was short of cash, so Larry made the payments to her starting in March. What is Larry's alimony deduction for 2006?

5. Sally incurred a ninety-mile round-trip commute every day, mainly because she could not get along with her supervisor at the sales office four miles from Sally's home. Sally works under a one-year contract, and her assignment to the nearer office is affirmed in the current year's contract, but management has allowed her to travel to the further location. How many deductible commuting miles does Sally accumulate on a work day?

6. Professor White operates a popular bar review course as a sole proprietorship. He charges $1,000 tuition to each student, and he guarantees a full refund of the tuition if the student passes an in-course exam but does not pass the actual bar exam on the first try. White is bold enough to do this because the first-time-pass rate is more than 80 percent for the bar exam (as opposed to less than 15 percent for the CPA exam). He collected $50,000 tuition for his Fall 2005 review section, but he reported the gross receipts on his 2006 Form 1040, because the grades for those taking the fall review are not released until February 2006. Thus, White asserted that he had no constructive receipt of the tuition until February 2006. Is this treatment correct?

7. Lisa, usually a stay-at-home mother, went to the hospital one day for some outpatient surgery. She hired a babysitter for $35 to watch her four-year-old son while she was gone. What tax benefits are available to Lisa for this cash payment?

8. Same as 7, except that Lisa paid the sitter while she worked as a scout leader for the Girl Scouts.

9. Joan, a traveling sales representative, kept no formal books and records to summarize her gross receipts for the year, but she retained copies of all customer invoices and reported her gross income for the year from these totals. Is she liable for a negligence penalty under § 6662 for failing to keep any books and records?

10. Tex's credit union has provided him with financing to acquire his $200,000 home. The loan is set up as a three-year note with a balloon payment, but the credit union always renews the loan for another three years at the current interest rate. This year, the credit union renewed Tex's loan for the third time, charging $3,000 in points. In what year(s) can Tex deduct this $3,000?

11. Barb and Bob were one-fourth shareholders of a C corporation. When the entity had negative E&P, Barb and Bob secretly withdrew $200,000 in cash, hiding this fact from the other owners. How much gross income do Barb and Bob report?

12. Detail the tax effects to the Prasads of making the election to include their seven-year-old daughter's $10,000 unearned income on their current-year joint return.

13. Eighty percent of the Willigs' AGI comes from their submarine sandwich proprietorship. In 2006, the Willigs lost an IRS audit and owed $12,000 in 2004 Federal income taxes, all attributable to inventory computations in their business. Interest on this amount totaled $3,200. All amounts due were paid by the end of 2006. How much of the interest can the Willigs deduct on their 2006 Schedule C?

14. Al and Amy are divorced. In which of the following cases can legal fees be deducted?
    a. Al pays $5,000 to get the court to reduce his alimony obligation.
    b. Amy pays $5,000 to get the court to increase her alimony receipts.
    c. Al pays Amy's attorney fees in part b, as required by the original divorce decree.

15. Katie is a one-third owner of an S corporation. After a falling-out with the other shareholders, Katie signed an agreement early in January 2005. Under the terms of the agreement, Katie took $200,000 of her capital from the corporation and had eight months to negotiate a purchase of the stock of the other shareholders. She did not complete this task by the end of August 2005. Thus, contrary negotiations began and on March 1, 2006, Katie sold all of her shares to the remaining shareholders for a $2.5 million gain. For how many of these months does Katie report flow-through income from the S corporation?

16. Can an individual make a contribution to an IRA based on unemployment compensation proceeds received?

17. Duane paid his 2001 Federal income taxes in January 2004 in the amount of $10,000, and then paid $4,000 interest and penalties on this amount in May 2005. In April 2007, Duane filed a claim for refund of the $14,000, due to a sizable operating loss from his business in tax year 2006. Can he recover the 2001–related amounts?

18. After an audit was completed, IRS agent van Court informed Harris of the latter's $10,000 Federal income tax deficiency by leaving a summary memo on Harris's e-mail account. Harris shared this account with his mother, who read the mail first and in a panic confronted Harris with a two-hour "What's this all about?" interrogation. Did van Court violate Harris's right to privacy by using e-mail in this manner?

19. SlimeCo spent $250,000 to build storage tanks for its waste by-products. This is a recurring expenditure for SlimeCo, because once the tanks are filled, new ones must be built. When can SlimeCo deduct the $250,000?

20. Prudence was named a shareholder in her law firm, which operates as an S corporation. Her payments into the capital of the firm were to start in about nine months, when an audit would determine the full value of the firm and a new corporate year would commence. Paperwork with

the pertinent state offices was completed, naming Prudence as a share-holder and director and adding her name to that of the firm. But Prudence left the firm eight months after the announcement, that is, before she paid any money for shares. Is Prudence liable for tax on her share of the entity's earnings for the eight months?

21. Laura deducted $8,100 in state income taxes on her 2004 Federal income tax return. Her refund, received in 2005 after all credits and the minimum tax, was $7,800 for these taxes.
   a. How much 2005 gross income must Laura recognize?
   b. How does your answer change if Laura's 2004 deduction was limited to $7,200, due to the application of IRC § 68?

22. Cal's son has been labeled a "can't miss" NBA prospect since junior high school. This year, while the son is a college freshman and classified as an amateur under NCAA rules, Cal spent $14,000 for special clothing, equipment, camps, and personal trainers to keep improving his son's skills. Can Cal deduct these items?

23. CPA Myrna forgot to tell her client Freddie to accelerate the payment of state income and property taxes in a year when Freddie was in an unusually high tax bracket. Upon discovering the error, the parties negotiated a $15,000 payment from Myrna (and her insurance company) to Freddie to compensate Freddie for Myrna's inadequate professional advice. Is this payment gross income to Freddie?

24. How much of the $100,000 interest that is paid on a loan from Everett National Bank can Ben deduct if he invests the loan proceeds in the following? Consider each item independently.
   a. South Chicago School District bonds.
   b. AT&T bonds, paying $125,000 interest income this year.
   c. Computer Futures, Inc., shares, a growth stock that pays no dividend this year.
   d. A life insurance policy on Betty, Ben's wife.

25. Lilly leases a car that she uses solely for business purposes. The car would be worth $40,050 on the market, and Lilly paid $7,400 in lease payments this year. How are these items treated on her tax return?

RESEARCH CASES

26. Lizzie filed a gift tax return for a sizable transfer to her nephew. The value of the gift exceeded the annual gift tax exclusion and used up $1 million of her transfer tax exemption equivalent, so Lizzie's later gifts and taxable estate would have a more likely chance of being taxed.

   Four years later, another relative won a court case against Lizzie and the nephew. Uncle Joe prevailed in showing the court that the gift property was his, not Lizzie's. It seems that title to the property actually was held by Uncle Joe, not Lizzie, so the property was not hers to give away. Uncle Joe recovered the property and associated income from the nephew. But what about Lizzie? Is the $1 million of her exemption equivalent now wasted?

27. You served as an expert witness in taxation in a recent Tax Court case, charging $400 per hour for your services. The LLC client who employed you prevailed in the decision against the government, so now the client is filing to recover your fees from the Treasury under § 7430(c)(1)(B)(iii). How much can the client collect?

28. Pete is an engineering professor at State University. Under his contract, Pete's inventions while employed at the university are the property of the Board of Regents, but Pete receives an addition to his salary equal to one-third of the royalties received by the university on his patents. This year, Pete received $75,000 on top of his salary, as royalties allocated to him. Does Pete recognize this amount as ordinary income or capital gain?

29. Tobey was late in filing his Federal income tax refund claim, but he requested an extension of the statute of limitations, citing the financial disability exceptions of § 6511(h). Tobey's mother is chronically ill, and he must make four-day-a-week trips to another city to care for her. Will the IRS grant Tobey's request?

30. Dean and Robin owned a family business, each holding the shares as community property. When they were divorced in 2000, the court did not force them to split the shares, citing damage to the business that could occur if the public learned that ownership of the enterprise was changing. Now it is 2006 and Robin wants to remarry. She and her new husband want to have the business re-title one-half of the shares in Robin's name only. The original divorce court agrees in 2006. Is this an income taxable transfer? Is it a gift taxable event?

31. Dave took a $100,000 cash withdrawal from his IRA. He bought $100,000 of Microcraft stock and, within the rollover period, transferred the stock to another IRA. Does Dave report any gross income?

32. Gold Partners wanted to complete a like-kind exchange just before it liquidated. Accordingly, it sold the real estate it meant to transfer to the other party, and a qualified intermediary held the resulting cash. When the intermediary found acceptable replacement realty, the intermediary transferred cash and the like-kind property directly to the partners, thereby liquidating Gold. Does § 1031 apply?

33. HelpCo pays Hank two $100,000 salaries per year, one through its WestCo subsidiary and one through its EastCo subsidiary. How do Hank and HelpCo treat his Social Security tax obligations?

34. Jack died three years after winning the lottery grand prize. He had elected to take the prize as a series of $500,000 payments for the rest of his life. Once the payment method was chosen, the annuity was not transferable to any other party, except for Jack's estate. According to IRS annuity tables, the present value of the remaining payments to be received by the estate was $8 million. How much should be included in Jack's Federal gross estate?

35. Karen files jointly in a year when she incurs $2,000 of job-related education expenses. No one else in her family incurred tax-favored education expenses this year. AGI is $80,000, and Karen's miscellaneous itemized deductions for employee business expenses total $400. How should Karen treat her education costs so as to maximize her Federal tax benefits for the year?

36. On December 6, Ed Grimely appeared on the game show, "The Wheel of Fate." As a result of his appearance, Grimely won the following prizes.

	Manufacturer's Suggested List Price	Fair Market Value	Actual Cost to the Show
All-expenses-paid trip to Hawaii	$8,432	$6,000	$5,200
One case of Twinkies	16	12	0
Seven music lessons for the calliope	105	35	0
One year of free haircuts	120	60	15

a. Assuming that Grimely received all of these prizes by the end of the year, compute his gross income from these prizes.
b. Will this amount change if Grimely refuses to accept the calliope lessons immediately after the program's taping session is completed?

37. Josh bought $120,000 worth of furnishings on his MasterCard in 2005, paying off the entire principal and interest in 2006. Interest charges of $7,800 relate to 2005 for the furnishings. How much can Josh deduct for interest relative to this transaction for 2005?

38. Rita's family had a history of heart disease. To reduce Rita's risk of future heart problems, and to enable her to lose about ten pounds, her physician recommended a rigid running program. Accordingly, Rita joined the Vic Tanny Health Club. One-fourth of her time at the club was spent on a supervised running program. How much of her $450 annual fee is deductible as a medical expense?

39. Ellie owned five apartment buildings, each worth $200,000. For three of the buildings, she worked with employees to keep the property in good repair. This entailed maintaining electrical and plumbing fixtures, common areas, and walls and roofs, and providing janitorial services such as garbage removal, vacuuming, and rest room supplies. For the other two buildings, Ellie's lease required the tenants to perform this work. Can her estate claim a § 6166 estate tax deferral for any of the buildings?

40. HardCo spent $4 million this year on a new graphic design for its product, a yo-yo. Under the prior design, HardCo's name and logo only

appeared on the box and wrapping paper, which were discarded by most customers once they started using the product. The new design displayed HardCo's name and newer, flashier logo on both sides of the yo-yo, with a paint that also made it glow in the dark. When can HardCo deduct the $4 million?

ADVANCED CASES

These items require that you have access to research materials other than the Federal tax law and related services. For instance, you might need to refer to an international tax or multistate service or to access Internet sources to prepare your solution for these cases. Consult with your instructor before beginning your work, so that you are certain to have available to you all of the necessary research resources for the case(s) that you choose.

41. Tony received some nonqualified and incentive stock options when he worked for his employer in Oregon. But when he took a two-year assignment in another country, the corporation employing Tony there granted him some options, too. Does Tony have gross income in the other country upon receiving or exercising the non-U.S. options? Assume that Tony was assigned to a corporation based in:
   a. Belgium
   b. Germany
   c. Hong Kong
   d. Russia
   e. The Netherlands

42. Chico is a corporation operating in several states on the accrual basis. Chico received a state income tax refund this year, in 2007, in the form of a check from the state. Based on the following sequence of events, in which tax year does Chico recognize the refund as gross income?

   2004: Generated the operating loss.
   2005: Filed the loss carryback form with the state.
   2006: Received notice that the refund was approved.
   2007: Received the refund check.

43. Rosemary's house just did not sell, after her employer transferred her to another town. After two years of Internet listings, open houses, repairs and improvements, and price cuts, a buyer finally came along. By this time, the house had sat empty for twenty-five months before the closing occurred, and Rosemary rented it out just to help with the mortgage payments. Rosemary claimed a $40,000 Schedule C loss with respect to the house. Do you agree with this filing position?

44. Edna is a well-paid executive with ADley, a firm that uses stock options and deferred compensation as well as high salaries, to compensate its most successful employees. When Edna and Ron were

divorced, Ron got the rights to a bundle of these deferred compensation rights. Complete the following table, indicating the required tax results.

Tax Year	Market Price for Edna's Option Transferred to Ron	Event	Tax Consequences to Edna	Tax Consequences to Ron
2004	$9	Divorce settlement		
2007	$14	Ron exercises options with $10 cash payment, then holds stock received.		
2010	$20	Edna terminates employment with ADley; $100 lump sum of deferred compensation is distributed to Ron.		
2012	$22	Ron sells shares received via option contracts.		

45. Wes and Donna were the only members of an LLC, and they fended off unwanted takeover suitors with a clause in the charter that shares could change hands only with unanimous approval from all of the other owners. Wes is now age seventy, so he wants to start phasing out of the business. He makes a gift of 10 percent of the LLC shares to his son Jeffrey as agreed to by Donna. The shares are worth $20,000. What is Wes's taxable gift in the year of the transfer to Jeffrey?

46. According to the Tax Foundation, what was Tax Freedom Day in 2005? How much of this time was spent with respect to tax liabilities and how much in meeting tax compliance costs? Which states bear the heaviest tax burden? The lightest? Per capita, how much annual total income and total tax does the U.S. citizen generate? What is the average U.S. citizen's average tax rate?

47. Chan's only transaction in the United States this year was to sell the biggest office building in Denver at a $100 million gain. Chan has no assets, offices, or employees in the United States. Can he be taxed on the gain? Why or why not?

48. As the result of a Federal audit, your 2004 Federal taxable income increased by $27,000. By when must you report this adjustment to your state's revenue department? What form is used for this purpose, where do you obtain it, and where is it to be filed?

49. Does your state provide a form with which to file for a manufacturer's exemption from sales/use tax? Which form is used for this purpose, where do you obtain it, and where is it to be filed?

50. For the current period, what is the short-term, quarterly compounded Federal AFR? Mid-term? Long-term exempt interest rate for computing loss carryforwards under § 382?

51. SalesCo sold Tom a prepaid phone card for $100 in 2005. Tom used the phone card for communications services in 2006. When can your state collect sales/use tax from SalesCo for the sale to Tom?

52. GoodCo donated $40,000 of goods from its inventory to the Red Cross. Does your state require GoodCo to collect or pay sales/use tax on these donated goods?

53. The Downtown Wellness Clinic, a tax exempt organization, sells memberships to corporations so that their employees can work out before and after office hours. Three blocks away, the Power Up Fitness Center has similar facilities and also wants to sell memberships to corporate neighbors. Is the Clinic subject to Federal income tax on its membership sales?

54. Does America Online owe any corporate income tax to your state? Don't compute the tax, but determine whether AOL is subject to any obligation for the current year.

55. How much state and local income tax did New York Yankee Alex Rodriguez owe to your state last year?

56. Find two government documents that discuss potential solutions to the so-called marriage penalty characteristic of the Federal income tax.

Chapter 11

Tax Planning

LEARNING OBJECTIVES

■ Identify several fundamental tenets of tax planning for optimizing tax liabilities.

■ Gain perspective as to the role of tax planning in tax practice.

■ Define and apply several key terms with respect to tax rate schedules.

■ Illustrate effective tax planning as found in today's tax profession.

CHAPTER OUTLINE

In this chapter, we return to that element of the tax practice consisting of tax planning, as it was introduced in Chapter 1. A working knowledge of tax planning concepts is imperative for the researcher, because tax avoidance constitutes both (1) an important part of tax practice and (2) a prime motivation in the "open-fact" research context.

For most practitioners, tax research and planning represent the "glamor" end of the business. Properly accomplished tax planning:

- Forces the client to identify financial goals and general means by which to achieve them.
- Allows the tax professional to exercise a higher degree of creativity than in any other part of the practice.
- Affords the practitioner the greatest possible degree of control over the prescribed transactions and the tax consequences.

The tax planning process finds the tax professional in the roles of technical expert, friend, seer, and confessor priest for the client. It offers an opportunity for the most psychologically and financially rewarding work possible, in the context of a tax practice.

ECONOMICS OF TAX PLANNING, AVOIDANCE, AND EVASION

From both the Treasury and the taxpayer viewpoint, taxes can modify individual decisions. Taxes represent an additional cost of doing business or of accumulating wealth. Assuming that economists are correct in speaking about the ways in which a rational citizen makes day-to-day decisions, taxpayers employ tax planning techniques to accomplish the overall goal of wealth maximization.[1] Because taxes deplete the wealth of the taxpayer, planning behavior is designed to reduce the net present value of the tax liability. This is not the same as a simple reduction of taxes in nominal dollar terms, an objective that is so often assumed by laypeople, the media, and others, including too many tax advisors.

Example 11–1 Sharon can choose between two business plans. One will cost her enterprise $1,000 in taxes today. The other will cost the business $2,000 in taxes ten years from now. The plans are identical in all other ways. Prevailing interest rates average 10 percent. Because the present value of the taxes levied with respect to the second alternative are about $800, Sharon should choose the latter plan, that is, the one with the higher nominal dollar tax cost.

If prevailing interest rates average 5 percent during the ten-year planning period, the present value of the taxes levied under the second alternative

---

1. We use "wealth" in its broadest sense here; that is, an individual may choose increased leisure time or other forms of so-called psychic income over traditional forms of wealth. Wealth, the accumulation of which constitutes the overall goal for the specified time period, thus can include measures of happiness, satisfaction, investment, and control over time and other resources.

would be about $1,225, so the first plan, the one that requires an immediate tax payment, should be adopted.

In one important sense, the Federal income tax is its own worst enemy. Taxpayers are rewarded more for finding ways to save taxes than for earning an equal amount in the marketplace. This incentive for tax planning is the result of two rules of tax law.

The first such rule is that the Federal income tax itself is not allowed as a deduction in determining taxable income. Consequently, reducing the amount of income taxes that are paid does not decrease one's allowable deductions and, hence, does not trigger any further increase in taxable income. Instead, the full amount of any tax that is saved increases after-tax income; that is, the tax savings themselves do not constitute taxable income. Unlike most profit-seeking activities, tax planning produces benefits that are completely exempt from income taxation.

The second such rule allows a deduction for any business-related expenses that are incurred in connection with the determination of a tax. Most tax planning costs are deductible by business owners and sole proprietors, but only a few employee-individuals qualify for such a deduction. The net cost of a tax planning project, then, is its gross cost minus the amount of the reduction in the tax liability that is generated by the attendant deduction. In concise terms, the after-tax cost of tax planning can be expressed as follows.

ATC = BTC × (1 − MTR)

where

ATC = after-tax cost
BTC = before-tax cost
MTR = marginal tax rate

In relating both rules to tax planning projects, one can see that such endeavors enjoy an economic advantage over most other profit-seeking activities. In evaluating most other investment projects, the decision maker must compare after-tax benefits with after-tax costs. Yet, for tax planning projects, the payoffs are tax free, while the costs usually remain tax-deductible. Thus, for tax planning activities, one effectively compares pretax benefits with after-tax costs.

Example 11–2 A corporate taxpayer, subject to a marginal state and Federal income tax rate of 40 percent, is considering two mutually exclusive alternatives. Alternative A is to hire a university accounting major for the summer at a cost of $2,000; his task would be to undertake research on a tax avoidance plan. If it is successful, the plan would save the corporation $1,600 in Federal income taxes. The probability of success for the plan is estimated at 80 percent. Alternative M is to hire a university marketing major for the summer at a cost of $1,800; her task would be to undertake research on a marketing plan. If it is successful, this plan would generate new revenues of $2,000. The probability of such success is estimated to be 85 percent. Which, if either, alternative should the corporation pursue?

	Alternative A	Alternative M
Before-tax cost	$2,000	$1,800
Tax reduction (40%)	−800	−720
After-tax cost	$1,200	$1,080
Possible pretax payoff	$1,600	$2,000
Probability of success	×0.80	×0.85
Expected pretax payoff	$1,280	$1,700
Tax on expected payoff (40%)	−0	−680
Expected after-tax payoff	$1,280	$1,020
Excess of after-tax payoff over after-tax cost	$ 80	$ (60)

Decision: Even though Alternative M offers a higher pretax payoff, a lower before-tax cost, and a higher probability of success, Alternative A should be accepted.

The facts of this example illustrate the apparent built-in economic bias of current tax law for tax planning projects, relative to other, seemingly more productive activities.

The analysis of Example 11–2, like most of the illustrations in this book, is based on a "marginal" viewpoint. Its purpose is to determine the effect of the transactions at issue, assuming that all other characteristics of the situation do not change. When it is viewed from this perspective, the after-tax cost of any deductible expenditure decreases if the marginal tax rate is increased. This fact may explain why lower income taxpayers, who are subject to lower marginal tax rates, engage in tax planning activities less often than do higher income taxpayers.

Example 11–3 Assume the same situation and opportunities as in Example 11–2, except that the corporation's marginal tax rate is 20 percent.

	Alternative A	Alternative M
Before-tax cost	$2,000	$1,800
Tax reduction (20%)	−400	−360
After-tax cost	$1,600	$1,440
Possible pretax payoff	$1,600	$2,000
Probability of success	×0.80	×0.85
Expected pretax payoff	$1,280	$1,700
Tax on expected payoff (20%)	−0	−340
Expected after-tax payoff	$1,280	$1,360
Excess of after-tax payoff over after-tax cost	$ (320)	$ (80)

Decision: Accept Alternative M, because it generates the lesser after-tax loss, or undertake neither (seemingly profitable) project.

SPOTLIGHT ON TAXATION: Observation

Sometimes it is difficult to get a taxpayer to think in "after-tax" terms, so "bad" decisions can be made. For other taxpayers, there is an impression that the government fully reimburses a deduction, i.e., a $1 "write-off" means that there is no cost to the taxpayer. The tax planner often must act as educator to eliminate both of these mistaken impressions.

TAX RATE TERMINOLOGY

The basic formula for computing a taxpayer's liability is

Tax Liability = Tax Base × Rate

Thus, in many respects, the function of a legislative body is to define adequately the appropriate tax base and construct a schedule of tax rates, so that the ensuing liabilities will be in accordance with the prevailing revenue and nonrevenue objectives of the tax system. Once a tax has been included in a society's tax structure, legislative efforts seem to focus on slight modifications of the existing tax base and rates; major overhauls, additions, or deletions to the structure rarely are considered. Tax reform legislation thus usually takes the form of "fine-tuning" the system rather than "changing channels" altogether.

TAX BASE

The income tax is the most modern of the taxes that are commonly found in contemporary industrialized societies. Allowing for the difficulties in constructing a definition for a virtually imaginary concept, most policymakers believe that a tax that is based on "ordinary taxable income," allowing deductions for the costs of earning such income and for certain personal expenditures, best reflects the capacity of the taxpayer to support government finance.

Previous efforts to base taxation on ability to pay have included taxes on individual consumption and wealth. Consumption taxes are supported by the rationale that the taxpayer receives personal benefit from society in accordance with the amount of goods and services that he or she exhausts during the period; thus, the government should appropriate its share of finances from what people take out of society's "kitty" for personal reasons, not from what they put into it, as is the case under income taxation.

Wealth or property taxes also have been structured to base levies on one's capacity to support the government. Most often, wealth taxes take the form of levies against the net holdings of tangible assets that are controlled by the taxpayer at a given time. In accounting terminology, the tax on the net tangible assets is assessed on what appears on the taxpayer's balance sheet at the end of the taxable year.

TAX RATES

Most tax scholars identify three distinct tax rate structures: proportional, progressive, and regressive, as illustrated in Exhibit 11–1. The classification of a rate structure depends on the trend of the tax rate as the tax base increases. Under a **proportional tax rate** system, the tax rate is constant; for example, it might stand at 29 percent of net wealth, over all possible values of the tax base. Most American sales and property taxes employ a proportional rate structure. Under a tax system with **progressive tax rates**, the applicable tax rate increases as the tax base grows larger. American income, estate, and gift taxes typically use nominally progressive rates. Finally, the tax rate decreases as the tax base grows larger under a system of **regressive tax rates**. Using the present scheme of classification, no significant American tax to date has employed a system of nominally regressive tax rates.

Example 11–4 In the typical year, Social Security taxes are imposed on employees at a flat rate (before credits), say, of 8 percent on all wages up to

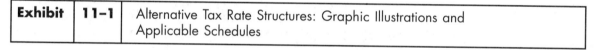

Exhibit	11–1	Alternative Tax Rate Structures: Graphic Illustrations and Applicable Schedules

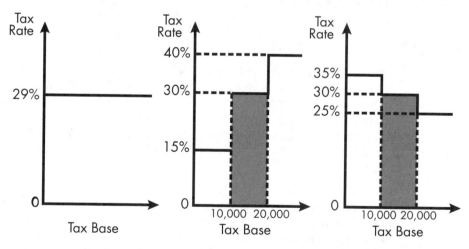

PROPORTIONAL RATES		PROGRESSIVE RATES		REGRESSIVE RATES	
Tax Base	**Rate**	**Tax Base**	**Rate**	**Tax Base**	**Rate**
All amounts	29%	1st $10,000	15%	1st $10,000	35%
		2nd 10,000	30	2nd 10,000	30
		3rd 10,000	40	3rd 10,000	25

$90,000. For wages in excess of $90,000, there is no additional tax. Technically, this tax is proportional, because all covered wages (the tax base) are subject to the same rate of tax. However, many people regard Social Security taxes as being regressive, presumably because they tend to relate their analysis to all of one's income and not just to the statutory tax base. Under this view, because the marginal tax rate is zero on wages in excess of $90,000 for the year, the tax is both effectively and nominally regressive.

Many taxpayers confuse the appropriate meaning of their **marginal tax rate**. Typically, they assume that if a taxpayer is subject to a 36 percent marginal tax rate (i.e., 36 cents is payable in tax on the next dollar of taxable income), he or she owes 36 percent of the *entire* taxable income. One often hears people fall victim to this fallacy, when they state, "I wish I hadn't gotten that raise, because it threw me into a higher tax bracket!" The truth is that even under a system of progressive tax rates, one is never left worse off by earning more money. The higher marginal rates that apply to additional income affect only those increments; the tax liability on the original income layers does not change.

Such comments reflect a confusion on the part of the taxpayer concerning marginal tax rate and average tax rate. The **average tax rate** is a simple division of the total tax liability by the corresponding tax base.

Example 11–5 Lydia earned $30,000 this year. After applying various deductions, exclusions, and exemptions, though, Lydia's statutory taxable income is $21,000; further, the middle tax rate system of Exhibit 11–1 is in effect. Lydia's tax is computed as follows.

$$
\begin{array}{rcl}
15\% \times \$10,000 &=& \$1,500 \\
30\% \times 10,000 &=& 3,000 \\
40\% \times 1,000 &=& \underline{400} \\
\text{Tax liability} & & \$4,900 \\
\end{array}
$$

Lydia's marginal tax rate is 40 percent, but her average rate is only 23.33 percent ($4,900 tax due ÷ $21,000 taxable income).

The reader should make sure that he or she understands this distinction between marginal and average tax rates, because all tax planning analyses should be based on the marginal tax that the individual will pay or save by adopting a particular course of action. The average tax rate is an interesting statistic, but it is solely the marginal rate that affects the change in tax liability and any corresponding changes in taxpayer behavior.

Of course, this definition of statutory taxable income allows for certain deductions, exemptions, and exclusions from total receipts in determining the tax base for the year. Often, because one has received tax-exempt income during the period and because of the tax base's exemptions and standard

Exhibit	11–2	Various Tax Rate Computations Illustrated

Lydia files a tax return for $30,000 of economic income and $9,000 of exemptions, exclusions, and deductions. Taxable income is $21,000. Tax liability is $4,900 under the prevailing rate system.

Marginal tax rate   40% (from tax rate schedule, middle system, Exhibit 11–1)

Average tax rates   Nominal average rate: $4,900/$21,000 = 23.33%
Effective average rate: $4,900/$30,000 = 16.33%

deduction, an individual controls more receipts than he or she legally must report as taxable income. In this case, the distinction between the nominal and effective average tax rates becomes important. The **nominal average tax rate** can be computed in Example 11–5 as the division of total tax liability by taxable income (i.e., 23.33 percent). However, before considering Lydia's exclusions, exemptions, and deductions, effectively she had command over $30,000 of income during the year, even though only $21,000 of this amount was defined technically as taxable income. Thus, Lydia's **effective average tax rate** of tax for the year can be found by dividing the total tax liability by "total," or economic, income. Here, the effective average rate of tax is only $4,900 ÷ $30,000 = 16.33 percent. Exhibit 11–2 summarizes the various tax rate computations that have been introduced in this section.

TAX PLANNING IN PERSPECTIVE

The entrepreneurial tax professional should not see tax planning as an end in itself. Rather, especially when dealing with individual clients, tax planning must be seen as part of two sets of major services provided by the practitioner, as illustrated in Exhibits 11–3 and 11–4. As we discussed in Chapter 1, tax planning is part of the entire menu of tax services that the tax professional makes available. Although the compliance and litigation aspects of the profession increasingly are shared with paraprofessionals (who prepare the bulk of tax returns for many professional firms) or attorneys (when a seemingly irresolvable conflict arises, usually between the client and the IRS), tax planning rightly is initiated by the well-educated and experienced tax practitioner.

Similarly, tax planning is but one of the various types of planning services that a tax professional offers to clients. As the U.S. population collectively ages, the importance of portfolio, estate, and retirement planning has increased. As the "baby boom echo" materialized in the early part of the twenty-first century, education planning again has taken center stage. Planning for cash and risk contingencies is mandatory for business clients, but even the

Exhibit	11–3

Tax Planning in the Typical Tax Practice, by Time and Effort of the Professional Staff

TAX COMPLIANCE		
Tax Research	**Tax Planning**	**Tax Litigation**

Exhibit	11–4

Tax Planning in the Client's Wealth Planning Process

EDUCATION PLANNING
Trusts for Minors
Special Investments

ESTATE PLANNING
Asset Management
Distributions and Control

RETIREMENT PLANNING
Qualified Plans
Nonqualified Plans
Distributions
Plans and Vehicles

INCOME TAX PLANNING
Timing
Tax Entity
Exclusions and Deductions
Income Classification
Special Taxes
Withholding
Interest and Penalties

INVESTMENT PLANNING
Risks
Rewards
Control
Purchases/Sales
Asset Allocation
Regulations

CASH PLANNING
Budgeting
Finance

RISK PLANNING
Insurance
Security

most modestly endowed of individual clients can benefit from an introduction to such planning.

Thus, to the extent that the tax professional offers tax planning and counseling services, he or she must be facile with the rudiments of the planning process and with the dynamic nature of the evolution of the tax law as it affects planning engagements.

FUNDAMENTALS OF TAX PLANNING

As we noted in Chapter 1, tax planning is a completely legal means for saving taxes.[2] The basic objective of such planning is to arrange one's financial activities in a way that will reduce the present value of tax costs, such that maximum wealth accumulation can occur in the time period specified.

2. Portions of this section are adapted from Raabe and Parker, *Tax Concepts for Decision Making* (St. Paul, MN: West Publishing Co., 1985).

Opportunities for effective tax planning almost always are greater when tax effects are given consideration before transactions are finalized, rather than after they are completed. Decision makers should constantly be alert for tax-optimizing alternatives in the everyday conduct of their affairs. In other words, the first requirement for effective tax planning is **tax awareness** on the part of decision makers, rather than tax expertise by tax professionals.

Example 11–6 Russell and Phyllis Cohen, a married couple subject to a 30 percent marginal tax rate, currently are negotiating the purchase of their first home with the Hacienda Heights Construction Company, a land developer. The company has offered to sell the Cohens a selected house and lot at a price of $60,000, with a 20 percent down payment and 10 percent interest on annual payments over a five-year period. Under these terms, payments would be as follows.

Year	Beginning Balance	Interest	Principal	Total
0	$60,000	$ —	$12,000	$12,000
1	48,000	4,800	7,862	12,662
2	40,138	4,014	8,648	12,662
3	31,490	3,149	9,513	12,662
4	21,977	2,198	10,464	12,662
5	11,513	1,151	11,513	12,664
Totals		$15,312	$60,000	$75,312

The Cohens are aware that mortgage interest payments are tax-deductible and that the purchase price of a home is not. Thus, they make a counter-offer to purchase the home at a price of $54,445, with $12,000 down and 15 percent interest on annual payments over a five-year period. Under these new terms, Hacienda Heights receives the same cash payments (and gross income) as it did under the original terms. However, the amount of allowable deductions to the Cohens would be increased, with no change in total cash payments.

Year	Beginning Balance	Interest	Principal	Total
0	$54,445	$ —	$12,000	$12,000
1	42,445	6,367	6,295	12,662
2	36,150	5,423	7,239	12,662
3	28,911	4,337	8,325	12,662
4	20,586	3,088	9,574	12,662
5	11,012	1,652	11,012	12,664
Totals		$20,867	$54,445	$75,312

These results are not uncommon in a robust tax planning context. Often, decision makers can benefit by recognizing how the rearrangement of a planned transaction can produce tax savings, even if the economic substance of the transaction is left unaltered (or altered very little). The key, of course, is to pay close attention to the structural and transactional categories that have been established by Congress and the courts. In Example 11–6, by reclassifying a portion of their housing expenditures as (deductible) interest, rather than (nondeductible) principal, the Cohens were able to increase their allowable deductions and save taxes. Stated differently, the taxpayer's ability to conceptualize actions or events within stated legal definitions is of utmost importance.

Tax planning behavior can be characterized as falling into one or more of the general categories enumerated in Exhibit 11–5. Virtually every tax planning technique employed by the tax professional fits one or more of these overriding planning objectives.

Exhibit 11–5	
Goals of Tax Planning Behavior	• Avoiding statutory income, obtaining deductions • Postponing income recognition, accelerating losses and deductions • Changing tax jurisdictions • Controlling the classification of income • Spreading income among related taxpayers

SPOTLIGHT ON TAXATION: Radical Tax Planning

"A well-timed death is the acme of good tax planning, better even than a well-timed marriage."

—(Former IRS Commissioner) Donald C. Alexander

AVOIDING INCOME RECOGNITION

Taxpayers often can reduce their exposure to taxation by avoiding the accumulation of gross income that must be recognized. This is not to suggest that a taxpayer should avoid accumulating real economic income. As long as marginal tax rates remain less than 100 percent, few people would be willing to go to that extreme. Rather, one usually should strive to obtain economic wealth in some manner that does not create recognized income under the tax law.

Example 11–7 Julie earned $3,500 when she sold the crop of fruits and vegetables that she grew, and she was subject to income tax on the full amount. Warren also grew a crop of produce of the same size, but he and his family ate the food. Thus, Warren recognized no gross income and paid no income tax relative to his gardening activities, but his family enjoyed $3,500 worth of fruits and vegetables.

Another method by which one can avoid obtaining recognized income is through the use of debt. Since neither the borrowing of money nor the receipt of funds that previously were lent generates gross income, taxpayers sometimes can use loans to avoid the recognition of taxable income on appreciated investments and enjoy the temporary use of the cash.

Example 11–8 Doug owns a tract of land that he acquired many years ago for $10,000. Currently, the land is worth $100,000. Doug needs $50,000 cash for a business venture. He is considering two alternatives: one is to sell half of the land and the other is to borrow the $50,000 by giving a mortgage on the land.

If Doug sells one-half of the land, he will recognize a $45,000 ($50,000 − 1/2 of $10,000) taxable gain. However, Doug recognizes no taxable income if he borrows the money, even though the amount that he borrows will be in excess of the basis of the land.

Example 11–9 Barbara Ward formed a new corporation by investing $100,000 cash. Following the advice of her tax consultant, Barbara designated $60,000 to be used for the purchase of corporate stock and $40,000 as a loan to the corporation. In this way, if Barbara wants to receive large amounts of cash back from the corporation in the future, the entity simply will repay part or all of the loan principal to her, tax free, rather than making a large (taxable and nondeductible) dividend payment. Barbara also can direct the corporation to pay interest on the loan; such payments are deductible by the corporation. Of course, both interest and dividends are taxable to Barbara when she receives them.

Still another, and perhaps more obvious, way in which one can avoid the recognition of income for tax purposes is to take advantage of the many exclusions that the law permits. For example, an employee might arrange to receive certain nontaxable fringe benefits (such as health insurance) from the employer, in lieu of an equivalent value in (taxable) cash salary. This relationship should affect all negotiations as to compensation arrangements: the employer is indifferent between the two choices because both salary and fringe benefit payments are fully deductible against gross income, but the employee's after-tax wealth increases more where tax-free benefits are received.

Example 11–10 Lee Schrader, who is subject to a 40 percent overall marginal tax rate, is better off if she receives a tax-free fringe benefit than if she receives an equivalent raise in her salary.

	If Salary Increases	If Fringe Benefit Is Chosen
Value of compensation received	$2,000	$2,000
Tax on employee's compensation	− 800	
After-tax increase in employee's wealth	$1,200	$2,000

POSTPONING INCOME RECOGNITION

By delaying the recognition of income, one also delays the payment of the tax and, hence, can continue to enjoy the use of that tax money. Given the relatively higher interest rates that are anticipated in coming years, this delay takes on increased importance. At 6 percent annual interest, the present value of a $1,000 tax that is postponed for ten years is only $558, a "forgiveness" of almost one-half of the tax "cost." For longer periods and/or higher interest rates, the economic significance of the delay would be even greater. Appendix A includes a series of tables computing factors to reflect the time value of money.

Example 11–11 Agatha Fraser paid $1,000 for 4,800 Euros. At the same time, her sister, Betty, put $1,000 into a U.S. bank savings account. By the current year, the value of Agatha's Euros had increased to $1,800, and Betty's bank account had increased, due to interest accumulations, to the same amount. Since the increase in the value of the Euros was unrealized, Agatha had not been taxed yet on her $800 increase in economic wealth. On the other hand, Betty's increase was realized from interest that was credited annually to her account. Under the tax doctrine of *constructive receipt*, Betty had recognized gross income, accumulated over the nine-year planning period, of $800.

Example 11–12 Janie Heller owns land adjacent to her home that appreciated in value by $5,000 this year. However, because she did not sell the land, the appreciation in market value was not realized in a market transaction or recognized for income tax purposes. Janie has no recognized income from the land for that year.

Example 11–13 Janie Heller, of Example 11–12, paid interest of $4,000 on a mortgage that was used to finance her home and land investment. Janie can deduct the interest amount to offset the income that she derived from other investment sources in computing her taxable income. In effect, Janie is able to achieve a deliberate mismatching of current-year costs and unrealized revenues.

Example 11–14 Janie Heller, of Example 11–12, constructed an apartment building on her land, at a cost of $500,000, of which $475,000 was borrowed. By electing accelerated depreciation, which is based on the total $500,000 cost of the building rather than on Janie's $25,000 equity therein, Janie is able to take a depreciation deduction of about $24,000 in the construction year alone, nearly equal to her entire cash outlay for the current year.

CHANGING TAX JURISDICTIONS

Tax systems are not universal in breadth, nature, or application. Taxes are adopted by governmental jurisdictions, to be collected from those who live and do business within their boundaries. Often, by moving assets or income out of one tax jurisdiction and into another, tax reductions can be effected. Over time, governments tend to modify their tax systems to prevent the "leakage" of tax revenues through such cross-border transactions. Yet, in an effort to attract businesses and resulting jobs into their jurisdictions, governments often retain or create border incentives in the form of tax reductions that are limited in time or scope.

Example 11–15 The island country of Ricardo meets its revenue needs with tariffs on the fishing industry. Ricardo never has adopted an income tax system. Harris, a U.S. corporation, could build its new assembly plant through a wholly owned subsidiary incorporated and doing business only in Ricardo, thereby reducing its costs of conducting business because there is no income tax on executive salaries or annual profits. Perhaps by design, Ricardo has attracted new business, profits, jobs, and other benefits through its tax policies.

Example 11–16 State A includes in its statutory definition of taxable business income the interest paid on U.S. Treasury obligations. OneBank holds billions of dollars in Treasury notes, bills, and bonds, so, in an effort to reduce its tax costs, it creates a wholly owned subsidiary incorporated and doing business only in State B, which does not tax interest income. The subsidiary "repatriates" the interest to OneBank through quarterly dividend distributions, not taxed under the laws of State A. The economy of State A has been depleted because of its tax policy, but the taxpayer has responded with rational behavior in accord with its overall financial goals through judicious tax planning techniques.

CONTROLLING CLASSIFICATION OF INCOME

For Federal income tax purposes, several distinct categories of income, deductions, and credits are recognized. The most important of these are (1) ordinary income, which is fully taxable, and ordinary deductions, which decrease the tax base dollar for dollar; (2) investment or "portfolio" income, which usually is fully taxable except for tax-exempt state and local bond interest, and related expenses, which typically can be subtracted only against investment income; and (3) income from passive activities, such as the ownership of rental or "tax shelter" assets, which usually is fully taxable, and related expenses, which can be subtracted only against passive income.

In addition, a fourth classification of income and expenses should be identified. If the taxpayer is subject to the alternative minimum tax, preference and adjustment items, such as accelerated depreciation deductions, may be included, and other expenditures may not be available as deductions.

Effective tax planning often includes the proper identification or reclassification of income or expenditure items, using these statutory definitions.

Example 11–17 Phil Jankowski is the sole shareholder of a management consulting corporation. In addition, he has invested in tax shelter entities that are generating $40,000 per year in passive losses for him. According to the Code, such losses from passive activities cannot be applied as deductions to offset fully taxable income, for example, from Phil's salary or capital gain transactions. Accordingly, Phil cannot reduce current taxable income by the $40,000 passive loss from his tax shelter.

As the dominant shareholder of his corporation, however, Phil may be in a position to salvage the $40,000 deduction. If he reduces his salary from the corporation by $40,000 and takes instead from the corporation a $40,000 properly structured lease payment for the use of specified personal or real property that he owns but the corporation uses, like office equipment or automobiles, he may be able to create $40,000 in passive income from rental activities, against which the tax shelter loss can be offset.

Example 11–18 Matt Young Eagle is subject to the alternative minimum tax for the first time ever this year because he exercised the incentive stock options of his employer. Nonbusiness taxes paid and miscellaneous itemized deductions, among other familiar items, are not allowed as deductions when computing alternative minimum taxable income. Only certain tax credits are allowed against the AMT. Accordingly, Young Eagle should defer the payments of his fourth-quarter state income tax estimates and of the real estate tax on his home until next year, when the usual definitions of taxable income will apply to him again.

SPREADING INCOME AMONG RELATED TAXPAYERS

Because different types of legal entities are taxed separately and at different rates, an individual often can produce an overall tax savings by conducting various business and investment activities within separate tax-paying entities. The progressive nature of the various tax rate schedules further tends to increase the advantage of income splitting. This benefit might result from shifting income, either among different economic entities that are owned by the same individual or among the individual's family members. Accordingly, tax considerations often play an important role both in the selection of organizational forms for a business enterprise and in family financial arrangements.

Example 11–19 Bob and Lorraine Whitehead are currently providing for Lorraine's parents' retirement out of after-tax income. Given the Whiteheads' marginal income tax rate of 30 percent, $1,000 of pretax income is needed to produce $700 of savings [$1,000 − (0.30 of $1,000) = $700]. Assuming that the parents have a marginal income tax rate of only 18 percent, a transfer to them of $1,000 of pretax income, say, by the placement of income-producing assets into an appropriate trust, would raise the after-tax contribution to the parents' retirement to $820 [$1,000 − (0.18 of $1,000)].

Example 11–20 Sally Campbell is the sole shareholder and only employee of the Newark Corporation. The corporation's operating income this year is expected to be $125,000. Sally is subject to an overall marginal income tax rate of 30 percent. Sally wishes to know, considering only the Federal income tax, what amount of salary payments to her would produce the smallest combined tax for both herself and the corporation. Sally's income from other sources is sufficient to meet her living expenses and it precisely equals her total income tax deductions, so her taxable income is exactly equal to any salary that she receives from the corporation.

Currently, marginal corporate income tax rates do not exceed the 30 percent marginal individual tax bracket until corporate taxable income exceeds $75,000.

Accordingly, the tax adviser should be certain to plan the corporation's compensation policy so that a corporate taxable income of at least $75,000 exists every year.

DEPARTING FROM THE FUNDAMENTALS

The general principles of tax planning that have been presented usually produce an optimal tax liability for the taxpayer. However, unusual circumstances may dictate that such principles should be violated purposely, to produce a desired effect. Again, however, the tax awareness of the parties is utmost in proper planning activities.

Example 11–21 Gretchen's manufacturing business is unincorporated. It has generated an operating loss of $265,000, which Gretchen can deduct on her tax return. Although there may be other tax uses for this loss, Gretchen may want to accelerate the recognition of other gross income into the current year, for example, by selling appreciated investments, exercising more sophisticated tax accounting elections, or simply sending out bills to customers in a more timely fashion. Economically, such income has been earned gradually by Gretchen, but it has had no tax effect yet because it has not been realized. Realization this year, however, will result in no tax liability for Gretchen because of the loss, so income acceleration should be considered.

Example 11–22 Brian's gross income is lower than he expected because of an unanticipated decrease in the sale of his homemade sandals. From a tax standpoint, it may be better to delay deductible expenditures of a discretionary or personal nature (e.g., advertising, medical expenses, and charitable contributions) until business picks up again. In this manner, the value of such deductions will increase, as will the marginal income tax rate to which he is subject.

Example 11–23 Dolores is subject to the alternative minimum tax this year, so her marginal tax rate is 24 percent, not the usual 36 percent. She might consider accelerating some gross income into the current year to take advantage of this structural decrease in her marginal tax rate. The tax adviser must be certain, though, to compare the present values of the resulting taxes, not just the nominal dollar amounts (i.e., the proper tax planning comparison is between the $32,400 and the $24,000), and Dolores should accelerate the gross income in this setting.

	If Regular Tax Applies, Taxed Next Year	If AMT Applies, Taxed This Year
Nominal tax liability	$36,000	$24,000
Present value of tax liability	32,400	24,000

SPOTLIGHT ON TAXES: Fruits of Tax Planning

"Tax planning is driven by the fact that under a non-neutral tax law, transactions or arrangements whose economic differences are minor can have significantly different tax consequences."

—James W. Wetzler

EXPLOITING INCONSISTENCIES IN THE STATUTE

Sometimes, especially when the tax planner can affect the behavior of more than one taxpayer, the tax planning goals can be accomplished by exploiting perceived inconsistencies in the tax system. Multiple taxpayers can exist in the form of family members or related corporations and their shareholders. Several types of systemic inconsistencies can be identified and used by the tax planner.

INCONSISTENCIES BETWEEN TRANSACTIONS

Most forms of self-provided in-kind income go unrecognized for tax purposes. Often, the same items are not deductible, however, when they are purchased in market transactions. Thus, providing for one's own needs can be an important technique in managing the recognition of taxable income.

Example 11–24 Jerry has $50,000 in savings. If the money were invested in securities, the yield on his investment would be taxable, although no deduction would be allowed for his "personal" expense of renting a home. If the $50,000 were invested in a home for his own use, however, the net rental value of the home would escape taxation, since such in-kind value is not recognized as gross income under the law.

INCONSISTENCIES BETWEEN TAXPAYERS

Inconsistencies often exist between Code sections that control the recognition of income and those that control the allowance of deductions for the same items. When a transaction is between related taxpayers, such inconsistent treatments sometimes can be used to the taxpayers' advantage. The objective in such a situation usually is to structure the terms of the transaction so as to decrease taxable income to the taxpayer group as a whole.

Example 11–25 Marilyn is the sole owner-employee of a corporation. To the extent that the corporation pays dividends to Marilyn, she will recognize gross income, but the corporation will receive no deduction. To the extent that Marilyn is paid a reasonable salary, she will recognize gross income and the corporation will receive a deduction. To the extent that she receives certain employee fringe benefits, such as medical insurance, Marilyn is not required to recognize taxable income, and the corporation is allowed an ordinary business expense deduction. In summary, the payment of dividends increases combined taxable income of a shareholder and the corporation, the payment of salary does not change combined taxable income, and providing qualified fringe benefits reduces combined taxable income.

Example 11–26 Don and Ann Evans operate a farm, producing a net taxable income of about $30,000 per year. Their nondeductible expenses for housing average $12,000 per year.

The Evanses should consider forming a corporation and making a tax-free transfer of all of the farm property to the corporation, including their personal living quarters. As shareholders of the corporation, they could hire themselves as employees, with a requirement that they live on the business premises. The value of the lodging would not be taxable to the Evanses as individuals, under § 119 of the Code, but it would be deductible as a business expense of the corporation, thus reducing the corporation's taxable income before salaries to $18,000 ($30,000 − $12,000).

The Evanses then should have the corporation pay them reasonable salaries totaling $18,000. In this manner, taxable income of $18,000 would be taxed directly to them as individuals, and the corporation's taxable income would be reduced to zero, thus avoiding any double taxation. By using this combination of income splitting and an employee fringe benefit, the Evanses could effectively reduce their taxable income (i.e., from $30,000 to $18,000) by the amount of their lodging costs ($12,000), even though such costs are generally nondeductible by both self-employed persons and employees.

This result is based on the assumptions that $18,000 is a reasonable salary for the work that they perform, and that the requirement for living on the farm is for a bona fide business purpose (other than merely for tax avoidance).

INCONSISTENCIES BETWEEN YEARS

Another form of inconsistency concerns timing differences in the recognition of income and deductions. Such inconsistencies may relate to the transactions of one taxpayer, or they may concern two taxpayers engaging in a single transaction. In both cases, careful planning to take advantage of tax law inconsistencies can result in a considerable delay in the payment of taxes.

Example 11–27 Sarah Carter uses borrowed funds to acquire non-dividend-paying corporate stocks. Appreciation on the stocks is not taxed until it is realized on the sale of the shares; yet, Carter might be able to claim investment-interest deductions for the interest that she pays on the borrowed funds.

Example 11–28 Harry Fischer is a 40 percent shareholder and junior executive of Able Corporation. Harry's performance incentive bonus is set at 30 percent of the corporation's pretax earnings for the year. It is payable on January 31 of the following year.

Because the corporation is an accrual-basis taxpayer, the bonus is deductible in the year in which it is earned. As a cash-basis minority shareholder, however, Harry need not recognize the income until the following taxable year (i.e., when he receives it). To the extent of Harry's bonus, the recognition of combined corporate and shareholder income thus is delayed for one year.

Example 11–29 Jane Summer is an employee of Orange Corporation and is covered by the company's qualified pension plan. The corporation makes a contribution to the plan for Jane's retirement, which will occur in 30 years. Although Jane will not receive any gross income from the pension benefits until her retirement in 30 years, the corporation is entitled to a current-year business expense deduction.

AVOIDING TAX TRAPS

Ever since the enactment of the first income tax law, taxpayers have been trying to find ways to avoid such taxes. Likewise, Congress, the IRS, and the courts have enacted rules and doctrines to prevent, or at least restrict, various avoidance schemes. As a result, current tax law includes a maze of tax traps for the unwary.

STATUTORY TAX TRAPS

Many of the statutory provisions encountered in a tax planning context can best be understood when they are viewed as preventive provisions, that is, as rules designed by Congress to prevent certain techniques of tax avoidance. However, remember that any transaction that falls within the scope of a given provision, whether or not it is intended as part of a tax avoidance scheme, is subject to that provision. Thus, a basic knowledge of the tax system is necessary for the tax planner if certain disastrous pitfalls are to be avoided.

As we noted earlier in this chapter, income splitting between related taxpayers often can generate significant tax savings. To be effective for tax purposes, though, the income actually must be earned by the separate entities and not merely assigned by means of artificial transactions between them. Section 482 gives the IRS the power to reallocate both income and deductions among certain related taxpayers so as to reflect "true taxable income."

In applying § 482, the regulations indicate that the IRS's right to determine true taxable income is not limited to fraudulent or sham transactions, but also situations where income inadvertently has been shifted between controlled parties. The courts have held, however, that there truly must be a "shifting" of income before the IRS's power comes into play. Bona fide business transactions that bring tax advantages in their wake should not subject the related parties to reallocation. In concept, at least, § 482 can be applied by the IRS only where there has been some manipulation of income or deductions by the taxpayers.

Thus, while its boundaries are, in practice, both broad and sometimes hazy, § 482 does not prohibit the use of multiple entities for the purpose of earning income. It does, however, give the IRS a potent weapon with which to combat the artificial shifting of income between those entities.

Example 11–30 X and Y are two corporations that are fully owned by the same individual. X operates an international airline, and Y owns several hotels that are located in cities served by X. In conjunction with the advertising of its airlines, X often pictures Y's hotels. Although the primary benefit of the advertising is to X's airline operations, Y's hotels also obtain patronage by travelers who respond to the ads. X does not charge Y for the advertising. Because an unrelated hotel operator presumably would have been charged for such advertising, the IRS may make an allocation of income from X to Y to reflect the fair market value of the advertising services that were provided.

The Code restricts the amount of unearned income that can be taxed at the (lower) marginal rates of one's dependent child who has not yet attained age 14, to less than $1,500 per year, an amount indexed for inflation. Any unearned income of the child that exceeds this amount is taxed to the child, but at the (higher) marginal rates of his or her parents. The purpose of this portion of the *Internal Revenue Code* is not to discriminate against children (who cannot vote in congressional elections), nor to place a higher tax burden on interest and dividend income, nor even to make the family the chief taxable unit in this country. Rather, the provision was enacted simply to discourage the shifting of taxable income from the higher tax brackets of the parent, through a temporary trust or some other accepted income-shifting vehicle, to the more favorable rates of the child, without any permanent loss by the parent of control over the use of the asset. Such tax planning techniques had been undertaken for many years, as a means (similar to that of Example 11–19) of accumulating after-tax contributions to an educational fund, by transferring income to the lowest marginal tax rates that were available within the family.

Whereas the objective of this part of the statute may be defensible by some, the broad provision that was enacted to implement it may create undue hardships in some circumstances, because it affects all taxpayers, not only those with the now-forbidden income-shifting motivation.

Example 11–31 Jimmy, age 7, received an inheritance from his grandmother's estate last year. Grandmother wanted Jimmy to attend a good graduate program in taxation someday, so she invested in high-income securities that produce about $12,000 in interest income annually. Jimmy's parents are to see that he accumulates this income for his education. The interest will be taxed at the parents' 40 percent marginal rate, however, and not at Jimmy's (zero and) 15 percent rate, so a smaller after-tax amount of this income will be available for this laudable educational purpose.

Judicial Tax Traps

In the final analysis, the words of the tax law mean only what the courts say that they mean. Often, judicial decisions must be consulted to determine the allowable limits of various Code provisions.

Example 11–32 An employee-shareholder of a 50 percent family-owned corporation received an annual salary in excess of $1 million, an amount greater than that then paid to the heads of such corporations as General

Motors and Sears.[3] Yet, despite IRS arguments to the contrary, the Tax Court upheld the entire amount paid as "reasonable" under the circumstances of the case because of the special talents and abilities that the employee brought to the corporation.

Example 11–33 A widow changed her will to disinherit her relatives and leave her assets to her attorney and his wife.[4] When the widow died, her relatives brought suit against the attorney, alleging that he had influenced the widow improperly through a personal relationship with her. The attorney paid them $121,000 to withdraw their litigation and deducted the payment as a business expense. The Tax Court upheld the deduction on the grounds that the payment was made for the purpose of maintaining the professional reputation of the lawyer.

On appeal, the Tax Court's decision was overturned. According to the appeals court, a taxpayer's reasons for paying do not determine whether the payment is deductible. Because the lawsuit arose from the attorney's personal relationship with the widow, the $121,000 settlement was deemed to be a personal, nondeductible cost.

Example 11–34 Housing is expensive in Japan. A unit of Mobil Oil owned the house that was used by its president, at his discretion, when he stayed in Japan.[5] The house would have rented for $4,400 a year in the United States, but in Tokyo its annual rental value was $20,000. The executive included it in income and paid tax on $4,400, the U.S. rental value. However, the IRS asserted that the full $20,000 should have been included in his gross income.

The U.S. Court of Claims agreed with the taxpayer, holding that the excess rental value was primarily of benefit to the company, rather than to the individual. The home's prestige value was held to be important to the employer because of social values that were peculiar to Japan, where, in the words of the court, "'face' is an almost tangible reality."

Two pervasive judicial doctrines that often limit the taxpayer's ability to employ effective planning techniques are the concepts of *business purpose* and *substance over form*. To be upheld for tax purposes, transactions must possess some nontax, or "business," purpose in addition to that of tax avoidance. Moreover, there is always the possibility that the court may ignore the form of a transaction if it perceives that such structural false colors cloud the actual substance of the arrangement.

Whenever a series of transactions results in significant tax savings, the IRS may attempt to apply the concept of substance over form by "telescoping" or "collapsing" several transactions into one. If it is upheld by a court, this *step-transaction doctrine* sometimes can negate what had been a good tax plan (where the steps were viewed as separate transactions). To guard against this possibility, the taxpayer should have a bona fide business purpose for

---

3. *Home Interiors and Gifts, Inc.*, 73 T.C. 92 (1980).
4. *William J. McDonald, Jr.*, 592 F.2d 635, 78-2 USTC ¶ 9631, 42 AFTR2d 78-5797 (CA-2).
5. *Faneuil Adams*, 585 F.2d 106, 77-2 USTC ¶ 9613, 40 AFTR2d 77-5607.

each individual step in the transaction. Of course, documenting nontax purposes is usually much easier if the various transactions are separated by reasonable time spans, since they are then less likely to be viewed as component parts of an overall plan.

Example 11–35 Sandra is the sole shareholder of a real estate development corporation. On January 15, she purchased ten additional shares of stock from her corporation for $100,000. On the same day, she sold a tract of undeveloped land to the corporation for its fair market value of $100,000. To the corporation, the land will be inventory. For Sandra, it had been a capital asset, having been held for investment purposes since its purchase ten years previously for $20,000. If these events are viewed as two separate transactions, Sandra will have increased the basis of her investment in the corporation by $100,000 and realized a fully taxable capital gain of $80,000 ($100,000 − $20,000). The corporation's basis in the land will be $100,000. Thus, if the corporation were to sell the land for, say, $110,000, its income therefrom would be only $10,000 ($110,000 − $100,000).

Alternatively, if these events are collapsed into a single transaction, Sandra's payment and receipt of cash would be ignored. Instead, she would be viewed as having given a tract of land in exchange for ten shares of stock of a corporation that she already controls. Under this single-transaction view, Sandra would recognize no taxable capital gain, and the corporation's basis in the stock would be the same as her prior basis, $20,000. Thus, if the corporation were to sell the land for $110,000, its ordinary income would be $90,000 ($110,000 − $20,000).

Taxpayers are restricted to the actual legal forms of the transactions in which they engage, but the IRS has the option of employing the step-transaction doctrine. Thus, the lack of any time lapse between the two transactions effectively gives the IRS its choice as to which interpretation it wishes to follow.

TAX PLANNING ILLUSTRATIONS

Consider several other examples of tax planning that are found in today's tax practice. Usually, a tax planning technique manifests at least one of the planning goals as listed in Exhibit 11–5. The best techniques meet two or more of those goals.

Example 11–36 Albert contributes the maximum amount for the year to an Education IRA for his daughter. No immediate deduction is allowed, but the earnings in the account never are taxed. Withdrawals similarly are excluded from gross income when they are used for education-related expenses. Result: *Avoiding statutory income.*

Example 11–37 Phil designates a portion of his monthly paycheck for medical and child care expenses. No payroll taxes are due on these amounts. Phil's employer reimburses him from these funds when it receives documentation from Phil that he incurred medical and babysitting expenses for the period. By using a "flexible spending plan" such as this one, Phil reduces his total tax liability and has more discretionary income for the year. Result: *Avoiding statutory income.*

Example 11–38 Mary Jane uses a depreciable asset in her business to generate net sales at a profit. The depreciation deductions shelter current sales income from tax, but because the tax basis of the asset is reduced accordingly, there is a greater gain computed when Mary Jane sells or retires the income-producing asset. Result: *Postponing income recognition.*

Example 11–39 Judy keeps a log of her travels so that she can document that she is a resident of Texas, not New York. As a result, Judy's state income tax liability is reduced significantly every year. Result: *Changing tax jurisdictions.*

Example 11–40 Because she is a citizen of the Cayman Islands and not the United States, Ingrid is subject to very low marginal estate and gift tax rates on her extensive portfolio and collectible holdings. Result: *Changing tax jurisdictions.*

Example 11–41 Fizzy Corporation holds some vacant land for potential expansion of its operating plant. By paving asphalt over the land and turning it into a parking lot, charging its executives a nominal fee so that they can park closer to their offices, Fizzy converts portfolio gain into passive income, which frees up deductions now suspended under the passive activity rules. Such passive income is taxed, however, only when Fizzy unilaterally decides to sell the vacant land. Result: *Controlling income classification. Postponing income recognition.*

Example 11–42 Ralph forms a partnership that borrows money and purchases an office building in Texas, which is the home state of none of the partners. The entity passes through net operating losses, made up chiefly of interest and depreciation deductions, which the partners use to offset their passive income from other sources. When the building is sold, state and local income and property taxes are relatively low under Texas law. Result: *Avoiding statutory income. Postponing income recognition. Changing tax jurisdictions. Controlling the classification of income. Spreading income among related taxpayers.*

Example 11–43 Carolyn sets up a charitable lead trust, under which the museum receives the trust's distributable net income for 15 years. Carolyn receives an immediate charitable contribution deduction, equal to the present value of the income stream that she has transferred to the museum. Then, the income-producing property of the trust is deeded to Carolyn's granddaughter, thereby likely deferring any estate tax on the property for another 50 years. Result: *Avoiding statutory income. Postponing income recognition (and transfer tax). Spreading income among related taxpayers.*

Example 11–44 George renovates a downtown warehouse and turns it into condos and apartments. Because the building has some historic significance, George undertakes the rehabilitation so as to maximize his state and Federal tax credits for rehabilitation expenditures. Result: *Controlling income classification. Avoiding statutory income (creating tax credits).*

Example 11–45 Richie makes certain that he makes gifts every year of $11,000 to each of his relatives, thereby using the entire statutory annual gift tax exclusion. Result: *Avoiding statutory income (using transfer tax exclusions). Spreading income among related taxpayers.*

SUMMARY

The study of taxes can be viewed as an examination of various ways to optimize one's tax liability. Tax rules that otherwise might seem as dry as a mouthful of sawdust have a way of becoming interesting, stimulating, and challenging when one realizes their economic significance and the resulting implications on human behavior. Tax optimization, therefore, can be viewed both as the heart of professional tax work and as the most important aspect of taxation for nontax specialists.

TAX TUTOR

Reinforce the tax research information covered in this chapter by completing the online tutorials located at the Federal Tax Research web site:

http://raabe.swlearning.com

KEY WORDS

By the time you complete your work relative to this chapter, you should be comfortable discussing each of the following terms. If you need additional review of any of these items, return to the appropriate material in the chapter or consult the glossary to this text.

Average Tax Rate

Effective Average Tax Rate

Marginal Tax Rate

Nominal Average Tax Rate

Progressive Tax Rate

Proportional Tax Rate

Regressive Tax Rate

Tax Awareness

EXERCISES

1. Using the following codes, identify the basic approach(es) to tax avoidance that are used in each of the cases described below.

Av = Avoiding income recognition

Cl = Controlling the classification of income or expenditure

Ju = Changing tax jurisdictions

Po = Postponing income recognition

Sp = Spreading income among related taxpayers

None = None of the above

a. Albert invests his savings in tax-exempt state bonds.

b. Betty invests in non-dividend-paying corporate stocks by using borrowed funds.

c. Chuck lends $100,000 to his daughter on an interest-free demand note.

d. Doris lends $10,000 to her son on a five-year note, bearing interest at the annual rate of 65 percent.

e. Ed invests $100,000 of his savings in a home for his own use.

f. Frankie invests in a mutual fund that purchases only the indebtedness of the state in which he lives.

g. Grace invests in a mutual fund that purchases only the shares of U.S. corporations that pay no dividends, but whose share prices increase in value over a five-year time period.

2. Using the codes from Exercise 1, identify the basic approach(es) to tax avoidance that are used in each of the cases described below.

a. Annie invests in a mutual fund that purchases only the shares of Colonnia corporations, a country that has no tax treaty with the United States.

b. Burt moves his manufacturing plant to Mexico. Mexico has a tax treaty with the United States, but its labor and utility rates are much lower than is the case where Burt's Ohio plant now operates.

c. Cheryl moves her manufacturing plant to Allegro. Allegro has no tax treaty with the United States, and its labor and utility rates are much lower than is the case where Cheryl's Ohio plant now operates.

d. Donna fails to report on her tax return the interest earned on her savings account.

e. Evelyn has her controlled corporation pay her a salary instead of a dividend during the current year.

f. Flip operates his business as a regular corporation because of his high marginal tax rate. He plans to sell the corporation in five years.

g. Georgia grows most of her own food instead of taking a second job.

3. With respect to the system of coding used in Exercises 1 and 2, create one new illustration in each tax planning category.

4. How do taxes fit into the general economic goals of most taxpayers?

5. How might a tax adviser ignoring the present value approach to tax planning arrive at an improper conclusion? Illustrate.

6. Give some examples of U.S. taxes that employ proportional, progressive, and regressive rate structures.

7. Give an example of a transaction between two taxpayers in which an inconsistent treatment is afforded the two taxpayers. Explain how related taxpayers might structure a transaction to take advantage of this inconsistency.

8. Give an example to show when a taxpayer might consider shifting income from the ordinary classification to capital.

9. Name two types of tax traps and give an example of each.

10. How does the typical tax practitioner divide his or her time among planning, compliance, research, and litigation?

11. What planning engagements can the tax professional offer? Why is he or she in an ideal position to offer these services?

12. Summarize the most important planning services that a tax professional can offer to a client.

13. Why does tax planning analysis focus on the marginal tax rate?

14. When might a taxpayer undertake transactions seemingly opposite to the usual tax planning principles?

15. Higher income taxpayers tend to engage in tax planning more than do lower income taxpayers. Why?

16. Is the objective of tax planning always to minimize taxes? Explain.

PROBLEMS

17. Examples 11–2 and 11–3 in the text concern a decision between the same two mutually exclusive alternatives under identical conditions, except for the corporation's marginal tax rate. In Example 11–2, where the marginal tax rate was 40 percent, the conclusion was to accept Alternative A. In Example 11–3, where the marginal tax rate was 20 percent, the conclusion was to accept Alternative M.

    Determine the marginal tax rate at which the two alternatives would be economic equivalents, that is, they would generate the same excess after-tax payoff over after-tax cost. Your answer should be based on all of the conditions and assumptions as stated in Examples 11–2 and 11–3.

18. On creating a new 100 percent owned corporation, Ben was advised by his tax consultant to treat 50 percent of the total amount that was invested as a loan and 50 percent as a purchase of corporate stock. What tax advantage does this arrangement have over structuring the entire investment as a purchase of stock? Explain.

19. Julia currently is considering the purchase of some land to be held as an investment. She and the seller have agreed on a contract under which Julia would pay $1,000 per month for 60 months or $60,000 total. The seller, not in the real estate business, acquired the land several years ago by paying cash of $10,000. Two alternative interpretations of this transaction are (a) a price of $51,726 with 6 percent interest and (b) a price of $39,380 with 18 percent interest. Which interpretation would you expect each party to prefer? Why?

20. George, a high-bracket taxpayer, wishes to shift some of his own taxable income to his fifteen-year-old daughter, Debra, and is considering two alternative methods of doing so. One is to make a gift of the interest on some corporate bonds that he owns. The other is to make her a gift of the full principal amount of the bonds. Evaluate the pros and cons of each alternative.

21. Betty Smith has two sons, Bob and Jack. List several tax planning techniques that would allow Betty to transfer her full ownership in the family dry cleaning business to Bob and Jack, maximizing the wealth of all four taxpaying entities (Betty, Bob, Jack, and the company).

EXTENDED CASES

22. Should Ferris Corporation elect to forgo the carryback of its $60,000 year 2005 net operating loss? Ferris is subject to a 15 percent cost of capital. Corporate tax rates are as in IRC § 11.

    a.

Tax Year	Actual or Projected Taxable Income
2004	$700,000
2006	700,000

    b.

Tax Year	Actual or Projected Taxable Income
2004	$ 70,000
2006	700,000

    c.

Tax Year	Actual or Projected Taxable Income
2004	$ 70,000
2006	(70,000)
2007	(70,000)
2008	(70,000)
2009	700,000

23. Should Harris Corporation accelerate gross income into 2006, its first year subject to the alternative minimum tax? Harris is subject to a 14 percent cost of capital. The corporate AMT rate is a flat 20 percent, and Harris exceeds the annual AMT exemption phase out.

    a.

Tax Year	Actual or Projected Taxable Income
2007	Regular Tax $700,000
2008	Regular Tax $700,000

    b.

Tax Year	Actual or Projected Taxable Income
2007	AMT $700,000
2008	Regular Tax $700,000

c.

Tax Year	Actual or Projected Taxable Income
2007	AMT $700,000
2008	AMT $700,000
2009	AMT $700,000
2010	AMT $700,000
2011	Regular Tax $700,000

24. Paris Corporation holds a $100,000 unrealized net capital gain. Should Paris accelerate the recognition of this gain, given a net capital loss carryforward in each of the following amounts? Paris is subject to a 14 percent cost of capital. Its marginal tax rate is 40 percent.
    a. $40,000
    b. $120,000
    c. Repeat parts a and b but assume that Paris is subject to a 6 percent cost of capital.

25. Maris Corporation put into service $100,000 of equipment that qualifies for its state's 10 percent research credit. To the extent that the credit is claimed, no cost recovery deductions are allowed. Maris is subject to a 14 percent cost of capital. If the credit were not claimed, the property would qualify for cost recovery deductions using a three-year life, straight line with no salvage value, and a half-year convention. The state's flat income tax rate is as follows.
    a. 2 percent
    b. 4 percent
    c. 8 percent

Chapter 12

Working with the IRS

LEARNING OBJECTIVES

- Understand the organizational structure of the Internal Revenue Service and administrative procedures relative to the audit and appeals process.

- Advise clients as to audit selection factors and probable litigation success.

- Develop decision guidelines as to audit etiquette, working through the appeals system, and constructing taxpayer defenses.

CHAPTER OUTLINE

We have discussed various aspects of tax practice throughout this text, including both the principles of tax research and the structure of the judicial decision-making process. In this chapter, we will examine in more detail the workings of the **Internal Revenue Service** (IRS) and the **Treasury Department,** with an eye toward an overview of the elections and other opportunities and pitfalls that face the practitioner in working with these administrative bodies.

After all, when the researcher has decided that his or her client should prevail with respect to a specified tax issue, a challenge to the IRS must be issued and implemented. In this chapter, we present some of the procedural aspects of this course of action.

ORGANIZATION OF THE INTERNAL REVENUE SERVICE

The Department of the Treasury is responsible for administering and enforcing the internal revenue laws of the United States. However, most revenue functions and authority have been delegated by the Secretary of the Treasury to the **Commissioner of Internal Revenue.** The commissioner is the chief executive officer of the Internal Revenue Service and is appointed by the President of the United States. The Commissioner holds the responsibility for overall planning and for directing, coordinating, and controlling the policies and programs of the IRS.

The Internal Revenue Service is one of about a dozen bureaus within the Department of the Treasury. It was established by Congress on July 1, 1862, to meet the fiscal needs of the Civil War. At that time, the name of the agency was the Bureau of Internal Revenue. In 1953 the name was changed to the Internal Revenue Service.

Since 1962 the agency has undergone a period of steady growth as the means for financing government operations shifted from the levying of import duties on outsiders to one of internal taxation on U.S. citizens and businesses. This expansion increased substantially after 1913 with the ratification of the Sixteenth Amendment, which authorized the modern income tax on noncorporate entities.

Until 1951 the agency was organized on a type-of-tax basis (i.e., with income, alcohol and tobacco, etc., divisions), with jurisdictionally separate departments that were responsible for administering these different revenue sources. Since 1952 the agency has undergone five major reorganizations, including one in 1998 aimed at reengineering the organization. The most important aspects of these structuring exercises have been the reorganization of the IRS along functional lines (i.e., into administration, operations, technical, planning, and inspection divisions), and the abandonment of the system of political appointments to positions other than that of the Commissioner and the Chief Counsel.

The latest restructuring effort was initiated as a response to perceived abuses by the agency. Recognizing that most Commissioners serve only a short tenure and that the Treasury Department carries myriad duties, Congress wants to use third parties to improve the chances for the development of consistent long-term IRS strategies and priorities. Private sector input is provided through the **IRS Oversight Board**, which functions as part of the Treasury Department. The Board has no authority to affect tax policy, to intervene in IRS personnel or procurement matters, or to affect the processing of individual tax cases. Its major duties include the following.[1]

- Review and approve IRS mission, strategic plans, and annual planning documents.
- Review IRS operational functions, including modernization, outsourcing, and training efforts.
- Recommend to the President candidates for Commissioner.
- Review the process of selecting, evaluating, and compensating senior IRS executives.
- Review and approve the IRS annual budget request.
- Ensure the proper treatment of taxpayers.

The Board is designed to function like a corporate board of directors. It is made up of six members of the private sector, appointed to five-year terms by the President, and of the Treasury Secretary, the IRS Commissioner, and a representative of IRS employees.

SPOTLIGHT ON TAXATION: Observation

The current IRS Commissioner has focused on the enforcement and compliance aspects of the agency's work, whereas the immediately prior executive was more market- and customer-oriented. It is a difficult balance to achieve in setting strategic and operational goals for the IRS. So many tax returns are filed that a customer-friendly approach seems right, however since "a little" cheating on returns is allowable under societal norms, a "get tough attitude" might be needed by the IRS.

IRS NATIONAL OFFICE

The IRS processes about 225 million tax returns every year, about 40 million of which are filed electronically. It collects almost $2 trillion in tax revenues and pays refunds to about 130 million taxpayers every year. Today, the IRS is an organization of about 100,000 employees. With the exception of the Department of Defense, it is the largest agency of the Federal government. It consists of a national office in Washington, D.C., and a large decentralized field organization. Its current mission statement is as follows, reflecting the more aggressive enforcement orientation that the agency now has implemented.

Provide America's taxpayers top quality service by helping them understand and meet their tax responsibilities and by applying the tax law with integrity and fairness to all.

1. § 7802.

Exhibit	12–1	IRS National Office

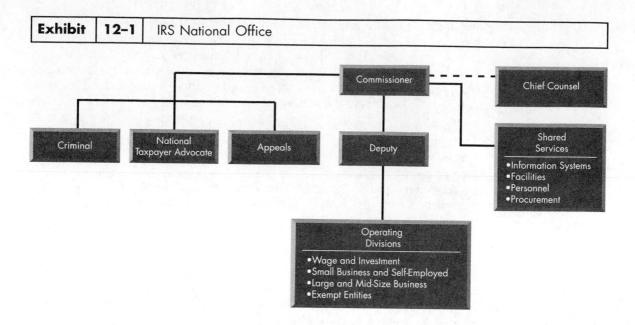

Guiding Principles

- Understand and solve problems from taxpayers' point of view.
- Enable IRS managers to be accountable to taxpayers.
- Use balanced measures of performance to measure taxpayer satisfaction; business results, and our employees' satisfaction.
- Foster open, honest communications.
- Insist on total integrity.

Exhibit 12–1 illustrates that the IRS is organized to facilitate both the processing of tax returns and the carrying out of its broader goals, using a "shared services" model like that used by most large businesses.

The IRS's national office is located in the District of Columbia. It is staffed by the office of the Commissioner of Internal Revenue, which includes a Deputy Commissioner and various chief officers and assistants to the Commissioner. The IRS Commissioner is appointed by the President to a renewable five-year term. He or she is the chief executive officer of the agency and is charged to administer, manage, conduct, direct, and supervise the execution of the Federal tax laws.[2] The Commissioner's nomination is reviewed by the Senate. He or she advises the President as to the person who should be named Chief Counsel. The Commissioner is the agency's final authority as to the interpretation of tax law.

The **Chief Counsel** is the agency's highest ranking legal adviser. He or she is appointed by the President and reports to the Commissioner, relative to the administration and enforcement of the tax laws. In effect, the Chief Counsel is the IRS's attorney. Rulings and other written determinations are prepared by the Chief Counsel's office.[3] The Chief Counsel represents the

2. § 7803(a).
3. § 7803(b).

agency in Tax Court cases and often assists in preparing proposed legislation, treaties, regulations, and executive orders. Associate Chief Counsels are assigned duties relative to litigation, technical matters, international transactions, and finance and management.

The **National Taxpayer Advocate** administers a taxpayer-intervention system, which is designed to resolve a wide range of tax administration problems that are not remedied through the agency's normal operating procedures or administrative channels.[4] The Advocate reports directly to the Commissioner and works through a system of local Taxpayer Advocates, one of which is located in each state.

The operating divisions of the IRS reflect the major types of tax return that the agency processes. Exhibit 12–2 provides estimates of the workload of each operating division.

Exhibit	12–2	IRS Operating Divisions

Tax Year 2000 estimates	Wage and Investment	Small Business and Self-Employed	Large and Mid-Size Businesses (Assets > $5 million)	Exempt Entities (Charities, Retirement Plans, Governments)
Type of return filed	1040 with only wage and investment income (no Schedules C, E, F, or Form 2106)	1040 Schedules C and F, Forms 1120, 1120S, and 1065	1040 Schedules C and F, Forms 1120, 1120S, and 1065	Form 990 and various payroll forms
Number of filers	90 million, 116 million taxpayers	45 million	210,000	3 million entities, 1.9 million pay tax
Annual income tax liabilities	$265 billion	$816 billion	$466 billion	$94 billion
Payroll taxes, withholdings paid	$38 billion	$562 billion	$712 billion	$198 billion
Notes	Fewer than half use a paid tax preparer Only 2% earn >$100,000 per year, 85% earn <$50,000, 28% earn <$10,000	Pay in over 40% of all cash received by the IRS 4–60 annual transactions with the IRS	Further organized into industry segments to handle complex filing requirements About 10% are audited every year, some deal with IRS agents year-round	Control about $7 trillion in assets

4. § 7803(c).

The IRS also takes on national-level projects in working with taxpayers. Some of the most important of these recent initiatives include the following.

- Document matching, allowing a lower audit rate because deficiencies or refunds are sent out when data listed on a tax return does not match that on a corresponding source document, like a Form 1099 or W-2.
- Electronic filing, again to reduce error rates and improve compliance with the filing requirements and to enact a modernization of the agency's data processing functions.
- Extending the reach of the Earned Income Credit to more of the targeted low-income employees.
- Educating cash- and tip-oriented workers to comply fully with their filing requirements.

IRS SERVICE CENTERS

The first **Internal Revenue Service Center** was established in 1955 in Kansas City on a pilot basis. Additional service centers were established during the 1960s to meet the processing needs of the various geographic regions of the country. A few were redeployed after 2000 to reflect the increase in electronic filing. Today, IRS service centers are located at

- Andover, MA
- Atlanta, GA
- Austin, TX
- Fresno, CA
- Kansas City, MO
- Memphis, TN
- Ogden, UT
- Philadelphia, PA

The primary function of the service centers is to process and perform mathematical verifications of the massive volume of Federal tax returns. **Computing Centers,** located in Detroit; Martinsburg, WV; and Memphis, manipulate data collected from tax returns at **Processing Centers** in Austin, Cincinnati, Kansas City, and Ogden. About twenty-five **Customer Service Sites** deal with telephone and electronic contacts from taxpayers, in working with electronic filing of returns, and in answering telephone and online taxpayer inquiries.

SPOTLIGHT ON TAXATION: Observation

More closings and downsizing of IRS processing facilities will be called for in the future, to better manage the agency's cost structure when electronic filing and deposits become the norm. Resisting these redeployments surely will be the personnel unions associated with IRS employees, attempting to slow down technology and protect their jobs, much as did those in print publishing before the document processing revolution was brought about by copy machines, faxes, and computers.

TAXPAYER ASSISTANCE ORDERS

The National Taxpayer Advocate can issue a **Taxpayer Assistance Order** (TAO) to suspend, delay, or stop actions where, in the determination of the Advocate, the taxpayer is suffering or about to suffer a significant hardship as a result of the manner in which the IRS is administering the revenue laws.[5]

"Hardships" refer to any circumstance that includes an immediate threat of adverse action for the taxpayer, his or her irreparable injury, a delay of more than 30 days in settling the taxpayer's account, or the incurring of significant costs (such as professional advisory fees) to handle the dispute.[6] The IRS action that is the subject of a TAO must be such that it would offend one's sense of fairness, given all the related facts.

Typically, the TAO requires remedial actions, such as a release from the IRS's levy of specific property or the cessation of a collection activity, or it gives the IRS a deadline for action. A TAO is binding on the IRS, short of its rescission by the Advocate, the Commissioner, or a Deputy Commissioner.

A taxpayer applies for a TAO by filing Form 911, Application for Taxpayer Assistance Order (Taxpayer's Application for Relief from Hardship), reproduced as Exhibit 12–3.

LOCAL TAXPAYER ADVOCATES

The IRS uses local Taxpayer Advocates in a system designed to help resolve taxpayer problems or complaints that are not being satisfied through regular agency channels. The primary objective of the Advocate system is to provide taxpayers with a representative within the IRS who has access to the pertinent regional, district, or service center official. In addition, the program enables the IRS to identify its own organizational, procedural, and systematic problems and to take corrective action as needed.

The system is not intended to circumvent the existing IRS channels of managerial authority, established administrative procedures, and formal avenues of appeal. Rather, it is designed to ensure that taxpayer problems or complaints that have not been resolved adequately through such normal procedures are referred and controlled within the program. When a case is referred to a member of the National Taxpayer Advocate team, he or she will ensure that the problem is not lost or overlooked, and that it will be resolved as promptly and efficiently as is possible. If a case cannot be resolved within five working days after receipt of the statement of the problem or complaint, the taxpayer will be contacted by telephone, advised of the status of the case, and given the name and telephone number of the IRS employee who is responsible for the resolution of the problem. Typically, the Advocate system is used to resolve billing, procedural, computer-generated, and other problems that taxpayers cannot correct after one or more contacts with the IRS office that is handling the matter.

5. § 7811.
6. § 7811(a)(2).

Exhibit	12–3	Application for Hardship Relief

OMB No. 1545-1504

Department of the Treasury – Internal Revenue Service

TAXPAYER ADVOCATE (SERVICE)

Application for Taxpayer Assistance Order (ATAO)

Form **911**
(Rev. 3-2000)

Section I.   **Taxpayer Information**

1. Name(s) as shown on tax return	4. Your Social Security Number	6. Tax Form(s)
	5. Social Security No. of Spouse	7. Tax Period(s)
2. Current mailing address (Number, Street & Apartment Number)	8. Employer Identification Number (if applicable)	
	9. E-Mail address	
3. City, Town or Post Office, State and ZIP Code	10. Fax number	
11. Person to contact	12. Daytime telephone number	13. Best time to call

14. Please describe the problem and the significant hardship it is creating. *(If more space is needed, attach additional sheets.)*

15. Please describe the relief you are requesting. *(If more space is needed, attach additional sheets.)*

I understand that Taxpayer Advocate employees may contact third parties in order to respond to this request and I authorize such contacts to be made. Further, by authorizing the Taxpayer Advocate Service to contact third parties, I understand that I will not receive notice, pursuant to section 7602(c) of the Internal Revenue Code, of third parties contacted in connection with this request.

16. Signature of taxpayer or corporate officer	17. Date	18. Signature of spouse	19. Date

Section II.   **Representative Information (if applicable)**

1. Name of Authorized Representative	3. Centralized Authorization File Number (CAF)
2. Mailing Address	4. Daytime telephone number
	5. Fax number
6. Signature of Representative	7. Date

Cat. No. 16965S

Form **911** (Rev. 3-2000)

Exhibit	**12-3**	Application for Hardship Relief—Concluded

Section III.   (For Internal Revenue Service only)

Taxpayer Name	Taxpayer Identification Number (TIN)

1. Name of Initiating Employee	2. Employee Telephone Number	3. Operating Division or Function	4. Office

5. How Identified & Received (Check the appropriate box)

IRS Function Identified Issue as Meeting TAS Criteria
☐ (r) Functional referral (Functional area identified TP/Rep issue as meeting TAS criteria)
☐ (x) Congressional correspondence/inquiry not addressed to TAS but referred for TAS handling

Taxpayer or Representative Requested TAS Assistance
☐ (c) Taxpayer or representative filed Form 911 or sent other correspondence to TAS
☐ (n) Taxpayer or representative called into a National Taxpayer Advocate (NTA) Toll-Free site
☐ (p) Taxpayer or representative called TAS (other than NTA Toll-Free)
☐ (s) Functional referral (Taxpayer or representative specifically requested TAS assistance)
☐ (w) Taxpayer or representative sought TAS assistance in a TAS walk-in area
☐ (y) Congressional corresp/inquiry addressed to TAS or any Congressional specifically requesting TAS assistance

6. IRS Received Date

7. TAS Criteria (Check the appropriate box)
☐ (1) Taxpayer is suffering or about to suffer a significant hardship
☐ (2) Taxpayer is facing an immediate threat of adverse action
☐ (3) Taxpayer will incur significant costs, including fees for professional representation, if relief is not granted
☐ (4) Taxpayer will suffer irreparable injury or long-term adverse impact if relief is not granted
☐ (5) Taxpayer experienced an IRS delay of more than 30 calendar days in resolving an account-related problem or inquiry
☐ (6) Taxpayer did not receive a response or resolution to their problem by the date promised
☐ (7) A system or procedure has either failed to operate as intended or failed to resolve a taxpayer problem or dispute with the IRS
☐ (8) Congressional Duplicate of any criteria or non-criteria case already in TAS or on TAMIS
☐ (9) Any issue/problem not meeting the above TAS criteria but kept in TAS for handling and resolution

8. Initiating Employee: What actions did you take to help resolve the problem?

9. Initiating Employee: State reason(s) why relief was not provided.

Section III Instructions (For Internal Revenue Service only)
1. Enter your name.
2. Enter your telephone number.
3. Enter your function (i.e.; ACS, Collection, Examination, Customer Service, etc.). If you are now part of one of the new Business Operating Divisions (Wage & Investment Income, Small Business/Self-Employed, Large/Mid-Size Business, Tax-Exempt/Govt Entity), enter the name of the division.
4. Enter the number/Organization Code for your office. (e.g.; 18 for AUSC, 95 for Los Angeles).
5. Check the appropriate box that best reflects how the taxpayer informed us of the problem. For example, did TP call or write an IRS function or TAS? Did TP specifically request TAS assistance/handling or did the function identify the issue as meeting TAS criteria?
6. The IRS Received Date is the date TP/Rep first informed the IRS of the problem. Enter the date the TP/Rep first called, walked in or wrote the IRS to seek assistance with getting the problem resolved.
7. Check the box that best describes the reason/justification for Taxpayer Advocate Service (TAS) assistance and handling.
8. Indicate the actions you took to help resolve taxpayer's problem.
9. State the reason(s) that prevented you from resolving taxpayer's problem and from providing relief. For example, levy proceeds cannot be returned since they were already applied to a valid liability; an overpayment cannot be refunded since the refund statute expired; or current law precludes a specific interest abatement.

Section IV.   (For Taxpayer Advocate Service only)

1. TAMIS CF#	2. BOD/Client	3. How Recd Code	4. Criteria Code	5. IRS Recd Date	6. TAS Recd Date
7. Reopen Ind	8. Func/Unit Assigned	9. Employee Assigned	10. Major Issue Code	11. ATAO Code/Subcode	12. PSD Code
13. Special Case Code	14. Complexity Code	15. Outreach	16. Local Use Code ☐TP _|_|_|_|_| ☐Case _|	17. Relief Date	18. TAS Clsd Date
19. Cust Satisfact Cde	20. Root Cause Code				

Hardship ☐ Yes ☐ No	Taxpayer Advocate Signature	Date

Cat. No. 16965S

Form **911** (Rev. 3-2000)

The National Taxpayer Advocate works through local team members who are responsible for the work that is conducted within his or her jurisdiction. Local advocates are independent from IRS examination, collection, and appeals functions. They are responsible only to the National Taxpayer Advocate.

TAXPAYER RIGHTS

Under three incarnations of the so-called *Taxpayer Bill of Rights*, taxpayers are guaranteed various rights to representation before the IRS, a recording of any proceedings, and an IRS explanation of its position relative to the pertinent disagreement. Specifically, the taxpayer has a right to know why the IRS is requesting information, exactly how the IRS will use the information it receives, and what might happen if the taxpayer does not submit the requested information. Accordingly, prior to an initial audit or collection interview, an IRS employee or officer must explain, orally or in written form, the pertinent aspects of the procedures to come.[7]

A taxpayer may be represented by an attorney, CPA, or other person who is permitted to represent a taxpayer before the IRS and who has obtained a properly executed power of attorney. Absent an administrative summons, a taxpayer cannot be required to accompany the representative to an interview.[8]

After meeting a ten-day notice requirement, the taxpayer is allowed to make a tape recording of the IRS interview, using the taxpayer's own equipment. Similarly, if the IRS intends to record an interview with a taxpayer or his or her representative, it must give a ten-day notice to the taxpayer. In addition, upon receiving a request from the taxpayer and a reimbursement for duplication costs, the IRS must make available to the taxpayer a transcript of the interview or a copy of its tape recording.[9]

To protect the rights of so-called innocent spouses on joint returns, the IRS must inform spouses of their joint and several liability for tax deficiencies, and both spouses must receive separately mailed notices as to audit, appeals, and Tax Court proceedings.[10] This may be especially important where the spouses have divorced or separated subsequent to filing the original joint return.

The Service must inform taxpayers of their rights to representation in carrying out a dispute with the agency. The taxpayer can suspend at any time an interview with IRS personnel so as to include a representative.[11]

With respect to noncriminal tax matters before the IRS or a Federal court, the common law privilege of confidentiality exists between a taxpayer and his or her tax practitioner, that is, one who is authorized to practice before the IRS. The privilege exists with respect to tax advice the practitioner has rendered. These provisions extend existing privilege protection previously

7. § 7521(b)(1).
8. § 7521(c).
9. § 7521(a); Notice 89-51, 1989-1 CB 691.
10. § 6103(e)(1)(B).
11. § 7521(b)(2).

only applicable between a taxpayer and his or her attorney. The privilege does not exist with respect to dealings with tax shelters. (See Chapter 5.)

THE AUDIT PROCESS

The U.S. Federal income tax system is based primarily on an assumption of self-assessment. All persons with taxable incomes that exceed a specific amount are required to prepare an accurate statement of annual income (i.e., an income tax return) and to remit in a timely fashion any amount of tax that is due. In a somewhat paternalistic sense, the IRS uses the examination of returns as an enforcement device to promote such voluntary compliance with the internal revenue laws. In a manner that is somewhat similar to the treatment by a parent of a child who is considering some forbidden behavior, the threat of an IRS audit encourages many taxpayers to report accurately their taxable incomes and to pay any tax liability that remains outstanding.

Because only a small number of tax returns can be audited each year, the IRS attempts to select for examination only those returns that will generate additional revenues for the Treasury. It primarily relies on sophisticated statistical models and computer technology to identify those returns that possess the greatest revenue return for the agency's investment of audit resources. However, in addition to this scientific selection process, a number of returns are manually selected for examination at an examiner's discretion.

PRELIMINARY REVIEW OF RETURNS

All business and individual tax returns are reviewed routinely by IRS personnel for simple and obvious errors, such as the omission of required signatures and Social Security numbers, at one of the service centers. After this initial (often computer-based) review, income tax returns are processed through the IRS Automatic Data Processing (ADP) program.

One of the most important functions performed by the ADP program is the matching of the information recorded on a return with corresponding data received from third parties, for example, from an employer on Form W-2. This procedure, which is referred to as the Information Document Matching Program (IDMP), has uncovered millions of cases of discrepancies between the amount, say, of income that recipients have reported on tax returns and corresponding deductions or other information that has been transmitted by payors. In addition, the IDMP provides the IRS with a means by which to detect taxpayers who fail to file any return at all. In the typical year, about five million taxpayers are sent such failure-to-file inquiries as a result of the matching program.

ADP is also used to conduct the Service's Mathematical/Clerical Error Program. This process is designed to uncover relatively simple and readily identifiable problems that can be resolved easily through the mail.

Mathematical/Clerical Error Program

The Mathematical/Clerical Error Program is one of a number of special programs that are conducted at the service centers. This program checks every return for mathematical errors, recomputes the tax due after properly applying the numbers that are included in the return, and summarily assesses any additional tax that is due or allows refunds or credits based on (previously) miscomputed deductions or credits. A summary assessment may be made concerning any deficiency that results from a mathematical or clerical error.[12] Consequently, the IRS need not send the taxpayer a formal notice of deficiency (i.e., a ninety-day letter, as discussed subsequently in this chapter) before the additional tax is assessed.

Almost 4 percent of all filed returns show an error of this type. When a mathematical or clerical error is identified by the service center, the IRS mails the taxpayer a corrected tax computation and requests that he or she pay the additional tax within ten days of the date of the notice, or twenty-one days if the tax underpayment is less than $100,000. If the deficiency is paid within this period, no interest is charged on the underpayment. However, if the deficiency is not paid in a timely fashion, interest is imposed on the unpaid amount for a period that begins on the date of the notice and demand and ends on the date of payment.

A taxpayer may not petition the U.S. Tax Court with respect to a deficiency that results from a mathematical or clerical error. However, other administrative procedures will allow the taxpayer to contest the summary assessment without first paying the tax.

The IRS must give an explanation of the asserted error to the taxpayer. After receiving this explanation, the taxpayer has sixty days within which to request that the additional tax be abated. If a request for abatement is made, the assessment will be canceled automatically. However, the return is then identified for further examination if the taxpayer cannot justify satisfactorily or substantiate the figures that were included on the original return.

When an error results in a taxpayer overpayment of the tax, the IRS usually sends a corrected computation of the tax, together with a brief explanation of the error and a refund of the excess amount that was paid.

The IRS does not consider such a contact that it makes with the taxpayer to be an examination. Therefore, a taxpayer who is contacted under the Mathematical/Clerical Error Program is not entitled to the administrative remedies that are available to taxpayers who are involved in a formal examination.

In addition to this testing of mathematical computations, the ADP program is useful for verifying one's compliance with estimated tax payment requirements. As a result of utilizing this system, the IRS has discovered that thousands of taxpayers have not been complying with the statutory estimated tax requirements, and that others collectively have been claiming millions of dollars in payments that actually never were made.

12. § 6213(b)(1).

Unallowable Items Program

The IRS conducts another program at each service center that is similar to the Mathematical/Clerical Error Program called the Unallowable Items Program. Under this program IRS personnel at each service center question items that have been included on individual income tax returns that appear to be unallowable by law. These items may be identified manually or on their face by computer, and include such return elements as an overstatement of the standard deduction, the claiming of an incorrect filing status, the deduction of Federal income taxes, or the deduction of lost (but not stolen) assets as a casualty loss.

If a return is identified as including an unallowable item, the IRS computes the seemingly necessary adjustment in taxes, and the taxpayer is notified by mail. Again, the IRS does not consider the contact that it makes with a taxpayer under the Unallowable Items Program to be an examination.[13] Consequently, it treats an adjustment in this circumstance as a correction of a mathematical or clerical error, and the taxpayer is not sent a formal notice of deficiency.

If the taxpayer is able to explain the questioned item adequately, the assessment is abated. However, the case will be continued as a correspondence or office audit if the taxpayer's response is deemed unsatisfactory.

SPOTLIGHT ON TAXATION: The Future

A new processing system, replacing the antiquated ADP system, is being phased in during the first decade of the 2000s. Because the IRS's appropriation for computer improvements is perpetually inadequate given the growth in the number of taxpayers and the sophistication of some of the transactions reported, though, most believe that this system will be obsolete before it is fully implemented.

SELECTION OF RETURNS FOR EXAMINATION

Each year the IRS determines the approximate number and types of returns that it intends to audit. The national office then prepares an audit plan to allocate its personnel to achieve the desired audit coverage. The primary goal of the IRS in selecting a return for examination is to review only those returns that will result in a satisfactory increase in the tax liability.

Computer and manual methods are used to select returns for examination. Computer programs select certain returns for examination, based on the potential that exists for changes in the tax treatment of certain items on the return. Generally, this is done through the use of mathematical models, including correlations and discriminant functions. IRS personnel also manually select returns

13. Rev. Proc. 94-68, 1994-2 CB 803.

that they believe warrant special attention. The Service describes in nontechnical terms its selection procedures in its annual Publication 1. Selection criteria for audits are not disclosed by the Treasury.[14]

Although most of the initial IRS screening of the returns for audit is performed by computers, a most detailed selection procedure is employed manually in the Examination Division of the local IRS office, where the classification staff ultimately selects those specific cases that will be examined. The number of returns that finally is selected by the staff is based on the examination resource (and other) capabilities of the respective offices.

Discriminant Function System

Once a return has been processed through the Service's ADP program, a magnetic tape that contains the information from each return, as prepared at the service center, is sent to the National Computer Center in Martinsburg, West Virginia. There, each return is rated by computer for its audit potential by means of a mathematical model, the **discriminant function formula** (DIF). This formula assigns numeric weights to certain (undisclosed by the IRS) return items, generating a composite score for the return. In this regard, the higher the DIF score, the greater the potential for a favorable-to-the-Treasury change to the return upon audit. Statistics provided by the Commissioner show a high correlation between DIF scores and such tax modifications, but the specifics of the formula are not disclosed.[15]

When the computer selects a return that has a high probability for an adjustment, as indicated by a high DIF score, an employee at the service center manually inspects the return to confirm its audit potential. If an acceptable explanation for the DIF score cannot be found after this manual examination of the return and its attachments, including explanatory data that the computer did not consider, the return is forwarded to the Examination Division at the appropriate local IRS office.

Taxpayer Compliance Measurement Program

The Taxpayer Compliance Measurement Program (TCMP) is a research program that is designed to furnish the IRS with statistics concerning the type and number of errors that are made on a representative sample of individual income tax returns. These statistics then are used to develop and update the DIF formulas. Under the TCMP procedures, perhaps 50,000 individual income tax returns are selected randomly for an extremely thorough examination, based on the ending digits of the taxpayer's Social Security number. These returns then are examined comprehensively to determine the degree of their accuracy as filed.

Unlike the treatment that is given returns that are selected for general audit, the TCMP examiner may not exercise any judgment in dealing with an item on the return selected for review. All errors are noted and corrected, regardless of their amount. This procedure is necessary to a determination of the

---

14. § 6103(b)(2); *Long v. U.S.*, 742 F2d 1173 (CA-9, 1984).
15. *Feltz v. IRS*, 79 AFTR2d 97-747 (DCWWis).

actual error patterns that individual income tax returns exhibit, so that the statistics that underlie the DIF procedure are free from any major bias. TCMP audits conducted between 2002 and 2004 updated underlying audit data that were almost a generation old.

Other Selection Methods

In addition to the previously discussed computerized methods for identification of returns for IRS examination, returns may be selected manually, for a variety of reasons. An examination may be initiated, for instance, because of information that is provided by an informant or because the selected return is linked to another return that is currently under examination, using the Coordinated Industry Case Program (e.g., a partner's return may be selected as a result of a partnership audit).

Moreover, some returns automatically are reviewed by IRS personnel because the reported taxable income, gross receipts, or total assets exceed a predetermined materiality amount. For instance, individual returns with total positive income of $50,000 or more, or partnership returns with gross receipts or gross income of $500,000 or more, can be selected in this manner. Finally, a return may be selected for examination because the taxpayer has filed a claim for refund or otherwise has indicated that an adjustment in the original amount of tax liability is necessary.

"Economic reality" factors can be considered by the IRS in selection of returns for audit, but only where the agency has some other evidence that the taxpayer has underreported taxable income for the year. For instance, manual selection of a return and an economic-reality review might occur when an IRS employee, reviewing data in three-filing-year periods, finds indications that income might be underreported or deductions might be overstated or misclassified. Some of the factors believed to be perused in an economic reality audit include the following.

- Significant increases in interest, dividend, and other investment income.
- Significant decreases in mortgage and other reportable interest paid.
- Significant variance in self-employment or farming income during the period, relative to industry norms.
- Business and other expenditures not seemingly justified by income levels.

Current IRS audit initiatives also include the following.

- Frivolous returns, usually involving tax protestors.
- Tax shelter investors and their advisers.
- Exempt organizations, looking for compliance with disclosure rules and for unrelated business taxable income.
- Large corporations.
- Specific issues related to market segments, often specialized in the local area, e.g., software companies on the West Coast.

Chances of Audit

Taxpayers often want to know what their overall probability of selection for an audit might be for a given year. In general, the IRS selects less than one percent of all returns for examination, outside of the mathematical error program. The chances for selection increase, though, if the taxpayer:

- claims tax shelter losses;
- operates a cash-oriented business, such as a restaurant (both as an owner, selling food and drink for cash, and as a waiter, collecting tips) or repair/construction trade;
- claims business deductions that are excessive for the income level;
- has had prior-year returns that were audited and found incorrect; or
- claims itemized deductions that are excessive for the income level.

Relative to the last point, one should not hesitate to claim all legitimate deductions, but it is useful to know what raises the IRS's "red flag" for itemized deduction amounts. The data in Exhibit 12–4 were current for calendar-year 2002 returns. They vary quite a bit from state to state, given differing income levels, types and deductibility of state and local taxes, and spending patterns.

| Exhibit | 12–4 | Average Itemized Deductions |

AGI ($000)	0–15	15–30	30–50	50–100	100–200	200+
Medical	$ 7,400	$ 5,890	$ 4,994	$ 5,672	$10,969	$28,305
Taxes	2,237	2,327	3,187	5,173	9,785	35,815
Contributions	1,423	1,890	2,006	2,530	3,875	17,354
Interest	7,043	6,453	6,850	8,364	11,825	21,998
Total	12,771	12,239	13,096	16,177	25,768	65,923
Percent Itemizing	5.1%	16.9%	39.6%	70.9%	91.5%	93.8%

Note also in Exhibit 12–4 the varying degrees to which taxpayers itemize deductions, approaching (but not attaining) 100 percent at upper income levels. Non-itemizers at upper income levels usually indicate the lack of a state income tax, a paid-up residence or rental arrangement, or the presence of comprehensive health insurance coverage.

The probabilities of selection for audit in a recent tax year were as shown in Exhibit 12–5.

EXAMINATIONS

After a return is selected for audit, an IRS agent schedules it for a review in either a correspondence, office interview, or field examination. The type of examination to which the taxpayer is subject generally is determined by the audit potential of the return, the nature of the asserted error, and the type of taxpayer.

Exhibit | 12–5

Various Audit
Statistics

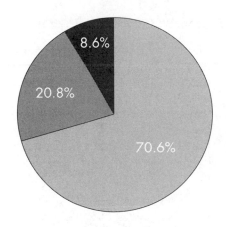

■ Correspondence Audit

■ Field Audit   ■ Office Audit

Individuals' returns filed	130,341,200	
Individuals' returns audited	728,003	0.56% of filed returns
Office audits	70,511	
Field audits	171,576	1.6% of Schedule Cs
Correspondence audits	581,662	1.1% of corporate returns

Chances of Audit

Individual's Total Positive Income ($000)	Nonbusiness Returns	With Schedule C
0–25	0.49%	2.44%
25–50	0.22	1.10
50–100	0.26	1.10
100+	1.49	1.34
S Corporation		0.40
Partnership		0.26
Gift Tax		0.5
Estate Tax, Gross Estate ($000,000)		
0–1		2.46
1–5		6.97
5+		25.02

Average proposed tax and penalty assessment, individuals' returns

Office audit	$ 4,591
Field audit	19,967
Compliance Center (math/clerical)	3,373

"No change" audit report

Office audit, individuals' return	24%
Field audit, individuals' return	20
Compliance Center correspondence	18
Office audit, corporate return	25
Field audit, corporate return	29

CORRESPONDENCE EXAMINATIONS

Many times, IRS personnel question only one or two items on a selected return. In these cases, an examination is typically conducted by telephone or mail. The IRS examiner will request that the taxpayer verify the questioned item of income, deduction, or credit by mailing copies of receipts, canceled checks, or other documentation to the district office or service center. If the taxpayer requests an interview, the issues become too complex, or the taxpayer is unable to communicate effectively in writing, the case is referred to the appropriate district office for resolution as an office or field examination.

Local office personnel usually conduct **correspondence examinations.** However, service center staff will conduct such a review if the questioned item is an itemized deduction on an individual taxpayer's income tax return.

A taxpayer who is subject to a correspondence examination is entitled to the same administrative and judicial appeal rights that are allowed to persons who are involved in office or field audits.

Issues that typically are addressed in the correspondence audit setting include itemized deductions for interest, taxes, charitable contributions, medical expenses, and simple miscellaneous deductions such as union dues.

OFFICE EXAMINATIONS

When a return that has been selected for examination involves one or more issues that will require some analysis and the exercise of the IRS personnel's judgment, rather than a mere verification of record-keeping requirements, the audit is usually conducted at the pertinent IRS office. An office interview also will be scheduled if the examiner believes that an office examination is necessary to guarantee that the taxpayer's legal rights will be respected.

If the IRS decides to conduct an office examination, the taxpayer is asked to come to the local IRS office for an interview and to bring any records and documents that will support the questioned items. Generally, the auditor is given very little time in which to prepare for the session, and the scope of the examination is limited to the items that are listed in the audit notification letter.

Office audits are usually confined to individuals' income tax returns that include no business income. However, in recent years, the IRS has increased the scope of some office audits to include a limited number of small business returns. Issues that typically are examined in an office audit setting include dependency exemptions; income from tips, rents, and royalties; income from partnerships, estates, and trusts; deductions for travel and entertainment; deductions for bad debts; and casualty and theft losses.

A field examination may be conducted in lieu of an office audit if it is difficult for the taxpayer to bring the requested records to the district office or if the taxpayer for some other valid reason requests that the audit be conducted on his or her premises.

FIELD EXAMINATIONS

Examinations that present complex issues that require more advanced knowledge of the internal revenue laws and accounting skills usually are conducted on the taxpayer's premises. A **field audit** is more comprehensive than a correspondence or office audit, and it usually is limited to an examination of corporation and individual business returns. In a field examination, the revenue agent reviews completely the entire financial operations of the taxpayer, including the business history of the taxpayer; the nature, amount, and location of taxpayer assets; the nature of the business operations; the extant accounting methods and system of internal control; and other financial attributes of the entity.

While an office audit ordinarily is limited to the items that are specified in the audit notification letter, a field examination may be open-ended. The agent is free to pursue any unusual items that are recorded in the tax return(s) or the records of the taxpayer (i.e., journals, ledgers, and worksheets) and to investigate other areas of which he or she may be suspicious.

The IRS prefers to conduct the field audit on the taxpayer's premises because the taxpayer's books and records may be more accessible and the agent will be better able to observe the taxpayer's business facilities and the scope of its operations. However, it is sometimes possible to have the audit conducted at the office of the taxpayer's representative instead. Only one such inspection of taxpayer books and records may be made for a tax year.[16] The Code includes a broad set of restrictions as to access to the taxpayer's physical office by the IRS.[17] Taxpayers refusing to admit IRS personnel are subject to a $500-per-refusal fine.[18]

The IRS uses a team approach in its field audits, known as the Coordinated Examination Program, when it examines the returns of large corporate taxpayers. During this type of examination, a large group of IRS agents will be used to investigate the operations of the taxpayer. Normally, such an investigation will span more than one IRS district as well.

DEALING WITH AN AUDITOR

Most practitioners develop over time a list of "dos and don'ts" in negotiating with a government auditor. In the very best case, one will have dealt with the same auditor many times and will have become familiar with the nuances of that particular auditor's mode of operation. Whether this is the case or not, the following guidelines, dictated as much by common courtesy and decorum as by ethics and hardcore negotiating techniques, are likely to be useful.[19]

• Do conduct yourself courteously and professionally, showing that you have prepared yourself for the audit.

16. § 7605(b).
17. § 7606.
18. § 7342.
19. Some of the material is adapted from a talk by Robert E. Dallman, "The Audit Process."

- Do review the strengths and weaknesses of your position before the agent arrives.
- Do cooperate with the auditor and promptly respond to all requests.
- Do establish internal timetables and responsibilities for completing the audit.
- Do provide the auditor with adequate work accommodations.
- Don't impede the audit process.
- Don't allow the auditor free access to and through the taxpayer's building.
- Don't let the agent browse through taxpayer information.
- Don't volunteer comments or information not requested by the agent.
- Don't attempt to bully or intimidate the auditor.
- Do assign one person to be the primary on-premises contact with the auditor—he or she cannot interview taxpayer employees on a random basis.
- Do verify the auditor's credentials before providing any information.
- Do request that all communications be in writing.
- Do keep track of time spent (by taxpayer, practitioner, and auditor) on the audit.
- Do meet at least daily with the auditor to review issues.
- Do agree to disagree on major irreconcilable issues.
- Do conduct a concluding conference to discuss audit recommendations.
- Do obtain copies of all government workpapers affecting the potential assessment.
- Do request clarification of the rest of the appeals process.

CONCLUSION OF EXAMINATION

Upon the conclusion of the examination, the IRS auditor or agent must explain to the taxpayer any proposed adjustments to the tax liability. A written **Revenue Agent's Report** (RAR) is prepared by the agent and is given to the taxpayer. The RAR contains a brief explanation of the proposed adjustments and lists the balance due or the overpayment.

The RAR also includes a waiver of the restrictions on assessment, which the taxpayer is asked to sign if he or she agrees with the proposed modifications. This waiver will permit the IRS to assess any deficiency in tax immediately, without sending the taxpayer a formal notice of deficiency.

Even though the taxpayer may agree with the proposed adjustments to his or her return and sign the form, thereby indicating acceptance of the proposal, the case technically is not closed until the agent's report is reviewed and accepted by the district office review staff. Therefore, it is possible that an agreement that is worked out with the agent may not be accepted by the IRS.

After the taxpayer agrees to any increase in tax, he or she may either make an advance payment of the deficiency and accrued interest, to eliminate additional interest charges, or wait for a formal request for payment from the service center.

If the taxpayer disagrees with the agent's proposals, the IRS will make an immediate attempt to resolve the disagreement. The taxpayer normally will be given an opportunity to discuss the proposed adjustments with the agent's group supervisor or with an appeals officer. If an immediate interview is not possible or if the issues remain unresolved after such an interview, the tax-payer will receive a preliminary notice of deficiency, which is also referred to as a "thirty-day letter."

THIRTY-DAY LETTER

When the taxpayer does not agree with the agent's proposed adjustments, a **thirty-day letter** is issued. This correspondence formally notifies the tax-payer of the examiner's findings, requests that the taxpayer agree to the proposed adjustments, and informs the taxpayer of his or her appeal rights. If the taxpayer does not respond to the notice within thirty days, he or she will receive a statutory notice of deficiency, also known as a "ninety-day letter," discussed later in this chapter.

The taxpayer has thirty days from the date of the thirty-day letter to request a conference with an appeals officer. This request may be made orally with respect to an office examination or if the total proposed additional tax and penalties total $2,500 or less. The taxpayer's appeal must be in written form if the total proposed additional tax and penalties exceed $2,500,[20] and a formal protest, setting forth the specific facts and applicable law or other authority in support of the taxpayer's position, is required if the proposed tax and penalties exceed $10,000.[21]

FILE A PROTEST OR GO STRAIGHT TO COURT?

In deciding whether to file a protest and request a hearing in the Appeals Office or to allow a ninety-day letter to be issued and skip directly to the courts for satisfaction, the taxpayer and his or her adviser must consider a number of factors.[22]

Factors in Favor of the Protest/Appeals Process

- An appeals officer can consider the hazards of litigation. This allows for the possibility of a settlement without the costs of litigation.
- The litigation path remains a possibility even if an appeal is pursued.
- The appeals process allows a further delay in the payment of the disputed tax. This can be an important criterion if (1) funds are not available with which to pay the tax, or (2) the taxpayer can earn more on the funds during the administrative period than is assessed in the form of interest.
- During the appeals process, the taxpayer will discover more of the elements of the government's position. In addition, the taxpayer will gain additional time in which to formulate or polish his or her own position.
- Recovery of some court costs and attorney fees is available if the court finds that the government's case was largely unjustified and all administrative remedies were attempted. Thus, working through the appeals process is required if any costs are to be recovered.

20. Reg. §§ 601.105(c)(2)(iii) and (d)(2)(iv).
21. Reg. §§ 601.105(d)(2) and 601.106(a)(1)(ii).
22. Saltzman, *IRS Practice and Procedure*, Warren, Gorham & Lamont; ¶ 9.05(1).

Factors in Favor of Bypassing Appeals

- The likelihood of the government finding and raising new issues during the appeal is eliminated.
- The government receives a psychological message that the taxpayer is firmly convinced of his or her position, and negotiating advantages for the taxpayer may result.
- The conclusion of the dispute, whether for or against the taxpayer, is expedited.

THE APPEALS PROCESS

To minimize the costs of litigation in both time and money, the IRS encourages the resolution of tax disputes through an administrative appeals process. If a case cannot be resolved at the examination level, the taxpayer is allowed to appeal to a separate division of the IRS, known as the **Appeals Office.**

The Appeals Office has the exclusive and final authority to settle cases that originate in a district that is located within its jurisdiction. This division is under the supervision of the Commissioner of the IRS, with input from the Chief Counsel. The appeals function provides the taxpayer with a final opportunity to resolve tax disputes with the IRS without incurring litigation. Its objective is to resolve tax controversies without litigation on a basis which is fair and impartial to both the government and the taxpayer.

APPEALS CONFERENCE

The conference with the appeals officer is an informal proceeding. Although the appeals office may require allegations to be submitted in the form of affidavits or declarations under the penalty of perjury, testimony typically is not taken under oath.[23] The taxpayer, or his or her representative, meets with the appeals officer and discusses the dispute informally. According to the IRS's conference and practice rules, the appeals officer is to maintain a standard of strict impartiality toward the taxpayer and the government.

The appeals officer has the authority to settle all factual and legal questions that are raised in the examiner's report. He or she also can settle a tax dispute on the basis of the hazards of litigation. However, no settlement can be made that is based on the nuisance value of the case to the government.

The appeals officer may use a considerable amount of personal judgment in deciding how to handle the disputed issues of a case. He or she can split or trade issues where substantial uncertainties exist as to the law or the facts. On the other hand, the appeals officer may defer action on, or refuse to settle, a case or an issue to achieve greater uniformity concerning the application of the revenue laws and to improve the overall voluntary compliance with the tax laws.

23. Reg. § 601.106(c).

NINETY-DAY LETTER

If the taxpayer and the IRS cannot agree on the proposed adjustments after an appeals conference, the regional director of appeals will issue a **statutory notice of deficiency.**[24] The statutory notice also is issued if the taxpayer does not request an appeals conference.

A statutory notice of deficiency, commonly referred to as a **ninety-day letter,** must be sent to the taxpayer's last known address by certified or registered mail before the IRS can assess the additional taxes that it believes are due.[25] Once a formal assessment has been made, the IRS is entitled to collect and retain the tax. However, a statutory notice is not required relative to deficiencies that result from mathematical errors or from the overstatement of taxes that were withheld or paid as estimated taxes.

After the statutory notice of deficiency is mailed, the taxpayer has 90 days (150 days if the letter is addressed to a taxpayer who is outside the United States) to file a petition with the U.S. Tax Court for a redetermination of the deficiency. If such a petition is not filed in a timely fashion, the deficiency is assessed and the taxpayer receives a notice and demand for payment of the tax.[26] Once this ninety-day period expires, the taxpayer cannot contest the assessment without first paying the tax, filing a claim for refund, and, if the claim is denied by the IRS, instituting a refund suit in a district court or the U.S. Court of Federal Claims.

Generally, no assessment or collection effort may be made during the ninety-day period, or, if a Tax Court petition is filed, until after the decision becomes final.

A mailing of the statutory notice to the taxpayer's last known address is sufficient to commence the running of the ninety-day period, unless the commissioner has been notified formally of a change of address.[27] The statute does not require that the taxpayer receive actual notice; therefore, a notice that is sent by certified or registered mail to the proper address is effective, even though it is never received by the taxpayer him- or herself.[28]

After a case has been scheduled (docketed) for review in the Tax Court, the taxpayer is invited to attend a pretrial settlement conference with an appeals officer and an IRS attorney. However, this conference typically is offered only if the case was not considered previously by the appeals office and if no related criminal prosecution is pending. If the taxpayer and the IRS agree to settle the dispute at this stage, they will enter into a written agreement stipulating the amount of any deficiency or overpayment. This stipulation is filed with the Tax Court, which will enter a decision in accordance with the agreement. The Tax Court can levy a penalty of up to $25,000 if it determines that

24. § 7522.
25. §§ 6212(a) and 6212(b)(1).
26. § 6213(c).
27. § 6212(b); *McIntosh v. U.S.*, 85 AFTR2d 98-6501 (SDOh).
28. § 6212(a); *Lifter*, 59 T.C. 818 (1973), and *U.S. v. Ahrens*, 530 F.2d 781 (CA-8, 1976).

| **Exhibit** | **12–6** | Income Tax Appeal Procedure |

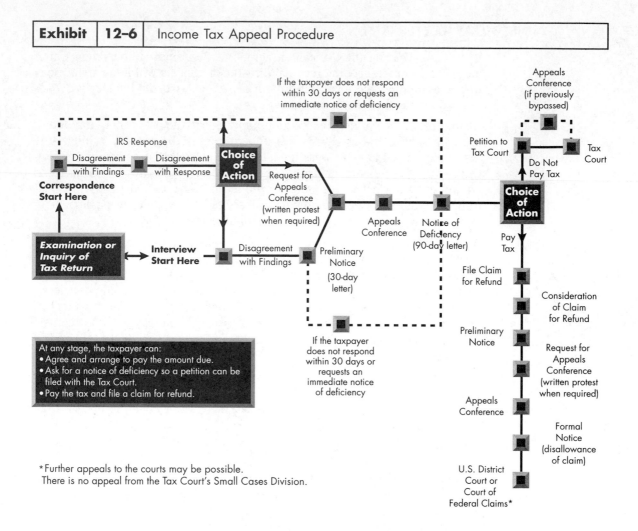

*Further appeals to the courts may be possible.
There is no appeal from the Tax Court's Small Cases Division.

the taxpayer did not pursue the available administrative remedies prior to approaching the court.[29]

Possibilities for appeal after completing the trial-level suit have been discussed in Chapters 2, 3, and 5. Exhibit 12–6 illustrates the appeals procedures, from the initial IRS examination to the hearing before the trial-level court. Exhibit 12–7 offers sample thirty- and ninety-day letters for the reader's perusal.

ENTERING THE JUDICIAL SYSTEM

If a taxpayer cannot resolve his or her dispute with the IRS administratively, he or she may seek judicial relief. As we have discussed throughout this text, the taxpayer can choose from among the U.S. Tax Court, the pertinent District

---

29. § 6673(a)(1)(c).

Exhibit	**12–7**	Sample Thirty- and Ninety-Day Letters

Notice of Adjustment—Thirty-Day Letter

Internal Revenue Service   Department of the Treasury
Date:
Social Security or Employee Identification Number:
Tax Year Ended:
Person to Contact:
Contact Telephone Number:
Contact Address:

Dear

Enclosed are two copies of our report explaining why we believe adjustments should be made in the amount of your tax. Please look this report over and let us know whether you agree with our findings.

If you accept our findings, please sign the consent to assessment and collection portion at the bottom of the report and mail one copy to this office within 30 days from the date of this letter. If additional tax is due, you may want to pay it now and limit the interest charge; otherwise, we will bill you. (See the enclosed Publication 5 for payment details.)

If you do not accept our findings, you have 30 days from the date of this letter to do one of the following:

1. Mail us any additional evidence or information you would like us to consider.
2. Request a discussion of our findings with the examiner who conducted the examination. At that time you may submit any additional evidence or information you would like us to consider. If you plan to come in for a discussion, please phone or write us in advance so that we can arrange a convenient time and place.
3. Discuss your position with the group manager or a senior examiner (designated by the group manager), if an examination has been held and you have been unable to reach an agreement with the examiner.

If you do not accept our findings and do not want to take any of the above actions, you may write us at the address shown above or call us at the telephone number shown above within 30 days from the date of this letter to request a conference with an Appeals Officer. You must provide all pertinent documentation and facts concerning disputed issues to the examiner before your case is forwarded to the Appeals Office. If your examination was conducted entirely by mail, we would appreciate your first discussing our findings with one of our examiners.

The Appeals Office is independent of the District Director. The Appeals Officer, who had not examined your return previously, will take a fresh look at your case. Most disputes considered by Appeals are resolved informally and promptly. By going to Appeals, you may avoid court costs (such as the United States Tax Court filing fee), clear up this matter sooner, and prevent interest from mounting. An Appeals Officer will promptly telephone you and, if necessary, arrange an appointment. If you decide to bypass Appeals and petition the Tax Court, your case will normally be assigned for settlement to an Appeals Office before the Tax Court hears the case.

Continued

| Exhibit | 12–7 | Sample Thirty- and Ninety-Day Letters—Continued |

Under *Internal Revenue Code* Section 6673, the Tax Court is authorized to award damages of up to $25,000 to the United States when a taxpayer unreasonably fails to pursue available administrative remedies. Damages could be awarded under this provision, for example, if the Court concludes that it was unreasonable for a taxpayer to bypass Appeals and then file a petition in the Tax Court. The Tax Court will make that determination based upon the facts and circumstances of each case. Generally, the Service will not ask the Court to award damages under this provision if you make a good faith effort to meet with Appeals and to settle your case before petitioning the Tax Court.

The enclosed Publication 5 explains your appeal rights.

If we do not hear from you within 30 days, we will have to process your case on the basis of the adjustments shown in the examination report. If you write us about your case, please write to the person whose name and address are shown in the heading of this letter and refer to the symbols in the upper right corner of the enclosed report. An envelope is enclosed for your convenience. Please include your telephone number, area code, and the most convenient time for us to call, in case we find it necessary to contact you for further information.

If you prefer, you may call the person at the telephone number shown in the heading of this letter. This person will be able to answer any questions you may have. Thank you for your cooperation.

Sincerely yours,
IRS Examinations

Enclosures:
Examination Report (2)
Publication 5
Envelope

Notice of Deficiency—Ninety-Day Letter

Internal Revenue Service Department of the Treasury
Date:
Social Security or Employer Identification Number:
Tax Year Ended and Deficiency:
Person to Contact:
Contact Telephone Number:

Dear

We have determined that there is a deficiency (increase) in your income tax as shown above. This letter is a NOTICE OF DEFICIENCY sent to you as required by law. The enclosed statement shows how we figured the deficiency.

If you want to contest this deficiency in court before making any payment, you have 90 days from the above mailing date of this letter (150 days if addressed to you outside of the

Exhibit	**12-7**	Sample Thirty- and Ninety-Day Letters—Concluded

United States) to file a petition with the United States Tax Court for a redetermination of the deficiency. To secure the petition form, write to United States Tax Court, 400 Second Street, NW, Washington, D.C. 20217. The completed petition form, together with a copy of this letter must be returned to the same address and received within 90 days from the above mailing date (150 days if addressed to you outside of the United States).

The time in which you must file a petition with the Court (90 or 150 days as the case may be) is fixed by law and the Court cannot consider your case if your petition is filed late. If this letter is addressed to both a husband and wife, and both want to petition the Tax Court, both must sign the petition or each must file a separate, signed petition.

If you dispute not more than $50,000 for any one tax year, a simplified procedure is provided by the Tax Court for small tax cases. You can get information about this procedure, as well as a petition form you can use, by writing to the Clerk of the United States Tax Court at 400 Second Street, NW, Washington, D.C. 20217. You should do this promptly if you intend to file a petition with the Tax Court.

You may represent yourself before the Tax Court, or you may be represented by anyone admitted to practice before the Court. If you decide not to file a petition with the Tax Court, we would appreciate it if you would sign and return the enclosed waiver form. This will permit us to assess the deficiency quickly and will limit the accumulation of interest. The enclosed envelope is for your convenience. If you decide not to sign and return the statement and you do not timely petition the Tax Court, the law requires us to assess and bill you for the deficiency after 90 days from the above mailing date of this letter (150 days if this letter is addressed to you outside the United States).

If you have questions about this letter, please write to the person whose name and address are shown on this letter. If you write, please attach this letter to help identify your account. Keep the copy for your records. Also, please include your telephone number and the most convenient time for us to call, so we can contact you if we need additional information.

If you prefer, you may call the IRS contact person at the telephone number shown above. If this number is outside your local calling area, there will be a long distance charge to you.

You may call the IRS telephone number listed in your local directory. An IRS employee there may be able to help you, but the contact person at the address shown on this letter is most familiar with your case.

Thank you for your cooperation.

Sincerely yours,

Commissioner

By

Enclosures:
Copy of this letter
Statement
Envelope

Court, and the U.S. Court of Federal Claims to initiate the lawsuit against the government.

The Tax Court will review the taxpayer's case, provided that he or she files a petition with the court within ninety days of the date of his or her statutory notice of deficiency. The District Courts and the Court of Federal Claims cannot hear the taxpayer's case unless he or she is suing for a refund. Consequently, the taxpayer first must pay the disputed tax, and then file an (unsuccessful) claim for refund to obtain a judicial review in either of these latter two forums.

SPOTLIGHT ON TAXATION: Deciding to Litigate

One should not consider tax litigation lightly. The additional costs to the taxpayer for attorney and accountant fees, in addition to filing and processing fees and the cost and time involved in gathering supporting documentation for the taxpayer's position, finding and coaching expert and other witnesses, and providing for one's own travel to the site of the hearing, make litigation a costly prospect. Given the right combination of facts and law, though, a suit might be the taxpayer's only chance to achieve an equitable solution.

Remember, nonetheless, that the IRS tends to litigate only cases that (1) it expects to win and (2) it expects will make good precedent to discourage other taxpayers. Moreover, because many taxpayers represent themselves before the Tax Court, procedural errors occur, usually to the detriment of the taxpayer. Thus, it is not surprising that the deck appears to be stacked against the taxpayer once he or she enters the judicial system, especially outside the Tax Court. The information in Exhibit 12–8 illustrates this situation.

| Exhibit | 12–8 | Taxpayer and Government Victories in Tax Litigation |

Forum	Percent of Partial Taxpayer Victories	Percent of Total Taxpayer Victories	Percent of Total Government Victories
U.S. Tax Court, Small Cases Division	49.0	5.0	46.0
U.S. Tax Court, all other	64.0	3.0	33.0
U.S. District Court	11.6	23.2	65.2
U.S. Court of Federal Claims	12.2	14.3	73.5

SUMMARY

In counseling clients, the tax professional must be aware of the organization and inner workings of the Internal Revenue Service. Strategic and tactical decisions as to how and when to appeal within the administrative system of the Service, assessing the strengths and weaknesses of the client's case, and determining available remedies can be made only with a thorough understanding of the agency and its operating style. Some of the most valuable advice that a client receives can be in the context of an audit selection letter or the handling of settlement alternatives thereafter.

TAX TUTOR

Reinforce the tax research information covered in this chapter by completing the online tutorials located at the Federal Tax Research web site:

http://raabe.swlearning.com

KEY WORDS

By the time you complete your work relative to this chapter, you should be comfortable discussing each of the following terms. If you need additional review of any of these items, return to the appropriate material in the chapter or consult the glossary to this text.

Appeals Office	IRS Oversight Board
Chief Counsel	National Taxpayer Advocate
Commissioner of Internal Revenue	Ninety-Day Letter
Computing Center	Office Audit
Correspondence Examination	Processing Center
Customer Service Site	Revenue Agent's Report
Discriminant Function Formula	Statutory Notice of Deficiency
Field Audit	Taxpayer Assistance Order
Internal Revenue Service	Thirty-Day Letter
Internal Revenue Service Center	Treasury Department

DISCUSSION QUESTIONS

1. Why must the tax professional be cognizant of how tax law administration works?
2. What are the major functions of the national office of the IRS?
3. What are the chief responsibilities of:
   a. The IRS Commissioner
   b. The IRS Chief Counsel
   c. The National Taxpayer Advocate
   d. Local Taxpayer Advocates
4. List three of the items included in one of the Taxpayer Bills of Rights.

5. Distinguish between the Math/Clerical Error program and the Unallowable Items program.

6. What are the chances of having a tax return audited this year?

7. What techniques other than the random selection of returns for audit does the IRS use in its enforcement function?

8. Why might it be desirable to settle with an agent, rather than to continue by appealing to a higher level within the IRS?

9. Relate some of the "audit etiquette" tactics that you have heard taxpayers or tax professionals discuss.

10. Which of the following methods is used to select tax returns for audit? More than one answer may be correct.
   a. DIF procedures
   b. Random samples
   c. Amount of gross income
   d. Type of income, for example, business or wages

11. Which type of audit is used most often to substantiate the reported items of income or deduction for individuals who have only wages?
   a. Field
   b. Office
   c. Correspondence
   d. Home

12. A revenue agent may do which of the following in an attempt to negotiate a settlement after the completion of an audit? More than one answer may be correct.
   a. Attempt to settle an unresolved issue based on the hazards of litigation.
   b. Settle a question of fact.
   c. Reach an agreement that will be accepted unconditionally by the IRS.
   d. Turn the case over to the Appeals Office.

13. When an agreement cannot be reached with a Revenue Agent, a letter is transmitted stating that the taxpayer has thirty days to do which of the following?
   a. File a suit in the U.S. Tax Court.
   b. Request an administrative appeal.
   c. Pay the tax.
   d. Find additional facts to support his or her position.

14. A statutory notice of deficiency gives the taxpayer ninety days to do which of the following?
   a. Pay the tax.
   b. Request an administrative appeal.
   c. File a suit in the U.S. Tax Court.
   d. File a protest.

15. Distinguish among the various means by which the IRS selects a tax return for examination. For this purpose, examine the criteria of:
   a. scope of review
   b. probability of selection
   c. preservation of taxpayer constitutional rights

16. Add two items to the "dos and don'ts" list included in the discussion of audit etiquette.

17. Suggest other information documents that the IRS computers could add to the IDMP.

18. Identify several items that you believe are included in the prevailing DIF model.

EXERCISES

19. Make a chart that distinguishes among the various types of examinations that the IRS conducts relative to individual income tax returns, namely, office, correspondence, field, and TCMP audits. For this purpose, examine the criteria of:
    a. scope of review
    b. type of documentation that typically is required of the taxpayer
    c. use of IRS personnel time and other resources
    d. opportunity for agent to use professional judgment in resolving issues

20. Respond to a client's comment: "We have a better than even chance of winning in the Tax Court, according to an article I read. Let's sue the government!"

21. With respect to the Small Cases Division of the U.S. Tax Court, which statement is true?
    a. The taxpayer (but not the IRS) can appeal a contrary judgment.
    b. The IRS (but not the taxpayer) can appeal a contrary judgment.
    c. Either the IRS or the taxpayer can appeal a contrary judgment.
    d. Neither the IRS nor the taxpayer can appeal a contrary judgment.

22. How should the tax professional advise a client whose charitable contributions are double that of the U.S. norm for his or her income level?

PROBLEMS

23. The President of the United States has hired you to assist in a trim-the-fat program with respect to the Federal government. He has asked you to recommend specific steps to downsize the bureaucracy of the IRS, from the national office through the district headquarters, by 15 percent. Draft a memo to the President summarizing your recommendations. Augment your memo with diagrams supporting your proposals.

24. The IRS has issued a summons for the tax file held by CPA Ann Whitman for her clients the Harberts. The file consists of paper and electronic spreadsheets in which Whitman detailed some tax computations using assumptions that the IRS would find to be "too aggressive." In addition, the file includes notes from meetings with the Harberts, income and balance sheet data as to their personal assets, and other technical correspondence, including e-mail messages. In a memo to the tax research file, summarize the current status of the law as to whether the privilege of confidentiality protects these documents from the government.

RESEARCH CASES

25. Your supervisor says that the U.S. Constitution forces the IRS to reveal the make-up of the DIF formula that it uses to select tax returns for audit. Prepare a file memo assessing the supervisor's assertion.

26. Max and Annie are roommates sharing an apartment. Although they know each other well, they have respect for each other's privacy. Thus, when Max's 2003 Form 1040 was audited by the IRS, he made no mention of the audit to Annie. When Annie was clearing the answering machine that they shared, she heard the following message: "Max, this is Richard, the IRS auditor. My figures show that you owe the government $10,000 in taxes and another $4,500 in penalties and interest."

    When Annie brought up the message during dinner conversation that night, Max was furious. How could the IRS be so careless as to broadcast this news to a stranger? Didn't he have any privacy and confidentiality rights? Max calls you to determine whether he might have a case against the IRS or Richard, the agent. Prepare a file memo assessing Max's position.

27. You have just rendered service for a taxpayer as an expert witness in a case heard by the U.S. Tax Court. The taxpayer is requesting reimbursement for your fees and for those amounts paid to her attorney in presenting the case. Your billing rate for this type of engagement is $200 per hour, the market rate for such services in your city, plus out-of-pocket expenses (e.g., auto mileage, computer charges). How much of your fee will the taxpayer recover?

28. Examine some tax journal articles and treatises to put together a checklist, "How to Prepare for a Tax Audit."

29. Examine some tax journal articles and treatises to put together a checklist, "How to Prepare for an Appeals Conference."

Chapter 13

Tax Practice and Administration: Sanctions, Agreements, and Disclosures

LEARNING OBJECTIVES

■ Identify various penalties that may be applied to tax practitioners who fail to perform as directed by the Internal Revenue Service, and related computations of interest charges.

■ Identify various penalties that may be applied to taxpayers whose returns reflect improper amounts, and related computations of interest charges.

■ Understand the application of the statutes of limitations, and taxpayer-government agreements that may be made with respect thereto.

CHAPTER OUTLINE

The adversarial nature of the Federal tax system has become apparent throughout this text, especially in Chapter 12. The revenue system is based on the notion of self-assessment, but the failure of the taxpayer to comply in detail with the requirements of the structure can lead to painful negotiations with the Internal Revenue Service and prolonged litigation.

Yet, the Treasury need not wait for a resolution of the disputed tax issues alone to collect revenues. Penalties and interest play an ever-increasing role in the makeup of the Federal tax system—in many cases, the accumulated penalties and interest assessed by the IRS equal 50 percent of the disputed tax or more.

Interest charges are made by the Treasury so that the taxpayer gains no advantage or disadvantage with respect to the time value of money in deciding how to handle a tax dispute—to the extent that interest rates are developed to parallel those of the rest of the financial market, both parties are indifferent as to cash flow issues, and the negotiations can center on the tax issues alone. In Chapter 11, we discussed the role of present values in assisting taxpayers to make these decisions in an economically prudent manner.

Penalties have become more prominent in the Federal tax system for several reasons. The tax professional must incorporate into the research model the penalty-based "costs" of being too aggressive in taking a tax return or litigation position, and convey the computations of those costs to the client.

- In an environment where nominal tax increases are politically unpopular, penalty increases can supplement revenues in a manner that is acceptable to the public.
- Politics aside, penalties increase the tax cost of negotiating with the Treasury and may discourage challenges to tax precedents that are not founded in sound tax law.
- Penalties can bolster the self-assessment process by discouraging taxpayers from behaviors that the Treasury wishes to repress, such as working with tax shelters and ignoring filing deadlines and requirements.
- As professional tax preparers and advisers play a more important role in the development of tax return positions, the behavior of such third parties also must be controlled, both in keeping a free flow of information between the government and the taxpayer and in interpreting the tax law in an objective manner.

We conclude this chapter with a review of alternatives and strategies available to taxpayers in making various compromises and other agreements with the IRS as a result of the examination process. In today's tax practice, the professional must have a full working knowledge of the details of the tax administration process, so as best to serve clients and the fisc.

TAXPAYER PENALTIES

To promote and enforce taxpayer compliance with the U.S. voluntary self-assessment system of taxation, Congress has enacted a comprehensive array of penalties. Tax penalties may involve both criminal and civil offenses.

Criminal tax penalties are imposed only after the usual criminal process, in which the taxpayer is entitled to the same constitutional guarantees that are given to nontax criminal defendants. Normally, a criminal penalty provides for imprisonment. Civil tax penalties are collected in the same manner as other taxes, and they usually only provide for monetary fines. Criminal and civil penalties are not mutually exclusive; therefore, a taxpayer may be liable under both types of sanctions.

CIVIL PENALTIES

The Code imposes two types of **civil penalties.** *Ad valorem penalties* are additions to tax that are based on a percentage of the delinquent tax. Unlike assessable penalties, ad valorem penalties are subject to the same deficiency procedures that apply to the underlying taxes. *Assessable penalties* typically are expressed as a flat dollar amount. Because of the lack of jurisdiction by the Tax Court or a specific statutory exemption, assessable penalties are not subject to review by the Tax Court. Note that the Code characterizes tax penalties as additions to tax; thus, they cannot subsequently be deducted by the taxpayer.

Civil penalties are imposed when the tax statutes are violated (1) without **reasonable cause,** (2) as the result of **negligence** or intentional disregard of pertinent rules, or (3) through a willful disobedience or outright **fraud.** The most important civil penalties include the following.

- Failure to file a tax return
- Failure to pay tax
- Failure to pay estimated income taxes
- Negligence, fraud, or substantial understatement of income tax
- Substantial understatement of the tax liability
- Failure to make deposits of taxes or overstatement of such deposits
- Giving false information with respect to withholding
- Filing a frivolous return

Failure to File a Tax Return

When a taxpayer fails to file a required tax return, a penalty is imposed unless it is shown that the failure is due to some reasonable cause and not to the taxpayer's willful neglect. The penalty is 5 percent of the amount of the tax, less any prior payments and credits, for each month (or fraction thereof) that the return is not filed. The maximum penalty that may be imposed is 25 percent (or five months' cumulative penalty).[1] A fraudulent failure to file is subject to a 15 percent monthly penalty, to a 75 percent maximum.[2]

If the taxpayer's failure to file is due to willful neglect, there is a minimum penalty for a failure to file an income tax return within sixty days of the due date, including extensions. This minimum penalty is the lesser of $100 or the full amount of taxes that are required to be shown on the return. The penalty

1. § 6651(a)(1).
2. § 6651(f).

does not apply if the failure is due to reasonable cause.[3] This penalty is applied in lieu of, rather than in addition to, some other penalty.

No statutory or administrative definition exists for the term "reasonable cause." However, some courts define it to include such action as would prompt an ordinary, intelligent person to act in the same manner as did the taxpayer, under similar circumstances. One of the most commonly encountered examples of reasonable cause is the reliance on the advice of competent tax counsel.[4] Other examples of reasonable cause that the *Internal Revenue Manual* describes include the following.

- A timely mailed return that is returned for insufficient postage.
- Death or serious illness of the taxpayer or his or her immediate family.
- Destruction of the taxpayer's residence, place of business, or records by fire or other casualty.
- Proper forms were not furnished by the IRS.
- Erroneous information was obtained from IRS personnel.
- A timely mailed return was sent to the wrong district.
- An unavoidable absence by the taxpayer.
- An unavoidable inability to obtain records necessary to compute the tax.
- Some other inability to obtain assistance from IRS personnel.

However, the penalty will not be excused for any of the following reasons.

- The taxpayer lacks the necessary funds with which to pay the tax.[5]
- The taxpayer was hospitalized and suffered from an illness that was not incapacitating.[6]
- Lost or destroyed records were not necessary to the completion of the return.[7]
- The taxpayer was incarcerated.[8]
- The taxpayer allegedly was ignorant of the laws.[9]

To avoid the penalty, the taxpayer must meet the burden of proof that the failure to file (or to pay) was due to reasonable cause. In these situations, the IRS's determination of the penalty is presumed to be correct.

SPOTLIGHT ON TAXATION: When Is a Return Filed?

To avoid the § 6651 penalty, a return must be "filed." Some taxpayers think that sending in a blank form, or neglecting to sign the return, is enough to avoid this penalty, but the tax law says otherwise. The taxpayer information must be included in a readable format, almost always on the correct IRS form, mailed by the due date, and signed by the

Continued

---

3. § 6651(a)(3).
4. See, for example, *Chamberlin*, TC Memo 2000-50.
5. *Langston*, 36 T.C.M. 1703 (1977).
6. *Hernandez*, 72 T.C. 1234 (1979).
7. *Long*, 37 T.C.M. 733 (1978).
8. *Jones*, 55 T.C.M. 1556 (1988).
9. *Lammerts Estate v. Comm.*, 456 F.2d 681 (CA-2, 1972).

appropriate parties. There must be enough information on the return so as to compute the correct amount of tax; thus, leaving lines or check-boxes empty will void the filing and the penalty will be assessed.

In the future, electronic filing requirements likely will be imposed, both to speed up the system, and to eliminate the possibility of errors, as the IRS software will not accept an incomplete or frivolous return. This is also a way to verify tax identification numbers, so as immediately to identify those with other delinquent accounts, or with inadequate filing credentials.

Failure to Pay Tax

If a taxpayer fails to pay either a tax that is shown on his or her return or an assessed deficiency within ten days of an IRS notice and demand, a penalty is imposed. The ten-day period becomes twenty-one days when the tax due is less than $100,000. The penalty is 0.5 percent of the required liability, after adjusting for any prior payments and credits, for each month (or fraction thereof) that the tax is not paid—but it increases to 1 percent of the under-paid tax per month after notice from the IRS.[10] The maximum penalty that may be imposed is 25 percent of the outstanding tax. This penalty does not apply if the failure to pay is attributable to a reasonable cause, or to the failure to pay an estimated tax for which there is a different penalty.

For this purpose, reasonable cause is defined in a manner that is identical to that discussed in conjunction with the failure-to-file penalty, except that, if an individual is granted an automatic filing extension, reasonable cause is presumed to exist, provided that the balance due does not exceed 10 percent of the total tax.[11]

The failure-to-file penalty is reduced by the 0.5 percent failure-to-pay penalty for any month in which both apply. Thus, no more than a 5 percent total (nonfraud) penalty typically can be assessed against a taxpayer for any month. Nonetheless, after rendering sufficient notice to the taxpayer, the IRS can assess both the failure-to-pay and the failure-to-file penalties.

A taxpayer can avoid the failure-to-file penalty if an extension of the return's due date is granted by the IRS. However, with the two exceptions that we just discussed, the failure-to-pay penalty is imposed when the total amount of the tax is not paid by the unextended due date of the return.

Example 13-1 John Gray, a calendar-year taxpayer, filed his 2005 income tax return on October 10, 2006, paying an amount due of $1,000. On April 1, 2006, John had obtained a four-month extension of time in which to file his return. However, he could not assert a reasonable cause for failing to file the return by August 15, 2006 (the extended due date), nor did he show any

---

10. § 6651(a)(2). The monthly penalty rate is cut in half for taxpayers paying delinquent taxes under an installment agreement. § 6651(h).
11. § 6654(d)(1)(B)(i).

reasonable cause for failing to pay the tax that was due on April 15, 2006. Gray's failure to file was not fraudulent. As a result, Gray is subject to a $35 failure-to-pay penalty and a $135 failure-to-file penalty, determined as follows.

Failure to pay

Underpayment	$1,000
Penalty percentage	× .005
Penalty per month outstanding	$ 5
Months (or fractions thereof) for which required payment was not made	× 7
Failure-to-pay penalty	$ 35

Failure to file

Underpayment	$1,000
Penalty percentage	× .05
Penalty per month outstanding (before reduction)	$ 50
Months (or fractions thereof) for which return was not filed	× 3
Unreduced penalty	$ 150
Less: concomitant failure-to-pay penalty (i.e., for August–October) [3 months × (.005 × $1,000)]	− 15
Failure-to-file penalty	$ 135

Accuracy-Related Penalty

Major penalties relating to the accuracy of the return data, including the existing negligence penalty and the penalty for substantial understatement of income tax liability, are combined in a single Code section. This consolidation of related penalties into a single levy eliminates the possibility of the stacking of multiple penalties when more than one type of penalty applies to a single understatement of tax.

The **accuracy-related penalty** amounts to 20 percent of the portion of the tax underpayment that is attributable to one or more of the following.

- Negligence or disregard of applicable Federal tax rules and Regulations
- Substantial understatement of income tax
- Substantial valuation overstatement
- Substantial overstatement of pension liabilities
- Substantial understatement of estate and gift tax valuation

The penalty applies only where the taxpayer fails to show either a reasonable cause for the underpayment or a good-faith effort to comply with the tax law.[12] When the accuracy-related penalty applies, interest on the penalty accrues from the due date of the return, rather than merely from the date on which the penalty was imposed.

Occasionally, a valuation overstatement penalty is encountered. This 20 percent penalty applies when an asset value has been overstated on a return, for example, to substantiate a charitable contribution deduction. It is assessed when the valuation used is 200 percent or more of the actual value, resulting in an underpayment of over $5,000 ($10,000 for C corporations).

12. § 6662.

Similarly, a 20 percent transfer valuation understatement penalty is assessed where the claimed value is 50 percent or less than the asset's actual value, resulting in an underpayment of over $5,000. The rate of both penalties is 40 percent if a gross valuation misstatement is made, that is, the income tax valuation was at least 400 percent of actual value, or the transfer tax value was 25 percent or less of actual.[13]

The practitioner is likely to encounter two of the elements of this penalty most frequently: (1) negligence or disregard of rules and (2) substantial understatement of tax. In the first penalty, "negligence" includes any failure to make a reasonable attempt to comply with the provisions of the Code.[14] This might occur when the taxpayer fails to report gross income, overstates deductions, or fails to keep adequate records with which to comply with the law. "Disregard" includes any careless, reckless, or intentional disregard of the elements of the tax law.

The negligence component of the penalty is waived where the taxpayer has made a good-faith attempt to comply with the law, as indicated by a full disclosure of the nonfrivolous position that may be contrary to that of the IRS. Such disclosure is made by completing Form 8275, reproduced as Exhibit 13–1, and attaching it to the return. If the return position is contrary to the language of a Regulation, Form 8275-R is used.

The second commonly encountered penalty, substantial understatement of income tax, occurs if the determined understatement exceeds the greater of (1) 10 percent of the proper tax liability or (2) $5,000 ($10,000 for a corporation other than an S corporation or a personal holding company).[15] The amount that is subject to this penalty is reduced if the taxpayer either has substantial authority for the position that was taken in the return, or makes a full disclosure of the position taken in the return, on Form 8275 or 8275-R.[16] More specifically, the taxpayer is not subject to this penalty where there is **substantial authority** for his or her position that supports a one-in-three likelihood of defeating contrary positions.[17]

For this purpose, "substantial authority" includes the Code, Regulations (proposed and temporary), court decisions, administrative pronouncements, tax treaties, IRS information and press releases, IRS Notices and Announcements, Letter Rulings, Technical Advice Memoranda, General Counsel Memoranda, Committee Reports, and "Blue Book" explanations of tax legislation.[18] Substantial authority does not include conclusions reached in tax treatises, legal periodicals, and opinions rendered by tax professionals.[19]

Clearly, greater weight will be placed on the Code and temporary Regulations than will be assigned to Letter Rulings and IRS Notices, but the derivation

---

13. § 6662 (e) through (h).
14. § 6662(c).
15. § 6662(d)(1).
16. § 6662(d)(2)(B). Tax shelters cannot use this provision.
17. § 6662(d)(2)(B).
18. Reg. § 1.6662-4(d)(iii).
19. Notice 90-20, 1990-1 CB 328.

| Exhibit | 13–1 | Disclosure Statement |

Form 8275
(Rev. May 2001)

Department of the Treasury
Internal Revenue Service

Disclosure Statement

Do not use this form to disclose items or positions that are contrary to Treasury regulations. Instead, use Form 8275-R, Regulation Disclosure Statement. See separate instructions.

▶ Attach to your tax return.

OMB No. 1545-0889

Attachment
Sequence No. **92**

Name(s) shown on return

Identifying number shown on return

Part I   General Information (see instructions)

(a) Rev. Rul., Rev. Proc., etc.	(b) Item or Group of Items	(c) Detailed Description of Items	(d) Form or Schedule	(e) Line No.	(f) Amount
1					
2					
3					

Part II   Detailed Explanation (see instructions)

1

2

3

Part III   Information About Pass-Through Entity. To be completed by partners, shareholders, beneficiaries, or residual interest holders.

Complete this part only if you are making adequate disclosure for a pass-through item.

Note: *A pass-through entity is a partnership, S corporation, estate, trust, regulated investment company (RIC), real estate investment trust (REIT), or real estate mortgage investment conduit (REMIC).*

1 Name, address, and ZIP code of pass-through entity	2 Identifying number of pass-through entity
	3 Tax year of pass-through entity / / to / /
	4 Internal Revenue Service Center where the pass-through entity filed its return

For Paperwork Reduction Act Notice, see separate instructions.   Cat. No. 61935M   Form **8275** (Rev. 5-2001) of a weighted average among all of the competing positions with respect to a given tax question is not likely to be easily obtained.

Civil Fraud

If any part of an underpayment of tax is attributable to fraud, a substantial civil penalty is imposed. In addition, the taxpayer may be liable for a criminal penalty, which we will discuss later in this chapter. The civil fraud penalty is 75 percent of the underpayment that is attributable to the fraud.[20]

The burden of proof in a fraud case is on the IRS—it must show a fraudulent intent for the underpayment. This usually entails more than mere negligence, but a plan to defraud the government, often including a series of actions over time to evade the tax.

SPOTLIGHT ON TAXATION: Proving Fraud

The courts factor in the education and experience of the taxpayer in determining whether fraud has occurred. Is the taxpayer "smart" enough, say in terms of business and accounting training, to construct a plan to defraud, and then to carry it out? In cases of a complicated tax law or tax-reduction device, the taxpayer might successfully plead ignorance and avoid the fraud charge.

Under an all-or-nothing rule, if the IRS establishes that any portion of an underpayment is attributable to fraud, the entire underpayment is treated as attributable to fraud, and the penalty applies to the entire amount due. If any part of an underpayment is attributable to fraud, only the fraud penalty may be imposed with respect to that amount.[21] Neither the failure-to-file nor the failure-to-pay penalty, nor the civil accuracy-related penalty, is assessed in these circumstances. However, the penalty for underpayment of estimated tax (discussed here) may still be assessed, and interest is assessed from the (extended) due date of the return.

Fraud is not defined in either the Code or the Regulations. One long-standing judicial definition of fraud describes it as ". . . actual, intentional wrong-doing . . . the intent required is the specific purpose to evade a tax believed to be owing."[22] This definition has been expanded to include acts that are done without a "bad or evil purpose." In *U.S. v. Pomponio,* the Supreme Court held that "willfulness," which is a crucial element of fraud, is present when the taxpayer's actions constitute ". . . a voluntary, intentional violation of a known legal duty."[23] Consequently, the taxpayer's deceptive or

20. §§ 6663(a) and (b).
21. § 6663(b).
22. *Mitchell v. Comm.,* 118 F.2d 308, 310 (CA-5, 1941).
23. 97 429 U.S. 10, S.Ct. 22 (1976).

misleading conduct distinguishes fraud from mere negligence, or from other actions that are taken to avoid taxation, and not the presence of some (inherent or documented) evil purpose.

If a taxpayer is convicted of criminal fraud, he or she cannot contest a civil fraud determination. However, a charge that the taxpayer is guilty of criminal fraud may be contested when a civil fraud determination has been upheld. In a criminal fraud case, the IRS must prove "beyond a shadow of any reasonable doubt" that the taxpayer's actions were fraudulent. In a civil fraud case, there must be "clear and convincing evidence" that the taxpayer committed fraud.

Ordinarily, the evidence that indicates that a taxpayer's conduct was fraudulent is circumstantial. Thus, the court must infer the taxpayer's state of mind from the evidence. Examples of fraud include the following.

- Keeping two sets of books, one in English and one in Japanese.[24]
- Making false accounting entries.[25]
- Destroying books or records.[26]
- Concealing assets or sources of income.[27]
- Consistently understating income or overstating deductions.[28]
- Purposely avoiding the making of business records and receipts.[29]

Failure to Make Estimated Payments

A penalty is imposed on both individuals and corporations who fail to pay quarterly estimated income taxes. This penalty is based on the amount and duration of the underpayment, and the rate of interest that currently is established by the Code. This rate, for instance, was 4 percent late in 2004. Unlike the similar interest computation, however, this penalty is computed without any daily compounding and is not deductible.

The penalty is calculated separately for each quarterly installment. Each penalty period begins on the date on which the installment was required, and it runs through the earlier of either the date that the amount is paid or the due date for filing the return. Any overpayment is first applied to prior underpayments and the excess is credited to later installments.[30] In this regard, the taxpayer must balance cash flow concerns with the payment requirements of the Code.

Example 13-2 The taxpayer is required to have $100 paid in as estimates for the year. Payment schedule A would likely incur an underpayment penalty, while schedule B would not.

24. *Noro v. U.S.*, 148 F.2d 696 (CA-5, 1945).
25. *U.S. v. Lange*, 161 F.2d 699 (CA-7, 1947).
26. *U.S. v. Ragen*, 314 U.S. 513, 62 S.Ct. 374 (1942).
27. *Gendelman v. U.S.*, 191 F.2d 993 (CA-9, 1952).
28. *Holland v. U.S.*, 348 U.S. 121, 75 S.Ct. 127 (1954) and *Ragen*, op.cit.
29. *Garispy v. U.S.*, 220 F.2d 252 (CA-6, 1955).
30. §§ 6654(b) and 6655(b).

Quarter	Schedule A	Schedule B
1	$ 10	$ 40
2	40	10
3	10	40
4	40	10
Total	$100	$100

Individuals

An individual's underpayment of estimated tax is computed as the difference between the amounts that were paid by the quarterly due dates, and the least of (1) 90 percent of the tax that is shown on the current year's return; (2) 100 percent of the prior year's tax; and (3) 90 percent of the tax that would be figured by annualizing the income that was earned during the year, up to the month in which the quarterly payment is due.[31] For this purpose, unless the taxpayer can prove otherwise, taxes that are withheld are considered to have been remitted to the IRS in equal quarterly installments.[32]

The underpayment penalty will not apply if less than $1,000 in underwithheld tax is due, or if the total payments that are made by the applicable installment date are equal to an amount that would have been required on that date if the estimated tax (1) was based on the tax that is shown on the previous year's return (i.e., using 100 or 110 percent), or (2) equaled 90 percent of the tax, computed on the basis of the annualized income for the period that ends on the installment date. In addition, an individual can avoid the estimated tax underpayment penalty if (1) the preceding taxable year included 12 months, (2) the individual did not have any tax liability for the preceding year, and (3) he or she was a citizen or resident of the United States throughout the preceding taxable year.[33]

The IRS can waive the estimated tax underpayment penalty (but not the penalty that is based on the outstanding interest attributable thereto) (1) if the failure to make the payment was due to a casualty, disaster, or other unusual circumstance where it would be inequitable to impose the penalty, or (2) if the failure was due to reasonable cause rather than willful neglect during the first two years after the taxpayer retires after reaching age 62, or becomes disabled.[34] The fourth installment penalty is waived if the corresponding tax return is filed with full tax payment by the end of the first month after the tax year-end (January 31 for calendar-year taxpayers).

Corporations

An underpayment on the part of a corporation is defined as the difference between the amount of the installment that would be required to be paid if

31. § 6654(d). The rule is 110 percent of the prior-year tax if that year's AGI > $150,000.
32. § 6654(g).
33. §§ 6654(e)(1) and (2).
34. § 6654(e)(3).

the estimated tax was equal to 100 percent of the tax that is shown on the return (or, if no return was filed, 100 percent of the actual tax that is due), and the amount that was actually paid on or before the prescribed payment date.[35]

The underpayment penalty will not apply if less than $1,000 in tax is due, or if the total payments that are made by the applicable installment date are equal to the least of:

1. 100 percent of the nonzero amount of tax that is shown on the corporation's tax return for the preceding year, provided that the preceding year contained twelve months;

2. 100 percent of the current-year tax liability; or

3. 100 percent of the tax that is due using a seasonal installment method, or annualizing the current year's income received for (a) the first two or three months, relative to the installment that is due in the fourth month of the tax year, (b) the first three, four, or five months, for the installment that is due in the sixth month, (c) the first six, seven, or eight months, for the installment that is due in the ninth month, or (d) the first nine, ten, or eleven months, for the installment that is due in the twelfth month as elected.[36]

Exception 1 does not apply to a "large corporation," that is, one that had a taxable income of $1 million or more in any of its three immediately preceding taxable years. To avoid an underpayment penalty, a large corporation must remit quarterly estimated tax payments that are equal to its current year's tax liability, or it must meet Exception 3, as discussed.[37]

Failure to Make Deposits of Taxes or Overstatements of Deposits

The Code requires employers to collect and withhold income and Social Security taxes from their employees. Amounts that are withheld are considered to be held in a special trust fund for the United States, and they must be deposited in a government depository on or before certain dates prescribed by the statute and Regulations. An employer who does not have either the inclination or sufficient funds with which to meet its deposit obligations may be tempted to postpone the making of these deposits, that is, to "borrow" from the government the cash provided by employees. Consequently, the Code imposes heavy civil and criminal penalties on those who are responsible for the failure to make a timely deposit of the withheld funds.[38] A responsible party may be an officer or board member of a corporation rather than the corporation itself, even for charities and other exempt entities.

If an employer fails to deposit on a timely basis taxes that were withheld from employees, a penalty equal to a percentage of the underpayment is imposed. This rate varies from 2 to 15 percent, depending on when the failure

---

35. § 6655(b)(1).
36. §§ 6655(d), (e), and (f).
37. §§ 6654(d)(2) and (g)(2). The prior-year exception can be used in making the first-quarter installment, however. § 6654(d)(2)(B).
38. § 6656.

is corrected.[39] The penalty may be avoided where the taxpayer can show that his or her actions were due to reasonable cause and not to willful neglect.

If any person who is required to collect, truthfully account for, and remit employment taxes willfully fails to do so, a penalty equal to 100 percent of the tax is imposed.[40] Therefore, when a corporate employer does not pay to the government employment taxes that it withheld from an employee, the IRS effectively may collect the tax from those who are responsible for the corporate actions, such as the corporate directors, president, or treasurer.[41]

In addition to the civil penalties that have been discussed, criminal penalties may be imposed in an aggravated case of nonpayment.

Giving False Information with Respect to Withholding

All employees are required to give their employer a completed Form W-4, Employee Withholding Allowance Certificate. This form notifies the employer of the number of withholding exemptions that the employee is entitled to claim. The employer then calculates the amount of tax that must be withheld from each employee. A civil penalty of $500 is imposed on any person who gives to his or her employer false information with respect to withholding status or the number of exemptions to which he or she is entitled. This penalty is not imposed where there was a reasonable basis for the taxpayer's statement. Moreover, the IRS may waive all or a part of the penalty if the actual income taxes that are imposed are not greater than the sum of the allowable credits and estimated tax payments.[42]

The Regulations require that employers who receive a Form W-4 from an employee, on which he or she claims more than ten exemptions, must submit a copy of the form to the IRS.[43]

Filing a Frivolous Return

A separate $500 civil penalty is assessed when the taxpayer is found to have filed a frivolous return.[44] Returns of this sort have been used to assert that the taxpayer's Fifth Amendment rights are violated by tax return disclosures,[45] that the taxpayer objects to the use of his or her tax receipts for defense or other uses,[46] that the government can collect taxes only in gold-based coins and certificates (which no longer circulate freely in the United States), or some other argument. Specifically, the penalty applies when the return:

- does not contain information by which to judge the completeness of the taxpayer's self-assessment (e.g., if the return is blank);

39. § 6656(b)(1).
40. § 6672(a).
41. § 7809(a).
42. § 6682.
43. Reg. § 31.3402(f)(2)-1(g).
44. § 6702.
45. *Welch v. U.S.,* 750 F.2d 1101 (CA-1, 1985).
46. *Fuller v. U.S.,* 786 F.2d 1437 (CA-9, 1986).

- contains information or statements that on their face indicate that the self-assessment requirement has not been met (e.g., a "tax protestor" statement is attached); or
- otherwise takes positions that are frivolous or are meant to impede the administration of the tax law, for example, it takes a return position contrary to a decision of the U.S. Supreme Court, or it is not presented in a readable format.

SPOTLIGHT ON TAXATION: Frivolous Returns

The $500 penalty will not be assessed in the course of a typical dispute over the amount of tax due, e.g., on an audit where both sides have defensible positions concerning the law. The penalty also is not applied in the case of a mathematical/clerical error. But the penalty applies to the taxpayer *and* the tax preparer, and it relates to the original return as filed, i.e., the penalty is not waived if the taxpayer "fixes" the problem by filing an amended return.

The frivolous return penalty applies even if the taxpayer legitimately owes a zero tax, and if the taxpayer was not required to file a return (e.g., due to low taxable income) but did so anyway.

Other Civil Penalties

A variety of other civil penalties may be imposed on taxpayers who fail to comply with the Code. Most of these penalties involve a specialized area of the tax law and ordinarily are not encountered by taxpayers. Consequently, one should be aware of the existence of such sanctions and refer to the Code and Regulations when working in such a specialized field to identify the events that might trigger such penalties.

Reliance on Written Advice of the IRS

The Secretary of the Treasury must abate any civil penalty or addition to tax that is attributable to the taxpayer's reliance on erroneous written advice furnished by an IRS officer or employee. This abatement is available only with respect to advice given in response to a specific request by the taxpayer, and it is negated if the IRS error was made due to a lack of information provided by the taxpayer.[47]

CRIMINAL PENALTIES

In addition to the civil penalties that we have discussed so far, the Code prescribes a number of **criminal penalties** for certain acts of taxpayer noncompliance. The criminal penalties are intended "to prohibit and punish fraud

47. § 6404(f).

occurring in the assessment and collection of taxes."[48] They are imposed only after the implementation of the constitutional criminal process, under which the taxpayer is entitled to the same rights and privileges as other criminal defendants.

SPOTLIGHT ON TAXATION: Tax Criminals

With Enron and other accounting scandals still destabilizing the economy, the question should be asked: What are the tax implications of these infractions? Are indictments of tax fraud and other tax-related criminal activities still to come?

Without knowing the workplan of the Treasury and Justice Departments, this question may not be answerable. But trends of the last decade or so would speak to a lack of interest by the federal government in pursuing corporate tax crimes. Criminal tax investigations tend to involve both of the above departments of the President's cabinet, and they reflect the existence of convincing evidence of a serious tax infraction, not just a "fishing expedition." Civil penalties, audits, and appeals in the normal administration of the tax law are put on hold when a taxpayer is under a criminal tax investigation.

Are corporate taxpayers more compliant with the tax laws than they were in the past? Are the investigations less aggressive than they have been in the past? Why?

How else to explain the change in the work patterns of the criminal tax investigators? Today they tend to concentrate on smaller, mundane cases, not the high-profile violations of the Al Capones and Spiro Agnews of the past. And the investigations have declined in absolute terms as well, according to a think tank at Syracuse University. Estimates for the 2002 work year are for about 360 criminal tax prosecutions.

	2002	1992 or 1993
Criminal tax investigations initiated	2,500	4,000
Prosecutions for tax crimes	500	1,000
Corporate civil fraud penalties assessed	159	555
Corporate negligence penalties assessed	22	2,376

The IRS was not part of President George W. Bush's post-Enron Corporate Fraud Task Force, leading some to conclude that the government is not currently interested in pursuing tax criminals. And, even though there are 12 percent more corporate tax returns than there were a decade ago, the number of revenue agents employed by the agency to follow these returns has fallen by a quarter.

Previous comments by IRS personnel have admitted that the agency pursues only 20–30 percent of the known tax criminal cases, and that about $280 billion per year escapes collection because of this limited enforcement. Another report estimates that there are about 7,500 known "tax protestors" whom the government does not pursue.

48. *U.S. v. White*, 417 F.2d 89, 93 (CA-2).

Prosecutions for tax crimes have brought down some highly visible individuals, including political and entertainment figures, but the penalties can be used against any taxpayer. Currently penalties are in public favor as part of "white collar" crime investigations. They can entail felony or misdemeanor infractions and are meant to punish the offender for evading the tax.

Nature of Criminal Penalties

Criminal and civil penalties are not mutually exclusive. Consequently, a taxpayer may be acquitted of a criminal tax offense, but still be liable for a corresponding civil tax penalty.

The IRS bears a greater burden of proof with respect to a criminal case. Moreover, the taxpayer holds the right to refuse to answer inquiries that are made by the IRS in a criminal setting if he or she would suffer a loss of some constitutional right by answering.

Ordinarily, criminal prosecutions are limited to flagrant offenses for which the IRS believes it is virtually certain to obtain a conviction. As a result, the IRS usually limits its charges to the civil penalty provisions. In the typical context, according to Section 100 of the *IRS Law Enforcement Manual IX,* criminal prosecutions are limited to cases in which (1) the additional tax that will be generated from a successful prosecution is substantial, (2) the crime appears to have been committed in three consecutive years, or (3) the taxpayer's flagrant or repetitive conduct was so egregious that the IRS believes that it is virtually certain to obtain a conviction. As a result, the IRS usually will not engage in a criminal prosecution when the taxpayer's noncompliance can be corrected by imposing civil penalties.

Criminal Tax Offenses

The principal criminal offenses that are addressed by the Code include the following.

- Willful attempt to evade or defeat a tax (i.e., tax evasion)—a felony offense that is punishable by a fine that is not to exceed $100,000 ($500,000 for corporations), reimbursement of the government's cost of prosecution, and/or imprisonment for a period that is not to exceed five years.[49]
- Willful failure to collect, account for, and remit any tax, by any person who is required to do so—a felony offense that is punishable by a fine that is not to exceed $10,000, reimbursement of the government's cost of prosecution, and/or imprisonment for a period that is not to exceed five years.[50]
- Willful failure to file a return, supply information, or pay tax or estimated tax—a misdemeanor offense that is punishable by a fine that is not to exceed $25,000 ($100,000 for corporations), reimbursement of the government's cost of prosecution, and/or imprisonment for a period that is not

49. § 7201.
50. § 7202.

to exceed one year (five years and felony status for returns relative to cash received by a business).[51]

- Willful making, subscribing, or aiding or assisting in the making of a return or other document that is verified by a declaration under the penalties of perjury, and that the person does not believe to be true and correct as to every material matter—a felony offense that is punishable by a fine not to exceed $100,000 ($500,000 for corporations), reimbursement of the government's cost of prosecution, and/or imprisonment for a period that is not to exceed three years.[52]

- Willful filing of any known-to-be-false or fraudulent document—a misdemeanor offense that is punishable by a fine that is not to exceed $10,000 ($50,000 for corporations) and/or imprisonment for a period not to exceed one year.[53]

- Disclosure or use of any information that is furnished to a person who is engaged in the business of preparing tax returns, or providing services in connection with the preparation of tax returns, for purposes other than the preparation of the return—a misdemeanor offense that is punishable by a fine not to exceed $1,000 and/or imprisonment for a period not to exceed one year.[54]

In addition to the penalties that we have just described, the Code prescribes a number of other criminal penalties that ordinarily are not encountered on a regular basis. Most of these penalties involve a specialized area of the tax law. Consequently, one should be aware of the existence of such sanctions and refer to the Code and Regulations when working in such a specialized field to identify them.

Defenses to Criminal Penalties

The standard for conviction in a criminal case is establishment of guilt beyond a reasonable doubt. With respect to criminal tax cases, taxpayers have had some success in presenting one or more of the following defenses—that is, to establish some doubt in the minds of the court or the jury.

- Unreported income was offset fully by unreported deductions.[55]
- Unreported income was in reality a gift or some other excludible receipt.[56]
- The taxpayer was confused or ignorant as to the applicable law—one cannot intend to violate the tax law if he or she does not know what that law is.[57]
- The taxpayer relied on the erroneous advice of a competent tax adviser.[58]

51. §§ 7203 and 6050I.
52. § 7206.
53. § 7207.
54. § 7216.
55. *Koontz v. U.S.*, 277 F.2d 53 (CA-5, 1960).
56. *DiZenzo v. Comm.*, 348 F.2d 122 (CA-2, 1965).
57. *U.S. v. Critzer*, 498 F.2d 1160 (CA-4, 1974). This is not a mere disagreement with the law, which is not an acceptable defense. *U.S. v. Schiff*, 801 F.2d 108 (CA-2, 1986), cert. den.
58. *U.S. v. Phillips*, 217 F.2d 435 (CA-7, 1954).

- The taxpayer has a mental disease or defect, so could not have acted willfully to violate the tax law.[59]
- The statute of limitations (discussed later in this chapter) has expired.
- The taxpayer enters a plea bargain and accepts conviction on a lesser offense.

PENALTIES ON RETURN PREPARERS

Individuals who prepare income tax returns or refund claims for compensation are subject to a number of disclosure requirements and penalties for improper conduct in the preparation of those documents. These provisions were added to the Code after Congress found that about one-half of all taxpayers utilized some form of professional assistance in preparing their income tax returns. Moreover, a significant percentage of returns that were prepared by return preparers indicated some fraud potential.

The return preparer penalties apply only to income tax returns. Most of them are mild, ranging from $50 for the failure to furnish an identification number to $1,000 for the aiding and abetting of an understatement of a tax liability. However, as these sanctions may be applied cumulatively, their magnitude can become more substantial. In addition, the criminal penalties that may be imposed on the return preparer provide for substantial monetary fines and jail terms.

We discussed some of these rules in Chapters 1 and 2. For both taxpayer and tax preparer, the penalty system "encourages" a lawful application of the tax rules by all, by raising the cost of the tax when specific requirements are violated.

DEFINITION OF RETURN PREPARER

An income tax **return preparer** (ITRP) is any person who prepares for compensation, or employs one or more persons to prepare for compensation, all or a substantial portion of a tax return or claim for income tax refund.[60] An ITRP can be an employer, employee, or a self-employed person. This distinction is important because certain penalties are imposed only on a selected type of preparer. For instance, only an employee preparer is subject to a negligence or fraud penalty, unless the employer participated in the wrongdoing. To determine whether the employer or employee return preparer (or both) is liable for a certain penalty, the Regulations that relate to that penalty must be consulted.

A person must prepare an income tax return for compensation if he or she is to be subject to the return preparer sanctions. If a return is prepared gratuitously, the preparer is not an ITRP. The preparer also must prepare all or a substantial portion of a return if the ITRP sanctions are to apply. In determining whether the work that has been performed by the party is substantial, a comparison must be made between the length and complexity of the prepared schedule, entry, or other item and the total liability or refund claim.

---

59. *U.S. v. Erickson*, 676 F.2d 408 (CA-10, 1982).
60. § 7701(a)(36).

The Regulations adopt two objective safe harbors in determining the constitution of a substantial portion of a return or claim. If a schedule, entry, or other item involves amounts that are (1) less than $2,000 or (2) less than $100,000 and also less than 20 percent of the gross income (or adjusted gross income, where the taxpayer is an individual) that is shown on the return, then the item is not substantial.[61]

DEFINITION OF RETURN PREPARATION

In constructing a definition of the ITRP, one first must define the domain of *return preparation.* Return preparation includes activities other than the mere physical completion of a return. The IRS asserts that tax advisers, planners, software designers, and consultants are all tax preparers, even though they may only review the return or give the taxpayer instructions on its completion. According to the Regulations, one who furnishes a taxpayer or other preparer with "sufficient information and advice so that completion of the return or claim for refund is largely a mechanical matter" is an ITRP.[62] However, an adviser is not an ITRP when the advice is given with respect to completed transactions or for other than tax return filing purposes.

A person is not an ITRP merely because he or she:[63]

- furnishes typing, reproducing, or other clerical assistance;
- prepares a return or refund claim of his or her regular employer or of an officer or employee of the employer;
- prepares as a fiduciary a return or claim for refund;
- prepares a claim for refund during the course of an audit or appeal;
- provides general tax advice to a taxpayer;
- is an employee or official of the IRS, while performing job-related duties;
- prepares the return for no compensation; or
- works for IRS-sponsored programs such as Volunteer Income Tax Assistance, Tax Counseling for the Elderly, or a Low-Income Tax Clinic.

Being classified as an ITRP is not directly based on the attainment of a certificate or degree, or the completion of continuing education requirements, but on the substantial completion of a tax return for compensation.

PREPARER DISCLOSURE PENALTIES

Five different **preparer penalties** may be imposed on those who do not comply with certain disclosure requirements.[64]

- A penalty of $50 for each return may be imposed on an (employer of an) ITRP if the taxpayer is not given a complete copy of the return when it is presented to him or her for signature.
- A penalty of $50 for each return may be imposed on an employee ITRP if he or she fails to sign the return.

61. Reg. § 301.7701-15(b)(2).
62. Reg. § 301.7701-15(a)(1).
63. § 7701(a)(36)(B) and Reg. §§ 301.7701-5(a)(2) through (7).
64. § 6695.

- A penalty of $50 for each return will be imposed on an (employer of an) ITRP if the preparer's identification number or that of his or her employer, or both, is not listed on each completed return.
- A penalty of $50 for each failure will be imposed on an (employer of an) ITRP if he or she does not retain a copy of all returns that he or she prepared. Alternatively, he or she may retain a list of all of the taxpayers and their identification numbers for whom returns were prepared for the previous three years.
- A penalty of $50 for each failure to retain, and $50 for each item that is omitted, is imposed on an (employer of an) ITRP who does not retain records that indicate the name, identification number, and place of work of each preparer who is employed during the twelve-month period that begins on July 1 of each year.

In each instance, the maximum penalty for any calendar year is $25,000.

PREPARER CONDUCT PENALTIES

The Code contains a number of civil and criminal penalties that may be imposed on return preparers relative to their misconduct. The civil penalties were added to the Code because Congress found that a significant number of return preparers were engaging in improper practices, such as guaranteeing refunds or having taxpayers sign blank returns. However, except for the criminal penalty of aiding and assisting in the preparation of a false return, there were no lesser sanctions that could be applied to return preparers who were guilty of misconduct.

Civil penalties that may be imposed on preparers relate to:

- endorsing or negotiating a refund check;
- negligent understatement or intentional disregard of rules and Regulations;
- willful understatement of tax liability;
- organizing, or assisting in organizing, or promoting and making or furnishing statements with respect to an abusive tax shelter;
- aiding and abetting the understatement of a tax liability; and
- disclosure or use of return information for other than return preparation.

Return preparers have always been subject to criminal prosecution for willful misconduct. The two principal criminal preparer penalties involve those who:

- aid or assist in the preparation or presentation of a false return, affidavit, claim, or other document,[65] or
- disclose or use information for other than return preparation purposes.[66]

Endorsing or Negotiating a Refund Check

An income tax return preparer may not endorse or otherwise negotiate an income tax refund check that is issued to another person. A preparer who violates this rule is subject to a $500 penalty.[67]

65. § 7206(2).
66. § 7213(a)(3).
67. § 6695(f).

Understatements Due to Unrealistic Positions

A tax preparer incurs a $250 penalty for each occurrence of an understatement of tax due to the taking of an unrealistic position in the return. This criterion is not subject to a materiality threshold. Rather, where there is no **realistic possibility** that the preparer's position will be maintained on its merits, the penalty simply applies.[68] The penalty is waived if the return includes a disclosure of the preparer's nonfrivolous position, or if the preparer has acted in good faith in preparing the return.

For this purpose, a realistic possibility exists where a reasonable and well-informed analysis by a person knowledgeable in the tax law would result in the conclusion that there was at least about a one-in-three likelihood that the position would be upheld on its merits. Thus, this criterion does not require certainty nor, indeed, even a preponderance of the evidence. Most likely, the party whose likelihood of sustaining the position is being measured is an appropriate judicial forum.

This penalty also is applied where the preparer fails to make adequate inquiries of the taxpayer relative to information that appears to be incomplete or incorrect.[69] The penalty is assessed only on the preparer who is required to sign the return.

Example 13-3 Josie's return includes the claiming of a deduction that is contrary to an extant Revenue Ruling. Because of a new court decision in another circuit that is favorable to the deduction, Josie believes that there is a 70 percent chance that she would prevail in a suit relative to the deduction. No substantial-understatement penalty will apply to Josie, whether she wins or loses in court, and she need not disclose in any way her variance from the government position on her return.

Example 13-4 Continue with the facts of Example 13-3, except assume that Josie believes the following probabilities exist with respect to a court's treatment of her deduction, as supported by substantial authority.

Full support for her position	40%
Partial deduction allowed	35%
No deduction allowed	25%

No substantial-understatement penalty will apply to Josie, whether she wins or loses in court, and she need not disclose in any way her variance from the government position on her return. There is a realistic possibility that her position will prevail.

Example 13-5 Return to the facts of Example 13-3, except assume that Josie believes that she has a 25 percent probability of success in a court hearing. To avoid any substantial-understatement penalty, Josie must attach a Form 8275 to the return, revealing where and how she has deviated from the government's position relative to the deduction.

68. § 6694(a).
69. § 6694(a)(2).

Example 13-6 Return to the facts of Example 13-3, except assume that Josie believes that she has a 5 percent probability of prevailing in court. Josie cannot take this filing position on any tax return. This is a frivolous position and would trigger a penalty on her and the tax preparer of the return.

This discussion begs the question of how the typical lay taxpayer would arrive at the table of probabilities necessary to determine whether an additional Form 8275 disclosure would be necessary. It is clear that the substantial-authority criterion needs refinement to make it applicable to all but the most educated of taxpayers.

Willful Understatement

A preparer is subject to a $1,000 penalty if any part of an understatement of a taxpayer's liability is attributable to the preparer's willful attempt in any manner to understate the liability, or to the reckless or intentional disregard of IRS rules or Regulations.[70] A preparer is considered to have willfully attempted to understate the tax in this manner if he or she disregards information that has been supplied by the taxpayer, or by any other person, in an attempt wrongfully to reduce the taxpayer's levy.

The willful understatement penalty is not imputed to the employer of the return preparer unless the employer also participated in the wrongdoing. The penalty focuses only on the conduct of the actual ITRP.

It is possible that both the willful and unrealistic position understatement penalties will apply to the same return. A penalty for willful understatement of liability may be based on an intentional disregard of the pertinent rules and Regulations. If a penalty is collected under the unrealistic-position penalty rule, the amount that may be collected under the willful-understatement penalty rule is reduced by a corresponding amount.

Organizing Abusive Tax Shelters

A civil penalty may be imposed on any person who organizes or assists in organizing, or (even indirectly) participates in the sale of any interest in, a tax shelter, and who makes or furnishes a statement regarding an expected tax benefit that the person knows or has reason to know is either false or fraudulent, or a gross valuation understatement.[71]

For this purpose, a gross valuation understatement is a statement of the value of any property or service that exceeds 200 percent of the amount that is determined to be its correct value, if the value of the property or service is directly related to the amount of any allowable deduction or credit.[72] Accordingly, there does not need to be an understatement of tax before this penalty can be applied. The penalty can be triggered without an IRS audit, and it can be based only on the shelter's offering materials.

The amount of the penalty is the greater of $1,000 or 100 percent of the gross income that is derived, or is to be derived, by the taxpayer from the project.

70. § 6694(b).
71. § 6700.
72. § 6700(b)(1).

The IRS may waive all or a portion of the penalty that is attributable to a gross valuation understatement if there was a reasonable basis for the valuation, and it was made in good faith.[73]

Although the penalty is not aimed specifically at tax preparers, but rather at the tax shelter industry itself, professional tax advisers may be subject to the penalty because they often assist in organizing tax shelter projects.

Aiding and Abetting Understatement

The Code imposes a civil penalty on any person who aids or assists, or procures or advises, in the preparation or presentation of any portion of a return or other tax-related document, if he or she knows or has reason to believe that the return or other document will be used in connection with any material tax matter, and that this use will result in the understatement of another person's tax liability.[74] This penalty may also be imposed on a person who acts in violation of the statute through a subordinate (e.g., an employee or agent) by either ordering or causing the subordinate to act, or knowing of and not attempting to prevent the subordinate from acting, wrongfully.[75]

The amount of the penalty is $1,000 ($10,000 for corporations) for each understating taxpayer. This penalty may be imposed only once per year for each understating taxpayer who is serviced by the ITRP. However, it may be imposed in addition to other penalties. Thus, the preparer may also be prosecuted under the criminal statutes.[76]

Aiding or Assisting in the Preparation of a False Return

A criminal penalty may be imposed on any person who willfully aids or assists in the preparation of a return or other document that is false as to any material matter. This penalty is the criminal equivalent to the civil penalty for aiding and abetting the understatement of any tax liability.

A person who is convicted of violating this statute is guilty of a felony and is subject to imprisonment for up to three years and/or may be fined an amount that cannot exceed $100,000 ($500,000 for corporations). This is one of the most severe tax preparer penalties under the Code.[77]

The persons who are prosecuted under this statute usually are accountants or other return preparers. However, a person who supplies false information that is used in the preparation of a return may also be subject to this penalty. The penalty can be assessed when it is merely a false tax-related document (like a Form 1099 or W-4), and not a tax return, that is prepared.

Disclosure or Use of Information by Return Preparers

The Code imposes a civil penalty on any return preparer who discloses or uses any tax return information for other than the purpose of preparing a

73. §§ 6700(a)(2) and (b)(2).
74. § 6701(a).
75. § 6701(c).
76. § 6701(b).
77. § 7206(2).

tax return. This penalty amounts to $250 per improper use; a preparer's maximum penalty for any calendar year is $10,000. The Code also imposes a criminal penalty on any return preparer who knowingly or recklessly discloses or uses any tax return information for other than the specific purpose of preparing a tax return. One who is convicted of violating this statute is guilty of a misdemeanor and is subject to imprisonment for not more than one year and/or may be fined an amount that cannot exceed $1,000.[78]

The definition of a tax return preparer for purposes of this criminal penalty is broader than that under the civil preparer statutes. For instance, a clerical assistant who types or otherwise works on returns that are completed by the preparer is a "tax return preparer" for purposes of this provision; however, he or she would not be considered to be an ITRP for purposes of the civil preparer penalty statutes.

The preparer, as here defined, may disclose information that is obtained from the taxpayer without being subject to the civil or criminal penalty if such disclosure is pursuant to any other provisions of the Code, or to a court order.

See Exhibit 13-2 for a summary of the most important of the civil and criminal penalties that may apply to taxpayers, preparers, and shelter distributors.

INJUNCTIONS

The IRS is empowered to seek **injunctions** against two classes of persons of interest to our discussion: (1) income tax return preparers and (2) promoters of abusive tax shelters. An injunction is a judicial order that prohibits the named person from engaging in certain specified activities. The courts have broad authority to structure any injunctive relief that is granted to fit the circumstances of the case as appropriate.

ACTION TO ENJOIN INCOME TAX RETURN PREPARERS

The IRS may seek an injunction against an ITRP who is guilty of certain misconduct to prohibit him or her from engaging in such misconduct or from practicing as a return preparer.

Before such an injunction can be issued, however, the preparer must have:

- violated a preparer penalty or a criminal provision of the Code,
- misrepresented his or her eligibility to practice before the IRS,
- guaranteed the payment of any tax refund or the allowance of a credit, or
- engaged in other fraudulent or deceptive conduct that substantially interferes with the administration of the tax laws.

In addition, it must be shown that the injunctive relief is appropriate to prevent the conduct from recurring. An injunction to prohibit the preparer from acting as an income tax return preparer may be obtained if the court finds that the preparer continually or repeatedly has engaged in misconduct, and that an injunction prohibiting such specific misconduct would be effective.[79]

78. §§ 6713 and 7216(a).
79. § 7407.

Exhibit	**13–2**	Summary of Tax-Related Penalties

Criminal and civil penalties are not mutually exclusive, so a taxpayer or a preparer may be liable for both. Unlike civil penalties, which are collected in the same manner as would be true for the regular tax, criminal penalties are imposed only after the completion of the normal criminal process, in which the defendant is entitled to a number of constitutional guarantees and other rights, i.e., he or she is deemed to be innocent until proven guilty.

IRC Section	Type of Infraction	Penalty
Civil Penalties		
6694(a)	Understatement due to unrealistic position	$250 per return
6694(b)	Willful understatement of liability	$1,000 per return
6695(a)	Failure to furnish copy to taxpayer	$50 per failure
6695(b)	Failure to inform taxpayer of certain record-keeping requirements or to sign return	$50 per failure
6695(c)	Failure to furnish identifying number	$50 per failure*
6695(d)	Failure to retain copy or list	$50 per failure*
6695(e)	Failure to file correct information return	$50 per failure to file; $50 per omitted item*
6695(f)	Negotiation or endorsement of refund checks	$500 per check
6700	Organizing (or assisting in doing so) or promoting and making or furnishing statements with respect to abusive tax shelters	Greater of $1,000 or 100% of gross income derived by preparer from the project
6701	Aiding and abetting an understatement of tax liability	$1,000 per return; $10,000 per return if taxpayer is a corporation
6713	Improper disclosure or use of return data	$250 per improper use; annual maximum $10,000

*Annual maximum penalty = $25,000.

IRC Section	Type of Infraction	Penalty
Criminal Penalties		
7201	Attempt to evade or defeat tax	Felony; fine of not more than $100,000 ($500,000 if a corporation) and/or imprisonment for not more than five years
7202	Willful failure to collect or pay over a tax	Felony; fine of not more than $10,000 and/or imprisonment for not more than five years
7203	Willful failure to file return, supply information, or pay tax	Misdemeanor; fine of not more than $25,000 ($100,000 if a corporation) and/or imprisonment for not more than one year (five years relative to cash received by a business)
7204	Fraudulent statement or failure to make statement to employees	Fine of not more than $1,000 and/or imprisonment for not more than one year
7205	Fraudulent withholding exemption certificate or failure to supply information	Fine of not more than $1,000 and/or imprisonment for not more than one year

Continued

Exhibit	13–2	Summary of Tax-Related Penalties—Concluded

IRC Section	Type of Infraction	Penalty
Criminal Penalties *(continued)*		
7206	Fraud and false statements	Felony; fine of not more than $100,000 ($500,000 if a corporation) and/or imprisonment for not more than three years
7206(2)	Aid or assistance in the preparation or presentation of a false return, claim, or other document	Felony; fine of not more than $100,000 ($500,000 if a corporation) and/or imprisonment for not more than three years
7207	Fraudulent returns, statements, or other documents	Fine of not more than $10,000 ($50,000 if a corporation) and/or imprisonment for not more than one year
7210	Failure to obey summons	Fine of not more than $1,000 and/or imprisonment for not more than one year
7212	Attempts to interfere with administration of internal revenue laws	Fine of not more than $5,000 and/or imprisonment for not more than three years
7216	Disclosure or use of information by preparer of return	Misdemeanor; fine of not more than $1,000 and/or imprisonment for not more than one year

ACTION TO ENJOIN PROMOTERS OF ABUSIVE TAX SHELTERS

The IRS may obtain an injunction against a person who is guilty of promoting abusive tax shelters, or of aiding and abetting an understatement of the tax liability, to prohibit him or her from engaging in such conduct or activities. Before such an injunction is issued, a court must find that injunctive relief is appropriate to prevent this conduct from recurring.[80]

INTEREST

The Code provides for the payment of interest on underpayments and overpayments of tax, at an adjustable rate, compounded daily. The objective of these provisions is to compensate offended parties for the use of their funds. Moreover, the interest charge eliminates the benefits that taxpayers (or the government) could obtain by adopting aggressive positions in the creation or processing of tax returns in order to postpone or avoid the payment of their taxes.

INTEREST-COMPUTATION CONVENTIONS

Interest on underpayments is payable at a federally specified rate, from the last date that is prescribed for the payment of the tax to the date on which the tax is actually paid. The last date that is prescribed for payment of the

80. § 7408.

tax is usually the unextended due date of the return that reports the amount of tax that is due.[81]

Interest is compounded on a daily basis.[82] Thus, given an interest rate that equals or exceeds about 15 percent, the obligation of the taxpayer or government could double in five years. The IRS has published interest-factor tables which automatically calculate the daily compounding for various rates of interest.[83]

The rate of interest that is used for underpayments and overpayments is adjusted quarterly to reflect the federal short-term interest rate for the first day of the quarter.[84] The new prevailing rate is published in a timely fashion, typically in a Revenue Ruling.

The interest rate on underpayments is set at one percentage point higher than that for overpayments. Thus, the taxpayer is subject to an interest rate that is higher than that which applies to the government. Large corporations add two more percentage points to the underpayment rate. Corporate overpayments in excess of $10,000 earn interest at only a discounted rate. Exhibit 13–3 documents the various IRS rates of interest that applied to over- and underpayments occurring through early 2005.

Where the taxpayer is subject to both underpayment and overpayment computations for the same time period, whether the prior disputes involve income, transfer, or employment taxes, the amounts due and payable to the government are netted and a zero interest rate applies to those amounts.

Example 13-7 Mary Brown, a calendar-year taxpayer, filed her 2003 tax return and showed a balance due of $1,000. The return was filed on June 30, 2004, pursuant to a properly executed extension of time to file, and the tax was paid in full with the return. The prevailing IRS interest rate that applies to Brown's underpayment was 5 percent. She must pay about $17 of interest with her return, determined as follows.

Total tax outstanding	$	1,000
Factor from Rev. Proc. 95-17, for 5% interest and		
76 days' late payment	×	.010464621
Interest assessed	$	10.46

If Brown does not remit the interest that she owes when she files the return, interest will accrue, on both the tax and the $10 of interest itself, until the obligation is paid in full. If this amount is paid within ten days of the receipt of an IRS notice and demand for payment, however, no further interest accrues.

Interest accrues on the full amount of the tax liability that is appropriate under the Code, regardless of the amount of tax that is entered on the return. Moreover, interest is imposed on an assessable penalty, additional amount, or addition to the tax if these amounts are not paid within ten days of the

---

81. §§ 6601(a) and (b).
82. § 6622(a).
83. Rev. Proc. 95-17, 1995-1 CB 556.
84. § 6621.

| Exhibit | 13–3 | IRS Overpayment and Underpayment Interest Rates |

Period			Rate
Prior to July 1975			6%
July 1, 1975	–	January 31, 1976	9
February 1, 1976	–	January 31, 1978	7
February 1, 1978	–	January 31, 1980	6
February 1, 1980	–	January 31, 1982	12
February 1, 1982	–	December 31, 1982	20
January 1, 1983	–	June 30, 1983	16*
July 1, 1983	–	December 31, 1984	11*
January 1, 1985	–	June 30, 1985	13*
July 1, 1985	–	December 31, 1985	11*
January 1, 1986	–	June 30, 1986	10*
July 1, 1986	–	December 31, 1986	9*

Period			Over- payment Rate*†	Under- payment Rate*†	Large Corporation Under- payment Rate*	Rate for Corporation Over- payments >$10,000*
January 1, 1987	–	September 30, 1987	8%	9%		
October 1, 1987	–	December 31, 1987	9	10		
January 1, 1988	–	March 31, 1988	10	11		
April 1, 1988	–	September 30, 1988	9	10		
October 1, 1988	–	March 31, 1989	10	11		
April 1, 1989	–	September 30, 1989	11	12		
October 1, 1989	–	March 31, 1991	10	11		
April 1, 1991	–	December 31, 1991	9	10	12%	
January 1, 1992	–	March 31, 1992	8	9	11	
April 1, 1992	–	September 30, 1992	7	8	10	
October 1, 1992	–	June 30, 1994	6	7	9	
July 1, 1994	–	September 30, 1994	7	8	10	
October 1, 1994	–	December 31, 1994	8	9	11	
January 1, 1995	–	March 31, 1995	8	9	11	6.5
April 1, 1995	–	June 30, 1995	9	10	12	7.5
July 1, 1995	–	March 31, 1996	8	9	11	6.5
April 1, 1996	–	June 30, 1996	7	8	10	5.5
July 1, 1996	–	April 15, 1998	8	9	11	6.5
April 16, 1998	–	December 31, 1998	7	8	10	5.5
January 1, 1999	–	April 15, 1999	6	7	9	4.5
April 16, 1999	–	April 15, 2000	7	8	10	5.5
April 16, 2000	–	April 15, 2001	8	9	11	6.5
April 16, 2001	–	June 30, 2001	7	8	10	5.5
July 1, 2001	–	December 31, 2001	6	7	9	4.5
January 1, 2002	–	December 31, 2002	5	6	8	3.5
January 1, 2003	–	September 30, 2003	4	5	7	2.5
October 1, 2003	–	March 31, 2004	3	4	6	1.5
April 1, 2004	–	June 30, 2004	4	5	7	2.5
July 1, 2004	–	September 30, 2004	3	4	6	1.5
October 1, 2004	–	March 31, 2005	4	5	7	2.5

*Daily compounding required.
†After 1998, noncorporate taxpayers use the second column for both under- and overpayments. Corporations still receive one percentage point less with respect to their smaller overpayments; i.e., the first column applies.

date on which the IRS requests its payment. Interest on penalties generally is imposed only from the date of this IRS notice and demand, and not from the due date of the return. However, the fraud, accuracy-related, and failure-to-file penalties run from the (extended) due date of the return.[85]

No interest is charged on criminal penalties or delinquent estimated tax payments. However, recall that a nondeductible penalty is imposed in lieu of interest with respect to delinquent estimated tax payments. This penalty is computed in the same manner as would be the required interest, except that daily compounding of the penalty is not required.

In general, the IRS has no authority to forgive the payment of interest. Consequently, a taxpayer will be required to pay the total amount of interest assessed on any underpayment, even though the delinquency was attributable to a reasonable cause, including an IRS loss of records and the illness, transfer, or leave of a pertinent IRS employee. However, the IRS can abate such interest where it is attributable to an error or delay caused by an employee or officer of the IRS in response to the taxpayer's filing a claim on Form 843. Such a delay cannot be traceable to an interpretation of the tax law, but rather must relate to nondiscretionary, administrative, or managerial duties of procedure or return processing, including an IRS loss of records and the illness, transfer, or leave of a pertinent IRS employee.[86]

The government is required to pay interest at the applicable Federal rate to any taxpayer who has made an overpayment of tax. Interest on an overpayment runs from the date of the overpayment to the date on which the overpayment is credited against another tax liability, or, in the case of a refund, to a date that is not more than thirty days before the date of the refund check.

However, the IRS is allowed a specific period in which it may refund an overpayment without incurring interest. This interest-free period runs for forty-five days after the unextended due date of the return or, if the return is filed after its due date, for forty-five days after it is actually filed. If the refund is not made within this forty-five-day period, interest begins to accrue from the later of (1) the due date of the return or (2) the date on which the return was actually filed.[87]

Example 13-8 Joan Jeffries, a calendar-year taxpayer, filed her 2004 Federal income tax return on October 1, 2005. Her return showed an overpayment of $2,500, for which Jeffries requested a full refund. If the IRS refunds the $2,500 overpayment on or before November 14, 2005, no interest will be due from the government. However, if the refund is paid after November 14, 2005, interest will accrue from October 1, 2005, through a date that is not more than thirty days before the date of the refund check. (In any event, interest does not accrue as of April 16, 2005, for Joan.)

The date that is stated on the government's refund check determines whether the overpayment is refunded within the forty-five-day interest-free period.

85. § 6601(e)(2).
86. § 6404(e); *Dormer*, TC Memo 2004-167; TD 8789 (1998).
87. § 6611(e).

The date on which the refund is actually received does not control for this purpose. Thus, an interest-free refund may be paid, even though it is not received by the taxpayer until the forty-five-day period has expired.

SPOTLIGHT ON TAXATION: Prepaying Interest

If interest rates are relatively high, some taxpayers consider prepaying the amount of tax in dispute, so as to stop the running of interest charges that will be due if the issue is found in favor of the government. A deposit of the tax (and perhaps of related penalty and interest charges) is set up with the Treasury. Such a prepayment might make sense because:

- The prepayment can trigger an immediate interest deduction.
- If the taxpayer prevails in the dispute, interest will be payable back from the government on the full deposit amount.

APPLICABLE INTEREST RATE

Different rates are used with respect to IRS overpayments and underpayments after 1986, as is evident in Exhibit 13–3. The overpayment rate (paid by the IRS) is two percentage points greater than the Federal short-term interest rate, compounded daily, and the underpayment rate (paid to the IRS) is three percentage points greater than the same Federal rate.

Large corporations pay interest at two percentage points higher than the usual underpayment rate. Corporations receive interest on overpayments at $1\frac{1}{2}$ percentage points lower than the usual overpayment rate, where the overpayment exceeds $10,000. Under- and overpayment rates are determined for the beginning of each calendar quarter, using the Federal rates in effect for the first month of that quarter.

STATUTES OF LIMITATIONS

The Code establishes a specific period of time, commonly referred to as a **statute of limitation,** within which all taxes must be assessed and collected and all refund claims must be made. After the pertinent statute of limitations expires, certain actions may not be taken, because the expiration establishes an absolute defense for the party against whom legal action is brought. In other words, a taxpayer cannot be required to pay taxes that he or she rightfully owes if these taxes are not assessed and collected within the time periods that the Code has established.

NATURE OF STATUTES OF LIMITATIONS

Although the statute of limitations appears to be a legal loophole that rewards delinquent taxpayers who avoid detection, Congress believes that, at some point, the right to be free of stale claims must prevail over the government's right to pursue them. If the statutes permitted the lapse of an extended period of time between the initiation of a claim and its pursuit, the defense could be jeopardized because witnesses might have died or disappeared, memories might have faded, and records or other evidence might have been lost. Moreover, some statutes of limitations are designed solely to protect the government (e.g., the statute of limitations on credits or refunds). A number of such statutes limit the time period within which assessment, collection, and claim for refund or credit activities must be conducted.[88]

ASSESSMENT

Assessment of an internal revenue tax generally must be made within three years of the later of the date that the return was actually filed or the unextended due date of the return. A return that is filed prior to its due date, for this purpose, is deemed to be filed on its due date. The assessment period for a return that is filed after the due date starts on the day that follows the actual filing date, regardless of whether the return is delinquent or the due date was extended properly.

The period in which a tax may be assessed is extended to six years if the taxpayer omits from his or her reported gross income an amount that is greater than 25 percent of the reported gross income.[89] For this purpose, § 61 gross income is used in the 25 percent computation, with two exceptions. First, the gross income of a business is *not* reduced by cost of sales. Second, income that is omitted from the return is ignored for purposes of constructing the base for the 25 percent test, if the omission is disclosed in the return or in an attached document.[90]

Although the limitations period will be extended for a substantial omission of income, it (surprisingly) is not extended where the taxpayer has overstated the amount of his or her deductions, regardless of the amount of the overstatement.

Irregular Returns

A tax may be assessed at any time when a taxpayer files a false or fraudulent return with the intent to evade tax liability.[91] Once the fraudulent return is filed, the limitations period remains open indefinitely. A later filing of a nonfraudulent amended return will not start the running of the three- (or six)-year limitation period.[92]

When a taxpayer fails to file a return, the tax may be assessed at any time. For this purpose, one's failure to file need not be willful. A taxpayer who innocently or negligently fails to file is still subject to an unlimited period of assessment for the tax.[93]

---

88. § 6501.
89. § 6501(e)(1)(A).
90. §§ 6501(e)(1)(A)(i) and (ii).
91. § 6501(c)(1).
92. *Badaracco v. Comm.,* 464 U.S. 386, 104 S.Ct. 756 (1984).
93. § 6501(c)(3).

Acceleration, Extension, and Carryback Effects

Generally, the filing of an amended return does not affect the length of the limitations period. However, the limitations period is extended by sixty days if the IRS receives, within sixty days of the expiration of the applicable statute of limitations, an amended return that shows the taxpayer owes an additional tax.[94] This provision was enacted to discourage taxpayers from waiting until the limitations period on an assessment was about to expire before submitting an erroneous amended return. Prior to the enactment of this provision, it was beneficial for the taxpayer to wait to file an amended return this way, because the IRS would not have enough time to assess more tax if an examination of the original return uncovered additional unreported errors or omissions.

The usual three-year assessment period can be reduced to eighteen months if a request for a prompt assessment is filed with the IRS.[95] This request usually is made for an income tax return of a decedent or an estate, or for a corporation that is in the midst of a dissolution. Generally, a prompt assessment is requested when all of the involved parties wish to accelerate the final determination of the tax liability.

A deficiency for a carryback year that is attributable to the carryback of a net operating loss, capital loss, or unused research or general business credit can be assessed at any time before the expiration of the limitations period for the year in which the loss occurred or the credit originated. This extension in the period of assessment for the carryback year is necessary to ensure that there is adequate time to process the refund claim and to allow the IRS to examine the return that gave rise to the carryback item.[96]

The period for assessment is not extended when a net operating loss, capital loss, or unused credit is carried forward.

IRS-Requested Extensions

An extension of the period of limitations typically will be requested by the IRS when an audit or an appellate review cannot be completed until after the statute of limitations expires. The taxpayer is not bound to agree with such a request, but such a refusal may prompt the IRS to stop negotiations prematurely and assess a deficiency against the taxpayer. Although the issuance of a statutory notice of deficiency does not preclude the taxpayer from obtaining a negotiated settlement with the IRS, he or she will be required to undertake a more costly procedure and file a petition with the U.S. Tax Court or pay the assessment and file a claim for refund. Consequently, a taxpayer normally should not refuse to sign a waiver of the statute of limitations, as requested by the IRS, unless the agent has completed the examination and there exist one or more unagreed-upon issues that the taxpayer is ready to litigate.

94. § 6501(c)(7).
95. § 6501(d).
96. §§ 6501(h) through (k).

COLLECTION

All taxes must be collected within ten years after a timely assessment has been made.[97] **Collection** can be made either by IRS levy or by the agency's commencement of an action in court. If the tax is not collected administratively by levy within the ten-year period, the IRS must commence an action in court to reduce the assessment to a judgment before the statute of limitation expires. Once a judgment for the assessed tax is awarded, the tax may be collected at any time after the normal period of collections has expired. Thus, collection is not barred after the ten-year period expires, provided that the IRS has obtained a timely judgment against the taxpayer.

The taxpayer and the IRS may agree to an extension of the normal collection period. The IRS will request such an extension whenever the taxpayer has agreed to extend the period of limitations for assessment of the tax. In addition, the taxpayer may request an extension to allow additional time in which to (raise and) submit any delinquent taxes. If the taxpayer agrees to extend the period of limitation on collections, the IRS may agree not to seize and sell the taxpayer's property to satisfy the tax liability.

The ten-year period of limitations begins only after an assessment is made. If an assessment can be made at any time, for example, because the taxpayer failed to file a return or filed a fraudulent return, the tax may be collected within ten years of the date of assessment, regardless of when it eventually is made.

CLAIM FOR REFUND OR CREDIT

A taxpayer must file a timely and valid claim at the service center for the district in which the tax was paid to receive a refund or credit of an overpayment of tax. The claim should be made by individuals on Form 1040X, Individual Amended Income Tax Return, and by corporations on Form 1120X, Corporate Amended Income Tax Return.

Generally, an overpayment can be refunded or credited only to the person who was subject to the original tax. However, the IRS can apply overpayments to delinquent support obligations and certain certified nontax debts that are owed to the Federal government. Refunds in excess of $2,000,000 may not be made until they have been reviewed by the Joint Committee on Taxation.[98]

A taxpayer who reports a net operating loss, capital loss, or credit carryback can accelerate the processing of the refund by filing an Application for Tentative Carryback Adjustment on Form 1045 (for individuals) or Form 1139 (for corporations). The IRS has ninety days from the later of the date on which the application was filed or the last day of the month in which the return for the loss is due to examine the application and accept or deny the claim.[99]

97. § 6502(a)(1).
98. § 6405(a).
99. § 6411(b) and Reg. § 1.6411-1(b).

However, if the application is denied, the taxpayer cannot bring a suit for recovery of the overpayment, because the IRS's determination is only tentative. Instead, the taxpayer must file a refund claim on the appropriate form and wait for six months from the date on which the claim was filed, or until the IRS denies the refund claim, before legal action can be started.

Before a refund or credit can be issued, the IRS must review the taxpayer's claim. Even if the Commissioner agrees that the taxpayer has overpaid a tax, he or she has no authority to refund or credit the overpayment unless the taxpayer files the claim within the allowable period. Any refund of an overpayment that is made after the period for filing a timely claim is considered erroneous and a credit is considered void.

Limitations Period

A taxpayer who has filed a return must file a claim for credit or refund within three years of the date on which the return was filed or two years of the date on which the tax was paid, whichever is later. If the taxpayer did not file a return (e.g., because taxes were withheld from the taxpayer's wages, but the taxpayer did not file a return because his or her taxable income did not exceed the applicable exemptions and standard deduction), the claim for credit or refund must be made within two years of the date on which the tax was paid.[100]

The period within which a claim for credit or refund may be filed is extended when the taxpayer and the IRS agree to extend the statute of limitations on assessments. A claim can be filed within six months after the expiration of the extended assessment period.[101]

Other Extensions

The limitations period also can be extended where an overpayment results from a business bad debt or from a discovery of worthless securities.[102] A claim for refund or credit that is attributable to losses sustained from worthless securities or business bad debts may be filed within seven years from the date that the return was due, without regard to any extension for filing the return. This period is extended further if the debt or loss increases a net operating loss carryback, since the taxpayer will be entitled to three additional years for the filing of a claim that is based on the carryback.[103]

This provision was enacted because the determination of the date on which a debt or share of stock becomes worthless is a question of fact that may not be determined until after the year in which the loss actually occurred. If taxpayers were not allowed additional time in which to file refund claims for these items, they could incur substantial losses without the receipt of any tax benefits, because the deductions must be taken in the taxable year of the loss, not in a later year.

The period for filing a claim for refund is extended when the claimed overpayment results from the carryback of a net operating loss, capital loss, or

100. § 6511(a).
101. § 6511(c)(2).
102. § 6511(d).
103. § 6511(d)(2)(A).

certain credits. If a claim for credit or refund is attributable to the carryback of a net operating loss, net capital loss, or business credit, it can be filed within three years of the extended due date of the return for the year in which the losses occurred or the credits originated, rather than within three years of the due date of the return for the carryback year. Again, this provision was enacted because the existence and amount of these items might not be known until after the expiration of the usual three-year period for filing the claim.

Amount of the Credit or Refund

If a claim for refund or credit is filed in a timely fashion, the amount of the taxpayer's refund or credit is limited to the portion of the tax that was paid during the three immediately preceding years, plus the period of any extension for filing the return.[104] The amount of tax that is subject to the claim may include amounts that were withheld and estimated payments that were made more than three years before the date on which the claim was filed, because these amounts are all deemed to have been paid on the due date of the return.

If a claim is filed after the three-year period, the amount of any refund or credit is limited to the portion of the tax that was paid during the two years that immediately precede the filing of the claim. This two-year period also is effective if a claim is filed for a year in which a return was not filed. Because this claim relates only to a two-year period, it may not protect payments that were made with the original return.

SUSPENSION OF PERIOD OF ASSESSMENT AND COLLECTION

Usually, a tax must be assessed within three years after the filing of a tax return, and it must be collected within six years of the assessment. However, under certain circumstances, the running of the statutes of limitations on assessment or collection is suspended.

When the IRS mails a statutory notice of deficiency (i.e., a ninety-day letter) to the taxpayer, the assessment and collection period is suspended for 150 days (210 days if the letter is addressed to a person who is outside the United States).[105] The statutes of limitations on assessment and collection also are suspended when a case is pending before the U.S. Tax Court. This suspension period begins when the taxpayer files a petition in the Tax Court contesting the deficiency, and it continues until sixty days after the decision of the Tax Court becomes final.

When a taxpayer submits an offer in compromise for consideration by the IRS, the statute of limitations on assessment is suspended. This suspension period begins when the offer is submitted, and it continues until one year after the offer is terminated, withdrawn, or formally rejected.[106]

104. § 6511(b)(2)(A).
105. § 6503(a)(1).
106. Reg. § 301.7122-1(f).

In addition to the circumstances just discussed, the statute of limitations also can be suspended when:[107]

- the taxpayer's assets are in the custody of the court;
- the taxpayer is outside the United States for six or more consecutive months;
- the taxpayer's assets are wrongfully seized;
- a fiduciary or receiver is appointed in a bankruptcy case;
- the IRS is prohibited under bankruptcy law from any assessment or collection of a tax; or
- the collection of excise or termination taxes on certain retirement plans or private foundations are suspended.

MITIGATION OF STATUTE OF LIMITATIONS

Generally, the IRS cannot make an assessment and a taxpayer cannot obtain a refund after the statute of limitations has expired. However, §§ 1311 through 1314 of the Code include a complex set of rules designed to prevent the taxpayer or the IRS from taking advantage of an oncoming expiration of the period of limitations on assessment, collection, or refunds.

When an error has been made in the inclusion of an item of income, allowance, or disallowance of a deduction or other tax treatment of a transaction that affects the basis of property, the mitigation provisions will allow a submission of the error to be corrected, even though the normal period of limitations has expired for that year.

STATUTORY AGREEMENTS

The Code provides for two types of agreements that may be used to resolve tax disputes, namely, closing agreements and offers in compromise.

CLOSING AGREEMENTS

A **closing agreement** is a formal, written agreement that is made between a taxpayer and the IRS. It is the only agreement that the Code recognizes as being binding. Once it is approved, a closing agreement is final and conclusive on the part of both the government and the taxpayer, unless there is a showing of fraud, malfeasance, or a misrepresentation of a material fact, by either party.[108]

The purpose of a closing agreement is either (1) to enable the taxpayer and the IRS to resolve, finally and completely, a tax controversy for any period prior to the date of the agreement and to protect the taxpayer against the reopening of the matter at a later date; or (2) to determine a matter in a tax year that arises after the date of the agreement.

---

107. §§ 6503(b) through (f). That section also contains other, less frequently encountered suspension possibilities.
108. § 7121(b).

The IRS is authorized to enter into a closing agreement in any case where there appears to be a benefit to the government in closing the case permanently and conclusively, or if the taxpayer demonstrates a need to close the case and the government's interests are not harmed. Typically, a closing agreement is used in cases where the IRS and the taxpayer have made mutual concessions relative to the case, and it is necessary or desirable to bar further actions by either party. Such an agreement also may be used when a corporation is winding up its business affairs or when a taxpayer needs some authentic evidence of his or her tax liability, say, to satisfy creditors.

As a matter of practice, the IRS discourages the use of closing agreements because of their finality. Moreover, the IRS would have a difficult time processing a large number of requests for these agreements. Consequently, it prefers to use a number of informal agreements that may not resolve conclusively the tax dispute that is under examination, or that may not provide for the same degree of finality as would a closing agreement.

OFFERS IN COMPROMISE

The Commissioner can make an **offer in compromise** for any civil or criminal case that does not involve sales of illegal drugs, prior to the time that the case is referred to the Justice Department for prosecution or defense. Once the case is referred to the Justice Department, however, the U.S. Attorney General has the final authority to compromise the case.[109] Compromise proposals entailing more than $50,000 in tax also must be supported by an opinion of the Chief Counsel.

In this context, the government will compromise a case only if there is doubt as to the liability or collectibility of the assessed tax. The IRS will not enter into a compromise with the taxpayer if the liability has been established by a valid judgment, and if there is no doubt as to the ability of the IRS to collect the amounts that are due.

A compromise agreement may cover the principal amount of tax, plus any corresponding interest or penalties. Ordinarily, the IRS will not compromise a criminal tax case unless it involves a violation of a regulatory provision of the Code or of a related statute that was not deliberately violated with an intent to defraud.

A compromise agreement relates to the entire liability of the taxpayer, and it conclusively settles all of the issues for which an agreement is to be made. It is a legally enforceable promise that cannot be rescinded unless there has been a misrepresentation of the assets of the taxpayer by falsification or concealment, or a mutual mistake relative to a material fact. Consequently, a taxpayer cannot decide later to bring a suit for refund with respect to any item that is so compromised. Moreover, if a taxpayer defaults on a compromise agreement, the IRS may collect the original tax liability, less any payments that were actually made, or sue to enforce the agreement.

109. § 7122(a).

An offer in compromise is typically made via Form 656, Offer in Compromise, and it must be accompanied by a comprehensive set of the taxpayer's financial statements. The offer may be revoked or withdrawn at any time prior to its acceptance. Form 656 is reproduced in Exhibit 13–4.

An offer in compromise is perhaps most appropriate in the following circumstances.

- There is doubt as to the taxpayer's liability for the tax (i.e., disputed issues still exist).
- There is doubt as to the collectibility of the tax (i.e., the taxpayer's net worth and earnings capacity are low).
- Payment of the disputed amount would constitute an economic hardship for the taxpayer. For instance, the taxpayer is incapable of earning a living because of a long-term illness or disability, or liquidation of the taxpayer's assets to pay the amount due would leave the taxpayer unable to meet basic living expenses.

The IRS investigates the offer by evaluating the taxpayer's financial ability to pay the tax. In some instances, the compromise settlement includes an agreement for final settlement of the tax through payments of a specified percentage of the taxpayer's future earnings. This settlement procedure usually entails lengthy negotiations with the IRS, but the presumption is that the agency will find terms upon which to enter into a compromise with the taxpayer. The IRS is charged to use a "liberal acceptance policy" in compromising with taxpayers and to increase educational efforts so that taxpayer rights and obligations are better known.

The IRS has statutory authority to enter into a written agreement allowing taxes to be paid on an installment basis if that arrangement facilitates the tax collection.[110] The agency encourages its employees to use installment plans, and an individual is guaranteed the right to use an installment agreement when the amount in dispute does not exceed $10,000. The taxpayer uses Form 9465 to initiate the installment plan.

The IRS provides an annual statement accounting for the status of the agreement. The agreement may later be modified or terminated because of (1) inadequate information, (2) subsequent change in financial condition, or (3) failure to pay an installment when due or to provide requested information.

SUMMARY

In dealing with tax underpayments, the stakes include more than just the disputed tax. Interest charges accrue, and both the taxpayer and tax adviser can be subjected to significant amounts of civil and criminal penalties. Restrictions on the actions of the taxpayer and practitioner are expressed using such ambiguously defined terms as *reasonable cause* and *substantial authority*, such that the lay taxpayer is expected to project accurately the final holding of a judicial forum. Such is the condition of a tax system under which tax rates

110. § 6159.

Exhibit	**13–4**	Offer in Compromise

IRS

Form 656

Offer in Compromise

Department of the Treasury
Internal Revenue Service

www.irs.gov

Form 656 (Rev. 7-2004)
Catalog Number 16728N

Attach Application Fee *(check or money order)* **here.**

IRS RECEIVED DATE

Item 1 — Taxpayer's Name and Home or Business Street Address

Name

Name

Street Address

City   State   ZIP Code

Mailing Address *(if different from above)*

Street Address

City   State   ZIP Code

DATE RETURNED

Item 2 — Social Security Numbers

(a) Primary   _____

(b) Secondary _____

Item 3 — Employer Identification Number *(included in offer)*

Item 4 — Other Employer Identification Numbers *(not included in offer)* _____

Item 5 — To: Commissioner of Internal Revenue Service

I/We (includes all types of taxpayers) submit this offer to compromise the tax liabilities plus any interest, penalties, additions to tax, and additional amounts required by law (tax liability) for the tax type and period marked below: (Please mark an "X" in the box for the correct description and fill-in the correct tax period(s), adding additional periods if needed).

❏ **1040/1120 Income Tax** — Year(s) _____

❏ **941 Employer's Quarterly Federal Tax Return** — Quarterly period(s) _____

❏ **940 Employer's Annual Federal Unemployment (FUTA) Tax Return** — Year(s) _____

❏ **Trust Fund Recovery Penalty** as a responsible person of (enter corporation name) _____

for failure to pay withholding and Federal Insurance Contributions Act Taxes (Social Security taxes), for period(s) ending _____

❏ **Other Federal Tax(es)** [specify type(s) and period(s)] _____

Note: If you need more space, use another sheet entitled "Attachment to Form 656 Dated _____ ." Sign and date the attachment following the listing of the tax periods.

Item 6 — I/We submit this offer for the reason(s) checked below:

❏ **Doubt as to Liability** — "I do not believe I owe this tax." You must include a detailed explanation of the reason(s) why you believe you do not owe the tax in Item 9.

❏ **Doubt as to Collectibility** — "I have insufficient assets and income to pay the full amount." You must include a complete Collection Information Statement, Form 433-A and/or Form 433-B.

❏ **Effective Tax Administration** — "I owe this amount and have sufficient assets to pay the full amount, but due to my exceptional circumstances, requiring full payment would cause an economic hardship or would be unfair and inequitable." You must include a complete Collection Information Statement, Form 433-A and/or Form 433B **and** complete Item 9.

Item 7

I/We offer to pay $ _____ **(must be more than zero)**. Complete item 10 to explain where you will obtain the funds to make this offer.

Check **only** one of the following:

❏ **Cash Offer (Offered amount will be paid in 90 days or less.)**

Balance to be paid in: ❏ 10, ❏ 30, ❏ 60, or ❏ 90 days from written notice of acceptance of the offer.

❏ **Short-Term Deferred Payment Offer (Offered amount paid in MORE than 90 days but within 24 months from written notice of acceptance of the offer.)**

$_____ within_____days (not more than 90 — See Instructions Section, **Determine Your Payment Terms**) from written notice of acceptance of the offer; and/or

beginning in the _____ month after written notice of acceptance of the offer $_____on the _____day of each month for a total of_____months. (Cannot extend more than 24 months from written notice of acceptance of the offer.)

❏ **Deferred Payment Offer (Offered amount will be paid over the remaining life of the collection statute.)**

$_____ within_____days (not more than 90 — See Instructions Section, **Determine Your Payment Terms**) from written notice of acceptance of the offer; and

beginning in the first month after written notice of acceptance of the offer $_____on the _____day of each month for a total of_____months.

virtually cannot be raised, yet revenue needs continue to escalate. The tax professional must include these sanctions in the research process, communicating their effects to the client as needed.

TAX TUTOR

Reinforce the tax research information covered in this chapter by completing the online tutorials located at the Federal Tax Research web site:

http://raabe.swlearning.com

KEY WORDS

By the time you complete your work relative to this chapter, you should be comfortable discussing each of the following terms. If you need additional review of any of these items, return to the appropriate material in the chapter or consult the glossary to this text.

Accuracy-Related Penalty
Assessment
Civil Penalty
Closing Agreement
Collection
Criminal Penalty
Fraud
Injunction

Negligence
Offer in Compromise
Preparer Penalties
Realistic Possibility
Reasonable Cause
Return Preparer
Statute of Limitations
Substantial Authority

DISCUSSION QUESTIONS

1. When should prevailing interest rates bear on tax decision making?
   a. The taxpayer is contemplating litigation in either the Tax Court or the Court of Federal Claims.
   b. An understatement of estimated tax payments is discovered late in the tax year.

2. What is the role of the statute of limitations in the Federal income tax system?

3. Indicate whether each of the following statements is true or false.
   a. The government never pays a taxpayer interest on an overpayment of tax.
   b. Penalties may be included as an itemized deduction on an individual's tax return.
   c. An extension of time for filing a return results in an automatic extension of the time in which the tax may be paid.
   d. The IRS can compromise on the amount of tax liability if there is doubt as to the taxpayer's ability to pay.
   e. The statute of limitations for assessment of taxes never extends beyond three years from the filing of a return.

    f. There is no statute of limitations relative to a taxpayer's claim for a refund.

4. Indicate whether, after both parties sign a closing agreement, the following result(s) occur. More than one answer may be correct.
   a. The taxpayer still may appeal to a higher level of the IRS.
   b. The interest on the assessment stops accruing immediately.
   c. The agreement is binding on both the taxpayer and the IRS.
   d. The tax must be paid, but a suit for refund can be filed in the District Court or U.S. Court of Federal Claims.

5. Ace filed her 2003 income tax return on January 25, 2004. There was no material understatement of income on her return, and the return was properly signed and filed. The statute of limitations for Ace's 2003 return expires on:
   a. January 25, 2007
   b. April 15, 2007
   c. January 25, 2010
   d. April 15, 2010

6. Blanche filed her 1998 income tax return on April 4, 2004. On December 14, 2004, she learned that 100 shares of stock that she owned had become worthless in 2003. Since she did not deduct this loss on the 2003 return, Blanche intends to file a claim for refund. This claim must be filed by no later than April 15,
   a. 2005
   b. 2008
   c. 2010
   d. 2011
   e. There is no expiration date for the statute of limitations in this context.

7. Carl purposely omitted from his 2003 tax return $40,000 of the gross receipts that he collected as the owner of a saloon. His 2003 return indicated collective gross receipts of $25,000. The IRS no longer can pursue Carl with the threat of a collection of the related tax, interest, and penalties, as of April 15,
   a. 2005
   b. 2008
   c. 2010
   d. 2011
   e. There is no expiration date for the statute of limitations in this context.

8. Diane accidentally omitted from her 2003 tax return $40,000 of the gross receipts that she collected as the owner of a saloon. Her 2003 return indicated collective gross receipts of $25,000. The IRS no longer can pursue Diane with the threat of a collection of the related tax, interest, and penalties, as of April 15,
   a. 2005
   b. 2008
   c. 2010
   d. 2011
   e. There is no expiration date for the statute of limitations in this context.

9. Describe the civil fraud penalties, the definition of fraud, and the all or nothing rule for civil fraud. What are differences in individual and corporate penalties for failure to make adequate estimated payments? What is a frivolous return?

10. Explain the imposition of criminal penalties. What is the relationship between criminal and civil penalties? What are the defenses against criminal penalties?

11. Discuss the penalties imposed on tax return preparers. Who is a preparer and what is defined as a tax return preparation and what is not preparation?

12. What is an injunction and when may the IRS seek an injunction?

13. What are the statutes of limitations for the IRS and taxpayers and why did Congress create them? When can they be shortened, extended, or suspended?

14. How has Congress used tax penalties to discourage the development of certain tax shelters?

15. Define and illustrate the following terms or concepts.
    a. Fraud
    b. Negligence
    c. Reasonable cause
    d. Lack of reasonable cause
    e. Civil penalty conviction
    f. Criminal penalty conviction

EXERCISES

16. Construct a scenario in which the tax adviser should recommend that the client terminate the challenge of the IRS with the following.
    a. Lawsuit
    b. Offer in compromise
    c. Closing agreement
    d. Appeals conference
    e. Office audit
    f. Correspondence audit

17. The client's return is found to include fraudulent data. Which of the following could the IRS charge with a preparer penalty?
    a. Taxpayer
    b. Partner of the accounting firm that prepared the return
    c. Employee of the client, who provided the accounting firm with the fraudulent data
    d. Staff member of the accounting firm, who used the fraudulent data to prepare the return and did not verify its accuracy
    e. Secretary of the accounting firm, who made copies of the fraudulent return

18. The client's return is found by the U.S. Tax Court to have included improper business deductions. The court agreed that the taxpayer's position had some statutory and judicial merit, but it held for the government nonetheless. Which of the following could the IRS charge with a preparer penalty?

    a. Taxpayer
    b. Partner of the accounting firm that prepared the return
    c. Employee of the client, who provided the accounting firm with the deduction data
    d. Staff member of the accounting firm, who used the deduction data to prepare the return
    e. Secretary of the accounting firm, who made copies of the return

19. Discuss which penalties, if any, the tax adviser might be charged with in each of the following independent circumstances. In this regard, assume that the tax adviser

    a. provided information about the taxpayer's Federal income tax returns to the pertinent state income tax agency.
    b. provided information about the taxpayer's Federal income tax returns to the pertinent county's property tax agency.
    c. provided information about the taxpayer's Federal income tax returns to the FBI, which was interested in gathering evidence concerning the client's alleged drug dealing activities.
    d. suggested to the client various means by which to acquire excludible income.
    e. suggested to the client various means by which to conceal cash receipts from gross income.
    f. suggested to the client means by which to improve her cash flow by delaying for six months or more the deposit of the employees' share of Federal employment taxes.
    g. suggested to the client means by which to improve her cash flow by delaying for six months or more the deposit of the employer's share of Federal employment taxes.
    h. kept in his safe deposit box the concealed income of item (e).
    i. suggested that the client invest in a real estate tax shelter.
    j. provided a statement of assurance as to the accuracy of the financial data that is included in the prospectus of a real estate tax shelter.
    k. suggested to the promoters of a real estate tax shelter that a specific accounting technique, not recognized by generally accepted accounting principles, should be used to construct the prospectus.
    l. failed, because of pressing time conflicts, to conduct the usual review of the client's tax return. The IRS discovered that the return included fraudulent data.
    m. failed, because of pressing time conflicts, to conduct the usual review of the client's tax return. The IRS discovered a mathematical error in the computation of the taxpayer's standard deduction.

PROBLEMS

20. Lefty, a calendar-year taxpayer subject to a 34 percent marginal tax rate, claimed a charitable contribution deduction of $15,000 for a sculpture that the IRS later valued at $10,000. The applicable overvaluation penalty is:

    a. $0
    b. $100 (minimum penalty)
    c. $340
    d. $1,700
    e. Some other amount

21. Righty, a calendar-year taxpayer subject to a 34 percent marginal tax rate, claimed a charitable contribution deduction of $170,000 for a sculpture that the IRS later valued at $100,000. The applicable overvaluation penalty is:

    a. $0
    b. $100 (minimum penalty)
    c. $4,760
    d. $5,950
    e. Some other amount

22. Shorty, a calendar-year taxpayer subject to a 34 percent marginal tax rate, claimed a charitable contribution deduction of $400,000 for a sculpture that the IRS later valued at $150,000. The applicable overvaluation penalty is:

    a. $0
    b. $17,000
    c. $21,250
    d. $10,000 (maximum penalty)
    e. Some other amount

23. Baldy, a calendar-year taxpayer subject to a 34 percent marginal tax rate, claimed a charitable contribution deduction of $600,000 for a sculpture that the IRS later valued at $100,000. The applicable overvaluation penalty is:

    a. $0
    b. $34,000
    c. $68,000
    d. $10,000 (maximum penalty)
    e. Some other amount

24. Slim, who is subject to a 50 percent marginal gift tax rate, made a gift of a sculpture to Red, valuing the property at $7,000. The IRS later valued the gift at $15,000. The applicable undervaluation penalty is:

    a. $1,000
    b. $800
    c. $100 (minimum penalty)
    d. $0
    e. Some other amount

25. Tiny, who is subject to a 50 percent marginal gift tax rate, made a gift of a sculpture to Blondie, valuing the property at $80,000. The IRS later valued the gift at $150,000. The applicable undervaluation penalty is:
   a. $8,750
   b. $7,000
   c. $1,000 (minimum penalty)
   d. $0
   e. Some other amount

26. Fuzzy, who is subject to a 50 percent marginal gift tax rate, made a gift of a sculpture to Pinky, valuing the property at $100,000. The IRS later valued the gift at $250,000. The applicable undervaluation penalty is:
   a. $10,000 (maximum penalty)
   b. $18,750
   c. $15,000
   d. $0
   e. Some other amount

27. Jumbo, who is subject to a 50 percent marginal gift tax rate, made a gift of a sculpture to Curly, valuing the property at $100,000. The IRS later valued the gift at $500,000. The applicable undervaluation penalty is:
   a. $10,000 (maximum penalty)
   b. $80,000
   c. $40,000
   d. $0
   e. Some other amount

28. Compute the overvaluation penalty for each of the following independent cases involving the taxpayer's reporting of the fair market value of charitable contribution property. In each case, assume a marginal income tax rate of 30 percent.

Taxpayer	Corrected IRS Value	Reported Valuation
a. Individual	$ 10,000	$ 20,000
b. C Corporation	10,000	30,000
c. S Corporation	10,000	30,000
d. Individual	100,000	150,000
e. Individual	100,000	300,000
f. C Corporation	100,000	500,000

29. Compute the undervaluation penalty for each of the following independent cases involving the executor's reporting of the value of a closely held business in the decedent's gross estate. In each case, assume a marginal estate tax rate of 50 percent.

	Reported Value	Corrected IRS Valuation
a.	$12,000	$ 15,000
b.	50,000	90,000
c.	50,000	150,000
d.	50,000	200,000

30. Kim underpaid her taxes by $15,000. Of this amount, $7,500 was due to negligence on her part because her record-keeping system is highly inadequate. Determine the amount of any negligence penalty.

31. Compute Dana's total penalties. She underpaid her tax by $50,000 due to negligence, and by $150,000 due to civil fraud.

32. Trudy's AGI last year was $50,000. Her Federal income tax came to $16,000, which she paid through a combination of withholding and estimated payments. This year, her AGI will be $170,000, with a projected tax liability of $46,000, all to be paid through estimates. Ignore the annualized income method. Compute Trudy's quarterly estimated payment schedule for the year, assuming that she wants to make the minimum necessary payments to avoid any underpayment penalties.

33. When Maggie accepted employment with Martin Corporation, she completed a Form W-4, listing fourteen exemptions. Since Maggie was single and had no exemptions, she misrepresented her tax situation in an attempt to increase her cash flow. To what penalties is Maggie exposed?

34. What is the applicable filing period under the statute of limitations in each of the following independent situations?
    a. No return was filed by the taxpayer.
    b. The taxpayer incurred a bad debt loss that she failed to claim.
    c. A taxpayer inadvertently omitted a large amount of gross income.
    d. Same as part (c), except that the omission was deliberate.
    e. A taxpayer inadvertently overstated her deductions by a large amount.

35. Kold Corporation estimates that its 2005 taxable income will be $900,000. Thus, it is subject to a flat 34 percent income tax rate and incurs a $306,000 liability. For each of the following independent cases, compute the minimum quarterly estimated tax payments that will be required from Kold to avoid an underpayment penalty.
    a. Taxable income for 2004 was ($100,000). Kold carried back all of its loss to prior years and exhausted the entire net operating loss in creating a zero 2004 liability.
    b. For 2004, taxable income was $200,000 and tax liability was $68,000.
    c. For 2003, taxable income was $2 million and tax liability was $680,000. For 2004, taxable income was $200,000 and tax liability was $68,000.

36. Mimi had $40,000 in Federal income taxes withheld in 2005. Due to a sizable amount of itemized deductions, she figured that she had no further tax to pay for the year. For this reason and because of personal problems, and without securing an extension, she did not file her 2005 return until July 1, 2006. Actually, the return showed a refund of $2,400, which Mimi ultimately received. On May 10, 2009, Mimi filed a $16,000 claim for refund of her 2005 taxes.
    a. How much of the $16,000 will Mimi rightfully recover?
    b. How would your analysis differ if Mimi had secured from the IRS an automatic four-month extension of time for filing her 2005 return?

RESEARCH CASES

37. The Bird Estate committed tax fraud when it purposely understated the value of the business created and operated by the decedent, Beverly Bird. Executor Wilma Holmes admitted to the Tax Court that she had withheld several contracts and formulas that, had they been disclosed to the valuation experts used by the government and the estate, would have added $1 million in value to the business and over half that amount in Federal estate tax liabilities. Summary data include the following.

	Reported on Form 706	Other Amounts
Gross estate	$12 million	$1 million understatement
Deductions on original return	$2 million	
Interest on estate tax deficiency, professional fees incurred during administration period		$400,000

Holmes asks you for advice in computing the fraud penalty. Ignore interest amounts. She wonders whether to take the 75 percent civil penalty against the full $1 million understatement or against the $600,000 net amount that the taxable estate would have increased had the administrative expenses been incurred prior to the filing date of the Form 706. Write Holmes, an experienced CPA with an extensive tax practice, a letter stating your opinion.

38. Blanche Creek has engaged your firm because she has been charged with failure to file her 2005 Federal Form 1040.

    Blanche maintains that the "reasonable cause" exception should apply. During the entire tax filing season in 2006, she was under a great deal of stress at work and in her personal life. As a result, Blanche developed a sleep disorder, which was treated through a combination of pills and counseling.

    Your firm ultimately prepared the 2005 tax return for Blanche, but it was filed far beyond the due date. Blanche is willing to pay the delinquent tax and related interest. However, she feels that the failure to pay penalty is unfair as she was ill. Consequently, she could not be expected to keep to the usual deadlines for filing.

    Write a letter to Blanche concerning these matters.

39. The Church of Freedom encourages its members to file "tax protestor" returns with the IRS, objecting to both (a) the government's failure to use a gold standard in payment of tax liabilities, and (b) its sizable expenditures for social welfare programs. These returns routinely are overturned by the tax court as frivolous, with delinquent taxes, penalties, and interest due, and the church has engaged in a long-standing,

sometimes ugly battle with the IRS over various constitutional rights. Meanwhile, church members continue to file returns in this manner.

Ellen overheard church members talking about "roughing up" the IRS agents who were scheduled to conduct an audit of various members' returns. She went to the IRS and informed them of the danger that they might encounter. At the IRS's direction, Ellen then took a key clerical job at church headquarters. In this context, she had access to useful documentation and over a period of a few months gave to the IRS copies of church mailing lists and computer disks. She also helped tape record key conversations among church leaders and search the church's trash for other documents. In other words, Ellen helped the IRS build a case of civil and criminal tax fraud against the church and various members.

All of these materials were given voluntarily to Ellen by church leaders in her context as an employee. Church members never suspected that she was working with the IRS. After delivering the various materials to the IRS, Ellen quit her job with the church and severed all communications with the IRS.

After the parties were charged with fraud, the government's case was found to be insufficiently supported by the evidence, and no penalties were assessed. Afterward, church leaders sued Ellen in her role as IRS informant, charging that she had violated their First Amendment rights of free association and their Fourth Amendment rights against illegal search and seizure. Government employees are immune from such charges, but Ellen was only an informant to the IRS and not its employee. Can the church collect damages from Ellen for informing on them?

40. Butcher attended meetings of tax protestors for many years in which the constitutionality of the Federal income tax and its means of collection were routinely challenged. Members of various protestor groups were provided with materials to assist them in preparing returns such that little or no tax would be due on the basis that, for instance, only gold- or silver-backed currency need be submitted to pay the tax or that a tax bill had originated in the Senate rather than the House of Representatives. Some of the groups maintained that no returns need be filed by individuals at all on the grounds that the current law supporting a Federal income tax violates various elements of the U.S. Constitution.

The U.S. Tax Court routinely overturned such means of avoiding the tax, charging that such protestor returns were frivolously filed and charging the protestors with delinquent taxes, interest, and a variety of negligence and other accuracy-related penalties, especially where taxpayers failed to file altogether. The results of these cases never were discussed in the meetings that Butcher attended, though. Thus, although he never joined any of the groups, Butcher felt comfortable with the arguments of the protestor groups and never filed a Federal income tax return for himself or his profitable sole-proprietorship carpentry business.

When the IRS discovered his failure to file and charged him with tax, interest, and penalties, Butcher went to the tax library and found that judicial precedent and administrative authority were stacked against him. He asked the court for relief from the civil fraud penalties related to his failure to file and failure to pay tax on the basis of his good-faith belief that the tax protestor information he had received was an acceptable interpretation of the law. Under this argument, a taxpayer cannot be found to willfully have failed to file and pay if he or she had a good-faith belief that no such requirement was supported by the Constitution. Should Butcher be required to pay civil fraud penalties?

41. Chang wants to claim a cost recovery deduction for the acquisition of masterwork paintings to be hung in the reception area of her dental office. The paintings were specially chosen because of their tendency to relax the patients who would be viewing them, thereby facilitating the conduct of Chang's business. Chang lives and works in the Fifth Circuit. A recent Eleventh Circuit case seems to support such a deduction, in limited circumstances. Complete the following chart, indicating for each independent assumption the actions that Chang can take without incurring the civil penalty for substantial understatement of taxes, but still maximizing her legitimate deductions for the year.

Probability of Success in Court	Claim the Deduction?	File a Form 8275 Disclosure?
80%		
40		
20		
2		

42. Continue with the facts of Research Case 41. Now assume that you are Chang's tax adviser. You wish to eliminate any chance of incurring a preparer civil unrealistic-position penalty. Indicate the actions that you would recommend that Chang take.

Probability of Success in Court	Claim the Deduction?	File a Form 8275 Disclosure?
80%		
40		
20		
2		

43. Your client, Lee Ann Harkness, has been accused of criminal tax fraud. A high school dropout, she received hundreds of thousands of dollars over the years from Bentley, an elderly gentleman, in exchange for love and companionship. When Bentley died and Harkness was left out of the will, she sued the estate for compensatory payments earned throughout her years of attending to Bentley. The government now accuses Harkness of fraud in failing to file income and self-employment tax returns for the open tax years. Construct a defense on Harkness's behalf.

44. The Scooter Company, owned equally by Julie (chair of the board of directors) and Jeff (company president), is in very difficult financial

straits. Last month, Jeff used the $100,000 withheld from employee pay-checks for Federal payroll and income taxes to pay off a creditor who threatened to cut off all supplies. To keep the company afloat, Jeff used these government funds willfully for the operations of the business, but even that effort was not enough. The company missed the next two payrolls, and today other creditors took action to shut down Scooter altogether. From whom and for how much will the IRS assess in taxes and penalties in the matter?

45. For the completion and filing of his 2005 Federal income tax return, Ron retains the services of a tax preparer. Because of a particularly hectic tax preparation season, the preparer does not complete and file the return until June 2006. Is Ron excused from the failure to file and pay penalties under the reasonable cause exception?

Appendices

Appendix A

Time Value of Money Tables

CONTENTS

Future Value of $1

Periods	4%	6%	8%	10%	12%	14%	20%
1	1.040	1.060	1.080	1.100	1.120	1.140	1.200
2	1.082	1.124	1.166	1.210	1.254	1.300	1.440
3	1.125	1.191	1.260	1.331	1.405	1.482	1.728
4	1.170	1.263	1.361	1.464	1.574	1.689	2.074
5	1.217	1.338	1.469	1.611	1.762	1.925	2.488
6	1.265	1.419	1.587	1.772	1.974	2.195	2.986
7	1.316	1.504	1.714	1.949	2.211	2.502	3.583
8	1.369	1.594	1.851	2.144	2.476	2.853	4.300
9	1.423	1.690	1.999	2.359	2.773	3.252	5.160
10	1.480	1.791	2.159	2.594	3.106	3.707	6.192
11	1.540	1.898	2.332	2.853	3.479	4.226	7.430
12	1.601	2.012	2.518	3.139	3.896	4.818	8.916
13	1.665	2.133	2.720	3.452	4.364	5.492	10.699
14	1.732	2.261	2.937	3.798	4.887	6.261	12.839
15	1.801	2.397	3.172	4.177	5.474	7.138	15.407
20	2.191	3.207	4.661	6.728	9.646	13.743	38.338
30	3.243	5.744	10.063	17.450	29.960	50.950	237.380
40	4.801	10.286	21.725	45.260	93.051	188.880	1469.800

Future Value of an Annuity of $1 in Arrears

Periods	4%	6%	8%	10%	12%	14%	20%
1	1.000	1.000	1.000	1.000	1.000	1.000	1.000
2	2.040	2.060	2.080	2.100	2.120	2.140	2.220
3	3.122	3.184	3.246	3.310	3.374	3.440	3.640
4	4.247	4.375	4.506	4.641	4.779	4.921	5.368
5	5.416	5.637	5.867	6.105	6.353	6.610	7.442
6	6.633	6.975	7.336	7.716	8.115	8.536	9.930
7	7.898	8.394	8.923	9.487	10.089	10.730	12.916
8	9.214	9.898	10.637	11.436	12.300	13.233	16.499
9	10.583	11.491	12.488	13.580	14.776	16.085	20.799
10	12.006	13.181	14.487	15.938	17.549	19.337	25.959
11	13.486	14.972	16.646	18.531	20.655	23.045	32.150
12	15.026	16.870	18.977	21.385	24.133	27.271	39.580
13	16.627	18.882	21.495	24.523	28.029	32.089	48.497
14	18.292	21.015	24.215	27.976	32.393	37.581	59.196
15	20.024	23.276	27.152	31.773	37.280	43.842	72.035
20	29.778	36.778	45.762	57.276	75.052	91.025	186.690
30	56.085	79.058	113.283	164.496	241.330	356.790	1181.900
40	95.026	154.762	259.057	442.597	767.090	1342.000	7343.900

Present Value of $1

Periods

	4%	5%	6%	8%	10%	12%	14%	16%	18%	20%	22%	24%	26%	28%	30%	40%
1	0.962	0.952	0.943	0.926	0.909	0.893	0.877	0.862	0.847	0.833	0.820	0.806	0.794	0.781	0.769	0.714
2	0.925	0.907	0.890	0.857	0.826	0.797	0.769	0.743	0.718	0.694	0.672	0.650	0.630	0.610	0.592	0.510
3	0.889	0.864	0.840	0.794	0.751	0.712	0.675	0.641	0.609	0.579	0.551	0.524	0.500	0.477	0.455	0.364
4	0.855	0.823	0.792	0.735	0.683	0.636	0.592	0.552	0.516	0.482	0.451	0.423	0.397	0.373	0.350	0.260
5	0.822	0.784	0.747	0.681	0.621	0.567	0.519	0.476	0.436	0.402	0.370	0.341	0.315	0.291	0.269	0.186
6	0.790	0.746	0.705	0.630	0.564	0.507	0.456	0.410	0.370	0.335	0.303	0.275	0.250	0.227	0.207	0.133
7	0.760	0.711	0.665	0.583	0.513	0.452	0.400	0.354	0.314	0.279	0.249	0.222	0.198	0.178	0.159	0.095
8	0.731	0.677	0.627	0.540	0.467	0.404	0.351	0.305	0.266	0.233	0.204	0.179	0.157	0.139	0.123	0.068
9	0.703	0.645	0.592	0.500	0.424	0.361	0.308	0.263	0.225	0.194	0.167	0.144	0.125	0.108	0.094	0.048
10	0.676	0.614	0.558	0.463	0.386	0.322	0.270	0.227	0.191	0.162	0.137	0.116	0.099	0.085	0.073	0.035
11	0.650	0.585	0.527	0.429	0.350	0.287	0.237	0.195	0.162	0.135	0.112	0.094	0.079	0.066	0.056	0.025
12	0.625	0.557	0.497	0.397	0.319	0.257	0.208	0.168	0.137	0.112	0.092	0.076	0.062	0.052	0.043	0.018
13	0.601	0.530	0.469	0.368	0.290	0.229	0.182	0.145	0.116	0.093	0.075	0.061	0.050	0.040	0.033	0.013
14	0.577	0.505	0.442	0.340	0.263	0.205	0.160	0.125	0.099	0.078	0.062	0.049	0.039	0.032	0.025	0.009
15	0.555	0.481	0.417	0.315	0.239	0.183	0.140	0.108	0.084	0.065	0.051	0.040	0.031	0.025	0.020	0.006
16	0.534	0.458	0.394	0.292	0.218	0.163	0.123	0.093	0.071	0.054	0.042	0.032	0.025	0.019	0.015	0.005
17	0.513	0.436	0.371	0.270	0.198	0.146	0.108	0.080	0.060	0.045	0.034	0.026	0.020	0.015	0.012	0.003
18	0.494	0.416	0.350	0.250	0.180	0.130	0.095	0.069	0.051	0.038	0.028	0.021	0.016	0.012	0.009	0.002
19	0.475	0.396	0.331	0.232	0.164	0.116	0.083	0.060	0.043	0.031	0.023	0.017	0.012`	0.009	0.007	0.002
20	0.456	0.377	0.312	0.215	0.149	0.104	0.073	0.051	0.037	0.026	0.019	0.014	0.010	0.007	0.005	0.001
21	0.439	0.359	0.294	0.199	0.135	0.093	0.064	0.044	0.031	0.022	0.015	0.011	0.008	0.006	0.004	0.001
22	0.422	0.342	0.278	0.184	0.123	0.083	0.056	0.038	0.026	0.018	0.013	0.009	0.006	0.004	0.003	0.001
23	0.406	0.326	0.262	0.170	0.112	0.074	0.049	0.033	0.022	0.015	0.010	0.007	0.005	0.003	0.002	
24	0.390	0.310	0.247	0.158	0.102	0.066	0.043	0.028	0.019	0.013	0.008	0.006	0.004	0.003	0.002	
25	0.375	0.295	0.233	0.146	0.092	0.059	0.038	0.024	0.016	0.010	0.007	0.005	0.003	0.002	0.001	
26	0.361	0.281	0.220	0.135	0.084	0.053	0.033	0.021	0.014	0.009	0.006	0.004	0.002	0.002	0.001	
27	0.347	0.268	0.207	0.125	0.076	0.047	0.029	0.018	0.011	0.007	0.005	0.003	0.002	0.001	0.001	
28	0.333	0.255	0.196	0.116	0.069	0.042	0.026	0.016	0.010	0.006	0.004	0.002	0.002	0.001	0.001	
29	0.321	0.243	0.185	0.107	0.063	0.037	0.022	0.014	0.008	0.005	0.003	0.002	0.001	0.001	0.001	
30	0.308	0.231	0.174	0.099	0.057	0.033	0.020	0.012	0.007	0.004	0.003	0.002	0.001	0.001		
40	0.208	0.142	0.097	0.046	0.022	0.011	0.005	0.003	0.001	0.001						

Present Value of an Annuity of $1 in Arrears

Periods

	4%	5%	6%	8%	10%	12%	14%	16%	18%	20%	22%	24%	26%	28%	30%	40%
1	0.962	0.952	0.943	0.926	0.909	0.893	0.877	0.862	0.847	0.833	0.820	0.806	0.794	0.781	0.769	0.714
2	1.886	1.859	1.833	1.783	1.736	1.690	1.647	1.605	1.566	1.528	1.492	1.457	1.424	1.392	1.361	1.224
3	2.775	2.723	2.673	2.577	2.487	2.402	2.322	2.246	2.174	2.106	2.042	1.981	1.923	1.868	1.816	1.589
4	3.630	3.546	3.465	3.312	3.170	3.037	2.914	2.798	2.690	2.589	2.494	2.404	2.320	2.241	2.166	1.879
5	4.452	4.330	4.212	3.993	3.791	3.605	3.433	3.274	3.127	2.991	2.864	2.745	2.635	2.532	2.436	2.035
6	5.242	5.076	4.917	4.623	4.355	4.111	3.889	3.685	3.498	3.326	3.167	3.020	2.885	2.759	2.643	2.168
7	6.002	5.786	5.582	5.206	4.868	4.564	4.288	4.039	3.812	3.605	3.416	3.242	3.083	2.937	2.802	2.263
8	6.733	6.463	6.210	5.747	5.335	4.968	4.639	4.344	4.078	3.837	3.619	3.421	3.241	3.076	2.925	2.331
9	7.435	7.108	6.802	6.247	5.759	5.328	4.946	4.607	4.303	4.031	3.786	3.566	3.366	3.184	3.019	2.379
10	8.111	7.722	7.360	6.710	6.145	5.650	5.216	4.833	4.494	4.192	3.923	3.682	3.465	3.269	3.092	2.414
11	8.760	8.306	7.887	7.139	6.495	5.988	5.453	5.029	4.656	4.327	4.035	3.776	3.544	3.335	3.147	2.438
12	9.385	8.863	8.384	7.536	6.814	6.194	5.660	5.197	4.793	4.439	4.127	3.851	3.606	3.387	3.190	2.456
13	9.986	9.394	8.853	7.904	7.103	6.424	5.842	5.342	4.910	4.533	4.203	3.912	3.656	3.427	3.223	2.468
14	10.563	9.899	9.295	8.244	7.367	6.628	6.002	5.468	5.008	4.611	4.265	3.962	3.695	3.459	3.249	2.477
15	11.118	10.380	9.712	8.559	7.606	6.811	6.142	5.575	5.092	4.675	4.315	4.001	3.726	3.483	3.268	2.484
16	11.652	10.838	10.106	8.851	7.824	6.974	6.265	5.669	5.162	4.730	4.357	4.033	3.751	3.503	3.283	2.489
17	12.166	11.274	10.477	9.122	8.022	7.120	6.373	5.749	5.222	4.775	4.391	4.059	3.771	3.518	3.295	2.492
18	12.659	11.690	10.828	9.372	8.201	7.250	6.467	5.818	5.273	4.812	4.419	4.080	3.786	3.529	3.304	2.494
19	13.134	12.085	11.158	9.604	8.365	7.366	6.550	5.877	5.316	4.844	4.442	4.097	3.799	3.539	3.311	2.496
20	13.590	12.462	11.470	9.818	8.514	7.469	6.623	5.929	5.353	4.870	4.460	4.110	3.808	3.546	3.316	2.497
21	14.029	12.821	11.764	10.017	8.649	7.562	6.687	5.973	5.384	4.891	4.476	4.121	3.816	3.551	3.320	2.498
22	14.451	13.163	12.042	10.201	8.772	7.645	6.743	6.011	5.410	4.909	4.488	4.130	3.822	3.556	3.323	2.498
23	14.857	13.489	12.303	10.371	8.883	7.718	6.792	6.044	5.432	4.925	4.499	4.137	3.827	3.559	3.325	2.499
24	15.247	13.799	12.550	10.529	8.985	7.784	6.835	6.073	5.451	4.937	4.507	4.143	3.831	3.562	3.327	2.499
25	15.622	14.094	12.783	10.675	9.077	7.843	6.873	6.097	5.467	4.948	4.514	4.147	3.834	3.564	3.329	2.499
26	15.983	14.375	13.003	10.810	9.161	7.896	6.906	6.118	5.480	4.956	4.520	4.151	3.837	3.566	3.330	2.500
27	16.330	14.643	13.211	10.935	9.237	7.943	6.935	6.136	5.492	4.964	4.525	4.154	3.839	3.567	3.331	2.500
28	16.663	14.898	13.406	11.051	9.307	7.984	6.961	6.152	5.502	4.970	4.528	4.157	3.840	3.568	3.331	2.500
29	16.984	15.141	13.591	11.158	9.370	8.022	6.983	6.166	5.510	4.975	4.531	4.159	3.841	3.569	3.332	2.500
30	17.292	15.373	13.765	11.258	9.427	8.055	7.003	6.177	5.517	4.979	4.534	4.160	3.842	3.569	3.332	2.500
40	19.793	17.159	15.046	11.925	9.779	8.244	7.105	6.234	5.548	4.997	4.544	4.166	3.846	3.571	3.333	2.500

Standard Tax Citations

Citations are presented for illustrative and prescriptive purposes.
They do not necessarily track to actual documents.

Statutory

Constitution

U.S. Const. art. I, § 8, cl. 2.

U.S. Const. amend, XIV, § 2.

Code § 101(b)(2)(B)(ii).

Public Laws P.L. 109-123 Act § 1563.

Administrative

Regulation	Reg. § 1.162-5(a)(1).
Treasury Decision	T.D. 9043, 2003-1 C.B. 453.
Temporary Regulation	Reg. § 1.469-4T(c)(2).
Proposed Regulation	Prop. Reg. § 1.1176(b)(2).
Revenue Ruling	Rev. Rul. 2005-7, 2005-1 C.B. 712.
Revenue Ruling (temporary)	Rev. Rul. 2005-7, 2005-9 I.R.B. 712.
Revenue Procedure	Rev. Proc. 2005-21, 2005-1 C.B. 742.
Letter Ruling	Ltr. Rul. 200530042.
Technical Advice Memo	TAM 200005006.
Notice	Notice 2005-30, 2005-1 C.B. 989.
Notice (temporary)	Notice 2005-30, 2005-14 I.R.B. 989.
Announcement	Announcement 2005-11, 2005-4 I.R.B. 432.

Judicial

Board of Tax Appeals:

GPO reporter *Estate of D. R. Daly,* 3 B.T.A. 1042 (1926).

Tax Court Regular:

(temporary citation) *Mehan, Marty,* 122 T.C. ___ , No. 5 (2004).

Tax Court Regular:

GPO reporter *Mehan, Marty,* 122 T.C. 396 (2004).

Tax Court Memo:

General (unpublished) *Dixon, Michel,* T.C. Memo. 1999-310.

CCH reporter *Dixon, Michel,* 78 TCM 462 (1999).

RIA reporter[1] *Dixon, Michel,* RIA T.C. Memo. ¶ 99,310.

Kleinrock's *Dixon, Michel,* T.C. Memo. 1999-310.

Tax Court Small Cases Division: *Brown,* TC Summary Opinion 2004-109.

District Court:

West reporter *Barber, Lori,* 85 F.Supp. 2d. 967 (N.D.C.A., 2000).

CCH reporter *Barber, Lori,* 2000-1 USTC ¶ 50,209 (N.D. C.A., 2000).

RIA reporter[1] *Barber, Lori,* 85 AFTR2d 2000-879 (N.D. C.A., 2000).

Kleinrock's *Barber, Lori,* KTC 2000-45 (N.D.C.A., 2000).

Court of Federal Claims:[2]

West reporter *Bennett, Courtney,* 30 Fed. Cl. 396 (1994).

CCH reporter *Bennett, Courtney,* 94-1 USTC ¶ 50,044 (Fed.Cl., 1994).

RIA reporter[1] *Bennett, Courtney,* 73 AFTR2d 94-534 (Fed.Cl., 1994).

Kleinrock's *Bennett, Courtney,* KTC 1994-647 (Fed.Cl., 1994).

Court of Appeal:

West reporter *Home of Faith,* 39 F.3d. 263 (CA-10, 1994).

CCH reporter *Home of Faith,* 94-2 USTC ¶ 50,570 (CA-10, 1994).

RIA reporter[1] *Home of Faith,* 74 AFTR2d 94-5608 (CA-10, 1994).

Kleinrock's *Home of Faith,* KTC 1994-564 (CA-10, 1994).

1. Before 1992 this reporter was published by Prentice-Hall (P-H).
2. This court has been known as the Claims Court and the Court of Claims.

Supreme Court:

GPO reporter	*Indianapolis Power & Light*, 493 U.S. 203 (1990).
West reporter	*Indianapolis Power & Light*, 110 S.Ct. 589 (1990).
CCH reporter	*Indianapolis Power & Light*, 90-1 USTC ¶ 50,007 (USSC, 1990).
RIA reporter[1]	*Indianapolis Power & Light*, 65 AFTR2d 90-394 (USSC, 1990).
Kleinrock's	*Indianapolis Power & Light*, KTC 1990-53 (USSC, 1990).

Books

Raabe, W., Whittenburg, G., and Sanders, D. 2006. *Federal Tax Research*, 7th ed. Mason: Thomson South-Western.

Journals

Whittenburg, G., Bunn, R., and Venable, C. New Law Expands Tax Breaks for Paying Education Costs. *Practical Tax Strategies* (August 2001): 79.

Internet Document

Soled, Jay A. and Charles E. Falk. 2004. Cost Segregation Applied. *Journal of Accountancy Online*. 198 (August). Retrieved 9/10, 2004 from AICPA at: http://www.aicpa.org/pubs/jofa/aug2004/index.htm

Capitalization

Proper nouns and words derived from them are capitalized while common nouns are not. The names of specific persons, places, or things are proper nouns. All other nouns are common nouns. Examples of proper nouns include:

the Congress
the Code
Section 172(a)
the Regulations
Regulations Section 1.102-1
the President
the Fifth Circuit
the Tax Court
a Revenue Ruling
a Private Letter Ruling

Italics

In handwritten or typed papers <u>underlining</u> represents italics. The titles of books, magazines, newspapers, pamphlets, court cases, and tax services are shown in italics. Examples of items that are italicized include:

The Wealth of Nations
Journal of Taxation
New York Times
AICPA Code of Conduct
Circular 230
Statements on Responsibility in Tax Practice

Gregory v. Helvering
Cumulative Bulletin
Standard Federal Tax Reports
Federal Tax Coordinator 2d

Note: Do not italicize the titles of legal documents such as the U.S. Constitution and the U.S. Code.

Lists

A list is an independent clause followed by a colon with each item in the list separated by a comma.

The College of Business Administration has five departments: Accounting, Finance, Information Systems, Management, and Marketing.

Displayed Lists

Displayed lists are used to make items easy to scan by the reader. Such lists should be introduced with an independent clause or by a complete sentence ending with a period. Examples of items that it would be appropriate to display in list form would include:

- steps to solve a problem,
- rules,
- proposals to be discussed,
- checklists,
- recommendations, and
- procedures.

Periods are not used in lists unless the items in the list are complete sentences. The items in a list should be in the same form (i.e., nouns, phrases, clauses, or sentences). If the items in a list are to be numbered, use an arabic number followed by a period for each item. If the items are not numbered, say, because the list is not prioritized or sequential, consider using a bullet to draw the reader's attention to the items in the list (as shown above).

Other Systems

Many professions and academic disciplines have developed unique systems of citing published material. Examples of the more common style manuals include:

U.S. Government Printing Office Style Manual
The Chicago Manual of Style
MLA Handbook for Writers of Research Papers
The Bluebook, A Uniform System of (legal) Citations
Publication Manual of the American Psychological Association

In addition to the manuals listed above, there are style manuals published for accounting, biology, chemistry, geology, linguistics, mathematics, medicine, and physics.

Appendix C

IRS Circular 230

Treasury
Department
Circular No. 230
(Rev. 7-2002)

Regulations Governing the Practice of Attorneys, Certified
Public Accountants, Enrolled Agents, Enrolled Actuaries,
and Appraisers before the Internal Revenue Service

Department
of the
Treasury
**Internal
Revenue
Service**

Title 31 Code of Federal Regulations, Subtitle A, Part 10,
revised as of July 26, 2002

For a current version, see http://www.irs.gov/pub/irs-pdf/pcir230.pdf

Regulations Governing
the Practice of Attorneys,
Certified Public
Accountants, Enrolled
Agents, Enrolled
Actuaries, and Appraisers
before the Internal
Revenue Service

Treasury
Department
Circular
No. 230
(Rev. 7-2002)

This publication contains the revision of Treasury Department Circular No. 230 appearing in 31 F.R. 10773, dated August 13, 1966, and includes the following amendments:

Amendment appearing in 31 F.R. 12638, dated September 27, 1966, which adds omitted section heading § 10.58.

Amendments appearing in 31 F.R. 13992, dated November 2, 1966, which add subparagraphs (b) and (c) to § 10.57 and add a sentence at the end, as a continuation, or paragraph (c) of § 10.51.

Amendments appearing in 31 F.R. 13205, dated August 19, 1970, which are intended primarily to clarify the language of certain provisions of the regulations, strengthen certain conflict of interest and disciplinary provisions, and update statutory references.

Amendment appearing in 36 F.R. 8671, dated May 11, 1971, which corrects error in the August 19, 1970, amendments, which incorrectly added a new sentence to subparagraph 10.3(c) rather than subparagraph 10.3(e).

Amendments appearing in 42 F.R. 38350, dated July 28, 1977, which eliminate outdated terms and provisions, and which increase the restrictions on practice by former Government employees.

Amendments appearing in 44 F.R. 4940, dated January 24, 1979, which prescribe rules permitting the expansion of advertising and solicitation provisions of the regulations governing practice by attorneys, certified public accountants, enrolled agents and others who represent clients before the Internal Revenue Service.

Amendments appearing in 44 F.R. 4944, dated January 24, 1979, which prescribe rules to permit enrolled actuaries to engage in practice before the Internal Revenue Service in connection with the provisions of the Internal Revenue Code involving pension plans under the Employee Retirement Income Security Act of 1974 (ERISA).

Amendments appearing in 49 F.R. 6719, dated February 23, 1984, which clarify who may prepare a tax return and furnish information to the Internal Revenue Service, and set standards for providing opinions used in the promotion of tax shelter offerings.

Amendments appearing in 50 F.R. 42014, dated October 17, 1985, which implement section 156 of the Deficit Reduction Act of 1984, 98 Stat. 695, to provide for the disqualification of appraisals and appraisers' testimony in connection with Treasury Department or Internal Revenue Service proceedings with respect to any appraiser who has been assessed an aiding and abetting penalty under 26 U.S.C. 6701(a) after July 18, 1984.

Amendments appearing in 51 F.R. 2875, dated January 22, 1986, which require that those who are enrolled to practice before the Internal Revenue Service renew their enrollment on a periodic basis. A condition of eligibility for renewal of enrollment will be the satisfaction of continuing professional education requirements. In addition, the amendments modify the regulations reflecting the transfer to the Office of Director of Practice of certain functions formerly performed by the Commissioner of Internal Revenue relative to the enrollment of individuals who wish to practice before the Internal Revenue Service.

Amendments appearing in 57 F.R. 41093, dated September 9, 1992, which relate to the provisions of the regulations addressing advertising and solicitation by those eligible to practice before the IRS, which were occasioned by judicial determinations impacting on the subject.

Amendments appearing in 59 F.R. 31523, dated June 20, 1994, which establish tax return preparation standards and prescribe the circumstances under which a practitioner may be disciplined for violating those standards, limit the use of contingent fees for preparing tax returns, clarify that certain existing restrictions governing limited practice before the IRS apply to all individuals who are eligible to engage in limited practice before the IRS, establish expedited proceedings to suspend individuals from practice before the IRS in cases in which certain determinations have been made by independent bodies, and permit attorneys and certified public accountants in good standing to obtain or retain enrolled agent status.

Title 31 Code of Federal
Regulations, Subtitle A,
Part 10, revised as of
July 26, 2002

Department of
the Treasury
**Internal
Revenue
Service**

List of Subjects in 31 CFR part 10

Accountants, Administrative practice and procedure, Lawyers, Reporting and recordkeeping requirements.

Adoption of Amendments to the Regulations

Accordingly, 31 CFR part 10 is amended as follows:

Paragraph 1. The table of contents reads as follows:

PART 10—PRACTICE BEFORE THE INTERNAL REVENUE SERVICE

Authority: Sec. 3, 23 Stat. 258, secs. 2-12, 60 Stat. 237 et.seq.; 5 U.S.C. 301, 500, 551-559; 31 U.S.C. 321; 31 U.S.C. 330.

§10.0 Scope of part.

This part contains rules governing the recognition of attorneys, certified public accountants, enrolled agents, and other persons representing taxpayers before the Internal Revenue Service. Subpart A of this part sets forth rules relating to the authority to practice before the Internal Revenue Service; subpart B of this part prescribes the duties and restrictions relating to such practice; subpart C of this part prescribes the sanctions for violating the regulations; subpart D of this part contains the rules applicable to disciplinary proceedings; and subpart E of this part contains general provisions including provisions relating to the availability of official records.

Subpart A—Rules Governing Authority to Practice

§10.1 Director of Practice.

(a) *Establishment of office.* The Office of Director of Practice is established in the Office of the Secretary of the Treasury. The Director of Practice is appointed by the Secretary of the Treasury, or his or her designate.

(b) *Duties.* The Director of Practice acts on applications for enrollment to practice before the Internal Revenue Service; makes inquiries with respect to matters under his or her jurisdiction; institutes and provides for the conduct of disciplinary proceedings relating to attorneys, certified public accountants, enrolled agents, enrolled actuaries and appraisers; and performs other duties as are necessary or appropriate to carry out his or her functions under this part or as are prescribed by the Secretary of the Treasury, or his or her delegate.

(c) *Acting Director of Practice.* The Secretary of the Treasury, or his or her delegate, will designate an officer or employee of the Treasury Department to act as Director of Practice in the absence of the Director or a vacancy in that office.

§10.2 Definitions.

As used in this part, except where the text clearly provides otherwise:

(a) *Attorney* means any person who is a member in good standing of the bar of the highest court of any State, territory, or possession of the United States, including a Commonwealth, or the District of Columbia.

(b) *Certified public accountant* means any person who is duly qualified to practice as a certified public accountant in any State, territory, or possession of the United States, including a Commonwealth, or the District of Columbia.

(c) *Commissioner* refers to the Commissioner of Internal Revenue.

(d) *Practice before the Internal Revenue Service* comprehends all matters connected with a presentation to the Internal Revenue Service or any of its officers or employees relating to a taxpayer's rights, privileges, or liabilities under laws or regulations administered by the Internal Revenue Service. Such presentations include, but are not limited to, preparing and filing documents, corresponding and communicating with the Internal Revenue Service, and representing a client at conferences, hearings, and meetings.

(e) *Practitioner* means any individual described in paragraphs (a), (b), (c), or (d) of § 10.3.

(f) A *tax return* includes an amended tax return and a claim for refund.

(g) *Service* means the Internal Revenue Service.

§10.3 Who may practice.

(a) *Attorneys.* Any attorney who is not currently under suspension or disbarment from practice before the Internal Revenue Service may practice before the Internal Revenue Service by filing with the Internal Revenue Service a written declaration that he or she is currently qualified as an attorney and is authorized to represent the party or parties on whose behalf he or she acts.

(b) *Certified public accountants.* Any certified public accountant who is not currently under suspension or disbarment from practice before the Internal Revenue Service may practice before the Internal Revenue Service by filing with the Internal Revenue Service a written declaration that he or she is currently qualified as a certified public accountant and is authorized to represent the party or parties on whose behalf he or she acts.

(c) *Enrolled agents.* Any individual enrolled as an agent pursuant to this part who is not currently under suspension or disbarment from practice before the Internal Revenue Service may practice before the Internal Revenue Service.

(d) *Enrolled actuaries.* (1) Any individual who is enrolled as an actuary by the Joint Board for the Enrollment of Actuaries pursuant to 29 U.S.C. 1242 who is not currently under suspension or disbarment from practice before the Internal Revenue Service may practice before the Internal Revenue Service by filing with the Internal Revenue Service a written declaration stating that he or she is currently qualified as an enrolled actuary and is authorized to represent the party or parties on whose behalf he or she acts.

(2) Practice as an enrolled actuary is limited to representation with respect to issues involving the following statutory provisions in title 26 of the United States Code: sections 401 (relating to qualification of employee plans), 403(a) (relating to whether an annuity plan meets the requirements of section 404(a)(2)), 404 (relating to deductibility of employer contributions), 405 (relating to qualification of bond purchase plans), 412 (relating to funding requirements for certain employee plans), 413 (relating to application of qualification requirements to collectively bargained plans and to plans maintained by more than one employer), 414 (relating to definitions and special rules with respect to the employee plan area), 419 (relating to treatment of funded welfare benefits), 419A (relating to qualified asset accounts), 420 (relating to transfers of excess pension assets to retiree health accounts), 4971 (relating to excise taxes payable as a result of an accumulated funding deficiency under section 412), 4972 (relating to tax on nondeductible contributions to qualified employer plans), 4976 (relating to taxes with respect to funded welfare benefit plans), 4980 (relating to tax on reversion of qualified plan assets to employer), 6057 (relating to annual registration of plans), 6058 (relating to information required in connection with certain plans of deferred compensation), 6059 (relating to periodic report of actuary), 6652(e) (relating to the failure to file annual registration and other notifications by pension plan), 6652(f) (relating to the failure to file information required in connection with certain plans of deferred compensation), 6692 (relating to the failure to file actuarial report), 7805(b) (relating to the extent to which an Internal Revenue Service ruling or determination letter coming under the statutory provisions listed here will be applied without retroactive effect); and 29 U.S.C. 1083 (relating to the waiver of funding for nonqualified plans).

(3) An individual who practices before the Internal Revenue Service pursuant to paragraph (d)(1) of this section is subject to the provisions of this part in the same manner as attorneys, certified public accountants and enrolled agents.

(e) *Others.* Any individual qualifying under paragraph (d) of § 10.5 or § 10.7 is eligible to practice before the Internal Revenue Service to the extent provided in those sections.

(f) *Government officers and employees, and others.* An individual, who is an officer or employee of the executive, legislative, or judicial branch of the United States Government; an officer or employee of the District of Columbia; a Member of Congress; or a Resident Commissioner may not practice before the Internal Revenue Service if such practice violates 18 U.S.C. 203 or 205.

(g) *State officers and employees.* No officer or employee of any State, or subdivision of any State, whose duties require him or her to pass upon, investigate, or deal with tax matters for such State or subdivision, may practice before the Internal Revenue Service, if such employment may disclose facts or information applicable to Federal tax matters.

§10.4 Eligibility for enrollment.

(a) *Enrollment upon examination.* The Director of Practice may grant enrollment to an applicant who demonstrates special competence in tax matters by written examination administered by, or administered under the oversight of, the Director of Practice and who has not engaged in any conduct that would justify the censure, suspension, or disbarment of any practitioner under the provisions of this part.

(b) *Enrollment of former Internal Revenue Service employees.* The Director of Practice may grant enrollment to an applicant who, by virtue of his or her past service and technical experience in the Internal Revenue Service, has qualified for such enrollment and who has not engaged in any conduct that would justify the censure, suspension, or disbarment of any practitioner under the provisions of this part, under the following circumstances—

(1) The former employee applies for enrollment to the Director of Practice on a form supplied by the Director of Practice and supplies the information requested on the form and such other information regarding the experience and training of the applicant as may be relevant.

(2) An appropriate office of the Internal Revenue Service, at the request of the Director of Practice, will provide the Director of Practice with a detailed report of the nature and rating of the applicant's work while employed by the Internal Revenue Service and a recommendation whether such employment qualifies the applicant technically or otherwise for the desired authorization.

(3) Enrollment based on an applicant's former employment with the Internal Revenue Service may be of unlimited scope or it may be limited to permit the presentation of matters only of the particular class or only before the particular unit or division of the Internal Revenue Service for which the applicant's former employment has qualified the applicant.

(4) Application for enrollment based on an applicant's former employment with the Internal Revenue Service must be made within 3 years from the date of separation from such employment.

(5) An applicant for enrollment who is requesting such enrollment based on his or her former employment with the Internal Revenue Service must have had a minimum of 5 years continuous employment with the Internal Revenue Service during which he or she must have been regularly engaged in applying and interpreting the provisions of the Internal Revenue Code and the regulations thereunder relating to income, estate, gift, employment, or excise taxes.

(6) For the purposes of paragraph (b)(5) of this section, an aggregate of 10 or more years of employment in positions involving the application and interpretation of the provisions of the Internal Revenue Code, at least 3 of which occurred within the 5 years preceding the date of application, is the equivalent of 5 years continuous employment.

(c) *Natural persons.* Enrollment to practice may be granted only to natural persons.

§10.5 Application for enrollment.

(a) *Form; address.* An applicant for enrollment must file an application on Form 23, "Application for Enrollment to Practice Before the Internal Revenue Service," properly executed under oath or affirmation, with the Director of Practice. The address of the applicant entered on Form 23 will be the address under which a successful applicant is enrolled and is the address to which the Director of Practice will send correspondence concerning enrollment. An enrolled agent must send notification of any change to his or her enrollment address to the Director of Practice, Internal Revenue Service, 1111 Constitution Avenue, NW., Washington, DC 20224, or at such other address specified by the Director of Practice. This notification must include the enrolled agent's name, old address, new address, social security number or tax identification number, signature, and the date.

(b) *Fee.* The application for enrollment must be accompanied by a check or money order in the amount set forth on Form 23, payable to the Internal Revenue Service, which amount constitutes a fee charged to each applicant for enrollment. This fee will be retained by the United States whether or not the applicant is granted enrollment.

(c) *Additional information; examination.* The Director of Practice, as a condition to consideration of an application for enrollment, may require the applicant to file additional information and to submit to any written or oral examination under oath or otherwise. The Director of Practice will, on written request filed by an applicant, afford such applicant the opportunity to be heard with respect to his or her application for enrollment.

(d) *Temporary recognition.* On receipt of a properly executed application, the Director of Practice may grant the applicant temporary recognition to practice pending a determination as to whether enrollment to practice should be granted. Temporary recognition will be granted only in unusual circumstances and it will not be granted, in any circumstance, if the application is not regular on its face, if the information stated in the application, if true, is not sufficient to warrant enrollment to practice, or if there is any information before the Director of Practice indicating that the statements in the application are untrue or that the applicant would not otherwise qualify for enrollment. Issuance of temporary recognition does not constitute enrollment to practice or a finding of eligibility for enrollment, and the temporary recognition may be withdrawn at any time by the Director of Practice.

(e) *Appeal from denial of application.* The Director of Practice must inform the applicant as to the reason(s) for any denial of an application for enrollment. The applicant may, within 30 days after receipt of the notice of denial of enrollment, file a written appeal of the denial of enrollment with the Secretary of the Treasury or his or her delegate. A decision on the appeal will be rendered by the Secretary of the Treasury, or his or her delegate, as soon as practicable.

§10.6 Enrollment.

(a) *Roster.* The Director of Practice will maintain rosters of all individuals—

(1) Who have been granted active enrollment to practice before the Internal Revenue Service;

(2) Whose enrollment has been placed in inactive status for failure to meet the requirements for renewal of enrollment;

(3) Whose enrollment has been placed in inactive retirement status;

(4) Who have been censured, suspended, or disbarred from practice before the Internal Revenue Service;

(5) Whose offer of consent to resign from enrollment to practice before the Internal Revenue Service has been accepted by the Director of Practice under § 10.61; and

(6) Whose application for enrollment has been denied.

(b) *Enrollment card.* The Director of Practice will issue an enrollment card to each individual whose application for enrollment to practice before the Internal Revenue Service is approved after July 26, 2002. Each enrollment card will be valid for the period stated on the enrollment card. An individual is not eligible to practice before the Internal Revenue Service if his or her enrollment card is not valid.

(c) *Term of enrollment.* Each individual enrolled to practice before the Internal Revenue Service will be accorded active enrollment status subject to his or her renewal of enrollment as provided in this part.

(d) *Renewal of enrollment.* To maintain active enrollment to practice before the Internal Revenue Service, each individual enrolled is required to have his or her enrollment renewed. Failure by an individual to receive notification from the Director of Practice of the renewal requirement will not be justification for the failure to satisfy this requirement.

(1) All individuals licensed to practice before the Internal Revenue Service who have a social security number or tax identification number that ends with the numbers 0, 1, 2, or 3, except for those individuals who received their initial enrollment after November 1, 2003, must apply for renewal between November 1, 2003, and January 31, 2004. The renewal will be effective April 1, 2004.

(2) All individuals licensed to practice before the Internal Revenue Service who have a social security number or tax identification number that ends with the numbers 4, 5, or 6, except for those individuals who received their initial enrollment after November 1, 2004, must apply for renewal between November 1, 2004, and January 31, 2005. The renewal will be effective April 1, 2005.

(3) All individuals licensed to practice before the Internal Revenue Service who have a social security number or tax identification number that ends with the numbers 7, 8, or 9, except for those individuals who received their initial enrollment after November 1, 2005, must apply for renewal between November 1, 2005, and January 31, 2006. The renewal will be effective April 1, 2006.

(4) Thereafter, applications for renewal will be required between November 1 and January 31 of every subsequent third year as specified in paragraphs (d)(1), (2) or (3) of this section

according to the last number of the individual's social security number or tax identification number. Those individuals who receive initial enrollment after November 1 and before April 2 of the applicable renewal period will not be required to renew their enrollment before the first full renewal period following the receipt of their initial enrollment.

(5) The Director of Practice will notify the individual of his or her renewal of enrollment and will issue the individual a card evidencing enrollment.

(6) A reasonable nonrefundable fee may be charged for each application for renewal of enrollment filed with the Director of Practice.

(7) Forms required for renewal may be obtained from the Director of Practice, Internal Revenue Service, 1111 Constitution Avenue, NW., Washington, DC 20224.

(e) *Condition for renewal: Continuing professional education.* In order to qualify for renewal of enrollment, an individual enrolled to practice before the Internal Revenue Service must certify, on the application for renewal form prescribed by the Director of Practice, that he or she has satisfied the following continuing professional education requirements.

(1) *For renewed enrollment effective after March 31, 2004.* (i) A minimum of 16 hours of continuing education credit must be completed during each calendar year in the enrollment term.

(2) *For renewed enrollment effective after April 1, 2007.* (i) A minimum of 72 hours of continuing education credit must be completed during each three year period described in paragraph (d)(4) of this section. Each such three year period is known as an enrollment cycle.

(ii) A minimum of 16 hours of continuing education credit, including 2 hours of ethics or professional conduct, must be completed in each year of an enrollment cycle.

(iii) An individual who receives initial enrollment during an enrollment cycle must complete two (2) hours of qualifying continuing education credit for each month enrolled during the enrollment cycle. Enrollment for any part of a month is considered enrollment for the entire month.

(f) *Qualifying continuing education*—(1) *General.* To qualify for continuing education credit, a course of learning must—

(i) Be a qualifying program designed to enhance professional knowledge in Federal taxation or Federal tax related matters, i.e., programs comprised of current subject matter in Federal taxation or Federal tax related matters, including accounting, tax preparation software and taxation or ethics; and

(ii) Be conducted by a qualifying sponsor.

(2) *Qualifying programs*—(i) *Formal programs.* A formal program qualifies as a continuing education program if it—

(A) Requires attendance. Additionally, the program sponsor must provide each attendee with a certificate of attendance;

(B) Requires that the program be conducted by a qualified instructor, discussion leader, or speaker, i.e., a person whose background, training, education and experience are appropriate for instructing or leading a discussion on the subject matter of the particular program; and

(C) Provides or requires a written outline, textbook, or suitable electronic educational materials.

(ii) *Correspondence or individual study programs (including taped programs).* Qualifying continuing education programs include correspondence or individual study programs that are conducted by qualifying sponsors and completed on an individual basis by the enrolled individual. The allowable credit hours for such programs will be measured on a basis comparable to the measurement of a seminar or course for credit in an accredited educational institution. Such programs qualify as continuing education programs if they—

(A) Require registration of the participants by the sponsor;

(B) Provide a means for measuring completion by the participants (e.g., a written examination), including the issuance of a certificate of completion by the sponsor; and

(C) Provide a written outline, textbook, or suitable electronic educational materials.

(iii) *Serving as an instructor, discussion leader or speaker.* (A) One hour of continuing education credit will be awarded for each contact hour completed as an instructor, discussion leader, or speaker at an educational program that meets the continuing education requirements of paragraph (f) of this section.

(B) Two hours of continuing education credit will be awarded for actual subject preparation time for each contact hour completed as an instructor, discussion leader, or speaker at such programs. It is the responsibility of the individual claiming such credit to maintain records to verify preparation time.

(C) The maximum credit for instruction and preparation may not exceed 50 percent of the continuing education requirement for an enrollment cycle.

(D) An instructor, discussion leader, or speaker who makes more than one presentation on the same subject matter during an enrollment cycle will receive continuing education credit for only one such presentation for the enrollment cycle.

(iv) *Credit for published articles, books, etc.* (A) Continuing education credit will be awarded for publications on Federal taxation or Federal tax related matters, including accounting, financial management, tax preparation software, and taxation, provided the content of such publications is current and designed for the enhancement of the professional knowledge of an individual enrolled to practice before the Internal Revenue Service.

(B) The credit allowed will be on the basis of one hour credit for each hour of preparation time for the material. It is the responsibility of the person claiming the credit to maintain records to verify preparation time.

(C) The maximum credit for publications may not exceed 25 percent of the continuing education requirement of any enrollment cycle.

(3) *Periodic examination.* (i) Individuals may establish eligibility for renewal of enrollment for any enrollment cycle by—

(A) Achieving a passing score on each part of the Special Enrollment Examination administered under this part during the three year period prior to renewal; and

(B) Completing a minimum of 16 hours of qualifying continuing education during the last year of an enrollment cycle.

(ii) Courses designed to help an applicant prepare for the examination specified in paragraph (a) of § 10.4 are considered basic in nature and are not qualifying continuing education.

(g) *Sponsors.* (1) Sponsors are those responsible for presenting programs.

(2) To qualify as a sponsor, a program presenter must—

(i) Be an accredited educational institution;

(ii) Be recognized for continuing education purposes by the licensing body of any State, territory, or possession of the United States, including a Commonwealth, or the District of Columbia;

(iii) Be recognized by the Director of Practice as a professional organization or society whose programs include offering continuing professional education opportunities in subject matters within the scope of paragraph (f)(1)(i) of this section; or

(iv) File a sponsor agreement with the Director of Practice and obtain approval of the program as a qualified continuing education program.

(3) A qualifying sponsor must ensure the program complies with the following requirements—

(i) Programs must be developed by individual(s) qualified in the subject matter;

(ii) Program subject matter must be current;

(iii) Instructors, discussion leaders, and speakers must be qualified with respect to program content;

(iv) Programs must include some means for evaluation of technical content and presentation;

(v) Certificates of completion must be provided to the participants who successfully complete the program; and

(vi) Records must be maintained by the sponsor to verify the participants who attended and completed the program for a period of three years following completion of the program. In the case of continuous conferences, conventions, and the like, records must be maintained to verify completion of the program and attendance by each participant at each segment of the program.

(4) Professional organizations or societies wishing to be considered as qualified sponsors must request this status from the Director of

Practice and furnish information in support of the request together with any further information deemed necessary by the Director of Practice.

(5) A professional organization or society recognized as a qualified sponsor by the Director of Practice will retain its status for one enrollment cycle. The Director of Practice will publish the names of such sponsors on a periodic basis.

(h) *Measurement of continuing education coursework*. (1) All continuing education programs will be measured in terms of contact hours. The shortest recognized program will be one contact hour.

(2) A contact hour is 50 minutes of continuous participation in a program. Credit is granted only for a full contact hour, i.e., 50 minutes or multiples thereof. For example, a program lasting more than 50 minutes but less than 100 minutes will count as one contact hour.

(3) Individual segments at continuous conferences, conventions and the like will be considered one total program. For example, two 90-minute segments (180 minutes) at a continuous conference will count as three contact hours.

(4) For university or college courses, each semester hour credit will equal 15 contact hours and a quarter hour credit will equal 10 contact hours.

(i) *Recordkeeping requirements*. (1) Each individual applying for renewal must retain for a period of three years following the date of renewal of enrollment the information required with regard to qualifying continuing professional education credit hours. Such information includes—

(i) The name of the sponsoring organization;

(ii) The location of the program;

(iii) The title of the program and description of its content;

(iv) Written outlines, course syllibi, textbook, and/or electronic materials provided or required for the course;

(v) The dates attended;

(vi) The credit hours claimed;

(vii) The name(s) of the instructor(s), discussion leader(s), or speaker(s), if appropriate; and

(viii) The certificate of completion and/or signed statement of the hours of attendance obtained from the sponsor.

(2) To receive continuing education credit for service completed as an instructor, discussion leader, or speaker, the following information must be maintained for a period of three years following the date of renewal of enrollment—

(i) The name of the sponsoring organization;

(ii) The location of the program;

(iii) The title of the program and description of its content;

(iv) The dates of the program; and

(v) The credit hours claimed.

(3) To receive continuing education credit for publications, the following information must be maintained for a period of three years following the date of renewal of enrollment—

(i) The publisher;

(ii) The title of the publication;

(iii) A copy of the publication;

(iv) The date of publication; and

(v) Records that substantiate the hours worked on the publication.

(j) *Waivers*. (1) Waiver from the continuing education requirements for a given period may be granted by the Director of Practice for the following reasons—

(i) Health, which prevented compliance with the continuing education requirements;

(ii) Extended active military duty;

(iii) Absence from the United States for an extended period of time due to employment or other reasons, provided the individual does not practice before the Internal Revenue Service during such absence; and

(iv) Other compelling reasons, which will be considered on a case-by-case basis.

(2) A request for waiver must be accompanied by appropriate documentation. The individual is required to furnish any additional documentation or explanation deemed necessary by the Director of Practice. Examples of appropriate documentation could be a medical certificate or military orders.

(3) A request for waiver must be filed no later than the last day of the renewal application period.

(4) If a request for waiver is not approved, the individual will be placed in inactive status, so notified by the Director of Practice, and placed on a roster of inactive enrolled individuals.

(5) If a request for waiver is approved, the individual will be notified and issued a card evidencing renewal.

(6) Those who are granted waivers are required to file timely applications for renewal of enrollment.

(k) *Failure to comply.* (1) Compliance by an individual with the requirements of this part is determined by the Director of Practice. An individual who fails to meet the requirements of eligibility for renewal of enrollment will be notified by the Director of Practice at his or her enrollment address by first class mail. The notice will state the basis for the determination of noncompliance and will provide the individual an opportunity to furnish information in writing relating to the matter within 60 days of the date of the notice. Such information will be considered by the Director of Practice in making a final determination as to eligibility for renewal of enrollment.

(2) The Director of Practice may require any individual, by notice sent by first class mail to his or her enrollment address, to provide copies of any records required to be maintained under this part. The Director of Practice may disallow any continuing professional education hours claimed if the individual fails to comply with this requirement.

(3) An individual who has not filed a timely application for renewal of enrollment, who has not made a timely response to the notice of noncompliance with the renewal requirements, or who has not satisfied the requirements of eligibility for renewal will be placed on a roster of inactive enrolled individuals. During this time, the individual will be ineligible to practice before the Internal Revenue Service.

(4) Individuals placed in inactive enrollment status and individuals ineligible to practice before the Internal Revenue Service may not state or imply that they are enrolled to practice before the Internal Revenue Service, or use the term *enrolled agent*, the designation "E. A.," or other form of reference to eligibility to practice before the Internal Revenue Service.

(5) An individual placed in an inactive status may be reinstated to an active enrollment status by filing an application for renewal of enrollment and providing evidence of the completion of all required continuing professional education hours for the enrollment cycle. Continuing education credit under this paragraph (k)(5) may not be used to satisfy the requirements of the enrollment cycle in which the individual has been placed back on the active roster.

(6) An individual placed in an inactive status must file an application for renewal of enrollment and satisfy the requirements for renewal as set forth in this section within three years of being placed in an inactive status. The name of such individual otherwise will be removed from the inactive enrollment roster and his or her enrollment will terminate. Eligibility for enrollment must then be reestablished by the individual as provided in this section.

(7) Inactive enrollment status is not available to an individual who is the subject of a disciplinary matter in the Office of Director of Practice.

(l) *Inactive retirement status.* An individual who no longer practices before the Internal Revenue Service may request being placed in an inactive status at any time and such individual will be placed in an inactive retirement status. The individual will be ineligible to practice before the Internal Revenue Service. Such individual must file a timely application for renewal of enrollment at each applicable renewal or enrollment period as provided in this section. An individual who is placed in an inactive retirement status may be reinstated to an active enrollment status by filing an application for renewal of enrollment and providing evidence of the completion of the required continuing professional education hours for the enrollment cycle. Inactive retirement status is not available to an individual who is subject of a disciplinary matter in the Office of Director of Practice.

(m) *Renewal while under suspension or disbarment.* An individual who is ineligible to practice before the Internal Revenue Service by virtue of disciplinary action is required to be in conformance with the requirements for renewal of enrollment before his or her eligibility is restored.

(n) *Verification*. The Director of Practice may review the continuing education records of an enrolled individual and/or qualified sponsor in a manner deemed appropriate to determine compliance with the requirements and standards for renewal of enrollment as provided in paragraph (f) of this section.

(o) *Enrolled Actuaries*. The enrollment and the renewal of enrollment of actuaries authorized to practice under paragraph (d) of § 10.3 are governed by the regulations of the Joint Board for the Enrollment of Actuaries at 20 CFR 901.1 through 901.71. (Approved by the Office of Management and Budget under Control No. 1545-0946 and 1545-1726)

§10.7 Representing oneself; participating in rulemaking; limited practice; special appearances; and return preparation.

(a) *Representing oneself*. Individuals may appear on their own behalf before the Internal Revenue Service provided they present satisfactory identification.

(b) *Participating in rulemaking*. Individuals may participate in rulemaking as provided by the Administrative Procedure Act. See 5 U.S.C. 553.

(c) *Limited practice*—(1) *In general*. Subject to the limitations in paragraph (c)(2) of this section, an individual who is not a practitioner may represent a taxpayer before the Internal Revenue Service in the circumstances described in this paragraph (c)(1), even if the taxpayer is not present, provided the individual presents satisfactory identification and proof of his or her authority to represent the taxpayer. The circumstances described in this paragraph (c)(1) are as follows:

(i) An individual may represent a member of his or her immediate family.

(ii) A regular full-time employee of an individual employer may represent the employer.

(iii) A general partner or a regular full-time employee of a partnership may represent the partnership.

(iv) A bona fide officer or a regular full-time employee of a corporation (including a parent, subsidiary, or other affiliated corporation), association, or organized group may represent the corporation, association, or organized group.

(v) A regular full-time employee of a trust, receivership, guardianship, or estate may represent the trust, receivership, guardianship, or estate.

(vi) An officer or a regular employee of a governmental unit, agency, or authority may represent the governmental unit, agency, or authority in the course of his or her official duties.

(vii) An individual may represent any individual or entity, who is outside the United States, before personnel of the Internal Revenue Service when such representation takes place outside the United States.

(viii) An individual who prepares and signs a taxpayer's tax return as the preparer, or who prepares a tax return but is not required (by the instructions to the tax return or regulations) to sign the tax return, may represent the taxpayer before revenue agents, customer service representatives or similar officers and employees of the Internal Revenue Service during an examination of the taxable year or period covered by that tax return, but, unless otherwise prescribed by regulation or notice, this right does not permit such individual to represent the taxpayer, regardless of the circumstances requiring representation, before appeals officers, revenue officers, Counsel or similar officers or employees of the Internal Revenue Service or the Department of Treasury.

(2) *Limitations*. (i) An individual who is under suspension or disbarment from practice before the Internal Revenue Service may not engage in limited practice before the Internal Revenue Service under paragraph (c)(1) of this section.

(ii) The Director, after notice and opportunity for a conference, may deny eligibility to engage in limited practice before the Internal Revenue Service under paragraph (c)(1) of this section to any individual who has engaged in conduct that would justify censuring, suspending, or disbarring a practitioner from practice before the Internal Revenue Service.

(iii) An individual who represents a taxpayer under the authority of paragraph (c)(1) of this section is subject, to the extent of his or her authority, to such rules of general applicability regarding standards of conduct and other matters as the Director of Practice prescribes.

(d) *Special appearances.* The Director of Practice may, subject to such conditions as he or she deems appropriate, authorize an individual who is not otherwise eligible to practice before the Internal Revenue Service to represent another person in a particular matter.

(e) *Preparing tax returns and furnishing information.* Any individual may prepare a tax return, appear as a witness for the taxpayer before the Internal Revenue Service, or furnish information at the request of the Internal Revenue Service or any of its officers or employees.

(f) *Fiduciaries.* For purposes of this part, a fiduciary (i.e., a trustee, receiver, guardian, personal representative, administrator, or executor) is considered to be the taxpayer and not a representative of the taxpayer.

§10.8 Customhouse brokers.

Nothing contained in the regulations in this part will affect or limit the right of a customhouse broker, licensed as such by the Commissioner of Customs in accordance with the regulations prescribed therefor, in any customs district in which he or she is so licensed, at a relevant local office of the Internal Revenue Service or before the National Office of the Internal Revenue Service, to act as a representative in respect to any matters relating specifically to the importation or exportation of merchandise under the customs or internal revenue laws, for any person for whom he or she has acted as a customhouse broker.

Subpart B—Duties and Restrictions Relating to Practice Before the Internal Revenue Service

§10.20 Information to be furnished.

(a) *To the Internal Revenue Service.* (1) A practitioner must, on a proper and lawful request by a duly authorized officer or employee of the Internal Revenue Service, promptly submit records or information in any matter before the Internal Revenue Service unless the practitioner believes in good faith and on reasonable grounds that the records or information are privileged.

(2) Where the requested records or information are not in the possession of, or subject to the control of, the practitioner or the practitioner's client, the practitioner must promptly notify the requesting Internal Revenue Service officer or employee and the practitioner must provide any information that the practitioner has regarding the identity of any person who the practitioner believes may have possession or control of the requested records or information. The practitioner must make reasonable inquiry of his or her client regarding the identity of any person who may have possession or control of the requested records or information, but the practitioner is not required to make inquiry of any other person or independently verify any information provided by the practitioner's client regarding the identity of such persons.

(b) *To the Director of Practice.* When a proper and lawful request is made by the Director of Practice, a practitioner must provide the Director of Practice with any information the practitioner has concerning an inquiry by the Director of Practice into an alleged violation of the regulations in this part by any person, and to testify regarding this information in any proceeding instituted under this part, unless the practitioner believes in good faith and on reasonable grounds that the information is privileged.

(c) *Interference with a proper and lawful request for records or information.* A practitioner may not interfere, or attempt to interfere, with any proper and lawful effort by the Internal Revenue Service, its officers or employees, or the Director of Practice, or his or her employees, to obtain any record or information unless the practitioner believes in good faith and on reasonable grounds that the record or information is privileged.

§10.21 Knowledge of client's omission.

A practitioner who, having been retained by a client with respect to a matter administered by the Internal Revenue Service, knows that the client has not complied with the revenue laws of the United States or has made an error in or omission from any return, document, affidavit, or other paper which the client submitted or executed under the revenue laws of the United States, must advise the client promptly of the fact of such noncompliance, error, or omission.

The practitioner must advise the client of the consequences as provided under the Code and regulations of such noncompliance, error, or omission.

§10.22 Diligence as to accuracy.

(a) *In general.* A practitioner must exercise due diligence—

(1) In preparing or assisting in the preparation of, approving, and filing tax returns, documents, affidavits, and other papers relating to Internal Revenue Service matters;

(2) In determining the correctness of oral or written representations made by the practitioner to the Department of the Treasury; and

(3) In determining the correctness of oral or written representations made by the practitioner to clients with reference to any matter administered by the Internal Revenue Service.

(b) *Reliance on others.* Except as provided in §§10.33 and 10.34, a practitioner will be presumed to have exercised due diligence for purposes of this section if the practitioner relies on the work product of another person and the practitioner used reasonable care in engaging, supervising, training, and evaluating the person, taking proper account of the nature of the relationship between the practitioner and the person.

§10.23 Prompt disposition of pending matters.

A practitioner may not unreasonably delay the prompt disposition of any matter before the Internal Revenue Service.

§10.24 Assistance from or to disbarred or suspended persons and former Internal Revenue Service employees.

A practitioner may not, knowingly and directly or indirectly:

(a) Accept assistance from or assist any person who is under disbarment or suspension from practice before the Internal Revenue Service if the assistance relates to a matter or matters constituting practice before the Internal Revenue Service.

(b) Accept assistance from any former government employee where the provisions of §10.25 or any Federal law would be violated.

§10.25 Practice by former Government employees, their partners and their associates.

(a) *Definitions.* For purposes of this section—

(1) *Assist* means to act in such a way as to advise, furnish information to, or otherwise aid another person, directly or indirectly.

(2) *Government employee* is an officer or employee of the United States or any agency of the United States, including a *special government employee* as defined in 18 U.S.C. 202(a), or of the District of Columbia, or of any State, or a member of Congress or of any State legislature.

(3) *Member of a firm* is a sole practitioner or an employee or associate thereof, or a partner, stockholder, associate, affiliate or employee of a partnership, joint venture, corporation, professional association or other affiliation of two or more practitioners who represent nongovernmental parties.

(4) *Practitioner* includes any individual described in paragraph (f) of §10.2.

(5) *Official responsibility* means the direct administrative or operating authority, whether intermediate or final, and either exercisable alone or with others, and either personally or through subordinates, to approve, disapprove, or otherwise direct Government action, with or without knowledge of the action.

(6) *Participate or participation* means substantial involvement as a Government employee by making decisions, or preparing or reviewing documents with or without the right to exercise a judgment of approval or disapproval, or participating in conferences or investigations, or rendering advice of a substantial nature.

(7) *Rule* includes Treasury Regulations, whether issued or under preparation for issuance as Notices of Proposed Rule Making or as Treasury Decisions; revenue rulings; and revenue procedures published in the Internal Revenue Bulletin. *Rule* does not include a *transaction* as defined in paragraph (a)(8) of this section.

(8) *Transaction* means any decision, determination, finding, letter ruling, technical advice, Chief Counsel advice, or contract or the approval or disapproval thereof, relating to a par-

ticular factual situation or situations involving a specific party or parties whose rights, privileges, or liabilities under laws or regulations administered by the Internal Revenue Service, or other legal rights, are determined or immediately affected therein and to which the United States is a party or in which it has a direct and substantial interest, whether or not the same taxable periods are involved. *Transaction* does not include *rule* as defined in paragraph (a)(7) of this section.

(b) *General rules.* (1) No former Government employee may, subsequent to his or her Government employment, represent anyone in any matter administered by the Internal Revenue Service if the representation would violate 18 U.S.C. 207 or any other laws of the United States.

(2) No former Government employee who participated in a transaction may, subsequent to his or her Government employment, represent or knowingly assist, in that transaction, any person who is or was a specific party to that transaction.

(3) A former Government employee who within a period of one year prior to the termination of Government employment had official responsibility for a transaction may not, within two years after his or her Government employment is ended, represent or knowingly assist in that transaction any person who is or was a specific party to that transaction.

(4) No former Government employee may, within one year after his or her Government employment is ended, appear before any employee of the Treasury Department in connection with the publication, withdrawal, amendment, modification, or interpretation of a rule in the development of which the former Government employee participated or for which, within a period of one year prior to the termination of his or her Government employment, he or she had official responsibility. This paragraph (b)(4) does not, however, preclude such former employee from appearing on his or her own behalf or from representing a taxpayer before the Internal Revenue Service in connection with a transaction involving the application or interpretation of such a rule with respect to that transaction, provided that such former employee does not utilize or disclose any confidential information acquired by the former employee in the development of the rule.

(c) *Firm representation.* (1) No member of a firm of which a former Government employee is a member may represent or knowingly assist a person who was or is a specific party in any transaction with respect to which the restrictions of paragraph (b)(2) or (3) of this section apply to the former Government employee, in that transaction, unless the firm isolates the former Government employee in such a way to ensure that the former Government employee cannot assist in the representation.

(2) When isolation of a former Government employee is required under paragraph (c)(1) of this section, a statement affirming the fact of such isolation must be executed under oath by the former Government employee and by another member of the firm acting on behalf of the firm. The statement must clearly identify the firm, the former Government employee, and the transaction(s) requiring isolation and it must be filed with the Director of Practice (and at such other place(s) directed by the Director of Practice) and in such other place and in the manner prescribed by rule or regulation.

(d) *Pending representation.* Practice by former Government employees, their partners and associates with respect to representation in specific matters where actual representation commenced before July 26, 2002, is governed by the regulations set forth at 31 CFR Part 10 revised as of July 1, 2002. The burden of showing that representation commenced before July 26, 2002, lies with the former Government employees, and their partners and associates.

§10.26 Notaries.

A practitioner may not take acknowledgments, administer oaths, certify papers, or perform any official act as a notary public with respect to any matter administered by the Internal Revenue Service and for which he or she is employed as counsel, attorney, or agent, or in which he or she may be in any way interested.

§10.27 Fees.

(a) *Generally.* A practitioner may not charge an unconscionable fee for representing a client in a matter before the Internal Revenue Service.

(b) *Contingent fees.* (1) For purposes of this section, a contingent fee is any fee that is based, in whole or in part, on whether or not a position taken on a tax return or other filing avoids challenge by the Internal Revenue Service or is sustained either by the Internal Revenue Service or in litigation. A contingent fee includes any fee arrangement in which the practitioner will reimburse the client for all or a portion of the client's fee in the event that a position taken on a tax return or other filing is challenged by the Internal Revenue Service or is not sustained, whether pursuant to an indemnity agreement, a guarantee, rescission rights, or any other arrangement with a similar effect.

(2) A practitioner may not charge a contingent fee for preparing an original tax return or for any advice rendered in connection with a position taken or to be taken on an original tax return.

(3) A contingent fee may be charged for preparation of or advice in connection with an amended tax return or a claim for refund (other than a claim for refund made on an original tax return), but only if the practitioner reasonably anticipates at the time the fee arrangement is entered into that the amended tax return or refund claim will receive substantive review by the Internal Revenue Service.

§10.28 Return of client's records.

(a) In general, a practitioner must, at the request of a client, promptly return any and all records of the client that are necessary for the client to comply with his or her Federal tax obligations. The practitioner may retain copies of the records returned to a client. The existence of a dispute over fees generally does not relieve the practitioner of his or her responsibility under this section. Nevertheless, if applicable state law allows or permits the retention of a client's records by a practitioner in the case of a dispute over fees for services rendered, the practitioner need only return those records that

must be attached to the taxpayer's return. The practitioner, however, must provide the client with reasonable access to review and copy any additional records of the client retained by the practitioner under state law that are necessary for the client to comply with his or her Federal tax obligations.

(b) For purposes of this section—*Records of the client* include all documents or written or electronic materials provided to the practitioner, or obtained by the practitioner in the course of the practitioner's representation of the client, that preexisted the retention of the practitioner by the client. The term also includes materials that were prepared by the client or a third party (not including an employee or agent of the practitioner) at any time and provided to the practitioner with respect to the subject matter of the representation. The term also includes any return, claim for refund, schedule, affidavit, appraisal or any other document prepared by the practitioner, or his or her employee or agent, that was presented to the client with respect to a prior representation if such document is necessary for the taxpayer to comply with his or her current Federal tax obligations. The term does not include any return, claim for refund, schedule, affidavit, appraisal or any other document prepared by the practitioner or the practitioner's firm, employees or agents if the practitioner is withholding such document pending the client's performance of its contractual obligation to pay fees with respect to such document.

§10.29 Conflicting interests.

(a) Except as provided by paragraph (b) of this section, a practitioner shall not represent a client in his or her practice before the Internal Revenue Service if the representation involves a conflict of interest. A conflict of interest exists if:

(1) The representation of one client will be directly adverse to another client; or

(2) There is a significant risk that the representation of one or more clients will be materially limited by the practitioner's responsibilities to another client, a former client or a third person or by a personal interest of the practitioner.

(b) Notwithstanding the existence of a conflict of interest under paragraph (a) of this section, the practitioner may represent a client if:

(1) The practitioner reasonably believes that the practitioner will be able to provide competent and diligent representation to each affected client;

(2) The representation is not prohibited by law; and

(3) Each affected client gives informed consent, confirmed in writing.

(c) Copies of the written consents must be retained by the practitioner for at least 36 months from the date of the conclusion of the representation of the affected clients and the written consents must be provided to any officer or employee of the Internal Revenue Service on request. (Approved by the Office of Management and Budget under Control No. 1545-1726)

§10.30 Solicitation.

(a) *Advertising and solicitation restrictions.* (1) A practitioner may not, with respect to any Internal Revenue Service matter, in any way use or participate in the use of any form of public communication or private solicitation containing a false, fraudulent, or coercive statement or claim; or a misleading or deceptive statement or claim. Enrolled agents, in describing their professional designation, may not utilize the term of art "certified" or imply an employer/employee relationship with the Internal Revenue Service. Examples of acceptable descriptions are "enrolled to represent taxpayers before the Internal Revenue Service," "enrolled to practice before the Internal Revenue Service," and "admitted to practice before the Internal Revenue Service."

(2) A practitioner may not make, directly or indirectly, an uninvited written or oral solicitation of employment in matters related to the Internal Revenue Service if the solicitation violates Federal or State law or other applicable rule, e.g., attorneys are precluded from making a solicitation that is prohibited by conduct rules applicable to all attorneys in their State(s) of licensure. Any lawful solicitation made by or on behalf of a practitioner eligible to practice before the Internal Revenue Service must, nevertheless, clearly identify the solicitation as such and, if applicable, identify the source of the information used in choosing the recipient.

(b) *Fee information.* (1)(i) A practitioner may publish the availability of a written schedule of fees and disseminate the following fee information—

(A) Fixed fees for specific routine services.

(B) Hourly rates.

(C) Range of fees for particular services.

(D) Fee charged for an initial consultation.

(ii) Any statement of fee information concerning matters in which costs may be incurred must include a statement disclosing whether clients will be responsible for such costs.

(2) A practitioner may charge no more than the rate(s) published under paragraph (b)(1) of this section for at least 30 calendar days after the last date on which the schedule of fees was published.

(c) *Communication of fee information.* Fee information may be communicated in professional lists, telephone directories, print media, mailings, electronic mail, facsimile, hand delivered flyers, radio, television, and any other method. The method chosen, however, must not cause the communication to become untruthful, deceptive, or otherwise in violation of this part. A practitioner may not persist in attempting to contact a prospective client if the prospective client has made it known to the practitioner that he or she does not desire to be solicited. In the case of radio and television broadcasting, the broadcast must be recorded and the practitioner must retain a recording of the actual transmission. In the case of direct mail and e-commerce communications, the practitioner must retain a copy of the actual communication, along with a list or other description of persons to whom the communication was mailed or otherwise distributed. The copy must be retained by the practitioner for a period of at least 36 months from the date of the last transmission or use.

(d) *Improper associations.* A practitioner may not, in matters related to the Internal Revenue Service, assist, or accept assistance from, any person or entity who, to the knowledge of the practitioner, obtains clients or otherwise practices in a manner forbidden under this section. (Approved by the Office of Management and Budget under Control No. 1545-1726)

§10.31 Negotiation of taxpayer checks.

A practitioner who prepares tax returns may not endorse or otherwise negotiate any check issued to a client by the government in respect of a Federal tax liability.

§10.32 Practice of law.

Nothing in the regulations in this part may be construed as authorizing persons not members of the bar to practice law.

§10.34 Standards for advising with respect to tax return positions and for preparing or signing returns.

(a) *Realistic possibility standard.* A practitioner may not sign a tax return as a preparer if the practitioner determines that the tax return contains a position that does not have a realistic possibility of being sustained on its merits (the realistic possibility standard) unless the position is not frivolous and is adequately disclosed to the Internal Revenue Service. A practitioner may not advise a client to take a position on a tax return, or prepare the portion of a tax return on which a position is taken, unless—

(1) The practitioner determines that the position satisfies the realistic possibility standard; or

(2) The position is not frivolous and the practitioner advises the client of any opportunity to avoid the accuracy-related penalty in section 6662 of the Internal Revenue Code by adequately disclosing the position and of the requirements for adequate disclosure.

(b) *Advising clients on potential penalties.* A practitioner advising a client to take a position on a tax return, or preparing or signing a tax return as a preparer, must inform the client of the penalties reasonably likely to apply to the client with respect to the position advised, prepared, or reported. The practitioner also must inform the client of any opportunity to avoid

any such penalty by disclosure, if relevant, and of the requirements for adequate disclosure. This paragraph (b) applies even if the practitioner is not subject to a penalty with respect to the position.

(c) *Relying on information furnished by clients.* A practitioner advising a client to take a position on a tax return, or preparing or signing a tax return as a preparer, generally may rely in good faith without verification upon information furnished by the client. The practitioner may not, however, ignore the implications of information furnished to, or actually known by, the practitioner, and must make reasonable inquiries if the information as furnished appears to be incorrect, inconsistent with an important fact or another factual assumption, or incomplete.

(d) *Definitions.* For purposes of this section—

(1) *Realistic possibility.* A position is considered to have a realistic possibility of being sustained on its merits if a reasonable and well informed analysis of the law and the facts by a person knowledgeable in the tax law would lead such a person to conclude that the position has approximately a one in three, or greater, likelihood of being sustained on its merits. The authorities described in 26 CFR 1.6662-4(d)(3)(iii), or any successor provision, of the substantial understatement penalty regulations may be taken into account for purposes of this analysis. The possibility that a tax return will not be audited, that an issue will not be raised on audit, or that an issue will be settled may not be taken into account.

(2) *Frivolous.* A position is frivolous if it is patently improper.

Subpart C—Sanctions for Violation of the Regulations

§10.50 Sanctions.

(a) *Authority to censure, suspend, or disbar.* The Secretary of the Treasury, or his or her delegate, after notice and an opportunity for a proceeding, may censure, suspend or disbar any practitioner from practice before the Internal Revenue Service if the practitioner is shown to be incompetent or disreputable, fails to comply with any regulation in this part, or with intent to defraud, willfully and knowingly misleads or threatens a client or prospective client. Censure is a public reprimand.

(b) *Authority to disqualify.* The Secretary of the Treasury, or his or her delegate, after due notice and opportunity for hearing, may disqualify any appraiser with respect to whom a penalty has been assessed under section 6701(a) of the Internal Revenue Code.

(1) If any appraiser is disqualified pursuant to this subpart C, such appraiser is barred from presenting evidence or testimony in any administrative proceeding before the Department of Treasury or the Internal Revenue Service, unless and until authorized to do so by the Director of Practice pursuant to §10.81, regardless of whether such evidence or testimony would pertain to an appraisal made prior to or after such date.

(2) Any appraisal made by a disqualified appraiser after the effective date of disqualification will not have any probative effect in any administrative proceeding before the Department of the Treasury or the Internal Revenue Service. An appraisal otherwise barred from admission into evidence pursuant to this section may be admitted into evidence solely for the purpose of determining the taxpayer's reliance in good faith on such appraisal.

§10.51 Incompetence and disreputable conduct.

Incompetence and disreputable conduct for which a practitioner may be censured, suspended or disbarred from practice before the Internal Revenue Service includes, but is not limited to—

(a) Conviction of any criminal offense under the revenue laws of the United States;

(b) Conviction of any criminal offense involving dishonesty or breach of trust;

(c) Conviction of any felony under Federal or State law for which the conduct involved renders the practitioner unfit to practice before the Internal Revenue Service;

(d) Giving false or misleading information, or participating in any way in the giving of false or misleading information to the Department of the Treasury or any officer or employee thereof, or to any tribunal authorized to pass upon Federal tax matters, in connection with any matter pending or likely to be pending before them, knowing such information to be false or misleading. Facts or other matters contained in testimony, Federal tax returns, financial statements, applications for enrollment, affidavits, declarations, or any other document or statement, written or oral, are included in the term *information.*

(e) Solicitation of employment as prohibited under §10.30, the use of false or misleading representations with intent to deceive a client or prospective client in order to procure employment, or intimating that the practitioner is able improperly to obtain special consideration or action from the Internal Revenue Service or officer or employee thereof.

(f) Willfully failing to make a Federal tax return in violation of the revenue laws of the United States, willfully evading, attempting to evade, or participating in any way in evading or attempting to evade any assessment or payment of any Federal tax, or knowingly counseling or suggesting to a client or prospective client an illegal plan to evade Federal taxes or payment thereof.

(g) Misappropriation of, or failure properly and promptly to remit funds received from a client for the purpose of payment of taxes or other obligations due the United States.

(h) Directly or indirectly attempting to influence, or offering or agreeing to attempt to influence, the official action of any officer or employee of the Internal Revenue Service by the use of threats, false accusations, duress or coercion, by the offer of any special inducement or promise of advantage or by the bestowing of any gift, favor or thing of value.

(i) Disbarment or suspension from practice as an attorney, certified public accountant, public accountant, or actuary by any duly constituted authority of any State, territory, possession of the United States, including a Commonwealth, or the District of Columbia, any Federal court of record or any Federal agency, body or board.

(j) Knowingly aiding and abetting another person to practice before the Internal Revenue Service during a period of suspension, disbarment, or ineligibility of such other person.

(k) Contemptuous conduct in connection with practice before the Internal Revenue Service, including the use of abusive language, making false accusations and statements, knowing them to be false, or circulating or publishing malicious or libelous matter.

(l) Giving a false opinion, knowingly, recklessly, or through gross incompetence, including an opinion which is intentionally or recklessly misleading, or engaging in a pattern of providing incompetent opinions on questions arising under the Federal tax laws. False opinions described in this paragraph (l) include those which reflect or result from a knowing misstatement of fact or law, from an assertion of a position known to be unwarranted under existing law, from counseling or assisting in conduct known to be illegal or fraudulent, from concealing matters required by law to be revealed, or from consciously disregarding information indicating that material facts expressed in the tax opinion or offering material are false or misleading. For purposes of this paragraph (l), reckless conduct is a highly unreasonable omission or misrepresentation involving an extreme departure from the standards of ordinary care that a practitioner should observe under the circumstances. A pattern of conduct is a factor that will be taken into account in determining whether a practitioner acted knowingly, recklessly, or through gross incompetence. Gross incompetence includes conduct that reflects gross indifference, preparation which is grossly inadequate under the circumstances, and a consistent failure to perform obligations to the client.

§10.52 Violation of regulations.

A practitioner may be censured, suspended or disbarred from practice before the Internal Revenue Service for any of the following:

(a) Willfully violating any of the regulations contained in this part.

(b) Recklessly or through gross incompetence (within the meaning of §10.51 (l)) violating §10.33 or 10.34.

§10.53 Receipt of information concerning practitioner.

(a) *Officer or employee of the Internal Revenue Service*. If an officer or employee of the Internal Revenue Service has reason to believe that a practitioner has violated any provision of this part, the officer or employee will promptly make a written report to the Director of Practice of the suspected violation. The report will explain the facts and reasons upon which the officer's or employee's belief rests.

(b) *Other persons*. Any person other than an officer or employee of the Internal Revenue Service having information of a violation of any provision of this part may make an oral or written report of the alleged violation to the Director of Practice or any officer or employee of the Internal Revenue Service. If the report is made to an officer or employee of the Internal Revenue Service, the officer or employee will make a written report of the suspected violation to the Director of Practice.

(c) *Destruction of report*. No report made under paragraph (a) or (b) of this section shall be maintained by the Director of Practice unless retention of such record is permissible under the applicable records control schedule as approved by the National Archives and Records Administration and designated in the Internal Revenue Manual. The Director of Practice must destroy such reports as soon as permissible under the applicable records control schedule.

(d) *Effect on proceedings under subpart D*. The destruction of any report will not bar any proceeding under subpart D of this part, but precludes the Director of Practice's use of a copy of such report in a proceeding under subpart D of this part.

Subpart D—Rules Applicable to Disciplinary Proceedings

§10.60 Institution of proceeding.

(a) Whenever the Director of Practice determines that a practitioner violated any provision of the laws or regulations in this part, the Director of Practice may reprimand the practitioner or, in accordance with §10.62, institute a proceeding for censure, suspension, or disbarment of the practitioner. A proceeding for censure, suspension, or disbarment of a practitioner is instituted by the filing of a complaint, the contents of which are more fully described in §10.62.

(b) Whenever the Director of Practice is advised or becomes aware that a penalty has been assessed against an appraiser under section 6701(a) of the Internal Revenue Code, the Director of Practice may reprimand the appraiser or, in accordance with §10.62, institute a proceeding for disqualification of the appraiser. A proceeding for disqualification of an appraiser is instituted by the filing of a complaint, the contents of which are more fully described in §10.62.

(c) Except as provided in §10.82, a proceeding will not be instituted under this section unless the proposed respondent previously has been advised in writing of the law, facts and conduct warranting such action and has been accorded an opportunity to dispute facts, assert additional facts, and make arguments (including an explanation or description of mitigating circumstances).

§10.61 Conferences.

(a) *In general*. The Director of Practice may confer with a practitioner or an appraiser concerning allegations of misconduct irrespective of whether a proceeding for censure, suspension, disbarment, or disqualification has been instituted against the practitioner or appraiser. If the conference results in a stipulation in connection with an ongoing proceeding in which the practitioner or appraiser is the respondent, the stipulation may be entered in the record by either party to the proceeding.

(b) *Resignation or voluntary censure, suspension or disbarment*. In lieu of a proceeding being instituted or continued under paragraph (a) of §10.60, a practitioner may offer his or her consent to the issuance of a censure, suspension or disbarment, or, if the practitioner is an enrolled agent, may offer to resign. The Director of Practice may, in his or her discretion, accept or decline the offered censure, suspension, disbarment, or offer of resignation by an enrolled agent, in accordance with the consent offered. In any declination, the Director of Practice may state that he or she would accept an offer of censure, suspension, or disbarment, or, if the practitioner is an enrolled agent, offer of resignation, containing different terms; the Director of Practice may, in his or her discretion,

accept or reject a revised offer of censure, suspension, disbarment, or offer of resignation by an enrolled agent, submitted in response to the declination or may counteroffer and act upon any accepted counteroffer.

(c) *Voluntary disqualification*. In lieu of a proceeding being instituted or continued under paragraph (b) of § 10.60, an appraiser may offer his or her consent to disqualification. The Director of Practice may, in his or her discretion, accept or decline the offered disqualification, in accordance with the consent offered. In any declination, the Director of Practice may state that he or she would accept an offer of disqualification containing different terms; the Director of Practice may, in his or her discretion, accept or reject a revised offer of censure, suspension or disbarment submitted in response to the declination or may counteroffer and act upon any accepted counteroffer.

§10.62 Contents of complaint.

(a) *Charges*. A complaint must name the respondent, provide a clear and concise description of the facts and law that constitute the basis for the proceeding, and be signed by the Director of Practice or a person representing the Director of Practice under § 10.69(a)(1). A complaint is sufficient if it fairly informs the respondent of the charges brought so that he or she is able to prepare a defense. In the case of a complaint filed against an appraiser, the complaint is sufficient if it refers to a penalty imposed previously on the respondent under section 6701(a) of the Internal Revenue Code.

(b) *Specification of sanction*. The complaint must specify the sanction sought by the Director of Practice against the practitioner or appraiser. If the sanction sought is a suspension, the duration of the suspension sought must be specified.

(c) *Demand for answer*. The Director of Practice must, in the complaint or in a separate paper attached to the complaint, notify the respondent of the time for answering the complaint, the time for which may not be less than 15 days from the date of service of the complaint, the name and address of the Administrative Law Judge with whom the answer must be filed, the name and address of the person representing the Director of Practice to whom a copy of the answer must be served, and that a decision by default may be rendered against the respondent in the event an answer is not filed as required.

§10.63 Service of complaint; service and filing of other papers.

(a) *Service of complaint.*

(1) *In general.* The complaint or a copy of the complaint must be served on the respondent by any manner described in paragraphs (a)(2) or (3) of this section.

(2) *Service by certified or first class mail.* (i) Service of the complaint may be made on the respondent by mailing the complaint by certified mail to the last known address (as determined under section 6212 of the Internal Revenue Code and the regulations thereunder) of the respondent. Where service is by certified mail, the returned post office receipt duly signed by the respondent will be proof of service.

(ii) If the certified mail is not claimed or accepted by the respondent, or is returned undelivered, service may be made on the respondent, by mailing the complaint to the respondent by first class mail. Service by this method will be considered complete upon mailing, provided the complaint is addressed to the respondent at the respondent's last known address as determined under section 6212 of the Internal Revenue Code and the regulations thereunder.

(3) *Service by other than certified or first class mail.* (i) Service of the complaint may be made on the respondent by delivery by a private delivery service designated pursuant to section 7502(f) of the Internal Revenue Code to the last known address (as determined under section 6212 of the Internal Revenue Code and the regulations thereunder) of the respondent. Service by this method will be considered complete, provided the complaint is addressed to the respondent at the respondent's last known address as determined under section 6212 of the Internal Revenue Code and the regulations thereunder.

(ii) Service of the complaint may be made in person on, or by leaving the complaint at the office or place of business of, the respondent. Service by this method will be considered complete and proof of service will be a written statement, sworn or affirmed by the person who served the complaint, identifying the manner of service, including the recipient, relationship of recipient to respondent, place, date and time of service.

(iii) Service may be made by any other means agreed to by the respondent. Proof of service will be a written statement, sworn or affirmed by the person who served the complaint, identifying the manner of service, including the recipient, relationship of recipient to respondent, place, date and time of service.

(4) For purposes of this paragraph (a), "respondent" means the practitioner or appraiser named in the complaint or any other person having the authority to accept mail on behalf of the practitioner or appraiser.

(b) *Service of papers other than complaint.* Any paper other than the complaint may be served on the respondent, or his or her authorized representative under §10.69(a)(2) by:

(1) mailing the paper by first class mail to the last known address (as determined under section 6212 of the Internal Revenue Code and the regulations thereunder) of the respondent or the respondent's authorized representative,

(2) delivery by a private delivery service designated pursuant to section 7502(f) of the Internal Revenue Code to the last known address (as determined under section 6212 of the Internal Revenue Code and the regulations thereunder) of the respondent or the respondent's authorized representative, or

(3) as provided in paragraphs (a)(3)(ii) and (a)(3)(iii) of this section.

(c) *Service of papers on the Director of Practice.* Whenever a paper is required or permitted to be served on the Director of Practice in connection with a proceeding under this part, the paper will be served on the Director of Practice's authorized representative under §10.69(a)(1) at the address designated in the complaint, or at an address provided in a notice of appearance. If no address is designated in the complaint or provided in a notice of appearance, service will be made on the Director of Practice, Internal

Revenue Service, 1111 Constitution Avenue, NW., Washington, DC 20224.

(d) *Filing of papers.* Whenever the filing of a paper is required or permitted in connection with a proceeding under this part, the original paper, plus one additional copy, must be filed with the Administrative Law Judge at the address specified in the complaint or at an address otherwise specified by the Administrative Law Judge. All papers filed in connection with a proceeding under this part must be served on the other party, unless the Administrative Law Judge directs otherwise. A certificate evidencing such must be attached to the original paper filed with the Administrative Law Judge.

§10.64 Answer; default.

(a) *Filing.* The respondent's answer must be filed with the Administrative Law Judge, and served on the Director of Practice, within the time specified in the complaint unless, on request or application of the respondent, the time is extended by the Administrative Law Judge.

(b) *Contents.* The answer must be written and contain a statement of facts that constitute the respondent's grounds of defense. General denials are not permitted. The respondent must specifically admit or deny each allegation set forth in the complaint, except that the respondent may state that the respondent is without sufficient information to admit or deny a specific allegation. The respondent, nevertheless, may not deny a material allegation in the complaint that the respondent knows to be true, or state that the respondent is without sufficient information to form a belief, when the respondent possesses the required information. The respondent also must state affirmatively any special matters of defense on which he or she relies.

(c) *Failure to deny or answer allegations in the complaint.* Every allegation in the complaint that is not denied in the answer is deemed admitted and will be considered proved; no further evidence in respect of such allegation need be adduced at a hearing.

(d) *Default.* Failure to file an answer within the time prescribed (or within the time for answer as extended by the Administrative Law Judge) constitutes an admission of the allegations of the complaint and a waiver of hearing, and the Administrative Law Judge may make the decision by default without a hearing or further procedure. A decision by default constitutes a decision under §10.76.

(e) *Signature.* The answer must be signed by the respondent or the respondent's authorized representative under §10.69(a)(2) and must include a statement directly above the signature acknowledging that the statements made in the answer are true and correct and that knowing and willful false statements may be punishable under 18 U.S.C. 1001.

§10.65 Supplemental charges.

If it appears that the respondent, in his or her answer, falsely and in bad faith, denies a material allegation of fact in the complaint or states that the respondent has insufficient knowledge to form a belief, when the respondent in fact possesses such information, or if it appears that the respondent has knowingly introduced false testimony during proceedings for his or her censure, suspension, disbarment, or disqualification, the Director of Practice may file supplemental charges against the respondent. The supplemental charges may be heard with other charges in the case, provided the respondent is given due notice of the charges and is afforded an opportunity to prepare a defense to such charges.

§10.66 Reply to answer.

The Director of Practice may file a reply to the respondent's answer, but unless otherwise ordered by the Administrative Law Judge, no reply to the respondent's answer is required. If a reply is not filed, new matter in the answer is deemed denied.

§10.67 Proof; variance; amendment of pleadings.

In the case of a variance between the allegations in pleadings and the evidence adduced in support of the pleadings, the Administrative Law Judge, at any time before decision, may order or authorize amendment of the pleadings to conform to the evidence. The party who would otherwise be prejudiced by the amendment must be given a reasonable opportunity to address the allegations of the pleadings as amended and the Administrative Law Judge must make findings on any issue presented by the pleadings as amended.

§10.68 Motions and requests.

(a) *Motions.* At any time after the filing of the complaint, any party may file a motion with the Administrative Law Judge. Unless otherwise ordered by the Administrative Law Judge, motions must be in writing and must be served on the opposing party as provided in §10.63(b). A motion must concisely specify its grounds and the relief sought, and, if appropriate, must contain a memorandum of facts and law in support. Before moving, a party must make a good faith effort to resolve with the other party any dispute that gives rise to, or is a concern of, the motion. The movant must certify such an attempt was made and state, if it is known, whether the opposing party opposes the motion.

(b) *Response.* Unless otherwise ordered by the Administrative Law Judge, the nonmoving party is not required to file a response to a motion. If the Administrative Law Judge does not order the nonmoving party to file a response, the nonmoving party is deemed to oppose the motion.

(c) *Oral motions and arguments.* The Administrative Law Judge may, for good cause and with notice to the parties, permit oral motions and oral opposition to motions. The Administrative Law Judge may, within his or her discretion, permit oral argument on any motion.

§10.69 Representation; ex parte communication.

(a) *Representation.* (1) The Director of Practice may be represented in proceedings under this part by an attorney or other employee of the Internal Revenue Service. An attorney or an employee of the Internal Revenue Service representing the Director of Practice in a proceeding under this part may sign the complaint or any document required to be filed in the proceeding on behalf of the Director of Practice.

(2) A respondent may appear in person, be represented by a practitioner, or be represented by an attorney who has not filed a declaration with the Internal Revenue Service pursuant to §10.3. A practitioner or an attorney representing a respondent or proposed respondent may sign the answer or any document required to be filed in the proceeding on behalf of the respondent.

(b) *Ex parte communication.* The Director of Practice, the respondent, and any representatives of either party, may not attempt to initiate or participate in *ex parte* discussions concerning a proceeding or potential proceeding with the Administrative Law Judge (or any person who is likely to advise the Administrative Law Judge on a ruling or decision) in the proceeding before or during the pendency of the proceeding. Any memorandum, letter or other communication concerning the merits of the proceeding, addressed to the Administrative Law Judge, by or on behalf of any party shall be regarded as an argument in the proceeding and shall be served on the other party.

§10.70 Administrative Law Judge.

(a) *Appointment.* Proceedings on complaints for the censure, suspension or disbarment of a practitioner or the disqualification of an appraiser will be conducted by an Administrative Law Judge appointed as provided by 5 U.S.C. 3105.

(b) *Powers of the Administrative Law Judge.* The Administrative Law Judge, among other powers, has the authority, in connection with any proceeding under §10.60 assigned or referred to him or her, to do the following:

(1) Administer oaths and affirmations;

(2) Make rulings on motions and requests, which rulings may not be appealed prior to the close of a hearing except in extraordinary circumstances and at the discretion of the Administrative Law Judge;

(3) Determine the time and place of hearing and regulate its course and conduct;

(4) Adopt rules of procedure and modify the same from time to time as needed for the orderly disposition of proceedings;

(5) Rule on offers of proof, receive relevant evidence, and examine witnesses;

(6) Take or authorize the taking of depositions;

(7) Receive and consider oral or written argument on facts or law;

(8) Hold or provide for the holding of conferences for the settlement or simplification of the issues with the consent of the parties;

(9) Perform such acts and take such measures as are necessary or appropriate to the efficient conduct of any proceeding; and

(10) Make decisions.

§10.71 Hearings.

(a) *In general*. An Administrative Law Judge will preside at the hearing on a complaint filed under paragraph (c) of §10.60 for the censure, suspension, or disbarment of a practitioner or disqualification of an appraiser. Hearings will be stenographically recorded and transcribed and the testimony of witnesses will be taken under oath or affirmation. Hearings will be conducted pursuant to 5 U.S.C. 556. A hearing in a proceeding requested under paragraph (g) of §10.82 will be conducted *de novo*. An evidentiary hearing must be held in all proceedings prior to the issuance of a decision by the Administrative Law Judge unless: the Director of Practice withdraws the complaint; the practitioner consents to a sanction pursuant to §10.61(b); a decision is issued by default pursuant to §10.64(d), a decision is issued under §10.82(e); the respondent requests a decision on the record without a hearing; or the Administrative Law Judge issues a decision on a motion that disposes of the case prior to the hearing.

(b) *Publicity of Proceedings*. A request by a practitioner or appraiser that a hearing in a disciplinary proceeding concerning him or her be public, and that the record of such disciplinary proceeding be made available for inspection by interested persons may be granted by the Administrative Law Judge where the parties stipulate in advance to protect from disclosure confidential tax information in accordance with all applicable statutes and regulations.

(c) *Location*. The location of the hearing will be determined by the agreement of the parties with the approval of the Administrative Law Judge, but, in the absence of such agreement and approval, the hearing will be held in Washington, D.C.

(d) *Failure to appear*. If either party to the proceeding fails to appear at the hearing, after notice of the proceeding has been sent to him

or her, the party will be deemed to have waived the right to a hearing and the Administrative Law Judge may make his or her decision against the absent party by default.

§10.72 Evidence.

(a) *In general*. The rules of evidence prevailing in courts of law and equity are not controlling in hearings or proceedings conducted under this part. The Administrative Law Judge may, however, exclude evidence that is irrelevant, immaterial, or unduly repetitious.

(b) *Depositions*. The deposition of any witness taken pursuant to §10.73 may be admitted into evidence in any proceeding instituted under §10.60.

(c) *Proof of documents*. Official documents, records, and papers of the Internal Revenue Service and the Office of Director of Practice are admissible in evidence without the production of an officer or employee to authenticate them. Any such documents, records, and papers may be evidenced by a copy attested or identified by an officer or employee of the Internal Revenue Service or the Treasury Department, as the case may be.

(d) *Withdrawal of exhibits*. If any document, record, or other paper is introduced in evidence as an exhibit, the Administrative Law Judge may authorize the withdrawal of the exhibit subject to any conditions that he or she deems proper.

(e) *Objections*. Objections to evidence are to be made in short form, stating the grounds for the objection. Except as ordered by the Administrative Law Judge, argument on objections will not be recorded or transcribed. Rulings on objections are to be a part of the record, but no exception to a ruling is necessary to preserve the rights of the parties.

§10.73 Depositions.

(a) Depositions for use at a hearing may be taken, with the written approval of the Administrative Law Judge, by either the Director of Practice or the respondent or their duly authorized representatives. Depositions may be taken before any officer duly authorized to administer an oath for general purposes or before an officer or employee of the Internal Revenue

Service who is authorized to administer an oath in internal revenue matters.

(b) The party taking the deposition must provide the deponent and the other party with 10 days written notice of the deposition, unless the deponent and the parties agree otherwise. The notice must specify the name of the deponent, the time and place where the deposition is to be taken, and whether the deposition will be taken by oral or written interrogatories. When a deposition is taken by written interrogatories, any cross-examination also will be by written interrogatories. Copies of the written interrogatories must be served on the other party with the notice of deposition, and copies of any written cross-interrogation must be mailed or delivered to the opposing party at least 5 days before the date that the deposition will be taken, unless the parties mutually agree otherwise. A party on whose behalf a deposition is taken must file the responses to the written interrogatories or a transcript of the oral deposition with the Administrative Law Judge and serve copies on the opposing party and the deponent. Expenses in the reporting of depositions will be borne by the party that requested the deposition.

§10.74 Transcript.

In cases where the hearing is stenographically reported by a Government contract reporter, copies of the transcript may be obtained from the reporter at rates not to exceed the maximum rates fixed by contract between the Government and the reporter. Where the hearing is stenographically reported by a regular employee of the Internal Revenue Service, a copy will be supplied to the respondent either without charge or upon the payment of a reasonable fee. Copies of exhibits introduced at the hearing or at the taking of depositions will be supplied to the parties upon the payment of a reasonable fee (Sec. 501, Public Law 82-137)(65 Stat. 290)(31 U.S.C. 483a).

§10.75 Proposed findings and conclusions.

Except in cases where the respondent has failed to answer the complaint or where a party has failed to appear at the hearing, the parties must be afforded a reasonable opportunity to submit proposed findings and conclusions and their supporting reasons to the Administrative Law Judge.

§10.76 Decision of Administrative Law Judge.

(a) As soon as practicable after the conclusion of a hearing and the receipt of any proposed findings and conclusions timely submitted by the parties, the Administrative Law Judge will enter a decision in the case. The decision must include a statement of findings and conclusions, as well as the reasons or basis for making such findings and conclusions, and an order of censure, suspension, disbarment, disqualification, or dismissal of the complaint. If the sanction is censure or a suspension of less than six months' duration, the Administrative Law Judge, in rendering findings and conclusions, will consider an allegation of fact to be proven if it is established by the party who is alleging the fact by a preponderance of evidence in the record. In the event that the sanction is disbarment or a suspension of a duration of six months or longer, an allegation of fact that is necessary for a finding against the practitioner must be proven by clear and convincing evidence in the record. An allegation of fact that is necessary for a finding of disqualification against an appraiser must be proven by clear and convincing evidence in the record. The Administrative Law Judge will provide the decision to the Director of Practice and a copy of the decision to the respondent or the respondent's authorized representative.

(b) In the absence of an appeal to the Secretary of the Treasury or his or her designee, or review of the decision on motion of the Secretary or his or her designee, the decision of the Administrative Law Judge will, without further proceedings, become the decision of the agency 30 days after the date of the Administrative Law Judge's decision.

§10.77 Appeal of decision of Administrative Law Judge.

Within 30 days from the date of the Administrative Law Judge's decision, either party may appeal to the Secretary of the Treasury, or his or her delegate. The respondent must file his or her appeal with the Director of Practice in duplicate and a notice of appeal must include exceptions to the decision of the Administrative Law Judge and supporting reasons for such exceptions. If the Director of Practice files an appeal, he or she must provide a copy to the respondent. Within 30 days after receipt of an appeal or copy thereof, the other party may file a reply brief in duplicate with the Director of Practice. If the reply brief is filed by the Director of Practice, he or she must provide a copy of it to the respondent. The Director of Practice must provide the entire record to the Secretary of the Treasury, or his or her delegate, after the appeal and any reply brief has been filed.

§10.78 Decision on appeal.

On appeal from or review of the decision of the Administrative Law Judge, the Secretary of the Treasury, or his or her delegate, will make the agency decision. The Secretary of the Treasury, or his or delegate, will provide a copy of the agency decision to the Director of Practice and the respondent or the respondent's authorized representative. The decision of the Administrative Law Judge will not be reversed unless the appellant establishes that the decision is clearly erroneous in light of the evidence in the record and applicable law. Issues that are exclusively matters of law will be reviewed *de novo*. In the event that the Secretary of the Treasury, or his or her delegate, determines that there are unresolved issues raised by the record, the case may be remanded to the Administrative Law Judge to elicit additional testimony or evidence. A copy of the agency decision or that of his or her delegate will be provided to the Director of Practice and the respondent contemporaneously.

§10.79 Effect of disbarment, suspension, or censure.

(a) *Disbarment.* When the final decision in a case is against the respondent (or the respondent has offered his or her consent and such consent has been accepted by the Director of Practice) and such decision is for disbarment, the respondent will not be permitted to practice before the Internal Revenue Service unless and until authorized to do so by the Director of Practice pursuant to §10.81.

(b) *Suspension.* When the final decision in a case is against the respondent (or the respondent has offered his or her consent and such consent has been accepted by the Director of Practice) and such decision is for suspension, the respondent will not be permitted to practice before the Internal Revenue Service during the period of suspension. For periods after the suspension, the practitioner's future representations may be subject to conditions as authorized by paragraph (d) of this section.

(c) *Censure.* When the final decision in the case is against the respondent (or the respondent has offered his or her consent and such consent has been accepted by the Director of Practice) and such decision is for censure, the respondent will be permitted to practice before the Internal Revenue Service, but the respondent's future representations may be subject to conditions as authorized by paragraph (d) of this section.

(d) *Conditions.* After being subject to the sanction of either suspension or censure, the future representations of a practitioner so sanctioned shall be subject to conditions prescribed by the Director of Practice designed to promote high standards of conduct. These conditions can be imposed for a reasonable period in light of the gravity of the practitioner's violations. For example, where a practitioner is censured because he or she failed to advise his or her clients about a potential conflict of interest or failed to obtain the clients' written consents, the Director of Practice may require the practitioner to provide the Director of Practice or another Internal Revenue Service official with a copy of all consents obtained by the practitioner for an appropriate period following censure, whether or not such consents are specifically requested.

§10.80 Notice of disbarment, suspension, censure, or disqualification.

On the issuance of a final order censuring, suspending, or disbarring a practitioner or a final order disqualifying an appraiser, the Director of Practice may give notice of the censure, suspension, disbarment, or disqualification to appropriate officers and employees of the Internal Revenue Service and to interested departments and agencies of the Federal government. The Director of Practice may determine the manner of giving notice to the proper authorities of the State by which the censured, suspended, or disbarred person was licensed to practice.

§10.81 Petition for reinstatement.

The Director of Practice may entertain a petition for reinstatement from any person disbarred from practice before the Internal Revenue Service or any disqualified appraiser after the expiration of 5 years following such disbarment or disqualification. Reinstatement may not be granted unless the Director of Practice is satisfied that the petitioner, thereafter, is not likely to conduct himself contrary to the regulations in this part, and that granting such reinstatement would not be contrary to the public interest.

§10.82 Expedited suspension upon criminal conviction or loss of license for cause.

(a) *When applicable.* Whenever the Director of Practice determines that a practitioner is described in paragraph (b) of this section, the Director of Practice may institute a proceeding under this section to suspend the practitioner from practice before the Internal Revenue Service.

(b) *To whom applicable.* This section applies to any practitioner who, within 5 years of the date a complaint instituting a proceeding under this section is served:

(1) Has had his or her license to practice as an attorney, certified public accountant, or actuary suspended or revoked for cause (not including a failure to pay a professional licensing fee) by any authority or court, agency, body, or board described in §10.51(i);

(2) Has, irrespective of whether an appeal has been taken, been convicted of any crime under title 26 of the United States Code, any crime involving dishonesty or breach of trust, or any felony for which the conduct involved renders the practitioner unfit to practice before the Internal Revenue Service; or

(3) Has violated conditions designed to promote high standards of conduct established pursuant to §10.79(d).

(c) *Instituting a proceeding.* A proceeding under this section will be instituted by a complaint that names the respondent, is signed by the Director of Practice or a person representing the Director of Practice under §10.69(a)(1), is filed in the Director of Practice's office, and is served according to the rules set forth in paragraph (a) of §10.63. The complaint must give a plain and concise description of the allegations that constitute the basis for the proceeding. The complaint must notify the respondent—

(1) Of the place and due date for filing an answer;

(2) That a decision by default may be rendered if the respondent fails to file an answer as required;

(3) That the respondent may request a conference with the Director of Practice to address the merits of the complaint and that any such request must be made in the answer; and

(4) That the respondent may be suspended either immediately following the expiration of the period within which an answer must be filed or, if a conference is requested, immediately following the conference.

(d) *Answer.* The answer to a complaint described in this section must be filed no later than 30 calendar days following the date the complaint is served, unless the Director of Practice extends the time for filing. The answer must be filed in accordance with the rules set forth in §10.64, except as otherwise provided in this section. A respondent is entitled to a conference with the Director of Practice only if the conference is requested in a timely filed answer. If a request for a conference is not made in the answer or the answer is not timely filed, the respondent will be deemed to have waived his or her right to a conference and the Director of Practice may suspend such respondent at any time following the date on which the answer was due.

(e) *Conference.* The Director of Practice or his or her designee will preside at a conference described in this section. The conference will be held at a place and time selected by the Director of Practice, but no sooner than 14 calendar days after the date by which the answer must be filed with the Director of Practice, unless the respondent agrees to an earlier date. An authorized representative may represent the respondent at the conference. Following the conference, upon a finding that the respondent is described in paragraph (b) of this section, or upon the respondent's failure to appear at the conference either personally or through an authorized representative, the Director of Practice may immediately suspend the respondent from practice before the Internal Revenue Service.

(f) *Duration of suspension.* A suspension under this section will commence on the date that written notice of the suspension is issued. A practitioner's suspension will remain effective until the earlier of the following—

(1) The Director of Practice lifts the suspension after determining that the practitioner is no longer described in paragraph (b) of this section or for any other reason; or

(2) The suspension is lifted by an Administrative Law Judge or the Secretary of the Treasury in a proceeding referred to in paragraph (g) of this section and instituted under §10.60.

(g) *Proceeding instituted under §10.60.* If the Director of Practice suspends a practitioner under this section, the practitioner may ask the Director of Practice to issue a complaint under §10.60. The request must be made in writing within 2 years from the date on which the practitioner's suspension commences. The Director of Practice must issue a complaint requested under this paragraph within 30 calendar days of receiving the request.

Subpart E—General Provisions

§10.90 Records.

Availability. The Director of Practice will make available for public inspection at the Office of Director Practice the roster of all persons enrolled to practice, the roster of all persons censured, suspended, or disbarred from practice before the Internal Revenue Service, and the roster of all disqualified appraisers. Other records of the Director of Practice may be disclosed upon specific request, in accordance with the applicable disclosure rules of the Internal Revenue Service and the Treasury Department.

§10.91 Saving clause.

Any proceeding instituted under regulations in effect prior to July 26, 2002, that is not final prior to July 26, 2002, will not be affected by this part and will apply the rules set forth at 31 CFR part 10 revised as of July 1, 2002. Any proceeding under this part based on conduct engaged in prior to July 26, 2002, which is instituted after that date, shall apply subpart D and E of this part, but the conduct engaged in prior to July 26, 2002, shall be judged by the regulations in effect at the time the conduct occurred.

§10.92 Special orders.

The Secretary of the Treasury reserves the power to issue such special orders as he or she deems proper in any cases within the purview of this part.

§10.93 Effective date.

Subject to §10.91, this part is applicable on July 26, 2002.

Glossary

The following definitions pertain specifically to the manner in which the identified terms are used in a tax research context. Other uses for such terms are not examined.

A

ABA The professional organization for practicing attorneys in the United States, namely, the American Bar Association.

Academic journals Scholarly publications of law schools, business schools, and academic organizations. These publications are edited either by faculty members or by graduate students under the guidance of the school's faculty. The articles appearing in these publications are usually written by tax practitioners, academics, graduate students, or other noted commentators.

Accuracy-related penalty Civil tax penalty assessed where the taxpayer has been negligent in completing the return or is found to have acted with a disregard of IRS rules and regulations, a substantial understatement of the income tax, a substantial valuation or pension liability overstatement, or a substantial transfer tax valuation understatement. A 20 percent penalty usually applies to the pertinent understatement, and related interest accrues from the due date of the return, rather than the date on which the penalty was assessed.

Acquiescence A pronouncement by the IRS that it will follow the decision of a court case to the extent that it was held for the taxpayer. Announced in the *Internal Revenue Bulletin*. Modifies the citation for the identified case.

Action on Decision A memoranda prepared when the IRS loses a case in a court that recommends the action, if any, that the IRS should take in response to the adverse decision. See also *acquiescence, nonacquiescence.*

Administrative proceeding A hearing between the taxpayer and an administrative agency of the government, typically the Internal Revenue Service, in an audit or appeal setting.

Administrative sources Federal tax law that is created by the appropriate use of power that is granted to the Treasury Department by Congress. These sources of the law have a presumption of the authority of the statute, but they are subject to taxpayer challenge. Such sources include regulations, rulings, revenue procedures, and other opinions that are used by the Treasury Department or the Internal Revenue Service.

AFTR The citation abbreviation for the tax case reporter, *American Federal Tax Reports*. The first series of the reporter includes cases concerning pre-1954 Code litigation, and the second and third series include cases that address issues relative to the 1954 and 1986 Codes, respectively. Includes most tax case opinions issued by Federal courts other than the Tax Court.

AICPA The professional organization of practicing Certified Public Accountants in the United States, namely, the American Institute of CPAs.

All State Tax Guide A concise state-by-state analysis of all major taxes, with citations to state materials published by RIA.

Annotated tax service A commercial tax research reference collection, i.e., a secondary source of Federal tax law. Includes Code, Regulation and ruling analysis, judicial case notes, and other indexes and finding lists, organized by Code section number. The two most important annotated services are published

by Commerce Clearing House and Research Institute of America.

Annotation An entry in (especially) an annotated tax service, indicating a summary of a primary source of the Federal tax law that is pertinent to one's research, e.g., a court case opinion digest or a reference to a controlling regulation.

Announcements and Notices The IRS issues Announcements and Notices concerning items of general importance to taxpayers.

Annual Proceedings A collection of papers presented at a yearly meeting of tax professionals.

Appeals Office The internal group of the Internal Revenue Service that has the greatest authority to come to a compromise solution with a taxpayer concerning a disputed tax liability. Can consider the "hazards of litigation" in its deliberations. Failure to reach an agreement at this level of the IRS's organization means that the only subsequent appeal by either party to the dispute must be before a court of law.

Assessment The process of the IRS fixing the amount of one's tax liability. Although the U.S. tax system exhibits some degree of self-assessment, the IRS has the ultimate authority to assess the liability of every taxpayer.

Auto-Cite A citator in Lexis. The primary objective of Auto-Cite is to provide accurate citations as soon as possible, within 24 hours of receipt of each case. Auto-Cite can also be used to determine whether cases, Revenue Rulings, and Revenue Procedures are still good law.

Average tax rate The percentage of a taxpayer's income that is paid in taxes (i.e., computed by dividing the current-year tax liability by the taxpayer's income). The average can be computed as a percentage of total taxable income (this generates the taxpayer's average nominal tax rate) or as a percentage of the taxpayer's total economic income (this generates the taxpayer's average effective tax rate).

B

Bittker & Lokken Federal Taxation of Income, Estates, and Gifts A topical tax service published by Warren, Gorham & Lamont in five volumes, dedicated to Federal income and transfer taxation. Supplemented annually, the service includes a topical index and Code section, Regulation, case name, and Revenue Ruling finding lists.

BNA *Daily Tax Report* A daily collection of the latest regulations, rulings, case opinions, and other tax law revisions, as well as news reports, press releases, congressional studies and schedules, interviews, and other items of interest to the tax practitioner. Available through the mail and on various electronic tax services. One of the most important tax newsletters published because of its breadth of topics and its quality of analysis. In addition, the newsletter provides interviews with government officials, articles reviewing the day's events, and the full text of key documents discussed in the newsletter.

BNA *Tax Management Portfolios* A topical tax service published by the Bureau of National Affairs in a collection of more than three hundred magazine-size portfolios, dedicated to U.S. income, foreign income, and estate and gift taxation. Prepared by an identified expert in the field, each portfolio includes a detailed analysis of the topic, working papers with which to implement planning suggestions, and a bibliography of related literature. Supplemented by a biweekly newsletter, the portfolio series includes a topical index and case name and Code section finding lists.

Board of Tax Appeals An earlier name for the U.S. Tax Court, which did not have full judicial status. Opinions are recorded in the Board of Tax Appeals reporter, the citation abbreviation for which is BTA.

Boolean A deductive logic search that allows for the intersection of terms by using connectors such as "or," "and," or "within # number of words."

Bureau of National Affairs (BNA) A subsidiary of Tax Management. It offers a wide range of products covering all areas of Federal taxes. However, it is best known as the publisher of the *BNA Tax Management Portfolios* (BNA Portfolios). BNA Tax Management also has three electronic tax services: Portfolios Plus Library, Tax Practice Library, and TaxCore.

C

Case brief A concise summary of the facts, issues, holdings, and analyses of a court case. Used in a tax research context to allow subsequent review of the case by its author or another party. Includes complete citations of the briefed case, and other items addressed in the brief, to facilitate additional review when necessary.

CCH Citator A citator published by Commerce Clearing House that is part of the CCH *Standard Federal Tax Reporter*. The volumes of this loose-leaf service are labeled A to L and M to Z with a Finding List for Rulings in the back of the M to Z volume. This service covers the Federal income tax decisions that have been issued since 1913.

CCH *Federal Tax Articles* A loose-leaf and bound index to Federal tax articles published by Commerce Clearing House. This index provides concise abstracts for each article cited in the index. The framework for organizing these abstracts is the *Internal Revenue Code*. More than 250 journals, law reviews, papers, and proceedings are included in the index.

CCH *Federal Tax Service* The topical tax service of Commerce Clearing House. Offered to new subscribers only on CD-ROMs or through the Internet. Explanatory text, called the analysis, is divided into sixteen major topic areas, designated A through P. The editors' comments and evaluations of the law are the basis of the main text, with footnotes used to direct researchers to primary sources.

CCH *Standard Federal Tax Reporter* The annotated service of Commerce Clearing House dedicated to Federal income, estate, and gift taxation. Includes a weekly newsletter, topical index, tax calendar, rate tables and schedules, practitioner checklists, and case name, Code section, Regulation, and Revenue Ruling finding lists. In addition, it provides a two-volume *Internal Revenue Code* and a two-volume *Citator*.

CCH Tax Research NetWork The Internet tax service provided by Commerce Clearing House. It can include all of the tax services available from CCH if the practitioner is willing to purchase these services.

CD-ROM system West, CCH, RIA, and several other vendors have made available a collection of tax statutes, Regulations, rulings, cases, and other primary-source materials readable by a computer in a CD-ROM format. The related software allows the researcher to conduct an electronic search of the pertinent materials without incurring online charges: subscribers receive a series of compact disks containing the source materials, and the software instructs the user which disks to insert into the CD-ROM reader at appropriate times.

Chief Counsel The chief legal officer of the Internal Revenue Service. Responsible for making litigation and acquiesce/nonacquiesce decisions, and for developing interpretive material of the agency, including rulings and memoranda.

Circular 230 A tax regulation detailing the requirements and responsibilities of those who prepare Federal tax returns for compensation. Includes educational, ethical, and procedural guidelines.

Citation A means of conveying the location of a document. Appendix B of this text offers a standard format for citations used by tax researchers.

Citator A research resource that presents the judicial history of a court case and traces the subsequent references to the case. When these references include the citating case's evaluations of the cited case's precedents, the research can obtain some measure of the efficacy and reliability of the original holding.

Citator 2nd Series Published by Research Institute of America (RIA). The *Citator 2nd Series* is composed of three bound volumes plus paperback supplements, which cover from 1954 to the present. This citator series includes the history of cases that have been decided since 1954 and updates for cited cases appearing in the previous series. Within each volume, the cases are arranged in alphabetical order.

Cite When one case refers to another case, it cites the latter case.

Cited case With respect to a citator, the original case, whose facts or holding are referred to in the opinion of the citing case.

Citing case With respect to a citator, the subsequent case, which includes a reference to the original (cited) case.

Citing Reference In the Westlaw citator, a listing of all cases that refer to the cited case.

Civil penalty In a tax practice context, a fine or other judgment that is brought against a taxpayer or preparer for a failure to comply with one or more of the elements of the Federal tax law. Examples include penalties for failure to file a return or pay a tax in a timely fashion.

Client letter A primary means by which to communicate one's research results to the client. Includes, among other features, a summary of the controlling fact situation and attendant assumptions, a summary of the critical sources of the tax law that led to the researcher's conclusions, specific implications of the results of the project, and recommendations for client action.

Closed transaction A tax research situation is closed when all of the pertinent transactions have been completed by the taxpayer and other parties, such that the research issues may be limited to the proper nature and amount of disclosure to the government on the tax return or other document, and to preparation activities relative to subsequent government review.

Closing agreement A form with which the taxpayer and the IRS finalize their computations of a disputed tax liability.

Collateral estoppel The legal principle that limits one's judicial exposure relative to a disputed item to one series of court hearings. In a tax environment, the principle can present hardships for the taxpayer who wishes to raise additional issues during the course of a judicial proceeding.

Collection The process by which the IRS extracts an assessed tax liability from a taxpayer. Usually takes the form of the receipt of a check or other draft from the taxpayer, but can include liens or other garnishments of taxpayer assets.

Commerce Clause of Constitution The clause of the U.S. Constitution indicating that Congress has the power to regulate commerce with foreign nations, among states, and with Native American tribes. It grants powers to Congress and places constraints on the states' ability to tax interstate trade.

Commissioner of Internal Revenue The chief operating and chief executive officer of the Internal Revenue Service. Holds the ultimate responsibility for overall planning and for directing, coordinating, and controlling the policies and programs of the IRS.

Committee Report A summary of the issues that were considered by the House Ways and Means Committee, Senate Finance Committee, or Joint Conference Committee, here relative to proposed or adopted changes in the language of the *Internal Revenue Code*. Useful in tax research as an aid to understanding unclear statutory language and legislative history or intent. Published in the *Internal Revenue Bulletin*.

Compare It A feature offered by RIA with its Checkpoint service. It enables the researcher to directly link to the same topic material from one state to another state and return. This feature is available only for explanatory materials and not for state statutes or regulations.

Compilation Broadly, a collection of primary sources, editorial comments, and annotations in a tax service (i.e., its collection of volumes).

Computing Centers IRS service centers that manipulate data collected from tax returns.

Connectors In using an online database or CD-ROM service, connectors are employed to link various parts of a search command using Boolean logic. For instance, "or," "and," and "within" are used as connectors in various research services.

Contingent fees The practice under which a professional bases his or her fee for services upon the results thereof. The AICPA has held that the performance of services for a contingent fee can be unethical; one exception is available, though, where (as in tax practice) the results are subject to third-party actions (here the government, in an audit setting). Several states are relaxing this restriction, allowing CPAs to mix the form of their compensation between fixed and contingent fees.

Correspondence examination An audit of one's tax return that is conducted largely by telephone or mail. Usually involves a request for substantiation or explanation of one or more items on a tax return, such as filing status, exemptions, and itemized deductions for medical expenses, interest,

taxes paid, charitable contributions, or miscellaneous deductions.

Court of Appeals A Federal appellate court that hears appeals from the Tax Court, Court of Federal Claims, or District Courts within its geographical boundaries. Organized into geographical circuits, although there are additional circuits for Washington, D.C., and for cases appealed from the Court of Federal Claims. Opinions are recorded in the *Federal Reporter*, various series, and in the AFTR and USTC tax case reporter series.

Court of Federal Claims A trial-level court in which the taxpayer typically sues the government for a refund of overpaid tax liability. Hears nontax matters as well in Washington, D.C. or in other major cities. Opinions are reported in the Court of Federal Claims reporter and in the AFTR and USTC case reporter series.

Create-a-Chart A feature offered by RIA with its state and local service. It facilitates the creation of charts from various state tax materials. This feature enables the practitioner to summarize pertinent multistate tax information in a convenient chart that can be exported to a word processing document.

Criminal penalty A severe infraction of the elements of the Federal tax law by a taxpayer or preparer. Felony or misdemeanor status for tax crimes can be accompanied by substantial fines or jail terms. Examples of tax crimes include tax evasion and other willful failures to comply with the *Internal Revenue Code*.

Cumulative Bulletin An official publication of the IRS, consolidating the material that first was published in the *Internal Revenue Bulletin* in a (usually semiannual) hardbound volume. Publication alters the proper citation for the contents thereof.

Customer Service Sites IRS service centers that deal with telephone and electronic contacts from taxpayers, in working with electronic filing of returns, and in answering telephone and online taxpayer inquiries.

D

Daily Tax Report Available from Tax Analysts, a daily summary of tax developments, cases, rulings, and other information of interest to the tax professional.

Determination Letter An IRS pronouncement issued by the local IRS office, relative to the agency's position concerning a straightforward issue of tax law in the context of a completed transaction.

Direct History In the Westlaw citator, a listing of the citations to hearings of the cited case by lower level courts.

Discriminant function formula A means by which, on the basis of probable return to the IRS in terms of collected delinquent tax liabilities, the Service selects tax returns for examination.

District Court A trial-level court that hears tax and nontax cases. Organized according to geographical regions. Jury trials are available. Opinions are reported in the *Federal Supplement Series* and in the AFTR and USTC tax case reporter series.

Due Process Clause of Constitution Found in the Fourteenth Amendment to the U.S. Constitution, it limits the territorial scope of a state's taxing authority, particularly in regard to interstate commerce.

E

Effective average tax rate The proportion of a taxpayer's economic income that was paid to the government as a tax liability (i.e., it is computed by dividing the tax liability by the taxpayer's economic income for the year). Economic income includes nontaxable sources of income, such as gifts and inheritances, and tax-exempt interest.

En banc When more than one Tax Court judge hears a case, the court is said to be sitting "en banc."

Enrolled agent One who is qualified to practice before the IRS by means other than becoming an attorney or CPA. Typically, one must pass a qualifying examination and meet other requirements to become an Enrolled Agent.

Equal Protection Clause of Constitution Found in the Fourteenth Amendment to the U.S. Constitution, it requires that similarly situated persons or property be treated in a similar manner by the law. Although the Equal Protection clause does not reference taxation specifically, it has been relied upon to determine whether tax provisions treat different taxpayers equally.

Ernst & Young Commonly Asked Questions A database of questions with answers that can be searched by keyword or the drill down method offered by CCH.

Ernst & Young Online Tax Advisor A CCH service that allows practitioners to fill out a form online providing relevant facts of the transaction. Ernst & Young will deliver a response within a time frame suggested.

Ethical standards Boundaries of social or professional behavior, derived by the culture or its institutions. Tax ethics are described in various documents of governmental agencies or professional organizations.

F

Fact issue A tax research issue in which the practitioner must determine whether a pertinent question of fact was satisfied by the taxpayer; e.g., was an election filed with the government in a timely manner? What was the taxpayer's motivation underlying the redemption of some corporate stock?

Federal Tax Baedeker Analysis and explanation of tax laws covering individuals, businesses, trusts, and estates. Included in the Tax Analysts tax service.

Federal Tax Library The searchable database of federal tax materials made available by Tax Analysts. Available in Basic and Complete versions.

Federal Taxation of Income, Estates, and Gifts An authoritative tax treatise available on Westlaw and the RIA tax service, often cited as a leading secondary source of tax law.

Field audit The review of a corporation or business tax return by an IRS agent. Typically involves more complex issues of law and/or fact than are the subject of a correspondence or office audit. Open-ended in nature. The agent who conducts a field examination reviews all of the taxpayer's business and financial operations, accounting methods, and means of internal control.

File memorandum A primary means by which to communicate the results of a research project to oneself, one's supervisor, and/or one's successor. Includes, among other features, a statement of the pertinent facts and assumptions, a detailed outline (and citations of) controlling tax law, a summary of the researcher's conclusions, and a listing of action recommendations for the client to consider.

Finding list An index to primary tax law sources, such as court cases or Revenue Rulings, typically arranged alphabetically, and referring to paragraph or division citations in the tax service's compilations.

Fraud In a tax practice context, a taxpayer action to evade the assessment of a tax. Criminal fraud requires a willful intent by the taxpayer. The IRS bears the burden of proof relative to fraud allegations.

Full-Text Document In the Westlaw citator, a tool that displays the full text and all versions of the citation for a case, a summary of the proceeding, headnotes, and Key numbers.

Full-text search A computerized version of a published index. A full-text search locates every occurrence of a word or phrase in every document available for the search.

G

General Counsel's Memorandum A memoranda generated upon the request of the IRS, typically as a means to assist in the preparation of Revenue Rulings and Private Letter Rulings.

General Regulation A regulation issued under the general authority granted to the IRS to interpret the language of the Code, usually under a specific Code directive of Congress, and with specific congressional authority.

Golsen **rule** Tax Court decisions are appealed to the Court of Appeals for the taxpayer's place of work or residence. The decisions of the Courts of Appeal are not always consistent. Thus, when a taxpayer whose circuit has ruled on a given issue brings a case that includes that issue before the Tax Court, the Tax Court will follow the holding of the pertinent Circuit, even if the Tax Court disagrees with the holding, or if another circuit has issued a contrary holding. This can lead to contradictory Tax Court rulings, based solely upon the state of the taxpayer's residence.

H

Headnote Numbered paragraphs in which the editors of the court reporter summarize the court's holdings on each issue. These paragraphs appear in the court reporters before the text of the actual court case.

Hypertext (Hyperlinked) A means of moving around within the documents of an electronic database by clicking on a mouse or keyboard where a special text color or character indicates that a related document is available. For instance, in reading a court case, the user might move to the opinion issued in another case cited in a footnote, or to a controlling Code section or Regulation that is cited in the document.

I

Independence The AICPA requires the CPA who renders an opinion relative to a client's financial statements to be (and to appear to be) independent from the client. This principle entails restrictions as to the CPA's direct and indirect financial dealings with the client, and its simultaneous role as financial auditor.

Indirect History In the Westlaw citator, a listing of the citations to those case opinions that refer to the cited case. The citator indicates whether the citing cases positively or negatively affect the precedential value of the cited case.

InfoTax Provider of a CD-ROM tax research service, including Code and Regulations, court cases, and administrative pronouncements.

Injunction The action by which the IRS or a court prevents (enjoins) a taxpayer, preparer, or tax shelter distributor from undertaking a specified action (e.g., preparing tax returns for compensation or offering a tax shelter for sale).

Internal Revenue Bulletin An official weekly publication of the Internal Revenue Service that includes Announcements, Treasury Decisions, Revenue Rulings, Revenue Procedures, and other information of interest to the tax researcher.

Internal Revenue Code The primary statutory source of the Federal tax law, a collection of laws that have been passed by Congress and incorporated in Title 26 of the United States Code. The Code was last reorganized in 1954. It presently is known as the Internal Revenue Code of 1986. The chief subdivision of the Code is the section.

Internal Revenue Service A division of the Department of the Treasury, the Federal agency that is charged with the collection of Federal taxes and the implementation of other responsibilities that are conveyed by the *Internal Revenue Code*.

Internal Revenue Service Centers Locations at which the IRS receives and processes tax returns, distributes tax forms, and performs other specified functional activities in the administration of the Federal tax laws.

Internet A means by which millions of remote computer stations are connected and can be used by individuals at any such station. Search engines assist in finding pertinent materials, and download features allow users to view and obtain files from the remote locations. The Internet is organized chiefly using the World Wide Web, bulletin board and newsgroup systems, and file transfer protocols. The Internet is useful to the tax researcher as a means of finding primary and secondary source documents in a timely fashion, sharing tax newsletters and spreadsheets, and transferring data to and from taxing jurisdictions.

IRS Oversight Board A group of at least nine individuals that acts as the board of directors of the IRS. Responsible for overseeing the agency's operational and internal control functions, approving mission plans and strategies, reviewing the agency's budget, and ensuring the proper treatment of taxpayers.

J

Joint Audit Program Allows the Multistate Tax Commission to perform a comprehensive audit of a business's taxes simultaneously for several states.

Judicial sources Certain Federal court decisions that have the force of the statute in constructing the Federal tax law. The magnitude of this authority depends upon the level and location of the courts that issued the opinions.

K

KeyCite (KC) A Westlaw citator that furnishes a comprehensive direct and indirect history for court cases. The indirect history includes secondary materials that have the cited case in their text. *KeyCite* allows the researcher to select a full history, negative history, or omit minor cases. This option is not available with the other citators.

KeySearch A search aid employing the West numbering system of the key issues in court cases. When a researcher identifies the legal topic applicable to the search, this search aid formulates a query based on the underlying terms for the topic based on the key numbers system.

Kleinrock's *TaxExpert* A CD-ROM and Internet tax research service provided by Kleinrock. It includes primary tax law sources plus an explanation of the law.

KWIC Key word in context, a means by which to display electronic search results.

L

Law issue A tax research question in which one must determine which provision of the Federal tax law applies to the client's fact situation. This entails the evaluation of various statutory, administrative, and judicial provisions with respect to the client's circumstances, e.g., is the client's charitable contribution subject to the 30 percent of adjusted gross income limitation?

Law reviews Scholarly publications of law schools. These publications are edited either by faculty members or by graduate students under the guidance of the school's faculty. Most law reviews also use an outside advisory board comprised of practicing attorneys and law professors at other universities to aid in selecting and reviewing articles. The articles appearing in these publications are usually written by tax practitioners, academics, graduate students, or other noted commentators.

Legislative Regulation A regulation by which the IRS is directed by Congress to fulfill a law-making function and to specify the substantive requirements of a tax provision.

LEXCITE A citator service of Lexis. For the case citation entered, it ascertains parallel citations and then searches for all of the cites in the case law documents. It will find embedded references to a variety of documents such as cases, law reviews, journals, Federal Register, and Revenue Rulings.

Lexis An Internet service for legal (tax) sources started in 1973 by LexisNexis.

LexisNexis One of the largest legal and news services available on the Internet. An online database resource that allows the researcher to access a database consisting of the text of court cases, administrative rulings, and selected law review articles and to search these files for tax (and other) law sources that may be relevant to the research problem.

Lexis/Nexis Academic A version of the LEXIS and NEXIS database services designed for use at public libraries, universities, and law schools.

Linking A method of moving among the documents of an electronic database, as indicated by the controlling software. See *hypertext*.

Local citation A citation that directs the researcher to the exact page where the cited case is mentioned in the citing case.

M

Marginal tax rate The proportion of the next dollar of gross income (or other increase in the tax base) that the taxpayer must pay to the government as a tax. Thus, the marginal tax rate conveys the proportionate value of an additional deduction, or the cost of an increase to the tax base. Tax-effective decisions must take into account the marginal (and not the average or nominal) tax rate.

Memorandum decision A decision of the Tax Court that, in the opinion of the chief judge, does not address any new issue of tax law. Accordingly, the government does not publish the opinion. Commerce Clearing House and Research Institute of America each publish annual collections of these Tax Court Memorandum decisions.

Mertens Law of Federal Income Taxation A topical tax service designed chiefly by and for attorneys.

Multistate Alternative Dispute Resolution Program Developed by the Multistate Tax Commission. It affords taxpayers the opportunity to resolve common tax issues with several states at once. The program also assists taxpayers in negotiating and drafting settlement agreements to be submitted to participating states.

Multistate Tax Commission (MTC) Created in 1967 by the Multistate Tax Compact. The MTC adopted the Uniform Division of Income for Tax Purposes Act (UDITPA) as part of its Articles, issued regulations interpreting the UDITPA and continues to issue apportionment rules. As of early 2005, there are 45 states participants in MTC. The five states not associated with MTC are Delaware, Indiana, Nevada, New York, Vermont, and Virginia.

Multistate Tax Compact An organization of state governments that created the Multistate Tax Commission in 1967.

N

National Conference of Commissioners on Uniform State Laws In 1957, it drafted the Uniform Division of Income for Tax Purposes Act (UDITPA) to create a greater uniformity and consistency in the measurements of business income.

National Nexus Program Developed by the Multistate Tax Commission. Its function is to facilitate information sharing among participating states.

National Taxpayer Advocate Empowered to achieve a temporary delay in the normal enforcement procedures of the IRS, as specified in a Taxpayer Assistance Order.

Natural language A search where a tax question is entered in standard English (natural language) words, phrases, (entered within quotation marks) or sentences. The program determines the key terms for searching and relationships among the words (i.e., connectors to apply). This type of search is useful when the researcher is unsure as to which keywords would be the most effective.

Negligence In a Federal tax context, a (nonwillful) failure to exercise one's duty with respect to the *Internal Revenue Code* or to use a reasonable degree of expected or professional care. Examples include the unacceptable failure to attempt to follow the IRS's rules and Regulations in the preparation of a tax return for compensation.

Nexis An Internet service for news, financial, and business information, started in 1979 by LexisNexis.

Nexus A sufficient business connection with a locality that gives taxing authority to the locality over the business.

Ninety-day letter A statutory notice from the IRS that the taxpayer has failed to pay an assessed tax. An issuance of such a letter usually indicates that the taxpayer has exhausted all of his or her appeal rights within the IRS and that the next forum for review will be a trial-level court. Strictly, the taxpayer has ninety days to petition the Tax Court to be relieved of the deficiency assessment. If no such petition is filed, the IRS is empowered to collect the assessed tax.

Nominal average tax rate Determined by an inspection of the applicable rate schedule. The average nominal rate at which the taxpayer's total taxable income is taxed is computed by dividing the taxpayer's total tax liability by his or her taxable income. Tax-exempt income is not included in the denominator of this fraction.

Nonacquiescence An announcement by the IRS that it will not follow the decision of a court in a tax decision that was adverse to the agency. Notation is included in the proper citation of the disputed case. Announced in the *Internal Revenue Bulletin*.

O

Offer in compromise The means by which the government offers to reduce the amount of an assessed tax, usually because of some doubt as to the "litigation-proof" magnitude or collectibility of the tax. A legally enforceable promise that cannot be rescinded, an offer in compromise relates to the entire liability of the taxpayer, and it conclusively settles all of the issues for which an agreement can be made.

Office audit The audit of a nonbusiness tax return that is conducted at an IRS district office. Usually requires some analysis and the exercise of the IRS personnel's judgment, rather than a mere inquiry or substantiation verification. Typically involves tip, rent, or royalty income, travel and entertainment deductions, and income from partnerships or other conduit entities.

OneDisc A Tax Analyst's single disc tax product similar to the Kleinrock service. It contains an extensive list of primary sources and the explanations of *Federal Tax Baedeker*.

Online system In a tax research context, a collection of the text of court case opinions, statutes, administrative rulings, and selected law review articles. These text files can be searched by the practitioner using an Internet connection in an extremely fast and efficient manner, to assist him or her in locating tax law sources that may be relevant to the disputed tax issue.

Open transaction A tax research issue is open when not all of the pertinent transactions have been completed by the taxpayer or other parties, such that the researcher can suggest to the client several alternative courses of action that will generate differing tax consequences.

Oral presentation A primary means of communicating the results of a research project to others by way of a telephone conversation or a more formal presentation system.

P

PH Citator The first series of citators, formerly published by Prentice-Hall and now published by Research Institute of America. The first series consists of three bound volumes that cover all of the Federal tax cases dated between 1863 and 1953.

Permanent citation A Tax Court citation issued to a Tax Court decision containing the case name, volume number, reporter page number, and the year of the decision.

Practice before the IRS The privilege to sign tax returns as preparer for compensation and to represent others before the IRS or in court in an audit or appeal proceeding. This privilege is granted by the IRS and controlled under *Circular 230*.

Practitioner journal Journals published by professional organizations and commercial companies. The objective of these journals is to keep tax practitioners abreast of the current changes and trends in the tax law.

Preparer penalties A series of fines and other levies by which the IRS encourages taxpayers and preparers to fulfill their responsibilities under the *Internal Revenue Code.* Examples include penalties for failure to sign returns, keep or furnish copies of returns, and provide required information to Federal agencies.

Primary authority An element of the Federal tax law that was issued by Congress, the Treasury or Internal Revenue Service, or a Federal court, and thus carries greater precedential weight than elements of the tax law issued by other parties.

Private letter ruling A written determination published by the Internal Revenue Service relative to its position concerning the tax treatment of a prospective transaction. Strictly, it cannot be applied to any taxpayer other than the one who requested the ruling. Text or summaries thereof are included in various commercial tax services.

Privileges and Immunities Clause of Constitution Grants citizens of each state all privileges and immunities of citizens in every other state. Note that the clause applies only to "citizens" of states. Since a corporation is considered a "person" but not a "citizen" under the law, corporations are not protected by the Privileges and Immunities clause.

Problem Resolution Program An organizational means by which the IRS attempts to satisfy taxpayer complaints, inquiries, and disagreements, short of the appeals process or litigation. The taxpayer can employ the Problem Resolution Program when the usual agency channels do not produce the desired results. Typically, the program is used to resolve billing, procedural, computer-generated, and other problems that the taxpayer has not resolved after one or more contacts with the appropriate IRS office.

Proceedings The published versions of conference presentations. These proceeding are distributed to the participants at the conference and later to the general public in the form of a collection of articles.

Processing Centers IRS service centers that process Federal tax returns.

Professional journals Synonym for practitioner journal.

Progressive tax rate If the marginal rates of a tax rate schedule increase as the magnitude of the tax base increases, the schedule includes progressive tax rates.

Proportional tax rate If the marginal rates of a tax rate schedule remain constant as the magnitude of the tax base increases, the schedule includes proportional tax rates.

Proposed Regulation An interpretation or clarification of the provisions of a portion of the *Internal Revenue Code,* issued by the Treasury and available for comment (and possible revision) in a public hearing.

Public Purpose Most state Constitutions require that tax revenues be imposed only for public purposes. Public purpose is rarely defined, however.

Q

Query A means of searching an electronic database. Includes a definition of the scope of the search and a specification of the targeted terms in which the researcher is interested, often employing connectors in the grammar of the query.

R

Realistic possibility The realistic possibility standard is met if analysis of the tax return position by a reasonable and well-informed person knowledgeable in the tax law(s) would lead such person to conclude that the position has approximately a one in three (or greater) likelihood of being sustained on its merits.

Reasonable cause A means by which a taxpayer or preparer can be excused from an applicable penalty or other sanction. For instance, if the taxpayer failed to file a tax return on a timely basis because of illness or if the underlying records were destroyed by natural cause, the taxpayer likely would be excused from the penalty (but not from the tax or any related interest) because of this reasonable cause.

Regressive tax rate If the marginal rates of a tax rate schedule decrease as the magnitude of the tax base increases, the schedule includes regressive tax rates.

Regular decision A decision issued by the Tax Court that generally involves a new or unusual point of law, as determined by the Chief Judge of the court.

Regulation An interpretation or clarification of the provisions of a portion of the *Internal Revenue Code*, issued by the Treasury under authority granted by Congress. Legislative Regulations directly create the details of a tax law. Both general and legislative Regulations carry the force of the statute, unless they are held to be invalid in a judicial hearing.

Return preparer Any person who prepares for compensation, or employs one or more persons to prepare for compensation, all or a substantial portion of a tax return or claim for income tax refund.

Revenue Agent's Report Prepared upon the completion of the examination of a tax return to explain to the taxpayer the sources of any adjustments to the reported tax liability. If the taxpayer agrees to this recomputation, the associated tax, penalty, and interest become due. Lacking such agreement, other aspects of the appeals process are undertaken.

Revenue Procedure A pronouncement of the Internal Revenue Service concerning the implementation details of a specific Code provision. Published in the *Internal Revenue Bulletin*.

Revenue Ruling A pronouncement of the Internal Revenue Service concerning its interpretation of the application of the Code (typically) to a specific taxpayer-submitted fact situation. Published in the *Internal Revenue Bulletin*. Can be relied upon as precedent by other taxpayers who encounter similar fact patterns.

RIA Checkpoint State & Local Tax (SALT) Comprehensive tax service providing analysis of state and local taxes for all 50 states and the District of Columbia. All taxes imposed by states and most enacted by localities are covered by the service. Editorial explanations and annotations are included in the service.

RIA Checkpoint Tax Reporter The Internet tax service provided by Research Institute of America. This is one of the most authoritative and well known Internet tax services available. All services available from Research Institute of America may be accessed by subscription through Checkpoint.

RIA Citators The citator service published by Research Institute of America. It includes two series of citators, the *PH Citator* and the *Citator 2nd Series*.

RIA *Federal Tax Coordinator 2d* Comprehensive topical tax service published by Research Institute of America. The editors comments and evaluations of the law are the basis of the main text with footnotes used to direct researchers to primary sources. One of its strong points is its general background discussions summarizing the major issues.

RIA OnPoint CD resource that allows the researcher to access a database consisting of the text of court cases, administrative rulings, and selected tax treatises and analytical articles and to search these files for tax law sources that may be relevant to the research problem.

RIA *United States Tax Reporter* The annotated service of Research Institute of America dedicated to Federal income, estate, and gift taxation. Includes a weekly newsletter, topical index, tax calendar, rate tables and schedules, practitioner checklists, case name, Code section, Regulation, and Revenue Ruling finding lists. This tax service has a unique and functional paragraph numbering system. All paragraphs pertaining to a particular Code section incorporate that section number into the paragraph number. A single digit is added to the end of the Code section number, indicating the nature of the material contained in the paragraph.

S

Scholarly Reviews Tax periodicals that are directed at an academic audience, and wherein articles are written by those working at universities and law schools.

Seamless Ability to perform a function with little or no effort. For example, the ability to retrieve references full-text through the computer by double clicking on the reference's title.

Secondary authority An element of the Federal tax law that was issued by a scholarly or professional writer, e.g., in a textbook, journal article, or treatise, and thus carries less precedential weight than elements of the tax law issued by primary sources.

Shepardizing Slang used in the legal profession used to describe the process of using a Shepard's citator.

Shepard's Citations The full coverage of Shepard's citators available through Westlaw.

Shepard's Citator The only major tax citator that is organized by case reporter series.

Shepard's Federal Tax Citator A citator available through Westlaw and Lexis, organized by reference to the case reporter and volume number in which the case is found. Thus, to use the citator, the practitioner must know the court reporter citation for the case of interest.

Small Cases Division The Tax Court allows taxpayers whose disputed tax liability does not exceed $50,000 to try the case before the court's Small Cases Division. Procedural rules of the division are somewhat relaxed, and taxpayers often represent themselves. The Small Cases Division decisions are not published, nor can either party appeal the holdings thereof.

Statute of limitations Provides the maximum amount of time within which one or both parties in the taxing process must perform an act, such as file a return, pay a tax, or examine a return. Various time limits apply relative to the *Internal Revenue Code*, although both parties can, by mutual agreement, extend one or more of these time limitations, if desired.

StateNet An RIA database consisting of all proposed and current enacted state legislation in full text. Proposed legislation's current status can be tracked on this database.

State Research Library The searchable database of state and local tax materials made available by Tax Analysts.

State Tax Reporters A CCH state tax service that combines detailed explanations, primary source materials, and practical compliance guidance. All of the major taxes imposed by states and localities are covered by the service. Explanations are organized by tax type with links to related primary sources.

Statutory notice of deficiency Synonym for a ninety-day letter.

Statutory sources The Constitution, tax treaties, and the *Internal Revenue Code* are the statutory sources of the Federal tax law. They have the presumption of correctness, unless a court modifies or overturns a provision in response to a taxpayer challenge. In this regard, legislative intent and history can be important in supporting the taxpayer's case.

Substantial authority A taxpayer penalty may be incurred if a tax return position is taken and not disclosed to the IRS where no substantial authority (generally, statute, Regulation, court decision, or written determination) supports the position.

Supremacy Clause of Constitution The clause in the U.S. Constitution that confers superiority to Federal laws over state laws. That is, Federal laws are "the supreme law of the land" and trumps state laws. If a state law or constitutional provision is in conflict with a Federal law, it is considered to be invalid.

Supreme Court The highest Federal appellate court. Hears very few tax cases. Approves a *writ of certiorari* for the cases that it hears. Opinions are reported in the *U.S. Supreme Court Reports* (citation abbreviation, US); the *Supreme Court Reporter* (SCt); the *United States Reports, Lawyer's Edition* (LEd); the AFTR and USTC tax case reporter series; and various on-line services.

T

Table of Authorities A service available through Westlaw and Lexis that lists cases that are cited within a case of interest.

Tax Analysts A nonprofit entity organized to provide literary forums for the discussion of taxation. It disseminates timely and comprehensive state, Federal, and international tax information through their daily, weekly, and monthly print publications, scholarly books, and electronic database services.

Tax and Accounting Sites Directory Internet site linking to various government, publisher, and academic web pages of interest to the accounting or tax professional. Often called "Tax Sites."

Tax authority Any source of the Federal tax law; in common usage, this term is used to refer to government agencies.

Tax avoidance The legal structuring of one's financial affairs so as to optimize the related tax liability. Synonym for tax planning.

Tax awareness The first requirement for effective tax planning on the part of decision makers. It requires decision makers to be alert for tax-optimizing alternatives.

Tax compliance An element of modern tax practice in which a practitioner works with a client to file appropriate tax returns in a timely manner and represents the client in administrative proceedings.

Tax Court A trial-level court that hears only cases involving tax issues. Issues regular and memorandum decisions. Meets in Washington, D.C. and in other major cities. Formerly called the Board of Tax Appeals. Regular opinions are reported in the *U.S. Tax Court Reports*. Memorandum opinions are published only by commercial tax services.

Tax ethics The application of ethical standards to the tax practice.

Tax evasion The reduction of one's tax liability by illegal means.

Tax Freedom Day The Tax Foundation uses this device to measure the impact of tax liabilities on citizens' budgets. Expressed in terms of days of work, rather than percentages of a total income amount. The measure computes the day of the year when taxpayers have earned enough money to pay for all of their taxes.

Tax journal A periodic publication that addresses legal, factual, and procedural issues encountered in a modern tax practice. As a secondary source of Federal tax law, analyses in tax journals can be used in support of a taxpayer's case before a government agency or, especially, before a court.

Tax litigation An element of modern tax practice in which a practitioner represents the client against the government in a judicial hearing.

Tax Management Portfolios See BNA *Tax Management Portfolios*

Tax newsletter A weekly, biweekly, or monthly publication or electronic document, often furnished as part of a subscription to a commercial tax service. Typically provides digest-style summaries of current court case rulings, administrative pronouncements, and pending or approved tax legislation cross-referenced to the organization system of the tax service. Helps the practitioner to keep current relative to the breaking developments in the tax community.

Tax Notes A weekly collection of the latest regulations, written determinations, case opinions, congressional studies, policy analyses, and other items of interest to the tax practitioner. Available through the mail and on various electronic tax services.

Tax Notes Today Version of the Tax Notes publication that discusses the latest developments in tax rulings, cases, transcripts, studies, and other documents of interest to the tax professional.

Tax planning Synonym for tax avoidance.

Tax practice Meeting the tax research, litigation, planning, and compliance needs of a client by a recognized tax professional.

Tax Practice Library A basic electronic tax service of BNA furnishing access to primary sources, practice tools, and limited news sources. Rather than relying on the BNA *Portfolio Series*, Tax Practice has developed its own explanatory analysis. Other than offering fewer databases (no BNA *Portfolio* or journals), this service is almost identical to Portfolio Plus in its searching methods.

Tax research An examination of pertinent sources of the state, local, and Federal tax law in light of all relevant circumstances relative to a client's tax problem. Entails the use of professional judgment to draw an appropriate conclusion and the communication of such conclusions or alternatives at a proper level to the client.

Tax service A commercial tax reference including statutory, administrative, and judicial sources of Federal tax law. Structured to maximize the practitioner's ease of use via a variety of indexes and finding lists. Often includes the text of the pertinent tax authorities and relevant scholarly or professional commentary.

Tax treaty An act of Congress that addresses the application of certain *Internal Revenue Code* provisions to a taxpayer whose tax base falls under the taxing statutes of more than one country. Published, among other places, in the *Internal Revenue Bulletin*.

TaxBase Electronic newsletter published daily by Tax Analysts. It covers Federal, state, and worldwide tax news as well as court petitions and complaints and highlights of the daily tax news.

TaxCore Subscribers to several of BNA's news services receive this service. It provides the hyperlinked primary sources and tax-related documents discussed and cited in the news reports.

Taxpayer Assistance Order The taxpayer uses this request to engage an IRS Taxpayer Advocate to delay the implementation of an IRS action, such as a collection or seizure activity, where it appears that the taxpayer has received less than fair treatment through the administrative procedures of the agency.

Taxpayer Compliance Measurement Program A means by which the IRS develops its discriminant function formulae. The taxpayer's return is selected randomly for an extensive review, during which every item of income, credit, deduction, and exclusion is challenged by the government. The results of such reviews are used (other than to adjust the examined taxpayer's liability) to delineate criteria by which other taxpayers' returns will be selected for examination.

Technical Advice Memorandum A pronouncement of the National Office of the Internal Revenue Service stating the agency's position relative to the tax treatment of a taxpayer whose return is under audit. Text or discussion thereof may be included in the body of a commercial tax service.

Technical Memorandum A memoranda prepared in the production of a Proposed Regulation.

Temporary citation A Tax Court citation issued to a Tax Court decision containing the case name, volume number, reporter, the case number, and the year of the decision. The page number is not included because the opinion has not yet been published.

Temporary Regulation An administrative pronouncement of the IRS, typically concerning the application of a recently enacted or detailed provision of the tax law, especially where there is insufficient time to carry out the public-hearings process that usually accompanies the Regulations process. Temporary Regulations carry the force of law, although citations differ from those for permanent Regulations with regard to the prefix.

Terms and Connectors The LexisNexis form of a Boolean search.

Thirty-day letter A notice from the IRS formally notifying the taxpayer of the results of an examination of the return and requesting that the taxpayer agree to the proposed modifications to the tax liability. A taxpayer's failure to respond to the letter triggers the statutory notice of a tax deficiency, i.e., the ninety-day letter demanding the payment of the tax or a petition to the tax court.

Topical tax service A professional tax research reference collection, i.e., a secondary source of Federal tax law. Includes Code, Regulation, and ruling analysis; judicial case notes; and other indexes and finding lists organized by general topic. The most important topical tax services are published by the Research Institute of America and the Bureau of National Affairs.

Treasury Decision A Regulation that has not yet been formally integrated into the published tax Regulation collection. Often issued in the *Internal Revenue Bulletin*.

Treasury Department The cabinet-level government agency that is responsible for administering and enforcing laws that affect the currency. The Treasury has assigned its responsibilities relative to the *Internal Revenue Code* to the Internal Revenue Service.

U

Unauthorized practice of law A prohibited aspect of modern tax practice by nonattorneys, entailing, e.g., the issuance of a legal opinion or the drafting of a legal document for the client, for which the practitioner could be subject to legal or professional penalties.

Uniform Division of Income for Tax Purposes Act (UDITPA) Drafted in 1957 by the National Conference of Commissioners on Uniform State Laws, to create a greater uniformity and consistency in the measurements of business income.

Uniformity Clause of Constitution Closely related to the Equal Protection concept. This clause requires that similarly situated persons or property be treated in a similar manner, including the taxation of property or person.

Universal characters Symbols that are holders for zero or more characters in searches. See *Connectors*.

U.S. Constitution Ultimate source of the Federal tax law.

USTC The citation abbreviation for the Commerce Clearing House reporter, *United States Tax Cases*. Includes most of the tax decisions of the Federal courts other than the Tax Court.

W

Warren, Gorham & Lamont's *Index to Federal Tax Articles* An index to Federal tax articles published by Warren, Gorham & Lamont. It provides citations and occasionally summaries for articles covering Federal income, gift, and estate taxation or tax policy that appear in over 350 periodicals. This index has permanent cumulation indexes provided in paperbound volumes and is updated quarterly by paperback cumulative supplements. Both the topic and the author indexes contain full article citations.

Weekly Report A tax newsletter published by BNA, expanding upon and summarizing materials that were included in the *Daily Tax Report*.

Westlaw An online database resource provided by West Group. Allows the researcher to access a database consisting of the text of court cases, administrative rulings, and selected law review articles and to search these files for tax (and other) law sources that may be relevant to the research problem.

Wildcard characters See *universal characters*.

World Wide Web A popular means by which to organize and present one's data to the Internet community. The IRS, various tax research services, and numerous law libraries offer home pages on the Web, such that tax professionals can find and search through the documents available on the computers of those hosting the Internet site.

Writ of certiorari Document issued by the Supreme Court indicating the Court will hear the petitioned case. If the case will not be heard, certiorari is said to be denied.

Written determination General description of IRS or Treasury pronouncements, including Revenue Rulings, Revenue Procedures, Private Letter Rulings, Technical Advice Memoranda, and Determination Letters.

Index